FDDI Networking

Planning, Installation, and Management

Martin A. W. Nemzow

McGraw-Hill, Inc.
New York San Francisco Washington, D.C. Auckland Bogotá
Caracas Lisbon London Madrid Mexico City Milan
Montreal New Delhi San Juan Singapore
Sydney Tokyo Toronto

Library of Congress Cataloging-in-Publication Data

Nemzow, Martin A. W.
   FDDI networking : planning, installation, and management / Martin A. W. Nemzow.
      p.   cm.— (McGraw-Hill series on computer communications)
   Includes index.
   ISBN 0-07-046322-0
   1. Local area networks (Computer networks)   2. Fiber Distributed Data Interface (Computer network standard)   I. Title.   II. Series.
   TK5105.7.N45   1993
   004.6'8—dc20   93-26465
                                                                              CIP

Copyright © 1994 by McGraw-Hill, Inc. All rights reserved. Printed in the United States of America. Except as permitted under the United States Copyright Act of 1976, no part of this publication may be reproduced or distributed in any form or by any means, or stored in a data base or retrieval system, without the prior written permission of the publisher.

1 2 3 4 5 6 7 8 9 0   DOC/DOC   9 9 8 7 6 5 4 3

ISBN 0-07-046322-0

The sponsoring editor for this book was Jeanne Glasser, the editing supervisor was David E. Fogarty, and the production supervisor was Donald Schmidt.

Printed and bound by R. R. Donnelley & Sons Company.

Information contained in this work has been obtained by McGraw-Hill, Inc., from sources believed to be reliable. However, neither McGraw-Hill nor its authors guarantee the accuracy or completeness of any information published herein, and neither McGraw-Hill nor its authors shall be responsible for any errors, omissions, or damages arising out of use of this information. This work is published with the understanding that McGraw-Hill and its authors are supplying information but are not attempting to render engineering or other professional services. If such services are required, the assistance of an appropriate professional should be sought.

Contents

Preface xi
Acknowledgments xv

Part 1. Overview 1

Chapter 1. Networks for Competitive Strategy 3
Advantages of Networks 8
Networks Reduce Costs 9
Networks Create Monopolies 10
Networks Optimize Data Flow 12
Networks Focus Distribution Channels 15
Networks Improve Information Flow 16
Networks Add Value to Products 16
Bulletin Boards Shift Purchasing Decisions 17
Information Distribution Supplants Processing 19
Networks Are Fundamental to Wall Street 19
Strategic Necessity of Networks 22
Shared Network Resources 23
Business Arguments for a LAN 24
Presenting Networking 26

Chapter 2. The Current and Future Place for FDDI 29

Chapter 3. Benefits of Networking 35
Definition of a Local Area Network 35
Benefits of Establishing an Internetwork 39
Operational Benefits 40
Economic Benefits 41
Network Topologies 42
The Problems of FDDI 49

Chapter 4. Network Health Risks 51
Acute Dangers 51
Electrical Safety 51
Ladder Safety 54
Indoor Pollution 57
Exertion Risks 57
Dangers from Laser Signals 58
Dangers from Electromagnetic Pollution 58
Cellular Communications 61
Inconclusive Evidence 62
FCC Emission Ratings 63

Prudent Precautions	64
Data Corruption	65
Safety Recommendations	66
Safety Testing Tools	69

Part 2. Software and Hardware — 71

Chapter 5. FDDI Standards — 73
The FDDI Protocol	73
The Definition of FDDI	84
FDDI Variations	85
Twisted-Pair	88
FDDI Compatibility	90
Operational Comparisons	91
Network Management Protocols	92
Comparison of SNMP, CMOT, and CMIP	97
Network Economies	99

Chapter 6. FDDI Hardware — 101
Hardware	101
Optical Fiber	102
FDDI Operations	104
Controller Functionality	106
Gateway Functionality	108
FDDI Physical Channel Limitations	108

Chapter 7. FDDI Software and Process — 113
Transmission Process	113
Frame Components	114
Frame Preamble and Overhead Components	118
FDDI Protocol Control Fields	119
How FDDI Transmits	120
Supplemental FDDI Features	122
Network-Level Software	124
Network and Transport Services	125
IPX/SPX	125
Protocol Comparison	128

Chapter 8. Planning an FDDI Network — 131
Design Criteria	133
Design Subject to User Needs	134
Physical Plant Limitations	137
Power Protection	139
FDDI Compatibility	141
Network Limitations	144

FDDI Network Components	145
Inventory Necessary Components	156
Blueprint the Planned Network	156

Chapter 9. Installing an FDDI Network — 159

Planning for Installation	159
Preparing for the Physical Installation	161
Installation Tool Kit	161
Installing Optical Fiber	164
Installing Twisted-Pair Wiring	165
Unshielded Twisted-Pair	168
Checkpoint Testing	181
FDDI Addressing	182
Shake Down New Installations	182
Securing the Components	183
Blueprinting: Confirming the Design	183
Common Installation Failures	184

Chapter 10. Expanding an FDDI Network — 187

Inspire Design Simplicity	188
Speeding up LANs	189
Expanding LANs	190
The Wiring Concentrator or Hub	191
Network Repeaters	192
Multipurpose Solutions and Devices	194
Network Bridges	196
Network Routers	201
Network Gateways	202
Gateways Integrate Networks Protocols	204
Essential Connections	213
X.25	215
Frame Relay	216
ATM Cell Relay	216
ISDN	217
VSAT	217
SMDS	218
FDDI-II	219
Wireless Networks	219
Extended FDDI Network Configurations	224

Chapter 11. FDDI for Enterprise-Wide Networks — 231

Network Communication Growth	231
Enterprise-Wide Potential	235
Downsizing to LANs	236
Client/Server Computing	240
Interconnectivity and Interoperability	241

Consolidation of Information Management	248
Enterprise-Wide Linkage Products	250

Part 3. Practical FDDI Management 253

Chapter 12. Managing an FDDI Network 255

Rules of Thumb	255
Network Administration	257
Understand Network User Desires	258
Resource Allocation	259
Financial Planning	260
Resource Allocation	261
Setting Priorities	261
Assessing Budgetary Allocations	262
Licensing and Warranty Issues	263
Security	264
Environmental Problems	265
Standards	266
Wiring Mechanical Integrity	266
Maintenance and Repairs	266
Downtime	267
Crash Policy	268
Planning for Catastrophe	269
Staging Upgrades	269
Upgrade Policy	270
Locate Failure Points	271
Pilot Projects	271
Long Lead Times	271
Replacement Parts	272
FDDI Monitoring	274
Maintain a Network Profile	274
Blueprint the Network	275
Managing Change	275
The Problems of New Networks	276
Log Work Requests and Network Changes	278
Backup	282
Coordinating Network Disruptions	282
Vendor Support	284
"Squeaky Wheel" versus Problem Resolution	285
Short-Term versus Long-Term Planning	285
Easier Said than Done . . .	287
Dos and Don'ts	288

Part 4. Network Troubleshooting   289

Chapter 13. Network Monitoring Tools   291
Media Testers   291
Optical Fiber Testers   293
Network Protocol Analyzer   295
CMIP and SNMP   296
Network Tool Application   296

Chapter 14. Media Testing   299
Twisted-Pair FDDI Tools   299
Optical Fiber FDDI   302
Interpreting Results   304
Blueprinting   308

Chapter 15. Debugging with the Protocol Analyzer   311
Network Management Protocols   312
Network Management Software   313
Protocol Analysis   313
Network Information   316
Network Performance Questions   316
Heisenberg Uncertainty Principle   317
Vendor-Specific Limitations   317
The Role of Network Monitoring   318
Understanding Network Performance   318
Frame Counts   321
Statistics for Network Planning   322
Network Traffic Composition   322
Global and Node-Specific Data Collection   324
General Purpose Network Flow Information   326
Network Performance Data   328
Network Load and Traffic Simulation   333
Network Usage Assessments   333
Capture and Store   334
Snooping with the Analyzer   335

Part 5. Network Management   337

Chapter 16. Statistics for an FDDI Network   339
Network Traffic   339
FDDI Bottlenecks   342
Rate Statistics   342
Definition of Abnormal States   343
Theoretical and Obtainable Capacity   346
Token Rotational Time   347

Transmission Efficiency	350
FDDI Modeling	352
The FDDI Model	353
Conclusion	355

Chapter 17. Tuning Performance — 357

Performance Solutions	357
Network Performance and Bottlenecks	358
Network Load and Performance Monitoring	364
Network Statistical Analysis	365
Verify Configuration to FDDI Specification	365
Component Consistency	366
Network Slowdown Solutions	366
Distribute Load	366
Provide Local Resources	368
Specialty Controller Hardware	369
Optimize Station Bottlenecks	370
Provide Alternative Channels	370
Remove Bridges	371
Buffer Networks with Store-and-Forward Gateways	374
Rechannel with Additional Rings	374
Expand Conservatively	375
Tuning Performance	375
Expand Reach with Wider Area Networks	375
FDDI	376
Solve Traffic Overloading Problems	377
Tuning Recommendations	377

Chapter 18. Network Security — 379

Security Overview	379
FDDI Lacks Inherent Security	380
Threats to the Network	381
Protection Countermeasures	385
Physical Network Isolation	386
Password Protection	387
Encryption	388
External Access	389
Occasional Policy Changeovers	390
Data Encryption	391
Access Control for Network Monitoring Devices	391
Application of Monitoring Devices to Detect Intrusions	392
Vandal Detection	393
Hierarchy of Access	394
Fall-Back Countermeasures	394
Network Backup	396

Chapter 19. Backup and Redundancy — 399
Network Backup — 399
The Value of Information — 400
Media Backup — 401
What to Save — 403
Who Provides Backup Services — 404
What Media — 405
How Often and When to Back Up — 406
Where to Store — 407
Recycling Policy — 407
Value of Stored Information — 408
Verification of Backup — 408
Hardware — 409
Labor — 410
Disasters — 411
Redundancy — 414

Chapter 20. Human Factors — 415
Network Management — 416
Required Management Skills — 416
Administrative Control — 416
Record-Keeping and Inventory-Tracking Skills — 417
Technical Skills — 418
Technical Managing Skills — 418
Interpersonal Communication Skills — 419
Making Decisions — 419
Setting Priorities — 420
Working around Staff Shortages — 420
Burnout and Recognition — 421
Employee Development Skills — 421
Team Building Skills — 421
Technical Knowledge — 423
Diagnostic and Analytic Skills — 423
Interpersonal Communication Skills — 423
Hierarchy — 423
Fear of Technology — 424
Squeaky Wheel versus Problem Resolution — 424
The Effects of Change — 425
Political Feasibility — 425
Easier Said than Done... — 427

Part 6. Troubleshooting Reference — 429

Chapter 21. FDDI Troubleshooting Sequence — 431

Isolation Techniques	431
Station Hardware and Software Failures	432
Network Hardware Failures	432
Progressive Search for Hidden Component Failure	433
Isolation Techniques for Enterprise-Wide Network Failures	433
Isolation Techniques for Network Failures	435
Decreasing Likelihood Search: Station Failed	436
Decreasing Likelihood Search: Network Software Failed	436
Decreasing Likelihood Search: Network Hardware Failed	437
Progressive Search for Hidden Component Failure	438
Chapter 22. Tool Usage Reference	**439**
Functionality of Network Tools	440
Troubleshooting Sequence for Software Failures	442
Troubleshooting Sequence for Hardware Failures	444
Appendixes	451
Glossary	**453**
Additional Reading and References	**483**
Index	**487**

Preface

Data communications and networks are often promoted as a "competitive weapon" and the means to solve computer problems and lower data processing expenses. Such approaches often misfire unless the network is carefully and intelligently administered. In today's competitive environment the lack of distributed data processing and wide area communications is tantamount to failed data processing. *Fiber Distributed Data Interface* (FDDI) is a transitional or supplemental protocol, best applied to solve internetworking problems on large campuses or to meet the need for increased data transmission bandwidth to the desktop for client-server database applications and imaging applications. FDDI will rarely be the primary single-site protocol that either Ethernet or Token-Ring are today. As FDDI component costs decrease in price and as FDDI-compliant twisted-pair wiring (category 5) supplant optical fiber, FDDI may displace Ethernet and Token-Ring as the low-end local area network wiring. As such, FDDI will then meet basic data processing requirements and furnish an organization with the means to maintain parity with the competition. However, outstanding applications of FDDI technology are required to currently justify the cost and complexity of FDDI and create a sustainable competitive advantage.

This book presents the practical knowledge needed to design, build, grow, and maintain a FDDI data communications network for most vendor equipment and software, whether AMP, BT&D, Cabletron Systems, Crescendo Communications, IBM, Interphase, Microsoft, National Semiconductor, Novell, Sun Microsystems, or many others. Issues such as interconnecting networks to form metropolitan and enterprise-wide networks and successfully achieving interoperability are addressed, as are the cost and benefits achieved through host mainframe downsizing and installation of client-server networks.

FDDI Networking is designed primarily to answer questions facing a consultant, network manager, and the network team. The specifications of the Institute for Electrical and Electronics Engineers (IEEE) 802 committee, the International Standards Organization (ISO) network standard 9314, and the American National Standards Institute (ANSI) FDDI X3T9.5 steering committee are used as a base for definition of key terms because most vendors try to adhere to these standards, and because they provide a consistent and credible basis for describing FDDI protocols and the proliferating derivative nonoptical media variants. Vendor-supplied FDDI documentation is supplemented and explained, and its practical ramifications are discussed. In addition, the nuts and bolts of planning for installation and cabling, capacity planning, physical maintenance, and statistical tracking are presented for the busy network administrator. Concise and specific illustrations and descriptions prepare even the novice for all stages of network administration to clarify the ambiguous and developing vendor FDDI documentation.

This preface presents the organization of *FDDI Networking*. As an acknowledgment of the reader's limited time, Figure 1 illustrates the design and flow of the knowledge contained within this book.

Chapter 1 presents the network in light of its connective power as a strategic resource in today's competitive resource-limited environment and suggests how to make a persuasive argument for network technology.

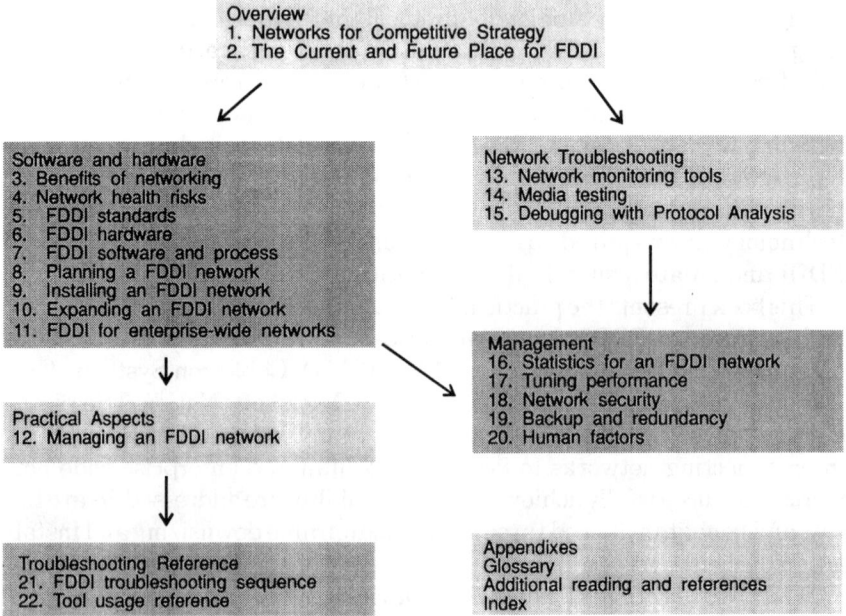

Figure 1 The organization of *FDDI Networking*

Preface

Chapter 2 speculates on the future of FDDI as a viable networking protocol for local area networking, backbone connectivity, distributed processing, and connectivity to enterprise-wide networks.

Chapter 3 discusses in overview the benefits of networking and describes what FDDI is, how it works, and the types of problems that can be encountered in a production environment.

Chapter 4 broaches health risks facing network personnel and users with copper-based twisted-pair derivative FDDI networks.

Chapter 5 presents the standard OSI networking model and the FDDI media variants. It describes standard optical cabling, voice-over data options, copper-based media variants, and other protocol enhancements.

Chapter 6 describes the hardware and the mechanical process of FDDI. The components of an FDDI network are described and illustrated to help the reader understand the ingenious simplicity of FDDI.

Chapter 7 explains the FDDI process. This includes the transmission methodology and characteristic features of network-level software.

Chapter 8 details the planning procedures for the mechanical components of FDDI networks, completing what spartan vendor instructions omit. This chapter outlines those issues that an experienced network manager considers before building or expanding an FDDI network, or interconnecting existing LANs with an FDDI backbone.

Chapter 9 explains the installation procedures for the mechanical components of FDDI networks, supplementing incomplete vendor instructions. This chapter suggests what steps an experienced network manager takes for testing and benchmarking a newly installed network.

Chapter 10 explains why bridges, gateways, and true routing stations are necessary on a large FDDI, and how these units are installed. Since organizational growth is likely to outstrip the capacity of any original network, bridges, gateways, and repeaters are also presented as solutions to overloaded networks.

Chapter 11 addresses the concept of the enterprise-wide network. Internetworking and network software issues are gaining importance. As client/server computing displaced antiquated mainframe data processing, local area networks are becoming integrated into distributed computing and enterprise-wide environments.

Chapter 12 presents practical rules of thumb and suggestions for successfully using FDDI. The formal IEEE and ISO specifications do little to explain the hows and whys of success and failure with FDDI; therefore Chapter 12 concentrates on operational management.

Chapter 13 suggests practical tools that test, monitor, and analyze network status. When the network fails there are various techniques to identify, locate, and repair problems. Some techniques require specialized tools like a twisted-pair wiring scanner or an optical time domain reflectometer, and a protocol analyzer.

Chapter 14 details the usage of a media testers and the practical steps to check the usability of network hardware, and to verify correct installation. These tools also provides a desirable method to benchmark a network.

Chapter 15 describes the necessity for network management software [such as Simple Network Management Protocol (SNMP), Common Management Information Protocol (CMIP), or CMIP over TCP/IP (CMOT)] and the network protocol analyzer and shows how to identify, locate, and isolate suspected network problems.

Chapter 16 calculates the statistics of FDDI transmission protocols. This information is useful to understand why bottlenecks and slowdowns occur and why performance becomes suboptimal even for a protocol providing 100 Mbits/s transmission rates.

Chapter 17 shows how to tune network performance. This builds upon the knowledge from the chapters on installation, configurations, network traffic, and statistics for the purpose. It also discusses optimal planning, network loads, and alternative solutions for overloaded rings. This single chapter can be invaluable when network trouble occurs, when no solutions are self-evident, and when there appear to be no options for locating network failures.

Chapter 18 discusses security issues, explains why the OSI networking model contains limited reference to either data or physical security, why FDDI provides limited security, and what precautions can be taken to protect a network from outside prying and unauthorized access. Because FDDI is a public network, packets are freely readable by any network station. As such, it is dependent on network software, specialized hardware, and judicious management procedures to maintain security.

Chapter 19 explains backup procedures and suggests what hardware, software, or operational procedures can be implemented to produce a nearly fault-tolerant network. Issues and redundancy for the important network services—files storage, printing, backup of network data as well as data and software on network clients, shutdown of failed segments—are discussed in this chapter.

Chapter 20 illustrates why trained and qualified people are an important resource for network administration. FDDI depends on people with expertise and experience. Without knowledgeable people, the network will perform below capacity, cause severe operational problems, constrain organization growth, and in extreme cases, even fail to function.

Chapter 21 summarizes the contents of this book with an FDDI tool usage manual. This chapter supplies ideas and information on when to analyze scanners, light meters, multimeters, an OTDR, and a protocol analyzer to solve network problems.

The appendixes include a glossary with data communication and FDDI terms defined and cross-referenced by the all-too-common acronyms.

Acknowledgments

FDDI Networking was made possible by the efforts of many people who provided technical information and supplied protocol specifications, reference materials, and collaborative support. I was helped by my two children, Gabriel and Sophie Esther, who sat on my lap and pressed occasional learned letters on the keyboard, and by Carol, who taught them their letters and read *their* books to them at so many other times and also provided me the wherewithall to research and write this book.

Martin Alan Wiesel Nemzow

About the Author

Martin A. Nemzow is currently executive vice president of Value-Finders, a database publishing company, and director of product deveopment for NPI. His previous books include *Ethernet Management Guide*, *The Token Ring Management Guide*, and *LAN Performance Optimization*, all published by McGraw-Hill.

Part 1
Overview

This section presents an overview of FDDI networking. Chapter 1 presents the network in light of its interconnective power as a strategic resource in today's competitive resource-limited environment and suggests how to make a persuasive argument for network technology. Chapter 2 speculates on the future of FDDI as a viable networking protocol for local area networking, distributed processing, and connectivity to enterprise-wide networks. Chapter 3 discusses in overview the benefits of networking and describes what FDDI is, how it works, the variations in FDDI protocols, and the types of problems that can be encountered in a production environment. Chapter 4 broaches health risks facing network personnel and users.

Chapter

1

Networks for Competitive Strategy

This chapter is intended to provide the sparks for new ideas so that readers can better utilize FDDI networking technology. It is also included to address and counter the threats that top management may perceive to be arising from the diffuse, complex, critical, and rapidly expanding technology of voice and data communications. This information is also provided to address threats perceived by host mainframe management colleagues who see the blurring of any distinction between mainframes and networks, local area networks (LANs), wide area network (WAN) linkages, and the private branch exchanges (PBXs). Strictly speaking, fiber distributed data interface (FDDI) is a metropolitan area network (MAN) spanning an area that could be 250 km in circumference; single links can be as long as 30 km. In addition, this chapter discusses the new emphasis upon interconnectivity and host mainframe access, workgroup tools, and data sharing issues.

Networking technology includes the simplest local area networks to those enterprise-wide endeavors that span large, multiple-site organizations. Although this book contains specific, hands-on information for managing FDDI networks, most readers doubtlessly may be deeply immersed within FDDI and already understand its potential. In general, FDDI is a LAN expansion protocol rather than an initial basic LAN topology; very few organizations will install FDDI as the first and primary protocol. It would be a considerable risk to trust a new team with a new technology when the technology is not well understood in the marketplace. A lack of network management experience and the brief track record of FDDI will tend to create a difficult enterprise.

As such, this chapter support situations in which management must be sold a specific course of action, LAN/WAN investment decisions, or technological change. This chapter is relevant when technical knowledge is insufficient to make a purely business or strategic decision; it is useful to frame equipment acquisition decisions in other terms when asking top management to sign a big check.

Networks in corporations, government organizations, and nonprofit associations no longer provide an unassailed advantage over competitors—even if used well. Local area networks (LANs) are necessary in virtually all organizational activities today. The economics of data processing (DP) are such that mainframes perform either specialized functions, process huge volumes of transactions, provide massive data repositories, or are being phased out with "downsized" client-server operations. Terminal service with minicomputers or LANs connecting personal computers (PCs) and workstations provide adequate and cost-efficient technology for all but the most specialized processing requirements. The UNIX minicomputer or engineering workstation supports large databases, client/server operations, and increasingly, specialized image processing for business, scientific, and medical research. LANs can support most DP functions. WAN linkages provide a wider geographic coverage, campus interconnectivity, and multisite cooperation and cost savings.

Today, LANs, MANs, and WANs provide mission-critical processing for daily accounts payable, accounts receivable, sales analysis, brokerage account tracking, and act as windows into distant data sources. When designed and managed properly, LANs, MANs, and WANs can be as reliable as mainframe hosts with WAN access and local terminals. Uptime without a single hardware, software, or management failure can exceed three months; backup channels, spanning trees, optical switches, and hot servers can produce an environment with nearly 100 percent uptime.

The cost and quality of standardized software for PCs and workstations has dramatically shifted the cost efficiency from singular central processing units (CPUs) to distributed computing environments. The availability of specialized database servers and "superservers" on networks has supplanted much of the traditional mainframe operations. The paradigms of the "glass house" and the "lights out computer room" for containing and maintaining the integrity and reliability of the mainframe are shifting into the client/server and networking environment. The inherent value provided by networks include the distribution of information, selected and controlled access to data, an economical means to store, share, and protect information, and also access to tools usable by people who are less than computer-literate. Thus, the computer processing technology is being pushed to the people who have the most need for it, but at the same time, this technology is also being given to those with the least computer skill and with the least available time for learning it. In other words, the technology is being simplified and disseminated in that new format.

Networks are providing the rudiments to construct the assembly lines for information manufacturing. The air drills and screwdrivers, power presses, rivet guns, and conveyer belts of this century will be paralleled by the spreadsheets, word processing, image preparation, information brokerage and arbitrage, voice generation, and groupware of the next century. Assembly lines are giving way to channels of paper flow, information attainment and serialized processing. Just as the assembly line become the concentration point for many small parts operations and the integration of those subassemblies, the data network channels are serving very much the same purpose. MANs and WANs are integrating the subnetworked LAN operations and providing a unifying cohesiveness for information. More application software, such as Lotus Notes, encourage a consistency in the organization output by enforcing quality standards and formats. Group tools improve work flow.

While LANs once may have provided a strategic advantage for an organization, distributed networks have become a virtual necessity today for many enterprises. Organizations are at a strategic *disadvantage* if they lack information networks. There is a DP cost disadvantage. There is a tool-quality disadvantage without networks. There is a steeper software development cost and higher user-training cost and less access to planning, tracking, and processing tools without networks. Corporate business nearly always requires software to meet specialized needs; the days of canned software other than utilities and generic processes is waning, although the paradigms for certain functions have been rigorously standardized. Examples include spreadsheets, word processing, and simple accounting. The information required to thrive in a globally competitive market cannot be forced into templates made of generic software. Business is based upon information and profits by making new information in a technical assembly line. The best information assembly line wins.

As such, there are still strategic advantages available through networking. These new advantages relate to cost cutting, labor reduction, information invention, informational-based arbitrage, consolidation of services, and improved operating efficiency. Specifically, downsizing DP operations and distributing resources is cost-efficient. Labor costs are reduced when paper files are optically scanned, centrally stored, always locatable for review or photocopies, and quickly available throughout an organization via networks. Electronic mail (E-mail) cuts delivery costs, provides list distribution, automated forwarding, message reply, and delivery redirection. Facsimile (FAX), voice, data, and video can be converted to analog signals for transmission on X.25, T-1 circuits, fractional T-1, E-3, T-3, or can even be packetized for delivery by frame relay and regional data services, such as ISDN, SONET, and the forthcoming cell relay ATM. Transmission can be prioritized and queued subject to available bandwidth for service cost reductions.

The complex business environment is challenging organizations to discover new ways to retain *any* competitive advantage. In addition to traditional physical and monetary assets such as equipment, buildings, and cash reserves, an organization has information and particularly networking data communications assets. Information management is better understood by most private-sector business administrators through the context of the value chain, market dynamics, distribution channel, and price points than it is through the context of computer technology, networking, management of information systems, or data processing. However, those represent information with a time value; those who can sift through them and craft good decisions survive and thrive. Production prices, delivery costs, product availability, international purchasing commitments, tariffs, local ordinances, environmental regulations, government subsidies, market opportunities, cartels and monopolistic practices all diminish opportunities for unsophisticated organizations and create new ones for the techno-elite. Size of the organization is not an issue; the quality of the competition is. Furthermore, disparities in access to information create opportunities. Consider the variations in the availability of, cost for, and access to capital by regions and economies. The ability to capture, analyze, and act upon such disparities creates opportunities in every industry, from wholesale food distribution, to consumer products, to commodity brokerage, to new product design and production, and to standardized medical procedures. When insurance carriers realize that some medical clinics or hospitals charge significantly lower rates for complicated operations while providing fewer complications and extended hospital stays, patients may be encouraged to travel to the lower-price, higher-quality provider. Similarly, when manufactured and packaged food products are cheaper in certain parts of the country when purchased in year-long commitments, we will see the continued growth of wholesale buying cooperatives to exploit those opportunities.

An organization also can leverage the creative uses of information and networking technology for strategic benefit. The aim of networking strategies is to move an organization to its potential while locking out its competitors and providing a sustainable competitive advantage which those competitors will find difficult to copy.

There is a continuum of complexity with computer and communications technology. For a small company, connecting just the inventory system with a LAN might be considered a strategic necessity, while a larger company might implement a MAN hub to link all workers at all locations for electronic mail, software disk storage consolidation, optical storage and retrieval, and shared access to corporate databases. Some might even include customers and suppliers. There is a learning curve attached to information and communications technologies. Even while the key to success is to learn faster and implement sooner than the competition, the internetworking trend is continuing. Each success raises the ante; more complex and intuitive applications of networking are required to sustain a competitive parity. The ante today is any network.

This proliferating new communications technology has redefined the marketplace because it has altered the competitive game for all organizations. Communications have become integral to most computer and business activities. Some organizations will fail to recognize the available opportunities, and others will fail to recognize how to adapt them to the new possibilities in their strategic planning. Technological changes improve the efficiency and enhance implementation of communication. Networking, in particular, is a sophisticated and deliberate strategy that can lower data processing costs, improve profits, productivity, market share, product distribution, and work environments by facilitating quick decisions, improving information flow and accuracy, and communicating such information and decisions rapidly to those who would benefit from them.

Specifically, networking provides an economy-of-scale through downsizing and distributing complex mainframe data processing operations. This push toward smaller, less expensive, and more responsive personal computers interconnected by means of an enterprise-wide network is driving the new data processing and communications paradigm. Note that LANs might be no less expensive than a mainframe solution. The transition period is in fact likely to be more expensive since both solutions must be maintained in parallel during the transition period. While it is perceived that the cost advantage is with the LANs, the real benefit is the reduced application development time and improved tools for LAN-based client-server sites. Furthermore, the problems of organizing and protecting the LAN assets may exceed host system costs.

Yet, LAN technology is inherently scalable. Therefore, on a measure for measure basis, initial costs are less, and the marginal costs for additional capacity is small. Networking also provides communal access to information and other networked resources. Additionally, networking provides a new shared access to previously unavailable corporate data in (database) views for many users. Furthermore, the technology vanguard is shifting from powerful Unix workstations to common personal computers, except for specialized imaging, drafting, and database services. The sophistication and ease-of-use for generic software means that specialized data applications are available in days rather than months or years.

If information and networking technology appear to furnish strategic solutions, this technology must be applied with foresight, forethought, and a critical understanding of the market. Clearly, the risk is not only to those who try new technology with its potential for clumsy and inefficient results; too many organizations have learned the painful consequences of limiting the reach and coverage of information exchange or overcommitting the organization to the success of a major MIS overhaul. The risk is also to those who watch and wait while others succeed first.

With the accelerating pace of change, the complexity of technology, and the increasing sophistication of those applying networking technology, there is little ascertainable difference between strategic initiative and a "hare-brained" idea; for a strategy to be effective it must be implemented correctly before the competition understands what that strategy is. Of necessity, effective strategies must precede the complete understanding of the applicable technology.

Advantages of Networks

Networks yield significant advantages that can overwhelm a nonnetworking competitor. Networking power can provide better service with fewer resources and expand the access to services beyond the local organization. Specifically, downsizing from mainframe technology to distributed personal computers is very cost-effective for many common organizational functions like bookkeeping, billing, and payroll. Data communications networking can also provide a medium in a research and development environment for cross-fertilization of ideas. This concept is presented in more detail in Chapter 11.

As particularly the case with FDDI and its large geographic coverage, networking can provide complete data access throughout an organization or speed the transfer of large data blocks. Furthermore, the possibility of priority delivery of voice and video over data in FDDI-II networks may provide a path of integration and cost consolidation in data and voice communications—if this enhancement becomes readily available.

Networking can streamline processes that are inherently slow or fragile, and automate these processes for higher integrity. While the financial planner is often severely challenged to quantify these benefits in terms acceptable to stockholders, trustees, and bankers, it has been proven that networks do generate cost-effective benefits, create significant economies of scale, boost worker productivity, and create unanticipated and imaginative results. The examples in this chapter attest to the success of networking.

Networks thus offer an applicable competitive strategy. Furthermore, as a business reaches beyond borders of states, countries, or continents, network communication is a critical component to success. The competitive parities created through networking and replacing mainframes are summarized in Figure 1.1.

It has been known for years that data processing is a viable competitive tool. Such systems have generated information that managers have applied to pare costs, simplify product design, identify excessive or expensive procedures, locate cost variances, reduce inventory, target

Networks for Competitive Strategy

- Higher worker productivity
- Integration of process and information
- Lower installation cost per device or user
- Sharing of expensive resources
- Consolidation of scarce resources
- Creation of critical channels for communications
- Increases in the speed of contact and transactions
- Global access to information
- Higher resource utilization
- R&D discovery
- Interaction between information workers
- Lower communication costs
- Globalization
- Acquisition integration and standardization

Figure 1.1 Networks provide competitive necessities.

customer preferences, and provide strategic product information required to capture a market segment. Data processing is most useful in capturing cost, inventory, pricing, and production information.

More sophisticated uses of computer networking power have been integrated directly into marketed products and services, and these products and services sell better because of that informational content. While computer-related products—hardware, software, information, published works, or research and development (R&D)—are often presented as products and services that strategically benefit from computer networking, many "unlikely" products and services benefit as well by providing wider information exchange and faster response, and by opening new areas and new sources. New examples that this book highlights include paperless transactions, manufacturing and customer tracking, price arbitrage, and replacement of legacy systems.

Networks Reduce Costs

The desktop metaphor has blossomed with the advent of MS Windows version 3.0 and version 3.1. Two major new categories of products, network fax and optical storage and retrieval (sometimes called *automated image management*), show great potential for many organizations. Network fax simplifies fascimile delivery by eliminating the printing and manual fax cycle. Network fax provides literally the ability to "print to a fax number" from a computer. Additionally, incoming fascimiles can be routed to individuals (albeit with great clumsiness given the current technology), and thus to some degree minimizing security leaks and lost faxes, while providing online copies, an automated storage facility, and optical character recognition capabilities, while eliminating curling, yellowing, and fading thermal output. Optical storage provides the ability to scan documents and store them on magnetic disks or optical drives. The LAN provides the means for a user to retrieve individual pages or entire documents. Once a document is scanned and filed, it is rarely lost. Users can review multiple copies simultaneously; rarely are folders misplaced or lost. Copies are easily printed or faxed. When documents (scanned or received as fascimiles) include important text, this text is optically scanned for character content. The text can be imported into WordPerfect, WordStar, MS Word for Windows, or any word processor or database.

DST of St. Louis created Optifile for in-house use to minimize the paper costs associated with handling mutual fund transactions. Mutual fund transactions are paper intensive, particularly when there are nearly twenty million customers. Furthermore, the SEC requires that all share purchases, conversions, custody transfers (401K and IRA), and redemptions be retained for seven years. Since customer paper files are easily misfiled, lost, retained offsite in bulk warehouse facilities, and not quickly accessible, optical storage and retrieval is extraordinarily cost-effective. Although retrieval may be slow—about twenty seconds initially for the first page, ten seconds thereafter, locating a person by cross-referenced name, address, telephone number, social security number, fund name, or employer is a boon. Locating a physical file required a platoon of file clerks. Furthermore, with optical storage, customer records are accessible not only from the processing site, but also almost instantly at any regional sales office via WAN. Data sharing and interconnectivity simplifies the supplanted manual procedure of photocopying source documents from microfiche and sending the paper by fax or express delivery.

Daily operations and labor requirements are simplified. Microfiche document copying for offsite backup is no longer needed. Manual folder creation and filing is no longer necessary. Documents are fed into a sheet feeder and coded by an operator as each document is scanned. Three people now perform the job of sixty. The benefits do not end there. Auditing is simplified since any transaction is directly supported by available evidence and documentation. Optical storage devices—not to be confused with optical storage and retrieval—provide a write-once permanent laser-burned record that meets SEC qualifications for security and permanence.

Networks Create Monopolies

TWA built the APOLLO flight reservation system, while American Airlines constructed the SABRE network. These two reservation system were integrated into the travel agent's selling cycle. They surpassed expectations because they offered precise and readily available information about flight times, seating availability on a selected flight, and

Networks for Competitive Strategy

connecting links. Once these flight reservations had widely replaced the mediocre travel agent, reinforced the knowledgeable agent, and circumvented other information channels, these systems monopolized the purchasing decisions by preventing travelers from seeing alternatives to TWA and American flights.

Cost information was filtered at the time of the presentation to the benefit of the airlines and detriment of the traveler. The reservation system bypassed alternative purchasing processes by providing time-critical information otherwise unavailable to the true decision maker, the agent, not the traveler. Figure 1.2 contrasts the functional simplicity of the flight reservation system with more complicated preprinted and quickly outdated flight schedules.

Competitors have not been idle in the ten years of SABRE operation. Two examples are presented here. Certified Vacations, which assembles packaged tours from unfilled transportation seats, vacant accommodations, and empty cruise cabins, also seeks to improve upon its data processing capabilities. Just as DST shifted to client-server processing, Certified Vacations is installing PCs to access new host-based database servers and provide simultaneous online information for many different categories of services (that is, airline flights, cruise cabins, hotel rooms, tours, and local services). The impetus is not to reduce costs. Rather, there is a lack of parts for aging traditional (or *legacy*) mainframes.

Furthermore, these systems can not provide the desired graphic user interface, the application development tool kits, the simultaneous access and automated updates of information desired. The impetus is to pro-

Preprinted Flight Schedule	Online Reservation System
Determine source and destination	
Locate flight options	Query terminal for
Direct flights	Flight times
Indirect flights	Seating
Connecting flights	Lowest fair or most commission
Competitor's connecting flights	Flight plan
	Check frequent flier bonuses
Repeat for each airline	
Determine seating availability	
Determine pricing (many options)	
Check alternatives	
Select option	Select option
Confirm with airline	Confirm with airline

Figure 1.2 Flight reservation purchasing process.

vide more and better information to the telemarketing sales representatives in order to either provide a less expensive vacation package, *upsell* the customer and provide a more luxurious vacation, or capture last-minute vacancies and opportunities otherwise lost with adequate information systems.

Similarly, a cruise company called Carnival Cruise Lines is seeking to bypass this network for its niche market. The cruise company is building its own system to track customers, provide point-to-point plane reservations, hotel accommodations, and track the actual cruise itself. The company seeks to optimize its revenue, share of the market, and control over the quality of its packaged vacations.

Networks Optimize Data Flow

American Airlines has not been idle to apply local area network technology either. Industry deregulation has lead to fare wars, the failure of significant competitors, and a relative realignment of the key players in that industry. Increased and unstable fuel costs (due to embargoes, oil price fixing, and war) have focused management attention on minimizing the significant operation costs. This includes jet fuel. Additionally, suboptimal airline downtime for maintenance increases effective cost per passenger mile while poor routing of planes idles planes where there are no passengers.

American Airline's System Operations Control at Fort Worth, Texas has installed an FDDI network of Sun database servers and remote processors and Apple Macintosh computers for clients. Data entry and data collection are stored on this network and communicated by X.25 wide area communications lines to IBM mainframes in Tulsa, Oklahoma. The data is also available in Fort Worth from Tulsa for detailed routing and statistical analysis. Time and money is saved by utilizing less costly and more intelligent data entry front ends.

Data entry errors are minimized (so that planes are not misplaced and mistakenly taken out of service) through the use of easier-to-implement data validation techniques found in generic low-end PC software. A data error could idle a misplaced or overlooked plane or schedule it for an expensive and unnecessary overhaul. A single bit error literally could cost four million dollars as maintenance records are digitized. Additionally, flight plan information is automatically radioed to local offices of the Federal Aviation Administration (FAA), which requires explicit flight plans before any commercial plane can leave the ground.

Such improvements are only the initial part to larger monetary gains. The availability and accessibility of data increases the airplane availability by 20 percent. With no increase in the number of airplanes in the fleet, this yields a dramatic boost to return on investment. The efficiency and utilization of these substantial assets were dramatically increased

Networks for Competitive Strategy 13

at minimal cost. Such benefits mean that the airline can lower airfare costs and challenge the competition on ticket price or reap a larger profit, either of which is a significant business advantage.

This same position, flight path, and maintenance data can be applied to minimize labor needs and optimize flight plans to account for anticipated weather patterns, jet streams, and air density at different altitudes. Routing optimization of planes, a rehash of the old "traveling salesman" problem, can add to fleet efficiency. This optimization translates into more opportunity to stress the competition. Figure 1.3 illustrates how Sun host-based FDDI network increases return on investment.

More to the point, FDDI can optimize data flow. Consider the example of Jackson Memorial Hospital in Miami. Not only does FDDI provide a campus-wide enterprise network for E-mail and messaging, coordinated patient accounting, it also makes it technically possible to apply computerized imaging and enhancement technology. Electronic medical imaging solves a few processing problems impossible without the bandwidth of FDDI. First, imaging processing is faster electronically since display on an electronic monitor bypasses the time and expense of processing silver-based film. Second, electronic storage and retrieval of images produces economies and virtual access similar to the scanning and storage of paper documents. Third, delivery costs and access times are reduced; a physician can review the scan in the operating room, recall scans from patients with similar problems, or ask a colleague in a different building to review the scan while they talk by phone. Fourth, marginal images can be enhanced for better visualization, while three-dimensional scans can be reconstructed with surgical incision paths in mind.

Computer-based imaging for medical purposes is not as simple as image storage and retrieval. The FDA has yet to approve image compression for medical scans. The reasoning is that since many data compression methods are not "lossless," the danger to the patient from misdiagnoses based upon missing image information must be prevented until it can be adequately addressed. As result, a CAT or PET scan can easily create several 50 Mbyte images (in 24 bit color or grayscale) that will *nominally* require 6 full seconds each of FDDI bandwidth to transmit (and probably 18 seconds to get from hard disk, or 14 minutes from an

- Data flow optimization
- Better development tools
- Faster prototyping
- Distributed access to information
- Disseminated expertise
- Support for organization growth
- Scalable architecture
- Support for high-bandwidth applications (i.e., imaging)

Figure 1.3 Benefits provided with client/server and FDDI networking.

optical platter). While prohibitive on Ethernet (27 *minutes*) or Token-Ring (35 *minutes*), transmitting these images becomes possible with FDDI.

Sun Microsystems also has applied FDDI technology to secure the fuure of its downsizing activities throughout the organization. Initially, the microcomputer-based workstation manufacturer used a minicomputer for internal accounting, budgeting, order entry, job tracking, and customer activities. Standard PCs proliferated throughout the financial support organization for budgeting in Lotus 1-2-3, Visicalc, Supercalc, and other similar spreadsheet software. Distribution of budgets in the many diverse formats were accomplished by paper and sneakernets. Financial controls were similar to any low-tech manufacturing organization, despite the high-tech nature of this fast-growing company.

When sales reached the $400 M stage, order backlog had reached 4 to 6 months. Furthermore, the budgeting and tracking process had become unwieldy and unmanageable. The management decision to resolve this crisis was to install four mainframe computers running packaged accounting software. The alternatives in 1988 were few; this represented the best possibility for sustaining the growth of the company.

However, within two years, the capacity of these top-end mainframes had been reached. The continued use of the sneakernet for tracking and budgeting and the inability to support more than 80 users on the mainframes at any time demanded a new solution. Larger mainframes and more of them promised only more fragmented financial databases and an uncertain data flow through the organization. The technology in part developed by Sun and vendors providing Sun-based software technology provided a better alternative.

Networking, client/server processing, distributed databases, and powerful microcomputer-based hosts (of course, finally Sun equipment) provided the necessary infrastructure to develop an integrated accounting, ordering, manufacturing, customer support, and information services throughout the organization. This changeover represents the vanguard for client/server downsizing. After two years into the project and approaching 90 percent completion, it represents a financial success in that most of the original objectives have been achieved, but also it is a public relations achievement as well in that Sun can demonstrate that their technology is successful, efficient, and cost-effective for downsizing.

The question now is how does this relate to FDDI. Basically, the Sun campus and the network traffic load required a backbone with more bandwidth and peak capacity than the existing Ethernet or Token-Ring networks could provide. Subnetting, gateways, routers, and store-and-forward could no longer effectively link the local organizations. FDDI was installed as the only feasible linkage. ISDN was employed where available for digital connections to remote sites. VSAT, T-1, frame relay, X.25, and other protocols augment the ISDN. The integration of nearly

120,000 people is almost complete. Mail, financial data, and access to information and knowledge bases is available throughout Sun Microsystems, both domestically and internationally.

Furthermore, new client/server applications, such as online human relations functions and employee retirement account management are being prototyped and tested throughout the organization as a means to disseminate information, provide a high level of expertise, and simplify many complex processes. The infrastructure provided by the client/server, distributed database technology, and networking environment provides a testbed for new solutions and better tools for prototyping, a means for implementing a solution faster than available in other MIS environments.

Networks Focus Distribution Channels

Hospital Supply Corporation of America (HSC) supplied hospitals with free video display terminals and connections to its headquarters. Not only were the connections mechanical, but also administrative. This computer link-up provided hospitals with information on both hospital and HSC inventory levels, product prices, alternative products, and an instantaneous ordering process with known delivery times. Hospitals were able to reduce in-house inventory, pare costs, and uniformly locate better products at better prices.

HSC planned its own inventory levels with more efficiency and analyzed what hospitals needed and when, thus offering automatic deliveries of basic commodities. Competitors of HSC who tried to install terminals for their inventory lines found desktop space lacking, users unwilling to learn a new computer ordering system, and hospital administrations unwilling to cover training costs for small improvements offered by HSC competitors. Once the ordering system was installed and proven successful, competitors lacked a sufficient infrastructure to compete.

When these systems were integrated into the daily workings of the hospitals and buying economies were passed along to them, then HSC raised prices and substituted higher priced products for commodity items. This yielded a stunning price advantage for HSC, an advantage that is both legal and sustainable. The influence of the computer purchasing systems in the buying process is presented in Figure 1.4.

In similar ways, organizations can link vendors, suppliers, and even customers into communications networks. Information Data Exchange (IDE) is inevitably replacing paper transactions. High delivery costs, the increasing expense of forms and subsequent paper handling and storage costs, and the errors introduced through transcription of customer purchase order numbers and ordering information only encourages more organizations to consider more efficient alternatives. This represents the installation of online network systems such as HSC's, or direct transfer of

- Automate inventory
- Determine product shortages
- Locate new and/or improved products
- Search for lowest price
- Locate sufficient quantity to complete order
- Order
- Backorder
- Expedite emergency shipments
- Arrange delivery
- Bill
- Return

Figure 1.4 The influence of computerized purchasing.

electronic data in compatible and standardized formats. The vital need for interchangeable formats initiated the concept of IDE.

Networks Improve Information Flow

Fedders, Incorporated, which supplies environmental cooling and heating systems for large commercial and industrial buildings, gave large customers personal computers with software. Architects and building engineers use this software to configure the cooling and heating needs for a planned building. The building engineer transmits this information to Fedders offices for processing, and naturally, the results specify selected Fedders components. Not only are the architects hard-pressed to gather similar specifications from competitors, but Fedders gains early knowledge of building plans. As a result, Fedders vigorously sells components to the contractors before the competition even knows about the proposed building and promotes architectural specification of Fedders equipment at the design stage.

Competitors of Fedders, like competitors of HSC, find themselves locked out of similar strategies because of the reluctance of architects to learn and simultaneously use a second though not necessarily superior computer product. Figure 1.5 positions this critical influence of a computer on the architect's decision-making cycle.

Networks Add Value to Products

Cosmetic companies are using computers to learn about potential customers from a data entry questionnaire process at department store counters. The questionnaire seeks such information as skin color and tone, skin dryness, skin problems, specific cosmetic color preferences, clothes style preference, and lifestyle. An "expert system," a computer program that simulates the skills of an expert cosmetologist, generates a report containing details about, and categorizing problems facing, the

Networks for Competitive Strategy

- Accept plan
- Design building per architect's concept
- Configure cooling and heating systems
- Determine equipment components and prices
- Search for lowest price
- Accept configuration and/or redesign
- Verify quantities and performance by vendor
- Select vendor
- Arrange delivery

Figure 1.5 Computers influence the architectural design cycle.

customer. A salesperson can use this focused and personalized information to make a good sale and suggest specific products for the customer.

Often the report contains specific instructions for the customer on product usage. This report sells products more successfully than other methods because the products are bundled into proper combinations and proper quantities. Not incidentally, the sales ticket is often higher. After a successful sale, customer data are sent to headquarters, and customers are contacted periodically by phone or mail, or in person, solicited for reorders, plied with new products that may appeal to them, and tracked for all future purchases. Figure 1.6 demonstrates how an integrated sales system augments the initial buying process, and later the remarketing programs.

Bulletin Boards Shift Purchasing Decisions

Online bulletin boards like the IBM and Sears joint venture, called Prodigy, or older versions including The Source and CompuServe, are dial-in computer services. This replicates for consumers what HSC did for hospitals. These bulletin boards services (BBSs) provide exchange of information in specialized forums, games, current news and weather, and

- Determine customer preferences stated subconscious
- Determine customer requirements
- Determine customer criteria for satisfaction
- Determine price ranges for sales ticket
- Determine customer impulse buying habits
- Generate a qualified lead
- Increase average sales ticket
- Information data exchange (IDE) decrease transaction costs
- Customers receive faster response
- Suppliers implement just-in-time (JIT) deliveries
- Inventory storage costs are reduced
- Inventory obsolescence and wastage are minimized

Figure 1.6 Integrated computer systems improve sales procedures.

consumer buying services. While the concept of the community bulletin board is alive and well primarily in order to list used and unneeded items for sale, it also advertises services, airline tickets, catalog sales, cars, and even homes.

These listings supplement the usual channels for goods and services advertising. TV, newspapers, magazines, and radio advertising encroaches on everyday life. This online service presents the image that the consumer can pick and choose what advertising to see; it is not an unwanted bombardment. This advertising medium is perhaps more insidious than that. Just as the Home Shopping Club suggests to TV viewers that an item is unique, limited in quantity, or at a bargain price, and also makes it very easy to make a purchase painlessly by credit card, these online services simplify the process and monopolize the consumer's time. The online service maintains up-to-date credit card information; press a few keys and a purchase is made. Delivery is by U.S. Postal Service, United Parcel Service, or overnight Federal Express.

The time online must displace something else. This includes TV time, listening to the radio, or reading periodicals. The user is shifting where advertising is gathered and analyzed. The potential for locating the lowest prices should be available on these huge consumer product databases. Instead, the strategic advantage for the merchandisers is higher or parity pricing. The merchandisers take from local retailers. This is a very significant advantage.

Figure 1.7 lists the business advantages of online marketing as provided through wide area networks. Because these services are on computers, advertising viewing preferences and actual purchase information can be explicitly tracked. While it is not clear to date whether these online services sell credit card sales information, they have yet to intelligently target online consumers with personalized sales pitches. Just as HSC could establish automatic deliveries and promote good deals for their customers, these online services do have the potential to send online electronic mail (or have merchandisers send mail) containing focused sales pitches.

- Online advertisement displaces other media
- Pricing need not be competitive
- Novelty increases sales
- Purchase and delivery is convenient
- Potential to track individual consumer preferences
- Potential ability for targeted marketing
- Online sales displaces local or other catalog sales

Figure 1.7 The benefits of online marketing.

Information Distribution Supplants Processing

All these computer-aided product sales are billed as "data processing" coups. The technology of the times has extended from corporate support services to front-line product enhancement. Additionally, process information converts the product marketing cycle into a value added at the time of sale. While, in fact, these computer information systems do apply data processing operations, a key component of their success is dependency upon data transmission networks.

The flight reservation systems coordinate global information over wide area telecommunication networks. The flight operations network lowers operating costs and provides significant economic return with local networks and enterprise-wide access. The hospital supply ordering system relies upon leased lines to connect hospitals with corporate computers. Both the air conditioning and cosmetic supplier initially used mail delivery of superior customer-supplied information to corporate headquarters for analysis and eventual targeted marketing. The air conditioning and cosmetic suppliers have since integrated on-site data collection with corporate in-house data processing. The online merchandising systems use technology to simplify the purchase and delivery of a product and have extraordinary potential for targeted marketing. In all phases of these processes, a network provides data transmission.

The information that made these results feasible was always available but difficult to accumulate in accurate or useful formats. Data processing made data collection possible, and networks made the information readily and easily available; this becomes the strategic necessity. Information that is readily gathered within a focused and familiar content with a clearly identified benefit to the end users (consumers) is apt to be more accurate than any information gathered from shopping mall or telephone surveys. Data can be delivered, without filtering, directly to the people who process such information and distributed to those who implement products or services.

Networks Are Fundamental to Wall Street

Financiers value information highly. Stock prices represent a forecast view of the future; they are information. Therefore, effectively, financiers buy and sell information. Not only does information have extraordinary value in terms of identifying takeover targets and estimating the purchase price range for an entire company, or a portion of its capital stock, but also information has become an important commodity in its own right. As a consequence, financiers are becoming more familiar with the data processing methodology and networking since better information is their strategic necessity.

Information processing and distribution systems provide the data with which the Wall Street brokers and bankers price stocks, anticipate the financial health of a company, and assign value to a company for the purpose of making loans. As price-arbitrage becomes a more readily accepted method to outperform the market, brokers and bankers want faster systems, more data, and better integration of the information processing and distribution channels. They need networks to survive.

As an example, the New York Stock Exchange (NYSE) processes during peak days over 300 million shares representing 500,000 individual transactions. The buying and selling of stock takes place at kiosks within the pit area of the exchange. Increasingly, exchanges are made in block transactions. These transactions are negotiated between buyer and seller in other buildings, in other cities, and need to be "posted" on the NYSE to provide the transaction price data for other buyers and sellers. A device called the *Universal Floor Device Controller* (UFDC) routes the data all over the the stock exchange floor, and exports it to ticker-tape machines and information brokers. The UFDC is a network of data entry points, displays, and printers that provides sales confirmations—it automates the outdated brokerage system first introduced in the cattle mercantile exchanges of Chicago in the 1880s. See Figure 1.8.

On October 19, 1987, when the market fell 508 points, the transaction volume exceeded the planned peak by 250 million shares. Some of the panic that day, and on subsequent days, can be directly attributed to delays in the processing and distribution of information. Because there were delays in communicating verbal information in the usual way, by telephone, brokerage firms found it difficult to predict stock prices and execute orders. Because trades failed to occur as rapidly as expected the price information was delayed.

Because trade confirmations were delayed or lost as the price dropped, brokers and consumers feared further price decreases and tried to sell more stock. This cycle deepened the panic; it was alleviated when the NYSE management halted trading early each day for 2 weeks to unburden the data processing facilities before the system could become undermined beyond recovery. The "system" refers not only to the data

- List buy and sell orders
- Announce transaction prices
- Print transaction confirmations
- Calculate transaction volumes
- Announce bid and ask prices
- Segregate odd lots
- Transmit confirmations to brokerage houses
- Transmit all information to distribution channels
- Disseminate corporate news and rumors

Figure 1.8 The functions of the Wall Street networks.

processing facilities but also the larger economic system already affected by the reduced valuation in public corporations. The stock transaction network was saturated with trades, and the solution was to reduce transmission volume and off-load the transactions to hours when the exchange was closed.

Various commissions have since determined that computer trading and its associated networks were a fundamental cause in the market panic; Wall Street now accepts the fundamental importance of data processing and these data transaction networks which bind together the financial fabric. Telephone networks cannot handle the information efficiently or accurately, and confirmation on paper has become a bottleneck as well; computer trading, trade processing, and distribution of transaction prices is now critically dependent on data networks. Not only was the telephone as a transaction medium effectively made obsolete in October 1987, but also the importance of the network was firmly and irrevocably established as the telephone's successor.

It is also worthwhile to note that the speed and complexity of financial transactions allowed many brokerage houses and corrupt workers to reap enormous gains by parking stock in computerized accounts. Others took advantage of trade delays and inside information masked in layers of computer systems, computerized paper trails, minor technical opportunities, and glitches in the flow of networked information to cheat. Although networks provide significant opportunity for legitimate economic gains, the leading edge of any technology also provides the knowledgeable insiders with an illegitimate opportunity for fraud.

Thus, the dark side of networking technology exists, too. Private or privileged information is more widely available and dispersed. Although security has always been a concern in the data processing (DP) community, downsizing DP operations, distributed processing with client-server networks, enterprise-wide networks, and global networks remove the limiting walls of physical security. Networks remove boundaries. While this is of extraordinary significance because it creates economic benefits, it also constitutes a new risk.

Another sign that the financial community is aware of the value of networks is illustrated by an example of a recent takeover. Scandia Airlines (SAS) decided to acquire British Caledonia (BC). The usual first step in a takeover attempt is for the acquiring company to purchase a large block of stock in the target company. This stock represents the power to change the board of directors and make new policy for the target company. In this example, SAS orchestrated a preemptive strike and hired many key British Caledonia DP managers and computer programmers prior to purchasing any of BC's stock.

Perhaps, even more interesting as the financial service sector consolidation continues, many DP operations are no longer necessary. The acquired "lights out" and sterile automated shops are closed, their workload acquired and processed by the new parent company. Mainframes are disappearing, downsized and replaced by LANs and wide area linkages. Any local networks can be folded into the new corporate structure. The cost advantage is with the LANs.

As the APOLLO and SABRE networks demonstrate, information and networking are the key control, management, and marketing tools in today's information-based economy. SAS manipulated the outcome of this takeover because BC was stripped of vital value; other companies which had sought to acquire BC clearly saw that BC was severely weakened by the loss of the DP department. In some ways, this maneuver was the ultimate "poison pill," although perpetrated by the aggressor in this case. Future takeover targets might consider the desire of selling a DP department to thwart acquisition.

Ultimately, whether these aggressive tactics are legal and acceptable will be determined by judges and legislators. In the interim, other corporate acquisitions will start with a purchase of corporate information, and the acquisition of the information department and the networks that distribute corporate information.

Strategic Necessity of Networks

FDDI is strategically necessary. There are economic advantages to FDDI, as well as process and informational improvements. More difficult to justify as advantages are interconnection, intercommunication, and project-worker interrelationship. Figure 1.9 outlines the necessity of FDDI networking.

The economic arguments are straightforward. FDDI is a low cost installation, less expensive than a PBX cell relay system (such as *automated transfer mode,* or ATM) utilizing switching networks and modems, that encourages sharing of expensive resources and constructs a critical communications channel. Furthermore, data storage and printing services can be consolidated; data storage is usually cheaper in bulk units, and printing services are usually sporadic so that one printing unit can usually provide adequate service for many users. Peripheral devices, specialized processors, and other services can be

- Integration of process
- Information
- Interconnection
- Intercommunication
- Interrelationship
- Influence (in the organization through access to data)

Figure 1.9 The strategic advantages of FDDI.

Networks for Competitive Strategy

shared enterprise-wide with ease of access to yield higher utilization rates and similar shared economies.

Networking provides a recognized cost minimization integrating disparate steps into a continuous cycle. This process improvement is often observed in automated production and manufacturing environments. It is also an advantage where information is gathered, processed, stored, and sold. Networks integrate software design processes, accounts processing, and computer-aided design (CAD) into computer-aided manufacturing (CAM). Electronic and desktop computer-aided publishing (CAP) gathers text and graphic components together in a single place—the computer—and integrates an awkward, time-consuming, and time-constrained process into a streamlined cycle.

A strategic network advantage includes the networked access to optical storage and retrieval systems that lessen the storage cost and access times while providing more effective use of the information. Memory-intensive multimedia, which is the inclusion of sound and video information within an application, sees improved performance and utility when it is networked. This streamlining of design, accounting, production, manufacturing, quality assurance, and ultimately the marketing process amplifies labor to increase worker productivity. Figure 1.10 shows production cycle steps, typically time-consuming, that are streamlined by networking.

Shared Network Resources

Shared resources is a catch-all phrase that means everybody accesses all the equipment, a concept usually perceived from the resource-rich viewpoint. However, the reverse is also true. A resource not purchased

- Plan
- Determine data collection requirements
- Collect data
- Filter and correct data
- Process data
- Generate reports
- Analyze
- Make decisions
- Produce results, develop information products
- Assure quality
- Market
- Sell
- Package and direct for shipment
- Deliver
- Bill
- Analyze the financial results
- Online help and expert systems

Figure 1.10 The steps streamlined by FDDI internetwork integration.

because it is too expensive, too specialized, or marginally utilized by a single person or group may be highly desirable when viewed as a global network resource. A marginal resource on a network can be used to capacity, rather than remaining idle and wasted. Processes and methods not otherwise attempted can be tried and perfected because these resources are accessible.

Shared information has value in three ways. The first of these is that information otherwise duplicated is consolidated for data collection, storage, and processing. Data are inherently inaccurate, but single sources of information tend to be more accurate than succeeding information. As data are duplicated, so are their inherent errors multiplied by the number of copies distributed and modified by the processing operations as errors that become second, third, or more generations removed from the original errors. EDI minimizes distribution errors. The second value of shared information is that information otherwise difficult to gather becomes readily available for planning, processing, analyzing, and decision-making. It might not otherwise be generated, but because it is available, it can be applied. Two people sharing information may uncover novel possibilities when they chance to meet and discuss their different views of the shared data. The value of users all sharing the same version (and release) of a spreadsheet program is that the information retains a shared and accessible format. The third of the ways that shared information is strategically important concerns its value in innovation, accidental discovery, and incidental research and development.

Business Arguments for a LAN

Data communications is an organizational Tower of Babel. The challenge, as senior-level personnel perceive it, is to regain control of data processing, desktop computing, and networking without exceeding already tight bud-gets. The goals of the network manager and the administration team are to maintain the network, resolve any complaints from the user community, keep pace with the ever-changing technology, and enjoy their work. Since senior management increasingly questions the productivity gains from information technology, a convincing case is necessary.

FDDI networks with multiprotocol routers can create order from chaos, as Figure 1.11 shows. LANs clearly interconnect a diverse array of machines, including personal computers, terminals, mainframes and minicomputers, CAD/CAM and CAP equipment, and specialized peripheral devices. A local area network coalesces the information and processing systems into a coherent environment with minimum duplication of resources; therefore, networks enable better management of resources. Additionally, a network streamlines connections, thus making separate or duplicate wiring systems unnecessary; creates new electronic mail pathways

Networks for Competitive Strategy

- Interconnection
- Integration
- Automation
- Control
- Economy
- Utility
- Stability
- Strategic value
- Supplemental values (voice and video channels)
- Resource sharing
- Flexibility
- More efficient communications
- Shared access to information

Figure 1.11 The business case for FDDI MANs and WANs.

for interpersonal communication that are faster, efficient, and egalitarian; and also readily constructs an infrastructure for integration.

A network aids in process control, resource allocation decisions, daily maintenance and operations, accessibility and monitoring workloads, faster results, and reduction of unwarranted activities. Control is centralized under one network manager or *information officer* in the newest terminology. The simplicity of network wiring saves on personnel moves and new equipment installation. Because many resources can be shared, a network is economical and utilitarian.

When resources are shared, data processing is independent of location, and machines and information become interchangeable for stability; most fault-tolerant systems rely upon networking technology. Any node station could, if necessary, provide access to information anywhere on the network. This flexibility is part of the attraction of networking technology. Valuable information can be duplicated.

These shared benefits and strategic values are nebulous. They are more difficult to quantify with hard financial evidence than they are to qualify with words and examples. Some of these reasons, like data accuracy and integrity, can be economically determined and become the logical arguments for justifying network costs, while an argument for a network based on accidental discovery and possible innovation is often emotional and instinctual. How does one prove that a worthwhile invention, a future finding, some as yet unknown data discovery, will recoup all network expenses? How does one justify the value of telephone systems and "networks" of contacts, or the value of friendships?

Networks can never be fully justified, nor proven to be a complete solution. Incidental benefits may provide adequate reasons for new peripheral devices and networks in a research and development organization, a think tank, or a university setting. However, budgetary constraints create pressure for careful selection of such projects as a network installation. As a consequence, the cross-fertilizing power is an argument stated as an aside, and carefully skirted thereafter. This benefit is too intangible to justify with economic arguments.

Whenever you are considering new network projects, communicate the idea to superiors, subordinates, and peers throughout the organization. This has the benefit of letting others plug into your idea and plan to accommodate it or benefit from it. You find yourself with new allies (or, unfortunately, new enemies). Not only does a network project have an effect on other groups—for example, it could require significant floor space for new file servers—it could also fulfill and solve their needs as well. Networks often provide and promote synergy. Frankly, one network is cheaper than two, and better advance planning can reduce internetworking costs when that becomes necessary.

Presenting Networking

The reasons listed in Figure 1.11 are a good starting point for framing a convincing economic argument to top management. The key function of a manager is communications. A network's key function is to promote communications. A presentation coordinating these two—the problem and the solution—is an appropriate strategy to win acceptance of a new (or expanded) network. Networking transforms the way an organization does its job by improving the quality and effectiveness of marginal communications. In those cases where such a proposition may frighten upper-level management, the analysis is best replaced by economic approaches.

For example, suggest that it is better to be the "bankrupter" than the "bankruptee." Successful exploitation requires creative management, thus aggressive leadership from the top of the organization. Therefore, the leaders must accept the plan and promote it. Shift the burden of the decision-making. As stated in later chapters, consensus rather than the lone-wolf attack is a powerful tool for accomplishing goals. A straightforward economic argument is also applicable.

Talk costs, not technology. Technology is often perceived as a solution in search of a problem. Instead, present clearly the financial expenses to be incurred, the initial investment outlay, reliability, service, and cost containment. Demonstrate that networking provides cost-effective efficiency. Present the risks of the operations involved, the risks of failure. Present the vendors, their equipment, why their equipment is the most cost-effective solution. Since FDDI is a generic and widely supported networking standard, explain why FDDI does not tie the networking technology to a specific vendor, or to a volatile industry. Extrapolate what transformations are required, what impact the network will have on the people of the organization.

Talk benefits, not technology. Present the savings to be accrued with the networking technology. Indicate the benefits, whether soft or hard.

Networks for Competitive Strategy

Explain where the organization will gain short term and long. Make clear the risk of not maintaining competitive information and communication technology, as well as the need for a strong posture in the marketplace. Figure 1.12 contrasts the costs and benefits of installing a new technology.

It is insufficient to tally up the numbers for the business managers who sign the checks. Blue-sky intangibles do not carry much weight when money can be spent on something else. Check signers want sophisticated cost-benefit analysis. Demonstrate the short-term return on investment (ROI). Calculate the net present value of the network over time. Show how downsizing DP operations by replacing the host mainframe and 200 terminals with three file servers, 250 PCs, plus the network interface cards and cables will actually generate money in the present year. Show how the return on the networking project exceeds the organization's cost of capital.

Contrast the costs and the benefits. The standard methodology is to outline a cost-benefit relationship. Quantify both costs and benefits within the same framework, usually economic, and make a direct comparison. Ascribing a monetary value in current dollars (all present and future income and expenses relating to a project, a present value formulation) is also an effective method to justify a network. However, many benefits are financially intangible. Justify one absolute improvement and explain the additional "free" resources acquired as well. This strengthens the argument because the tenuous benefits are not erroneously subjected to the same stringent analysis as that of the basic design solutions.

Management acceptance for a networking project is not complete despite an approved budget and the proper go-ahead. Acceptance is always contingent; it could be revoked at any time and the project

Costs	Benefits
Financial	Financial
Risk of failure	Cost savings
Downtime	Flexibility
Human disruption	Strategic gains
Time	Reliability
Change	Efficiency
Security	Control
	Support
	Enterprise connectivity
	Better communications

Figure 1.12 The costs and benefits for FDDI networking.

canceled. While you might have convinced management that the project is critical to the long-term strategic success of the organization, tenure can be a short-term event. Carte blanche funding does not mean nor imply carte blanche development. Be receptive. Bewildered people may marvel at the idea, agree with the concept, and provide just enough leeway for you to construct an incomplete and nonfunctioning network. Understand that new technology frightens, more so when it appears to be a black art. Recognize that strategic networking projects that are too complex for users to understand and utilize will fail.

Avoid projects that cannot be demonstrated in short-term, discrete steps. Implement in small steps. For example, install E-mail. Interconnect diverse and campus networks with FDDI and multiprotocol hubs. Do not forget to train the users and respond to their complaints. Add more networks. Lastly, interlink the many networks that are required for the enterprise-wide finale. Each step represents a discrete success than can be evaluated for its own merits. Realize that projects must be justified as viable at all times. Progress reports and demonstrations maintain credibility, an important aspect in showing that the networking concept remains sound, viable, desirable, and beneficial.

Most strategic advantages are soft and intangible until someone bushwhacks the way. The path is murky, uneven, dangerous, anxious for those at the cutting edge. This is why there is little ascertainable difference between strategic initiative and a "hare-brained" idea. It has been said that for a strategy to be effective it must be implemented correctly before the competition even begins to understand what that strategy is and how the technology can be applied.

When the jungle path is clear—if the explorers have been successful—the results may already have been achieved, thus frustrating the hopes of those who follow in safety. Innovation is risky, benefits and opportunities shadowy except to the visionary few. The strategic advantages provided by networks inhabit this same jungle world. The dangers are clearly seen, the simple economic benefits are quantifiable and justifiable, whereas the more intangible aims—securing a market niche, accessing critical information before a competitor, automating production processes, simplifying the purchasing process for a customer, and capturing that customer's business—are available only for those willing to risk innovation. The alternative is a weak parity with your competitors. It is a floating crap game with rules tempered by experience, changing costs, performance, and technological breakthroughs. Seize the opportunity on your own terms rather than being driven to it by others' successes and pressures.

Chapter

2

The Current and Future Place for FDDI

This chapter is included here merely to help network administrators, MIS directors, and other managers make sound arguments for specifying a particular network architecture, selecting a hardware and software vendor, and FDDI. All too often, choices are second-guessed and vociferously questioned after the fact. It is important to know how to justify and quantify local area networks benefits and expenses.

Once, FDDI was viewed as the only next generation of local area networking in the mid-1980s. The limitations of the popular Ethernet and Token-Ring protocols in terms of contention, transmission speed, coverage area, security, and reliability demanded a next-generation product. During that time, it became obvious that increases in microcomputer processing power and the demands of computer-aided design and imaging required a networking protocol with an order of magnitude increase in power. However, today the power of desktop networked machines is at least several orders of magnitude faster than the seminal IBM PC AT. As a result, FDDI may not be fast enough as a long-term strategy; yet, it is the *only* viable standardized fast protocol available in the marketplace for local and campus-based networks. Additionally, to place FDDI in context, this protocol was viewed as a standardized communication technology that could help bridge the hodge-podge of operating systems, network software, and communication protocols.

Instead, FDDI is not the monolithic standard originally envisioned. There are now FDDI and FDDI-II variants. FDDI-II, which is the newer protocol, promises to support priorities for integration of data, voice, and full-motion video. Where FDDI is used as an internetworking connection, two major transitional technologies exist, namely packet encapsulation and protocol translation. Furthermore, the expected operational and performance benefits provided by optical fiber are under attack by the lower cost and more flexible FDDI protocols on copper-based twisted-pair solutions. With FDDI protocols on copper leading the way, other vendors are looking to provide the same 100 Mbits/s with existing protocols and current wiring plants. The costs for replacing software, drivers, network attachment units, and cabling are extraordinary for many networks; there are so many entrenched Ethernet and Token-Ring sites. Alternatives, such as FastNet (100 Mbits/s Ethernet, 802.3GV) are also promised as transitional products with performance equivalent to FDDI.

Yet, such alternatives are dwarfed by other developing data protocols. For example, asynchronous transfer mode (ATM) is envisioned as a PBX-type service. This protocol will offer cell relay transfer of data with speeds up to 4 Gbits/s for LAN, MAN, and WAN connections. Connection may be as simple as a RJ-11 phone-type connector. Just as the differences between ARCNet, Ethernet, and Token-Ring have been minimized by network operating systems—so much so that wiring and protocols are selected based upon convenience and price—little reason exists to develop other comparable protocols or support unusual protocols.

These alternatives represent future solutions. FDDI is a current solution where something greater than 16 Mbits/s is needed. Furthermore, the costs for FDDI technology have dropped with the introduction of single chip sets and vendor competition. Network access hardware for FDDI is now available at 10 percent of its initial costs. The inconvenience and extra expense of running FDDI over optical fiber has been addressed with copper-based twisted-pair schemes that reduce the cabling costs and simplify long-term network planning. It is basically cheaper to install a single wiring plant for telephone, serial lines, 10- and 16-Mbits/s LANs, and also provide an upgrade path to 100-Mbits/s technology. The cost for running parallel but separate cable for voice, low-speed data, and high-speed data run increases installation and maintenance costs.

Optical fiber is more expensive than copper media; the costs for acquiring another set of tools for installing, maintaining, and repairing a different media increases cost as well. However, optical fiber does provide certain substantial benefits. Fiber provides a clearer upgrade path for higher bandwidth transmission technology, is lighter in weight, and unaffected by electrical or radio disturbances. These benefits are useful in vehicles; Boeing is designing the next generation of planes with FDDI controls. Thusly, FDDI provides a current and available next-generation technology, whereas other protocols do not.

The utility of FDDI partially results from the wide acceptance of Unix and Ethernet personal computers and engineering workstations and its simple star-based architecture. By all accounts, FDDI provides a good transition for subnetting overloaded sites and linking sites too distant for acceptable performance with FIORL Ethernet or Token-Ring Repeaters, or sites where local T-1 links are just too expensive. Overloaded LANs and distributed LANs demand a hub router and gateway technology. FDDI provides this linkage technology with a ten fold channel speed boost and the ability to support sites at 2-km intervals or 32 km with single mode optical fiber and full-lasing extender equipment. It is a good choice for linking LANs on a campus. At a single site, the power of a "collapsed backbone" can provide the FDDI protocol with the installation and maintenance issues of actually stringing new optical cabling. Part of the success also can be attributed to the development and economics of twisted-pair and improved transmission speed which provide a transition for the low speed LANs. Any organization that requires this increased bandwidth has very few choices—FDDI being the most likely.

Furthermore, the high costs of choosing the wrong emerging network technology may encourage users of networks to opt for the more conservative path of known and generally accepted technologies. However, demands for higher software performance, enormous distributed data files, channel clogging multimedia sound, scanned images, and full-motion video beg for faster protocols. This technology is already relevant and gathering momentum for use in these premier applications and as a backbone to interconnect distributed buildings and university campuses. The economics will certainly improve. Just as FDDI hardware originally cost upward of $5000 and now is available at 20 percent of that cost, $800 copper-based FDDI connections can be expected to show a similar cost curve when many sources produce single-chip sets for this protocol. Do not discount the future of FDDI and assume that it merely will be bypassed by technological change. Change and higher performance generally come with a cost. Just as FDDI is relatively costly now, cell relay protocols are likely to be initially very costly. Token protocol networks (of which FDDI is one) provide inherently consistent response time, reasonable throughput, although with higher overhead than the comparable TCNS or Fast Ethernet. A slower response time (usually measured in ms) is provided in exchange for consistency and predictability of token protocols. The Open Systems Interconnection (OSI) communication structure provides the means to alter protocol layers independently of the others while maintaining global node and routing addressing and internetworking with as-yet-undeveloped protocols.

While many forward-thinking product developers and strategic planners might be aghast at this blasphemy, it is also important to realize that applications and user work flow patterns are very difficult to upgrade. Installed bases of software, computer equipment, and dedicated processes provide a conservative drag on the quickening pace of technical development. Retraining and retooling people is more difficult, expensive, and time-consuming than replacing hardware. Furthermore, personal preferences endure as many network managers can attest as they install yet another character-based word processor into graphical user interfaces (GUI) such as X Windows and MS Windows.

Yet, this very conservatism is a major reason for the success of FDDI and its continued applicability. As many organizations realize the value and necessity for comprehensive data communications, the merit of enterprise-wide networks emerges. Unfortunately, the diversity of installed bases of PCs, workstations, and file servers, as well as mainframes precludes most organizations replacing all existing systems. In fact, that is absurd and unnecessary. FDDI and Novell NetWare provide a foundation for linkage. Similarly, Sun Microsystems Network File System (NFS), although inherently Unix- and Ethernet-based, transparently supports Token-Ring, UDP, ISDN, and FDDI as native communication protocols. That is a sufficient and an efficient method to connect disparate computers, operating systems, and network protocols.

While most people may view new technology as a threat to existing ones, sometimes, instead, it can amplify the value of older technology. The sudden availability and prominence of interconnectivity, and interoperability, and development of user-level tools only increases the importance of existing networks. Existing networks are unlikely to be replaced very quickly by faster or merely new technology; instead, they will be integrated into organization-wide networks. This data access and linkage process has opened many eyes to utility of PCs with MS Windows or X Windows-based GUIs, and the possibility for real organization-wide client/server computing. OSI and Motif standards provide uniform front ends for users to gather, construct, and process networked data. This, too, drives efforts to rightsize data processing operations.

Similarly, while Novell predominantly supports IPX/SPX protocols, Novell also created the Network Device Independent Specification (NDIS) which allows software vendors to build applications that are virtually independent from the underlying network protocols. This includes FDDI. FDDI is a preference for the scientific and research and development community with overloaded but entrenched Ethernets.

Furthermore, a major stumbling block to all network technology is the difficulty to manage and control the communication channels and the attached resources. This is particularly the case with such common network protocols which lack a network control center feature. Network management is in its infancy and tools exist merely to capture information. Few tools provide assessments or intelligently help analyze this information, and fewer yet can make automated decisions. Despite the codification of Simple Network Management Protocols (SNMP) for TCP/IP networks or the long-awaited Common Management Information Protocol (CMIP) under OSI FDDI, management remains in its infancy. The nature of compound networks, backbones, interconnectivity, bridging, and routing and the problems of ensuring network reliability and balancing performance without doubt will increase with FDDI. While better throughput may solve some traffic bottlenecks,

The Current and Future Place for FDDI

faster speeds and additional protocols merely increase the complexity of networks and the importance of resolving bottlenecks at network interconnections. The infrastructure must be developed to manage network complexity.

FDDI remains the protocol of choice for expansion because of the new availability of shielded (STP) and unshielded (UTP) twisted-pair FDDI components. Furthermore, the tools, experience, and compatibility issues are expanding. It is not the protocol for simple LAN wiring, but is the choice when specific situations demand higher transmission speeds. FDDI provides increased capacity for overloaded LANs, interconnecting LANs, or providing a bandwidth a magnitude higher for imaging and client/server transaction processing. FDDI is positioned as just one supplement. Other supplements and enhancements are just "vapornets." Do not discount FDDI until we can compare it to the full costs for frame relay, SONET, and ATM. The current though small installed base ensures its survival for some more years.

Additionally, the OSI structuring of most high-level protocols allows software developers to rethink, rebuild, and rebundle network services. This FDDI technology also provides a good starting point for linking small network installations that can gradually expand to routed rings connecting concentrations of other installations. Networks were once the domain of software developers, universities, and large corporations. Small businesses now use LANs as an efficient alternative to minicomputer-based applications and for enterprise-wide communication. FDDI networks supporting client/server processing also provide an important downsizing opportunity since this environment provides better development tools, faster development times, and competitive advantages no longer available with mainframe data processing. (Note that this environment may be as expensive as mainframe computing—or more so—and thus not show any cost savings in downsizing.) Furthermore, connectivity is still king; FDDI provides a plug-and-play intercompatibility otherwise unavailable. Its major limitation is the 100-Mbits/s transport speed and the effective throughput with 30 nodes providing traffic at 3 Mbits/s. While FDDI promises a faster standard, it perhaps provides only a transitional product proprietary in nature because it is limited to 100 Mbits/s. That order of magnitude is not a great difference in the scheme of the computing world and may be insufficient to warrant wholesale replacement of existing networks. The ATM networks will soon be developed and may find an audience for LAN interconnection and WAN; nonetheless FDDI is reality now.

The FDDI implementations both encapsulate and translate other packets for delivery. Implementations of routers, packet switches, and gateways in hardware will boost the integration of small networks into enterprise-wide endeavors. Furthermore, high-bandwidth optical links will add credibility to construction of effective enterprise-wide networks, while electronic exchange of data and online storage and retrieval of documents will supplant more paper transactions. Additionally, the requirements of internetworking, distributed databases will change the emphasis from peer-to-peer networking to client/server models. Although Ethernet, Token-Ring, and FDDI support this, the winner in any network protocol race will be that providing the most effective management and control tools. The emergence of the OSI model and vendor realization that interconnectivity, interoperability, and network management are crucial to technology sales and constitute both a major design and development effort and important aspects to highlight in marketing liturature and presentations. As a result, more quality network management tools are available which provide architecture- and protocol-independence and support for large architectures.

Chapter

3

Benefits of Networking

This chapter gives an overview of FDDI. It defines the concepts of networks, local area networks, metropolitan area networks, wide area networks, and backplanes. It then describes the benefits of the networking environment. Common network configurations and transmission protocols are expounded upon and compared to FDDI configurations and protocols. The final section of this chapter describes the problems with FDDI.

Definition of a Local Area Network

A *processor* is anything with computing power such as a microcomputer, a mainframe computer, or an intelligent workstation. A *device* is anything that performs processing, input and/or output services, such as a computer, a printer, a terminal, or a plotter. A device may be either a *node* or a *station*. Within the FDDI terminology, a station is any device attached to a main network; this is generally a *dual attached station* (DAS) which accesses the dual counterrotating optical fiber ring. A node is any device connected to the network as a *single attached station* (SAS); this can be a device attached to one the rings in a FDDI dual-ring architecture, or a device attached on a subnet or to a concentrator which in turn on attached to the main network. This book refers to devices on a dual rings as stations, devices on concentrators, hubs, or FDDI subnet trees as nodes.

A *network* exists whenever two or more processors are connected to one another with a cable and with networking software (software that directs the flow of information between processors and that monitors requests for access to devices). A network connects processors that may have been isolated from one another.

A *local area network* transmits large amounts of data at high speeds over limited distances. A local area network generally services a single room, a single floor, a building, or a two-building facility, as shown in Figure 3.1. The LAN is generally limited to a compact geographic area

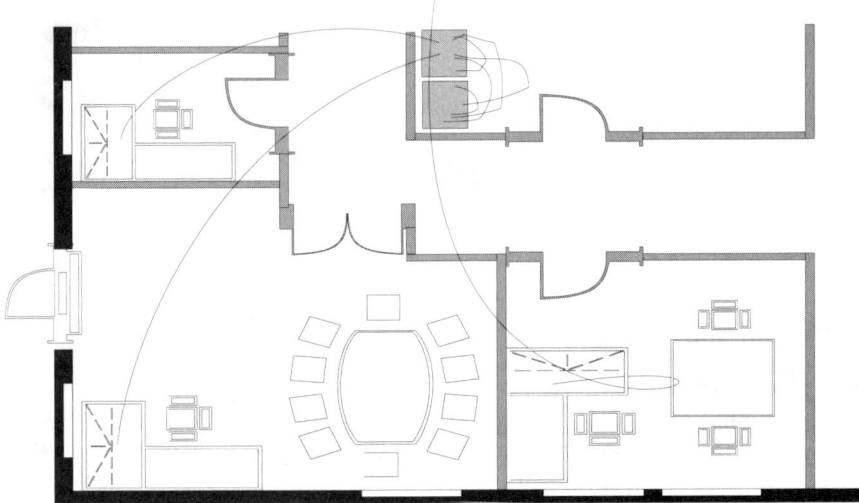

Figure 3.1 A local area network (LAN) services a "local area."

(perhaps a 1500-m circumference). FDDI limits the geographic area to 50 km. It is not, per se, a LAN.

A mainframe servicing remote terminals provides centralized processing while a LAN is decentralized. On a LAN, the network processing power is distributed among all the processors and peripheral devices. While a mainframe that serves remote terminals may structurally look like a local area network, the LAN differs because each workstation and processor operates independently. Usually, an inexpensive and general-purpose cable provides a trunk cable that forms the network's *ring* or *backbone*. In fact, the network is only a utility that uses all the devices. See Figure 3.2 for a definition of a LAN.

A LAN is designed to benefit a group with a common cause, common equipment, and similar and shared needs. A local area network should interconnect equipment from different manufacturers, as shown in Figure 3.3. This capability is termed *peer-to-peer exchange*. A LAN

- Limited geographic area [0.1 to 1 kilometer (km)]
- Moderate to high data rate (0.1 to 100 Mbits/s)
- Inexpensive medium ($0.60 to $10.00 m)
- High interconnectivity and access
- Decentralized control
- Interconnectivity between manufacturers
- Device and control independence

Figure 3.2 The definition of a local area network.

Benefits of Networking

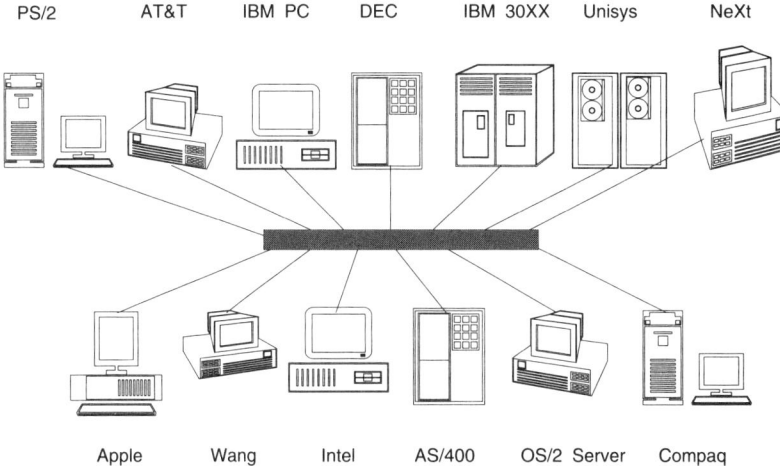

Figure 3.3 LANs provide peer-to-peer vendor intercompatibility.

interconnects equipment with many specific functions, allowing resources to be shared by all network users as shown in Figure 3.4. Information can be shared across the network and stored on disk. Programs can be stored in a single location and made available to multiple users, thus saving expensive disk space and increasing availability of data and tools.

Peer-to-peer *exchange* is also a term used to refer to a network with stations or nodes of equal capacity. *Client/server* exchange refers to the network situation where a server computer provides specialized services not available (or configured to be available) on the client computers. *Servers* provide various concentrated functions like printing, file storage, application software storage, database data storage, optical storage and retrieval,

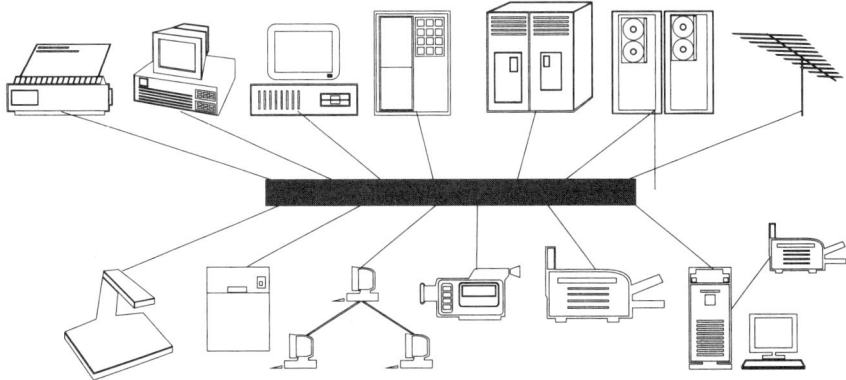

Figure 3.4 A local area network provides many services.

network fascimile, electronic mail functions, and gateways to other networks. Figure 3.5 lists typical server functions. Chapter 11 discusses client/server processing in the context of enterprise-wide networks.

An *internetwork* is a network of networks. Internetworks are typically more complex than a single network because they must service numerous topologies, protocols, transmission media, and a larger number of devices, stations, and nodes. Internetworks are represented by wide area networks and enterprise-wide networks. FDDI is positioned as the product for interconnecting many LANs across a campus.

A *wide area network (WAN)* represents the interconnection of multiple local area networks or the attachment of remote stations to a host mainframe. This usually refers to the connection of LANs within different buildings, but it as easily could refer to the connection of LANs within the same building. WAN connectivity is often provided by dial-up phone lines (analog signaling), public data networks (digital signaling on T-1 or ISDN), private branch exchanges and lease lines (usually digital networks), microwave transmissions, packet switching and routing, FDDI on optical fiber, and satellite communications.

A *metropolitan area network (MAN)*, as defined by IEEE 802.6, represents the interconnection of users and LANs within a campus-wide area, as shown in Figure 3.6. The predominant MAN protocol is manufacturing access protocol (MAP), as defined by General Motors for CAD/CAM integration. MANs are indeed common for college campuses, universities, large commercial facilities, and government installations.

- Network printing
- Specialized output
    - Typesetting
    - Transparencies
    - Film
    - Tape
    - Punch cards
    - Plotters
    - Color output
- Data backup
- File services
    - Database data
    - File storage
    - Application storage
- Electronic mail (E-mail)
- Gateways
- Network management tools
- Shared access to database files
- Time-share computer access

Figure 3.5 Client/server functions.

Benefits of Networking

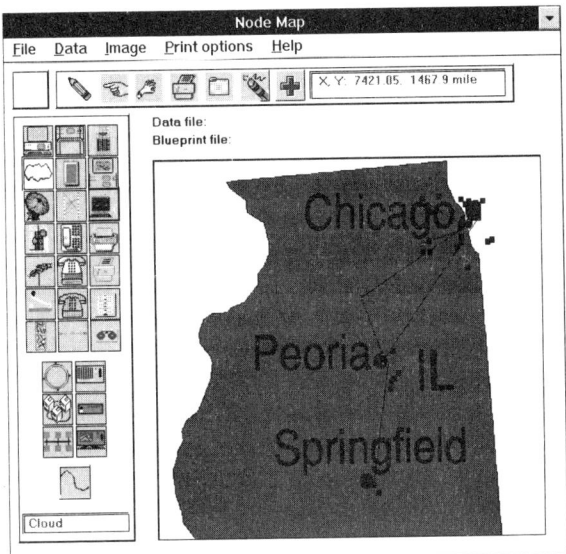

Figure 3.6 A metropolitan area network (MAN) services a "campus" area. This bitmap image from WANCAD shows an enterprise network. (NPI)

Both of these wider geographically distributed networks fall within the definition of an *enterprise-wide network*. Given the geographic reach of FDDI, it is a MAN protocol. The enterprise-wide network also may connect dispersed geographic sites. Chapter 11 is devoted to the issue of enterprise-wide networks, although the next section will discuss it briefly.

Benefits of Establishing an Internetwork

There are both operational and economic benefits to internetwork a distributed organization. Operational benefits include wider access to devices, more productive software, greater access to shared information, and reduced transmission errors. Electronic mail drives internetworking, as does the downsizing transition from host mainframes. While it may have been easy to dial into a mainframe for access to data, dialing into a LAN is not as desirable. The tools and overhead are much different; direct access via routers or gateways is preferable for performance, control, and security. Economic benefits include fewer equipment purchases, more equipment available to each user, decreased warranty costs, and lower cost per device. Additionally, once installed, there may be no external communications costs as there are with central office telephone switching services or megalink T-1 lines. See Figure 3.7.

- Wider access to devices
- Greater independence
- Faster access to devices
- Shared information
- Reduced transmission errors
- Specialized communications
- Fewer purchases
- Extra processing power
- Lower cost per workstation
- Simplified wiring

Figure 3.7 A network provides many services.

Operational Benefits

A network provides wider access to peripheral devices because all devices become available to all processors on the network. On a network, a user whose workstation is running off processor A can use a printer on processor B. Printers, plotters, typesetters, CAD/CAM workstations, facsimiles, scanners, video entry systems, and specialized disk and tape storage devices can be shared.

Network access can facilitate remote usage of a peripheral device otherwise accessible only through data transfer by magnetic medium, a slow and irksome process. A network therefore provides faster access to devices.

With a network, distributed processing permits stand-alone microcomputer workstations to function undisturbed by such things as remote failures, peak loads, and limited resources; the processors are not dependent on the availability of one mainframe. Note, however, that clients of a client/server processor are completely dependent upon that server. The distribution of workload requires at least the same aggregate central resources as any mainframe environment, but with networking the processing occurs at greater speeds, with more flexibility, and greater independence. The distribution of peripheral loads also frees the central mainframe for more important jobs.

Many distributed processing sites that are not on a network experience problems in providing data file backup, in sharing information, or in coprocessing. Tasks that were formerly isolated on individual processors can be consolidated to improve operational efficiency. For example, computer-aided design, publishing, and manufacturing processes can reside on one network. Programs can be made available to more users with less disk space across a network, and specialized processors are easily accessible. Networks make possible electronic mail for internal communications. Electronic mail is a "free" network service that provides rapid delivery, high success of delivery, message broadcasting, and automatic reply options. Network facsimile minimizes paper handling, prints incoming faxes to LAN printers, and adds security features.

Benefits of Networking 41

Telecommunications via private branch exchange (PBX) modems is inherently slow and error-prone unless expensive error-checking and correcting equipment is used, whereas a network has fewer transmission errors. Telecommunications is also a simplex (unidirectional) transmission in that only one workstation can talk at any time to only one other workstation, in one direction. A local area network allows two-way (duplex), simultaneous connection to all facilities from all facilities, at transmission speeds thousands of times faster. Networks with optimized architecture provide high data rates on tuned channels that often interconnect supercomputing processors or scientific data acquisition equipment, offering access to specialized communications.

Economic Benefits

Rather than support each workstation with local data storage and local printing, plotting, typesetting, and tape facilities, a network permits sharing of these resources among multiple processors and users. This is the function and justification for the client/server configuration. Fewer purchases are necessary and there may be some consolidation of resources. In a distributed processing environment that does not use networking, growth means that many basic resources like printers, storage media, and modems need to be duplicated whereas networks provide these critical services more economically. The per seat cost tends to decrease as the LAN or MAN grows, whereas this is typically not the case with WANs until a new host processor is required. Resources that might not be cost-effective to purchase for a single purpose may become attractive when a network makes them available to multiple network users. Often, extra processing power, which is like an empty airplane seat because it has little value, can be accessed across a network and used.

The economics of LANs are similar to those of any mainframe environment. There is a high fixed cost for initial installation but an increasing economy for additional network devices. An example of this economy is presented in Figure 3.8. The shape of the curve emphasizes the decreasing costs for marginal additions. The basic network wiring cost is a fixed asset that must be provided independently of the number of stations and nodes. While the initial network wiring installation costs $10,000 and the first node costs $8000 with printer, modem, and local data storage, the tenth unit costs a marginal $3000 for a total expenditure of $80,000; peripheral devices are shared rather than duplicated for each additional unit and network costs are amortized over a wider base, as the concave graph indicates. The effect is a lower cost per additional workstation and a cost that is less than for a centralized processing environment such as a host mainframe.

In summary, networking logically divorces the workstation from the file structure, the disk storage, and the CPU. MAN communications and

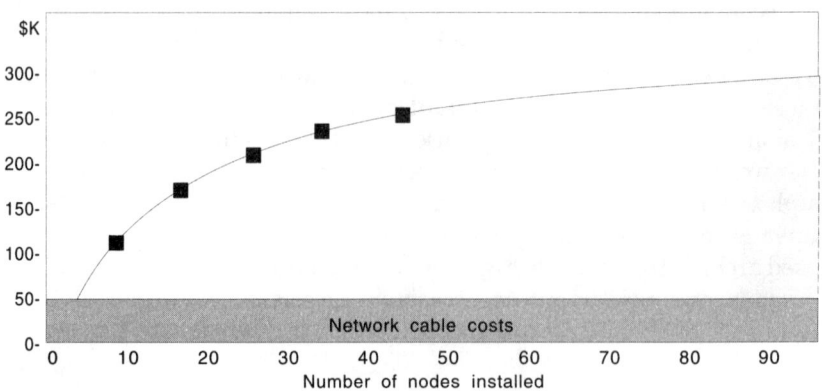
Figure 3.8 Networks provide economies-of-scale.

LAN interconnection further divorces station location from the LAN; users may be anywhere on a large campus. A novel application of this concept is network computing, which means that underutilized CPUs will broadcast their status and provide automatic parallel computer power; this technology is available with specialized Unix workstations. Network databases are a specialized application of network computing. The IEEE parallel processing group seeks to define a Network Interface Definition Language (NIDL) to promote parallel processing and logical process partitioning, although the complexity to date defies solution on even single CPU processors.

Network Topologies

A *topology* describes the geographic relationship of the network devices. The three most prevalent topologies include the bus, ring, and star configurations. See Figure 3.9 for representations of these architectures.

Star Topology

The star network is often the choice where many units are dependent upon a single processor, as in a typical mainframe situation where personal computers require frequent access to a mainframe. In this situation all cable connections are separately wired to a centralized patch panel. Although the mainframe environment is not strictly a "network," most mainframe computer is wired from a central point.

Multiplexing units, hub concentrators, and wiring pairs only reduce wiring requirements without eliminating them, and this topology provides few economies unless it is wired in parallel with a phone system. It is cheap when well-planned, but increasingly expensive for each additional device, particularly for any devices that exceed planned

Benefits of Networking

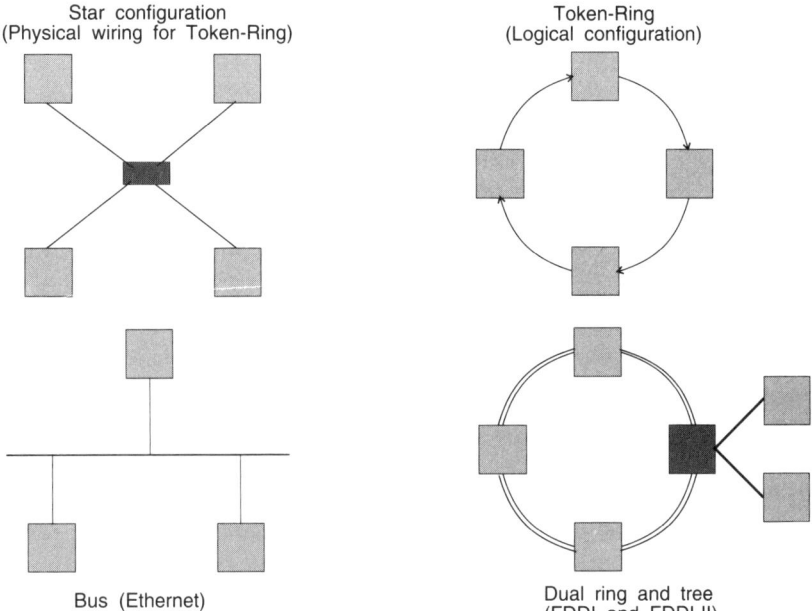

Figure 3.9 Common local area network topologies.

capacity, as each added unit will require wiring from the device location to the central location. Physical movement of a device can be a very simple process since changes could be performed at a central patch panel. It is, however, a stable design in that any failed node would affect few, if any, other nodes, although centralized failure would affect all attached nodes.

In fact, the twisted-pair FDDI, or *TP-DDI*, technology uses this topology. The hubs, or concentrators, provide multiple ports that are wired with the standard *voice-grade* telephone cable or special data *data-grade* communications cable. The *data-grade* is preferable. In fact, standards have defined for 100-Mbits/s transmission on copper media. Twisted-pair FDDI provides a cost-effective alternative to optical fiber. The downside to the applying standard voice-grade twisted-pair for FDDI is very real and should be considered carefully; specifically, signal crosstalk undermines clarity, external signal noise increases transmission error rates, and radiation may cause health problems.

The star-wired twisted-pair design is the most convenient topology for wiring data communication networks. In the star topology all nodes are wired to a central site. This is generally called the wiring closet. Phones, IBM Token-Ring, Ethernet 10Base-T, and copper-based FDDI are generally wired to a central wiring closet. Note that Token-Ring and FDDI are logically rings, that 10Base-T is logically a bus, but that all are generally physically wired as stars. Most organizations and standards encourage this structure because it simplifies wiring and provides centralized maintenance; it also conforms to the recently introduced Telecommunications Industry Association (TIA) and Electronic Industry Association (EIA) site wiring standards, TIA/EIA 568 and TIA/EIA 569. On a optical fiber FDDI network, dual access stations (DAS) are generally physically wired in a dual close ring, while single attachment stations (SAS) are wired from a DAS with star topology twisted-pair copper wire. The health consequences from copper-based FDDI are unknown; their reputed risks remain to date unsubstantiated, as Chapter 4 explains.

Ring Topology

The ring configuration is designed as just that, a circular architecture, with each device directly connected to two other devices. All network traffic passes through each network device in series on the ring until it reaches the intended receiver. This wiring scheme demonstrates few economies over the star design. It is also complicated and requires meticulous care to wire correctly. The ring is easily expanded to insert more devices, although this process is disruptive since the ring is broken while a new unit is installed.

Also, physical movement of a devices requires two separate steps: disconnection to remove a device and again to install the device in its new location. Likewise, should any single device fail, the network fails just as the failure of one decorative tree light causes the whole string to

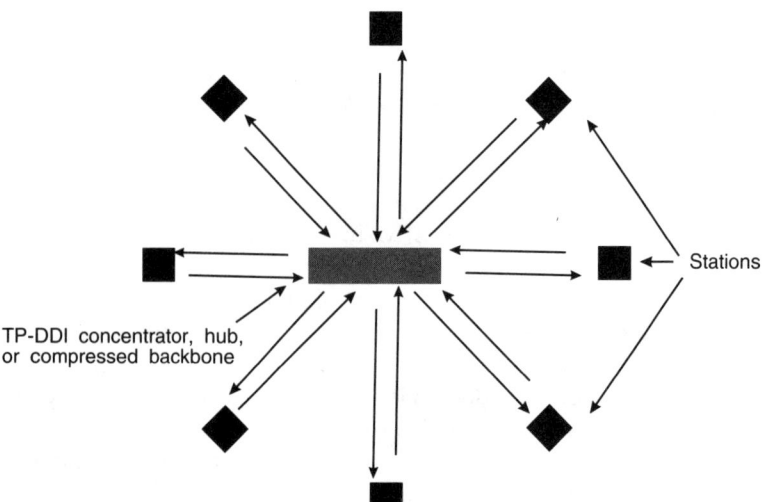

Figure 3.10 FDDI is a ring; TP-DDI is wired as a physical star.

Benefits of Networking

fail. It is a fragile design despite the addition of various automatic mechanisms designed to bypass failed cable sections or nonresponsive devices. FDDI is in fact a ring structure when wired with optical fiber, although it is wired as a star with TP-DDI, as Figure 3.10 illustrates. Furthermore, FDDI includes "ring wrap" and "lobe isolation" techniques to somewhat minimize the fragility of the ring. Bypass switches can ensure FDDI uptime and provide a mission-critical environment.

The FDDI optical technology and FDDI twisted-pair is based upon a dual-ring topology. Two rings with counterrotating transmission channels to some degree overcome the basic limitations of the ring design. When a station fails, as in FDDI, it is supposed to remove itself, that is, "self-heal," from the ring until repair. The dual ring becomes a single ring at the failure point. Additionally, physical failures in a segment of fiber are supposed to be removed from service by applying this fail-safe mechanism. FDDI in a ring structure is useful for interconnecting individual FDDI networks or LANs across a campus.

Bus Topology

The bus design is an open architecture. All nodes connect in parallel on a single cable section, and this design is perceived as a simple architecture that is more difficult and expensive than star-wired twisted-pair. It is a common configuration, often used for Ethernet. One or more coupled sections and the nodes on it form a complete stand-alone network segment. One single segment usually forms a backbone and connects to all other segments and individual or multiple Ethernet buses. While this division of the network into separate segments improves traffic flow and increases reliability, it also allows all nodes to reach all other nodes. Ethernet was originally a bus technology, although now it is usually wired as a star by applying the 802.3 10BASE-T extensions.

Available Protocols

The last section described physical topologies. Networks also vary by transmission protocol, which is the method used to transmit data. The common networking protocols include RS-232, CSMA (Carrier-Sense Multiple-Access), CSMA/CD (Carrier-Sense Multiple-Access with Collision Detection), token bus, FDDI, and optimized token bus. Figure 3.11 shows which protocols can be used on each network topology.

Protocols range from simple one-way or two-way transmissions, as on an RS-232 network, to controlled token-passing and polling schemes or probabilistic broadcasting schemes. FDDI is a token passing protocol, and this protocol will be described in explicit detail. Each protocol has certain benefits and efficiencies as well as limitations. Benefits include simplicity, speed, and compatibility. Efficiencies are reflected in computer processor overhead, transmission timing, and loading factors. Limitations lie in the lack of a class of computers to accept that protocol,

Configuration	Available Protocols
Bus	CSMA/CD, token, optimized token
Star	FDDI, CSMA/CD, RS-232, token, polling
Ring	FDDI, token, polling, priority enforcement, OSI

Figure 3.11 Available network protocols.

the relative difficulty of installing or maintaining a specific protocol, relative speed, and relative cost.

RS-232 is generally run on twisted-pair, which is better known as *telephone wire*. RS-232 often can run on existing telephone cabling, and if not, this common wire is simple to install. Modems (sound *mo*dulator/*de*modulator) alter digital voltage changes into an analog sound pattern that is transmitted over twisted-pair. RS-232 is often used for mainframe to dumb-terminal communications, because such communication is relatively low load and slow speed. Two-way connections are established between a destination and a source, and this link is inflexible during the transmission session. RS-232 is often bundled into a T-1 network framework, or supplanted with digital attachment devices on T-1 lines. T-1 is a dedicated high-speed digital link that connects distant locations. This wide area network (WAN) differs from the LAN because of the lack of distance limitations between devices. T-1 is served via PBX and common carriers like AT&T. Speeds of communication on a single T-1 channel—and there are 24—range from up to 64,000 bits/s. Usable bandwidth per channel may correspond to 56,000 bits/s. This corresponds to approximately 30 to 600 characters per second. Generally, a limit of 9600 baud is achieved on voice-grade phone lines due to limitations inherent in this technology. New bit compression with error detection and correction technology is bringing higher speeds (14,000 and 115,400 baud) to market, although higher speeds often create disproportionately higher error rates.

Carrier-sense multiple-access with collision *detection (CSMA/CD)* is the protocol for Ethernet and 10BASE-T. The conflict from interfering signals is termed a *collision. Collision detection* is a euphemistic description of a busy network unable to handle the transmission volume. Collisions occur when two or more units transmit simultaneously, a factor usually indicative of the significant two-way transmission delay over the full network length, or, of channel overloading. This protocol *saturates* when the traffic level becomes too high, thereby preventing any communications whatsoever. Collisions are handled by rebroadcasts. Figure 3.12 outlines how CSMA/CD works.

Token protocols are more orderly than Ethernet CSMA/CD protocols. Token passing is the protocol for FDDI. If the analogy of CSMA/CD is the swinging door, token passing is analogous to a revolving door. Token

Benefits of Networking

protocols provide a consistent and controlled network load. No matter the traffic volume on the network, all stations get equal access to the network. The network will remain functional under the heaviest load. The delays waiting for permission to transmit will increase linearly with loading. Figure 3.13 charts how the token protocol works.

Rather than having each transmitter compete for a window in which to broadcast a message, a token is passed from one network device to the next. The token conveys the permission to transmit; no workstation can transmit without the token. Figure 3.14 illustrates the token-passing protocol and the mechanics of token permission in operation.

While the token passing scheme in Figure 3.14 seems more orderly, it suffers certain inefficiencies. For example, the token can get lost and not be regenerated for a time long by communication protocol standards, or duplicate tokens could be mistakenly generated. Token-passing pro-

CMSA/CD	Characteristics
Carrier sense	Listen before transmitting
Multiple access	Transmit when channel is free
Control process	Persistent
	Signal speed allows collisions
	Collision detection and retry transmission
	Delays a random length of time
	Equal access (no priorities)
	Algorithm generates delay
Advantages	Efficient with workload less than 30 percent capacity
Disadvantages	Nondeterministic; jams under heavy loads

Figure 3.12 Carrier-sense multiple-access with collision detection protocols (CSMA/CD).

Token passing	Characteristics
Carrier sense	Ring poll; token acquisition; repeated signal
Channel access	Acquire token for permission to transmit
Control process	Nonpersistent
	Ring poll; beacon
	Maximum token hold time; maximum token rotation time
	Equal access (no priorities)
Advantages	Does not saturate under ultimate loading
Disadvantages	High overhead; latency delay; transmission slows with load

Figure 3.13 Token passing protocols.

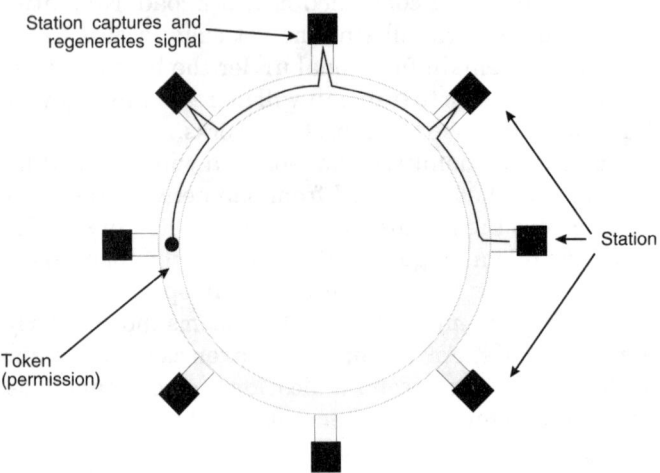

Figure 3.14 Token grants transmit permission to only one node at a time.

tocols limit the maximum time a workstation can actually hold the token, and this scheme assumes a uniform traffic level and penalizes high-volume users. Unfortunately, too, a workstation with a defective network access interface can hog the signal and "jabber" useless noise. Also, time is lost in the protocol of passing and accepting the token when a workstation may simply pass the token along without a need to communicate. This protocol is effective at very high traffic loads since it does not saturate; it is predictable and merely gets slower. All the protocols have best uses. Sometimes the choice is dictated by the higher initial expense of one protocol and the equipment it requires, a protocol's incompatibility with existing equipment, the cost of retrofitting an existing building for one type of network, the recommendations of an equipment vendor, or the availability from a vendor of a specific protocol. Other times, the software, production, or intercompatibility issues dictate the choices. A protocol is usually chosen in conjunction with many competing considerations.

FDDI has a higher initial cost than RS-232. However, RS-232 cannot provide adequate file transfers in the necessary timeframe, support the overhead for the pixelated screen pagination necessary for most desktop workstations, or service graphic manipulation at transmission rates consistent with current technology. These two, and several other protocols, are compared for speed, costs, and installation flexibility in Figure 3.15.

FDDI is often selected because it provides high speed and is compatible with the equipment of many manufacturers and software vendors. Additionally, the extended media topologies of twisted-pair star provide flexibility in network design, extension, maintenance, and preferences. Not only are communications achievable among different vendors; often

Benefits of Networking

Protocol	Rate (Mbits/s)	Cost per node	Flexibility
RS232	.0003 to .012	200 to 600	low
X.25 (star)	.0003 to .0019	200 to 600	low
Ethernet (bus)	10	950	high
Ethernet (star) 10BASE-T	10	800	medium
Token Ring	4 to 16	800	medium
FDDI	100	1850	low
TP-DDI	100	1450	medium

Figure 3.15 Comparisons of various protocols in common usage. Note the additional cost per node ($), not including workstation or amortized network backplane expenses.

different machines can talk and share information in a transparent manner. This magic is possible because FDDI is an official networking standard and also conforms to the structure of the generic network design specified by the International Standards Organization communications model, as described in Chapter 5.

The Problems of FDDI

The problems with FDDI include the lack of built-in resources for debugging and testing in spite of industry acceptance of network management protocols. These problems encompass the likelihood of electrical failure or optical failure, the inability to track network traffic and predict overloading problems in advance, and the difficulty in expanding network capacity beyond 100 Mbits/s. Tools to debug optical cabling plants are also expensive and difficult to justify and acquire when similar tools may already exist for Ethernet and Token-Ring. These are common problems often created in the initial installation or by creeping growth of an internetwork. It is prevalent for the far-reaching strategically implemented campus- and enterprise-wide network. Use of the wrong grade of wire and extending lobes beyond qualified lengths will cause constant or intermittent transmission errors. Constant construction and renovations across a large campus are likely causes for exposing and cutting the optical cable links. While a dual-ring optical fiber FDDI will self-heal to provide complete rings for the severed parts, the parts may still be unable to access distributed hosts and global E-mail services. Such limitations are resolved and hidden from an organization by good vendor installation teams or good administrative management and a large network budget. Unfortunately, networks do grow, equipment does age and fail, and random events do unfold that can break a network. Repair times range from minutes to months.

Most of these problems plague the inexperienced manager, while the seasoned network manager can forecast with ease the problems that will arise, and will know how to dispatch them quickly. The experienced network manager will have acquired the necessary tools and hired competent people who understand how to operate these special network tools, interpret findings, and apply expedient solutions. The problems of FDDI are not insurmountable with knowledge and experience; a good book guides the inexperienced along the path to learning.

Most mechanical problems, once understood, are quickly recognized by symptoms. Mechanical problems are also categorized by frequency and likelihood of occurring. Since FDDI is a ring where each station must repeat every signal, the failure of a single station can defeat the ring. This remains true even when a failed station is removed from the ring if it does not have automatic or passive bypass capabilities; it just becomes a dead point.

A partially failed network, single malfunctioning station, and long waiting times rates, all, for example, point to high traffic loads, shorts, or breaks. Continuous shutdowns of the network suggest failed transmitting gear or improper component installation. High traffic loads and slow service rates suggest improperly installed wiring, a network overloaded with traffic or stations, or faulty software. Cabling connections can be checked to solve such problems, and if the problem is an overburdened network, various options exist to first verify this theory and then reduce load or provide alternative communication routes. More rings can be installed to match capacity, or bridges, routers, and collapsed backbones can isolate and partition large rings into manageable groupings. Software problems are resolved by system restarts, programming repairs, or replacement of corrupted file systems.

The common network problems masquerade as either hardware or software failures. Without guidelines, it is often impossible to distinguish one from another. Network testing and monitoring provide the means to identify the root causes of FDDI problems, the understanding of how to isolate or remove the problem, and the experience to repair it. FDDI networking addresses these issues and provides a practical approach to FDDI network problem-solving and the related internetworking to other protocols.

Chapter 4
Network Health Risks

Computer professionals increasingly express concern about the possible health consequences of networks. Overt and acute dangers include electrical current used to power computer equipment and the risks from climbing ladders to reach lofty ceiling cables. Frequently, computer professionals lift heavy laser printers, servers, or furniture, which may result in a hernia, lower back pain, or pulled muscles. However, there is also a growing concern about the circumstantial but unsubstantiated long-term health consequences from exposure to radio-frequency and magnetic field pollution emanating from computer and telecommunication equipment. When this book was initially planned, it seemed as though the energy pollution issue was irrelevant for FDDI since optical fiber emits nothing but coherent light from the cable ends. However, the emergence of electrical transmission of FDDI OSI protocols on copper-based shielded and unshielded twisted-pair reinvigorates the issue due to the possible danger of energy pollution. Unfortunately, the health risks have not been resolved. This chapter will cover the obvious health issues and discuss more insidious danger from energy pollution.

Acute Dangers
The danger of electrocution or a fall from a ladder are the more likely physical dangers facing network support people. In most organizations, people are relocated an average of once every six months. Computer equipment and the associated networking access must be changed to accommodate the dynamics of the organization. This exposes the network team to various acute hazards like exposure to the computer power supplies, electrical connections, and the common ceiling-mounted cabling.

Electrical Safety
In general, FDDI on optical fiber solves a number of electrical problems. Optical fiber is carries no current and is itself no risk to installers and

network management. Thus, it is inert and safer than copper cabling. The nonconductive fiber reduces the risks from interbuilding electrical potential buildups—generally static electricity—and the conductance of lightning strikes. Since this cable is inert and nonconductive, it is a wise choice for interbuilding connections. Avoid steel-encased or steel-reinforced cable, since that would defeat the purpose. Many contractors do like to armor the cable within a steel pipe or installed armored cable since it can be located even underground with a metal detector. Installing the cable within a steel conduit or pipe is the better idea since the fiber will thus be electrically isolated. Since installation problems like stray voltage, electrical or communication crosstalk interference, and ever-present static electricity can span network segments, optical fiber can reduce the electric ground potential between network nodes. Internetworks and MANs are prone to NIC destruction caused by lightning diffusing throughout a copper coax or twisted-pair line. However, optical fiber bundled with standard copper lines or sheathed with steel to protect it from general damage does introduce the same dangers as other copper communication lines. Copper-based FDDI does introduce the same dangers as other copper communication lines also. Therefore, review the site and do not assume that the FDDI lines are safer because they are inert glass or plastic unless they are not armored and do not share the same packaging with copper lines.

Occasionally in the networking industry someone does get burned or badly shocked. In general, the danger from electrocution is minimal. Internal computer circuitry voltages utilize 12-V direct current and are for the most part harmless. Power supplies, transformers, and direct power connections transport more dangerous US 120-V alternating current or European 230 V. Currents over 40 V, nonetheless, should be considered hazardous; this includes phone lines. The shock risk is minor because Underwriters Laboratories and other private testing groups have checked for electrical hazards in consumer products; these standards and safety concerns have been incorporated in many commercial and exempted products like personal computers, workstations, and peripheral devices. The frequency of access to the internal power transformers, connectors, and cables, however, exposes the networking team members to a better chance of doing something wrong or finding a defect. Mainframe environments with large peripheral devices like reel-to-reel tape backup and removable "washtub" disk drives frequently have more significant power demands of 240 V. There is a corresponding increase in risk of course, although this technology is rapidly becoming specialized and obscured by microcomputers. For most personal computers or engineering workstations only the 120 V power supply itself presents a real danger. Video monitors do, however, have very high internal voltages—on the order of 10,000 V.

Network Health Risks

The best precautions to minimize the risk of electrical burns and shocks is common sense. Do not open cases unless you have sufficient knowledge to repair or diagnose the contents. This is particularly true for video display equipment where voltages exceed 10,000 Vs. Check the integrity of power cords; plug equipment into properly wired wall, floor, or desk-mounted electrical sockets; verify grounds and plug computer equipment into grounded receptacles; and repair damaged equipment to minimize this risk. Power off equipment before moving it or making physical configuration changes. Figure 4.1 outlines a robust electrical safety policy.

Most network cable carries only a small voltage—less than 12 V—with a small current. There is virtually no danger from those voltages. There are secondary electrical dangers. Twisted-pair bundles frequently share the same wiring conduit as phone lines and electrical power cables.

"Stray" electricity leaks from substantially overloaded or ancient wiring onto the nearest and largest ground. This does include network wires. Network wiring also can acquire an induced current with simple proximity to nearby power lines that could be significant. It is important that any FDDI shield or armor-sheathing bleed off these unwanted currents for safety reasons (and also for communications reliability and network equipment integrity). Jacketed cables could carry a substantial electrical potential. Since many UTP FDDI networks are built to conform with modular phone wiring specifications, it is possible that some network lines will be crossed with 48 V phone circuits. Phone-ringing voltages approach 100 V DC. Although this does not pose a substantial hazard to people because the amperage is minimal, network equipment (such as NICs, hubs, and routers) is liable to assault.

It is also possible that breaks in an electrical power cable leak electricity to a cable sheath because it provides the path of least resistance. Mistakes can happen when electricians or other mechanical installers make changes to the building wiring. Computer room air conditioning units lacking an unobstructed water discharge could create an immediate shock hazard or a slow corrosive problem eventually exposing power cables. Installations may not be complete or safe. Never

- Turn equipment off before moving
- Turn equipment off before installing or reconfiguring options
- Check the integrity of power cords
- Replace or repair defective or damaged equipment
- Do not open the cases of computers
- Do not open the cases of video monitors
- Minimize the use of power extension cords
- Verify electrical grounds
- Do not defeat 3-wire plug grounds (by cutting ground prong)

Figure 4.1 Electrical hazard precautions.

hold two sections of a network in separate hands until you are certain of their safety, as Figure 4.2 shows. First touch connectors together (and watch for a spark) or check connections with a multitester.

Additionally, UTP FDDI wiring is often installed into a building as a retrofit rather than as a planned part of the new construction process. As a result, it is rarely installed in a special conduit or wiring ladder. Instead, the wiring is rigged through the air-return or forced-air ceiling plenums. Air, particularly when very dry, blowing over the length of the shielded wiring also can induce a current. This static charge is highly unlikely to be dangerous; yet a static shock can surprise the unwary and dislodge a person atop a tall ladder. This raises another serious risk, that of the risk of a fall.

Ladder Safety

Falls from ladders are an occupational risk for network staff. Unfortunately, a fall from a ladder is not considered preventable until you or a member of your staff falls and breaks an ankle, shatters a pelvis, or lands in the hospital with a concussion. Take this risk very seriously. A fall could cause grave personal injury, damage to network installations, and subsequent downtime. There is the additional loss of productivity while the person heals. There are also financial consequences to the organization such as sick time salary, workman's compensation, and perhaps OSHA (see Appendix A) inspections and fines. Workman's compensation does not compensate the person injured for pain and suffering, or any lifelong problems as a result from that fall. Acquire safe ladder skills. Insist on ladder safety.

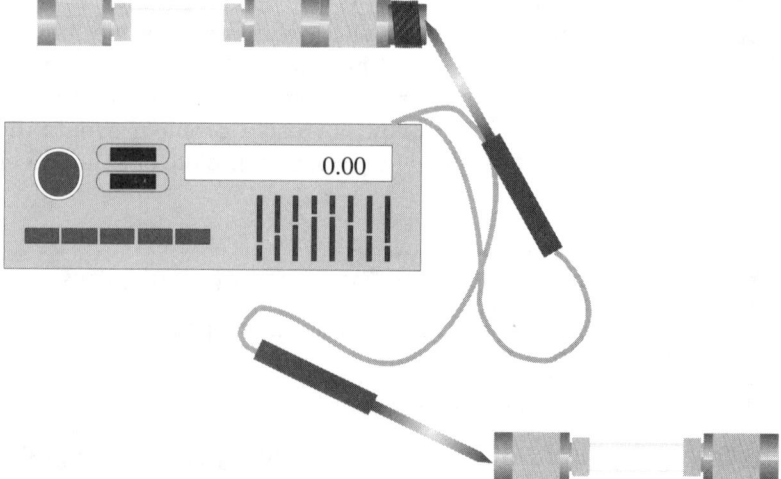

Figure 4.2 Electrician's safety precautions.

Network Health Risks 55

The art of climbing ladders is not taught to most people nowadays; it is a skill from yesteryear. Furthermore, network management is often a white-collar profession and there is a blinding perception that computer-related jobs are safe. Learn to climb ladders properly. Park the ladder on level ground, lock the ladder's folding supports, and never reach out so that your center of gravity is off the ladder. Never overextend your reach. Avoid the top step of folding A-shaped stepladders. The T-bar, found in most office buildings in the standard suspended ceiling, that you think will help you balance or support your weight will probably give way.

If you cannot reach, step down. Move the ladder. Remount the ladder and continue your work. Just because a few jumps from the top of the ladder or many steps from the top of the ladder seem okay, one misjudgment could break an ankle, cause shin splints, bruise the arches in the feet, or break a leg bone. Do not jump down from the ladder; climb down instead. Also, the fancy leather dress shoes may not provide sufficient support, cushioning, or grip when climbing a ladder. Keep a pair of moccasins or rubber sneakers at work. Not only will these feel more comfortable in general, they provide better grip and electrical insulation as well.

Install tool caddies or hooks to keep important tools within reach, or provide belt-mounted or vest tool carriers. Avoid painter's extension-type ladders since they do not provide stability. Add a "bear hug" gripper to the top of your ladder for additional stability, as Figure 4.3 shows. Consider the condition and utility of your ladders. Maintain ladders in safe condition. Tighten bolts. Replace rickety ladders. Since network management often begins as an ad hoc process, that old maintenance ladder is often the only available ladder. Do not chance it. Purchase a new ladder. Wooden rather than aluminum stepladders are inherently safer

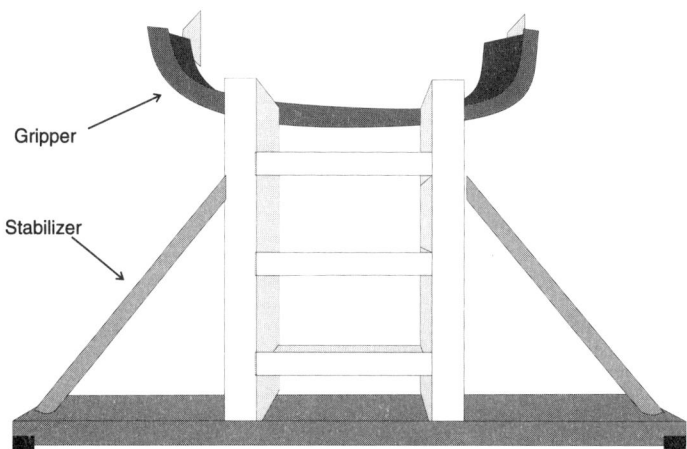

Figure 4.3 Ladder safety extension (or stabilizer) attaches to standard ladders.

since they do not conduct electricity. Fiberglass is stronger and is another good choice since it is electrically nonconductive. Beware of carbon fiber laminates since they do conduct. Multijoint ladders, which can assume a variety of articulated shapes, tend to be more stable, utilitarian, and safe although they are usually made from aluminum. Additionally, ladders vary in quality and strength as well as composition. They are graded as Classes I, IA, II, and III. Class III ladders are inexpensive. They are generally intended for intermittent household use and for persons under 200 lbs. Class I and Class IA are industrial strength reinforced ladders for constant use. Consider the legal and moral liability of an insufficient ladder.

Ladders are not the only tools to extend your reach. Library-style rolling stairs are inherently safer than ladders because of their larger silhouette and side railings. If the ceilings are unusually high, acquire scaffolding. Hydraulic lifts, sometimes called "cherry pickers," have safety cages. For industrial complexes, factory manufacturing floors, and space buildings with extended ceilings obtain a rolling platform (perhaps even motorized) to reach those heights. Platforms are inherently safer than long ladders and provide immediate tool access. Some people attach safety lines with quick release clips to roof trestles for added precaution. Remember that falling tools can injure bystanders below. Remember, too, that extension cords to power your tools are a risk atop the ladder both for the electrical potential and their chance of snaring you with a dangling cord. Figure 4.4 summarizes practical ladder precautions. These precautions are equally valid for all networking protocols since the cabling is often run from stations, upwards through ceiling plenums, from building to building on aerial poles, and finally to a terminating wiring closet.

- Set up the ladder on level ground
- Lock the ladder's folding supports
- Maintain center of gravity over ladder silhouette
- Never overextend your reach
- Do not move suddenly—move deliberately and carefully
- Do not balance on ceiling components
- Move the ladder directly beneath your work area
- Avoid the top step of folding A-shaped ladders
- Select a ladder tall enough to safely reach your work area
- Carry tools on a belt or vest
- Avoid extension-type ladders
- Add a bear hug gripper to the top of the ladder
- Maintain ladders in safe condition
- Replace rickety ladders
- Select wooden or fiberglass rather than aluminum ladders
- Acquire scaffolding or a rolling platform
- Attach safety lines with quick release clips
- Ground the ladder

Figure 4.4 Checklist for safe ladder usage.

Indoor Pollution

Most people would laugh aloud that the major health risk from a computer career would comprise lumbago, paper cuts, and overweight from a sedentary lifestyle. Whatever the reality of that view or the on-call lifestyle of a user and network support person, computer equipment does create substantial indoor pollution. Laser printers (and photocopiers) create ozone, a highly active form of oxygen (natural in our environment in low concentrations) that is corrosive to eyes and lungs. Ozone exposure is known to induce asthma and other respiratory disorders. It is thought to muddle thoughts and make people tired and lethargic. Long-term risks from elevated ozone exposure are unknown. Most people do not realize that laser printers and photocopiers have ozone filters. Replace the filters at the recommended intervals.

Although in reality computer equipment cases, the paint on the case, the fiberglass substrate used for computer circuitry, and other plastic materials may leach volatile resin solvents into the air, this is a minimal concern. Computers do create substantial energy pollution; the risk and extent of this energy pollution is the topic for the next several sections.

Exertion Risks

Basically, users who sit in front of a computer most of the day are likely to develop carpal tunnel syndrome and eyestrain. Neither are life-threatening or serious risks, although both may be painful and restrict future work. Carpal tunnel syndrome is a muscle and tendon affliction which results from repetitive activity—usually from typing on a computer keyboard. You might also know this problem as "tennis elbow," which results from the jarring and repetitive action of hitting a tennis ball. The cure is to avoid the activity that caused the problem initially; avoid typing. This is usually difficult for computer professionals. Prevention usually reflects the current understanding in ergonomics: for example, setting keyboard heights at 32 in (66 cm) rather than the standard tabletop height, providing arm and wrist supports to lessen the impact and effects of typing on the keyboard, and taking work breaks on an hourly basis.

Eyestrain results from viewing a flickering, low-resolution, or poorly adjusted display, viewing a computer screen in bright or reflective light, and reading a display with type that is too small to beeasily read. These problems can be simply corrected by reducing backlighting, putting computer terminals in different electrical circuits so that fluorescent lights will have a different flickering cycle than the displays, adjusting contrast between the text and the display background, and increasing the size of the objects displayed on the terminal.

Dangers from Laser Signals

Optical fiber generally transmits a coherent light produced by solid state laser diodes or light-emitting diodes. The light is *coherent* because the wavelength is consistent and because light particles are traveling in the same direction. Two optical fiber formats exist for FDDI; single mode fiber and multimode fiber. The single mode fiber is designed to carry a signal within a narrow bandwidth of light. The multimode fiber—the general FDDI standard is multimode fiber 62.5/125 mm in thickness— carries many wavelengths over a broader range. Both media require coherent signals. Coherence gives the light its enormous power and its utility for data communications. Typical risks from coherent light include burns. While the standard FDDI signal is not per se very powerful because of its wavelength, strength, and diode-based source, it can be dangerous when magnified. Specifically, coherent light of the magnitude produced in some optical networks can create retinal (eye) burns. Do not look into the light, or stare in a focused beam (that is, from a microscope). Even though light is invisible because the color is infrared, the beam can burn spots into the retina, the light-collecting portion of our eyes. These burns are painful and create dead vision in the eyes.

Laser safety necessitates ascertaining the status of a fiber and the signaling characteristics. Ascertain the power level of the signal and its inherent ability to cause burns. Never view it head on unless you are certain the signal is disconnected. Never view the magnified active signal for polishing the fiber ends. A magnifier or microscope can concentrate even safe coherent life in a burning ray.

Specifically, standard FDDI networks with multimode 62.5/125 micrometer fiber produce insignificant light, according to Dave Frattura of Codenell. On the other hand, single mode fiber with category 2 transmitters designed for 32 to 36 km segments are full lasers. They produce 1300 nanometer wavelength signals, and these are dangerous. Although safety interlocks are required on all optical fittings, careless actions or determined efforts to defeat the safety interlocks may result in painful and debilitating retinal burns.

Dangers from Electromagnetic Pollution

Energy pollution is a waste by-product of extracting energy from electricity. Such pollution is suspected to cause a variety of serious illnesses. Concern is warranted because more people are expressing their fears about this issue. Networks that connect computer systems also generate radiation and their risks should not be overlooked, either. In fact, that risk may be greater because the network wiring is invisible and therefore forgotten. Moreover, wireless network NICs and hubs broadcast not only radio signals to transport the UTP FDDI packets but also produce a fairly constant carrier signal. Cables and wireless networks discharge

Network Health Risks

radiation over a wider physical area than a singular personal computer. Thus, people usually not considered at risk are exposed to this hazard.

Fear over the dangers of the computer and network environment is derived from a higher incidence of serious and unusual illnesses for people living near other known sources of electromagnetic pollution. Illnesses and disorders include leukemia and other cancers, miscarriages, headaches, eyestrains, immune system problems, and juvenile growth disorders. Additionally, an observed increase in cataracts (deterioration and discoloration of the eye's lens) for mainframe data entry operators raises the direct suspicion that computers are not as safe as first perceived.

Suspected sources include the massive electrical power lines linking power generating plants with substations, radio stations, power stations, airports, and electric train lines. Even residential power lines and electric blankets are suspect. The problems are attributed to radiation generated by the flowing electricity itself. The force of electricity at very high voltages forcing its way through and over the high tension wires creates radio noise and localized but powerful magnetic fields. As computer operators have *attributed* similar health problems to longterm exposure to video display terminals (VDTs), concern grows over the health consequences of working near the ever-growing legions of personal computers and engineering workstations. Even at the lower voltages associated with computers, electricity can create pollution, too, albeit at lesser levels than caused by power lines. Electricity passing through the silicon paths on a computer chip or a wire (or coiled wire as found in a power transformer or electron beams within a video display terminal) creates an emanating energy field, as Figure 4.5 shows. Personal exposure even to this lower-level pollution is higher within the typically confined work areas of offices and cubicles.

It is important to realize that all forms of electromagnetic pollution are suspected to induce human illness. There are two basic types of electromagnetic pollution, either radio-frequency (RF) emissions or electromagnetic fields (EMF or EMI). Radio-frequency emissions like x-rays, infrared signals, microwave emissions, radio and television signals (and even sunlight) are all forms of light with different wavelengths, as Figure 4.6 denotes. Light is part unseen particle called a *photon*, and part wave energy. The spectrum varies with the energy context. X-rays are very short, intense signals that pass through most materials, whereas infrared is a very long and less powerful energy source that tends to bounce off things like air, people, and walls. Magnetic fields are not forms of light but rather are unseen rivers of electrons, a particle much larger than the photon. In general, RF pollution can be shielded with enough material to reflect or absorb the energy. On the other hand, magnetic energy is not easily shielded with

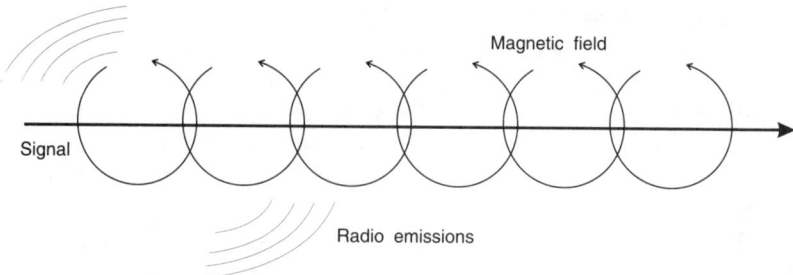

Figure 4.5 Flowing electricity creates electromagnetic interference (EMI) and magnetic field pollution.

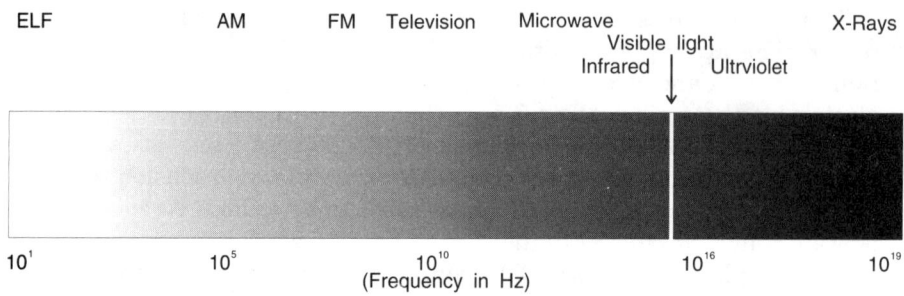

Figure 4.6 The electromagnetic spectrum.

solid materials although it can be dampened by creating new magnetic fields to counteract them.

Dr. Carol Weingrod, Medical Director of New Vistas, explains the reputed risk factors from exposure to radio-frequency pollution. She states that the energies of the electromagnetic spectrum are propagated waveforms with particle properties. This energy is inversely proportional to the wavelength; the longer the wavelength, the less energy associated. Nonionizing, or lower-level radiant energy (including microwave and radio-frequency), generally is thought to produce biologic hyperthermia. (In other words, cells get cooked.) The effects of radiant energy on biologic systems depend on the degree to which the energy particles penetrate the system and the chemical changes undergone by the molecules of the system once exposed to the energy. At issue is the seriousness of these biological changes and the ramifications of long-term, low-level exposure to energy pollution. Prudence clearly dictates an attempt to limit penetration of this energy into the biologic system.

There is no proof that magnetic fields have a health risk, merely causal connections. Magnetic energy is not wave or particle energy; rather, it is fields of flowing electrons and magnetic force. However, like radio-frequency emissions, the danger from this energy is inversely proportional to proximity. The best research suggests that magnetic energy is thought to accelerate chemical reactions within cells and perhaps create ozone, a triple-molecule form of oxygen that is highly reactive. This speeds the aging process, damages the DNA, and defeats the cell's ability to repair itself. Such biological changes are believed to cause cell failure or promote rampant cellular growth such as leukemia and other cancers. Prudence clearly dictates an attempt to limit exposure of this energy.

The concerns about RF and EMF to a lesser degree have become so important to the electrical generation and delivery industry and the cellular phone industry that both have formed research organizations and funded them heavily. This action may demonstrate the lessons learned from the effects of the tobacco industry categorically denying any healths risks from smoking and consuming tobacco. Pennsylvania Power and Light (PP&L) has hired a full time EMF consultant, Bernard Bernowski, solely to manage the placement of new residential power and high-voltage grids, serve as a community liaison on this issue, and research the issue. Motorola alone has funded $1 million for research and prodded the US government into reviewing its own research. The electrical generation industry has funded the Electric Power Research Institute and the Magnetic Research Lab. These organizations have built an uninhabited 8 acre subdivision in the Berkshire Mountains (Massachusetts, US) to explore the effects of radiation pollution.

To date, the results show that household appliances inside the house create create more radio and magnetic radiation than external high-voltage power lines. A clock radio—given its "proximity" to a person in bed—creates more pollution than house wiring, and much more than the distant power grid. That represents the official findings. Perhaps the lesson for computer workers is that office equipment, lighting, and computer equipment do represent a qualifiable risk. Mr. Bernowski did suggest the possibility that any risk may not be directly related to electrical transmission or usage, but rather from secondary environmental factors. While measurements have been made on steady-state voltages and loads, the danger (if any) may be caused by transient pulses and spikes or other consequences to which we are unaware.

Cellular Communications

The increasing use of cellular phone technology to connect portable network nodes and provide on-the-road links to office networks raises the issue of the dangers of cellular phone technology. While there have been a statistically-significant increase in the number of brain cancers in the U.S. during the past 15 years, the position of these cancers (for example, in the lower brain stem or behind the ears) relative to the positioning of the handheld phone antennas is not statistically relevant. In other words, people who hold cellular phones against their ears may be at an increased risk of brain cancer behind the ears, but it is remains unproven.

Since proximity to the radio signal does remain the issue, plan for mounted cellular phones and modems with external antennas rather than the handheld units. If you expect to use a cellular modem for long periods of time, use an antenna with a long cord that can be placed outside a hotel window or mounted on the roof of building. Since this is a new issue, the issues of secondary magnetic radiation (EMI) have not been addressed yet. Mostly, though, the concern with cellular communications is the same for other RF and microwave transmissions; proximity and duration.

Inconclusive Evidence

Results to date on the dangers of energy pollution remain inconclusive despite the government agencies, insurance companies, and private organizations that have commissioned studies. A coherent refutation of the dangers comes from John Baler, a consultant to the *New England Journal of Medicine*. He states, "If EMF was a problem, we would see more results of it." However, this denies any risk merely by alluding to the lack of hard evidence. That is not acceptable to most scientists. Simple reasons for the lack of hard evidence include the difficulty in excluding other environmental factors like lifestyle, diet, family background, the long periods required for illness to manifest itself, and other risk factors. Additionally, most hot sites that have been investigated are not "statistically significant"; although many residents alongside major power grids have experienced serious illness, the mathematical variances from what are considered the normal incidences of these maladies are too small to prove a definitive cause.

Furthermore, many of the studies are funded by groups with a vested interest in the study results. Computer manufacturers see increased product costs for equipment radiating less energy. Power companies do not want to be inundated with wrongful-injury lawsuits. Insurance companies certainly want to absorb fewer medical and liability claims. Radio stations broadcasting from within metropolitan districts atop the tall buildings and within residential neighborhoods have few other alternatives. Cable TV is a new and expanding industry that wants to maintain its profitable status. Airports and airplanes use powerful forward and downward viewing radar to provide passenger safety. The U.S. government as well has large military grids for broadcasting radar and special extremely long frequency (ELF) communication signals.

FCC Emission Ratings

The Federal Communications Commission (FCC) rates computer equipment for its potential to create RF pollution. All equipment designs are supposedly tested prior to commercial or consumer sale. Computer equipment is rated as Class A and Class B. Class B is suitable for use in a residential neighborhood, while Class A is for industrial zones only. This classification refers to the computer's ability to interfere with neighboring radio and television reception. Class B emits less RF pollution. Do not be fooled by the incorrect assumption that Class A equipment must be better than equipment with a Class B rating. There is no merit to the letter designations. These ratings detail nothing about the levels and signatures of magnetic fields; they explicitly state only that the magnitude of the radio signal emitted by these machines must fall within acceptable broadcasting noninterference standards. In other words, the FCC warrants that a certified item will not create "snow" on a nearby TV set. There is nothing stated about the health risks of sitting directly in front of a radio transmitter for hours each day over many years. Although RF pollution is assumed to be an unsubstantiated health risk, it is not within the jurisdiction of the FCC to qualify health risks; it merely manages use of the radio-frequency spectrum. Additionally, the FCC ratings provide no information about the magnitude or danger of emanating magnetic fields. It is likely that no 100-Mbits/s network will conform to a Class B rating.

It is important to note that the power of these fields, both RF and magnetic, are proportional to the size of the electrical load. Basically, RF and magnetic pollution are a direct by-product of the amount of electricity consumed. The more electricity consumed, the more energy pollution. The less electricity consumed, the less energy pollution. RF and EMI are also proportional to the force, or voltage, of the electricity. The higher the voltage, the more energy pollution. The lower the voltage, the less energy pollution. Practically, this means that video displays and power transformers create more hazard than the actual computer circuitry. This also means that the higher the protocol frequency (that is, the transmission speed), the more energy pollution.

Exposure is inversely proportional to distance and therefore dissipates rapidly with distance from its source. In other words, the smaller the power supply and the further from the equipment, the safer a person will be. This is true for both RF and magnetic field pollution. For example, a video monitor tends to have a larger envelope reaching out behind it because of its higher internal voltages than, say, a personal computer. Larger monitors have larger envelopes and color monitors with three or four electric beams broadcast to a larger area than do monochrome monitors with single beams. Monitors with higher scan rates have larger fields in general because they consume more electricity. Monitors that can display super video graphics array (SVGA), multisynch, and multiscan signals with resolutions above 1024 x 768 pixels are more powerful than monitors supporting the video graphics array (VGA) 800 x 600 standard. CAD and image stations may emit substantial EMI and RF. The VGA display monitor emits more energy than enhanced graphics array (EGA) with resolutions of approximately 480 x 320. The EGA-compatible monitor in turn broadcasts more extensive energy than color graphics arrays (CGA) with resolution of 320 x 240 pixels. The increasing use of 1600 x 1280 displays for CAD, publishing, and graphics should generate concern until these concerns are resolved. Early monochrome character-based monitors vary widely in their technology and safety. (Some even may emit more powerful and dangerous x-rays. It is wise to check older equipment carefully.) Under U.S. Federal law, detectable levels of ionizing (x-ray) radiation from VDTs have not been allowed since 1970.

Prudent Precautions

Despite a lack of conclusive proof for these health risks, sufficient circumstantial evidence exists for the prudent network manager to take precautions. (Although cigarette smoking was known to have health consequences, only recently have scientific studies actually proved and defined this risk for the primary smokers and those who breathe the secondary smoke. Only recently has this evidence been sufficient to cause restrictions in tobacco advertising and public consumption. Yet, risk-conscious people stopped smoking long ago.) Automobiles in metropolitan areas are the leading cause of ozone pollution and this should be balanced against the minimal levels produced by laser printers. Note, however, that most "modern" energy-efficient buildings are inadequately ventilated so that ozone does accumulate to levels exceeding regulations. It is equally important to place the risk of these radiation dangers into appropriate perspective. Because exposure to a higher level of background energy pollution from all other sources is greater than that from computers and networks, the risk is the constant exposure and proximity to emitting computer equipment.

Although the FDDI signal is high-frequency [125 megahertz (MHz)], the voltage and hence the electromagnetic emission levels are relatively low. The shield on the standard *shielded* twisted-pair is also designed to minimize RF emission (to improve reliability). Although RF radiation from wireless networks is less powerful than the ambient radiation from radio and television signals, these wireless signals are designed to penetrate walls and reflect around corners—and pass without distortion through people, too. Infrared is a relatively weak light signal unless transmitted as a coherent laser beam; its major danger is causing immediate retinal burns and not biological cell changes. Additionally, magnetic radiation or magnetically induced electrical fields surround

Network Health Risks

us from fluorescent light fixtures and high-voltage, high-frequency lighting (halogen and the like). Moreover, the amount of energy pollution is in proportion to the amount of electricity consumed by the electrical equipment and its proximity. The real danger of these energy fields is that we normally position ourselves close to the sources when we sit in front of a computer workstation. This magnetic radiation is insidious because it is most pervasive, invasive, and continuous when we sit within two feet of a computer screen. These fields radiate outward in various circular patterns from computer equipment and cabling, as Figure 4.7 illustrates. Although the patterns are consistent and maintain their shapes (they may surge outward when you first turn on the equipment), every piece of equipment will have its own signature.

Standards for acceptable levels of extremely low frequency (ELF)—2 kHz to 400 kHz and very low frequency (VLF)—5 Hz to 2000 Hz—signals and magnetic radiation have been set by the Swedish National Board for Measurement and Testing (e.g., MRP-I and MRP-II regulations). Other governments have proposed or enacted similar legislation, but the reality of enforcing these rules limits effectiveness. Tools for testing are not widely available, however. Furthermore, it remains unclear what is a safe exposure to radiation and what emission safety legislation can be enforced.

Data Corruption

Although the health risks of high-energy pollution are suspect, the effects of crosstalk and signal interference are well known. Because of this, many cars now are controlled by fiber optic subassemblies not

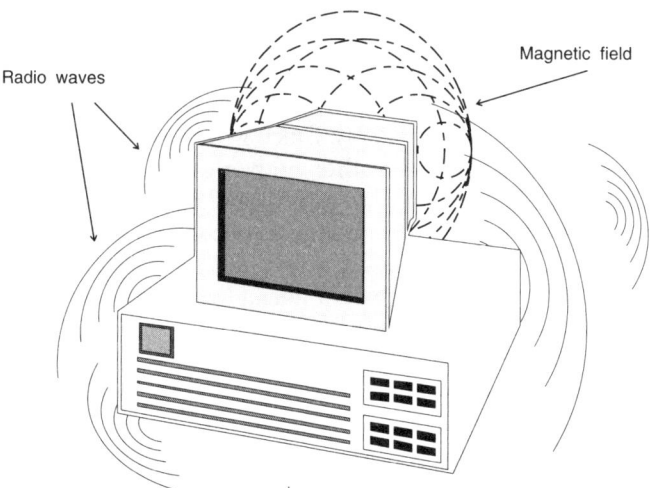

Figure 4.7 Computer equipment energy emission signatures.

subject to external signal interference; these subassemblies control car speed, servo motors, and other secondary functions. The danger is that external signals will corrupt and otherwise change data communications signals and send a car out of control. As such, consider installing optical fiber in mission-critical or dirty environments. When data controls critical functions, even one stray bit in a million (acceptable in ANSI FDDI X3T9.5) might well send a white-hot crucible spilling on the factory floor, or suggest that a shadow on a medical image represents a medical problem and not a data communications error. The legal ramifications of data corruption error caused not by human error but by transmission error represent a whole new legal specialty. This is particularly true as more products and production include a data component or rely upon information technology.

Safety Recommendations

There are four basic safety provisions. Figure 4.8 lists some possible solutions. First, isolate laser printers (and photocopiers) in a well-ventilated area. This will minimize exposure to ozone by distancing the source of this gas from people and also provide a cost-effective and energy-conservation means to ventilate a major source of indoor pollution. (The other major source of indoor ozone pollution is smoking.)

Second, shield people from radio energy by buying Class B equipment and position it as far from people as possible. That lessens exposure to RF (and magnetic energy to a lesser degree by proxy). Do not assemble or upgrade PC motherboards or power supply components within a computer since these components may not be FCC-certified and may not be certified within your particular hardware configuration. Also, since obstructions like metal-clad walls effectively reduce the energy dispersion, consider concentrating remote computing equipment in limited-access computer rooms and placing computer workstations in a computer work area away from desks, meeting rooms, and common areas. Consider replacing copper-wired networks with optical fiber networks. In many cases, such actions are impractical or costly. Since FDDI is a low-voltage medium, it is less of a risk than most other network-related computer equipment. The only risk, and also an unsubstantiated one, is the chance that the copper-based cabling itself will provide a conduit for energy and "beam" it, if you will, to users. Optical cabling (without metallic shielding for physically caused damage) is desirable for aerial links between buildings since it will not conduct a lightning strike. Route cabling, both electrical and network twisted-pair, away from users. For the most part, the real risk is the high voltage components like display monitors, and to a lesser degree, the computer circuitry, including the FDDI network interface controllers that should be considered the real health risks. For these reasons, position workstations and the video monitors as far physically from users as they will tolerate.

Network Health Risks

- Ventilate laser printers
- Power off equipment when not in use
- Minimize the use of power extension cords
- Concentrate remote equipment away from people
- Provide file servers
- Provide limited access to computer rooms
- Place wiring closets and hubs as far from people as possible
- Provide adequate electrical power cords
- Route network cables away from people
- Choose workstations with internally mounted options
- Position equipment as far as physically possible from user
- Select low-energy consumption equipment
- Install diskless workstations
- Choose equipment with lower capacity power supplies
- Limit installation of options:
  Modems
  Tape drives
  Extra memory
- Choose FCC Class B equipment
- Choose newer equipment with reduced magnetic emissions
- Verify FCC ratings compliance
- Assess the emission levels of RF networks
- Replace electrical networks with optical fiber

Figure 4.8 Network safety precautions.

Third, because magnetic field pollution is a direct function of energy usage, select computer equipment with lower energy requirements. Do not rely merely on the FCC Class B rating and assume that the equipment is safe. Ratings could be wrong and, furthermore, are significantly increased by installation of option cards (q.v., NICs, hard disk controllers, and memory boards). While radio signals can be shielded by design and by thicker equipment cases, magnetic fields are impervious to normal shielding techniques and can be diverted only by other magnetic fields. Since the concern of the health consequences of magnetic pollution is a new phenomenon and still unproven, effective designs and safer products are not yet available. Instead, use your discretion. (Select equipment with smaller power supplies and fewer options. Although this produces less powerful magnetic fields, it also provides less margin for voltage fluctuations; in some rural areas this may be a serious shortcoming to this approach.)

When deciding where to position computer rooms and wiring closets, see if people will be exposed to electrical signal. TP-DDI wiring concentrators and multiprotocol devices are likely to create considerable high-frequency radiation. Position such areas so that walls are exterior, upper-level atrium, vertical conduits, elevator shafts, lavoratories, and stair shafts. Exposure is an issue of proximity and *duration*; people pass through these areas and would not be exposed throughout the workday.

Video monitors are the primary cause of magnetic field pollution because of their high internal voltages. Install black-and-white (B&W) monitors with its single electron beam rather than color monitors with multiple beams. Do not assume that single beam color grid-masked color monitors are safer; the electron beam scan rate may be 300 percent faster and thus require a higher internal voltage. Choose equipment promising lower magnetic pollution. It is possible to counteract the magnetic field pollution by creating an equal and opposite magnetic field. Video monitors are available with countercyclical windings (cancellation yolk) designed to decrease this pollution (the NEC 4FG is one such monitor). Most new monitors conform to the Swedish EMF and RF pollution standards. Liquid crystal display (LCD) or gas plasma provide no radiation other than the minimal amounts generated from the computers chips.

Alternately, select smaller monitors with lower energy consumption. Choose monochrome monitors or select units conforming to the MPR Level I or lesser Level II emission standards. Where possible, install equipment as far from people as practical; since the strengths of magnetic fields decay rapidly with distance, the purported biological risk will also decrease with distance. Consider the video monitor carefully. SVGA monitors and other high-resolution displays cause an increased dosage of energy exposure. Not only do these devices emit more energy pollution, they also increase exposure to energy pollution because the type size and image size itself is smaller, thereby forcing the user to sit closer to the monitor to read the type. The dosage is increased exponentially by sitting closer. Microsoft Windows, for example, supports various screen resolutions including VGA, and EGA. X-Windows also supports workstations with higher resolutions and monitors with scan rates for 164 x 1320. Icons and text at set point sizes will appear progressively smaller at the higher resolutions. The higher resolution is a mixed health blessing since you need to be closer to the screen to discern the small letters.

Fourth, carefully weigh technology that is new or untested for its safety aspect. Manufacturers of radio-frequency networks say that the signal is 1000 times less powerful than a radio station. Transmitters emit several watts of power. Recall, however, that exposure is an issue of proximity, and it may be undesirable to bathe your work environment with a constant low-level signal. Practical matters may outweigh this concern; the simplicity of adding wireless FDDI may be safer than adding cabling to a building already wire-bound. Or, wireless may in fact pose a less serious health risk than installing twisted-pair wire in an asbestos-clad ceiling.

Fifth, use judicious planning when wiring a remote site with cellular modems or providing traveling sales people with cellular modems and laptops. Provide antennas with long cords or external car mountings.

Network Health Risks

Provide the option of connecting into a copper phone line when the connection will be lengthy and a standard phone line is available.

Safety Testing Tools

Few formal safety tools are available. Those that are available include gauss meters, radio-frequency analyzers, gas chromatography equipment, spectrum analyzers, x-ray detectors, and ozone detectors. A light meter (specifically designed for infrared) can measure the strength and danger from optical transmitters. Not only are these sensitive laboratory instruments, they are also prohibitively expensive for most network sites. If you foresee that the concern for employees becoming a company ethic and formal policy, acquire these tools *and* learn how to use them. Test for magnetic fields, radio-frequency pollution, x-rays from monitors, and indoor air pollution. If you suspect a substantial health risk hire a consultant to test your facilities. This will be cost-effective and it is more practical.

There are also cheaper routes and ones more likely to get approval from upper management. Buy instant film. Buy an AM radio. Get a compass. Film fogs in the presence of hard radiation like x-rays (however, computer equipment including VDTs is highly unlikely to produce x-rays). The radio will not tune in clear radio stations proximate to radio emitting equipment. The compass will indicate magnetic fields and their relative strengths by deflecting the needle from pointing northward.

A portable radio is a good and inexpensive tool for measuring radio emission from computer equipment. Noise that drowns out bona fide radio stations indicates poor shielding. The static will decrease with distance from the radio source. You may choose to replace such equipment. Some manufacturers took shortcuts and sold equipment lacking thorough certification. Not only is this a health risk, but it also has consequences for network functionality. As stated later in the book, FDDI network performance can also be adversely affected by unshielded radio sources, including a renegade personal computer (non-FCC-compliant).

A magnetic compass is a useful tool for evaluating the power of magnetic fields. Use it to plot the size, shape, placement, and intensity of the fields emanating from the computer equipment and cabling. This tool could suggest which equipment is better not purchased. The plot will show how to position a workstation, for example, to minimize the risk for a user. Figure 4.9 illustrates a typical plot and how to position a personal computer and the FDDI lobe cable to minimize the risk to the computer user. Note the placement of the video monitor against the walls with the backside positioned so as not to expose people.

Note that the computer chassis containing the motherboard, hard disk, FDDI NIC, and other accessories is placed as far from the body as possible. The keyboard obviously requires a convenient location;

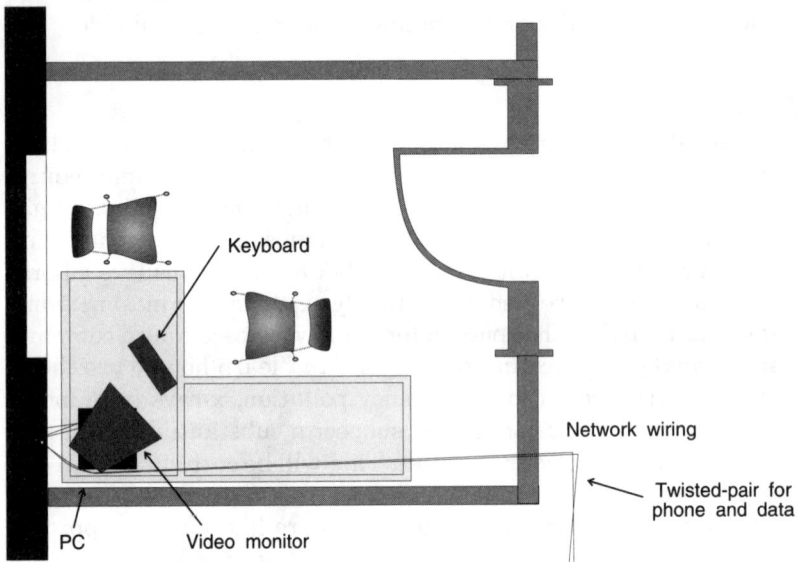

Figure 4.9 Optimal safe workstation placement.

this should be of lesser concern since it has a very low quotient of energy pollution produced *only* when a key is pressed. In this example, a large display monitor was placed on a higher platform, pitched forward, and moved as far from the user as tolerable. The limitation to video monitor placement is often the size of the office (or cubicle) and the user's visual acuity.

Part 2
Software and Hardware

This section describes the mechanical processes of FDDI networking: the hardware, the software, the installation, and the expansion process. It builds a basis of understanding for the operations and management of an FDDI network. Chapter 5 presents the standard Open Systems Interconnection reference model and FDDI variants. It describes the standard optical-fiber FDDI and twisted-pair variations; this includes full-lasing 32 km point-to-point linkages.

Chapter 6 describes the hardware and the mechanical process of FDDI. The components of an FDDI network are described and illustrated. Chapter 7 explains the FDDI process. This includes the transmission methodology and characteristic features of network-level software. Chapter 8 details the planning procedures for the mechanical components of FDDI networks, completing what vendors' spartan instructions omit. This chapter outlines those issues that an experienced network manager considers before building or expanding an FDDI network. Chapter 9 explains the installation procedures for the mechanical components of FDDI networks, supplementing vendors' incomplete instructions. This chapter suggests what steps an experienced network manager can take for testing and benchmarking a newly installed network. Chapter 10 explains why bridges, routers, and gateways are necessary on an FDDI internetwork, and how these units are installed. Since organizational growth is likely to outstrip the capacity of any original network, bridges, routers, gateways, and matrix switching technology are also presented as solutions to overloaded networks.

Chapter 11 addresses the concept of the enterprise-wide network, particularly relevant to the utility and coverage provided by large campus-wide FDDI networks. Internetworking, legacy system replacement, and network software issues are gaining importance as crucial transition issues. Client/server computing is displacing host mainframe data processing, and local area networks are becoming integrated into distributed computing and enterprise-wide environments. Although local area networks may preoccupy the efforts and attentions of many network managers, linking multiple LANs and host computers at distant sites is becoming an important FDDI topic.

Chapter

5
FDDI Standards

Conformity to a network standard represents important progress. Standards promote reliability, product growth, compatibility, and interconnectivity for local area networking. Standards are of prime importance for interconnectivity of heterogeneous local area networks, as well as necessary for development of effective network management tools. Although FDDI is standardized, there are at least two physical permutations. FDDI transmits a 125 megahertz signal for a signal speed of 100 Mbits/s; 4 bits are encoded into 5 signal transitions. Transmission media can utilize either shielded twisted-pair or unshielded twisted-pair wiring or the originally specified optical fiber. Furthermore, FDDI is supported on optical fiber as either a dual or single ring.

The FDDI standards are based upon standards codified by the Institute for Electrical and Electronic Engineers (IEEE) 802.6 (topology), by the American National Standards Institute, and also by the International Standards Organization (ISO). This chapter uses the ISO OSI model as a reference to describe the functions of FDDI data communications. This model is gathering widespread international acceptance while network hardware vendors recognize that conformity to these standards supplies an important selling merit. This chapter also describes four types of transmission media: shielded twisted-pair wiring, unshielded twisted-pair wiring, and optical fiber. FDDI network configurations conclude this presentation.

The FDDI Protocol

FDDI was proposed in 1984 to provide a network protocol an order of magnitude faster than existing technology. Various standards define the protocol. Specifically, ANSI X3.166 (1990) defines the physical layer, the medium dependent layer, and multimode fiber. The physical layer is referred to as PMD. The corresponding ISO specification is ISO 9314-3. The physical layer protocol (PHY) is defined by ANSI X3.148 (1988) and ISO 9314-1 (1989). Media access control (MAC) is defined by ANSI

X3.139 (1987) and ISO 9314-2 (1989). The station management (SMT) facility is defined by ANSI X3T9.5 and ISO WD 9314-6, unpublished and working documents at this time. These standards and proposed enhancements are listed in Figure 5.1.

The FDDI design conforms to this layered architecture model of networking, and represents one of the first communications protocols designed to conform to OSI standardization (others merely have been adapted or overlaid onto the OSI networking model for presentation purposes). The OSI model was developed by the International Standards Organization (ISO) as a generic model for data communication.[1]

Because modularity of communication functions is a key design criterion in the OSI model, vendors who adhere to the standards and guidelines of this model can supply FDDI-compatible devices, alternative FDDI media, and bridging protocols that easily and reliably interconnect other types of data networks to FDDI. Additionally, conformance to the ISO OSI model

FDDI Layer	Standard
PMD (physical layer)	ANSI X3.166 (1990)
	ISO 9314-3 (1990)
TP-PMD (twisted-pair)	No document yet (draft)
LCF-PMD (low cost fiber)	ANSI X3T9.5 (draft)
SMF-PRM (single mode)	ANSI X3.184 (1991)
	ISO 9314-4
SPM (SONET mapping)	No document yet (draft)
PHY (physical layer protocol)	ANSI X3.148 (1988)
	ISO 9314-1 (1989)
PHY-2 (enhancements)	ANSI X3T9.5 rev 4.1 (draft)
	ANSI X3T9.5 rev 5 (draft)
HRC (hybrid ring control)	ANSI X3.184 (draft)
	ISO 9314-5 (draft)
MAC (media access control)	ANSI X.139 (1987)
	ISO 9314-5 (1989)
MAC-2 (enhancements)	ANSI X3T9.5 (committee)
SMT (station management)	ANSI X3T9.5 rev 7 (1992)
	ISO 9314-6 WD
LLC (logical link control)	IEEE 802.1
	IEEE 802.2

Figure 5.1 FDDI Standards as of February 1993.

[1] *Datapro Network Reports* includes information on the OSI plenary groups and frequently prints the membership lists of standards-setting organizations.

FDDI Standards

means that the latest software monitoring and management software will simplify network management. Conformance to the OSI model offers remote management that will work even across bridges and other devices usually not viewed as FDDI-compatible.

The OSI model specifies seven layers of functionality as shown in Figure 5.2. It defines the functions layers but does not define the protocols that implement the functions at each layer. That is important for compatibility, protocol independence, and the future growth of network technology. Layer 1 is the physical layer (electrical, mechanical, or optical). Layer 2 is the data link layer (flow, standards, connections). Layer 3 is the network layer (routing and switching of the actual transmission). Layer 4 is the transport layer (transmission and transfer of data). Layer 5 is the session layer (administrative control of transmissions and transfers). Layer 6 is the presentation layer (interpretation and data transformation). Layer 7 is the application layer (system computing and user applications).

Implementations of the OSI model provide for a protocol for communication at each layer on two processors (that is, session to session) and an interface for communication between layers on one processor (that is, presentation to session). Physical communication occurs only at layer 1 (the protocol for electrical transmission on the transmission medium, bit by bit). The protocols for the other layers define virtual connections in the software. In other words, only layer 1 physically connects to layer 1. All communication, even from upper layers, transpires through a

Layer:			
7	Application	User application process and management functions
6	Presentation	Data interpretation, format, and code transformation
5	Session	Administration and control of sessions between nodes
4	Transport	Transparent data transfer and transmission control
3	Network	Routing, switching, and flow control
2	Data link	Maintain and release data; link, error, and flow control
1	Physical	Control of data circuits; physical media definition

Figure 5.2 The International Standards Organization (ISO) Open Systems Interconnect (OSI) model.

chain of layered control. Peer-layer communication is not possible in this model. Repeaters, bridges, routers, and gateways all must conform to this, too. All other layers communicate downward to lower levels in steps, or in the OSI terminology, communicate through *protocol stacks*. While OSI creates a distinct loss of efficiency in building and decoding each layer, the benefit is generic interconnectivity and interoperability. The following paragraphs describe the functions of each layer. Noncompliance causes compatibility problems and complications with network management software.

Layer 1, the *physical layer*, specifies the electrical, optical, and mechanical control of the actual data circuits. This function is managed by the FDDI NICs and station hardware (or hubs), and the optical cabling or twisted-pair wiring between them. While the transmission medium is formally defined by the ANSI standards, it is generally included in the OSI definition, and it can be thought of as the underlying layer of the OSI model. The model does specify (and limit) the media; enhancements to the protocol are in committee or draft for consideration. This is an important factor since many vendors provide STP and UTP support. For example, vendors have implementations of FDDI on twisted-pair. Crescendo has the CDDI trademark for a shielded twisted-pair network although this formerly meant copper-based FDDI, Synoptics and IBM have coined the SDDI term for FDDI on shielded twisted-pair, and FDDI committees refer to copper-based FDDI as TP-PMD and TP-DDI, or twisted-pair distributed data interchange. DEC created a "Greenbook" specification for its FDDI efforts. Other vendors, such as Codenoll, are substituting less costly plastic optical fiber for glass, and are part of the LCF-PMD committee.

The transmission media layer specifies the physical medium used in constructing the network, including size, thickness, and other characteristics of the actual medium. The electrical, mechanical, wireless infrared or radio frequency, or optical pulses travel along a transmission medium, which may be unshielded twisted-pair telephone line (which FDDI cannot effectively use for distances longer than 30 m), a special data-grade twisted-pair wire, or optical fiber. It is important to realize that FDDI is specified for use on multimode optical fiber with an internal diameter of 62.5 μm and an outside diameter of 125 μm. This does not preclude the use of fiber ranging in internal diameter from 50 to 100 nm, or the use of single mode fiber (SMF-PMD) for longer distances. The applications for these fiber variants are discussed in Chapter 7. For reference the ISO OSI reference model layer 1 corresponds to the PMD, PHY, PHY-2, SPM, and SMT (partially).

Layer 2, the *data link layer*, is software that manages transmissions, error acknowledgment, and recovery. The mechanical devices, such as NICs, are mapped data units to data units, to provide physical error

FDDI Standards

detection and notification, and link activation and deactivation of a logical communication connection. This is the media access control layer (MAC), and the NICs maintain station FDDI addressing at this level. For reference the ISO OSI reference model layer 2 corresponds to the MAC and MAC-2, HRC, and SMT (partially). Layer 2 also encompasses the IEEE 802.1 dependencies and 802.2 LLC.

Layer 3, the *network layer*, is the borderline between hardware and software. At the network layer, the protocol mechanisms activate the data routing by providing network (station) address resolution and flow control in terms of segmentation and blocking. The network layer also provides service selection, connection resets, and expedited data transfers. Typically, the Internet protocol (IP) is transported at this layer. Other network layer protocols in use include network layer drivers for Appletalk and NetWare.

Layer 4, the *transport layer*, controls data transfer and transmission. Routing and data encapsulation of non-OSI protocols occurs at this layer. Transport of packets via alternative routes is performed at this level. FDDI conforms to the IEEE802.1 routing protocols.

Layers 5, 6, and 7 are generally supplied by vendor-specific software and are not part of FDDI per se. These layers are part of the network operating system and the application. Layer 5 recognizes the active nodes on the network and sets up the tables of source and destination addresses. It also establishes, quite literally, a handshaking for each session between different nodes and processes. Technically, services at layer 5 are called *session connection, exception reporting, coordination of send/receive modes*, and, of course, the actual data exchange.

Layer 6, the *presentation layer*, transfers information from the application software to the network session layer to the operating system. The interface at this layer performs data transformations, data formatting, syntax selection [including American Standard Code for Information Interchange (ASCII), Extended Binary Code Decimal Interchange Code (EBCDIC), Tagged Image Format (TIF), and other numeric or graphic formats], device selection and control, and finally, data compression or encryption.

Layer 7, the *network application layer*, supports identification of communicating partners, establishes the authority to communicate, transfers information, and applies privacy mechanisms and cost allocations. It may be a complex layer. The application layer supports file services, print services, and electronic mail. Electronic data interchange (EDI) occurs at this layer since it is based upon a file format and various gateway transmission methods. These "applications" are not to be confused with user applications. The application layer is the network system software that supports user-layer applications, like word or data processing, CAD/CAM, and image scanning. Figure 5.3 lists specific examples of standard protocols for each layer of the OSI model.

RS-232 and RS-449 are twisted-pair network standards. DDCMP is Digital Data Communications Message Protocol. LAP-B is Link Access Control-Balanced. SDLC is an acronym for Synchronous Data Link Control, whereas HDLC is an acronym for High-Level Data Link Control. UDP 2 is User Datagram Protocol. ARP is Address Resolution Protocol. IPX is internet packet exchange. This predominant network management technology is SNMP and SNMP-II. These TCP/IP- based protocols are not OSI-compliant and compete with the more rigorously defined CMIP management protocol. These are presented later in this chapter. However, since so many network devices now include SNMP-aware functions, and because SNMP is far simpler than CMIP, this management protocol is becoming the prevailing convention. It is certainly interesting that FDDI, which is an OSI ISO-compliant protocol, is usually provided on NICs, hubs, or concentrators with SNMP management firmware (i.e., chip microcode) and software. Soon it may include the next revision of this TCP/IP derivative software, SNMP-II.

The ISO standards also specify how repeaters, bridges, routers, and gateways are established to extend the topology of a network. The simplest of these OSI definitions is the LAN repeater, which receives, regenerates, and amplifies the transmission signal from one network segment onto another network segment.

OSI Repeaters

Repeaters extend signal. They represent active devices; FDDI stations are repeaters. In effect, every DAS node on FDDI is a repeater since each station captures and retransmits the token or frame. See Figure 5.4 for the ISO repeater model. Signals are amplified to reach the next DAS nodes or DAS/SAS hubs beyond the normal lobe or trunk length. If MAC-layer routing occurs, this will filter FDDI packets for higher

ISO	Example Architecture
Layer 7	X.400, SNMP, NFS, NetWare, PC LAN, SNA, vendor-specific
Layer 6	NAPLPS, MAP, vendor-specific
Layer 5	Vendor-specific
Layer 4	ARP, IPX, TCP (as in TCP/IP), vendor-specific
Layer 3	FDDI SMT, X.25, UDP and IP (as In TCP/IP), DECnet, SPX
Layer 2	FDDI, IEEE 802.2, DDCMP, LAP-B, NetBIOS, SDLC, HDLC
Layer 1	FDDI, IEEE 802.1, RS-232, RS-449, Token-Ring, V.22, V.32, V.42 bis

Figure 5.3 Examples of standard protocols in the ISO architecture.

FDDI Standards

traffic rates by maintaining a MAC-level or ring address routing table for SAS devices.

OSI Bridges

The *bridge*, as shown in Figure 5.5, interconnects network rings. A simple bridge, for example, might connect a Token-Ring 4 Mbits/s with an Ethernet or with an FDDI fiber network. A bridge can convert a

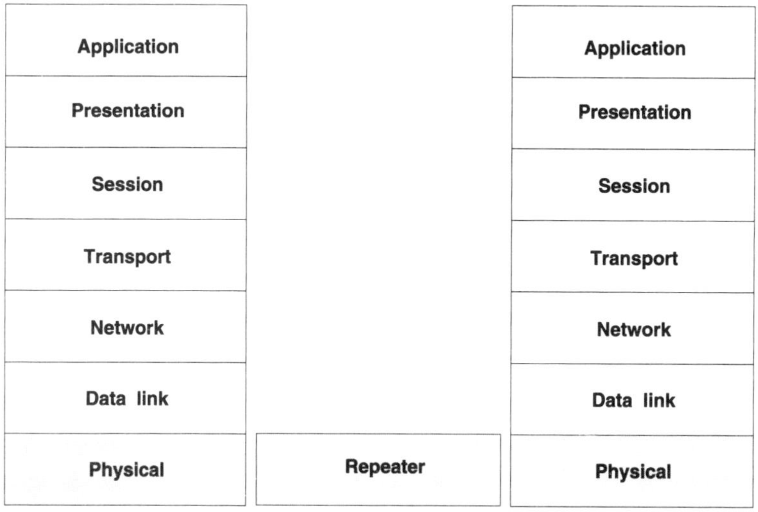

Figure 5.4 The OSI repeater model.

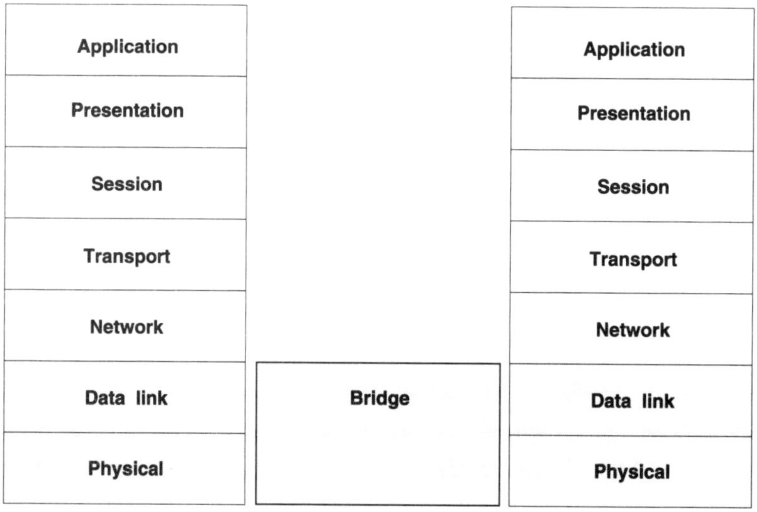

Figure 5.5 The OSI bridge model.

digital signal into a frequency-modulated electrical signal or a diode laser signal. Network, transport, session, presentation, and application layers are not affected by the bridge, so the bridge is totally transparent to the user. A bridge converts TP-DDI signals to the optical FDDI signal. For reference, most SAS devices are media bridges as well as signal repeaters. A bridge does not examine the protocol header above OSI layer 2. The protocol, per se, is not bridged; only the transmission medium itself is so connected. A bridge can interconnect two Ethernet-based networks with a third FDDI ring in the middle that cannot understand the packets traveling through it (unless they are translated at the routing layer). The bridges see only the middle segment as a routing path, important when FDDI is traditionally applied to link multiple LANs in a distributed campus setting or within the vertical structure of a high-rise corporate building.

There are also intelligent bridges that limit traffic between network segments. These bridges learn addresses, filter packets, and forward a subset of packets based upon the contents of a routing table. As such, these bridges are actually level 3 routers. Dual-port bridges isolate segments in just this manner and only forward packets addressed to devices on the other segments. Multiport while SAS bridges provide an effective solution to interconnect LANs and WANs to an FDDI backbone. These performance-enhancing features are becoming desirable and more available as SAS and multiple protocol hubs are designed as compressed backbones (i.e., a ring in a box). An intelligent bridge can function as a packet switch to eliminate multiple hops between segments with similar characteristics. They provide better performance, but also more flexibility in network design.

OSI Routers

The *router*, as shown in Figure 5.6, interconnects network segments at OSI layer 3, the network layer. It is protocol-dependent. In fact, the major failure in connecting networks to FDDI is that NetBIOS, UDP, and NFS protocols are not routable, and that most node addresses in other protocols do not conform to the 64-bit OSI station address. Routers read the protocol header and forward packets to other segments which request forwarding to those other segments. Routers often support multiple protocols and provide either data encapsulation or translation. They can interconnect networks with different physical and/or data link protocols. Transport, session, presentation, and application layers are not affected by the router.

There is some confusion between the definition of the bridge and a router. A router is a device that spans the media, data link, and transport layers of the OSI model. It receives only those packets addressed to it by a transmitting node or another router. It does not forward packets transparently as the bridge does; instead, the router

FDDI Standards

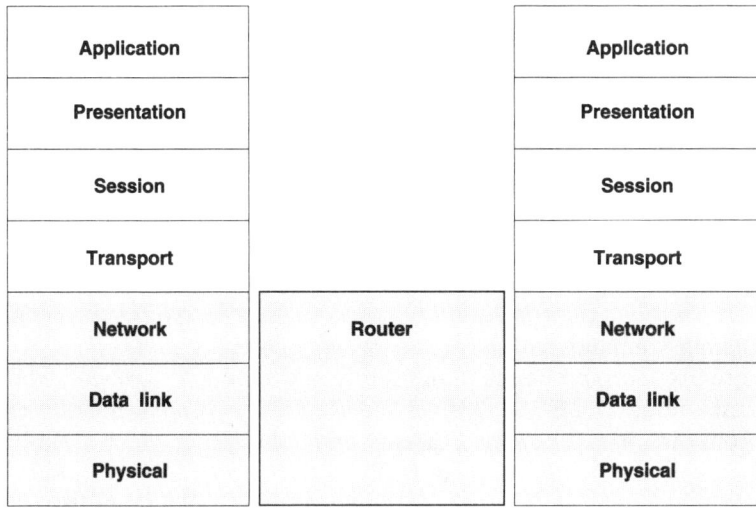

Figure 5.6 The OSI router model.

requires other routers for this task. Additionally, spanning-tree routers determine the best transmission path when there are active loops. This functionality requires extensive routing tables and preferences to determine the best route.

Multiprotocol routers provide an effective solution to interconnect LANs, optical fiber, FDDI, and long-distance connections where there are multiple network protocols such as Ethernet, Token-Ring, FDDI, and T-1. They provide more flexibility for network design but are difficult to configure and complex to maintain. Campus sites with multiple routers represent a demanding management task because configuration options are compounded by the dispersion of the routers; they represent performance issues because FDDI generally provides more bandwidth than most routing equipment, because many competing protocols for maintaining alternate routing paths exist and are often incompatible, and because packets routed across an FDDI span may not be in a native FDDI format.

It is appropriate at this point to discuss the differences between data encapsulation and translation. Since routing devices may connect different LANs together across an FDDI linkage, the data may require a rearrangement for delivery. The station addresses certainly do. Ethernet provides for 1024 station address. Token-Ring provides for 255 ring address and 255 separate rings. ARCnet provides for 256 nodes on each network. OSI addresses provide 64 bits of addressing with an option for 128 bits. FDDI addresses are optional 16 or 58 bits. All stations need to understand and respond to addresses in either format. Generally, the first 12 bits are assigned by equipment manufacturers.

The remaining 48 bits are split into two segments for local and internetwork station address management. The router matches addresses for the different protocols. To some degree this may overcome protocol differences.

However, this may not provide for delivery of an Ethernet packet or Token-Ring frame to an FDDI desktop. Routers may simply place these packets inside of a larger FDDI frame for delivery to another routing device; this process is called *encapsulation*. Alternatively, the addresses, check sums, and data components can be extracted for insertion into an FDDI frame for native mode delivery to an FDDI desktop; this process is called *translation*. Encapsulation tends to require less CPU time but more transmission bandwidth for faster delivery than translation.

But there are more problems than merely addressing differences. The data formats differ. The FDDI OSI vehicle is called a *frame*. This differs slightly from the terminology for Ethernet and Token-Ring which equally refers to packets and frames, or generically to *datagrams*. All represent a data component and a packaging for safe delivery. The FDDI OSI term for the data component is called the *data payload* rather than the data "field." These data components vary in size. ARCNet has less than 507-byte and fixed 1143-byte data fields. Ethernet allows packets with up to 1500 bytes of data. Token-Ring provides for data fields up to 18,432 bytes at 16 Mbits/s, but only 4600 bytes at 4 Mbits/s transmission speed. FDDI specifies a maximum data payload of 8978 symbols (of 9000 symbols for the total frame), each of which represents 4 bits of transport-level data. Network operating systems may impose additional restrictions.

For example, Novell NetWare IPX typically limits packet sizes to 1024 bytes for simplified compatibility, but further limits data field sizes to 512 bytes when they are "hopped" across NetWare routers. In effect, translation is an operating system dependent issue. How would an FDDI server send a datagram to a Ethernet node across an NetWare router in native OSI mode? Transmission would require a large number of 512-byte packets. This is true even if the burst mode enhancement is enabled—the sending station can just send more than one 512-byte packet on each token acquisition. Alternatively, how would a 17,563 byte LAN Manager Token-Ring frame be delivered in any form to an FDDI station? Surely, it would need to be divided into smaller encapsulation payloads and reassembled there. For the most part, encapsulation is faster and simpler, but translation more desirable for true interoperations to the desktop and internetworking with other protocols and network operating systems.

OSI Gateway

A *gateway* in the OSI model interconnects networks and equipment with different characteristics. Information, presentation (ASCII to EBCDIC for example), source and destination addressing, and physical

FDDI Standards

connections are translated by the gateway. A gateway might, for example, translate a file into a stream to be directed over a frame relay link or translate that same file into an IBM file format and X.400 interconnection. Gateways frequently *decouple* communication from the application. As likely as not, when FDDI rings are interconnected, a buffered gateway will be the interconnection mechanism for performance reasons.

See Figure 5.7 for an example of this translation. The gateway is a strict definition within the context of the OSI model and differs from the common connotation of a "software" repeater, which is a workstation interconnected to two different network rings. In some cases, a gateway may encapsulate or translate one protocol within another for transport as with FDDI backbone.

It is becoming more common to encapsulate packets into the 9000 symbol FDDI frame because it is technologically simpler and faster than extracting the data from the frames of other protocols and decoupling those transmissions. Although encapsulation is usually faster, it can become a performance bottleneck when large frames are divided into small blocks for delivery. As such, substantial overhead would be wasted encapsulating the frame with FDDI. Additionally, this same technique can be modified for Novell NetWare, Banyan Vines, Ethernet, PC LAN Server, LAN Manager, and the myriad of proprietary network operation system protocols. Compare this with packing thousands of individual postal letters into containerized crates for ocean shipping.

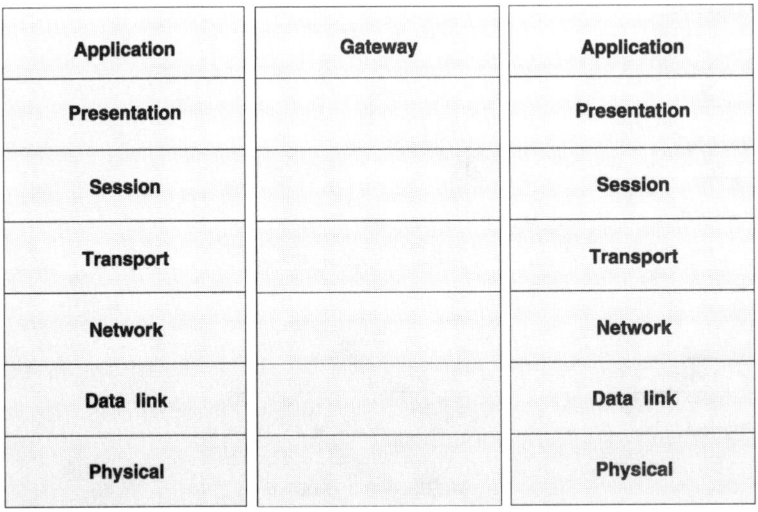

Application	Gateway	Application
Presentation		Presentation
Session		Session
Transport		Transport
Network		Network
Data link		Data link
Physical		Physical

Figure 5.7 The OSI gateway model.

The Definition of FDDI

Fiber Distributed Data Interface (FDDI) comprises only layers 1 through 3 of the OSI model. FDDI is also defined by the ANSI X3T9.5 and the other standards, as previously listed in Figure 5.1. FDDI is represented by hardware and media access protocols, transmissions, error acknowledgment, and recovery. The mechanical devices, like NICs, are mapped station units to station units, to provide physical error detection and notification, and link activation and deactivation of a logical communication connection. This is the media access control layer (MAC), and the NICs maintain a universal OSI station FDDI address at this level. FDDI, like a telephone, will handle different application software. Just as with any phone that accesses a network of other phones, it must adhere to certain standards. These standards are the protocols described in Chapter 6.

Any disparity between the OSI model and other data communications protocols is likely to fade as multinational communications increases the premium on interoperability and simplicity. Although some people correctly show that the many functional layers of the OSI stack increase channel overhead and CPU overhead for encoding and decoding, the simplicity of applying one uniform protocol across many LANs, WANs, MANs, and computing platforms will ease the transition to true internetworking and distributed client/server processing. Figure 5.8 shows the mapping of the FDDI standard to the OSI model. The bi-annual Interop and Network World Shows salute the possibilities available when equip-

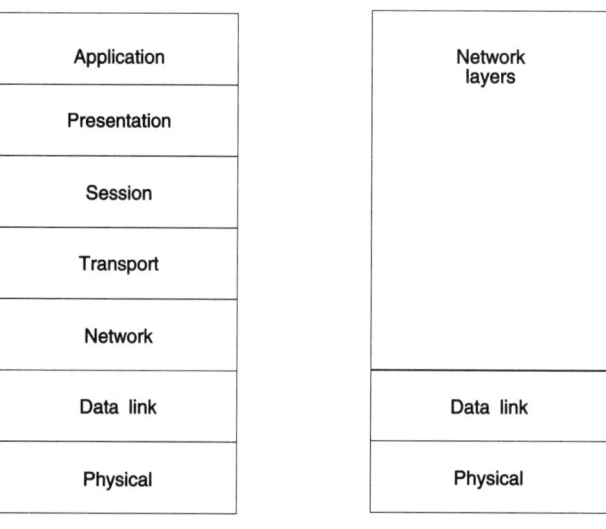

Figure 5.8 Comparison of the OSI model to the FDDI standard.

ment from different vendors can in fact interoperate. Buyers at these shows encourage vendors to create uniform standards, adhere to them, and demonstrate the openess of any interoperability claims. As a result, cisco routers, Apple Macintoshes, Sun workstations, and PC clones work well together sharing the same FDDI ring.

FDDI Variations

FDDI is not the monolithic OSI standard is appears to be. There are media and hardware variants. There are even protocol variants. This section defines those media, hardware, protocols, and the physical differences among them. It also describes mechanical standards for the various transmission media, shielded and unshielded twisted-pair, and optical fiber.

Optical fiber technology is the original technology, and the standard against which all variants are compared, although it remains more expensive and a demanding technology. Fiber cable is difficult to extend, comparatively difficult to splice and repair, severely tests those expecting to add new nodes and rearrange locations of existing nodes, and suffers transmission degradation over time. Expansion and contraction, and extremes from heat and cold fracture the cable. Heat and cold and particle radiation discolor the optical qualities and gradually decrease the bandwidth and transmission efficiency. Managers at several nuclear sites with very large installations have discovered this firsthand after five or ten years with fiber. Additionally, the infant technology to bridge FDDI networks to other LANs and WANs remains ill-defined and not standardized, although FDDI multiprotocol routers are changing this.

Briefly, FDDI is specified for optical fiber with an internal diameter of 62.5 mm and an external diameter of 125 mm. The fiber itself is a multimode glass that is capable of transporting various wavelengths of light. Actual transmission wavelength is infrared from diodes transmitting light in phase at 850 or 1300 nanometers (nm). Signal loss is specified at 3.5 dB or less.

However, most of the technology will work with other sizes of optical fiber. Some installations will specify fiber with an internal diameter of 50 mm. The reason for this selection is that signal loss is lowered to 3.0 dB, hence distance between transmitters can be greater or attention to connection can be less. The downside is that creating connections for this smaller fiber is significantly more difficult. Standard FDDI fittings will work with this fiber, but ensuring that the fiber is centered on the coupling is tedious. For these reasons the U.S. military specifies a larger fiber with 100 mm glass fiber conduit and an exterior diameter of 150 mm. Signal loss is higher at 4 dB. The requirements for polishing the connectors are also less stringent because there is more surface area in the fiber ends to transfer the optical signal. Training is minimized, time for installation is reduced, and repairs are simplified under battlefield conditions.

In all cases, actual FDDI signaling is provided by an on/off transition. Another optical fiber–based media variant exists for special 32- to 36-km connections. If you recall the section from Chapter 4, this enhancement requires transmission with full lasing capability and a more powerful light beam. Signaling is also provided by the same on/off transition.

There are two variants for copper-based FDDI network. Both require two pairs of wires. One variant requires shielded twisted-pair (STP); the other one functions with unshielded twisted-pair (UTP). Because many buildings are wired for telephones and mainframe terminal data lines using voice-grade unshielded twisted-pair, this other UTP option will be discussed as well. Many corporate downsizing strategies begin with a transition based upon the suitability of UTP as the LAN medium. The hazards for this transition will be discussed in Chapter 7. It is important to note that the FDDI protocol is the not same for all media; the actual signaling method does vary. Optical fiber and STP employ the non-return to zero invert on ones (NRZI) encoding method, while UTP uses MLT-3. These will be defined in the next chapter. Figure 5.9 presents the FDDI family tree. Figure 5.10 lists the formal conventions for FDDI transmissions.

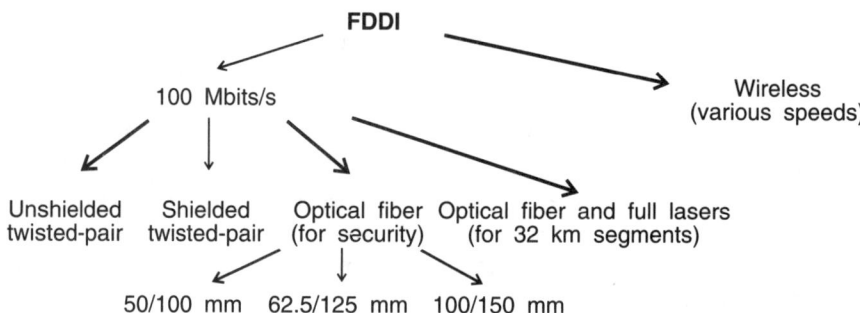

Figure 5.9 The FDDI media and transmission speed family.

Medium	Optical fiber or twisted-pair wire
Optical	830 or 1300 nm NRZI-encoded signal
Electrical	4.5 V DC NRZI- or MLT-3-encoded signal
Signal technique	Digital
Protocol	ANSI X3T9.5
Conventions	Token passing

Figure 5.10 The FDDI standards.

FDDI Standards

FDDI on Optical Fiber

Optical fiber is the basis for the current ANSI FDDI X3.139 standard. FDDI is normally transported by optical fiber. Optical fiber represents the typical method for building enterprise-wide networks. The distance between nodes can be as high as 2 km without the use of repeaters or signals boosters, and 32 to 36 km for full lasing single mode optical fiber. Additionally, as many as 1000 DAS units can be installed on the dual ring. The dual ring does not increase transmission capacity from 100 Mbits/s. The second ring is a called a *counter-rotating ring* since the token is passed in the reverse direction. This second ring provides an automatic wrap and backup in the event that the primary ring fails. This represents an important facility for campus networks and mission-critical activities.

Actual installation of fiber networks either that cable is pulled through existing conduit to interconnect floors, buildings, and LANs. When FDDI is retrofitted to an existing site or applied to link many LANs, trenches are dug between buildings or under parking lots, or cable is installed along with steam, gas, or water piping. Single, dual, or multiple fibers may be packaged together within a bundle. Some manufacturers provide UTP, STP, coaxial TV cable, and optical fiber in a single packaging. Special components and bundling can also be ordered. Some optical fiber cables are "armored" with a woven steel jacket. This protects the bundle from accident, security breaches, and careless installation. Nonetheless, very little can protect even an armored cable from an errant backhoe or bulldozer. Note that the use of armored optical cable run between buildings above ground is inadvisable. First, this creates a lightning rod that may redirect the power of the lightning strikes directly to sensitive computer equipment. Second, the failure to adequately ground the armored cable can cause a differential in ground potential between sites and equipment that is both hazardous to people and equipment. In such circumstances, an overload will travel the armor to the most effective ground—but not before overloading equipment in that path.

Optical fiber networks are more expensive and more difficult to debug, maintain, and expand than electrical networks. New test instruments and installation tools are required. However, it provides flexibility, greater reliability, faster transmission speeds, and a larger geographic reach for the LAN; it is one-third the weight of copper twisted-pair; it is not susceptible to electronic noise or signal crosstalk; and provides excellent security. Optical networks also easily provide 50- to 250-km rings. Figure 5.11 shows the composition of a fiber cable and its advantages and disadvantages.

Local area networks rarely service just a handful of users. Often, a small network has grown rapidly to encompass 50 or 100 users, and as is often the case with Ethernet or Token-Ring, becomes a traffic bottleneck. The most common and effective solution is to partition the network into rings

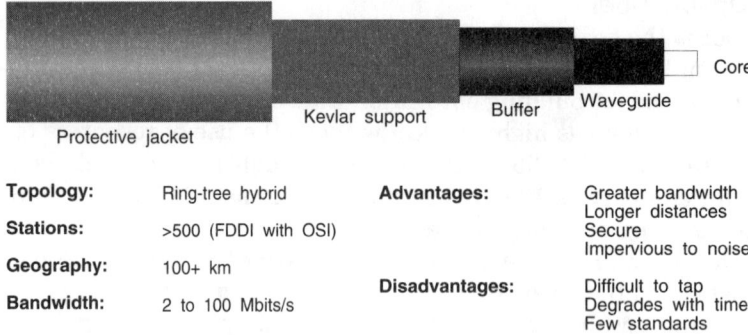

Topology:	Ring-tree hybrid	Advantages:	Greater bandwidth
			Longer distances
Stations:	>500 (FDDI with OSI)		Secure
			Impervious to noise
Geography:	100+ km		
		Disadvantages:	Difficult to tap
Bandwidth:	2 to 100 Mbits/s		Degrades with time
			Few standards

Figure 5.11 Optical fiber cable.

with fewer users and connect these segments to an FDDI backbone, multiprotocol router, or packet switch. Not only does optical fiber (FDDI) provide a greater bandwidth over longer distances; it also promises a precocious upgrade path and priority traffic support. Optical fiber is suitable with multiplexing equipment, concurrent phone links, and fiber optic interconnect repeater link (FOIRL) equipment with other protocols.

The FOIRL is a physical layer standard consisting of a 100 Mbits/s token ring using 62.5 and 125 μm twin optical fibers. The modal bandwidth at 850 nm should be 160 MHz/km. Cable attenuation at that distance should be -3.5 to 5.0 dB/km. The FDDI connector is a polarized duplex connector housing two ferrules within a single shell. One connector transmits; the other receives. The connector polarization prevents mismatching. An FDDI network has a ring topology with concentrators providing branches to achieve a physical star configuration with special node attachment requirements, as Figure 5.12 lists. Transmission is via a single or dual fiber (or four-wire copper) counter-rotating ring. The ring itself is self-healing and will link itself together to bypass a failed station when a fault is detected.

Twisted-Pair

FDDI can perform with at least four types of twisted-pair (TP) cable. Mixing types of TP is inadvisable. Generically, this consists of shielded and unshielded twisted-pair. Unshielded twisted-pair consists of either voice-grade telephone wiring, datagrade wiring, and composites. To

- DAS–dual-attachment station (workstations)
- SAS–single-attachment station (secondary networks)
- Wiring concentrators–DAS devices to connect multiple SAS devices

Figure 5.12 FDDI ring topology. FDDI supports three devices that attach to the dual ring to form a ring and star configuration.

FDDI Standards

further confuse this issue, there are at least three significant standards for grading wiring. TP is measured in gauges of thickness, by composition as defined by IBM, and by quality as measured in terms of transmission speed support and transmission distance. The most reliable and standardized method today is based upon the Telecommunications Industry Association and Engineering Industry Association (TIA/EIA).

IBM type 1 STP will support FDDI to a maximum distance of 298 ft (92 m); this provides for patch panel and jumper connections made from a lower quality cable at each of the connection. TIA/EIA category 3 UTP is suitable for speeds to 10 Mbits/s (Ethernet 10Base-T) and lobe lengths to 298 ft (92 m), category 4 UTP is suitable for speeds to 16 Mbits/s (Token-Ring) and lengths to 298 ft (92 m), while category 5 UTP is suitable for speeds up to 155 Mbits/s (FDDI and ATM) and 298 ft (92 m) lobe lengths. The use of category 3, category 4, or voice grade UTP, while inadvisable is possible for FDDI, although lobe lengths should be kept under 30 m. Since the quality is asserted by the manufacturer, it is wise to test the performance of the wiring before installation with a handheld scanner *before* network installation. Use of the these scanners are described in Chapter 14. Physically, the Type 1 cabling consists of two pairs of 22 gauge (AWG) vinyl-clad copper wire. These pairs indeed twist about themselves three times per foot to minimize the affects of signal crosstalk. It is called "twisted-pair" because the bundles of wires containing four, six, or eight direct current (DC) wiring pairs twist around each other. The wires are twisted to minimize crosstalk, signal attenuation, and susceptibility to stray noise. The pairs are color coded. One pair of wire supports receive (RX) signals (input to the NIC), while the other pair of wires supports transmit (TX) signals (output to the hub). These two pairs of wires are surrounded by a metal foil that is the ground (negative potential). The foil in turn is surrounded by a braided wire tube that is called the shield, and serves to both contain internal signals and exclude external false signals. This is surrounded by an extruded vinyl jacket. Building or fire code may mandate that the fluorinated ethylene propylene (FEP, trade name, Teflon) be used in place of vinyl for plenum and wall installations. Figure 5.13 illustrates the composition of IBM Type 1 shielded twisted-pair. STP jumpers (Type 6) have a similar composition but the wires are smaller and not twisted as frequently. This wire should not be applied for trunks or lobe runs longer than 30 m. There is a special STP product called Type 2 that also includes four unshielded twisted-pairs for voice (telephone) communication.

Unshielded and datagrade twisted-pair is a very different media. The wire is vinyl clad 24- or 26-gauge copper wire. Four pairs are twisted four or five times per foot. The four pairs are color-coded with candy stripes. A gray vinyl insulating jacket surrounds this group, in turn. Generally, twenty-five pairs are bundled into a larger bundle and vinyl

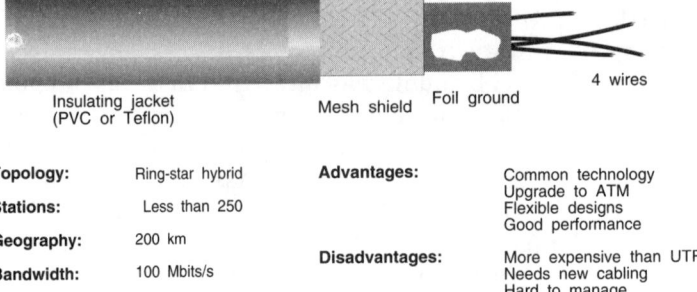

Topology:	Ring-star hybrid	Advantages:	Common technology
Stations:	Less than 250		Upgrade to ATM
Geography:	200 km		Flexible designs
			Good performance
Bandwidth:	100 Mbits/s	Disadvantages:	More expensive than UTP
			Needs new cabling
			Hard to manage

Figure 5.13 IBM Type 1 shielded twisted-pair wire.

clad as well. Building or fire code may mandate that Teflon be used in place of vinyl for plenum and wall installations. Figure 5.14 illustrates the composition of a typical unshielded twisted-pair.

The major differences between these media variations are the trunk and lobe lengths supported. Different NIC and hub units usually support different STP and UTP media—the transmission protocol and signaling characteristics may be very different. Some devices automatically sense (or are manually set for) the different media characteristics and boost signal strength and signal receive gain for UTP installations.

FDDI Compatibility

FDDI is consistent with the ANSI X3.139 standard for the physical interconnection of nodes on a network. Signaling characteristics are not the same for the various variants. Figure 5.15 lists the FDDI signaling characteristics. FDDI on optical fiber applies the NRZI encoding standard defined in the next chapter. FDDI on STP also uses NRZI. On the other hand, FDDI on UTP applies the MLT-3 standard and may require two pairs or four pairs of wires to communicate the data signals; UTP is more susceptible to noise and wiring resistance loss and more likely to cause interference.

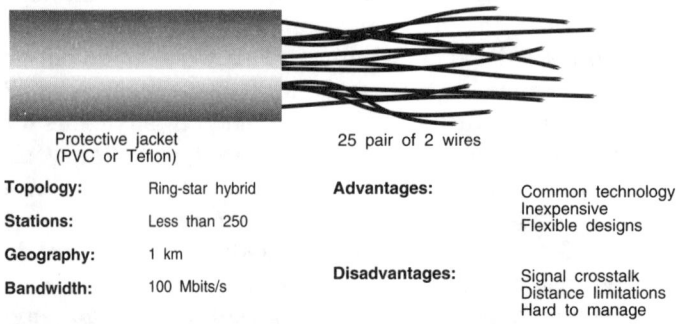

Topology:	Ring-star hybrid	Advantages:	Common technology
Stations:	Less than 250		Inexpensive
Geography:	1 km		Flexible designs
Bandwidth:	100 Mbits/s	Disadvantages:	Signal crosstalk
			Distance limitations
			Hard to manage

Figure 5.14 Typical UTP twisted-pair wiring bundle.

FDDI Standards

- DC to upper-frequency limit
- One channel per pair of twisted-pair
- Token and ring poll provides "carrier"
- NRZI and MLT-3 encoding scheme
- Digital transmission (no modem translations)

Figure 5.15 FDDI signaling characteristics.

Network compatibility is also a function of network length and length of individual node connections. FDDI transmission is based upon a statistical signal and ranges of signal acceptance. Violation of those specifications does not per se mean that a network will not work; it merely means that the network could function, albeit erratically. Exceeded point-to-point lengths, concentrator-to-node copper lobe lengths, twisted-pair connections, too many optical fiber splices or connections, inserting unshielded twisted-pairs stress the network. Compatibility should be viewed in these terms as well. Chapter 6 illustrates these limitations.

Note that while NetBIOS, Appletalk, DECnet, and IPX/SPX are supposed to provide a consistent application-layer function, these definitions leave enough gray area for different vendors to define inconsistent software standards. This is rapidly changing as vendors see a reason to agree with competitors on compatibility. However, FDDI and TCP/IP do provide a migration path to other ISO protocols and perhaps the application of 155 Mbits/s or greater asynchronous transfer mode protocols (ATM) to the desktop for LAN and WAN capabilities.

The OSI model has become generally accepted by industry due to the globalization of telecommunications and data communications; it is a de facto standard. Despite the many vendors' claims that OSI architecture and compatibility are priorities for new products, implementation shortfalls plus the massive weight of the existing installed base of noncompliant hardware and software are delaying complete transition. Standardization implies comprehensive testing for conformity to OSI, and this is a monumental undertaking. However, the growing need for enterprise-wide networks, corporate networks excluding few employees, and multiple-site installations are increasing the complexity of network management. The desire for new network tracking and control tools as promised by the OSI CMIP network management protocol will speed transition to the OSI standards and encourage full vendor compliance.

Operational Comparisons

FDDI functions more or less the the same regardless of the media. Most network managers who have installed FDDI to supplement and expand existing networks report a "plug-and-play" success with FDDI. Their experience over the years with Ethernet and Token-Ring provides experience to handle most problems with FDDI, and they see very few. In fact, FDDI provides an immediate and effective bandwidth boost. Although optical fiber may represent a new technology, installation is simple even when vendors do not provide supply ready-made cable with connectors already installed. Few managers have sought to use existing UTP wiring for FDDI, if only to prevent the possible fiasco of spending budget on NICs, concentrators, optical bypass units, and the other components required with FDDI only to fail because the media is substandard. Even the use of many vendors, optical DAS devices, and STP and UTP SAS devices, rarely creates a problem. Most vendors have adhered to all the standards, have made provisions for conforming to the standards if they offer special features, and will work with customers to secure complete and successful interoperability.

FDDI Reliability

FDDI is a reliable medium when it is designed, installed, and maintained according to specification. In fact, FDDI is designed for perfect transmission operation. A frame error rate greater than 0.02% is deemed unacceptable and activates a network management alarm feature. When a node fails electrically or optically, the NIC or hub will try to isolate that lobe by wrapping the ring. In the worst case, that NIC will isolate itself from the ring. When that fails, other devices automatically try to ring wrap by isolating that failed unit from the ring. This "fail-safe" operation is not perfect, but for intents and purposes is effective. The active design of FDDI connections requires that most devices provide an automatic optical bypass when the node is powered down, disabled, or rendered defective. Note that when a ring is large and many nodes are so disabled, there may be no nodes online to repeat a signal within the length parameters between nodes. Under those unfavorable conditions, a ring will fail. The addition of optical bypasses and signal extenders or enhancers (repeaters) are a prerequisite for mission-critical FDDI networks. Review new installations or upgrades that are not working for improper installation techniques, connector and connection failures, bad components, as well as configuration settings for nodes. Typically, an FDDI node set for the wrong media or UTP protocol at the NIC will disable the entire LAN since that node must repeat every other node's signal. Similarly, different buffer sizes, packet sizes, or memory mapping for buffers could disable one node, and thus the entire network.

Network Management Protocols

Management and control functions are perceived as a major requirement for the continued success, increased complexity, and advanced technical development of networking standards, protocols, and transmission media. This is particularly relevant to the development of heterogeneous networks, enterprise-wide installations, and distributed

FDDI Standards

networks. Since the FDDI protocol actually defines very few network management functions other than station management, token passing, ring poll, beaconing, and ring-wrap, network management is usually seen as a feature of the network software. Two important network management protocols are currently defined but only partially available to service these needs. The acronyms are SNMP and CMIP. A further enhancement and refinement of SNMP, called SNMP-II, is undergoing final review during 1993.

SNMP
Simple Network Management Protocol (SNMP) is an network management protocol released in a 1988 Request for Comment by the Internet Activities Board. This de facto protocol was constructed to address the long lead times facing review and acceptance of more formal standards drafted by either ANSI or ISO. SNMP is implemented by many network hardware and software vendors. Clearly, vendors are trying to address the complex and increasing user need for managing and maintaining networks and communicate to customers that they do understand the need for conforming to network standards.

SNMP definition is one of simplicity, flexibility, and current availability. This has made it attractive. It is consistent with TCP/IP networks (most FDDI sites), which makes sense since it was defined by Internet. Some proponents tout this standard as realistic as well. It consists of three parts. This includes the structure of management information (SMI), the management information base (the MIB database), and the SNMP protocol itself, as Figure 5.16 indicates.

The SMI and MIB specify the information database structures and network alert conditions, and actually store this data. The SNMP protocol transports the information to and from SNMP agents at the MAC datagram level; a logical link does not even have to be established.

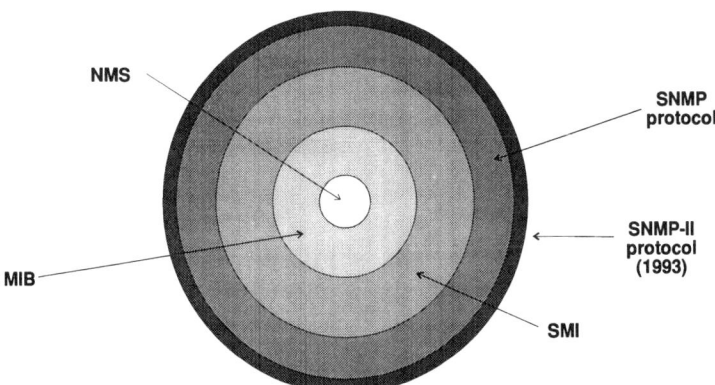

Figure 5.16 The Simple Network Management Protocol (SNMP).

This implies that data capture is simple and passive. SNMP agents are any network devices that capture, maintain, and forward MIB data to a management station. Agents include intelligent hubs, bridges, routers, gateways, specialized remote monitors, and computers at any legal node location. Agents have also included household toasters, mechanized toy animals, and other gadgets automated by vendors to demonstrate the flexibility of their own extensions to the SNMP function-call library. Since these extensions are by no means standardized, there is substantial risk of nonconformity, noncompatibility, and selection of the wrong network management software. The SNMP database and the delivery of its data can provide global network management or control of selected subsections.

A centralized network management station (NMS) is the master repository for all managed agents and the MIBs. It controls network agents via commands issued and transported at the datagram level. No logical connections are maintained between the NMS and any agents; this lowers network overhead. SNMP can trigger alarms on the basis of captured agent information and unsolicited alert information from a network agent. However, the implementation of SNMP does not detract from the more rigorous goal of a comprehensive network management tool to provide management information on complex networks. Ordinarily, SNMP does not provide information across bridges and gateways since it is a TCP/IP derivative and not OSI-compliant. Novell's IPX/SPX is also a derivative protocol and is not fully OSI-compliant. To meet this limitation, vendors are providing remote management tools (hardware and software) as an interim compromise. These tools collect and transport network performance data over various communications channels to bypass bridge or gateway limitations.

SNMP-II, the forthcoming revision and enhancement, seeks to overcome the enterprise limitations of SNMP. Primarily, SNMP requires 40 percent or more of the channel bandwidth just to provide the distributed management services required for bridges, routers, stations, and network segments. Since most networks with extended architectures tend toward full bandwidth utilization, any management overhead in excess of 5 percent is undesirable. SNMP-II represents not only a means to minimize intersegment traffic, but also an enhanced MIB for managing new devices and providing better information.

CMIP

The *Common Management Information Protocol (CMIP)* is a model formally accepted by the International Standards Organization (ISO) for network management in 1990. Despite the acceptance of FDDI and codification of CMIP by ISO, widespread implementation of CMIP is unlikely; SNMP is well-entrenched perhaps because it is compatible and under current use with other LAN and WAN protocols. Thus, the major

FDDI Standards

obstacle to acceptance and implementation is that CMIP requires the network hardware and software including upper-level protocols to provide complete compliance to the Open Systems Interconnect seven-layer network model. Many networks do not adhere to segmentation of the OSI model and allow layers to bypass the chain of layered control and communicated directly with other layers. Additionally, due to its increased power and complexity, the storage requirements for the CMIP database are least 3 times larger and code is 2.5 times larger.

The CMIP management protocol functions at the highest layer of the OSI model. Many widely accepted networks do not comply with this standard since it is not part of the formal FDDI station management protocol. TCP/IP does provide an overlapping mesh with these standards, but lacks clear demarcations within or between OSI layers 2 and 3. It does not maintain a clear chain of layer control. This structure for CMIP, CMOT, and SNMP are illustrated in Figure 5.17.

Additionally, developers state that the OSI network model requires code segmentation and "bloat." While SNMP requires only 8.7 K for protocol and 63 K of computer memory for message code/decode instructions, in comparison, CMOT instead requires 127 K for protocol and 182 K for code/decode. This results in extensive code, even duplicate code for each layer, and severe performance degradation on most network nodes. Few personal computers yet have the necessary CPU capacity to be OSI-compliant. This is an even more serious concern where smart

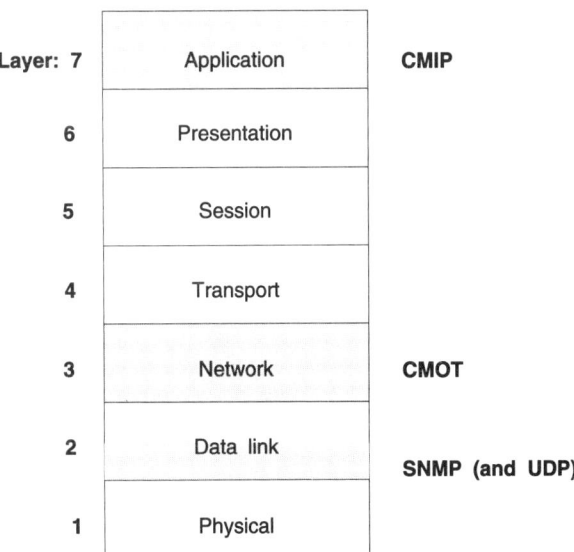

Figure 5.17 CMIP is activated at the application layer, whereas SNMP functions only partially at the data link level as datagrams. CMOT is a network-level compromise that allows User Datagram Protocol (UDP) frame inclusions within FDDI frames.

repeaters, bridges, and gateways must reprocess frames in real time for retransmission. Note that FDDI networks frequently provide management from the hub with FDDI's station management protocol in lieu of SNMP or CMIP.

Because both IPX/SPX and TCP/IP and SNMP derived from the Internet organization, there is a realistic symbiosis for this new management tool. However, vendors promise to supply SNMP and add the more rigorous CMIP functionality in transitional steps. Furthermore, many vendors will likely provide both within the same software to manage traditional NetBios networks bridged from OSI networks. Old protocols endure for many years and must be somehow integrated with advancing technology.

The OSI and CMIP models provide four aspects of network management. This model is mapped in Figure 5.18. These are network security, naming, addressing, and actual network management functions. The network manager interacts with the Management Application Process (MAP), or simply the *Network Manager AP*. These software applications are the *Management Specific Application Service Elements (MSASEs)* and the *Common Management Information Service Element (CMISE)*. The MSASEs are global-application functions, while the CMISE interacts with a set of *Local Management Application Entities (LMAEs)*. LMAEs are peer-to-peer objects that are managed. The bulk of the information is contained in the MSASEs and the CMISE. LMAEs only

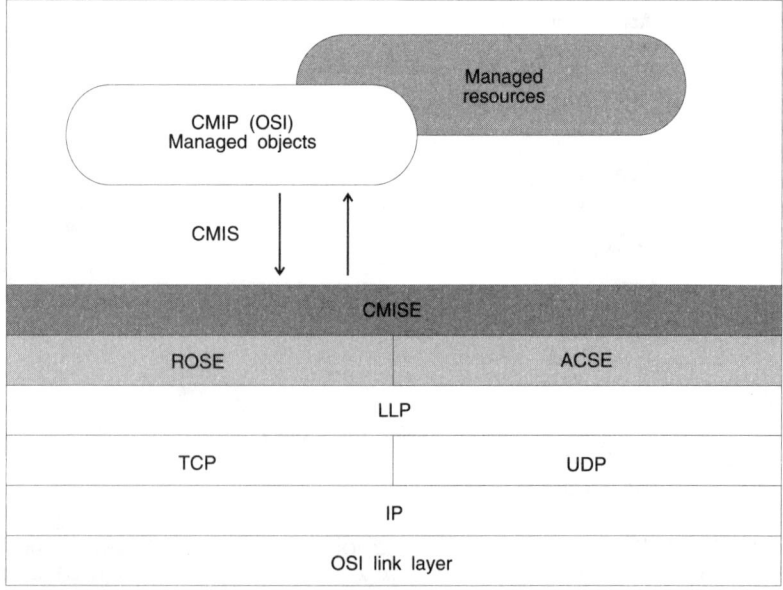

Figure 5.18 The CMIP layer representation.

FDDI Standards

allow the means to obtain or control operational parameters used within each OSI protocol layer. Note that not every layer must have a LMAE, but LMAEs must respond to commands from the MSASEs.

There are five MSASEs residing on top of the CMISE. These include *Account Management (AM), Configuration and Name Management (CM), Fault Management (FM), Performance Management (PM),* and *Security Management (SM)*. These tools must respond to commands from a MSASE component. The *Association Control Service Element (ACSE)* is a software application entity programmed with sufficient information to access an appropriate LMAE. The ACSE also obtains and transfers information to the *Remote Operation Service Elements (ROSEs)*. Remote objects include repeaters, routers, bridges, gateways, nodes, and other devices that have been recognized as OSI management agents. These agents are known as *OSI resources*. Remote-object control and management is particularly relevant for extended networks of networks including enterprise-wide networks. Essentially, CMIP is useful when there are a linked set of LANs which are called *domains* in the OSI CMIP terminology.

Once an association has been established between the CMISE and any LMAE (using the services of the ACSE), network data can begin to flow. This information provides event reporting, information transfer, and control. *Event reporting* is used to initiate transfer of information from an agent (LMAE) to the CMISE. In other words, the managed agents send their information back to the network management database. *Information transfer* is the operation where the network management software requests specifically statistical data from the managed agents. *Control* is the terminology used where the CMISE initiates selected actions by the LMAE agent. Figure 5.19 lists the CMIP MSASE and their functions. Response to these commands are actions, entries into the CMIP database (once the flow of information is initiated), or information displayed directly to the network manager's console. The MSASE is the network manager's interface to the MAP. It is either interactive or embedded in operations that can occur as automatically required. Information that can be captured is included in Chapter 16.

Comparison of SNMP, CMOT, and CMIP

CMIP is a connection-oriented protocol, while SNMP is connectionless. This means that CMIP-managed networks require that managed agents must establish communication links and maintain these conversations. This requires network resources in the form of packet transmissions. On the other hand, SNMP also requires network resources in the form of UDP/IP frame transmissions. The difference is that CMIP management is assured that messages, alarms, and data will be delivered unless there is a break in the network, while the comparable SNMP protocols are

CMIP MSASE	MSASE actions
AM	Initialize request
	Abort request
CM	Manage primitives
	Reset
	Load
	Time
	System print
FM	TCP
	Event
	Confirm event
	Linked
	Confirm get
	Set
	Confirm set
	Action
	Confirm action
	Terminate action
	Quit
PM	Get information
	Put information
SM	Username
	Password

Figure 5.19 MSASE commands to CMISE services.

not guaranteed. SNMP alarms, messages, collision, and packet counts are like junk mail; they may or may not arrive, and if the management station is offline even if they arrive, that transmitted information is lost. SNMP has a limited trap capability to catch unsolicited error messages and sends out only six types of unconfirmed asynchronous messages. SNMP is statistically efficient much as CMSA/CD is more efficient than token ring but not as reliable. CMIP requires much more overhead. However, SNMP alarms and traps of network failure may go unacknowledged, nor can it provide authentication. SNMP requires approximately 300 bytes per managed device and network management host structure. CMOT implementations require about 500 bytes.[2] Since CMOT has become arcane and implemented only within a test environment, you should avoid any vendor purporting to provide CMOT-compliant de-

[2] *Communications of the IEEE*, July 1990, Network Management of TCP/IP.

vices. CMIP can synchronize operations and perform multiple requests with a single transaction. CMIP operations can be linked for the same performance and efficiency effect. It can also browse MIB (managed devices) databases, whether the devices are newly installed or under prior management. While SNMP cannot review multiple objects at a time, CMIP can do wildcard searches. Since CMIP must poll to get data, there could be a maximum of 4500 managed devices against the 180,000 or so that SNMP could invisibly track. CMIP might be able to poll only 750 devices on a WAN because of the slower transmission speeds. SNMP cannot perform actions. CMIP does allow for the direct and imperative management of devices. In conclusion, SNMP is more useful as a protocol analyzer for monitoring network performance than as an active network management tool. While CMIP is the better solution, to date it has not been implemented sufficiently, and since most FDDI networks support UDP and connect to existing SNMP-managed networks, SNMP will probably endure as the management protocol of choice.

Network Economies

The economies-of-scale for STP, UTP, and optical fiber networks are significantly changing as technology develops and matures. STP provides a moderate-cost LAN. Initial cost is moderately high, although each additional node is inexpensive. It is highly flexible. UTP is almost identical, although the media cost runs about two thirds the cost of STP. All other component costs are the same. UTP is rarely feasible in sites with existing phone wiring; given the cost of other FDDI components the savings on wiring expenses can be easily lost managing failures from substandard wiring. Tread carefully, because subsequent installation and management costs often make UTP more expensive than STP. It also may not provide any upgrade path for cell relay and ATM protocols. Fiber networks provide higher speeds and even multiple-channel capacity, although the greater bandwidth is available at high initial costs. The differential between the more expensive optical NICs and electrical units is approaching parity. Optical is the best choice where station spacings exceed 100 m. STP FDDI is more common than UTP FDDI or optical fiber networks. STP- and UTP-based networks are likely for new FDDI installations because of cost, availability, existing cabling options, performance, and compatibility considerations. Economizing with unshielded twisted-pair is clearly effective, although distance and performance limitations are apt to create reliability problems without careful attention to installation, specification, and network maintenance.

Chapter 6
FDDI Hardware

This chapter describes the hardware commonly employed to construct FDDI networks, and the physical channel limitations inherent in FDDI. FDDI is often selected to resolve bottlenecks to the desktop on existing networks, augment the capacity and backbone connectivity between LANs, or internetwork a large campus or vertical high-rise building site. The protocol is defined primarily by ANSI standards. Furthermore, hardware is interchangeable to some extent among vendors. This provides a high degree of compatibility between the equipment of different manufacturers. FDDI is often selected because it is the only generally available high-speed LAN and WAN protocol. Relative to other network building blocks, the hardware for FDDI is simple, reliable, and uniform, and varies very little from vendor to vendor.

Hardware

The hardware required for the actual FDDI network is elementary. The most minimal configuration is made up of two stations and a closed loop of network wiring. The more usual configuration is a *star-based* wiring scheme with a central focal point provided by a single attached station (SAS) hub or concentrator. It is important to recognize that while FDDI is logically configured as a ring or loop with computer nodes—hence the "ring" nomenclature—the actual physical wiring is a ring when wired with optical fiber, but the configuration is a star when wired with twisted-pair. When FDDI is wired as a dual ring as defined by the original specifications, the second ring provides an automatic ring wrap to maintain the integrity and continued operation of the network. All devices which attach to the dual optical ring must be dual attached stations (DAS) with four connectors. Each ring requires a ring in and ring out connection. (They are labeled as A, B, C, and D lines.) These DAS stations can be gateways, servers, workstations, hubs, or concentrators that connect to other networks or a continued tree of SAS.

This configuration comprises the root hub and spoke wires, called *lobes*, to interconnect all nodes. The central hub, is an active device or intelligent device which provides star-configured wiring to multiple nodes. Intelligent devices may provide bus slots for up to 16 boards supporting eight nodes apiece. The connecting wire consists of twisted-pair wire bundles, using standard IBM Token-Ring genderless (hermaphroditic) connectors, and telephone modular jumpers. [Optical fiber dual 100/140 mm of course supports FDDI, although this is rarely implemented except where NSD A1 level security is sought by a government agency. See Chapter 17.] Shielded twisted-pair (STP), and to a lesser degree unshielded twisted-pair (UTP), are most commonly used because of their performance characteristics, extensive vendor experience and product support, and pricing.

Optical Fiber

Optical fiber consists of a single (simplex) or dual strand (duplex) of fiber normally not to exceed 2 km. Each strand can contain a single homogeneous fiber, may be constructed from segments mechanically connected together, or fused into single segment. The strand or strands may be bundled with many other fibers, with coaxial cable, telephone wire, and other special-purpose components. The bundle may be plastic coated, Teflon wrapped, or armored with nylon and steel. It is usually reinforced with Kevlar for strength. Connectors are available in two formats, bayonet or dual connectors with protective shrouding. These two formats are governed by the ANSI specifications. Although the dual ring may appear as a four-lane, two-way highway, the transmit cable is really only a continuation of the receive cable to complete the ring structure. Transmission for each is unidirectional.

Twisted-Pair

STP consists of dual pairs of wire twisted about themselves three to six times per foot; this twisting minimizes crosstalk. It is then surrounded by a foil and woven strand shield. It is often designated as as IBM Type 1, IBM Type 2, IBM Type 3, IBM Type 6, and IBM Type 9. Type 1 is the most prevalent grade. Type 6 is used for jumpers. Type 2 is identical to Type 1 but with the addition of four UTP pairs for voice communications. Alternatively, the *Electronics Industries Associations / Telecommunications Industries Association* (EIA/TIA) has ratified a premise wiring standard called EIA/TIA-568 provides precise guidelines defining communications wiring (data, image, and voice). It formalizes category 3 100-ohm unshielded twisted-pair wire with four copper pairs as suitable for transmission speeds to 10 Mbits/s, category 4 100-ohm unshielded twisted-pair wire, also with four copper pairs as suitable for transmission speeds to 16 Mbits/s, and category 5 100-ohm unshielded twisted-pair wire with four

FDDI Hardware

copper pairs as suitable for transmission speeds to 100 Mbits/s. STP with 150-ohm dual pairs is rated up 155 Mbits/s and thus suitable for the low-end ATM cell relay. STP-3 is comparable to Type 9, but is often used for Ethernet 10Base-T; STP-3 is adequate for FDDI subject to some significant length limitations.

It is important to recognize that IBM STP Type 3 represents a different designation system from category 3 wire. The wire itself is typically 24-gauge copper wire with a PVC or Teflon coating. A better grade of UTP-3 performs 100 percent better than a low-quality version. UTP-4 is more expensive and recommended by many twisted-pair suppliers. There is a quality difference between voice-grade and data-grade UTP. Qualify the one you install. STP performs better than UTP because it has better insulation against insertion capacitance and resistance to low-frequency electromagnetic noise—which means that it shields the signal and is rarely affected by external interference or internal crosstalk for the intended applications. The EIA/TIA specifications are intended to circumvent the market confusion and spurious claims for the many different types of wiring.

Rigorous manufacturing specifications and true adherence to EIA/TIA wiring and connector ratings will help ensure a reliable network and ensure a generally accepted conformity among different lots of cable and different manufacturers. Shielded wire provides dramatically improved service and longer run lengths than unshielded wire bundles because crosstalk is minimized, signal disruption is less, and signal attenuation is decreased. The transmitting characteristics for an STP or UTP wiring bundle are comparable but notably different. Specifically, vendors providing STP-based FDDI use the NRZI signal, while vendors providing UTP-based FDDI apply MLT-3 to minimize crosstalk and RFI problems.

The signals on twisted-pair are DC current fluctuations. Twisted-pair is actually two pairs; one for transmission and the other for reception. These pairs cross over so that a transmitter circuitry to the receiver circuitry and the receiver connects to a transmitter for each node pair to form the ring architecture. Although this may appear as a two-lane, two-way highway, the transmit pair is really only a continuation of the receive pair to complete the ring structure. Transmission is unidirectional. One of the reasons shielding is so important for copper-based networks is that the FDDI NIC functions as a repeater. The stronger and more stable outgoing signal has a tendency to distort the weaker incoming signal since the two pairs are in such close proximity, as Figure 6.1 indicates.

This explanation is pertinent to the understanding of why STP performs better than UTP. FDDI was designed to be a modulated optical signal corresponding to a digital waveform. The differences between media and quality of media are reflected in the overall achievable

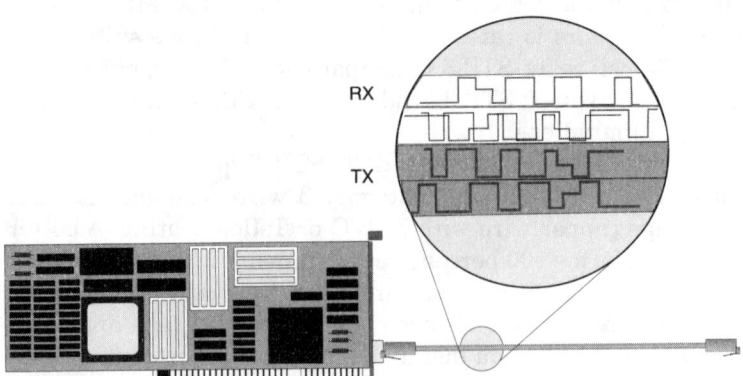

Figure 6.1 Incoming signals tend to be distorted.

network lengths and lengths between nodes. Shielded is better than unshielded twisted-pair because it provides less signal distortion, timing irregularities, and strength loss.

As explained above, FDDI specifies a logical ring design with SAS tree extensions. The hub device is the root of the SAS tree. Nodes connect independently. Independent wires or composite bundles traverse a facility, and special bridging hardware interconnects stand-alone segments and other twisted-pair hubs, and extends the geographic reach of the network. Figure 6.2 shows a typical network configuration with a simplified representation of the FDDI hardware.

A copper-based FDDI network consists of wire; connectors, including modular connectors and jacks; and the individual node network interface controllers. Often, the wiring is connected through a central wiring closet with a patch panel and jumpers. This is true whether the network is optically or electrically based.

The network has active components limited to stations, hubs, and controllers at each node location. The difference between typical Token-Ring MAUs and FDDI hubs are that MAUs tend to be passive devices (not powered by external AC). Hubs are active (powered by AC) and intelligent devices that monitor the nodes for activity and conformance to specification. When a hub is inactive, a bypass must be provided to guarantee that the FDDI signal will reach the next station.

FDDI Operations

Conceptually, FDDI is simple. The ring provides one-way channel connectivity between communicating parties (computer nodes) like daisy-chained Christmas tree lights; the ends of the chain connect together, however, to form a closed ring. The channel is the data communications

FDDI Hardware

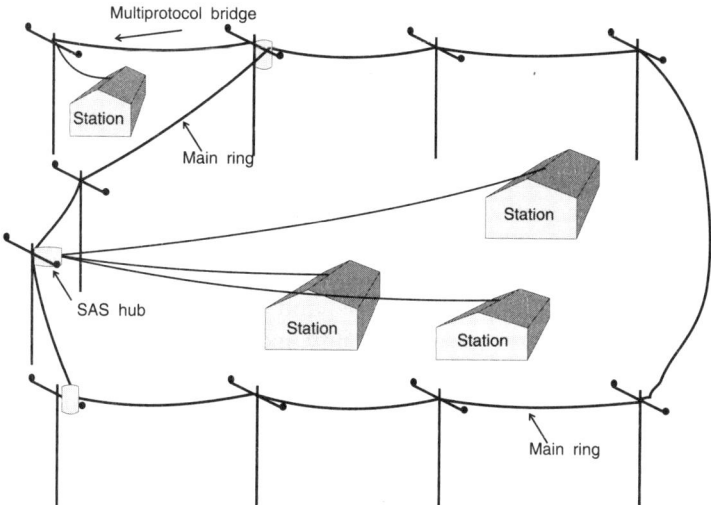

Figure 6.2 Representation of an FDDI network.

pathway. An FDDI frame is the transmission vehicle. While FDDI is a line waiting for a single phone booth (only a single transmission can proceed at a time), the transmission token protocols, which are rules of privacy or silence, accomplish an orderly transition for deciding who can transmit. Figure 6.3 pictures this analogy.

Each node has transmission and reception hardware, telephone handsets, if you will, and generally a supplemental set in case in failure in the primary. This hardware controls access to the communications channel and monitors traffic. Additionally, each node has hardware that

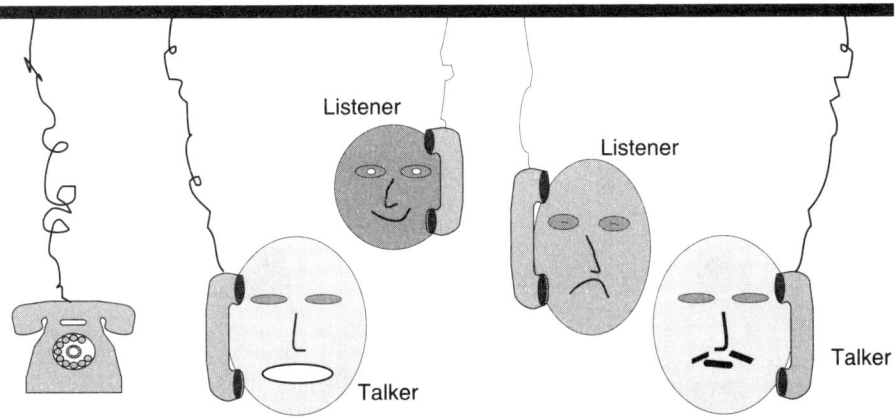

Figure 6.3 The party-line telephone analogy.

builds the messages to match the required FDDI frame format. The transmission-reception hardware is called a *network interface controller* (NIC) or *network adapter*. This is analogous to the earphone and microphone. There is traffic control hardware that is built into the controller, called the station management functions. Traffic control is handled totally by the hardware; packet destination information—analogous to the box and dialing mechanisms of a phone system—is provided by the variable address fields within each packet. The adapter for each node connects directly into the ring or through a concentrator just as a telephone cable stretches to the overhead wire from each house. At the other end, the FDDI controller connects to the workstation hardware via the computer bus, and interfaces with system software. The single component raises reliability and lowers hardware cost. Since most optical NICs provide connections to two rings—few electrical NICs do—it is possible and preferable to connect these channels to two separate rings or SAS devices. When a station connects to the ring through two separate channels at two separate points on a ring, this is *dual homing*. Dual homing represents an important facility for client/server support and mission-critical networks, as Figure 6.4 indicates.

Controller Functionality

Continuing the telephone analogy, the adapter (and network software described in Chapter 5) limit access to the telephone to one caller at a time and direct the transition from one transmission direction to another. The adapter waits for a token. A *token* is a fixed sequence of digital bits. It is also an FDDI frame without source address, destination address, or any data. "Capture" of this token provides the permission for a node to send data. A frame, which is assembled by the controller either in workstation memory or in special buffer memory on the controller board itself, is then broadcast on the outgoing transmission

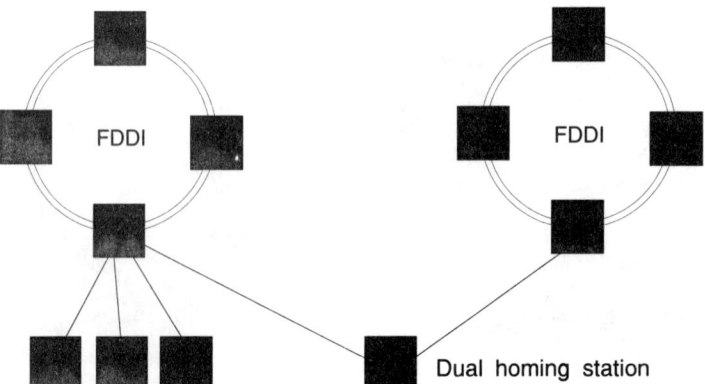

Figure 6.4 A critical station connected to the network with dual homing.

FDDI Hardware

line. This frame is either a series of digital optical pulses (i.e., on/off) or electrical pulses (within a range -3.0 V to +3.0 V DC) called a *signal*. The optical signal is transmitted at nearly the speed of light (3×10^9 meters per second). Although the signal is optical, the speed of light in optical fiber is less than the speed of light within a vacuum. The electrical signal is transmitted at approximately 52 to 57 percent of the speed of light. The signal is sent to the next downstream node. This node in turn receives, retimes, and repeats the signal to the next downstream node. This sequence is replicated until the signal returns to the originating node where only the token (e.g., an empty packet) is then returned to the network. Note that multiple frames may be sent to the same or different addresses while the token is held. Frames addressed to intermediate nodes will be copied into frame buffers by those nodes.

The FDDI adapter dials the number and builds the metaphorical phone call that is actually transmitted. This *frame*, as the packet is usually called, must conform to a rigorous format that ensures that party calls are minimal and that the transmitted packet is addressed to a designated node; by analogy the caller dials the number assigned to the person intended to receive the call. The *network interface card* (NIC), or network adapter, also disassembles packets and transfers this information to the receiving workstation's operating system. Figure 6.5 charts the functionality flow provided by the FDDI adapter.

This NIC, also called a *network access unit* (NAU), provides additional services to increase reliability. First, the NAU bypasses failed stations or wraps when it senses a failed source or destination line. Second, NAU

- Receive signal
- Transmit signal
- Test for reception
- Test for transmission
- Generate beacon signal
- Convert serial-parallel and parallel-serial
- Transmit and receive buffering
- Frame packets
- Encode and decode broadcast signals
- Recognize addresses
- Detect errors and collisions
- Generate and parse preamble
- Provide ring poll sense and deference
- Generate and verify frame check sequences
- Filter signal noise and lack of signal differentiation
- Filter alignment errors and overruns
- Limit data rate to prevent overruns
- Manage receive and transmit links
- Build and disassemble frame
- Request retransmission

Figure 6.5 FDDI station controller (NIC) functionality.

circuitry on the *wiring concentrators*, which are also called hubs, actually boost signal strength and gain (the difference between the signal highs and lows) to accommodate marginal transmission or reception quality. FDDI adapter functionality is specified by the OSI model and by the ANSI X3.139 specification as layers 1 and 2. Station management inhabits layer 3.

The usual causes for any incompatibilities are wiring violations or installation flaws, mixing STP and UTP within the same network, transmission speed differences, packet and buffer size inconsistencies, or application software differences. Only rarely will vendor implementation of software, NIC drivers, or hardware design errors be at fault. Where network data and voice lines are intertwined, investigate the possibility that telephone ringing voltages (48 V to 96 V) may have damaged hubs or NICs. Because FDDI is a universal standard, such specification integrity adds to the desirability of FDDI.

Gateway Functionality

The FDDI *gateway*, as presented by the OSI model in Chapter 5, provides network expansion capabilities for network connectivity and packet repetition. The gateway unit provides multiple-segment access, signal retransmission, and medium or software presentation conversions among networks with differing protocols. This mechanism is normally part of an FDDI network since FDDI is usually added to augment or link existing networks. By analogy, the gateway is either a long-distance switchboard or a telephone call to Western Union Telegram Services which translates format for retransmission to another medium.

FDDI Physical Channel Limitations

Token protocols place certain limitations on the physical channel. These limitations specify maximum signal propagation times and primary station counts, and as a consequence, maximum TP-DDI lobe lengths, since lobe lengths and propagation time affect the slot time, or TRT. While the precise ring specifications are provided in Table 6.1 at the conclusion of this chapter, these same physical configurations are presented below. These commonly stated limits were derived from the actual optical (and consequently electrical by proxy and conformity to the X3T9.5 FDDI standard) specifications of the ANSI X3.166 FDDI model.

These limitations are determined by the clock rates, the speed of optical transmissions, and lobe and adjusted ring lengths, although throughput is limited by node counts, signal delays, and frame overhead. These limitations are explored in greater depth in Chapters 16.

Despite this enormous signal propagation velocity, the *token rotation time* (TRT) is measurable in μs. In fact, the protocol requires that the

FDDI Hardware

TRT must be no more than 1.617 µs. This corresponds to the time required for a 24-bit token packet to propagate around the longest possible ring and accommodate the electronic signal repeater delay inherent in active stations. There are two other timer calculations maintained for FDDI. The maximum station physical insertion time can be no more than 25.0 µs. The maximum signal acquisition time for a station can be no more than 1.0 µs. This later figure represents the time required for the station to synchronize with the preamble signal.

Other important times include the token time at 0.00088 µs, the maximum transmitter set up time to begin transmitting after capture of the token at 0.0035 µs, and the transmission time for the longest FDDI frame at 0.361 µs. The claim frame consists of 16 bits of preamble and 48-bit addresses requires 0.00256 µs. The guaranteed maximum TRT time is 8.0 µs.

The ring is composed of two types of paths, the ring and secondary lobes. Rings connect primary stations, which generally consist of concentrators and hosts. There can be no more than 1000 primary station devices on the on this ring, and each device can be separated by no more than 2 km. This section of optical fiber may be one or more pieces of fiber that are linked with mechanical connectors or splices and fused with heat. The total loss for all such connections should not be more than 3 dB. If jumpers are used, the loss attributed to each jumper should be measured and the total loss should remain with these same tolerances. However, it is better if optical connections are built specifically to length. If stations apply full lasing transmitters and single mode fiber, the distance between such devices can be increased to 36 km. However, for the network to remain within specification and timing tolerances, there must be a limited number of such extended links. Lobes connect secondary nodes to a primary station. This lobe connection may consist of many spliced sections or jumpers, the smallest unit of cable. One or many jumpers, connect through a primary station to the main ring. These tree-shaped networks can constitute either a stand-alone network or require access to the main ring for operation.

The overall *drive distance* for STP and UTP is the limit of reliable signal transmission. This distance is the length for each lobe cable. The drive distance represents the distance an active node must force that signal through a lobe cable to the next active node or hub, as Figure 6.6 details. The maximum shielded twisted-pair (IBM Types 1 and 2) drive distance is 92 m. This decreases to about third to a half for UTP.

An FDDI ring cannot be composed of a single length of wire or optical fiber. When fiber is used to connect stations on ring, each connection is called a *trunk*. Each station forms an arc (or spoke) of the FDDI ring when a star-configured copper-based network is indicated. This arc or spoke is generally called a *lobe*. Very often wiring patch panels and multiple jumpers constitute each lobe. Figure 6.7 illustrates this archi-

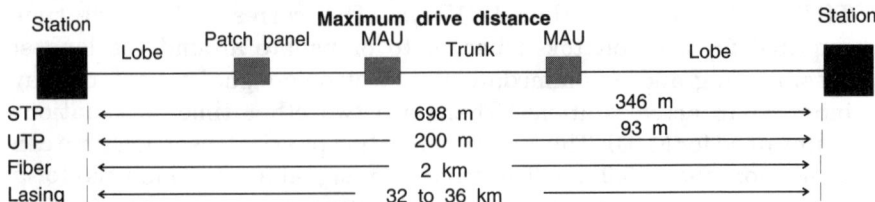

Figure 6.6 Maximum FDDI signal drive lengths.

tecture. Many jumpers can be spliced to construct a FDDI lobe. These, in fact, ease the burden of debugging most types of network hardware faults. However, in contrast, too many splices will increase the signal distortion and degrade signal quality. FDDI connectors fall into several categories. Optical connectors are either ST bayonet connectors or dual shrouded connectors. Electrical connectors are either standard IBM Token-Ring hermaphroditic media connectors or nine-pin D-connectors typically used with STP, or 6 pin RJ-11J-11 or 8 pin RJ-45 with UTP. While an electrical FDDI signal requires only four signal lines just like a standard telephone, the different design prevents cross-wiring phones and network equipment. (Some UTP MLT-3 implementations require eight wires for signaling.) The hermaphoditic plugs provide a self-connecting capability so that jumpers can form their own extension cords without the need for a gender changer. UTP connectors, jacks, and plugs are male or female. Moreover, networks utilizing UTP wiring may require a media filter to retime and adjust the distortions caused by unshielded wiring.

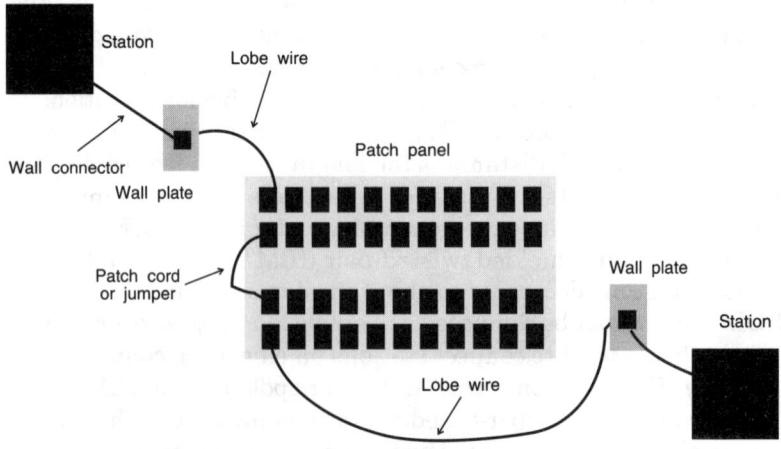

Figure 6.7 Maximum FDDI adjusted ring length of 250 km.

FDDI Hardware

Frame Size

Frame size is a maximum of FDDI 9000 symbols. This includes preamble, starting delimiter, frame control, ending delimiter, source and destination addresses, frame check sequence, and the data field. Each FDDI symbol represents a 4-bit unit of data. These four bits are encoded at the hardware level into a special 5-bit code called the *nonreturn to zero, invert on ones*, or abbreviated as NRZI. The NRZI symbol coding provides a polarity transition which represents a "1" and the absence of a polarity shift indicates a "0." The five-bit code provides for all data and hexadecimal symbols, as well as delimiters, line state values, control indicators, and halts. Some sequences do not yield consecutive code bit zeros and are not valid. ANSI standard X3.148 details the encoding standards.

Because 4 bits of data are coded as 5 bits for actual transmission, the data transmission rate of 100 Mbits/s corresponds to the true FDDI 125 Mbits/s signaling rate. This coding technique provides an effective FDDI efficiency rate higher than that of Ethernet or Token-Ring. Because these other protocols use Manchester or modified-Manchester coding, the signal transmission rate for these protocols are twice as high as the actual data rates. In the case of Ethernet, the clock time is 20 Mhz, and for Token-Ring, either 4 or 32 Mhz. Hence FDDI provides a five- or ten-fold performance improvement not only because it is signaling faster, but also because the FDDI symbol encoding is 80 percent more efficient.

Upper-level protocols, encapsulations, and protocol translations will affect packet (or frame) sizes. Since ARCnet limits frames to 507 bytes, Ethernet to 1518 bytes, 16-Mbits/s Token-Ring frames can be as long as 18,453 bytes (18,432 bytes of data), FDDI limits its data contents to 4478 bytes (8956 encoded symbols) and the FDDI will need to adjust accordingly. As such, interconnected FDDI networks will need to adapt to packets of different sizes. Of note, IBM LAN Server and MS LAN Manager on Token-Ring can create those longer frame lengths. Novell limits bridged hops to 512 bytes, although it can enable the burst mode protocol. Novell IPX frames are always 4202 bytes or less. Since Novell NetWare, IP, and Appletalk are the predominate FDDI NOSs, the frame limit is a pertinent limitation.

Twisted-Pair Specifications	Fiber	STP	UTP
Maximum station drive distance	2/36 km		
Maximum hub to node distance		100 m	30 m
Maximum trunk segment	2 km	200 m	100 m
Maximum number of primary stations	1000		
Maximum lobe length	200 m	100 m	100 m
Maximum packet size (in symbols)	9000	9000	9000
Minimum TRT (in μs)	0.0025	0.0025	0.0025
Maximum TRT (in μs)	1.6120	1.6120	1.6120
Signal progagtion speed (c)	0.9400	0.5800	0.5400

Table 6.1 Important FDDI specifications.

Chapter 7

FDDI Software and Process

This chapter explains the FDDI data communications process in terms of the operational mechanics. First, data transmission process and structures are outlined. Second, the transmission and reception procedures are presented. Third, transmission deficiencies are described. Last, layer protocols are described.

Transmission Process

FDDI transmits a single digital channel. Transmission is digital because the information is shipped in a cyclic representation, the cornerstone of digital representations. Analog transmission, on the other hand, would convert each digital bit into a voltage representation that parodies the analog value. For example, 0 might require 1 nanoseconds (ns) of no voltage, whereas 1 might require 2 ns of positive voltage. Alternatively, sound could be employed to represent data, whereas gaps might represent lack of data.

FDDI generates an encoded optical signal based upon the nonreturn to zero, invert on one (NRZI) code described in the preceding chapters. All encoding is performed at the hardware level to offload the CPU with this simple, but time-consuming translation. FDDI on STP also uses the same NRZI protocol for direct compatibility and simple media bridging. Typically, vendors provide NICs with interchangeable modules for optical and twisted-pair connections; the electronics remains the same. FDDI on UTP uses MLT-3, a Manchester encoding scheme, to minimize the chance that crosstalk disables communications and to lessen radio frequency interference on this lower quality media. Note that these two protocols do not coexist on the same twisted-pair networks; they must be bridged. Whatever the protocol, communication is similar for all FDDI networks.

The transmitting node propagates a digital signal wave outward in a single direction to the next logical downstream node. Figure 7.1 demonstrates this signal process. The receiving node "sees" or "hears" the

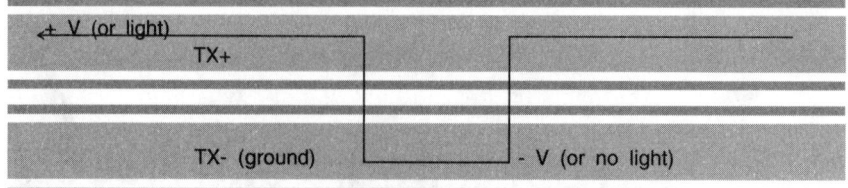

Figure 7.1 Digital signal wave transmission.

preamble and synchronizes the bit and timer clocks. The receiving electronics at this node convert this signal and interpret the data, or repeat on the transmitting electronics to its own downstream neighbor. The cycle time for each partial transmission is 0.008 ns, thus the time to send each individual bit is 0.001 ns due the efficient symbol encoding method. It is important that the highs and lows of either the optical signal wave or DC voltage modulation be well differentiated, as Figure 7.2 shows. Signal interference, optical scatter, media clarity, signal crosstalk, signal attenuation, or the length of the drive distance itself will degrade the signal and smooth the shape of the signal. This leads to transmission errors. Every active primary station is a repeater which interprets and regenerates signals for retransmission to the next downstream node on the FDDI ring. Bad signals only get worse and are less likely to be interpreted correctly. Note that the frame checksum and SMT features provide an integrity check. Failing devices immediately test the secondary ring or are isolated by upstream and downstream stations that sense that their neighbor is not conforming to protocol.

Frame Components

FDDI transmits information in a "packaged" format. This means that individual bits are not transferred from location to location without

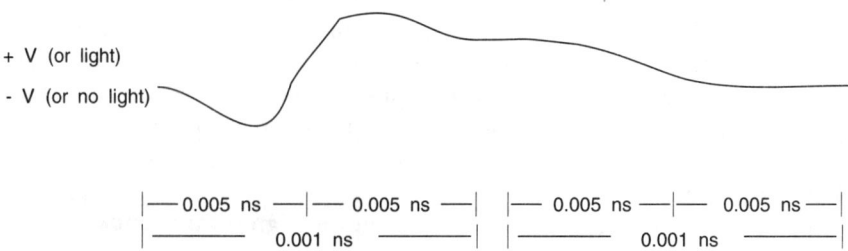

Figure 7.2 Signal shape must be well-differentiated.

FDDI Software and Process

preamble or explanation as they are in a dedicated link between mainframe and terminal or between modem-connected DTEs. The information to be transferred, however small or large, must be packaged, weighed, mailed, and checked upon receipt for proper delivery. This packaged format is called an information *frame*. This corresponds to Ethernet or Token-Ring packets. Like any postal letter, this frame contains a destination (the destination address), a return address (source address), a delivery weight (control field), the letter contents (actual data field), and a registered receipt (frame check sequence field) as pictured in Figure 7.3. Encapsulation of non-FDDI packets for FDDI transport requires a secondary format that also must retain the internal characteristics of that other packet.

Since FDDI is an electronic letter carrier, and letter transits can occur simultaneously, an agreed-upon handshaking between transmitting and receiving network devices prevents letters from crashing into each other and being scrambled (the token passing protocol). When the network is not busy, the token circulates the ring endlessly. The token is a 6-symbol signal with 16 symbols of preamble. It can also be visualized as a frame without address information or data. A token is not informationless, however. It provides information that the ring is functional, and it conveys permission to transmit. The frame and token are represented in Figure 7.4.

Optical and voltage information will be referenced in later chapters, specifically for cable testing and troubleshooting. More specific information is contained in Chapters 13 and 14, which detail the troubleshooting tools and techniques. Rather than concentrate on optical- or voltage-level representations of data, the frame format is presented pictorially in Figure 7.5. The actual encoded transmissions are handled by the transmission media and the lower layers of the OSI model: media, physical, and minimally within the data link layers. Above these layers, data are handled within the structure of the frame format. The frame consists of ten components: preamble, starting delimiter, controls, addresses, data, check sequence, ending delimiter, and frame status.

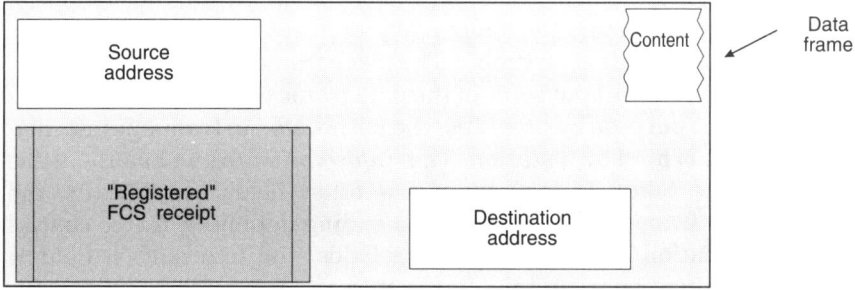

Figure 7.3 The FDDI frame.

Software and Hardware

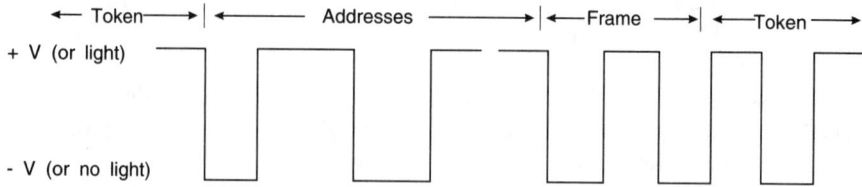

Figure 7.4 The digital FDDI signal.

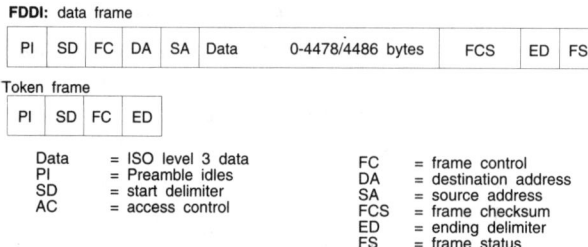

Data	= ISO level 3 data	FC	= frame control
PI	= Preamble idles	DA	= destination address
SD	= start delimiter	SA	= source address
AC	= access control	FCS	= frame checksum
		ED	= ending delimiter
		FS	= frame status

Figure 7.5 The FDDI frame, delimiters, and control fields.

Other FDDI signals include MAC beacon frame, a MAC claim frame, an LLC frame, SMT next station addressing frame, an implementer frame, and a termination frame. The beacon frame is transmitted for the purpose of indicating that corrective action is required on the ring in the event of serious ring failure. The claim frame indicates which station will create a new token and initialize the ring after recovery. An LLC frame is an information frame used for asynchronous transmission when priorities transmission levels have been established. The SMT frame is sent only to the next addressed station on the ring. The implementer frame is FDDI-implementation specific; consider it a reserved format. The termination frame halts traffic. It is a reserved function.

Token and Data Components

FDDI has two types of frames, but also other transmission signals as well. The *token frame* consists of three components: a starting delimiter, frame control field, and the ending delimiter. It is also preceded by the timing synchronization preamble. The token frame is basically an empty information field without some of the data frame control fields. It serves an important purpose by providing the permission to transmit information when it is held by a station. The *information frame* has the same fields as the token frame plus a few other fields. Specifically, the information frame has a starting and ending delimiter, frame control field, destination and source address fields, the information field, a frame check sequence, and the frame status.

Address Components

The *address fields* of an information frame consist of source and destination. FDDI-compatible devices are assigned either a 48-bit or 16-bit individual address. The leading two bits are usually reserved for manufacturer-assigned information. All stations should be able to interpret and repeat either 16-bit or 48-bit addresses. 48-bit addresses have the most significant bit reserved for individual or group identification (I/G), and the next most significant bit reserved for universal or local usage (U/L). The next most significant 12 of the 48 bits are designed to represent separate ring addresses. 16-bit addresses have the most significant bit reserved for individual or group identification (I/G). A special 16-bit address of all ones is a network-wide broadcast address (for both primary stations and secondary nodes). The I/G and U/L addresses provide for group and local multicast addresses. Local addresses are administered locally by the network administrator. The potential 32-byte savings is irrelevant and unwarranted to support.

The FDDI transmission software directly accesses this address. IPX and TCP/IP, for example, use a 2-byte Internet address, IPX/SPX uses a similar scheme, while OSI employs a full 64- or 128-byte address. Upper-layer protocols build symbol tables to reference this address and may include *media access control* (MAC) or *logical link control* (LLC) addresses within the actual information field. When a frame is transmitted, these logical addresses are resolved to the actual hardware source and destination FDDI addresses.

Addresses are important for all FDDI communications. The source station will recognize its own token and remove it from the ring. Destination station(s) will recognize frames as directed to them, copy the information field data, and reset the frame status field. Routers, bridges, and gateways broadcast requests for information in order to build and maintain their routing address tables. Of note, many routers and bridges create a substantial amount of network traffic that can be a bottleneck. The multicast addressing scheme is useful for maintaining router tables. It is also of particular relevance for distributed processing applications. For example, a user might request a specific data item but the application might not know which database on which file server has it. A single multicast request frame to all likely file servers is an efficient use of the FDDI channel.

The Data Field

The *data field* contains up to the maximum 4456 8-bit bytes. This size represents the FDDI 9000 symbol limitation less the preamble, address, and other overhead components. Since each typical byte has 8 bits, two symbols are required to transport each 8-bit byte. Although the physical token ring specifications provide these maximum sizes, FDDI as implemented by many NOS vendors (Novell, for example) limits frames to 4202 bytes or 512 bytes when the LAN is bridged. (The data field itself is 21 less due to the bytes allocated for ring addresses.) The minimum data field size holds 0 bytes. A byte may be referred to as an *octet* to confirm that it is an 8-bit byte. Transmissions of data streams longer than maximum data field size, as in a file transfer, a bit-mapped screen display, or document printing, require multiple frames. Since many stations contend for channel time, a large transmission might not be a contiguous signal. The upper levels of FDDI protocol understand this. In fact, most computers cannot accept a full 100 Mbits/s because they need time between frames to disassemble and process received data. The upper-layer protocols on a receiving machine accept such block data communications and modify the rate of frame transmissions to prevent overload.

The Frame Check Sequence

The *Frame Check Sequence* (FCS) is an error detection scheme designed to indicate transmission problems. FCS is sometimes referred to as a *Cyclic Redundancy Check (CRC)*, or simply as a checksum, since the FCS field contains a CRC checksum value. The encoding is defined by a standard generating polynomial, where x is frame length and the generating polynomial is a one's complement remainder obtained from the modulo two division. The polynomial is generally presented as:

$$G(x) = X^{32} + X^{26} + X^{23} + X^{22} + X^{16} + X^{12} + X^{11} + X^{10} + X^{8} + X^{7} + X^{5} + X^{4} + X^{2} + 1$$

Frame Status

The frame status provides an accessible update as to the disposition of the frame. This field usually shows whether the destination station has received the data and whether the frame is a valid frame. It is three symbols.

Frame Preamble and Overhead Components

There are two more related frame items. The starting delimiter and ending delimiters are two symbols. The starting field serves to synchronize clocks and base transmission timings for the receiving stations. The active monitor uses this field to reset the TRT time counter and other hardware clocks. After unreasonable delays without data or token frames, a station would send out a request to reinitialize the network. This starting delimiter also serves to forewarn NICs that a frame is headed in their direction. The ending delimiter resets the THT.

The first 4 bytes of the data field are reserved for the 802.2 logical link control (LLC) table. The DSAP is the destination service address port while SSAP is the source service address port. The LLC field contains

FDDI Software and Process

the frame field control information. The rest of the data field contains the actual information transferred by level 3 of the ISO model.

FDDI Protocol Control Fields

The data field is not strictly application-oriented data. FDDI also conforms to IEEE 802.1 and 802.2 protocols. Data link layers require control information to initiate, maintain, and conclude any conversation. TCP/ IP and IPX/SPX requires a logical link control. The user datagram protocol (UDP) is connectionless, although most UDP-based "connections" and processes expect a confirmation of message received by means of another UDP packet. This field often contains additional source and destination addresses and status codes. These status codes are called *service address points*. Figure 7.6 maps these service address points. Two addresses define the link level source and destination, and monitor the framing and synchronization of network transmissions.

Logical Link Fields

The *logical link control field* specifically provides framing and synchronization, error control and recovery, message acknowledgment, link initialization and disconnection, and addressing. Additionally, this field varies in format depending upon its function. When the data field contains instructional information, this field is called a *supervisory frame*. As stated previously, most receiving stations cannot accept data at the sustained FDDI rate of 100 Mbits/s; one of these supervisory control field functions synchronizes frame transfer rates. When the data field contains acknowledgments and control information, this field is called an *information frame*. Otherwise, when the FDDI frame contains only user application data, this field is called an *unnumbered frame*. All logical link control fields contain 16 bits.

Usage-Specific LLC Frames

Logical link control is also represented by the IEEE 802.2 standard; it is applied no differently from Ethernet or Token-Ring. It is important for transparent frame connectivity and network interconnectivity. The supervisory frame differs in format from both the information frame and

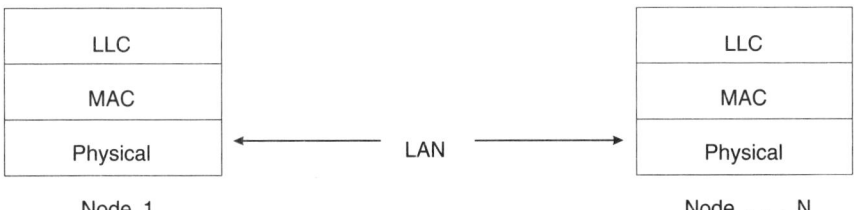

Figure 7.6 802.2 service address ports of the logical link control field.

the unnumbered frame. It contains a 4-bit reserved field, a 2-bit supervisory command code, and 2 bits indicating the control field format. Seven bits define the transmitter and receiver sequence numbers, and 1 bit serves as both a poll and a final bit. The control field for an unnumbered frame is only 8 bits, and the data field contains an extra byte of application-level data. Five modifier bits define the function code. This information is mapped in Figure 7.7.

Depending upon the FDDI physical implementation and network operating system software chosen, the data link layer may do the initial address recognition. Other connection-oriented communications functions may be provided at this level, including message acknowledgment, link initialization, and disconnection. An important feature is the Simple Network Management Protocol (SNMP), which functions at this datagram level to collect frame information for network management services. The upper layers provide additional link control, to be discussed in the next section.

How FDDI Transmits

The data and other frame components are built into a special buffer or coprocessing capabilities on the FDDI controller. This buffer is a critical component of the controller. In fact, the FDDI controller should have multiple buffers for better performance. As an example, most personal computers process information at only 1.3 to 3.8 million instructions per second (MIPS). If the PC processor were exposed to the FDDI transfer rate and not buffered by means of the control field within each information frame, it would soon be swamped with frames. Even a workstation capable of 40 MIPS or more may be unable to maintain the full throughput of FDDI. Figure 7.8 represents the importance of the NIC controller buffer in a PC. Of note, many high-end station devices, such as a Sun

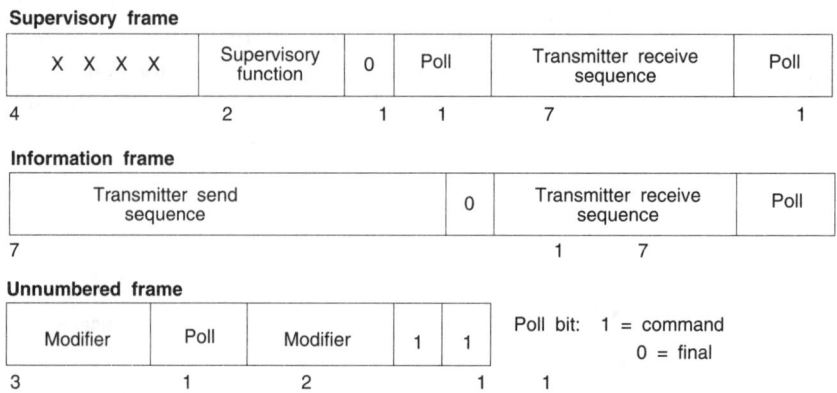

Figure 7.7 The 802.2 control field format.

FDDI Software and Process

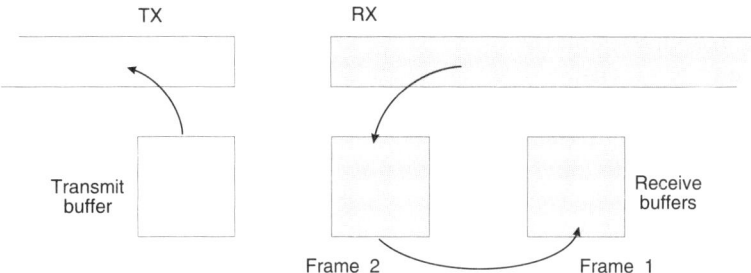

Figure 7.8 FDDI controllers require frame buffer space or coprocessors.

Microsystems workstation, may have a communications coprocessor to handle multiple NICs at full Ethernet and Token-Rings speeds with 20 Mbits/s of FDDI traffic simultaneously. Mission-critical applications may be configured so that overloads, primary server-to-server linkages, or failsafe connections are maintained in a dual homing state. This is both a function of a fiber optic NIC with A/B and C/D connections, two or more standard NICs, and adequate software to support this OSI routing function.

Once the data set is packaged into a frame, the FDDI controller awaits a token. Upon capture of a token, the NIC then transmits the information frame. The frame signal propagates to the next downstream neighbor. Each node, in turn, hears the transmission, synchronizes its clock, and repeats the frame. This clock synchronization is important to delineate the beginning and the end of the frame, as illustrated by Figure 7.9; the starting delimiter provides this frame alignment, as shown. If the frame were misaligned the FCS checksum would show an alignment error indicated by the power line. Nodes which see a frame error modify the status field, but still repeat the signal with the error. Some minor corrections are sometimes made if the error is nothing more than the preamble overshooting the NIC. The frame would be discarded by the destination node(s) and depending upon the network system software, the source node might retransmit the frame.

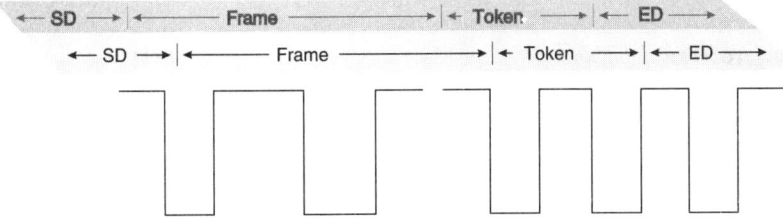

Figure 7.9 Synchronization prevents mistiming transmissions.

Every node on the network reads the address information. When a frame destination address matches the FDDI address of a node, the NIC for that destination node transfers the FDDI signal into the receive buffers on its FDDI controller. The signal is repeated by every station. The source station will recognize the source address as its own address; it does not repeat the signal. It returns the token to the ring upon passage of the token holding time or upon completed transmission, whichever comes first. This process is identical to the 802.5 Token-Ring early token release (ETR) option. This process is displayed in Figure 7.10.

The received frame is disassembled and decoded by the FDDI controller into three major components: the information frame, the data frame control, and the CRC checksum. The controller verifies that the length of the data message matches the value in the frame control field, and generates its own CRC to compare against the transmitted CRC value. Any discrepancies are passed to the software protocols. IPX and TCP/IP, for example, will request a rebroadcast of the damaged frame. IPX/SPX also reports receipt confirmation to the transmitting node via that logical link control field, whereas FDDI does not do so directly. If the transmission has been successful, the data field contents are passed to the software protocols and eventually transferred to the application level for its ultimate use. Note that all 4-bit data to 5-bit symbol encoding is performed within the controller on the fly, as is MLT-3 encoding for UTP media. It is basically invisible to a user or network administrator without a sophisticated protocol analyzer.

Supplemental FDDI Features

FDDI has a few wrinkles. Each station serves as network an active monitor. Any primary station can indicate ring failure or initiate a ring recovery. When a station is removed from the ring or the ring wraps and the token is lost, a primary station will issue a demand for the token. Other nodes can issue a request for the token. Upon acknowledgment of ring recovery—this means the ring is functionally complete though perhaps smaller with fewer nodes—a new token is issued.

Frame: received   rejected

8D   (a node address)   02
__   (broadcast)   04
8_   (multicast)   B3
8D   (direct to node)   7_

Figure 7.10 FDDI receives a signal.

FDDI Software and Process

Downstream nodes waiting for a token that never arrives, receiving a signal that is clearly incomplete, sensing two or more overlapping transmissions, or sensing some physical error on the ring will issue a *beacon* signal. This transmission overrides all other events. Usually the beacon is indicative of a node insertion. It could indicate more serious problems such as a failed lobe or trunk, a cut in the wiring, or power lost to a hub and other critical active components. The beacon usually indicates to all still-receiving ring stations that the ring is broken or that a station is not generating or repeating signals properly. This beacon initiates a sequence called the *ring recovery*. A failed station, hub, or section of ring may be removed from the greater ring or may wrap and seclude other hubs that seem to be failing.

A frame is almost certainly corrupted when a new station inserts itself into the ring. The noise and lack of signal retransmission and caused by the brief loss of the ring structure will with near certainty corrupt a token or information frame. This is normal. As a result, a ring with 120 stations should show approximately 120 errors related to "station insertion." Every time a PC is rebooted, power cycled, or the NOS reloaded, that station will reinsert itself into the ring. This is a normal process and to be expected. Note, that in general, most FDDI primary stations should be available 100 percent of the time. Primary stations are repeaters and critical to the integrity of the ring. Unless passive optical bypass switches are provided integral to each station NIC or installed to supplement the stations in the event of a power failure, station crash, or other occurrences, the ring will not be as reliable or failsafe as possible.

Soft errors are ring failures that do not generate a beacon. They are rare for FDDI. A soft error may include corrupted frames, lost tokens, overlapping signals, stations that run on beyond the THT limit, or a signal that is not stable. A *jabber* is a signal caused by a station that exceeds the allotted THT limit. Abundant soft errors are indicative of installation or software flaws in the FDDI ring. They degrade performance, waste channel capacity, and increase the average waiting times. There should be very few, if any at all, such soft errors because the FDDI specifications do not tolerate them. Most points of failure have been identified and formalized with defined actions and responses. The FDDI ring will either work or not. Typically, errors at the station level will cause the ring to wrap or crash, but rarely function in an intermediate states.

FDDI can be likened to a one-line phone system. You wait in line to make the call. When you are first in the line (grab the token), you ask for the operator to connect the call (transmit). The call is placed and the phone line is now busy. Only the person receiving the call is supposed to listen. The call has a time limit that is preset and a function of the transmission speed. No priority is enforced to get the line after a transmission; it is on the sequential basis of the token circulating about the ring. Asynchronous (i.e., priority) access to FDDI is not yet codified. Thus, FDDI, like the party-line, is public, and all stations and nodes can listen to every call as it is repeated around the ring; hence, the "party-line" moniker. FDDI is, however, very fair and even with the highest levels of traffic, every station and node will get a chance to hold the token and transmit data.

Network-Level Software

The last sections of this chapter describe the network layer software corresponding to OSI layers 3 through 7. For the purposes of this book, the functionality of these layers will be compressed into administrative and content layers. The administrative layer directs the frames and deals with traffic problems independently from frame content, whereas the content layer controls content, decides what should be transmitted, and processes the transmitted information.

The administrative layer software provides the functionality to know what devices exist. Some systems map network workstation names into logical Internet addresses, which are in turn matched with physical FDDI addresses. The network software also provides the interface between the FDDI process and the network software processes. This interface, additionally, maps user data into the frames. In other words, failed transfers are indicated for retry.

A station is considered "dead" if retransmissions continue to fail or if a station continuously transmits (jitters). Some network software has blind spots to failed transmissions, and this software will continue to load the network in error. Compare the role of this administrative layer to that of the telephone operator. The operator provides connections, distributes telephone numbers and verifies wrong numbers, retries the connection after a "busy" signal, switches connections onto other networks when the main network fails, troubleshoots the mechanical connection, and informs the calling party of network problems. Figure 7.11 demonstrates the operator role in terms of FDDI.

This network content software can be likened to the language and the grammar, and any cultural standards applied to phone conversations. The role that the calling party assumes is presented in Figure 7.12. Just as the telephone transmits language transparently, the FDDI administrative software transmits frames without inquiring into frame content. Content depends on the two parties communicating.

The network software builds, accepts, and interprets the frames, and applies the information. The range for FDDI data application is as large as that of the telephone. Not only can many languages be spoken over a telephone, but each can be encrypted. The language could convey news about the weather, be a sales call, contain a request for help, or provide an

FDDI Software and Process

- Resolve data location into a NetBIOS address
- Resolve LLC address into a NetBIOS address
- Resolve "domain" address to node address
- Accept data set
- Build protocol frame:
    Include addresses (source and destination)
    Insert data
    Calculate frame length
    Calculate checksum
- Encode frame
- Send frame to controller
- Wait until "circuits" are not busy; hold token
- Await successful transmission
- Inform calling party of network problems

Figure 7.11 The "operator" role.

- Request a connection
- Initiate a connection
- Await the connection
- Handshake ("say hello")
- Build the data for insertion into data frame
- Decode frame
- Pass data to administrative level software
- Await results
- Process responses
- Process errors

Figure 7.12 The "party" role.

explanation or the solution to a problem. In just such a manner, the content and logical composition of FDDI frames can vary.

Network and Transport Services

Protocols also initiate system and network operations. Just as a phone call to the fire station precipitates a frantic rush to save a burning building, an FDDI frame can contain information that initiates events. Network software, consequently, will provide such functionality as system boot, network initialization, electronic mail and bulletin boards, transfer file data, simple message routing, file services and print services, and system monitoring. Figure 7.13 shows this upper-layer network functionality.

IPX/SPX

Simple networks build upon IPX, which is derivative of the TCP/IP protocol. IP, Internet packet exchange (IPX), UDP, and NetBIOS protocols are the predominant FDDI software due to the success of Novell

- Remote workstation boot
- Network software initialization
- Internode addressing
- Electronic mail and network facsimile
- Computer bulletin boards
- File services
- Print services
- System monitoring
- Network performance monitoring

Figure 7.13 Upper-layer network services.

NetWare and the use of high-end Sun Microsystems servers and workstations on FDDI. These protocols provide intercommunication between nodes for messages, cumbersome file exchange, and terminal services. Such a network configuration would appear to be a mainframe computer serving dependent terminals, although the hardware wiring scheme has been simplified through the application of FDDI. More complicated networks simplify the file transfer operations, provide electronic mail instead of message capabilities, network fax services, and add bulletin board operations. Improvements to this include block file transfers, remote workstation operations, system kernel services (that is, the "remote boot"), file interchange capabilities, multiple-node access, multiple-file sourcing, single sourcing of network-wide software (for example, word processing, databases, and engineering programs), and remote device access and services, such as printing.

These user-layer applications are represented by such vendor offerings as Appletalk, NetWare, NFS, and other proprietary and nonproprietary network systems. Due to FDDI's robust error handling and reliability, more of a manager's time will be devoted to network software problems such as interoperability than hardware issues. As a consequence, manuals describing specific vendor networks need to be reviewed for the specific details of upper-level software. While hardware problems are easily diagnosed (see Chapters 12 through 14), network software problems can be narrowed to specific nodes with software tools and protocol analyzers, as explained in Chapter 16. However, many specific software failures often need to be resolved with vendors' own technical support people, because the additions to the basic TCP/IP are extensive and complicated. Figure 7.14 illustrates the relation between the FDDI frame, IP, and TCP.

The *Internet protocol* had its roots in communications addressing scheme known as *Address Resolution Protocol* (ARP). This formed the basis of the Department of Defense's Advanced Research Project (DARPA) four-node network called Arpanet. Arpanet evolved into Internet during the 1970s as TCP/IP was adapted for LANs. This now

FDDI Software and Process

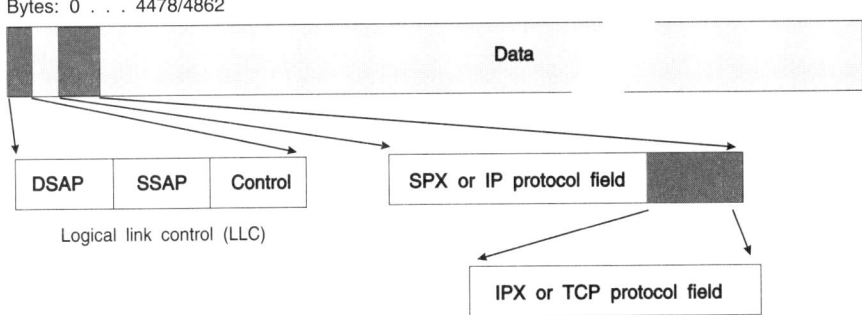

Figure 7.14 TCP/IP mapping from the FDDI frame data field.

forms the major connectivity effort for interchanging data between Ethernet, FDDI, WANs, and many other network protocols. A serious limitation of TCP/IP is that the Internet address is limited to 32 bits (while OSI provides to 128 bits). This is simply insufficient space to provide unique addresses for growing numbers of network nodes. The IP address contains a network and host address divided into parts; the first two components of "145.150.102.10" represent a network, and the rightmost two entries designate the host node. The *Domain Name System* (DNS) maps host names for nodes (such as "mickey," "donald," "field com," "T1F99S56," or "Marty@SST") into the IP and node addresses.

LLC Protocol

Internet protocol provides the lowest level of software access and interface to the FDDI environment. This protocol provides the link initialization and termination, node recognition, and frame control operations. The Internet control field, part of the LLC unit, resides within the first few bits of the FDDI frame data field. Figure 7.15 maps its components. This datagram is sometimes called the *MAC-level format* and is the primary information field for SNMP network management. It is important to note that system software utilizing the UDP implementation under TCP/IP will not be routable, and this will severely limit attempts to interoperate TCP/IP networks. Although TCP/IP supposedly conforms to the OSI model, there are gray areas.

TCP Protocol

Transmission Control Protocol (TCP) is a higher level communication protocol. This protocol sequences data transfers and the actual frame transmissions. It exists within the IP data field. In fact, TCP resides at the OSI layer 4, whereas IP is OSI layer 3. Figure 7.16 illustrates the components of this control field.

Internet protocol field

| V | HL | TS | LN | ID | FO | TL | PR | CS | Source | Dest | Option | Data |

```
V   = version              PR     = protocol
HL  = header type          CS     = header checksum
TS  = type of service      Source = source address
LN  = total length         Dest   = destination address
ID  = identification       Option = option
FO  = flag and offset      Data   = ISO level 4 data
TL  = time to live
```

Figure 7.15 Internet protocol.

TCP protocol field

| SP | DP | SN | AN | OF | W | CS | UP | Option | Data |

```
SP = source port           W      = window
DP = destination port      CS     = checksum
SN = sequence number       UP     = urgent pointer
AN = ACK number            Option = option
OF = flag and offset       Data   = ISO level 5 data
```

Figure 7.16 Transmission control protocol.

Protocol Comparison

Token-Ring running at either 4-Mbits/s or 16-Mbits/s has an extensive share of the personal computer networking market (40 percent share), and is particularly prevalent within the corporate world. Ethernet, the other major LAN protocol, has a 46 percent share of the PC market, but an 80 percent share of the workstation and scientific market. Thus, FDDI, Token-Ring, and Ethernet frequently need to interoperate. Many vendors provide bridging hardware or internetworking software solutions to connect these two important network standards. At a minimum, networks must intercommunicate. The Ethernet datagram, mapped in Figure 7.17 and the Token-Ring datagram, mapped in Figure 7.18, indicates why protocol interoperability remains a thorny problem. These data fields could contain 0 to 18,432 bytes of information, as compared to FDDI's maximum data field size of 4478 bytes. The additional overhead required by IP, TCP, and the LLC or any other MAC-level addresses will profoundly slow the transition from an Ethernet or Token-Ring frame to complete FDDI delivery. Also note that FDDI and Token-Ring have two types of frames, the token and the data frame to Ethernet's single frame format. This duality must be represented within the multiprotocol environment.

Another serious network concern is that the IBM LAN Server or MS LAN Manager program could require almost 600 K from the 640 K of DOS server memory. Since DOS itself can require 40 to 80 K, fitting the network software into memory is a significant and sometimes a lengthy

FDDI Software and Process

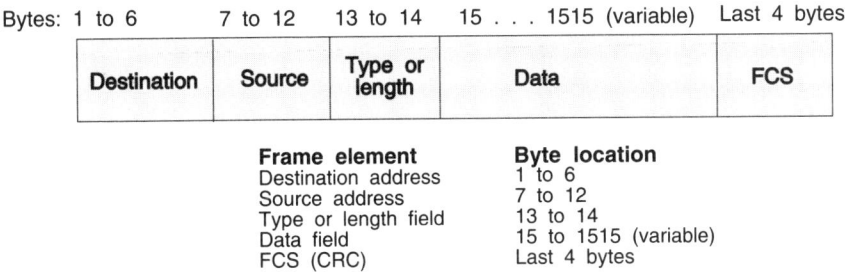

Figure 7.17 Ethernet packet (IEEE 802.3).

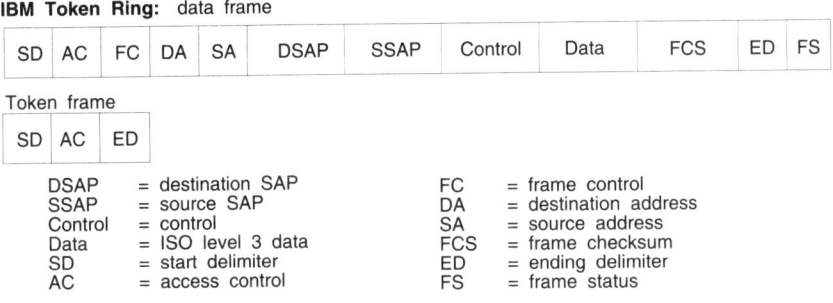

Figure 7.18 IBM Token-Ring packet (IEEE 802.5).

task. Unix or OS/2 can provide multiple concurrent sessions; this allows for a gateway function. Special extended or expanded memory management software, including HIMEM.SYS, EMM.SYS, and proprietary memory software, may allow network software to load. This memory shortage can be more pronounced when multiple protocols are loaded simultaneously to provide gateway services, as Chapter 11 describes. Of note, Sun Microsystems' Unix translates between FDDI, Token-Ring, and Ethernet almost transparently. It is easy to run all of these protocols from the same server. The server only needs at least one NIC for each protocol.

Chapter

8

Planning an FDDI Network

FDDI installation encompasses both planning and physically connecting the media-level hardware. This chapter describes the planning process and the components that must be included in the plan. The components and the support required vary depending upon media selected. Components for twisted-pair based networks include twisted-pair wire bundles; wire fittings like modular connectors, hermaphroditic media connectors, nine-pin D-connectors, or modular connectors; jacks and plugs; hub concentrators; wiring patch panels; jumpers; and network adapter units or NICs. Optical cable networks will require optical cable, suitable connectors, epoxy, signal splitters, bypass switches, and optical NICs and concentrators. This discussion also addresses cable hangers and cable tie mechanisms. It also addresses a valid concern about the physical and dimensional stability of the wire or optical fiber itself. An experienced network manager understands the value of blueprinting the installation, and this chapter describes how and when to blueprint. This presentation serves to augment vendor-supplied technical documentation. Figure 8.1 illustrates FDDI components described within this chapter.

- Blueprints
- Project plan
- Cable ladders or wiring conduits
- Wiring concentrators (hubs)
- Station controllers
- Optical fiber or twisted-pair wire (STP or UTP)
- Bypass switches and optical signal splitters
- Armored casings or below-ground conduits
- Packet switches
- Modular jacks and connectors
- Punchdown panels
- Bridges, routers, and gateways

Figure 8.1 Typical items required in FDDI network installation.

The first step in planning any installation is to analyze the user requirements and understand the network technology. The network plan should address both current and future needs by allowing for expansion at a later date. If at all possible, it is wise to begin with a small network and expand over time. While a small network will simplify the learning process and minimize the complexity of problem-solving, FDDI is rarely a physically small network. FDDI is usually the choice for campus connectivity and is a solution for Ethernet or Token-Ring capacity bottlenecks. As such, FDDI may be initially tried in a test environment but soon be placed in a mission-critical role.

Designing and planning the network configuration builds the foundation for long-term success of that network. Both under- and overdesign constitute network management failings. An overdesigned network—one built to accommodate more traffic, more network stations, and more users than foreseeably possible—constitutes a costly network. An underdesigned network constitutes the more serious flaw; a network that does not match minimal traffic volume need is unreliable, and provides negligible room for expansion. Instead, improper estimation of network loading and user requirements at this stage will lead to poor network management by overloading the staff with problems. Consider this fundamental reality: poor network performance is the key issue that forms the basis for a negative operational evaluation of the network administrator. However, performance is dependent upon the foundation of network design and many networks are inherited or built ad hoc. While operation and implementation issues addressed in Chapter 10 ultimately make or break a manager, design and planning concerns addressed in this chapter ultimately define the complexity of daily network implementation and operation. These basic items are expanded in Figure 8.2.

- Network design configurations
- Network user needs
- Physical plant limitations
- Power protection
- Network installation
- Compatibility
- ANSI, CCITT, IEEE, and OSI standards
- Connector integrity
- Network profiling
- Network blueprinting
- Network security
- Equipment energy and cooling requirements

Figure 8.2 Practical network design concerns.

Planning an FDDI Network 133

Design Criteria

The design of a network is a complex problem, with far-reaching ramifications. Insufficient capacity, incorrect media, and inadequate loading characteristics frequently cause performance lags. These design shortcomings are avoided by understanding organizational needs and network performance issues before contemplating a network. Break the analysis into small pieces. Understand who will use the network, what load each user will place upon the network, what access to devices each user requires, and how growth or organizational change might strain resources. See how competitors or other LAN customers are applying networking technology and what loads are transported by these networks. Compare this to your organization's needs.

Lease versus purchase decisions hinge upon financial concerns and useful component lifespans, as well as the lease vendor's attentiveness to customer support. This matter is not addressed here, although the reader might consider lease or rent as a viable alternative to outright purchase. Additionally, turnkey systems and professional installation save time, money, and personnel without the need to hire people normally associated with a network. Also consider the availability of spare parts and outside expertise to solve internal network problems. Figure 8.3 shows these network design and maintenance questions.

Construct the network from small, separable building blocks. Concentrators, backplanes, wireless "modem" linkages, NICs, and wiring panels are just some of several mechanisms to segment and extend the network. Complement these devices with gateways, matrix switches, repeaters, and subnetworks to divide the size and complexity of the network into comprehensible units. Such segmentation adds reliability, durability, and design simplicity, and may, in extreme cases, provide the only means to trace FDDI problems to their source.

When designing a network, insist that all classes of components come from the same manufacturer. Slight interpretative differences in ISO, ANSI, CCITT, IEEE, or FDDI specifications could mean that parts are

- Who will use the network?
- What load will each user place upon the network?
- What access to devices should each user have?
- What individual growth is anticipated?
- What centralized resources are needed?
- What load or peak loads can the network sustain?
- What spare parts are needed?
- What outside expertise is available?
- What other networks must connect to FDDI?
- How will a network conform to physical plant limitations?

Figure 8.3 Network design and maintenance questions.

not compatible. This issue is expanded within a following section. When it is unfeasible to select uniform network components, segregate the parts that differ. Avoid mixing network interface cards, workstations of different purpose and manufacture, and even cable or fiber. If station equipment includes personal computers and engineering workstations or different network operating systems, consider placing these units on separate rings. At the least, install a DAS station on the primary ring functioning as a true router to insulate heterogeneous devices on the secondary SAS network. Even with the full 100 Mbits/s bandwidth of FDDI, the traffic from PCs paging MS Windows, graphic stations scanning 32 Mbyte photographs, medical imaging stations creating incompressible patient scans, or client/server accounting can quickly saturate the FDDI backbone and mask the true source of the overload unless these secondary networks are subnetted and logically isolated. Thus, segmentation is an appropriate design criterion.

Last, do not overstate the capacity of a single FDDI channel, or of the FDDI system as a whole. Capacity saturates eventually at 100 percent of theoretical rated capacity (see Chapter 17), although performance grows slower with more network stations and higher traffic loads; waiting time increases and slows network performance to the ultimate FDDI token response limits—the maximum ring latency, as described in Chapter 6, is 1.612 ms, and 8 ms before ring recovery is initiated. Unlike Ethernet, FDDI does not fail with too much traffic. It simply gets slower until the TTRT, TRT, and maximum ring latency provide unacceptable response times.

Install capacity sufficient to match predicted needs. Be certain that vendors have provided the necessary references to verify not only their implementations of FDDI but also the expected quality of after-sale support. FDDI is at its best for occasional file transfers, electronic mail, communication, and internetwork linkages. It will support high loads of distributed client/server databases—subject to protocol overheads, channel capacity, the transmission content of the actual work. It may not be appropriate for massive file backups without dedicated channels, data transfers, or single-keystroke remote terminal support. Understand the limitations of this medium and the organizational needs. Where one medium is insufficient, research the benefits of another. Understand how expansion can be effected to support user and traffic growth, and technological change.

Design Subject to User Needs

When designing a network, it is important to envision the purpose of the network, the type of traffic it will accommodate, the distances between areas that need to be serviced, and the total load to be placed upon the network. Understand how design, configuration, segmentation, dual homing, and secondary support channels can affect perform-

Planning an FDDI Network

ance. Realize that FDDI specifications may inhibit or hinder your design; consider distance limitations and station counts, as well as repeater, or full lasing station placements. Figure 8.4 outlines issues to consider when designing a network, some of which are considered in this chapter. Because FDDI is a token-passing medium, it will handle a maximum of 100 percent of its rated transmission speed under ideal conditions, minus tokens, preamble, beacons and polling, ring inserts, jitter and misalignment, minus the results of all suboptimal hardware and software, minus a small, random error rate. Application-level protocols, semaphores indicating receipt and acceptance of transmissions and packet overhead also lower the true throughput. Since TCP/IP and UDP are the predominate transport- and network-layer protocols on FDDI, correctly estimate the true load from connectionless message packets. Effective usage may yield 50 to 75 percent of the rated 10 Mbits/s capacity. Furthermore, FDDI seems to lose about 20 percent efficiency (in terms of user-perceived response time) through the layered protocol stacks before any user data is transmitted.

Consider the very suitability of FDDI. A bus configuration network with a random access scheme may be better suited than the token-based FDDI for various reasons. For example, an engineering shop may get improved customer support with a matrix switch, an Ethernet backbone-in-a-box, or FastNet than with FDDI for the simple reason that the technical support staff is more familiar with Ethernet.

From a technical standpoint, a network with consistently low peak loads, centralized file access, and centralized computer processing may benefit from the bus wiring scheme and a single corporate network. FDDI may be precisely the proper medium, in cases like client/server mission-critical accounting to the desktop, medical imaging, connectivity for many, distributed LANs, or LANs supporting a downsizing transition from a mainframe environment. Networks of few users or

- Network purpose
- Traffic volume
- Peak traffic volume and traffic composition
- Network size and configuration
- Network user community size
- User workload
- Network functionality
- Security
- Reliability
- "Mission-critical" requirements
- Suitability
- Alternatives
- Installation, maintenance, and upgrade costs
- Performance enhancement and upgrade paths

Figure 8.4 Network design issues.

minimal requirements might better be served by ARCNET or a "zero-slot" LAN such as LANtastic or a peer-to-peer network such as MS Windows for Workgroups, both low-end networks.

Many factors increase the cost of FDDI; these should be established prior to the actual installation process—as part of the initial budgeting process. Optical fiber itself is an expensive proposition at several dollars per foot installed, possibly more if local building codes specify special "fire-safe" riser cable which ignites at a higher temperature and will not release toxic gas when it does burn. However, optical fiber is the only viable choice for segments longer than 100 m. This may suggest installing STP or upgrading existing IBM STP Token-Ring networks to TP-DDI, or substituting UTP twisted-pair wiring bundles or using the already available and unused wires in the telephone bundles. Match these needs against station-to-station lengths, and growth requirements. The NICs, concentrators, and other related FDDI hardware also present expenses. While FDDI hardware is an expense to consider, installation and maintenance are other cost factors, usually ten times larger than initial installation costs. Large FDDI configurations are physically difficult to maintain on campus-wide spaces, and therefore costly. Also, new tools to qualify and debug the media—particularly if the network is based upon optical fiber—will be expensive. They must support the media, the significantly higher transmission speeds, and support all the transport and network protocols transmitted on the network. The interaction of large networks, disparate hardware, and disparate loading are prime considerations in defining costs, because problems increase rapidly as a network grows in complexity and load.

For lower-volume serial lines, cheaper and lower-capacity networks are options worth consideration. This encompasses T-1, RS-232 connections with CCITT V.32 data compression modems, LANtastic, direct serial connection, or repeated parallel lines, as well as other proprietary PC networks. Note that FDDI management can become sizable and require the organizational resources of a dozen full-time staff. RS-232 networks are a very mature technology, both in terms of the hardware and management techniques. An IBM mainframe computer network may support 40 users each on 100 separate channels. This means that a single network will support 4000 terminals. That is, by the numbers, a very large management problem, because there would be at least 4000 users, maybe as many as 12,000 with channel multiplexing and multiple users sharing each terminal. Each user requires a log-in, accounts, and file storage space. Often, each account must be billed, and this creates a need for an accounting organization.

An FDDI network can be as complex, with 1000 primary DAS stations, and 1024 nodes on Ethernet networks indirectly attached to the FDDI stations. FDDI is far more difficult to manage because it is relatively

Planning an FDDI Network

newer, has a shorter track record, and has not demanded the vendor support applied to the more developed serial line technologies. FDDI can be just as demanding if it supports terminal servers (wiring concentrators linked to FDDI stations or Ethernet devices attacking to FDDI stations which then fan out to multiple RS-232 lines) and IRMA links to a host mainframe. Not only is the hardware still developing, but also management tools are less developed than in the mainframe environment. While initial FDDI traffic load is unlikely to saturate the 100 Mbits/s channel capacity, it is likely that increased network integration and new technologies will stress even that seemingly large bandwidth. While the physical and administrative demand is numerically greater, the frame in an RS-232 environment is also transmitted from the mainframe to the terminal. Characters are returned only to the mainframe. An FDDI environment is a true interconnected network, perhaps even a network of networks, not a hierarchical tree of decreasing importance. The topology is very different and loads distribute differently as illustrated in Figure 8.5. The mainframe network provides link-to-link access from the dumb terminals to the mainframe. A user at one such "node" seeking access to another such "node" must connect through the mainframe, and the interconnecting power is more limiting than in FDDI. On the other hand, every packet broadcast on FDDI is repeated by every DAS station. Although this does not require station CPU effort (or very minor activity), it does subtract from available network bandwidth and decreases the overall network response time.

Physical Plant Limitations

Sharing computer resources and exchanging electronic mail through a built-in computer network is not reserved for well-funded start-up ventures in newly built industrial parks. Older buildings, unplanned sprawling complexes, and high-rise buildings can have networks, too.

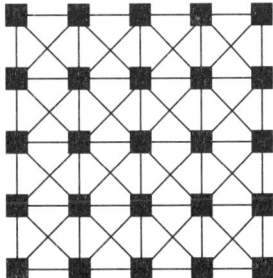
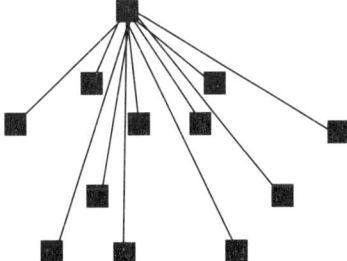

Figure 8.5 FDDI (left), although a star-wired network, is an interconnected network unlike a host star topology.

No building, no matter how old or how modern—no ship or plane, for that matter—will seemingly discourage you in your efforts to install the installation of the type your organization wants. Rarely will it be impossible. Even where overhead or underfloor wiring conduits seems full of cable, a dual FDDI fiber with a 3 mm connector diameter can probably fit. It is also one third the weight or less of comparable copper wire. Furthermore, noninvasive tools which locate wire and cable no longer in use and thus no longer needed can indicate how room can be made for new cable. While it is possible that the layout of the building may constrain the wiring efficiency, neither the building design nor the lack of space will limit the kind of network that you can install. If your building is of an older design, examine the premises more carefully because there may be additional costs for installing network wiring because the ceiling is inaccessible. Hanging ceilings or return-air plenums may be small or nonexistent. Existing pathways between floors or buildings may be unsuitable for new wire, or filled with old installations. In such cases, new conduits or cable trays may provide part of the answer. PVC cable produces a toxic gas when it burns, and is often banned from return-air plenums, the space above the hung grid ceiling. Teflon wire, although more expensive than PVC, exceeds most building codes without any restrictions.

Twisted-pair, the cable most often existing in old buildings and now in new installations, may provide a ready means to network a new or expanded LAN. Qualify the wiring for its ability to adequately convey FDDI traffic at 100 Mbits/s; this is very relevant for copper-based UTP media originally intended for voice grade applications. If growth, large numbers of far-linked machines in different directions, or video imaging are required, it may not be economical to reroute, add, or maintain twisted-pair. Rather, line-of-sight wireless infrared networks or the technology of radio- frequency (through the walls and floors) Token-Ring or Ethernet networks may be a good accommodation, with FDDI providing an interbuilding, aerial, or interfloor linkage.

Both STP and UTP have distinct disadvantages. STP must be run from central wiring hubs to each station. It does not provide flexibility. When a contractor has to drill holes through walls, ceilings, and beams, in order to route single through narrow plenums, it often makes more sense to pull a duplex or break out bundles of optical fiber through a facility from floor to floor. UTP, existing or new, may limit node lengths from a concentrator to satellite stations to 30 m. In electronic noisy environments it may be inappropriate, due both to the external noise and the crosstalk it creates. Note that EIA/TIA has endorsed the concept of a modular and centralized star wiring plant.

Locations of computer rooms may be suboptimal but possible in many locations. Select the location with the best cable access and most stable

Planning an FDDI Network

climatic environment, and one that will provide security to meet design requirements. Computer facilities are best if locked and if the temperature remains constant. Overheating and low humidity, which increases static, cause component failures. Climate-control equipment generally solves these problems. However, these concerns are best addressed during the planning stages rather than as retrofitted necessities.

Consider how best to schedule installation. If cabling conduits, optical fiber, and STP are installed as part of new construction, the work is just one more item for the building contractors. Cabling an existing facility may require working around physical limitations and the office hours. If your organization cannot be closed during the network installation, the contractor may have to coexist with employees and customers. Additionally, scrap, dirt, and constant traffic may create a need for frequent cleanings. Acquire a good vacuum cleaner with extension hoses. A vacuum is a good tool for removing dust from circuit boards, and grime from workstation air filters and inlet cooling ports on all electronic network components.

Remember one last point. Any cabling—optical fiber, UTP, or STP—is often installed within a ceiling plenum that is about 8 ft above the network connection for most stations. When planning cable runs from blueprints add the necessary height drop or you will find that estimates are significantly short—and the network may be longer than planned. While 8 ft (or 16 ft, representing up and down) may not mean much in terms of buying more wire, accumulations of such extra lengths could station-to-station or lobes lengths beyond specification.

Power Protection

Most network managers are aware of the danger of lightning striking outside wiring and sending a jolt down the line or down its armor jacket to damage anything unfortunate enough to be plugged into the outlet. Most managers are also aware of power surges and spikes that can cause premature failure of computer chips and magnetic media. Network wiring can also acquire induced or live voltages from proximity to power lines, not to mention the possibility that network wiring can be accidentally switched into live power. Some have experienced the slow degradation that occurs during a power brownout when voltage levels decay. Everyone knows the effects of a power blackout. The problem for the network manager is what can be done about these disabling situations.

Wiring errors are particularly relevant as data and voice lines are routed in pairs to offices. The higher telephone ringing voltages, although usually just a nuisance to people, are often fatally damaging to LAN equipment. Figure 8.6 lists the typical problems that can create network havoc. Also, *radio-frequency interference* (RFI) and *electromagnetic interference* (EMI) can travel through the power lines, phone lines, dedicated T-1, frame and cell relay lines with disastrous results to sensitive computer equipment.

The damage from such events is not limited just to damaged computer equipment itself, data loss or corruption, and downtime. Modems, phone equipment, CSU/DSUs, and PBXs can be damaged too. There are also lost opportunity costs, aggravation from frequent crashes, and additionally, the certainty that other damage will be spawned. A crash can destabilize a chemical reaction or an in-process clinical test, damage patient records and lose critical allergy information, or ruin a part in a computer-controlled manufacturing process.

It is important to weigh the importance of uninterrupted service and the cost of downtime. Frequent downtime affecting order entry, order processing, or accounts payable may be of little consequence, but it may represent the germinal stages of a bad customer-relations problem. The cost of the computer equipment is apt to exceed significantly the cost of protection, although the purchasing decision rests on the risk that the organization is willing to assume.

There are solutions to these problems. Specifically, filters screen out electrical noise from the incoming power, while suppressers level out the wave crests of power surges. Protect power lines, phone lines, data lines, and any other spanning connection. Isolation equipment provides capacitance to level out the wave troughs of low power. Voltage regulators filter the electrical power so that the voltage is stable. Standby battery supplies and uninterruptible systems provide the same emergency power function. *Uninterruptible power systems* (UPS) (usually) provide electricity automatically when the sensing apparatus detects power problems. Since UPS provides temporary emergency power only, most network managers allocate UPS capacity for an orderly and rapid server shutdown; monitoring software can track the performance of a UPS and initiate an orderly file server or client station shutdown when power reserves are depleted. If UPS should support continuous operations, acquire a generator that will handle capacity including the starting surges of several machines. Blueprinting AC wiring and routing of network wiring, and careful labeling of any network bundles can minimize errors. One important note to realize is that most surge suppression technology is based upon on a metallic oxide varister (MOV) which

- Power surges
- Power spikes
- Power sags
- Brownout
- Blackout
- Lightning strikes
- Stray voltage
- Static electricity
- Differential ground voltage potentials

Figure 8.6 Electrical problems that threaten networks.

Planning an FDDI Network 141

degrades with each voltage spike. These should be replaced—at least tested—annually before they fail to provide equipment any protection. Most UPS systems include surge suppression; these suppression components may lose effectiveness and need replacement too. Figure 8.7 lists commonly available electrical computer protection devices.

FDDI Compatibility

FDDI provides compatibility for optically based networks, and is generally compatible for STP-based networks. Check with vendors for any compatibility issues that might arise with UTP equipment; the prototypes are in flux. The transmission encoding speed, wiring requirements, and FCC qualifications are in all in flux. However, FDDI does offer a certain mechanical consistency; many vendors sell products to interface disparate "FDDI" components. Compatibility is often used as a selling point, as attendees to *InterOp* and *Network World* have seen. However, this doesn't always mean that FDDI-compatible equipment will transmit to other FDDI-compatible equipment; different NOS protocols on the same network can blindly share the network with each other.

Surpisingly, an accelerating area for incompatibility is the fiber connectors. Not all FDDI connectors are alike. At least three significant types of FDDI optical connectors exist. There is the single fiber bayonet connector, the dual fiber media interface connector as described in the FDDI specifications, and the Enterprise System Connector (ESCON) as developed by IBM. Although mating connectors do exist, the idea of inserting another entity in a fiber link is not great. Mating UTP and STP is a minor problem as this would occur at a hub or other connectivity unit.

There is a potential for interfacing problems. While the physical media and the transmission standards may be exact or similar, software discrepancies (at the NOS level) may make the FDDI versions listed in Figure 8.8 functionally incompatible. Mixes of optical, UTP, and STP are the key questions.

If you recall, FDDI is defined as a optical medium as well as the media access method (e.g., token passing). The extensions defining FDDI as a protocol for STP are not fully completed yet, while FDDI on UTP is merely in a draft format. Signaling differences between NRZI (optical fiber and

- RF and EMI filters
- Surge suppressors
- Isolation transformers
- Voltage regulators
- Hot standby battery backups
- Uninterruptible power systems

Figure 8.7 Power protection devices.

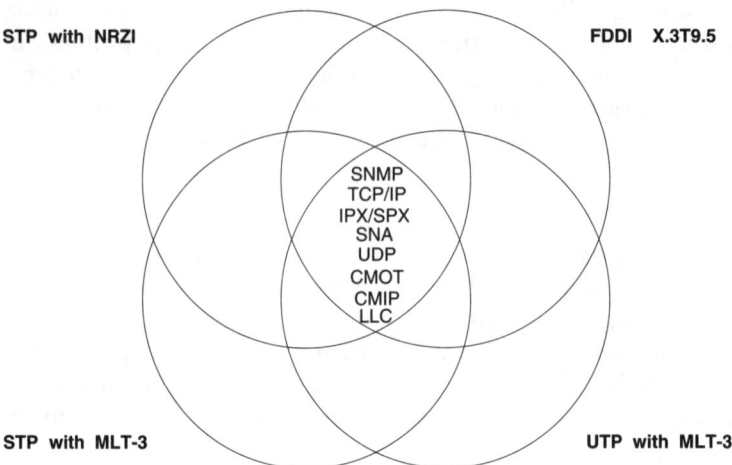

Figure 8.8 FDDI version compatibility.

STP) and MLT-3 (most UTP implementations) are not comparable, but can interoperate with a special bridge. This means that these versions will communicate to a standard network through a specified mechanism; it does not mean that these alternative networks are electrically compatible, or software-compatible with standard FDDI. An ISO bridging or gateway mechanism, sometimes called a *linkage product*, connects totally separate networks for enterprise-wide communications.

In order for any third-party vendor products to function correctly with the existing network, all transmission and reception hardware must synchronize timing; FDDI does state concise synchronization guidelines and limitations. NIC crystal clocks are not always accurate. Frame preambles are, however, precise. Subtle differences will become more apparent as the network grows in size and loading factors; these differences should be understood and the ramifications explored prior to actual purchase or installation. Be aware that prime vendors may substantially alter their equipment or software over time for any number of reasons, including bug fixes, better performance, a new sales strategy, or an attempt to undermine other vendors. As a consequence, third-party solutions may no longer be ideal.

In any event, get verified customer references from *both* happy and unhappy customers. Assess compatibility and the eventual upgrade and customer support policies. Vendors must support not only their own products, but also other network items that will interface with them.

Compatibility must be supported on the first three ISO layers for machines to share the same physical transmission highway. Compatibility must be supported on layers 3 and 4 for differing hardware to even

Planning an FDDI Network

acknowledge another protocol. Layers 5 and 6 must be identical for machines to interconnect. Layer 7 is only the application layer, and compatibility at this level is necessary only insofar as different machines need to share code, mail, network software, access directories of files, and run user-level application software.

A network ideally requires hardware and software components that match a single specification. Where components deviate from a single design criterion, isolate those unique components with subnetworks, bridges, routers, or gateways, as Figure 8.9 suggests. The backbone (trunk network) performing as subnet bridges, multiport bridges, or high-speed packet switching bridges interconnects LANs which are thus isolated.

Since FDDI is a physical specification for a communication network, this network design only specifies the media and the optical (or electrical) transmission standards; it does not define file transfer, mail systems, or other upper-layer protocols. These processes are supplied by UDP, NetBIOS, IPX, or TCP/IP, Appletalk, and other such ISO layer 3 definitions; differences in the programmer's implementation of IPX cause one major incompatibility. Figure 8.10 outlines possible FDDI discrepancies.

Different vendors supply their own interpretations of FDDI and especially NetBIOS. Furthermore, Unix operating systems, TCP/IP stacks, and UDP messaging protocols are usually provided on tape in source for compilation on the target machines. Anything can happen, and many problems do occur during the compilation, module linking, and setup of such a large operating system as Unix. While FDDI should be robust enough to provide access to all devices, in practice, slight differences are indeed likely to create transmission problems. Such

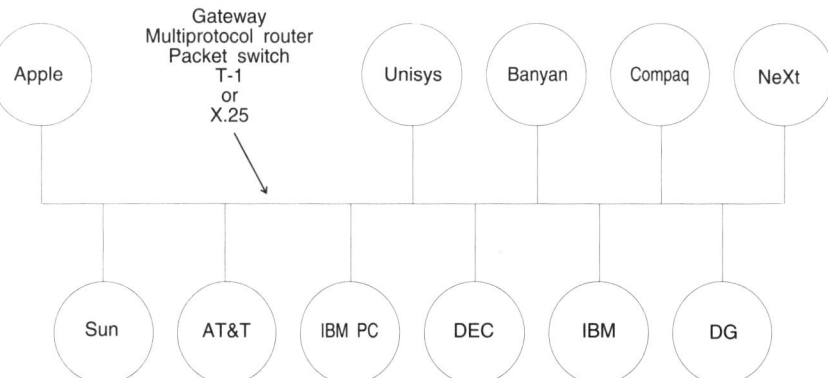

Figure 8.9 Isolate different equipment on separate rings.

- Transmission speed or media dissimilarities
- Transmission encoding dissimilarities
- Electrical or optical timing differences
- Controller buffering limitations
- Frame incompatibilities
- Logical link control differences (as in IPX or UDP)
- Error-handling discrepancies (at NOS level)
- Acknowledgment differences (at NOS level)

Figure 8.10 Possible FDDI incompatibilities.

incompatibilities are more likely on saturated networks. Different networks should isolate different types of equipment—until that equipment is proven to be well-behaved and fully compliant of FDDI protocols.

There is only one FDDI transmission speed, but three major wiring versions, and an erratic migration to OSI stacks. Each equipment and component vendor can redesign the functionality to minimize costs or maximize features. Small details, such as controller buffer parameters, coprocessor synchronization, bus-mastering efficiencies, quality of NIC drivers, or how upper-layer software device drivers will access physical devices, can make difficult-to-trace problems. Furthermore, vendor-supplied components can vary in small ways. While these minor deviations may not disrupt communications, incompatibilities may mean machines from different vendors can share a network without the ability to talk to each other. More ominously, such small differences can cause serious application-level shortfalls. For example, application software might not recognize the network printers, could crash suddenly and sporadically, corrupt data files, or fail to load within the PC or workstation memory.

Network Limitations

The FDDI specifications outline the requirements for a functioning network. Most of these specifications present maximum configurations for the following: total number of DAS stations, the maximum length between stations, minimum and maximum clock and timing values, number of secondary nodes, and numbers of protocols running concurrently on the network. As previously mentioned, FDDI never fails except for physical flaws; it will always transmit data although at increasingly slower rates—up to the specification maximums. FDDI is surprisingly robust and resilient, as might be expected for the first next-generation networking protocol. It is wise to plan a network with enough capacity for growth and *not* assume that the specifications can be stretched to accommodate that growth. Therefore, Figure 8.11 reiterates the FDDI configuration parameters on the next page.

Planning an FDDI Network

Parameter	Optical Fiber	STP	UTP
Data rate	100 Mbits/s	100 Mbits/s	100 Mbits/s
Max network span	250 km	984 m	200 m
Max stations/primary ring	1000	1000	1000
Max stations/network	Unlimited	Unlimited	Unlimited
Wiring:			
Type	Optical fiber	Type 1 or 2	UTP-3 or UTP-4
			Datagrade UTP
Connectors	ST, MIC, ESCON	Genderless	Modular
	Dual shroud	Modular	Modular
		Patch panel	Patch panel
Characteristics	830 or 1300 nm	8 ohms	12 ohms
Lobe wire:			
Type		Type 1 or 2	UTP-3 or UTP-4
			Datagrade UTP
Connectors		Genderless	Modular
		Modular	Modular
		Patch panel	Patch panel
Impedance		8 ohms	12 ohms
Jumper wire:			
Type	Optical fiber	Type 1 or 2	UTP-3 or UTP-4
		Type 6	Datagrade UTP
Connectors	ST, MIC, ESCON	Genderless	Modular
	Dual shroud	Modular	Modular
		Patch panel	Patch panel
Characteristics	830 or 1300 nm	8 ohms	12 ohms
Hubs:			
Ports		8, 12, 16	4, 8, 12, 16, 24, 48, by vendor
Ring wrap	Yes (if duplex)	Yes	Yes
Lobe isolation	No (if duplex)	Some	Some

Figure 8.11 FDDI network parameters.

FDDI Network Components

Because planning requires an understanding of the FDDI components, this chapter continues with a discussion of the options available for basic network components. Figure 8.12 outlines items of importance when

- Network cable sectioning
- Multiprotocol routers
- Concentrators (hubs)
- Patch panels
- Punchdown blocks
- Trunk cables
- Lobe cables
- Jumper cables (patch panel and wall)
- Twisted-pair wire
    Network interface cards (NIC)
    Modular connectors
- FDDI cable routing
    Avoidance of water, high-voltage, and temperature extremes
    Cable ladders and cable supporting logical routes
- Inventory necessary components
- Wireless networks
- Selection of components
- Project plan
- Blueprints

Figure 8.12 Planning considerations addressed in this chapter.

planning a network. Components required for even the simplest installation include wiring, connectors, cable ties, NICs, and hubs.

Network Station Sections

A network does not require a single continuous length of either optical fiber or twisted-pair wire station cabling. The network will work adequately if it is sectioned into convenient lengths and jumpered at central patch panels. There will be almost no detectable degradation if all the connections are properly installed. While optical fiber should be continuous, segments may be created with suitable connectors or fusion splicing. Optical bypass switches can be employed to segment and bypass segments in the event of a segment failure or security breach. Signal degradation should be benchmarked with a stabilized optical light source and light meter. Also, it is common practice for twisted-pair networks to route the wire bundles through several patch panels for configuration convenience. Many network managers might assume that such construction of a network hodgepodge with segments is in poor form. However, installation of shorter segments will not only prove easier, but installation costs will probably be less, installation time will be faster, and verification of the new network will proceed smoothly.

In fact, such segmentation demonstrates good planning. FDDI does experience transmission problems. Problems become more prevalent on longer and busier networks. Larger rings often span rooms, run vertically through ceilings and walls, and traverse floors and even buildings. There is limited practical benefit to installing long runs with contiguous cable;

Planning an FDDI Network 147

costs increase, availability of cable decreases, and cable may have flaws that otherwise can be repaired. It is awkward to string a bulky, inflexible cable through tight bends, and pull long lengths through the ceiling and through underground tunnels. The weight of the cable makes such practice difficult, and the friction along its length makes it virtually impossible. It is likely that the weight of the unsupported cable will break.

Another important reason for segmenting the ring is that certain test instruments, such as a time domain reflectometer (see Chapter 12), work poorly if the network segments are sectioned in lengths exceeding 100 m. (Note: lobes longer than 30 m for UTP and 100 m for STP generally fail to meet vendor recommendations, while segments longer than 2 km for optical fiber generally violate FDDI specifications.) This tool sends a radar-like electrical or optical signal down the network cable and illustrates blockages or breaks. This signal dissipates over distance, thereby providing less accurate information.

Ideally, a manager would section lengths of runs, and conveniently section these at critical junctures. Too many connections and segments increase signal reflection. This reflection is often referred to as *impedance*. It may also be referenced as *light scatter* or *signal decay*.

Connectors

FDDI has standardized parts that simplify and improve the reliability of the network, and ease problem-solving. Optical parts include single strand bayonet connectors (ST connectors), fixed duplex-shielded dual-fiber keyed connectors (Media Interface Connectors or MICs), and inline signal splitters and enhancers. Optical fiber is mechanically simple as there are actually few parts in the network. The IBM ESCON connectors are a modification on the standard MIC connectors.

Optical Fiber

Optical fiber is the only medium than can reliably transport data at rates faster than 100 Mbits/s given the current technology. It is the only technology that can multiplex multiple signals on the same channel at those speeds. While the EIA/TIA category 5 wiring standard presumes an upgrade path for ATM to the desktop at 155 Mbits/s, it remains unclear that copper connections will support such speeds and meet with FCC approvals. Also, existing fiber should provide a viable upgrade path for the European Fibre Channel 1 Gbits/s networking proposal. Therefore, consider installing optical fiber if you expect to require higher bandwidths or access to ATM, cell relay, frame relay, SONET, or similar type networks.

Optical fiber consists of various amorphous (i.e., glass and plastic) materials extruded into two concentric tubes. The innermost most tube is the actual transmission media; it carries the light signal. The next outer layer reflect any stray signal back into the core. Other outer layers provide signal isolation and structural support. The fiber is not really sharp like the edge of a broken glass; it feels more like a hard, flexible plastic. It doesn't shatter like a glass will either. The fiber itself is quite strong, although it will snap and break with enough force or by creating too tight a radius. Since it is made from an amorphous material, doped glass and plastic, it will eventually sag just as old glass windows run. However, the usable life of the optical fiber is likely to be longer than the useful life of this technology.

Several variants of optical fiber exist. These consist mostly of packaging differences. There is a standard indoor "tight buffered" cable optical fiber plenum (OFNP) in either simplex (one fiber) or duplex (two fibers) bundles. Riser cable, optical fiber riser (OFNR), is typically Teflon. "Breakout" cable is packaged such that there are multiple fibers with individual fibers easily accessible for separate termination. "Distribution" packaging consists of many tightly-packed individual fibers intended for long runs. Outdoor optical fiber cabling is usually gel filled, rather than foamed, for aerial installation, buried, or ducted through underground conduits.

Fiber is available in any length since it is extruded at the manufacturing process. It is usually sold in standardized lengths, such as 500 m or 2 km. Longer lengths can consist of segments connected together with couplings, although the norm for creating longer lengths is to splice cable together using a fusion tool that melts the glass fiber together.

FDDI X3.169 defines single and dual ring architectures. The single ring uses a single strand of fiber. The dual ring uses two strands of fiber. These two concentric rings are usually created with an optical fiber bundle that has at least two fibers. Two types of connectors are available, as shown in Figure 8.13. The common single fiber connector called a *bayonet* or *ST style* connector. This connector may also be referred to as a 2.5 mm connector. These connectors may also be used for dual ring network connections. Additionally, many vendors sell plugs that convert ST connections to the other type. The other type of connector is the *fixed shroud duplex* connector or the media interface connector (MIC). A new alternative to the MIC is the IBM enterprise connector called the ESCON. The connector is keyed plug that contains two optical fibers

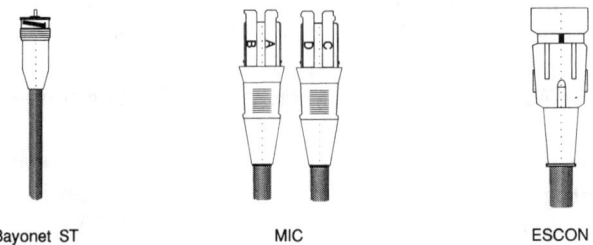

Bayonet ST MIC ESCON

Figure 8.13 FDDI ST, MIC (FSD), and ESCON connectors.

Planning an FDDI Network

recessed inside the connector's tip. It is advisable to employ this connector in FDDI networks for four reasons. The keyed (A/B and C/D; AMP differentiates the connector sets as type A and B, and additionally as master and slave) connectors prevent incorrect installation, while the recessed fibers generally prevent damage to the polished end of the fiber. Duplex connectors can also mate together without requiring an additional coupling as ST connectors do. Additionally, the duplex connector is more rugged. By the way, the ESCON connector is just a variation on the MIC; some ESCON and MIC connectors may mate properly. On the other hand, some will not.

FDDI may also contain two other devices, called an *optical splitter* and an *optical bypass*. See Figure 8.14 for a photograph of the optical signal splitter, and Figure 8.15 for a photograph of the optical bypass switch. The splitter takes a single and converts it into two identical outgoing signals. It is usually a passive, non-powered device such as a partial (half-silvered) mirror. The bypass is an effectively an optical transistor. Or, visualize it as a train track switch. This passive or active device can reroute signals from one destination to another. Some vendors provide banks of these switches in a single box to provide rapid network reconfiguration. Both switches and splitters can compromise the security of an FDDI network. But, they can also provide remote facilities for maintaining the mission-critical operations despite various network failures. Both of these devices reduce the signal strength of the source signal. More active devices will be available in the future as the technology of current-induced coatings matures.

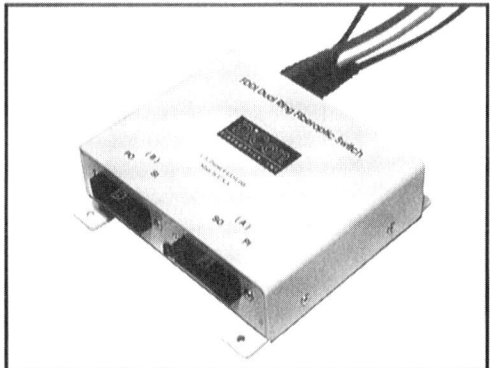

Figure 8.14 Optical signal splitter.

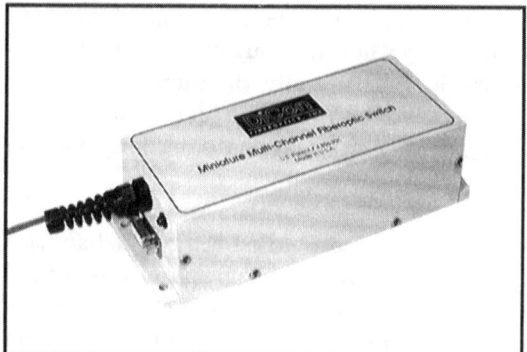

Figure 8.15 Optical signal bypass switch.

STP and UTP

If you think that there seems to be a similarity between FDDI on STP or UTP and the IBM Token-Ring, you are correct, and for some clear reasons. Vendors want to provide a simple FDDI upgrade path for existing Token-Ring networks. Twisted-pair parts include modular and genderless connectors and type 66 or type 110 punchdown blocks. For instance, Figure 8.16 contrasts the differences between the modular and genderless connectors.

Modular phone UTP wiring is a very simple installation medium and is finding favor for installation in new buildings and for many network extensions and retrofits. While more difficult to install correctly and maintain conformance to the rigid FDDI specifications, twisted-pair is effective. Twisted-pair bundles usually contain 25 "pairs" of wires in internal bundles of six or eight wires. FDDI utilizes only four wires in most vendor UTP offerings. The wires within each set are twisted around each other for the entire length to minimize signal interference

 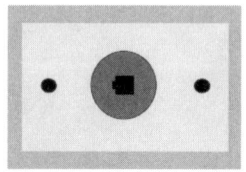  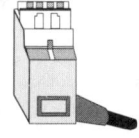

Figure 8.16 Modular and genderless connectors.

Planning an FDDI Network 151

and crosstalk from the other pairs. Wire is routed from a patch panel through walls or wiring conduits to modular jacks in walls or modular office furniture. RJ-11 and RJ-45 connectors crimp onto ribbon-like jumper cables (also called "twisted-pair" for convenience) that are not wiring bundles or even twisted. These are flat ribbon cables without and crosstalk-minimizing wire twists. Minimize jumper cable usage since it does not conform to the twisted noise- canceling specification. Note that the modular connectors are not easily installed on either STP or UTP; the bundle and each wire must be stripped individually. These four, six, or eight wire cords connect the wiring concentrator hubs or the NIC to the modular jacks as Figure 8.17 illustrates. The actual wiring connections are "straight through" as is standard with phone connections. Where the wires cross should be carefully controlled since you do not want to cross an odd number of times, or twist the standard phone connections and confuse the telephone system, either. (Some phone systems will "work" but not ring.)

Twisted-pair wiring is not only a simpler technology because it uses wire rather than coaxial cable or optical fiber, and it is also a packaging advance. A four-wire assembly connects the NICs directly to a comparable assembly in the wiring hub. This is a star configuration conforming to the EIA/TIA site-wiring standards. The one important element to remember is that the connecting wires should not cross over; although transmitting electronics send signals to the receiving electronics, the physical wiring transition is furnished internally. Some NIC interface boards either indicate a *polarity* error or perhaps even correct for the irregular wiring cross-over. The NIC and each port on the hub or multiport (8 on average) has separate transmitter and receiver circuitry. Figure 8.18 lists the wiring scheme for the 6-pin RJ-11 and 8-pin RJ-45 FDDI modular connectors; these are all the same for Ethernet, Token-Ring, and FDDI. Figure 8.19 lists the wiring scheme for genderless connectors. Note that twisted-pair installations that make full use of the wiring bundle for long runs, or intermix its use with RS-232 serial lines, are apt to increase crosstalk problems and expose pairs to excessive noise. Limit bundle utilization to 50 to 75 percent.

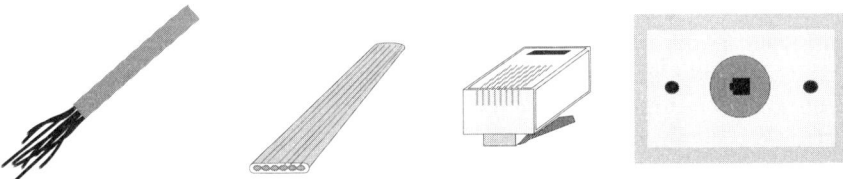

Figure 8.17 STP and UTP is stripped first for modular connector installation.

RJ-45 Pin Number	Function	Function
1	Unconnected	Unconnected
2	Unconnected	Unconnected
3	Transmit-	Receive+
4	Receive+	Transmit+
5	Receive-	Transmit-
6	Transmit+	Receive-
7	Unconnected	Unconnected
8	Unconnected	Unconnected

RJ-11 Pin Number	Function	Function
1	Unconnected	Unconnected
2	Transmit-	Receive+
3	Receive+	Transmit+
4	Receive-	Transmit-
5	Transmit+	Receive-
6	Unconnected	Unconnected

Figure 8.18 Modular connector wiring scheme for STP and UTP.

Genderless pin position	Genderless	DB-9
Black	Transmit+	Receive-
Orange	Transmit-	Receive+
Green	Receive+	Transmit+
Red	Receive-	Transmit-
Shield	Ground	Ground

Figure 8.19 Genderless connector wiring scheme.

Cable Routing

The next planning step is to define the route that the cable will take through the building. This route should provide ready accessibility to all workstations to minimize lobe lengths or twisted-pair lengths. This route should also provide adequate expansion capability. Specifically, a route that minimizes cable for the current installation may be insufficient for any expansion. The cable should also be easily accessible in case of malfunction. For example, a path that follows a corridor is superior to a diagonal route over cubicles.

Planning an FDDI Network

Avoid Water, High-Voltage, Temperature Extremes

Optical fiber and twisted-pair are both inert. Optical fiber is generally nonconductive. However, it is prudent to keep them away from water sources since these can short the electrical transmissions if water seeps along the cable and into a connector, and from high-voltage electrical sources which can interfere with and disrupt the signal.

Electrical or magnetic fields may conflict with the copper-based FDDI transmission and introduce high error counts. High-frequency radio sources disrupt communications. High-frequency lighting—vapor lighting—lab or medical apparatus that transmits—can disrupt network traffic. Even though optical fiber is inert and also nonconductive, be aware that any armor or shielding may be metallic. While optical FDDI transmission itself may be immune to signal carried by external metal cladding, this shielding may act as an antenna and carry signal to disrupt CPU or NIC coprocessor functions, or transport ground voltage differentials, electrical shorts, or lightning strikes for fatal results. If possible, route main cables away from the sources shown in Figure 8.20. Continual expansion and contraction from a heat source such as the air conditioning ductwork near the cabling plenum will cause micro-fractures in the copper cores and accelerate metal fatigue or discolor optical fiber. Fractures and optical discoloration will slow the speed of transmission; increase electrical impedance, causing high jitter rates; or completely disrupt communications. Slowing the transmission speed is not necessarily a problem unless the network is generally heavily accessed, in which case even a 0.1 percent transmission speed degradation can disrupt the NIC timing and cause transmission to fail.

Figure 8.20 Sources of EMI.

Installation Routing Options

Standard practice suggests that wire is best installed in cable ladders or wiring conduits. A cable ladder is a metal open-rung ladder for securing cables and wiring. Wiring conduits are sometimes called cable trays and are metal U-formed channels for concealing wire. Both items are best installed at the time a building is initially built since false ceilings and ductwork usually preclude retrofitting ladders or trays. J-hooks provide adequate support for retrofitted cable. J-hooks bolt to a stud shot into steel or concrete support beams. See Figure 8.21 for samples of hooks, ladders, and the plastic cable tie.

Cable routing depends in great part on the building design, the available financial resources, and networking goals. Wire can be routed through underfloor ducts, through cellular floors with trench headers, or beneath raised plenum floors as found in the standard computer room. The cable tie is an important item to ensure that wire, once installed, stays where intended. Since optical FDDI is often used to span buildings and cross campuses, cable routing may mean that optical fiber is run underground through steam conduits and power conduits, passageways, or buried in concrete or earth. Realize that high temperature steam can melt optical fiber, that people may attach accessible communication lines, and that insects and rodents might gnaw on underground connections. A common failure of long links occurs when new construction unearths the old links.

Local options include conduit systems in modular office furniture (so long as bend radii are not exceeded), surface raceways, or installation within a ceiling plenum. PVC cabling has a minimum bend radius of 3 in—a circle diameter of 6 in, while Teflon cabling requires double that measurement. Observe vendor specifications for optical fiber and armored optical fiber. Network routing should address the need for growth and change, equipment relocation, and expansion of basic network services. A good design is patterned on the voice networks which have confronted and solved most of the same issues now affecting data networks. This analogy explains the explosive acceptance of UTP twisted-pair wiring; it does *nominally* coexist and use the same wiring as the telephone voice networks. Nonetheless, twisted-pair for networking is a better grade than generally installed for

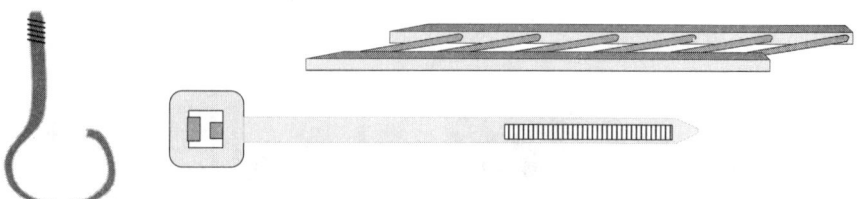

Figure 8.21 Hook, cable tie, and cable ladder.

Planning an FDDI Network

telephone lines. Two reasons that some organizations denounce the UTP technology are their own failure to install the specified quality of twisted-pair wiring bundles (category 3 or better) and their failure to adhere to rigorous length limitations. Substitution of "satin" wire, or the flat ribbon-like patch cord designed for telephone jumpers, defeats the noise canceling property of true twisted-pair wire and STP vendor recommendations. These failures represent installation errors.

Install Wire in Straight Runs

In general, it is better planning to avoid distance-minimizing wire routing. Stair-step patterns, wave or sawtooth zigzag are brilliant ideas whose time has passed, as shown in Figure 8.22. Odd routing patterns create a problem with pursuant connectivity malfunctions and more at operational time; simple, straight runs are better. Odd wiring routes and lax documentation will generate problems when backhoes, jackhammers, and earthmovers chew into underground conduits. The 2 km optical fiber limit is quite robust; conform to corridors. The 100 m STP and 30 m UTP function limitations can be overcome with concentrators, careful worksite analysis, and smart placement of an optical backbone.

While it is best to patch optical fiber directly into the end station (NIC) and avoid the use of jumpers to minimize signal loss, often the copper lobe cable will run to a standard modular (or genderless) wall plate. The copper cable can be segmented at a wall plate, although this shortens maximum lobe length slightly as a result of signal impedance. EIA/TIA standards actually specify the maximum twisted copper pair at 92 m, with 3 m patch cables at each end. A separate cable, possibly with a media filter, will connect from the wall plate to the computer device. Shorter cables can be used like extension cords and plugged together for longer lengths up to approximately the maximum specified length. Both UTP and STP are available in PVC or Teflon. It is best practice to install it in straight runs supported by hooks, ladders, or conduits; avoid securing wire and optical fiber to pipes, ductwork, lighting fixtures, or electrical lines. Simple paths endure longer and are easier to document.

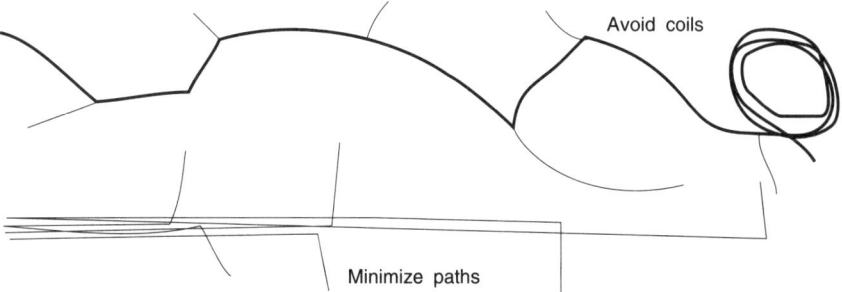

Figure 8.22 Avoid zigzag cable runs or coiling excess STP or UTP.

Inventory Necessary Components

Once the route the cable will take is defined, it is appropriate to select the type and quantity of the components. Use the discussion of components presented earlier in the chapter as a guide. Refer to Figure 8.23 for the component quantities required for building a network. Additionally, this chart lists some simple rules for component selection. Some commercial tools provide automated methods to create the parts, materials, and time requirements for successful installation. LANBuild from Network Performance Institute is one such product that supports FDDI with both optical and electrical components; it also includes support for dual homing stations and full lasing connections.

Blueprint the Planned Network

A wiring installation should be precisely blueprinted. Fiber or wire placement is one of the most critical items. Location can be lost in the false ceiling plenum, thus making shorts and breaks difficult to find and fix. Important items to document are changes in wire direction, endpoints, and places where the cable is jumpered. This is important in order to locate the places where failures are likely to occur and where a time domain reflectometer or scanner might connect to the network wiring. Another method for above-ceiling installations is to photograph the ceiling with the tiles removed and wiring exposed. A photograph can show the position and orientation of cable trays.

Installations that have CAD/CAM systems can computerize illustration; computerization improves the access to copies and allows for the construction of overlays. For example, one level might show only the main trunk cables, while other layers may show subnetted rings, paths of cables, and location of bridges, routers, and stations. See Figure 8.24 for a sample of blueprinting that illustrates wiring, and lobe-cable routing, as well as twisted-pair connections.

Pictures of the internal cable dynamics (compiled in reports generated by serial downlinking from a scanner, such as the the Microtest Ring Scanner or fiber feature detector) can be compared against views when malfunctions are disrupting network communications. Discrepancies suggest malfunction location. At a minimum, the cable length should be measured. It is folly to underestimate the network length and later discover that network wiring expansion has extended the network length beyond maximum length specifications. While optical-based FDDI is quite robust—20 times longer than other network limitations—it is folly to assume that this robustness will cover all sins. Networks are certain to fail sometimes; information about where the cables are located, stations are placed, and extenders, splitters, or bypass switches are installed, while expensive to generate initially, will be more expensive to gather later when there are problems.

Planning an FDDI Network 157

\	A LANBuild Design and Planning Tool Report Network Installation Bill of Materials for FDDI network *B-2 design backbone*			
Unit	**Description**	**Quantity**	**Notes**	**Spares**
network	KW electricity	170		35
network	dedicated circuits	300		61
network	tons BTU A/C capacity	151		38
network	patch panel	4		1
network	patch panel blocks	33	6	1
network	patch panel hydra bundle	105	6	6
network	wiring rack	3		1
network	patch panel jumpers	1179	2	68
node	NIC (dual units)	393	2, 9	20
node	station to station cable	394	2, 9	60
	Likely length is: 7.00 to 32.80 m			
network	optical bypass switches	0		1
network	hubs w/32 ports	28	2	2
network	trunk cables (for hubs)	29	2	2
	Average likely length is: 5.00			
node	station	215		11
node	server	71		22
node	support station	107		33
	Longest likely ring circumference is: 2797 m			
	Dual ring requires two optical rings with 5594 m wiring			
	Average likely segment is: 729 m			
node	single mode fiber extenders	393	2, 9	20
node	conditioned AC power	206	2, 7	42
node	cable ties	1072		
node	network software licenses	393		
node	network software drivers	393		
node	NIC device drivers	393		
Optional				
node	wall conduit	393		1
node	wall wiring box	393		1
node	wall box plate cover	393		1
node	wall plate to NIC jumpers	393	2	20
node	UPS power supply	178	7	36

Figure 8.23 Component quantities required for the basic FDDI network. Structural components and underground variants are not shown here. (LANBuild bill of materials report courtesy of Network Performance Institute.)

158 Software and Hardware

A LANBuild Design and Planning Tool Report
Network Installation Bill of Materials
for FDDI network *B-2 design backbone*

Note 2: Most hub nodes require AC electrical power for operation. Very few local nodes operate from workstation DC power. Although transmitter power requirements are fairly low, plan for adequate conditioned power in the desired locations. The same is true for servers, support nodes, and other critical powered components.

Note 6: A hydra connects easily into most standard patch panels and simplifies installation while increasing operating reliability.

Note 7: Uninterruptible power supplies (UPS) are battery-backup devices to provide needed service in case of power failures or spikes. Also, it is best to install isolated/grounded circuits for all critical computer equipment, active hubs, routers, and gateways.

Note 8: The FDDI station address must be set by software configuration.

Note 9: Dual fiber FDDI must be supported by the hardware and the NOS.

Note 11: LAN to LAN connectivity via modem lines, T-1, dedicated lines, ATM, SMDS, frame relay, or even serial lines often requires common carrier phone lines. Assess this need and plan for installation accordingly.

Figure 8.23 *(continued)* Component notes. (LANBuild bill of materials report courtesy of Network Performance Institute.)

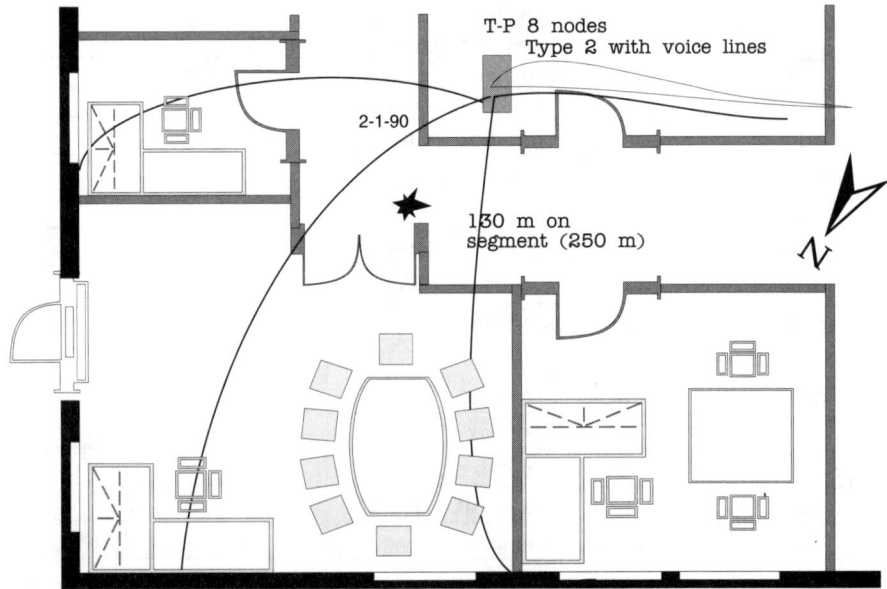

Bldg. 4, North Corner, 2nd floor   (8-15-1992)

Figure 8.24 Architect's style for network blueprint. (LANCAD screen courtesy of Network Performance Institute.)

Chapter

9

Installing an FDDI Network

A network design blueprint, project plan, a capacity and performance report, and a list of the required components and installation process steps are sufficient precursors to the installation process. This chapter describes the steps you must take and the tools you will need to put an FDDI network together.

Planning for Installation

Installation requires a qualified design and a good project plan. Network blueprints should be detailed enough to represent all the network hardware components required for a complete installation. This should comprise the actual physical components for the LAN and *also* ancillary factors such as electrical power requirements, cooling needs, and software. There are an increasing number of products that provide network design, capacity planning, and time and material estimates for LANs. While such tools are not absolutely required, they will minimize the chances for designing and building a flawed network. Examples include Bones or Planet, both from Comdisco; and NET·CAD, LANModel and LANbuild, all from Network Performance Institute. Many project planning and management tools will increase the odds that the network will be installed correctly and on time. While many people chaff at using such tools since they require significant training, the time invested both in learning and preparing a product plan is worthwhile. On one hand, the project plan ensures the timely synchronization of installation, the project plan is also an important communication tool to inform users and other affected parties what will take place, when, and how it will burden them.

If the vendor does not supply full plans or provide complete network parts and installation services, it is vital to coordinate the arrival of all the network components. The network will not work without wiring concentrators, or hubs, station lobe cables, or any number of other components, not the least of which is functioning network software.

Insufficient electrical power or inadequate cooling resources for 100 workstations drawing 720 watts at 4 amps per unit could easily stress a standard office environment. Any problems arising may not become apparent immediately. The installation can certainly be staged, since many installation procedures can be completed concurrently. Just about any missing part can, no matter what its simplicity or general insignificance, become a critically needed component.

Therefore, plan your installation timetable with an eye to the steps in network installation and coordinate delivery of components to ensure a smooth process. Figure 9.1 illustrates critical steps and a logical progression for network installation.

Each step encompasses several individual stages not included in the figure. STP, or wiring bundles, for example, requires cutting to length, applying media connectors or jacks and attaching the these into stations or patch panels; and installing the actual connection media in its final location. Installation is a mechanically simple process but a challenging experience if the technology is new to the organization. This is quite the case with optical fiber. Sufficient skills may not have been developed to adequately identify and repair network problems.

Therefore, consider the benefits in hiring the vendor or an experienced contractor to string the network cabling. Gather as much outside experience and expertise as possible to augment the internal network administrative team. Any failures or delays on such a visible project as an FDDI internet will undermine organization trust in the network team, give ammunition to nay-sayers to curtail the project, and unduly stress key supporters. The installation procedure requires a shakedown period. Premature acceptance of a new installation is unwise, and making or disseminating promises of network availability before most of the problems have been resolved will devalue the reputation of the network administration team. Budget sufficient time for overruns, problems, and missing components. Be certain to negotiate preconditions for any final acceptance with the vendors. An installation may provide marginally

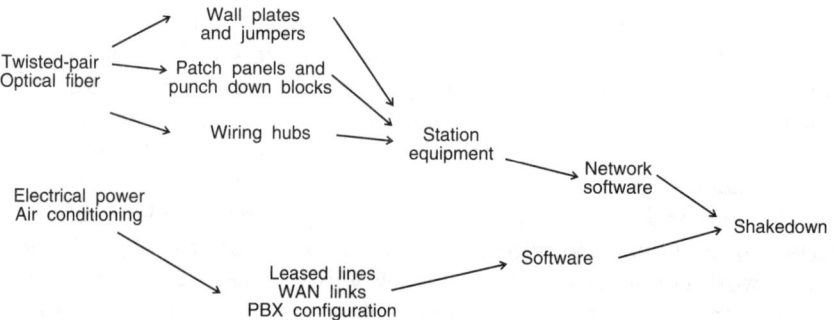

Figure 9.1 Critical paths for network installation.

Installing an FDDI Network

acceptable operations, but fail to perform the level of service desired. To forestall any future problems, define clearly what your expectations are. This is critical for successful vendor relations and achieving your organization's network goals.

Preparing for the Physical Installation

Installation of a new network goes smoothly if you gather the preliminary blueprints and all the equipment and components before beginning, and if you proceed in the order listed in Figure 9.2.

Installation Tool Kit

Installation requires a sizable tool kit. The contents are enumerated here solely to provoke some ideas. This kit should contain screwdrivers; pliers (including needle-nosed); diagonal cutters; a cable cutter; a wire stripper; a bright flashlight, preferably rechargeable; crimping tools; a soldering iron and silver solder; desoldering device; asbestos (or heat resistant) pad; a small mirror on a flexible handle; a shorting plug (a connector with a wire soldered to short the core conductor); and various spare parts like modular connectors, probe tips, junction boxes, and wall plates. Include specialty tools such as a manual or electric (vibrating) punchdown tool for modular patch panels.

Installations using optical fiber will require specialized tools which are not normally obtainable at hardware stores, and are also quite different from those required for coaxial Ethernet installation or

#	Steps	Equipment
1	Inspect cable (or wire) visually	Cable (fiber, STP, UTP)
2	Test cable	Cable and test equipment
3	String cable and label	Cable, tool kit, blueprint, and tape
4	Secure cable	Cable ties
5	Install connectors	Tool kit, connectors, insulation
6	Test connectors	Test equipment
7	Install network adapters	Adapters and tool kit
8	Test adapters	Software loopback test
9	Install other components	Tool kit, test equipment, and ladder
10	Secure network components	Cable ties
11	Update blueprint	Preliminary blueprint
12	Configure PBX for WAN	PBX technician, list of lines
13	Activate lease and WAN links	PDN activation order

Figure 9.2 Steps and equipment required for installation.

twisted-pair 10BASE-T or Token-Ring. This includes a fusion splicer, a stabilized light source with the appropriate light frequency (generally 1300 nm), a light meter sensitive to the same frequencies, and a scanner or optical time domain reflectometer. It is also good to have access to a protocol analyzer with sufficient capacity to decode FDDI at speed and full channel capacity, support all protocols and encapsulation technologies, and also be able to create traffic at the full 100 Mbits/s to test the network and attached devices. A microscope is useful to check fiber endpoints for proper polishing. A polishing kit is inexpensive. An epoxy connector kit is necessary only if you manufacture your own connections or need to repair a damaged connection; consider obtaining one for all building sites.

Another tool specific to optical fiber is a signal detector that can indicate which fibers are active without cutting or breaking the FDDI loop. This is illustrated in Figure 9.3. A similar and inexpensive device is available for electrical lines that light up when in proximity to active electrical circuits. Obtain one sensitive to UTP and STP voltage levels (10 volts DC), telephone voltage levels (48 volts DC), and for AC power lines (110 volts AC and up). This later range is useful to correctly identify dangerous power lines before physically touching them.

Less obvious tools include a rechargeable vacuum cleaner, ladders, a stud finder, walkie-talkies, and a radio. A powerful vacuum cleaner is invaluable for retrieving screws dropped inside a computer chassis, for clearing shards from a tap core that might short the coaxial cable, and for clearing accumulating dust that shortens the life of all electronic components. Avoid magnets for this purpose since they destroy integrated circuits and erase magnetic media. In a clever application of a standard carpenter's tool, the electric stud finder or electrical power proximity checker (much like the stud finder) also locates active cables

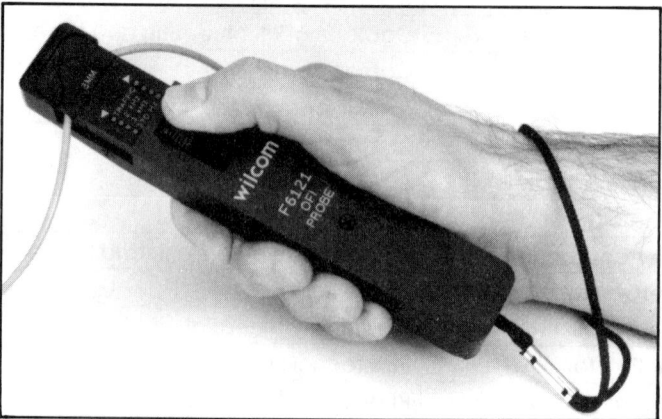

Figure 9.3 A fiber optic signal detector. (Courtesy of Wilcom, Inc.)

Installing an FDDI Network 163

and wires. This can be useful to find AC lines so as not to route network cable too close to the electrical power lines.

A portable AM/FM radio not only serves to relax hard-working installers but also provides cheap testing of any audible EMI sources that might disrupt network communications. Given the location of most cabling, a ladder or scaffold is suggested; a special multiple jointed ladder that acts like a scaffold fills both needs. A floor tile lifter for extracting raised floor panels may be another choice. Walkie-talkies or similar mobile communication devices provide a simple way to keep the installation or repair team in touch. Acquire alphanumeric beepers (pagers) and network paging software; the software can automatically call the correct beepers when improper status values or problems occur on the network. Include a standard No. 2 pencil, or an abrasive block eraser; it cleans edge connectors of circuit boards, chips, and Molex connectors, which corrode with time to cause intermittent problems. Add a spray can of an electrical contact cleaner and lubricant. Some sprays chemically improve electrical contacts. A multitester, a ring scanner, and various other test equipment are suggested. Figure 9.4 illustrates a robust tool kit. Chapters 12 through 16 describe these network-specific tools in more detail.

Another highly useful tool is the electronic tape measure. This device sends out an infrared signal (beware since it has the same wavelength as wireless infrared) to measure distances within an accuracy of centimeters (or inches). It is particularly useful as a planning tool to estimate

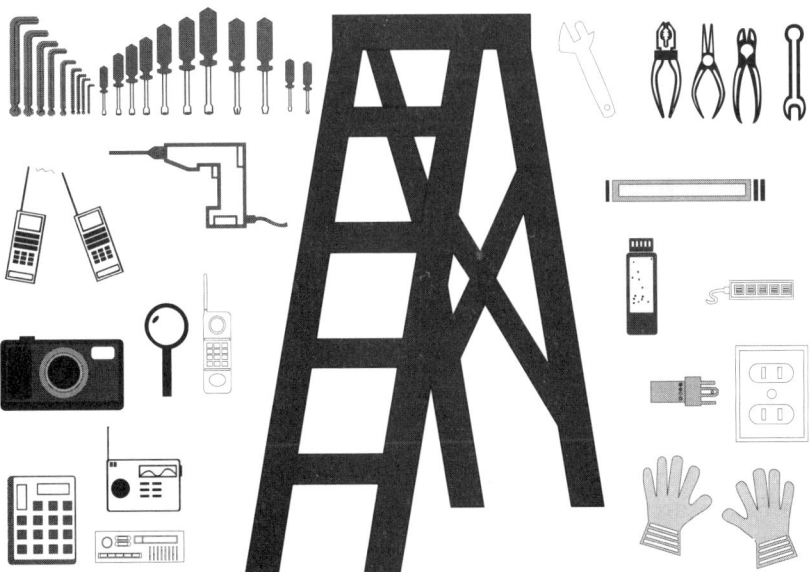

Figure 9.4 Typical installation tools.

wiring requirements very accurately. When measuring cable runs, do not overlook the vertical heights between nodes, wiring hubs, and other devices, and the possibly circuitous channels where the wire or cables will actually be installed.

Installing Optical Fiber

Optical fiber is available in many variations for FDDI; it varies by length, thickness, packaging, and modality. The standard and recommended optical medium is 62.5/125-mm fiber single mode, packaged as dual fibers. If you buy fiber cut to length, buy it with connectors installed and tested. If a vendor is installing the fiber, they will install the connectors on site and test them then. Other fiber is delivered in spools. Cut it with clippers to length. Polish it and attach connectors with the crimping tool, epoxy, or by whatever method indicated by the connector vendor.

Optical fiber is available in various thicknesses. The thickness measurements are paired. The first measurement refers to the internal transmission-carrying fiber; the second refers to the outer diameter. The measurements are important since connectors must match the sizes to fit properly and securely. Typically, FDDI fiber is 62.5/125 mm. Other sizes are 50/100 mm and 100/125 mm. The smaller the internal dimension, the better the fiber signal transmission properties provided by the fiber. In other words, the connections and polishing can be sloppier with 50/100-mm fiber, there can be more splices and jumpers, or the point-to-point connection can be longer. Conversely, the military typically specifies 100-mm fiber so that troop training time and the time to repair connections in the field is minimized.

Modality refers to the signal "color" transmitted by the fiber. Different wavelengths of light can be transmitted on multimode fiber to carry simultaneous or spread-spectrum transmission channels. Single mode supports only one wavelength and one channel. Typically FDDI is multimode, however, 32-to 36-km point-to-point links with full lasing transmitters require single mode fiber. Packaging is usually dual fibers in a single bundle. Two fibers of the same type can also be used. However, the difficulties involved in telling which is the primary ring and which is the secondary ring usually push veterans to choose the simpler dual fiber packaging. FDDI fiber can also be obtained with multiple pairs (20 pairs or more) in the same bundle. It can also be packaged with CATV cable, telephone UTP, and datagrade or STP cable. Manufacturers do fill special orders.

Optical fiber wiring is typically point-to-point. One station connects to the next station. Jumpers are rarely used in order to minimize the number of connections. Each connection reduces signal strength as measured in decibels (dB); each physical connection causes a -1.5-dB

Installing an FDDI Network

loss or greater. A splices causes a 0.25-dB loss or greater. These vary by the connector, the connector method, and the skill of the installer.

Single bayonet connectors are used for attaching test leads and stations on SAS or single rings. The duplex connectors are more common and are the preferred method for DAS stations. Note that the connectors are keyed as A/B and C/D. The A line is the primary ring signal input, while B is the primary ring signal output. C refers to the input from the secondary (backup) ring, while D refers to the output to the second ring. The key for these two types of connections is provided by *four* different connectors. This prevents mismatches. A forced mismatch at the ring will disable the FDDI ring until corrected. Figure 9.5 illustrates the various FDDI connectors.

Installing Twisted-Pair Wiring

Twisted-pair wiring is available in at least two major variations for FDDI; shielded twisted-pair (STP) and unshielded twisted-pair (UTP). The standard and recommended medium is shielded twisted-pair, or IBM Type 1 as used for IBM Token-Ring. This consists of two pairs of wires (four color-coded wires), a foil ground, a braided signal shield. A variant, IBM Type 2, wire has identical characteristics, but also contains four pairs of voice grade twisted-pair. IBM Type 6 is not as heavily built, shielded, or twisted. It is useful for jumpers only.

These shielded twisted-pair variants are wired from a central wiring hub to individual offices or cubicles. The data communications wires are pressed into a hermaphroditic media connector at the hub end and either a female 9-pin D-socket, a female RJ-11 jack, or a female RJ-45 jack at the station end. Voice lines, if any, are either crimped into standard RJ-11 or RJ-45 plugs, or punched down into a patch panel at the wiring closet and crimped into a female RJ-11 or RJ-45 jack at the office. A jumper cable with accommodating connectors will interconnect with the phone equipment and the NIC. Figure 9.6 illustrates the various modular connectors.

Unshielded twisted-pair is usually installed as a 25-pair bundle. Since each data or voice line usually requires two pairs, the bundle is sufficient for a mix of 12 voice and data lines. Do not mix a spare pair from one bundle

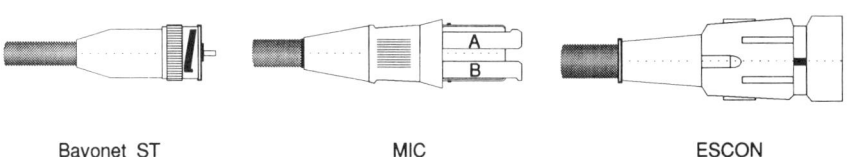

Bayonet ST   MIC   ESCON

Figure 9.5 Optical FDDI connectors.

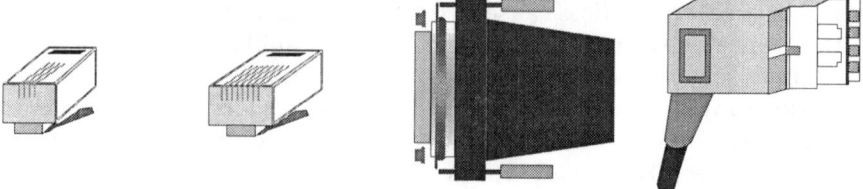

Figure 9.6 Modular, DB-9, and genderless connectors.

with a spare pair from another bundle; it is too difficult to document correctly. Save the spares in case lines fail. Unshielded twisted-pair is also available as a set of two pairs. Grade, quality, and wire diameter is important for data communication reliability. FDDI performs better with a bigger gauge and wires with a more frequent data-canceling twist. Note that 22-gauge wire is actually larger than 26-gauge wire; the gauge numbering system is inverted so that smaller numbers represent wires with thicker copper cores.

Most UTP networks require a media filter to retime, filter, and passively correct distorted signals. In older networks, these devices are often incorporated into the wall jack. Make certain that these components are FDDI-compliant when upgrading from UTP Token-Ring or 10BASE-T. Media filters that connect between NIC and a wall jack are a better alternative since they do not specify how a particular wire run from the wiring closet will be used. This provides more flexibility in that a dual jack could conceivably support two phone lines, two network nodes, a fax line and a serial line, TP-DDI and a phone, or any combination thereof. A media filter incorporated as part of the jumper cable provides a more modular approach to UTP wiring. Some intelligent hubs or UTP-compatible NICs include active media filter circuitry. Beware of upgrading or expanding an existing UTP network and using more than one media filter on each lobe; the resulting signal loss can create a very difficult-to-debug failure. While one media filter is good and necessary for some UTP installations, more than one filter is *not* better.

Generally, twisted-pair is not a satin ribbon cable (often used to patch a phone to a wall jack) that can be stripped, inserted within a connector, and crimped tight in one simple step. Installation is usually more labor intensive. First, the outer skin on the bundle is slit. This reveals from 2 to 25 pairs. The many individual pairs are then separated from the clump. Each pair of wires is then individually stripped for about 40 mm. Carefully—according to the color-coded wiring scheme—the bare ends are inserted into modular connectors, jacks, or hermaphroditic plugs. This process is described in detail later in the chapter.

Installing an FDDI Network 167

Optical Fiber Installation

Before installing any new, repaired, or additional twisted-pair wiring, the bundles should be inspected for visual defects. Scratches in optical fiber will leak signal or cause the fiber to break. The bundle should have no obvious physical defects such as cuts, tears, or bulges in the outer jacket. Optically, the individual fibers in each pair should transport signal without discontinuities. Each should be isolated. Techniques for testing with a multitester, optical time domain reflectometer, the signal generator, and the light meter are presented in Chapters 13 and 14. To install the cable you will need the tool kit, the preliminary blueprint, the cable, cable ties, and colored electrical tap for labeling the bundle.

Begin installation by extending the cable along the route mapped out in the blueprint, although it is wise to label the wire first. Any deviation made from this planned path should be noted on the blueprint. Obviously, special provisions must be made when cable is to be placed in a trench in the earth. A digging crew must be on hand to prepare the trench and refill it. These steps should be part of the project plan. Deviations might be needed to avoid rivers, lakes, and canals, buildings, sewers, elevator control cables, heat sources, high-tension lines, or steel beams. There are several details that the installer must not overlook. Avoid jacket abrasion, excessively bending the wire, and installing the wire with too extreme a radius. Avoid installing the wrong wiring grade, packaging, or type of cable on any segment. All the cable looks about the same and violations of building code or protocol specification are expensive and time-consuming to repair later. Cable with cracked insulation becomes brittle sooner and may snap. In general, prudent concern and attention to these details will yield a successful FDDI installation.

Twisted-Pair Installation

Twisted-pair is rarely installed as single wires. Instead, a *wiring bundle* containing multiple sets— often 25 pairs—is pulled through wiring conduits or the ceiling plenum. Two wire pairs are connected to a data set or combination phone and data set jack. IBM Type 1 STP is four wires (two pairs not bundled as pairs); one such cable must be pulled separately for each node. This conforms to the established norms for installing phone systems. However, do not make a mistake and assume that data communications wiring is identical to that used for phone systems. The grade must be of a higher quality. The modular connectors must match the exact gauge of the twisted-pair wire. Otherwise, modular connectors work loose from the wires over time to cause hard-to-trace intermittent network failures.

The wiring bundle should have no obvious physical defects like cuts, tears, or bulges in the outer jacket. Electrically, the individual wires in the bundle should conduct electricity without discontinuities. Each should be electrically isolated and not short out to each other. Techniques for testing with a multitester, time domain reflectometer, and the twisted-pair scanner are presented in Chapters 13 and 14. To install the twisted-pair wiring bundle you will need the tool kit, the preliminary blueprint, the cable, cable ties, and colored electrical tap for labeling the bundle.

Begin installation by extending the wire along the route mapped out in the blueprint, although it is wise to label the wire first. Any deviation made from this planned path should be noted on the blueprint. Deviations might be needed to avoid a ceiling light, an air conditioner, or a steel beam. There are several details that the installer must not overlook. Avoid bundle jacket abrasion and excessively bending the bundle. Avoid cable jacket abrasion, excessively bending the wire, and installing the wire with too extreme a radius (the minimum approximates a 3-in radius for PVC, and 6-in for Teflon). Wire with cracked insulation becomes brittle sooner, which causes electrical short circuits. In general, prudent concern and attention to these details will yield a successful copper-based FDDI installation. An AM/FM pocket radio, a simple and cheap as well as readily available tool, can locate radio interference that would affect twisted-pair transmissions.

Each IBM Type 1 cable is usually shielded enough so that cross-interference will not create a problem. However, since standard unshielded twisted-pair wiring for voice is not shielded, it is affected by both external and internal interference. Note, however, that high-traffic situations actually generate enough traffic that bundled cable may experience inductance problems. Voice grade bundles lack any shielding whatsoever and are susceptible to electromagnetic interference from nearby devices. Therefore, space the bundles and do not create a compact bunch. Buildings with radio transmitters on the roof or nearby may necessitate special insulation or substitution of STP for UTP; the extra shielding may be required. When actually wiring the individual pairs, maintain polarity and do not cross the pairs over; the wires should at all times be "straight through" from plug to plug. This is true for all phone lines (or the bell will not ring), RS-232 serial, FDDI on UTP, Ethernet 10Base-T, and the STP twisted-pair standard. The twisted-pair wire is used to connect the actual nodes to the wiring concentrator.

Unshielded Twisted-Pair

UTP Token-Ring cable segments use four unshielded wires that connect to ports 1, 2, 3, and 6 of an ISO standard physical interface. This is typically made up of an RJ-11 or RJ-45 telephone-type plug and jack. The plug and jack are not normally compatible with phone equipment. They are similar, but different enough to protect the network and baffle the unwary installer. The wires are typically 22- to 26-gauge copper wire. Wires 1 (red) and 2 (green) correspond to tip and ring receive, while wires 3 (yellow) and 6 (black) correspond to tip and ring transmit. While

Installing an FDDI Network

the vendor TP-DDI specifications do not actually limit networks connections to 100 m—they say that lobes lengths are "normally limited to 100 m." In other words, a higher grade of wiring—shielded wiring is one possibility—could support greater segment lengths as the specifications indicate in Chapter 5.

Labeling Cable

As you string the fiber or wire, label it with some identifying marks. Optical fiber is usually jacketed with a monocolor black or gray plastic. Fibers are not differentiable. Primary and secondary rings are not always easily distinguished. Multiple bundles are confusing; all should be labeled.

Although the unshielded twisted-pair jacket is color-coded—each pair contains some combination of two colors—red, green, yellow, and black, red and white, or blue and yellow—in candy cane spirals. Each of the jackets for these pairs has a different color and hash mark to identify the individual "pair" at each end of the bundle; multiple bundles are confusing and should be labeled. Shielded twisted-pair is usually a black cable with an extruded groove pattern. One cable is indistinguishable from the next. Color-coded electrical tape at 15 ft intervals helps sort out the spaghetti. Do not obscure any printed markings on the cable. Medical supply houses also carry alphabetic labels useful to indicate more specific information. Fluorescent marking tapes provide exceptionally effective identification above false ceilings when you are perched on a ladder 3-m high; visibility is often impaired by ductwork, supports, and wiring.

Securing the Cable

Once the fiber or wire is properly routed and installed in the trenches, through steam conduits or underground passageways, cable trays, ladders, and J-hooks, or draped over the suspended ceiling supports, the cable should be tied with plastic ties to prevent damage. (See Figure 9.7.) Velcro is effective for securing cable bundles and individual wire.

Installing Connectors

To install connectors, you must have already installed the cable (or at least measured and tested the cable). Sometimes, it is expedient to cut the cable and jumpers to length and install connectors on a bench before stringing it. Most vendors do this with optical fiber since testing requires a source light on one end of the cable and a light meter at the distant

Figure 9.7 The cable tie provides extra support for bundles and connectors.

end. Generally, this is pertinent only for short runs under 30 m that are not pulled through the ceiling, conduits, or modular tracks. Avoid stressing the installed connectors if they are pulled through the ceiling; tape them with duct tape to protect the connector and the optical end for fiber, if you must pull it through the ceiling or vertical conduits. You will need the blueprint and tool kit to complete this step. The tools required to install the fiber optic connectors include cutters, an insulation stripper, emery cloth or a polishing wheel, and epoxy or crimping tools. The tools required to install the connectors include cutters, a wire stripper, and crimping tools for copper wire.

There are seven basic types of FDDI connections: bayonet ST connectors, media interface connectors, which are sometimes called dual shrouded connectors, modular plugs, modular jacks, genderless (hermaphroditic) connectors, D-plugs, and wire ends that connect into the clips in a punchdown rack. The next sections detail these items and how they are installed.

Bayonet ST Connectors

These are the original optical fiber connectors, similar to the positive lock BNC connectors used for cable TV connections and thin Ethernet. The dual fiber is split into individual fibers. Each single fiber is stripped 4.12 cm (1.625 in). The glass (or plastic LDC wire) component is cut square. A heat shrink tube is placed over the fiber end. An eyelet with the flared end outward is placed over the end. Mix the two-part epoxy glue. 1.5 cm (.625 in) is removed from the still buffered fiber. Wash the fiber with isopropyl alcohol and epoxy the connector to the fiber. Make certain the Kevlar fibers will pass through and extend beyond the connector body. Crimp the eyelet. Apply the heat gun until the epoxy turns a dark brown. When the epoxy is cured, heat the shrink tubing. Screw the outer body of the connector onto the eyelet.

Polishing is performed by hand in three stages. Lapping paper is used for the first stage, and finer lapping film is used for the second and third stages. Each is less abrasive and finer than the prior one. Use a smooth surface for supporting the polishing materials and scribe a long figure eight. The connector and the fiber are polished at the same time. Chips at the outer edge are acceptable, but not in the center of the fiber face. No scratches should evident even with magnification. The quality of the polishing can also be tested with a stabilized light source and meter or a special device that shines a light and measures the scatter from the fiber end. The fiber end is inserted through the connector and protrudes from the connector.

Check that the fiber is centered in the body of the connector. Note that a connector with a ceramic ferrule is superior to the older design stainless steel connector since it is manufactured to size and requires no polishing. It also insures better face-to-face fiber alignment.

Installing an FDDI Network

Media Interface Connectors and Fixed Shroud Dual Connectors

These enhanced MIC connectors are better fiber connectors since the shrouded fiber is protected from external damage and also because the four dual FDDI ring connections cannot be improperly made. The dual fiber is split into individual fibers for about 2 cm (.75 in). Each single fiber is stripped .25 cm (.15 in). Polish each fiber. Polishing is performed as described for the ST connector. Be certain you provide proper support for the fibers since they are not supported by an eyelet or ceramic ferrule. Polish both fibers together so that the are exactly the same length. After polishing, remove the Kevlar strands and center each of the two fibers in the ceramic alignment grooves. The end of each fiber should uniformly reach the end alignment within the connector; this is important so that each fiber face will mate with ones in the mating connector. Install the alignment tubes (ferrules) on *each* fiber. Snap the connector together. Test each connection separately using the techniques described in Chapter 13.

Modular Plugs

Modular plugs were developed by AT&T to streamline the installation, maintenance, and repair of phone systems. This technology has been adapted for use with LAN data communications as well. In the simplest terms, an *unstripped* ribbon cable is inserted into a plug blank. A crimping tool forces a plastic tab into the jacket securing the cord. At the same time, four, six, or eight brass contacts pierce this outer jacket and the insulation on the inner conductors. Figure 9.8 shows the crimping tool attaching a jack. This procedure is almost impossible to perform without a tool specially designed for the job. A screwdriver and hammer do not work reliably. Recycling used plugs is a guarantee of future problems. Furthermore, plugs are available in many sizes and keyed shapes (RJ-3, RJ-11, RJ-22, and RJ-45, for example) and wire gauges. They are not compatible or interchangeable, although some may fit the same jacks. Verify the exact part designation.

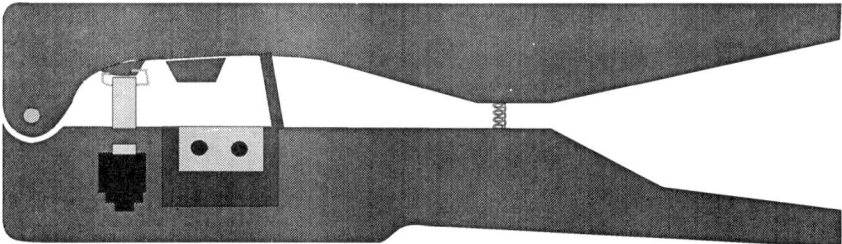

Figure 9.8 The crimping tool attaches a modular plug to STP and UTP.

Modular plugs also fit onto the wire with two orientations, up and down. The springy latches on both ends of the wire should always face the same direction. On long lengths of wire, the wire may coil, twist, and make it impossible to tell if the plug is installed correctly. The wires should run straight through and not twist. Instead, orient the color-coded wires such that the colors line up in the plugs as Figure 9.9 illustrates.

Shielded twisted-pair does not install as easily into modular connectors as the unshielded wire. Individual wires usually must be stripped individually and each wire of the two pairs must then be inserted into the modular plug. The gauge is thicker and the wires do not line up like the ribbon cable. As such, there are at least 15 ways (more with six or eight wires and with plugs with six or eight positions) to incorrectly insert them. Once all the wires (four, six, or eight) are inserted, crimp tight. Some phone systems require more than four wires for voice mail, paging, intercom, and other special functions. Therefore, the wiring may be designed for interchangeability and quick setup from a central patch panel. Consider creating a color chart to show where each wire belongs and memorize it.

Modular Jacks

Modular jacks are the female counterpart to the plugs. NICs, MAUs, patch panels, and wall sockets are usually female jacks. The only ones a network team is likely to encounter are the wall jacks. Since STP or bundles of UTP are strung to these jacks, the wires must be stripped individually. The most expedient jacks are identical in concept to the plugs; wires are held in place by crimping. The most common jack requires a screwdriver to tighten the individual screws which hold each stripped wire in place. Since the four wires carrying the RX/TX lines may be buried with a total of eight wires, know the color code. Telephone lines usually apply the red, green, yellow, and black wires. Normally, use these lines for RX and TX for consistency in use with fax, data, phone, serial lines, or TP-DDI as needed in the future. The candy-striped pairs are auxiliary lines; in a pinch or mixed for voice and data applications, use all eight wires.

Figure 9.9 Line up plugs to prevent twisted-pair crossover.

Installing an FDDI Network

Hermaphroditic Connectors

These *genderless media interfaces* connectors were defined by IBM for use in Token-Ring. A major source is AMP. They are the STP standard. The STP wire contains four and only four wires. These outer cable jacket is stripped exposing about 1.5 cm (1/2 in) of wire. Slide the plastic ring that is part of the housing over the STP cable. The shield is then cut and wrapped back along the outside of the cable jacket and a metal band is wrapped on top of this shield. The band is slid into place. This provides the ground and a fair method to protect the pairs from lateral force. The inner wires do not need to be individually stripped. They should merely be placed into the clear plastic retaining cover. Note the red, green, orange, and black color codes on this clip. The twisted-pairs should correspond to this color scheme. When the twisted-pairs do not conform—they might be yellow, gray, green and pink—but nonetheless maintain a uniform pattern and document it. When all four wires are placed into the cover, force the cover over the c-shaped wire retainers. The design is such that the metal retainers slit the insulation on the individual pairs and make a good electrical contact. The wires should not be stripped. Verify that no stray pieces such as foil, shield, or little wire chaff remain in the housing; these could move about and short the connector. Slide the plastic ring into the connector shell housing and snap the cover into place. This process is partially detailed by Figure 9.10. Avoid recycling these components since the metal fingers tend to wear and deform with usage.

Male and Female D-plugs

D-plugs are usually the NIC end of jumpers connecting a hermaphroditic wall plate connection to a IBM Token-Ring NIC. This is somewhat archaic, although many TP-DDI NIC manufacturers provide this facility for compatibility with preexisting networks. This connection is the end that the user usually sees, as Figure 9.11 shows. Strip 2 cm (3/4 in) from the end of the STP cable. Crimp or screw the retaining ring to the end of the outer jacket of the cable. This protects the cable from lateral force. The shield must be soldered or crimped to the connector shell ground. This ground is important for safety, signal integrity, and minimizing

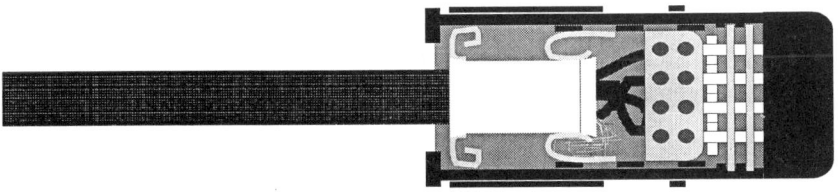

Figure 9.10 Installation of genderless STP connectors (cover removed).

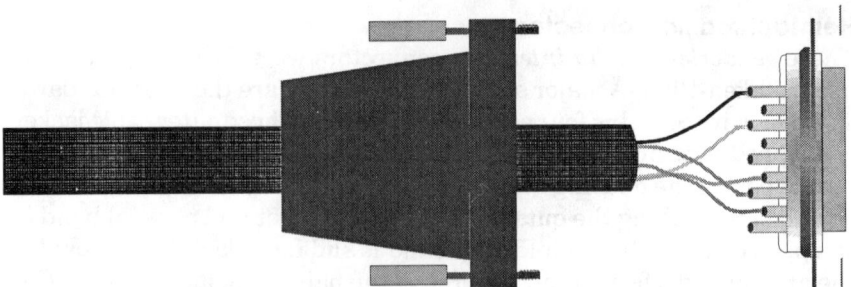

Figure 9.11 Installation of DB-9 connectors..

crosstalk. The black wire goes to pin 5, the red wire to pin 1, the orange wire to pin 8, and the green wire to pin 6. This is true for both male and female connectors. Soldered connections are usually more reliable and durable than crimped ones (since lead solder resists corrosion better than the zinc crimping material). Adjust for color code differences, but do so consistently. Document any such variances. Place the two retaining screws into their channels. These screws ensure that the male plug is not easily dislodged from the NIC socket in an accessible slot in the PC or from the wall. The outer connector shell snaps or screws together.

Punchdown Blocks

Punchdown blocks are not relevant for optical fiber networks, only for twisted-pair networks. However, infrequently, networks reconfigured with with optical switches may have a central wiring closet with a patchboard. This is rare since the idea is to minimize the number of optical connections between points.

Wiring pairs, shielded or unshielded, can be connected into a modular punchdown block. Since the components are modular, failed components are easily bypassed or replaced. A punchdown block snaps into punchdown panel. A typical block (type 66) contains 50 rows of four claw connectors or eight claw connectors. Some block designs feature five rows of *dual* sets of ten claws. The horizontal type 110 block is usually installed for small sites. However, choose a punchdown block that has been certified for data communications usage. Units with gold-plated contacts tend to be more reliable over time. Avoid installing voice-grade components and recycling available parts.

The four connector block is wired into four *hydra* or *50-pin champ* connectors on each side of the block, as Figure 9.12 details. When wiring bundles are connected to a hydra on each side of the block, there are no individual wires. In the more usual format, each set of two pairs is held in the punchdown claws across a row. Wires individually attach to the claw connectors. Without a punchdown tool, wires must be stripped and

Installing an FDDI Network

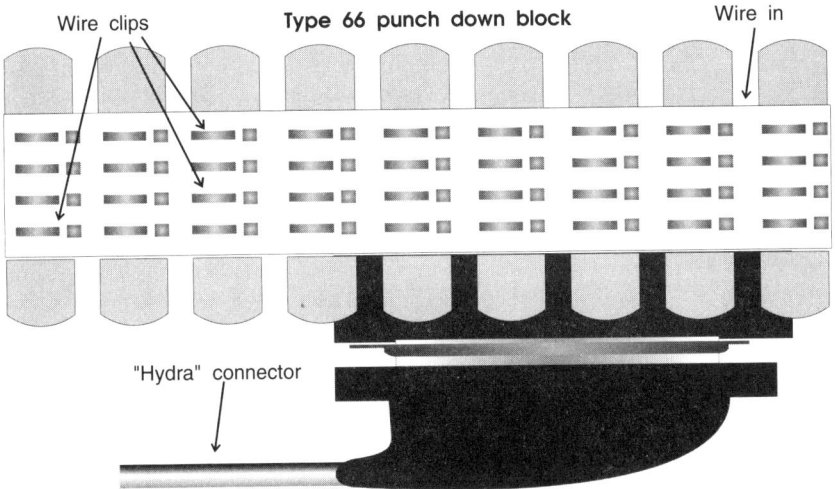

Figure 9.12 Punchdown block shown with 50-pin champ, or hydra connector.

forced into the teeth with a small screwdriver. This is labor-intensive and is best employed only for emergency field fixes.

Manual attachment is as follows. The pairs are stripped individually and inserted into the claws. Maintain the color code, which is commonly black, yellow, green, and then red. Twenty-five-pair bundles rarely contain single colors; instead, there are candy cane-striped jackets. A punchdown tool, hand-powered or battery-powered, separates the claws and forces the wire into place without the need to strip wires. The claws notch the insulation to establish a good electrical contact. Punchdown tools are inexpensive and improve the accuracy and speed of installation dramatically. Realistically, this tool is a necessity for installation.

Grounding the Network

At all steps during installation of both wire and connectors, be aware that all metallic outer casings, shields, and fittings that connect to an STP shield should be insulated with a nonconducting sleeve—a potential source of ground-induced noise. Avoid any possible accidental grounding. Figure 9.13 shows these critical points. Installation of rubber sleeves—if necessary—prevents random grounding. Differential grounding—when there is an electrical potential difference between grounds on the network—creates both static and surge problems. Typically, equipment should be attached to a common ground within the same building and isolated between buildings. All exposed conductive fittings should be insulated with a rubber boot or wound with insulating electrical tape to prevent a random ground. The hub or the workstation provides the necessary ground. Since STP and UTP are protected by vinyl or Teflon jackets, accidental groundings to cable trays, ductwork, and steel sup-

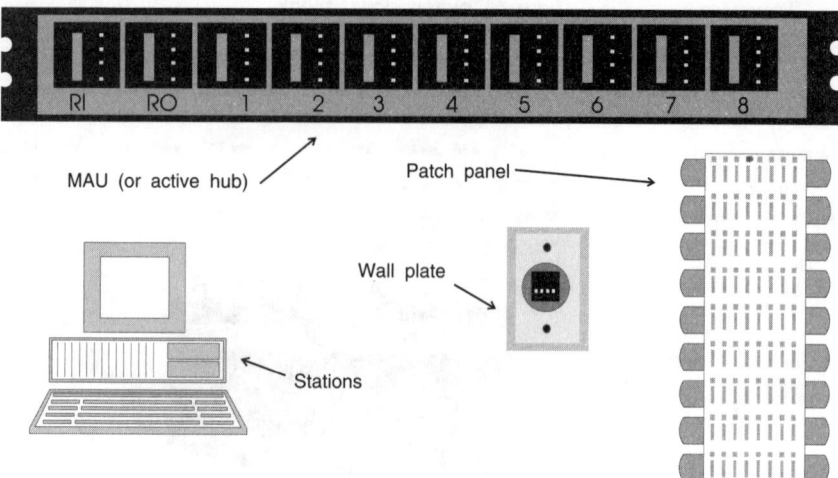

Figure 9.13 Avoid random (or differential) grounding of network components.

port beams are rare. One simple and inexpensive solution is to purchase a rubber coating dip (often sold at hardware stores) and brush abrasions.

Testing Connectors

A quick check with a multitester as explained in Chapter 13 or a ring scanner as explained in Chapter 14 will verify that the end connectors are not shorting and have a sufficiently good contact with the wire to actually carry the electrical signal. Modular wire is best tested with a phone line tester and a ring or pair scanner. Since these tests work only when there is something at the other end—live telephone line or network hub—test with the appropriate tool. Vendors will usually verify installation as part of the process. Insist on that.

As with any installation, a check that the connectors are properly installed is good policy. Verification with a multitester and a wire scanner should be standard practice, as outlined in Chapters 13 and 14.

Observe Distance Limitations

Optical point-to-point for FDDI DAS multimode connection is 2 km. This can be extended to 36 km with full lasing, single mode equipment. Most sites will not require this full length, but it is obtainable. Additionally, longer lengths are possible by installing single lengths of extruded cable, using powerful transmitters, sensitive receivers, or a thinner fiber. Also, select more transparent fiber, that is, one with better transmission characteristics for the selected transmission frequency. All fiber is not the same or the same quality. Even within lots, quality may vary.

Specifications for twisted-pair allow a maximum of 100 m between the wiring closet (where the wiring concentrator is placed) and the

Installing an FDDI Network

actual node devices for STP; this falls to 30 m for UTP. This conforms to EIA/TIA 658. These lengths are actually for perfect conditions. Perfect conditions are rarely obtainable. Twisted-pair is apt to be routed alongside AC electrical lines, near to radio-frequency emitters, and other wiring bundles which will distort the signal. Transformers and other energy sources can alter the impedance of the wire. Minimize the wiring bundle lengths, and do not leave tails of wire (coils of extra wire) above the wiring closet; cut the wiring bundle to the shortest possible length but leave sufficient slack for temperature-induced expansion and contraction as well as for the possibility that wiring punchdown panel or office partitions may get moved a few feet.

If you anticipate that the distance limitations or external interference may cause transmission problems, select the highest quality of UTP. Do not overlook vertical heights in estimating all cable or wiring measurements. As an alternative, select a higher grade. The normal grade is UTP-3. Substitute UTP-4; this corresponds to UTP category 4. Shielded 25-pair twisted-pair is available at a substantial premium since it is not as widely used or as common. STP-4 will perform better for all network applications since crosstalk, signal degradation, and insertion to capacitance are improved. Synoptics and UTP substitutions for FDDI STP may have different wiring grade requirements. In all cases, check with the NIC or hub vendor for recommendations, or verify wire utility with a pair scanner that measures attenuation, impedance, and crosstalk.

Patch Panels

FDDI STP is modular, although UTP is modular and centralized. The installation differences are distance limitations and that one STP cable is required per node while each UTP bundle provides service for at least eight nodes. The star configuration encourages installation of a patch panel for centralized wiring. Additionally, since twisted-pair networks and telephone circuits often share the same wiring, the common telephone wiring schemes are used. Punchdown patch panels separate and differentiate the 25 pairs of wires from each UTP bundle. The wires within the bundles are usually differentiated with two striped colors for the insulating jacket as opposed to solid vinyl insulation for single phone lines and modular jumpers.

Since FDDI (also, Ethernet 10BASE-T, and TP-DDI) requires four wires, each bundle yields 12 connections; you might want to use no more than eight to minimize crosstalk and keep some wires as spares. Transmission is most reliable when each bundle is used for only eight connections. The patch panel is marked (which is highly recommended) with the locations of the other ends of each pair, and each individual wire is snapped into a retaining clamp, generally with a punchdown tool. Acquire a specialized punchdown tool which will speed installation of pairs in the panel and increase the chance that the connection is true. When actually wiring the individual pairs, maintain polarity and do not cross the pairs over; the wires should at all times be "straight through" from plug to plug. The NICs and hubs handle the RX-to-TX crossover. Note that for network applications it is best not to overutilize the wiring bundle; many vendors suggest leaving at least 25 percent of the pairs unused to lower the crosstalk that will occur on the higher voltage, higher frequency employed even by 4 Mbits/s FDDI than by normal telephonic circuitry. Also, beware of mixing FDDI and serial lines within the same bundle. This may happen where terminal servers, FDDI, 10BASE-T, and serial printer connections coexist. Signal crosstalk *may* distort these four types of communication channels. Figure 9.14 illustrates a common punchdown or patch panel with modular wall jacks and jumpers. Jumpers are constructed to connect each pair on the panel into the wiring concentrator. Figure 9.15 illustrates a common punchdown or patch panel with DB-9 and genderless connectors typical for existing IBM type 1 Token-Ring STP installations.

A few problems need to be solved for FDDI to work on UTP. The cabling must not be too susceptible to electromagnetic noise (from transmitting devices, fluorescent lights, etc.); other devices transmitting similar frequencies; crosstalk between twisted-pair sets; or jitter, which occurs when preamble or packet signals are out of phase. Performance is a function of the signal-to-noise ratio. Higher-quality cable, better cable installation, shielded cable, low utilization of cabling bundles, superior wiring connections, shorter wiring runs, and superior hardware including hub concentrators and the controller cards improve the chance that the signal will reach its destination. It is important to remember that FDDI is a sequential delivery since every node repeats the transmission signal; the management game is to improve that chance for consistent transmission.

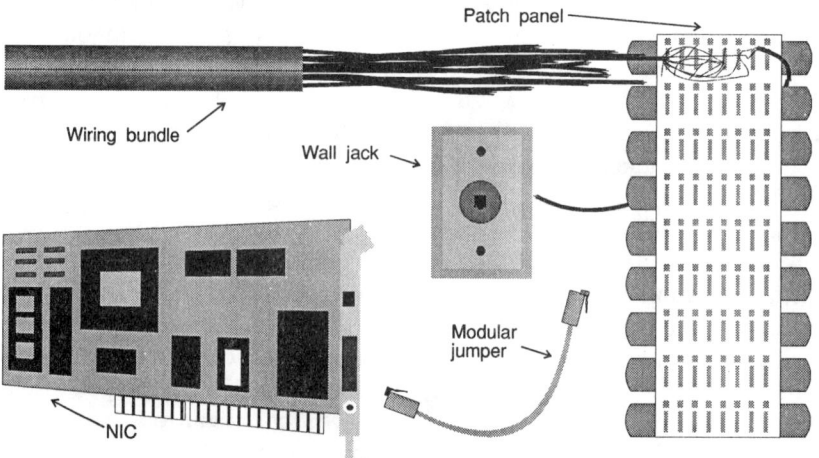

Figure 9.14 Twisted-pair patch panel and modular components.

Installing an FDDI Network

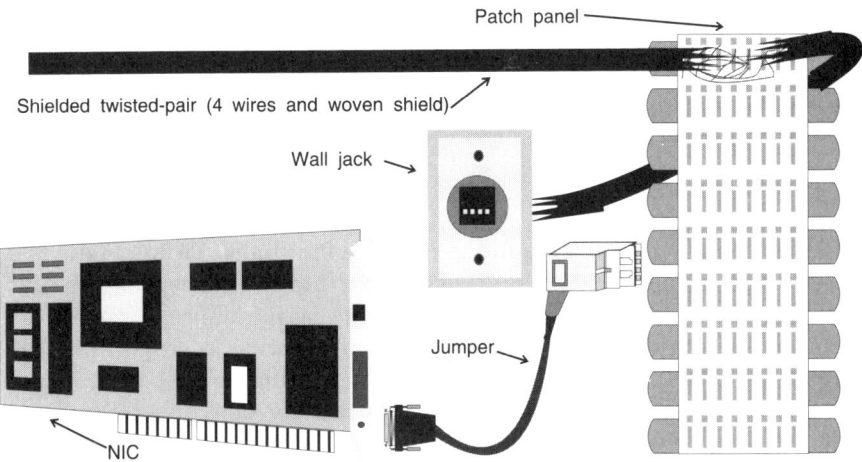

Figure 9.15 Twisted-pair patch panel and genderless components.

It is important to label all the connections carefully and maintain up-to-date records for each wiring pair. Neatness counts for time saved when later adding new lines, debugging problem lines, and resolving interconnected phone and data lines. If you interconnect a hub or network node with a telephone circuit, the network device *usually* will shut down and not operate. This is a good safety feature. The alternate is for the node or hub to assume that the high voltage is a jittering peer. Constant signals or requests for retransmission will substantially degrade network performance. Usually, downstream nodes will beacon, thereby indicating the incorrect lobe and perhaps removing it from the ring. If the single bad element is taken out of service, it is possible that the twisted-pair hub will still function and ignore the failed node.

The wiring closet and patch panel together provide a centralized location for connecting FDDI into Token-Ring or Ethernet, modems, or VSAT. In organizations with enterprise-wide networking, wiring closets quickly develop into phone maintenance space, computer rooms, and multimedia concentrators and adapter space. Plan ahead. Provide enough AC power and cooling capacity to support the devices anticipated for this space. Provide enough physical space for the hardware and for people to work. Route cables directly to this wiring closet, or provide enough slack in cables and optical fiber to later loop them into the room.

Optical Fiber Tips

Few problems should occur with optical fiber installation. It should work the first time. However, to be certain you get those results, get references as part of the initial vendor process. Qualify a vendor. Qualify the lot of cable. Qualify the connections and splices. Verify the quality of the installation before going live and connecting operative LANs into the FDDI ring. By and large, a quality optical fiber installation will be "plug and play." FDDI is quite robust and few problems will occur when it is installed properly.

Twisted-Pair Wiring Tips
Twisted-pair wiring is ubiquitous in office buildings. Twisted-pair is a cheap and an old technology. Twisted-pair fits the concept of the star topology for ease of installation and network maintenance. Rarely is the existing telephone cabling suitable for data networks, especially 100 Mbits/s FDDI. Shielding is nonexistent, routing is suspect and not documented, and the telephone cable probably does meet the more rigorous specifications required by data connections (category 3, 4, or 5). If you want your network to be reliable, the road to twisted-pair networking should begin with a new cable job. Of note, there are specialty tools available for qualifying the utility of existing UTP cable. The Next Scanner and FDDI pair scanners from Microtest are handheld devices which measure signal decay, crosstalk, capacitance, and attenuation. This information is necessary to determine whether existing UTP wiring will support a stable LAN, and also how long the trunk and lobe cables can be. It is important to differentiate unshielded twisted-pair from shielded twisted-pair wiring bundles. A pair scanner will perform the assessment directly. Poor wire could increase jitter, jabber, and chatter. (See Figure 9.16 for twisted-pair wiring installation tips.)

- Ensure that straight-through polarity is maintained
- Use wiring that meets operating specifications
- Use wiring that meets fire code specifications
- Maintain uniform color code
- Maintain 9-ohm/100 m impedance
- Avoid use of flat cable on any connection
- Install UTP matched to media filters or active hubs
- Avoid the use of standard punchdown panels
- Route twisted-pair away from RF and electromagnetic radiation
  6 in from standard power lines
  12 in from fluorescent lighting
  36 in from transformers
- Do not overallocate the twisted-pairs in a wire bundle for carrying data signals to minimize signal crosstalk
- Check for loose connections
- Use RJ-45 (not RJ-11) connectors matched to the wire gauge
- Observe pair polarity
- Apply a conductive spray to connections when installed
- Hire a qualified data cable installer

Figure 9.16 Twisted-pair wiring tips.

Installing an FDDI Network

You can estimate lengths of existing wire by measuring DC resistance with a multimeter. For example, 1000 ft of 24-gauge wire will measure 16 Ω. It is important to note that RJ-11 plugs and jacks are interchangeable with the RJ-45 counterparts. However, the wires will not match up correctly. There are also variations on RJ-45 connectors to account for shielded and unshielded twisted-pair sets and flat ribbon cables. Most STP installations require that the connectors are installed manually since each wire must be stripped individually, although a power punchdown tool speeds insertion of wires at the patch panel.

When installing FDDI, be certain that the cable installer recognizes that there are indeed differences and installs the correct RJ-45 connectors for data communications lines. Consider acquiring a large supply of RJ-45 components in a nonstandard color to provide immediate and effective visual differentiation from standard telephone connectors. Also, for the same reasons, avoid intermixing standard telephone punchdown panels and data communications punchdown panels for three reasons. They are not always reliable for data connections and they encourage incorrect wiring and possible cross connections with active telephone circuitry. Also, telephone ringing voltages, which range from a minimum of 48 V to more than 100 V with normal line surges, can cause considerable crosstalk effects on 4.5 V-data lines. This causes hubs to shift into a *link failure mode* and not transmit on the faulty lines.

Checkpoint Testing

It's a good checkpoint in the installation process because the network is now functionally complete. The tools required and how to use them are explained in Chapters 12 through 16.

If the network is broken, disassemble it, and restart the process. Assuming the network is still functioning and there is no indication of an optical or electrical short, measure light or resistance between the pairs. If the fiber is broken or defected, there will be no light. However, qualify a working segment for signal-carrying capability. A multitester should read approximately 16-Ω resistance per 100 m of twisted-pair on a completed network. A scanner or OTDR as outlined in Chapter 12 is the best tool to use. Readings should not fluctuate if pressure, twisting, and hard knocks are applied to connections. FDDI connections should match the either the two-pair polarity scheme for SAS connections, or the four-way polarity scheme for DAS connections. Twisted-pair should be tested for correct polarity and no crossover of the pairs. While many NIC and wiring concentrators do switch contacts automatically in instances of polarity exchanges for pairs, they cannot handle miswiring of the both pairs. Check genderless connectors for mechanical functionality.

FDDI Addressing

There is a quasi-formal FDDI hardware addressing scheme. 48 bit or 16 bit addressing is supported. Internetworks should use the 48 bit address. A NIC does have a two-bit vendor number. Rings have 30 bit significant addresses, and stations use the least significant 16 bits. The FDDI station address is assigned by network management.

Usually, the NetWare active monitor will assign a sequential node number when a station inserts into the ring and match this node number to the FDDI hardware station address. The hardware addresses are established by the system administrator in boot files. Session addressing is a function of the LLC (IPX, TCP, UDP, and NetBEUI), upper-level connections, and applications.

In all cases, make certain that there are no duplicate addresses, a situation which could immobilize the network or confuse stations that capture misaddressed packets. Furthermore, some NOSs will ignore packets even though addressed to them when the receive flag has been set since the station will believe it has already received the packet.

Shake Down New Installations

New installations, retrofits, additions, and any changes to the network all require a shakedown period. It is foolhardy and unprofessional to assume that any new installation will, from the start, work as promised. This is particularly the case for extensions and retrofits with new, upgraded, or untried components. There are always surprises, like a loose connection, vibration from an elevator shaft, overheating, marginal components, vendor incompatibilities, lot incompatibilities, and overloading. Premature assurances sap credibility. Certainly, basic testing of those items listed in Figure 9.17 is, at a minimum, appropriate.

- Fiber optic and twisted-pair wiring and connectors
- Controller installation
- Controller electronics
- Hub units
- Patch panels and punchdown blocks
- Bypass switches
- Dual homing nodes
- Signal splitters
- Node equipment
- File servers
- Network software
- User network access
- Peak load operations

Figure 9.17 Shakedown network components.

Installing an FDDI Network

A shakedown period should be initiated when additions, major network configuration changes, and physical relocations are effected. This requires that additional material and time resources be allocated. Allow half a day for each primary station of a network for new installations, and an hour for each secondary station when a network is segmented, rerouted, or extended. Figure 9.18 represents a core network that has ballooned to support new groups, multiple protocols, and wide area services.

Securing the Components

Once fiber optic cabling or twisted-pair wiring is properly installed in the underground passageways, cable trays, ladders, and J-hooks, or fitted to the suspended ceiling supports, all connecting wire should be tied with plastic ties. This ensures that the wire will not get damaged, and that connections will not be unplugged accidentally. The cable tie, as illustrated previously in Figure 9.5, is useful to attach lobe cables to the NIC, hubs, or workstations. This also relieves connector strain.

Blueprinting: Confirming the Design

Once a network is measured and tested, and connectors installed, it is good policy to benchmark it. The pair scanner with serial data downlink capability or a time domain reflectometer and an instant film camera

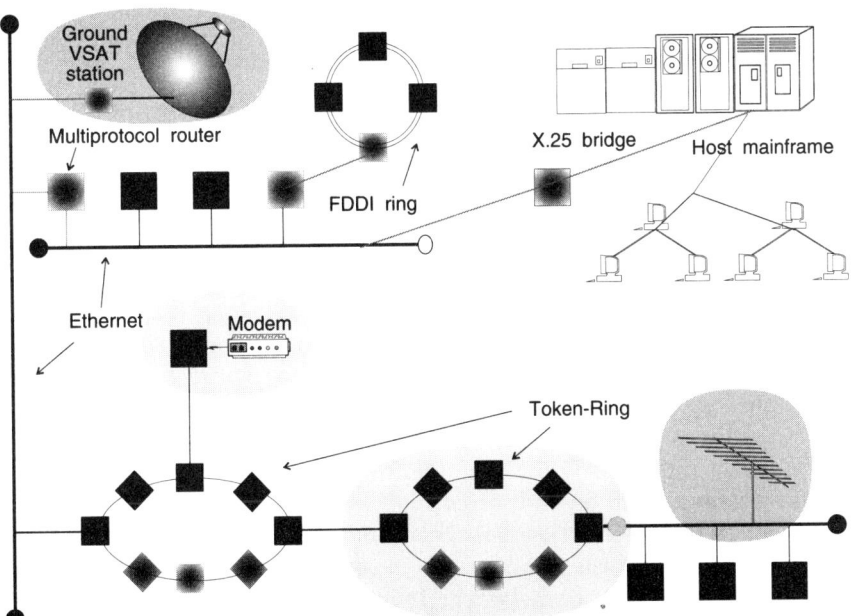

Figure 9.18 Shakedown additions, changes, and retrofits. This gradual network growth provides for focused testing of network additions.

or oscilloscope recorder provide extraordinary blueprinting. This is an important benchmark against which to compare at later times when network problems occur. While the wire is accessible, it can be purposely shorted at the connectors for benchmark photography. An instant camera also can blueprint physical wiring and deviations from the original plans. Any subsequent changes should also be added to the network blueprint to maintain an accurate view of the network.

Common Installation Failures

Slipshod work will complicate the installation and subsequent network management problems. Cable jacket abrasion can cause optical fiber to snap with pressure or cause excessive impedance on twisted-pair. Overbending or installing cable with an excessively tight radius may fracture fiber and break or short out the twisted pairs.

ST or FSD connectors may not snap into the receiving mount. The face of the mating fibers may not meet correctly, meet at a slight angle due to polishing deviances, or not meet at all when incorrectly installed in the connectors. Furthermore, ST connectors are prone to damage when not connected since the fiber face is exposed. Face polishing could also be imperfect. An RJ-11, RJ-45, D-plug, or hydra connector may not make a good contact. Frequently RJ-11 jacks and modular plugs are often mistakenly substituted for RJ-45 when installation is performed by telephone people. Although each connector is physically interchangeable, RJ-11 has only four contacts instead of six; the pairing is also slightly different, as shown in Chapter 8. While hubs and NICs often handle pair polarity errors, only *some* components may accommodate this wiring flaw while others do not. Complete crossover of the twisted-pair is usually a fatal defect for network functions (telephones will work although the ringer will not). Polarity problems with optical fiber are rare since dual optical connectors help maintain correct four-way polarities. If you are building your own cables and jumpers, you could install the connector with the polarity inverted. Also, when repairs are made to NICs or hubs, it is possible that the internal wiring is replaced improperly.

Optical fiber fails in limited ways. It can break or be broken. It can be damaged. A connection or fuse can fail. While its color may degrade over time, this is rare. It is more common where cable is exposed to alpha and gamma radiation, as in a radiation lab or in a nuclear power plant. Wires and connectors fail in a limited number of ways. The cable or the NIC electronics can be bad, or can fail over time. The likeliest reason for error is poor installation. Either the individual wires don't make good contact with the connector contacts, internally cross, or stray wires in the connectors short the network. Twisted-pair wiring presents a myriad of hazards. The most likely problems include connections between the hub and nodes that exceed specified length. The cable from the

Installing an FDDI Network

wiring closet may be looped or coiled. Not only does this lengthen the segment, but it also has the potential to induce significant crosstalk. Poor-quality (or the wrong cable and wire types) cable attenuates the signal too rapidly to cause signal distortion, loss in signal strength, or insufficient voltage spread between the highs and lows. Also, the modular connectors could be improperly installed, the transmit-receive pairs may cross over, or individual pairs may switch polarity at either end. Since FDDI frequently shares the wiring bundle with live telephone circuits, other likely failings include connection of an FDDI line into a live telephone circuit, or overuse of the pairs in the wiring bundle. The last point of installation failure is the D-plug. Half a connection is worse than a completely severed connection because the NIC might receive signal correctly but transmit a continuous signal onto the network or no signal whatsoever, thus, jamming the network completely.

In this chapter, installation procedures for optical fiber, shielded and unshielded twisted-pair, connectors, punchdown blocks, and modular components have been examined. Chapters 10 and 11 discuss devices and methodologies that expand FDDI service and topology.

Chapter

10

Expanding an FDDI Network

The FDDI specifications normally limit the optical fiber station-to-station drive distance to 2 km. The comparable STP drive distance is 100 m. This drive distance is conservatively reduced by UTP cabling to 30 m. Primary rings with optical fiber supporting *routed* secondary STP or UTP rings or trees represent a superb architecture. However, primary rings with mixed wire (STP and UTP) are inadvisable. If long distances between stations are required, intermediate stations can repeat the signal. Clearly the cost for doing this for copper-based cabling is unreasonable—even though a FDDI NIC now costs less than the actual computing station. For distances longer than 100 m, optical fiber is the media of choice.

There are other possibilities, since FDDI provides a consistent, adaptable, and robust architecture. For example, it is possible to push the optical FDDI signal further than 2 km by selecting more sensitive receivers, more powerful transmitters, and choosing the most transparent fiber for the given signal wavelength. Generally, you would place a light meter in front of the transmitting diodes until you found one with the most powerful output. Similarly, you would see which is the most sensitive receptor by placing a light source in front it and adjusting the light source until it was as dim as possible. Check all receptors until you locate the most sensitive one. Since receptors and receivers are paired (or installed in units of four) you would need to make a best choice on which NIC is best; the alternative is to disassemble NICs.

Choosing cable is a little bit more direct. Place a stabilized light source at one end of the cable and the light meter at the opposite end. Choose the cable with the least light scatter and the least loss in signal strength.

Using the leap-frog approach, it is possible to reach stations up to 50 km apart; this represents the maximum FDDI coverage. If there is a requirement for intermediate stations, this is reasonable. However, there is another alternative for distances beyond 2 km. This book has discussed the use of full lasing stations and single mode fiber in prior chapters. This hardware provides a point-to-point link from 32 to 36 km. This distance can perhaps be lengthened by increasing the signal strength and selecting the highest quality fiber available. Since this linkage is not line-of-sight—it is conducted by the fiber—you will not have to worry about aligning transmitters, airplanes or tall buildings obstructing the endpoints, or the curvature of the Earth as with RF, infrared, or microwave linkages, which are discussed later in this chapter. Also, fiber is immune to weather and signal interference.

If this limitation still poses a problem, it can be circumvented by special design or by installing an expansion device, such as the router, the bridge, and the gateway and connecting it to a true WAN link. WAN linkages are discussed later in this chapter.

Inspire Design Simplicity

One network management generality to consider meticulously when building, enhancing, and expanding LANs or providing an FDDI campus backbone is to avoid the novel and unusual enhancement products. This includes all expansion devices, NICs, wiring concentrators or hubs, specialty bridges and gateways, and enterprise-wide linkage hardware and software. This is particularly relevant when networks are essential to internal application or production and manufacturing operations. Complexity and fragility in any component decreases the overall reliability of the network. This rule is strengthened by the realization that FDDI is a logical ring where the failure of any node in the series may cause the whole ring to fail. Ring wrap is not also assured; the wrap or the counterrotating secondary ring could pose it own problems. Assess the reliability and integrity of intelligent hubs to handle failures.

The logic for this assertion is the premise that maintaining reliable network operations takes precedent over all over other concerns including cost, ultimate performance, upgrades, user satisfaction, efficiency, austerity measures, personnel reductions, and ego gratification. While these other concerns frequently arise in the political structures of most corporations, the absolute need to keep the network reliable is tantamount. When the network is crucial to business and functionally replaces traditional mainframe DP operations, such mission-critical applications require absolute reliability. All other LAN issues should be subordinated.

As such, the simplest configuration for the network (that meets requirements) will by nature have the fewest parts to fail, be simple, and easily replaced in part or repaired in whole when inevitable failures occur. Specialty hardware that improves cost, performance, and the myriad of other facets comes with a price of oddity, complexity, and increased failure rates. In time, odd parts may not be serviceable.

Expanding an FDDI Network

Even spanning trees, dual homing, redundancy, redundant disk storage, fault-tolerance or mirroring components do not necessarily decrease the statistical chance for downtime—that is a complex calculation requiring expert consultation. Also, more complex solutions require more elaborate management, or perhaps tax the abilities of any person or team to maintain large local and enterprise-wide networks that support critical DP activities. Instead, keep it simple and retain skilled people *always available* to resolve catastrophes.

Recognize, too, that anything that binds small, unique pieces together to form the whole is critically dependent upon each of those pieces being available, operable, and correct. Local networks, distributed computing, client/server interaction, file component linkages, and other binding computer events become more fragile as they become more complex. Duplication, redundancy, and application mirroring is frequently unattainable. Keep it simple.

Speeding up LANs

Most network bottlenecks are not caused by channel usage or speed limitations. Bottlenecks are usually caused by poor installation, improper configuration, mismanagement, and mismatched components. Bottlenecks are usually station-dependent. It is rarely the network channel. For example, slow client/server processing is more likely to result from a slow client, lack of client resources, poor client/server application software, or an inadequate server. A server may have insufficient cache, insufficient memory, slow disks, a slow NIC, or an overloaded bus. Bottlenecks are also caused by a chokepoint, a restriction in the channel, such as an overloaded router, 9600 baud modem link, or a mismatched network address that forces a station to route and translate received frames in a smaller packet size rather than simply repeat them. Packet sizes can be increased for an additional performance gain; this depending upon the NOS. Also, see if the "window"—the number of frames sent before a confirmation is required—between multiple frame transmissions and a confirmation of receipt can be increased.

If a LAN channel itself is overwhelmed, run FDDI to the desktop. Install a SAS concentrator. Eliminate the intermediate repeaters, bridges, routers, and gateways. Put network nodes on an FDDI concentrator, rather than 10BASE-T or Token-Ring hubs. FDDI is not just for internetwork backbones. It is also a LAN replacement option. Other sections in this chapter show how a cascaded LAN and a LAN partitioned with bridges, routers, and gateways to solve performance problems in the past can in fact become performance problems themselves. Traffic jamming up at bridges, routers, gateways and other such transition points can spill back on the other attached networks, causing those pathways to jam as well. The chokepoints can be resolved many times by widening the highway at all points and eliminating those transition points.

If the FDDI channel is overwhelmed, there is no substitute protocol that is faster than FDDI. ATM at 155 Mbits/s through 6.134 Mbits/s is not yet available. It might also not be cost effective when it does come to market. However, if performance is analyzed with a capable protocol analyzer and bottlenecks do show, separate FDDI channels can be installed to bypass these bottlenecks. In other words, link the stations that talk to each other on a private line.

If the FDDI channel in an internetwork is overwhelmed, review the traffic composition with a protocol analyzer. Look for SNMP or other network management data exceeding 10 percent of channel capacity. Five percent is an ideal management overhead, although rarely achieved. Routers and devices that maintain routing tables can saturate the network with broadcast storms when they request information about active network devices and stations. Although a 50 percent network or even channel saturation for a minute every half hour does not seem outrageous, the results from such transmission blackout to other ongoing tasks is significant. Consider making automatic routing table generation a manual activity. Also, routers use one or more of a dozen different routing algorithms to direct frames to the ultimate destinations. Some of these are more efficient for large internetworks because hops will be minimized, segments with high loads will be bypassed, and the fastest delivery channel will be selected.

Expanding LANs

An extensive network can be constructed with a complex, nonlinear geometry to serve high concentrations of users, longer distances, and the global OSI network maximum of 2^{64} addressable FDDI nodes. Wiring hubs provide dense service immediately from 8 to 1024 nodes; it doesn't necessarily need to be FDDI. The hubs could provide Ethernet or Token-Ring. Multiple hubs and racks with hubs in one wiring closet can connect an arbitrarily large number of nodes. By interconnecting subnets, the full FDDI address limit is conceivable. The *bridge* interconnects different networks into FDDI, albeit with the possible performance hit of irrelevant traffic. The *router* interconnects different networks with even different protocols and WAN linkages. It too has a disadvantage in that it may be unable to keep it with the incoming traffic and route it in real time. The *gateway* interconnects separate FDDI rings or segments with other protocols to one or more FDDI network; it also can provide a software, protocol, and application translation. Gateways can provide multihop services. The gateway shares the routing problems with the router, while also supporting considerable translation overhead.

Expanding an FDDI Network

There is no free ride, no perfect solution, no clearly superior choice. Any choice must be balanced against subnet loads, primary ring traffic, and time factors. Note, too, that the correctness of any choice changes over time as the network evolves. There are also other devices including the *network switch* (packet or matrix switch hub) and the IEEE 802.1d *spanning-tree bridge* which are useful for creating mission-critical and fault-tolerant networks since they provide alternate channels and multiple point-to-point routes. In general, bridges, routers, and gateways do not simplify networks or network management. They tend to add to the topological and managerial complexity. As such, they should be applied only when performance improvements or expansion requirements demand them.

The Wiring Concentrator or Hub

Although the *wiring concentrator* provides base-level service for an FDDI network, the hub also serves as an effective expansion unit. These devices usually support from 4 to 16 nodes each. Many multiple access units support two or eight lobes on a single adapter card which installs into a multiprotocol router or hub. It is basically comparable to a 10BASE-T hub or Token-Ring MAU; it may support all the protocols with different mix and match adapters. In fact, that is what it could be—even on an FDDI network. Figure 10.1 illustrates a typical twisted-pair wiring concentrator.

If you recall, twisted-pair IBM FDDI is not a true ring-configured network. It is a star or tree topology, and as such, all signals are

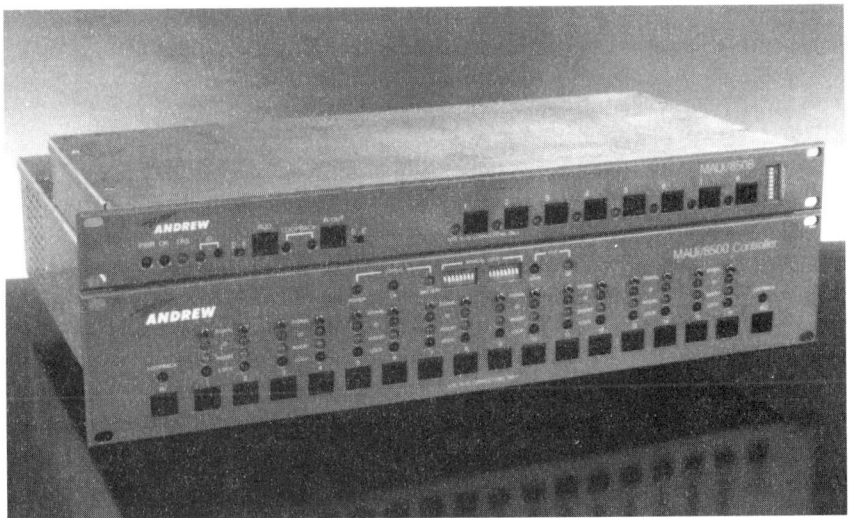

Figure 10.1 Typical twisted-pair concentrator or hub.

transmitted from each node to the hub, which then actively switches the signal to the other nodes. Smart hubs check the destination address, presence of errors, and defective frames before repeating them. Since the electrical signals on twisted-pair must be regenerated by all NICs, signal errors do arise. Also, defective frame are repeated to the nodes for the obvious reasons that the receiver and sender must see that a problem exists.

The easiest solution to high-concentration nodes is to place a hub at location. The hub would a primary DAS station connection to a dual FDDI trunk; all nodes on location would be SAS connections. This placement is subject to all timing limitations and the TRT and THT calculations. The use of such "outboard" hubs yields other economic and reliability benefits. Not only is the connecting wire from the node to the hub minimized but also the reliability of the local connections is superior. The disadvantage is that the concept of the centralized wiring closet is defeated, simple reconfiguration from the wiring closet is made complicated, and the possibility for similar additional expansions is remote. These problems can all be overcome by wiring all concentrated nodes to a local wiring closet are creating a local ring. Bridge that new ring to the existing FDDI network.

Some of the newer products include multiport NIC and access ports contained within a single PC expansion board. This component is essentially both a NIC and a hub for an additional number of ports. In such an architecture, this board fits within a personal computer and provides its own coprocessing CPU. A lobe cable from the hub connects to this machine. Other PCs with special client expansion boards attach locally to the expansion board with twisted-pair ribbon cable. Expansion and growth within a concentrated area is easily met by establishing a local ring or standalone network to the main trunk.

Network Repeaters

A *repeater* unit boosts the transmission signal for wiring runs which are longer than specification. A common unit is represented by Figure 10.2. FDDI is limited to a maximum drive length of 30 m and 36 km (depending upon the cabling and signaling variation), and the repeater can augment this length subject to the maximum FDDI TRT. Many repeaters can be used on a network—every station on FDDI is a repeater, of course. There are three variations on repeaters: the simple repeater, the smart repeater, and the half repeater.

The *simple repeater* just extends the signal, as shown in Figure 10.3. Note that the repeater unit connects into a trunk or lobe cable. If these are primary station devices, the repeater uses a station location and subtracts from the maximum network configuration. Repeaters will increase the TRT and ring latency.

Expanding an FDDI Network

Figure 10.2 A typical repeater.

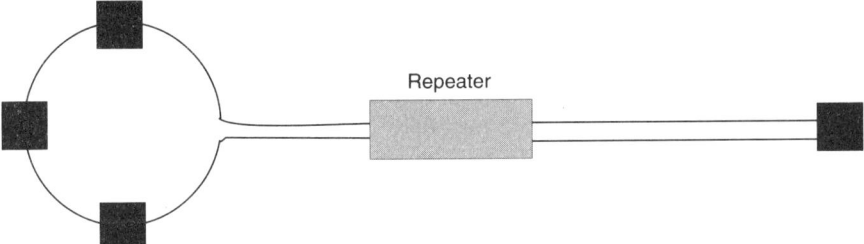

Figure 10.3 Nodes linked with a repeater.

The *smart repeater,* or *learning repeater,* filters packets by destination. This hybrid device is actually an ISO bridge because this functionality is supported at the OSI data link layer. If a packet were destined for another ring, the repeater captures and transmits the packet when that other network is free. A common error for such bridges connecting saturated rings or Ethernet segments is to create a performance bottleneck. Other packets are ignored. This smart repeater reduces the probability for decreased performance since a fraction of packets are filtered and not forwarded. This is relevant when using FDDI as a backbone to interconnect Ethernets on a campus. It is unwise to pass all the local traffic to the backbone. Repeating a topic presented earlier in this chapter, even at 100 Mbits/s, FDDI will saturate with the unfiltered noise from too many subnetworks. Figure 10.4 illustrates these two principles. Only packets sourced from node 4, 5, or 6 destined for node 1, 2, or 3 are repeated across this gateway. Likewise, only packets sourced from node 1, 2, or 3 destined for node 4, 5, or 6 are repeated. Internetwork traffic is thereby reduced for an effective performance gain.

Half repeaters transmit signals from one building to another. A half repeater might utilize an Ethernet baseband or broadband coax, fiber

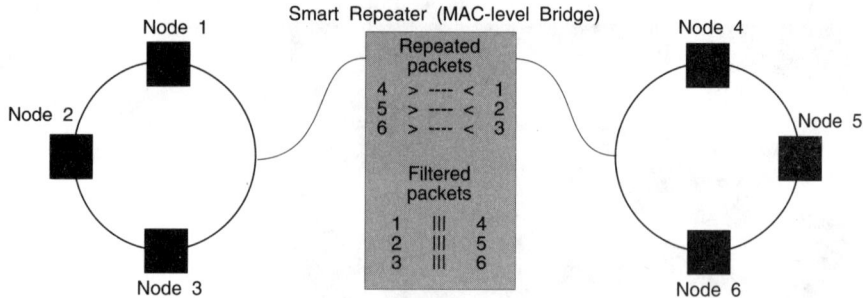

Figure 10.4 Two rings linked with a smart repeater.

optics, PBX network, infrared or microwave, or satellite transmission medium. The half repeater is often a long-haul link between distant networks. Specialized hardware filters, decouples, and synchronizes transmission and reception in order to eliminate increased TRT. *Decoupling* is the intertwined process of informing the sender that transmission has been logically and properly delayed to allow that sending process to continue processing. When transmission is finally completed, the sender receives a confirmation message within the scope of the *proper* network protocol. A half repeater, as illustrated in Figure 10.5, effectively joins two distinct networks.

Microwave interface units often include a store-and-forward buffer to decouple the microwave transmission. The buffer must prevent packets from colliding, or both coupled networks could exhibit a constant state of collision and saturation. Extra software is required to belatedly indicate transmission completion.

Multipurpose Solutions and Devices

Multipurpose devices economically expand FDDI. These units are frequently called *concentrators, wiring hubs, bridges, routers,* and *gateways.* Multipurpose devices interconnect multiple networks and handle incom-

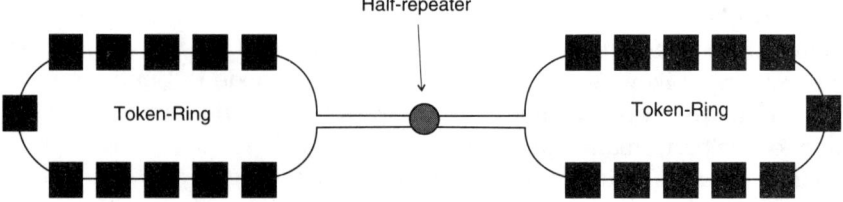

Figure 10.5 Full lasing repeater connects rings.

Expanding an FDDI Network 195

patible media. Multipurpose devices like concentrators are critical for building enterprise-wide networks since the network media is likely to include baseband Ethernet, Token-Ring, ARCNET, workgroup peer-to-peer networks, twisted-pair FDDI, RS-232, T-1, SNA, proprietary optical fiber, and other FDDI networks. Concentrators provide a single focus for connecting these disparate media and protocols. In addition to the physical connectivity and the centralized focus, these devices also include management tools such as CMIP or SNMP for managing these complex interconnected networks.

Synernectics, Chipcom, Shiva, Racal Interlan, BICC, and Cabletron are among the many vendors providing these complex connections. Most vendors now produce so called hub devices that integrate disparate networks into a central wiring closet, and then provide twisted-pair service from a star configuration. These products provide a focal point for controlling a network and asynchronous and synchronous networking services. Additionally, some concentrators provide multiple-channel routing and bridging that locates the fastest, shortest, or only available route between nodes. This technology is complex, difficult to install and maintain, but invaluable for networks suffering from overloading. It is presented later in this chapter. Cabletron and Synernectics, among a growing field, produce such units. They provide local area connectivity for asynchronous and synchronous networks, terminals, and peripherals. Specifically, these devices provide access to a modem pool, frame relay, ATM, Fibre Channel, printer support, terminal concentration, host computer concentration, synchronous protocol conversion, Ethernet, FDDI, and Token-Ring access—all from the same box. In many cases, these units contain multiple power supplies, hot swap capability, and fail-safe operation. This is unusual in that repairs and configurations can be performed while the hub remains in operation.

Another important multipurpose device is the *terminal server* which services from 8 to 64 RS-232 lines for data entry terminals, serial printers, or modems. The terminal server looks very much like any hub; output, however, does not propagate FDDI signals, but separate RS-232 serial lines. Frequently, these servers are employed where client/server distributed processing is not required for all users since less expensive dumb terminals can provide appropriate user access to host databases, mail services, network fax, network optical storage and retrieval of scanned documents, and typical desktop applications. Where a site conforms to the EIA/TIA wiring standards, a change from an RS-232, Ethernet, Token-Ring, or TP-DDI represents only a patch cable change in the central wiring closet and a node and possibly a NIC change. More esoteric hardware includes advanced *rings-in-box* technology. Hubs eliminate the requirement for trunk networks while hubs with *switched backplanes* and *cross-point switches* provide intermediate methods to reconfigure networks in real time for fault-tolerant operation. These uncommon devices for FDDI—most are designed to overcome saturation problems with Ethernet—are designed for high-volume and critical networks. Networks constructed with trunk service provided by a hub frequently experience capacity bottlenecks at this central hub. These newer technologies endeavor to bypass the bottlenecks. Of relevance, too, vendors are producing more multipurpose, multiprotocol bridge and hub devices that utilize Reduced Instruction Set Computing (RISC) chips, Complex Instruction Set Computing (CISC) chips, and Application Specific Integrated Circuits (ASIC). These are important in terms of providing adequate network performance for routing and gateway operations since each routing operation can require between 50 and 250 instructions to route a packet.

Despite this complexity and uniqueness, specialty products may provide the only solution for saturated large LANs and enterprise-wide networks. For example, the faster processing time becomes important when real-time protocol translation rather than frame encapsulation is required so that client-server distributed processing can occur with heterogeneous protocols. Protocol translation often requires multiple outgoing frames for each incoming one and perhaps complex address conversions, in addition to any simpler routing decisions.

Network Bridges

The simple *bridge* connects different types of networks together and promotes interconnectivity between multivendor networks. Figure 10.6 shows a node that bridges two networks. A bridge is either a specialized

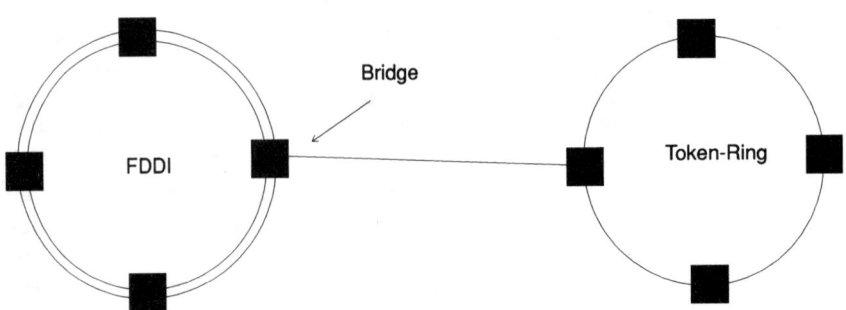

Figure 10.6 An FDDI bridge to a Token-Ring network node.

Expanding an FDDI Network

type of hardware that converts transmissions from one type of network into a medium required by another, or a computer computer device that is compatible with two communication device that interfaces with two communications networks. A bridge is totally transparent to the devices on the network. A bridge is also protocol-independent. *Protocol independence* means that packet signals are converted for transmission on another medium and the data format is invisible to the bridging device. The two media may be the identical or different. The most common bridging mechanism is a modem that converts digital baseband signals into a broadband format for long-haul or multiple-channel transmission. Figure 10.7 illustrates this bridging technology.

As larger organizations require enterprise-wide networks and integrate microcomputer technology and microcomputer networks, the importance of the microcomputer grows. Users find the microcomputer less restrictive than mainframes, and more available. It provides software unavailable on mainframes. File server networks present a viable downsizing opportunity, as Chapter 11 details. Uploading and downloading of information between mainframe and microcomputer is a growing requirement, and bridges establish a common link, common

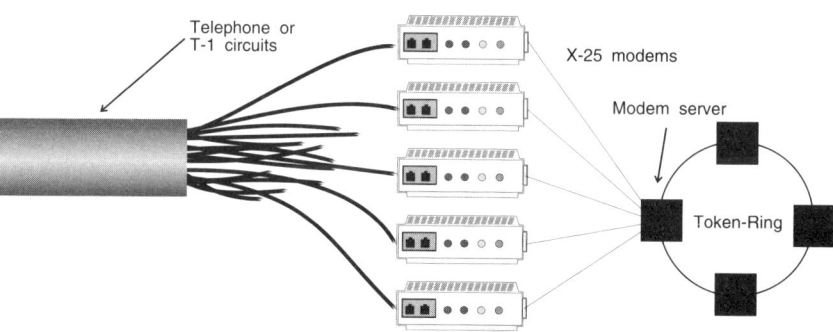

Figure 10.7 Modems bridge FDDI to remote nodes.

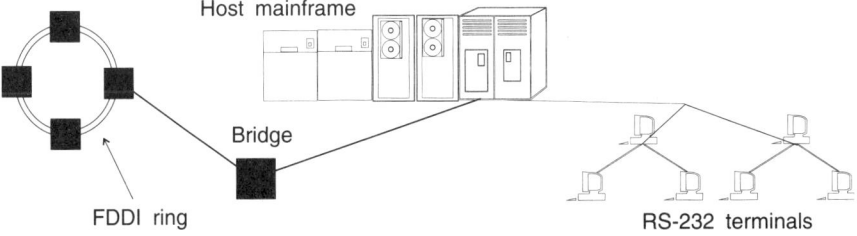

Figure 10.8 A bridge connecting a mainframe to an FDDI ring.

transmission formats, and increasingly, common data formats. The mainframe to microcomputer bridge is explained by Figure 10.8.

Bridges provide access to T-1 and networks like Tymnet and Telenet, which are public data networks (PDNs), or private branch exchanges (PBXs), which are no-dialing-required lease lines. However, transmission protocols must decouple the packet transmission since transit time will exceed the expected FDDI roundtrip delay of 1.617 ms. Solutions such as *frame relay* or protocols including *network block transfer protocol* (NETBLT) encapsulate or interpret the frame for the linkage. The encapsulation technique is protocol-independent. Note that while a mainframe can be a node on FDDI, mainframe communication protocols typically differ from the FDDI protocol, and a router or gateway (something above the OSI data link level) is required to translate and interface incongruous protocols. For example NetWare SNA or DCA IRMA would provide the software and the actual hardware gateway to connect a network server or user through to the host mainframe. Note that LAN to mainframe performance is limited both by the host, the gateway, the network traffic load, and only marginally by the speed of the required terminal software. Figure 10.9 shows a large network.

Although bridges do support the expansion of networks into a network of networks, they can also limit that same expansion. Bridges must be fast since they read every packet. FDDI networks approaching packet saturation may overwhelm the capacity of a bridge to forward packets. If a bridge

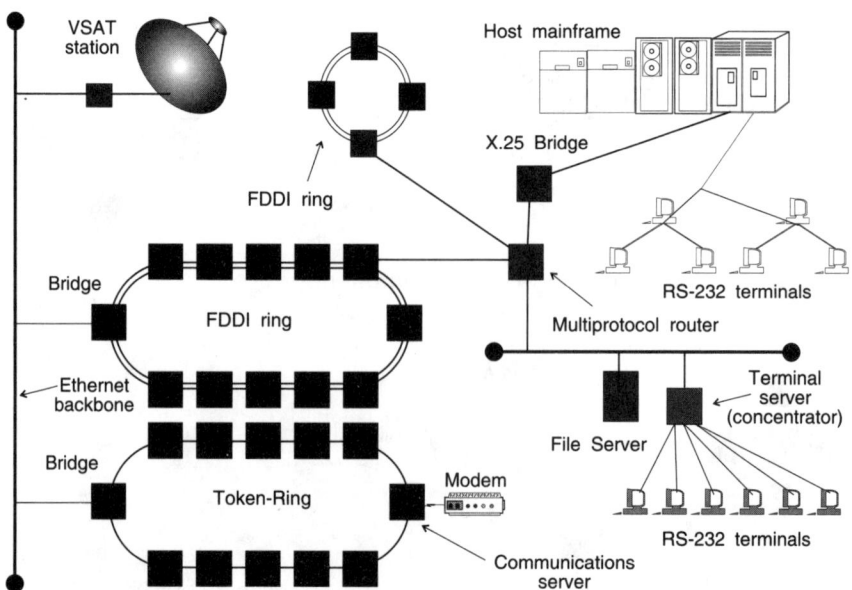

Figure 10.9 An expanded network topology.

Expanding an FDDI Network

cannot accommodate the network load, it will lose frames. Not only will performance suffer directly; the lost frames will have to be retransmitted as an added load. Although bridges are transparent to network devices, the same is not always true for software applications. Bridges are not the solution for every network expansion. In fact, *intelligent bridges* also create traffic when they poll devices to maintain routing tables and unleash a *broadcast storm* when they cannot accommodate a lower-level protocol. This happens when some broadcast LAN protocols cause frames to be passed through from all stations to each port. In the event of a malfunction or an improperly set parameter, this traffic can create a bottleneck on the entire network and render it inoperable.

Hybrid devices such as intelligent bridges provide a destination-filtering component to improve network performance. This overlaps the definition of the smart repeater and the router, and performs an identical function while also bridging different media types. Just as some smart repeaters often build their own routing tables, intelligent bridges learn addresses of devices on the network. This means that a new device can be added to the network without any special configuration. Intelligent bridges offer the added capability to selectively filter traffic. Security for a network segment can be enforced by establishing a set of nodes that cannot traverse the bridge or be reached from the other side of the bridge. *Source explicit forwarding* (SEP) allows the establishment of privileges by defining addresses in the routing table as either accessible or inaccessible for sets of users and node devices. Open shortest path first (OSPF) tries to match a need with the shortest available connection; this is not necessarily the fastest. Intermediate to intermediate (IS-IS) is an OSI routing protocol, while source route transparent (SRT) is useful for TCP/IP networks, and interior gateway routing protocol (IGRP) is a cisco Systems router protocol. Standard TCP/IP routing is accomplished with routing information protocol (RIP). Newer and more complex routing protocols include boundary routing, data prioritization, least-cost routing. Other routing algorithms do exist; about ten different ones exist. Most where designed to block competitors from a market niche. Some where designed to overcome some technological bottleneck. None are perfect. Most routing protocols tend to be proprietary, or in a state of definitional transition. We can hope that within a few years, a single routing protocol will emerge and the others will fade to obscurity. Note that the use of multiple routing algorithms will create a performance bottleneck on most hybrid networks.

Bridging Media

Bridges frequently interconnect different networks. A bridge could interconnect multiple networks. These networks are often FDDI or Ethernet. The bridges merely duplicate all signals originating from all source networks to the other networks for NetBIOS, NetBEUI, or LLC (802.2) protocols; otherwise frame and diffferences complicate the transition and protocol routers are required. This holds true for all simple bridges. Packets are not filtered before retransmission. The primary benefit of this process is that the junction bridges maintain throughput with minimal packet loss. The most substantial disadvantage is that all the interconnected networks experience a traffic level that is the sum of all interconnected networks. This is likely to yield severe network jams. For this reason, vendors have developed and enhanced hybrid devices including smart repeaters, intelligent bridges, complex routers, brouters, and packet switches. Packets switches effectively share the operating characteristics of multiport routers. Reduced instruction set computing chips (RISC), recently engineered for network routing, have resulted in the construction of switched backplane and cross-point switches that are not only more reliable but also perform faster so that packet routing can be optimized for reduced network loading.

Bridges also couple different media sharing the same protocols. A bridging device shuttles packets between the different media. For example, a bridge converts 4 Mbits/s Token-Ring to 16 Token-Ring. Some wiring hubs perform transmission speed conversions. Although the token protocol is identical for each, packet sizes may be larger within the faster environment. A bridge is required to convert UTP MLT-3 to NRZI on a fiber loop because there is a signaling difference; some might argue that this encoding represents a protocol difference, but really this is a only media-dependent signal transmission difference. When these devices bridge media, for example from optical FDDI to FDDI on STP, the protocol is not transformed in any way. Bridges are protocol independent. The LLC protocol must be the same at each end of the bridge for a bridge to be the proper connectivity device.

Spanning Tree Algorithm

Most FDDI networks, in fact most networks, are configured such that there is only a single path between any two devices. Even FDDI networks provide only a single path between devices since the signal is unidirectional. (FDDI provides multiple paths in event of cable failure because it is a dual ring, although the end result is that there is really only one path through the network.) Common network failures therefore can disable the entire network. Intelligent bridges can partition the internetwork into still functioning segments. However, this does not maintain network functionality for critical operations that might retain that functionality if other paths were available. FDDI does not normally allow two segments to be connected with more than a single device, repeater, bridge, router, or gateway. However, multiple bridges could be installed if they support the IEEE 802.1 Spanning-Tree Algorithm (STA). A *spanning tree* is any unique device-to-device path within the

Expanding an FDDI Network

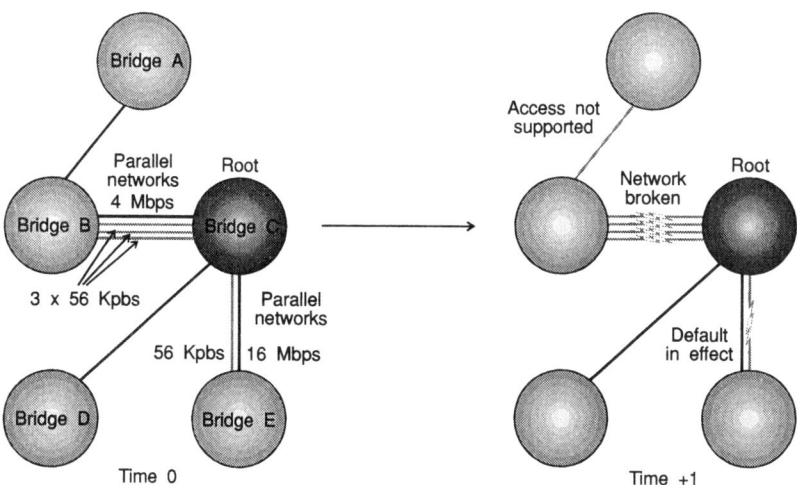

Figure 10.10 Spanning trees provide redundancy without active loops.

network, as Figure 10.10 illustrates. Several could exist. STA negotiates the optimum path (least time for transmission) and establishes one path as the forwarding path; all other paths are blocked. This guarantees a single active path between all node pair combinations so that there will be no active loops. Additionally, STA tracks for path failures and automatically establishes an alternative path in the event of failure. STA provides redundancy for critical operations.

Frequently, the alternate paths lack the bandwidth for normal throughput. The alternate paths guarantee only that a connection (such as RS-232 or X.25) is available within a specified interval (ranging from milliseconds to minutes). The spanning trees are frequently fail-safe alternatives for priority data communications and mission-critical DP. Of note, the use of dual homing connections on FDDI represents the use of a spanning tree.

Network Routers

A *router* is a bridge that is not protocol transparent. It must be addressed directly by a device on the network. Routers require routing tables that contain device addresses to identify network segments, the paths to these segments, and the relative efficiency of these paths. A router does not use the tables to locate specific devices on the network; rather, it relies on other routers. A router uses this information to determine the optimum route for each FDDI packet. *Static* routers require explicit routing table maintenance when devices are added, subtracted, or relocated on an internetwork, whereas *dynamic* routers automatically configure the tables. Dynamic routers usually require less maintenance although they are inadvisable for large networks. Nonetheless, routers are difficult to install and require specialized knowledge and a high level of network knowledge for performance optimization. Routers increase the complexity of network management dramatically, and make troubleshooting in the event of network failure that much more difficult. There is less control, and the process of automatically maintaining the routing tables increases the network traffic. Routers are not the solution for every network expansion. In fact, they also create traffic when they poll devices with a broadcast storm to maintain their automatic routing tables or check the operational status of the extended network.

Routers are one of the prime devices included within SNMP or CMIP management protocols. They are good agents for assessing traffic, TRT, latency, and timing errors. Some routers include priority network management software and display SNMP statistics directly. An intelligent router can improve network performance with various methods. They perform the functions of a smart repeater. They store, save, and forward packets at a later time. Intelligent routers also prioritize packet transmission by device address or inform a device that it will not transmit packets from a device *(source quench)* until the network traffic is lower.

Hybrid Bridges, Routers, and Brouters

Brouters are hybrid devices combining the functionality of bridges and routers. They are effective for complex, compound, or busy networks, or where an enterprise-wide network is warranted. They are devices best installed by the vendor since they are difficult to install and require specialized knowledge and a high level of network knowledge for performance optimization. Brouters increase the complexity of network management dramatically, and make troubleshooting in the event of network failure that much more difficult.

Network Gateways

Specialized *gateways* interface between different FDDI protocols and translate the transmission before retransmitting, as per the ISO definition. The gateway also has a software connotation, which is not to be confused with the ISO hardware definition. A software gateway performs the same function as a repeater, although it usually provides a routing mechanism that transmits only those packets clearly destined for that segment in the same way as a smart repeater routes packets. It relays traffic to the proper destination. More typically, a gateway is a software tool that provides interoperability functions at the OSI application and presentation layers. Such functionality includes data conversions, data presentations, protocol conversions and translations, encapsulation, and actual user file transfers.

Expanding an FDDI Network

A typical gateway has two or more controllers to connect separate networks. The most usual form of a gateway is a workstation or computer processor with two separate FDDI controllers. (A gateway represents more than a single optical NIC configured for dual homing.) Each controller connects into separate networks. This is not a bridge, although the node performs a bridging function. This is a true gateway because data interpretation occurs at all levels of the OSI model. The gateway unit supports two FDDI addresses, but one, two, or more Internet or IPX addresses. Most computer workstations support multiple controllers but require specialized software to function as a gateway. (See Figure 10.11.) Network gateways and foresighted network planning can localize groups and functional units on different networks for significant performance gains.

This subnetting isolates problems to each ring and allows loads, demand, and storage requirements on file servers and print servers to be controlled by the people who use those services, averting the possibility of developing a politically tense situation. Subnetting isolates a group to a subnet while lowering overall network traffic. It is one solution to overloading problems induced by cascaded networks.

This is a manageable approach to controlling resources by group and division, as well as by individual subnets throughout the institution. As an example, a backplane FDDI network would provide interconnection through multiple hops to all local rings and buses and supply network-wide access to expensive and low-usage specialized peripheral devices such as typesetters, image scanners, video entry cameras, pen plotters, coprocessors, and tape storage or disk storage devices. Subnets would concentrate each group onto a single network, so that excessive demand for services could be controlled, analyzed, and prevented from interfering with processing and traffic on other rings or the campus backbone.

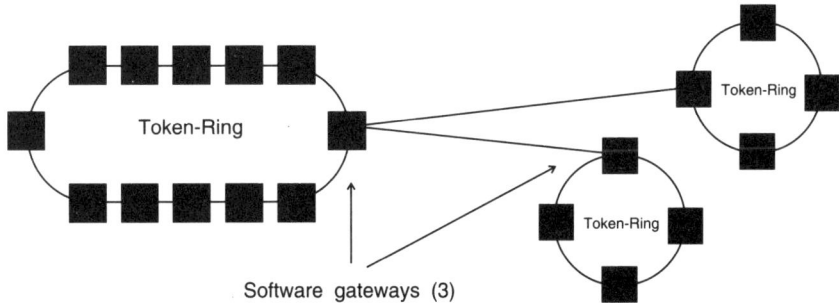

Figure 10.11 Station serving as gateway to interconnect three rings.

Gateways Integrate Networks Protocols

Gateways frequently form the primary prerequisite for building enterprise-wide networks. Existing ad hoc networks often represent multiple media and protocols and the gateway is required solely to interconnect these disparate parts into a cohesive whole. Replacing incompatible networks with the organization-sanctioned standard is often an unsatisfying and expensive alternative. Replacing functional networks with another type is one of those projects upper management is likely to quickly veto. Furthermore, suggesting such an inclination may make your stable network management positions suddenly tenuous. That is a tough battle to win, best accomplished in slow, concealed, and incremental steps.

While a growing number of vendors offer multiprotocol bridges, routers, and packet switches, nonetheless these network connectivity tools often yield insufficient utility. They might seem too difficult to install and manage. They might appear too expensive. They also function only at the lower protocol levels (OSI layers 2 and 3). Protocol translation at OSI level 7 is typically required to interconnect networks with incompatible protocols. Frankly, where possible, a single-purpose stand-alone gateway will perform better. It will actually be less costly overall than improvised solutions using a computer as a gateway (due to administration and maintenance costs). At the present time, Novell NetWare will support ARCNET, Ethernet, FDDI, and Token-Ring media, Macintosh Appletalk, OS/2, DOS, Unix, and connections to other client operating systems. When a commercial gateway does not exist, the only solution is a homemade software gateway.

The *software gateway* is a computer that runs two or more network protocols simultaneously. This is rarely a peer FDDI-to-FDDI connection since either a bridge or router can reroute and redirect FDDI packets at a lower protocol level. When LLC protocols do not mesh—examples include UDP, NetBIOS, NetBEUI, and OSI—the software gateway is appropriate. Sometimes, multiple low-level protocols (such as TCP/IP, UDP, IPX/SPX, NetBIOS, and NetBEUI) will coexist within the same FDDI channel, but these must be translated and rerouted across a gateway for protocol and presentation conversion. Figure 10.12 lists typical translations.

In addition to bidirectionally translating FDDI, it is also relevant to bidirectionally translate other protocols as well. For a classic Fortune 100 consider this situation: several departments need to interconnect Token-Ring LAN Server to LAN Manager. Research and development environments might translate FTP to NFS or to Ethernet and Novell. A database server running on Novell IPX/SPX might need to communicate with an Ethernet client. Although the larger network software vendors seek to establish standards for high-level interoperability and interconnectivity, these "standards" are just proliferating this translation problem. There are both commercial and technical reasons why vendors do not adhere to a

Expanding an FDDI Network

- FDDI<— | |—>Banyan
- FDDI<— | |—>Ethernet
- FDDI<— | |—>Frame relay
- FDDI<— | |—>GOSIP
- FDDI<— | |—>MAPS
- FDDI<— | |—>Novell IPX/SPX
- FDDI<— | |—>OSI
- FDDI<— | |—>Proteon Token Ring
- FDDI<— | |—>TCP/IP
- FDDI<— | |—>TCP/IP with UDP
- FDDI<— | |—>Token-Ring with LAN Manager
- FDDI<— | |—>Token-Ring with LAN Server
- FDDI<— | |—>Token-Ring with Novell NetWare
- FDDI<— | |—>Token-Ring with OS/2 Comm MGR
- FDDI<— | |—>X.25
- TCP/IP with UDP<— | |—>NFS

Figure 10.12 Typical gateway protocol translations.

full OSI network implementation and rely upon interoperability at the datagram level. Frequently, establishing an improvised gateway remains the only viable solution.

Configuration of the Software Gateway

The software gateway is a computer, typically a PC or engineering workstation, running two (or more) protocols and containing two (or more) network interface cards. Multiprotocol routing is certainly feasible. Notwithstanding, it is typically a complex installation. Each network protocol software requires memory-resident device drivers with controlling software. Each set of device drivers activates a single type of network interface card. The controlling software codes and decodes information, builds the protocol, and often provides application-level services like remote file access, print services, and electronic mail. The network software may set *hooks* into the underlying operating system to intercept interrupts and service requests (for redirecting directory requests, port outputs, and the like).

The number of possible ways of providing a protocol gateway with just the 16 options listed in Figure 10.12 is 16! combinations, a number too large to print here. While some network vendors may provide some direction for successfully building a gateway or providing connectivity to selected competing products, it is often an unsupported task. Technical support services might say, "Good luck! Let us know how it works out."

Memory Competition

When both sides of a protocol link do not support homogeneous protocol, the unorthodox loading of two very similar applications into computer memory simultaneously can create significant obstacles. Each driver and protocol set may exceed 100 K of system memory. This is usually not a problem for host mainframe, servers running OS/2 or Unix operating systems since they generally support linear mapping of memory and partition applications with ample protection. Difficulties arise when multiple network operating system programs fill memory or overlap the same memory addresses. This produces ruinous results. A solution may entail repeated time-consuming, trial-and-error reinstallation to determine the correct combination of installation sequences, device drivers required, bus and NIC IRQ interrupt settings, as well as memory allocations. It is likely that certain network software functionality (including print services, disk and file redirection, security, and even the network menu system) must be disabled to free needed memory. Note that if you must disable password and user login security—one of the least liked network features—do so only with full recognition of possible consequences.

PC-DOS or MS-DOS, currently limited by 640 K of addressable memory space, often yields a marginal gateway. Furthermore, DOS establishes discontiguous segments of memory. Low memory is the space from 0 K to 640 K where the MS-DOS or PC-DOS operating system and MS-DOS application software is loaded. High memory represents the space from 640 K to 1024 K (1 MB). High memory is also some composite of *expanded* and/or 16 K selectable blocks of *extended* optional memory above 1024 K. Memory discontinuities slow paging performance, complicate conflict resolution, and seriously hamper successful establishment of a functional dual- or multiprotocol gateway.

Note that even a paired-down MS-DOS with the requisite network drivers takes the first 50 K, leaving 590 K of free operating system memory. Now consider as an example, two network drivers and two network operating systems such as Banyan and TCP/IP can easily consume at least 200 K of that 590 K available memory leaving only a meager 390 K of free memory whereas IBM LAN Server might require up to 590 K all to itself. This leaves nothing for another protocol without disabling some LAN Server features such as the redirector, print services, and security.

Assuming that multiple network protocols will load and not conflict, the PC can access both networks sequentially. However, automatic translation and rerouting applications must fit within the remaining operating system memory area. Still, insufficient memory may frustrate even loading simple user-level applications accommodating the manual transfer of files (or bits and bytes) and mail. LAN Server or LAN Manager in conjunction with an FDDI-compatible protocol (such as TCP/IP, Novell, or NFS) might not even load concurrently within memory as implied above. When they do fit, it is likely that the DOS BIOS device calls will overlap and so entangle DOS as to disable one or both network protocols since they are so much alike. Together, they may even destabilize DOS causing it to "hang." Furthermore, both softwares with DOS overlapping interrupt vectors may create

Expanding an FDDI Network

a conflicting NETBEUI or NETBIOS function, thereby disabling the network NICs at a hardware level.

Memory management tools including QEMM, 386MAX, and QRAM remap DOS memory and enhance expanded and extended memory ranges (from 640 K to 64 M) for greater utility. While this often permits relocating operating system code, hardware drivers, and network software into high memory, this does not always provide for the concurrent usage of two or more network protocols. Each protocol may still demand absolute overlapping of DOS low memory locations. If the network operating system can be relocated to different memory addresses, either one protocol or another can run selectively. This may prevent a gateway from working concurrently as intended. A network operating system is much like a DOS *terminate and stay resident* (TSR) program. It stays in memory and fills memory although it may require less when deactivated. A network, analogously to a TSR, takes full control of the computer and temporarily disables all other operations or TSRs. Similarly, it frequently destabilizes the underlying operating system.

Just as third party memory managers do, MS-DOS 5.0 provides a more robust operating system with the ability to load drivers into high memory ranges. Network operating systems may fail with this (or other) progressive operating system due to compatibility problems. In fact, Novell had to effect substantial changes to NetWare for it to coexist within MS-DOS 5.0. Add one or more additional network protocols and problems are compounded. This does not mean that MS-DOS cannot support a gateway. It only means seek commercial solutions first before committing to undertaking a complex and by no means certain path.

When a concurrent MS-DOS gateway is not possible, consider a momentary gateway to gain connectivity for an application or for file transfers. Commercial and shareware programs such as CONFIG.EXE, REBOOT.COM, and REBOOT.EXE provide a simple method to select from various boot configurations. Alternative copies of the operating system boot files CONFIG.SYS and AUTOEXEC.BAT files (from a *backed up* subdirectory) replace these two files while the system is powered cycled or merely rebooted with a DOS call to memory address 03. These alternative configuration files can activate ARCnet, FDDI, or FDDI and install a zero-slot LAN, FDDI, LAN Manager, LAN Server, NetWare, or Vines. It is only necessary that the NICs are installed in the computer; generally, they are always physically installed in the machine. They do not conflict when their system drivers are not installed at boot time. Additionally, these files might establish different \ETC\HOST listings, a variant Internet address, X.400 and X.500 global naming services, different exportable disk partition names, or even a different workstation or server name.

The primary advantage of this method is that it always can be accomplished. While possibly difficult to establish initially, once the alternate boot files are built, they can be invoked at will. It is easier than struggling to get network stacks to be co-resident within a single gateway host or user node. First, files are copied from one network. Second, the PC is reconfigured and rebooted. Third, the files are then available to another network. This is relevant for mail access, availability to specialty printers compatible with one network protocol only, and connection to mainframes, host servers, and source code control systems. The disadvantages are that this represents no true gateway, solely momentary linkages. It is unwieldy; configurations must be backed up and sometimes all must be changed to reflect a new hardware driver or the peccadilloes of a newly installed obstinate software such as MS Windows. Because the linkage is only temporary, it is not reliable nor always available to other network users. This may mean that they cannot send mail, annotate files, or access files or another network resource. It is also costly in terms of the idle process time needed to shut down the applications, reconfigure the boot files, halt the system, and finally reinitialize it for each momentary need.

Unix and OS/2 Gateway Solutions

As mentioned in the last section, Unix and OS/2, unlike MS-DOS, map memory within single contiguous blocks. They also provide concurrent multiple software applications and protect each such application in its own segment. This is called *multiprocessing* on Unix and *threading* on OS/2. Multiple drivers and multiple sessions share the processor and coexist without conflict. In fact, it is possible under these operating systems to load multiple copies of even a single network protocol and associated device drivers to provide automatic routing services. Since the multitasking and concurrent operations are better managed by Unix and OS/2, these platforms are a better choice for gateways. Additionally, many client-server network protocols are only fully functional under Unix or OS/2. This includes Sun Microsystems NFS and LAN Manager.

Notwithstanding, each protocol needs a separate NIC card to run concurrently. Do not overlay duplicated or different protocols on the same NIC memory space unless this connection is momentary. Although the gateway may provide peer-to-peer FDDI-to-FDDI bridging, separate memory stacks must be built for the gateway to function. Note that the gateway could provide a four-way FDDI-to-Ethernet connection and FDDI-to-Token-Ring simultaneously. As each FDDI frame is captured on one side of the gateway, it must be rebuilt for retransmission to the other side. In fact, the gateway may receive a frame from one network while simultaneously sending a packet to the other network(s). A card and the protocol stacks therefore cannot be shared. Peer-to-peer examples include translating NFS to Novell on FDDI, Token-Ring LAN

Expanding an FDDI Network

Server to Token-Ring LAN Manager, and Novell IPX/SPX datagram packets to TCP/IP.

Although boot configurations can be altered for OS/2 and Unix using a similar method as that for MS-DOS, the time requirements to safely shut down and restart these more complex disk file systems may make this less practical. It is very unwise to terminate OS/2 or Unix file services by stopping the machine with a sudden change of the power switch. Multitasking and threading expose many temporary and permanent files to unstable states. Failure to flush database records or sectors of files that reside in cache memory and close these files may unchain (damage) them. These operating systems may require a more complex approach to establishing multiple protocol connectivity.

Installation of multiple protocols, while easier under Unix and OS/2, may still retain the same trial-and-error approach required for an MS-DOS-based gateway. Configurations such as device addresses, setting priorities for Unix multitasking, or OS/2 LIB, PATH, and DPATH might require careful tuning to get multiple protocols to install on the hard disk, much less even load. Executable code files could require hexadecimal editing so that addresses, paths, or file names are altered to prevent conflicts. Installation sequences and selected subdirectory names might need alteration. You might need duplicate driver files with different gateway node names or addresses so that each network will see the gateway server under a different node name; this prevents circular routing errors where a packet would never be captured and thus not be retransmitted or terminated.

Gateway Duality and Automation

Sometimes, multiprotocol translation is an either/or proposition, particularly the case under MS-DOS. The PC is configured to install NFS over FDDI to capture a file. Then, the PC is reconfigured (booted with alternate AUTOEXEC.BAT and CONFIG.SYS files) to move that file to another network such as FDDI, Banyan, or FTP TCP/IP. When multiple protocols load and function concurrently under Unix or OS/2, the mechanism for moving mail files or data files from one network to another may also require a similar sequenced manual transfer. The process would proceed like this: access one network and fetch the file, access the other network and transfer the file. This might represent a remote copy or a capture of a mail message. The resulting file might require character conversion or new mail header information to be useful on the destination network. There might even be a need to route that packet through translation on a second gateway. For example, Unix line endings differ from the MS-DOS counterpart, because of backspaces, linefeeds, new line characters (ASCII 8, 10, and 13), and because host mainframe EBCDIC differs from PC ASCII. Also, few mail message formats conform to the X.400 standards.

A medium akin to a routing mechanism is required to translate and route information across the gateway, whether manually or automatically. Sometimes a low-level protocol like TCP/IP or NETBEUI is available on both sides of the gateway. Then, the Internet address or another type of native address is sufficient to speed the information to the ultimate destination. Otherwise, a process must capture the packet and analyze the contents to determine what to do with it. The IPX/SPX client-server process is one example of a gateway translation process. Internet address routing is another. Although this routing function occurs due to OSI level 3 and 4 datagram functionality, the transfer must be achieved at OSI level 7. The translation is an application-level job because the datagram must be converted within the context of the application to which it is directed. For example, the transfer of a Lotus 1-2-3 data file is straightforward unless it gets to its destination blocked out of sequence. The file will not load into the spreadsheet program, and is unusable with any amount of effort. The only solution is to acquire a better copy. Basically, an automated process replicates what a user would do by remotely copying bytes from one network and then remotely copying them to another network within a new mail message or duplicating file structure.

Gateway Performance

The interoperability and interconnection provided by gateways comes with a steep price. A gateway is either a specialized device that is expensive, or it is a computer that serves that singular gateway purpose and was installed, configured, and optimized over a lengthy period. Gateways rarely are fast. This is a serious performance limitation. While repeaters tend to retransmit everything with only several milliseconds delay, bridges might rebroadcast only 11,000 of the 13,000 packets received with several hundred milliseconds of delay. Nothing is filtered, merely rebroadcasted.

Routers are even slower. A router first must capture all arriving packets (or create a LAN bottleneck). It decodes it for the destination address. If this address is contained in a routing table, the packet is retransmitted to a new network segment. Otherwise, the packets are discarded. The router may assign new addresses from the routing table (since routers only recognize other routers or packets addressed to addresses in the routing table or even reformats the information to the same or an alternate frame format). Finally, the router broadcasts it to another router or the ultimate destination node. The routing delay may approach a half second with 9000 of 18,000 packets received and 5000 rejected. Newer algorithms based upon hardware solutions rather than software may decrease the transit time and increase packet throughput. When FDDI can transport hundreds of thousands of frames per second, these limitations seem all the more substantial.

Expanding an FDDI Network 211

The discrepancy between packets received and packets transmitted represents failed delivery. This is an important statistic. Failed delivery is about 2000 packets for a bridge and 4000 packets for a router on a busy network. Generally, successful transmission for each packet requires that the receiver return a message to the sender. After the specified delay, lost packets are retransmitted until the sending process responds to them or the sender "times out" concluding that there is a network failure or that the recipient node is unavailable.

Gateways are slower yet since they embody the repeater, bridge, and routing functions with potentially more complicated translation and rebroadcast functions. Frequently the gateway is not expected to work in real time and transmission is decoupled, as previously defined for routing operations. In other words, an FDDI node does not expect an extended delay from a node across a gateway. For example, FDDI does not expect a gateway to translate a packet into VSAT format, transmit the packet to a station 9 seconds distant, and receive a reply within 3.2 milliseconds (twice the FDDI round-trip delay plus interpacket spacing delays and the typical network-configured retransmission delay). Transmission must be decoupled. A gateway might process 2000 packets of 18,000 received, while rejecting the 14,000 not directed to it. The 2000-packet overflow creates a serious network problem. Consider the problems when an FDDI network transports 100,000 frames each second; that places routing technology into perspective. As another example this is very obvious to users of distributed client/server databases. Applications that query a remote database intensively stress a gateway by requesting complex SQL SELECT statements which often are not processed at the remote database server. Massive numbers of data records are transmitted to the users' local nodes for local processing. If the network demand on the gateway exceeds its ability to translate and route that massive amount of information, it creates a bottleneck. Chapter 19 provides more detail on improving performance with gateways.

Gateway Traffic Jams

Lost packets are normally retransmitted within a few hundred milliseconds. If they collide with new packets, the sending network exhibits a traffic jam. Because most networks provide two-way transmission with a single channel only (dual ring FDDI is the one exception), the receiving network across the gateway sees the traffic jam as well. It cannot reply to packets received because it cannot get them through the traffic blockage. As a result, outgoing receipt messages on that recipient network collide with incoming packets. The sending network doesn't realize that packets have actually transversed the gateway because the transmission wasn't yet acknowledged, and it tries to send them again. This gridlock escalates into network channel saturation; recovery requires that all processes must be halted and restarted with reduced demand. That traffic level must be restrained or the obstruction will perpetually reoccur.

Gateway Routing Tables

Furthermore, a gateway requires routing information for true efficiency. It is unproductive for a gateway to replicate packets across a gateway unless they are destined for a device there. That would degrade the performance of the gateway and add an unnecessary load to the other networks. If those other networks were rings, the gateway could conceivably translate multiple copies of the original packets back to the originating network. This could escalate traffic to a virtual standstill. A routing table is essential. It is nothing more than a list of nodes with network locations relative to the router or gateway. A gateway can be manually provided with a routing table or build its own dynamically. Refer to Figure 10.4 again for a simplified illustration of a routing table.

Manually supplied tables tend to accumulate errors. Nodes and devices get moved (as expressed previously, about 50 percent of all workstations and PCs are moved annually at corporations). Consequently, many addresses or node names are changed. The Internet address once 123.45.678 might become 123.44.678, or a workstation called "Spooky" might be relabeled as "Marty." Old entries accumulate and bloat the table dimming performance. New entries get added when users complain about lack of enterprise-wide network access. On the other hand, dynamic tables require that the multiport or multiprotocol gateways poll the separate networks for node names, addresses, and locations. As an aside, this is as equally true for simpler multiport and multiprotocol routers. The routing table building process is achieved by broadcasting a request to all devices to identify themselves and their addresses. Routing table entries resolve to actual network locations. This broadcast storm often collides with normal network traffic causing a performance hit. This broadcast request for active nodes and node addresses must be repeated at intervals to see if machines have been turned on, and therefore connected to a network or physically relocated. In the likely event of a glitch, manual power cycle, power failure, software error, or some other random occurrence, the routing table must be rebuilt from scratch. Also, when multiple paths through the network exist, the operational or optimal path often changes as a result of which nodes are active, which paths are active, which internetwork linkages are active, and the traffic levels on subnetworks and linkages. Various algorithms are available for optimizing these linkages; they vary by vendor and LAN or NOS configuration. Traditionally, the complexity of maintaining multiple paths leads most network managers merely to choose whichever protocol works reliably rather than optimize performance; even IEEE 802.1 spanning bridges are slow and not always reliable.

Expanding an FDDI Network

Essential Connections

Internetworking and interoperability are frequently difficult to achieve. Commercial gateways are too costly to acquire while the improvised variety may require too much hardware, too many resources, and perform unreliably. It may be impossible even to establish a functional peer-level gateway at all. Additionally, the gateway may not be practical because transferring mail and files may require a convoluted effort. The format of mail messages may necessitate a program to route the mail message to the gateway, another program to translate the header information, and another process to remail the message on the new network segment. Similarly, files may require text conversion to reflect the differences in system storage formats, as previously conveyed.

Nonetheless, access to files on other networks are frequently imperative. Under these conditions, while peer-level gateways are not practical, another, simpler type of linkage is feasible. This type of gateway requires no bus slots, minimal software, minimal system memory, and frequently coexists with network operating systems. Examples include an IRMA FDDI to twinax AS/400 linkage, terminal emulation software with text capture performed via a dial-up modem, serial or parallel links, or a zero-slot LAN. Public domain products include Xmodem and Kermit. Complete MS-DOS commercial products also are readily available. IRMAtrac or IRMA WorkStation for Windows from DCA supplies host access for a PC whereas LYNX 3270/X provides a 3270 emulation with a host computer for X Windows workstations and terminals. Crosstalk captures text and files via modem and a serial port. Brooklyn Bridge, LapLink, and WinLink connect communication ports on two PCs for file transfer and some remote control features. Zero-slot LAN requires only a communication port that is built into virtually every PC.

When it is not possible to link an IBM 30XX host into a LAN using TCP/IP for FDDI compatibility, an IRMAtrac communication board provides a narrow access into the network. This is one option presented here that requires an interface board. The IRMA WorkStation for Windows otherwise can connect with an asynchronous connection, DFT, FDDI, and SDLC. Similar mainframe connectivity may be implemented through gateway software on a LAN connectivity host either on a NetBIOS FDDI, a separate X.25 connection, or by installing FDDI adapters in the mainframe. Many networks, since they are not PC-based, cannot receive an IRMA linkage board since most such cards are built for IBM AT, *Micro-Channel Architecture* (MCA), or *Extended Industry Standard Architecture* (EISA) bus slots. Some do exist for multibus. Nor do they support 3270 or 5250 terminal emulation for data capture. Although these network nodes cannot match mainframe protocol, they can host a client IBM-compatible PC connected to the mainframe. A single PC, when running suitable MS-DOS or MS Windows software, can capture text screens, select single database records, and obtain entire files. Files then can be distributed by the local network to needy users.

Shareware and public domain software, such as the Clarkson TCP/IP drivers, provide Internet and Unix-to-Unix system copy (UUCP) mail connections for any platform supporting a C-language compiler. Once Internet is supported, the common *remote copy protocol* (RCP) and mail with attached files provide rudimentary interconnectivity for that platform. Internet mail is widely supported and generally available in most cities worldwide through a central mail facility. Stanford University in Stanford, California assigns Internet Class A, B, or C Internet addresses when requested. These addresses provide unique identifications for Internet users, and consequently all TCP/IP and most FDDI users.

Other options are simpler and more commonplace. These options require only a serial or parallel connection. Conflicts over IRQ interrupts or memory addresses are rare since both PC- and MS- DOS, OS/2, Unix, and most network operating systems recognize the serial or parallel ports as vital for printed output. These programs sometimes conflict with mouse-input devices, graphics tablets, and unusual input or output devices. Supporting multiple ports, or conflicts over whether the print spooler, the modem, a null modem, or the printer ports represent the likely conflicts. Just note that A-B switch selector boxes for multiple connections generally defeat communication links; the printers may work, yet the send-receive signals for data transfer are defeated.

A modem with a text capture and file transfer capability provides linkage independent from distance, independent from machine protocol, and independent from platform. A PC can talk to another PC, an engineering workstation, a second-hand minicomputer, and most mainframe RS-232 serial ports. Only the transfer speed is limited to the modem's baud rate, of course, as stated previously. Speed limitations and transmission reliability faults can be partially resolved with X.25 data protocols, MNP modems, CCITT V.32 and V.42bis data compression, and error checking modems. Where nodes on different networks share a common area, a null modem cable (wires 1 and the ground connect, wires 2 and 3 cross over) can link these two computers. A parallel port connection is also supported. File transfer and remote control software easily copy files from one computer to the other. These MS-DOS programs, though simpler than network operating systems, infrequently conflict with configurations and systems drivers. When they do, the solution could require minimizing the CONFIG.SYS or AUTOEXEC.BAT files or rebooting with alternate versions. WinLink was designed to overcome the inherent MS Windows memory problems by relocating itself anywhere in memory. It works within the MS Windows environment.

Expanding an FDDI Network

Although MS-DOS communication software rarely works in the OS/2 compatibility box due to conflicts over multithreading and access to ports, OS/2 and Unix versions are frequently available rewritten specifically for these operating systems. Modem text and file capture programs are also available for these operating systems, as well as for AS/400, VMS, and IBM OS. Some are available from the public domain, thereby providing wide accessibility; examples include Xmodem and Kermit.

In all cases, transfer speed is limited since the parallel or serial channel capacity peaks around 125,000 bits/s. Such solutions are not true gateways, merely narrow conduits for getting bits and bytes across the gulf of incompatible protocols. Serial, parallel, RS-232, and X.25 connections bridge these protocol differences when it is essential to provide something less tedious than media conversions and "sneakernets."

X.25

CCITT X.25 (1988 revision) is public data delivery service that provides packet relay. User information is broken into small packets for transmission, sent individually through the network and perhaps even travel different routes, and reassembled at destination in the original format. Data is delivered through a packet switching network provided by a carrier such as Telenet. X.25 lines generally require dedicated analog lines to the point of presence of the service, generally a central office.

The connection is either the datagram or a virtual circuit (much like a phone conversation). There are also options to dial into an X.25 network via a standard telephone line and modem. X.25 is very effective for connecting equipment of different types, different operating systems, and different applications. The X.25 switching network can dynamically handle high temporary loads by buffering the packets in transit.

Connection establishment times range from 20 seconds to several minutes. X.25 transmission speeds range from 9.6 Kbits/s to 56 Kbits/s. Overhead required to packetized, address, and track delivery of information is substantial. X.25 Furthermore, most implementation require acknowledge of delivery for each packet before the next packet is sent.

As a result, X.25 tends to be slow. The use of leased lines can be expensive. These problems notwithstanding, X.25 can provide a very cost-efficient and effective method to provide WAN connectivity for E-mail, limited file transfers, and remote login access to file servers or hosts. It is simple, effective, and efficient when bandwidth is not an issue. Although it is an old technology, expect the pricing to adjust to the competition from newer technologies, such as frame relay, ISDN, and cell relay.

Frame Relay

Frame relay is public data delivery service whereby packetized data is routed from the source to the destination on a switched network, much like X.25. What this means is that a circuit is not dedicated or established as a point-to-point link. Rather packets are shuttled from point-to-point by whatever circuits are available. Those paths vary over time and from packet to packet. In fact, sequential packets may arrive at the destination by different routes and in a time sequence difference from the source transmission. The difference between X.25 and frame relay is the frame relay format is much simpler and more efficient. The addressing scheme requires less processing and overhead, while the error-checking is not as extensive so as to provide more efficient use of the connection. (Error checking is performed by higher level protocols.) There is also more sophisticated congestion control.

Frame relay transmission speeds range from 56 Kbits/s to 1.536 Mbits/s. Many carriers provide expandable capacity based upon available capacity. In other words, a user can contract for 56 Kbits/s with expansion to 224 Kbits/s. The extra capacity is not guaranteed at all times; it is contingent upon the carrier have the capacity at the instant when it is requested. Frame relay is as much a paper tiger as a real product. It garners more press information because it is an emerging technology than it may warrant. Perhaps only 1000 companies in the United States used this technology in 1992. Primary, great disparities in pricing, reliability, and availability in the target locations discourages many users from installing it. Nonetheless, it does provide useful digital communications for some needs.

ATM Cell Relay

Asynchronous transmission mode (ATM) transmits streams of 53 byte packets through a PBX-like switching system at speeds greater than 150 Mbits/s. The paths for each packet may vary, but arrival is guaranteed. This is a copper-based protocol using equipment with much in common to a central telephone switch. Not only will this protocol provide data communications and LAN-to-LAN connectivity, it will also integrate voice, full-motion video, and other data that can be packetized. The technology is expected to be prohibitively expensive when initially offered during the next two years. However, costs should drop with competition and competition fromthe other high-speed WAN options. Cell relay is public data delivery service whereby packetized data is routed from the source to the destination on a switched network, much like frame relay. Unlike frame relay which is based upon existing T-1 and DS3 technology, cell relay is more like X.25 packet switching networks.

Cell relay transmission speeds range from 155 Kbits/s on STP twisted-pair to 6.144 Mbits/s. As of yet, ATM is much like frame relay, a much

Expanding an FDDI Network

ballyhooed service with many vendors promising products and few takers. It is quite expensive where it is locally available. Nonetheless, like frame relay, it does provide useful digital communications for high-end LAN-to-LAN communication.

ISDN

Integrated Services Digital Network (ISDN) has been a product in search of vendors and a use for 10 years. IBM pushed this standard for years as the present and future WAN architecture. Primary it has become a product with the availability of digital lines as analog lines have been replaced by fiber and carrier-based digital switches (mostly Northern Telecomm). ISDN is two unidirectional 64 Kbits/s bearer (B) channels and a 16 Kbits/s controlling line (D channel). It is sometimes referred to as the basis rate interface (BRI). In other words, one line goes one way, the other line goes the other way, and the third, small line tells the computers what each line does. ISDN communication is a point-to-point connection, much like a standard telephone call. Unlike modem-initiated telephone calls, it may take as little as 1/10 s to establish a connection. ISDN is cheap where available—in some cases less costly than three comparable analog lines—and because it is asynchronous in two directions simultaneously, provides robust service. It is very effective for E-mail, low load WAN connections, and intermittent service. As Chapter 1 described, Sun Microsystems relies on ISDN services in California for connecting corporate and manufacturing sites. They also provide an ISDN adapter. It is comparable in price to FDDI NIC adapters.

VSAT

Satellite networks utilizing *very-small-aperture terminal* transmission (VSAT) connect host mainframes and LANs into an enterprise-wide network. This is a practical and effective technology to link multiple sites (more than 100) across long distances, or for a small number of sites when a local carrier can provide an inexpensive "piggyback" service on its existing network. While it is about the same cost as a comparable dedicated T-1 10-mi phone link, it is also a third of the price of a 1000-mi phone link. The cost of a satellite link is independent of distance, unlike a phone line. (Note that phone costs are becoming less price sensitive to distance because the public carriers also utilize VSAT.) Initial costs for the ground hub, antennas, and remote stations can run $1 million, but with a lease operating costs can average $500 per month. Also, a satellite user might provide incentives for others to piggyback on that preexisting capacity. This is available in most major metropolitan areas. Additionally, VSAT provides about 10 times the bandwidth (hence 10 times the data throughput) as a T-1 line, with increased reliability.

A ground-based hub transmits either a *time-division multiplexing access* (TDMA) or *frequency-division multiplexing access* (FDMA) radio-frequency signal to a satellite in geosynchronous orbit around the earth. FDMA combines and splits the channel into multiple TDMA channels for data, voice, and video conferences. The C-band uplink frequency (to the satellite) is around 4 GHz, while the downlink (from the satellite) is around 6 GHz. These bandwidths are shared with terrestrial microwave systems. Signal interference is a serious problem. Alternately, the Ku-band uplink frequency (to the satellite) is around 14 GHz, while the downlink (from the satellite) is around 16 GHz. This bandwidth is allocated *only* for satellite transmissions. For both bands, though, VSAT in the neighborhood can cause a conflict. In either case, the FCC regulates both bands and limits antenna size, performance, transmission characteristics, and satellite separation. The satellite repeats the signal to star-configured, remote earth stations, or to mesh configured stations. A *mesh* design allows peer-to-peer access without communicating to the central hub on the star configuration and is appropriate when all sites regularly talk to each other. The hub controls the protocol, network management, and channel rerouting.

A risk when relying upon a satellite link is that the satellite could fail. Quick repair or replacement is unlikely, although simple circuit failures are solved by shifting the failed channel to other spare circuits. There is a good deal of spare capacity because there are alternatives for satellite channels and there are many competing organizations with satellite communication capacity. For critical links, research how the satellite channel vendor handles downtime. Consider installing land-based fiber or traditional T-1 connections with spanning-tree bridges to automatically reroute transmission in case the main link fails.

SMDS

Wide area linkages are generally slow or expensive. T-1, T-3, PBX, PDN, and VSAT fall within those two categories. *Switched Multimegabit Data Services* (SMDS) is a high-speed digital link that provides shared service to cheaply connect remote sites. AT&T is beginning to introduce this service, as are other vendors. The key problem for this LAN to WAN to LAN connectivity is that the protocol is split for multiple users and shared uses. As such, there are interface inconsistencies and vendor inconsistencies. In other words, while sites can be connected physically with this service, the data must be framed with a recognizable format for translation or encapsulation.

The current protocol is called *SMDS interface protocol (SIP)* and it is a mix of OSI levels 1, 2, and 3. SMDS provides concurrent T-1 (1.544 Mbits/s)

Expanding an FDDI Network

and T-3 (50 Mbits/s). The physical protocol is either *High Speed Serial Interface* (HSSI), HDLC encapsulation, V.35, or RS-449. Because the interfaces and communication protocols can coexist, transmission of critical data can be prioritized, something seriously lacking within FDDI.

FDDI-II

FDDI-II is an upward-compatible (and perhaps backward-compatible) enhancement for FDDI. This is best grasped as a bandwidth allocation mechanism. While prearranged synchronous transmission expects a channel within two standard revolutions of the token, FDDI-II allocates bandwidth based upon the cycle clock, typically set at a 125 Mhz frequency. Subdivision of the delivery channel is the primary benefit of this refinement. T-1, video, voice, images, and network traffic can coexist. While connection to FDDI is available, the FDDI frame is transported as a "payload" without full FDDI station-to-FDDI station interoperability. Additionally, FDDI-II, like SMDS, will support priority transmissions with isochronous (nonpacketized) data for simultaneous data and full-motion video transmission, and prioritized transmission of critical data.

FDDI and FDDI-II are not the only optical fiber standards. *Synchronous optical network* (SONET) is a standard designed by the long-distance carrier community (for example, AT&T, MCI, and Sprint) and uses the previously mentioned TDMA protocol. SONET conforms to the IEEE 802.6 metropolitan area network (MAN) specification and provides bandwidths from 50 Mbits/s up to 18 billion bits per second when multiplexed. Furthermore, SONET is designed to be a "survivable" network by mixed bandwidths and channels. Selecting SONET may be relevant when planning enterprise-wide networks since the optical fiber LAN and VSAT connection should be compatible. Bridging is possible, but the address and packet must be encapsulated for the "payload," as a VSAT packet is termed.

Wireless Networks

Wireless Ethernet, FDDI, and Token-Ring minimizes the need for wiring. A wireless network does not require twisted-pair hubs and the wire, or patch panels. Bandwidth ranging from 19.2 Kbits/s to less than 3 Mbits/s is far less than FDDI; it is also less than what is normally seen even on Ethernet and Token-Ring. This option, albeit slow, is included here because speed of transmission is not always the key issue for network expansion. Sometimes speed and simplicity of installation or network access when rewiring is impossible or politically impossible represent more difficult management problems. As such, wireless is an effective expansion media. Wireless may provide an effective method to attach notebook and portable computers to the network. A technician repairing a ship or plane, for example, would find the lack of a tether highly desirable. Also, physical inventories on site in warehouses could be simplified with wireless connectivity.

Sudden growth in users or a requirement for a special task force suggests this type of solution. One of the big benefits of this technology is that the wireless hardware can be literally taken along when groups and their equipment are moved. The cabling portion for traditional networks is usually abandoned in the ceiling when the network is moved since it is expensive to retrieve and unwise to recycle UTP or even more durable STP. That part of the network investment is eliminated with wireless networks. As stated previously in this book, computer shows are good places for these networks, assuming that others are not using the same frequencies.

A wireless network is not totally wireless, however, in that it does require a connection from the transmitter-receiver units to be physically wired into the each workstation node. Some NIC cards provide external antennas that protrude from the PC card. Infrared networks work on the principle of modulating a light beam. The transmitting and receiving units must be in line of sight. Although the light beam diverges and brightness decays over distance, alignment is not critical but distance is. The BICC InfraLAN networking system is one example of a modular Token-Ring wireless network. This system is effective in areas under 800 square feet, a coverage similar to the NCR WaveLANNCR and Motorola Altair products. Note that coverage is not only for extending network services on a small site; vendors, including NCR, are also producing a directional antenna for bridging distances up to five miles and Cylink provides a point-to-point wireless SST modem with data rates to 256 Kbits/s with a range to 30 miles.

The distance limitation is not only a function of signal strength and antenna efficiency, it also derives from the slower transmission speeds of RF or infrared networks. Ethernet and Token-Ring wireless networks typically accommodate between 1 Mbits/s and 2 Mbits/s transmission speeds. Protocol specifications are based upon maximum signal transit times and not necessarily distance per se. Slower bit transmission speeds (not signal transmission speed) therefore shorten the overall length of a wireless network segment. InfraLAN Technologies, Inc. intends to market Ethernet and FDDI versions of the BICC InfraLAN product.

Radio-frequency units are best installed as high above people as possible. Until the evidence on health risks is finalized, assuming extra precautions is humane and legally advisable. Also these units should be installed with as few obstructions as possible. Although RF does penetrate objects, the effort does weaken and distort the signal. Note that

Expanding an FDDI Network

users may require FCC licenses to install RF units since they do broadcast within the bandwidth, power levels, and extended periods of time specified for jurisdiction by the FCC. Vendors usually complete the licenses and submit them for each installed site as part of the sales process. Many vendors also have joined the IEEE plenary committee to generate a standard. This active IEEE committee, designated 802.11, is seeking to codify transmission for data and real-time voice using isochronous RF signals.

Wireless networks are infrequently installed at new network sites. Without actual installation experience, most managers reject the extra hardware expense and rue the slower transmission throughputs. Since most wireless networks are installed at sites with existing network investments, interconnection of wireless with the hard-wired networks requires a bridging mechanism. Typically, a wireless server would have a secondary wireless controller and a primary standard NIC. This represents a routing configuration. Since configuration of home-made routers and gateways tends to be complex and unreliable, vendors like NCR Corporation and Persoft, Inc. provide specialized concentrators.

Another technology is under development for network inclusion of mobile stations. Cellular digital packet data (CDPD) provides packet-switched transmission at speeds up to 19.2 bits/s on existing cellular phone networks. RAM Mobile Data and Ardis are also building a packet radio network for wide area data transmissions with transmission speeds up to 9.6 bits/s. Meanwhile, Motorola is planning to install 66 low earth-orbit satellites for worldwide wireless coverage in the Dick Tracy wrist radio concept.

A very serious limitation to RF networks is that they can be tapped, jammed, or transmission altered unless encoded or multiple frequencies are applied. Wireless RF shares the same frequencies as garage door openers, cordless phones, and baby monitors. Although the 1986 Electronics Communications Privacy Act makes it illegal to intercept or jam wireless signals, this security can be breached with almost legal impunity. This is a ripe opportunity for industrial spying. If your organization services privileged information, recognize this limitation. Ordinary frequency scanners can listen to wireless broadcasts. Although it is difficult to decipher these signals, an astute spy can establish a wireless receiver and funnel the signal into a protocol analyzer. If your organization provides financial transaction processing, there may be SEC rules governing the security and integrity of data.

Another serious limitation to wireless networks is that they rarely support SNMP, CMIP, or CMOT network management protocols. Vendors providing low throughput transmission networks hardly want to further impede that performance with the overheads associated with management protocols. If customers are unhappy that some FDDI devices are not managed while most other devices are, vendors in time will update the software and hardware with the required agents. Note, however, that tuning performance on partially managed wired and wireless networks may represent an herculean task. Proceed cautiously before committing to mixed networks.

Sideband and Multifrequency Wireless

Most wireless units broadcast on a single wavelength. This is called *narrow-channel transmission,* and it provides the possibility for multiple networks to coexist with different channel frequencies within the same envelope. However, many vendors have discovered that there may be clashes over the channel. Instead, there is a technology called *spread-spectrum technology* (SST) which is applied to increase reliability, boost transmission speeds, lower power requirements, and bypass the need for a user license. No FCC license is required because the signal strength on any channel is below regulation limits.

SST broadcasts multiple copies of the data signal over a broad frequency range. In fact, NCR's WaveLAN broadcasts uses spread spec-

Figure 10.13 The simple ring structure.

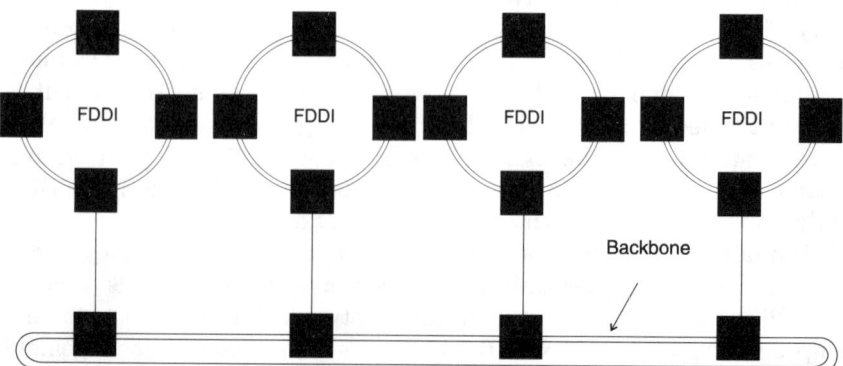

Figure 10.14 A ring structure expanded with bridged backbone.

Expanding an FDDI Network

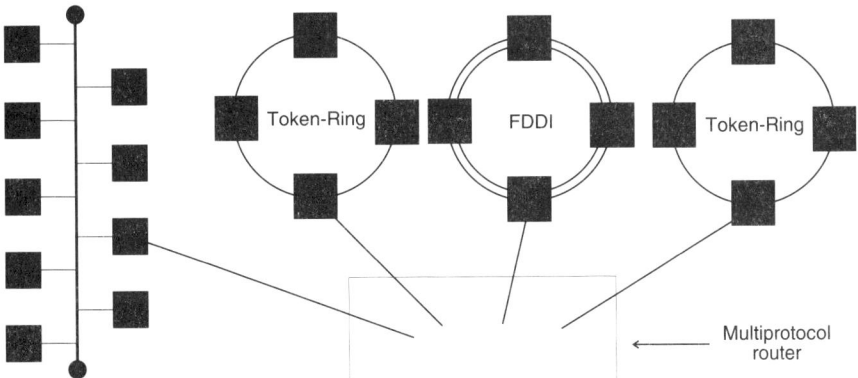

Figure 10.15 The ring structure with multiprotocol routers.

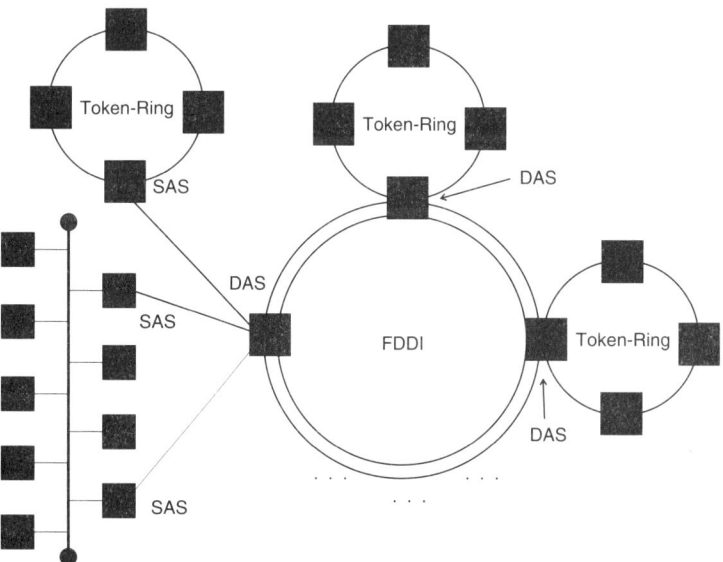

Figure 10.16 A multidimensional enterprise-wide network.

trum. This technology has been around since the 1940s in military applications to minimize enemy jamming, eavesdropping, or even interference from natural sources. It may be appropriate for secure networks.

Another cellular technology, called *code-division multiple access* (CDMA), is an SST broadcast for transmission of multiple channels at the same time. This is even more secure than a single channel and less susceptible to deliberate jamming or environmental noise. Operations where remote data entry, point-of-sales (POS) inventory activities, or shipping and receiving are required might benefit with hand-held network-connected nodes. This is an available technology for hand scanning and similar activities. There are some concerns that the nonlicensing of SST may cause crowding of the airwaves, a low limit to the number of user services within a cell area, and network performance degradation with increasingly heavy traffic.

Extended FDDI Network Configurations

Figure 10.13 shows the simple ring structure. Figure 10.14 expands this design with the inclusion of multiple rings to provide clusters which isolate traffic for workgroups. Figure 10.15 contrasts those simple networks with a network expanded by multiprotocol routers.

Figure 10.16 presents a configuration that might provide service to an entire building, with a backplane FDDI segment serving as the connecting link between all ring subnets. This last illustration suggests the communications power inherent within the FDDI network.

Multiple channels provide an easily implemented method of expansion for overloaded networks. A segregated network also isolates the effects and interruptions inherent in a network. Furthermore, subnetworks ease accountability, while providing a measure of increased data security. Few alternatives exist to subnets; the most readily available is, of course, broadband cabling. Optical fiber provides the most security.

The listings in Figure 10.17 summarize the differences among the alternative devices, and suggests their uses. Now that the details for FDDI process, installation, and network expansion methodologies have been explained, the next chapters apply this information to practical day-to-day management.

Expanding an FDDI Network

Twisted-Pair Networking
Advantages:
Is less expensive than optical fiber
Is easier to install than optical fiber
Makes node relocation simple
Disadvantages:
Serves a smaller geographic area
Has less tolerance to crosstalk and interference
Makes fault isolation more difficult
Is not as secure as optical fiber

STP Networking
Advantages:
Has better tolerance to crosstalk and interference than UTP
Is more durable and reliable than UTP
Disadvantages:
Is harder to install than with UTP
Is more expensive than UTP

UTP Networking
Advantages:
Is cheaper than STP
Is easier to install than STP
May be able to use preexisting phone wiring
Disadvantages:
Is less reliable than STP
Is harder to maintain and debug
Is sensitive to interference and may itself cause interference

Networking with FDDI Trunk Backbones
Advantages:
Provide better performance than cascades
Provide simple expansion possibilities
Provide the means to segment failed networks
Are easier to troubleshoot
Disadvantages:
Are hard to trace and blueprint
Are costly
Do not necessary provide the desired bandwidth

Wireless Networking
Advantages:
Is simple to install
Makes node relocation simple
Disadvantages:
Is expensive
Has a realistically limited distance
May provide slower transmission speeds
May have health consequences
Is susceptible to eavesdropping
Has poor tolerance to interference

Figure 10.17 Comparison between network expansion devices.

FDDI (optical fiber) Networking
Advantages:
Has exceptional tolerance to crosstalk
Has exceptional tolerance to interference
Is durable
Is light
Is reliable
Provides security from eavesdropping
Disadvantages:
Is harder to install
Is more expensive than other media
Is an immature technology

TP-DDI Networking
Advantages:
Provides 2 to 3 times the throughout of FDDI
Can run on existing STP Token-Ring wiring
Is reliable
Disadvantages:
Is harder to install
Is an immature technology

Hub Networking
Advantages:
Provide high-density service
Are easily installed
Do not require AC power
Can increase the size of a network
Are transparent to network devices
Disadvantages:
Extend hub to node lengths beyond limitations
Does not always offer good fault isolation
Increases the complexity of network management
Do not offer distributed management capabilities
Requires AC power at the hub

Modems, PBXs, and PDNs(RS-232, V.32, X.25, etc) for Internetworking
Advantages:
Are easily installed
Can provide LAN to WAN connections
Support several common protocols
Provide interconnectivity
Provide interoperability
Can support error checking and correction
Disadvantages:
Are slow
Are prone to signal interference
Do not provide security from eavesdropping

Figure 10.17 Comparison between network expansion devices. (*continued*)

Expanding an FDDI Network

Frame Relay for Internetworking
Advantages:
Is faster than X.25
Can provide LAN to WAN connections
Supports several common protocols
Disadvantages:
Is slow; reserve bandwidth is unreliable
Does not have frame error checking
Protocol interfaces are not standardized
Provides delayed transmissions
Does not provide security from eavesdropping
Not available in all areas

SMDS for Internetworking
Advantages:
Has adjustable bandwidth
Can provide FDDI WAN connections
Has good tolerance to interference
Supports priority transmission
Supports several common protocols
Disadvantages:
Media interfaces are not standardized
Protocol interfaces are not standardized
Provide delayed transmissions
Does not provide security from eavesdropping
Not available in all areas

VSAT Internetworking
Advantages:
Is distance independent
Has good tolerance to interference
Is durable
Is rarely affected by disasters
Is reliable
Disadvantages:
Networks are harder to install
Provide delayed transmissions
Is expensive
Is difficult to internetwork with FDDI
Does not provide security from eavesdropping

Figure 10.17 Comparison between network expansion devices. (*continued*)

Intelligent Hubs for Internetworking
   Advantages:
   Can integrate incompatible media
   Can integrate incompatible protocols
   Provide high density service
   Provide localized management
   Can increase the size of a network
   Might provide protocol translation
   Might provide fault-tolerant networking
   Disadvantages:
   Are complex to manage
   Increase the complexity of network management
   Do not offer good localized fault isolation
   Increase the chances for complete centralized network failure
   Requires AC power

Repeaters for Internetworking
   Advantages:
   Are simple to install
   Require no configuration
   Are transparent to network devices
   Can increase the size of a network
   Disadvantages:
   Do not provide significant fault isolation
   Do not offer distributed management capabilities
   Might constrain performance of the entire internetwork
   Increase the complexity of network management
   Make networks more difficult to troubleshoot

Bridges for Internetworking
   Advantages:
   Are simple to install
   Require no configuration
   Are transparent to network devices
   Adapt automatically to the environment
   Can connect networks running different high-level protocols
   Are flexible and adaptable
   Connect networks of any speed
   Can provide network management functionality
   Disadvantages:
   Cannot take advantage of multiple paths to a network
   Can constrain the topology of the internetwork
   Create transmission delays
   Can limit the size of a bridge-based internetwork
   Do not provide significant fault isolation
   Do not offer distributed management capabilities
   Might disable software applications
   Might constrain performance of the entire internetwork
   Increase the complexity of network management
   Make networks more difficult to troubleshoot
   Requires AC power

Figure 10.17 Comparison between network expansion devices. (*continued*)

Expanding an FDDI Network

Routers for Internetworking
Advantages:
Are configurable
Can be fine-tuned to improve internetwork performance
Are simpler if they automatically update routing tables
Provide security protection
Are easier to maintain than bridge-based equivalents
Provide protection between segments
Are not susceptible to the time delay constraints
Do not limit network topology
Permit more complex networks
Permit active loops
Offer distributed management capabilities
Disadvantages:
Require a considerable configuration
Are more difficult than bridges to install
Are protocol-independent
Cannot route low-level protocols
Are complex
Cannot interconnect different high-level protocols
Are more expensive than bridges
Create transmission delays
Might disable software applications
May limit performance of the entire internetwork
Increase the complexity of network management
Make networks more difficult to troubleshoot
Requires AC power

Brouters for Internetworking
Advantages:
Offer all the advantages of bridges and routers
Provide flexibility of bridging, routing, or both concurrently
Disadvantages:
Offer all the disadvantages of bridges and routers
Are more complex to install and maintain

Figure 10.17 Comparison between network expansion device. (*continued*)

Gateways for Internetworking
Advantages:
Are configurable
Can be fine-tuned to improve internetwork performance
Provide security protection
Provide protection between segments
Do not limit network topology
Permit more complex networks
Can connect networks running different high-level protocols
Can route low-level protocols
Permit active loops
Offer distributed management capabilities
Disadvantages:
Require considerable configuration
Are difficult to install
Create transmission delays
Are susceptible to the time-delay constraints
Are protocol-independent
Are complex
Are more expensive than bridges
Might disable software applications
Might constrain performance of the entire internetwork
Increase the complexity of network management
Make networks more difficult to troubleshoot
Requires AC power and extensive management support

Figure 10.17 Comparison between network expansion device. (*continued*)

Chapter

11

FDDI for Enterprise-Wide Networks

The complexity of enterprise-wide networks, interoperating applications, and network management overshadows the relative triviality of physically connecting the components into a larger whole. Often disparate local area networks, grown through hodgepodge efforts, appear as a serious organization constraint. The common vision that construction of an enterprise-wide network will reduce the chaos is mistaken unless firm controls and directed network management are provided. Comprehensive networking management is crucial for success of expanded networks.

The issues of enterprise-wide networks often encompass downsizing host mainframes; substituting PC- and network-based client/server processing; supporting distributed processing, interconnectivity, and interoperability; and performing information and network management. In fact, enterprise-wide networks frequently underlie any efforts to downsize data processing (DP) operations, create enterprise-wide E-mail and network facsimile (FAX) services, and build mission-critical networks. This chapter addresses such topics while the final section lists the components essential to forge enterprise-wide networks. For a review of the strategic issues relating to corporate-wide networks, refer to Chapter 1.

Network Communication Growth

The interconnection of many networks into a single entity has become a critical issue for many organizations. Networks of networks and the replacement of host mainframes with local area networks have warranted the construction of large networks. Connectivity for multiple platform product development, software application porting (rebuilding and optimizing software built for one operating system for usage within another), *executive information systems* (EIS), optical storage and retrieval systems, organization-wide electronic mail and computerized facsimile services, and operational consolidation (including personnel reduction) drive this strategy. Extended networks sustain transactions in the event of an emergency when primary sites have failed. There is

Software and Hardware

also a visible shift for responsibility and control of information more in line with the usage and source of that information—to the end user. Such a transition is very prevalent with peer-to-peer networks including LANtastic and Windows for Workgroups. While such inherently insecure and unmanaged technologies confound professional DP, MIS, and networking management groups, this impetus drives the installation of enterprise-wide networks.

The realization that information is one of the strategic assets has increased the demand that these networks function together. This appetite for global access to corporate information and the desire to prevent corporate information from fragmenting into small, useless pieces has propelled the enterprise-wide network into the forefront of local area networking. Large organizations cannot thrive with LANs as islands, isolated and unreachable.

The concepts and the jargon of enterprise-wide networks mask the complexity and confuse the underlying issues. Many consider an enterprise-wide network to be nothing more than terminals and modems linking a mainframe for data access; this is a misuse of that term for what is really a collection of host connections, or even possibly a wide area network (WAN). While is is possible to debate that definition, it misses the issue that enterprise-wide networking remains a complex and confusing current topic.

For the purposes of this book, an *enterprise-wide network* is a network that interconnects LANs at multiple sites and could provide, *in addition*, other types of communication services throughout the distributed sites of the organization. It could also include the live interconnection of customers and suppliers into the corporate network. This type of facility is also termed a *premises network* or simply an *enterprise network*. Figure 11.1 illustrates the possibilities for an enterprise-wide network.

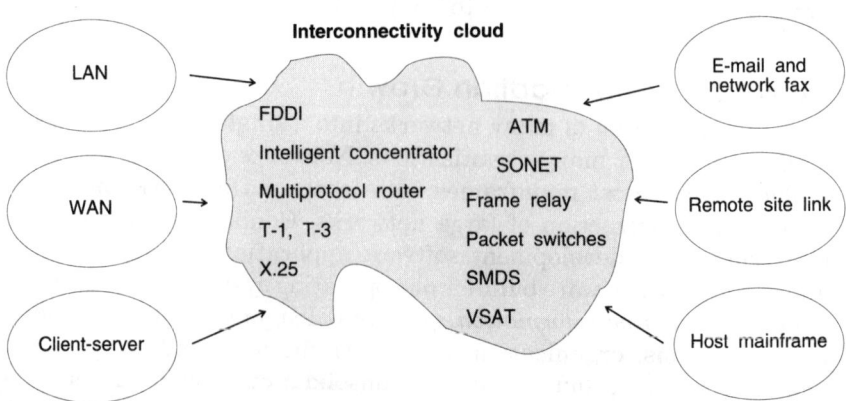

Figure 11.1 The enterprise-wide network.

FDDI for Enterprise-Wide Networks

Enterprise-wide networks frequently must interconnect and interoperate. *Interconnectivity* embodies the physical attachment of local area networks, devices, and processes that are not necessarily peers, not necessarily compatible, and do not necessarily conform to the same standards or methods of functionality. *Interoperability* means that despite the physical, logical, or functional differences, networks, devices, and processes can share network services, data, and processing power. Interconnection remains relatively easy to obtain with bridging hardware. OSI bridges, simple modems, and long-haul transmission techniques provide physical network interconnection. Interoperability, however, is more elusive. Terminal emulation software, screen capture routines, data conversion programs, and shared media (as in a "sneakernet") facilitate the logical sharing of network resources. When networks, devices, or processes are homogeneous peers (in that they use the same protocols), interoperability is immediately available through bridging. While network management, resource access (through passwords, establishment of user password accounts, or share rights), and security are valid concerns, operability is straightforward. Networks frequently incorporate heterogeneous protocols such as those listed in Figure 11.2 and maintain data and software code in incompatible formats.

Typically, on an FDDI network where the FDDI provides enterprise-wide backbone, protocols will include NetBIOS, NetBEUI, UDP, IP, and Appletalk with network connectivity software including NetWare, Sun NFS, FTP TCP/IP, Macintosh Appletalk, LAN Server and LAN Manager. With heterogeneous protocols, data formats, and incompatible software code, interoperability necessitates complex gateways and translation software so that multiple processes can share data. This may well entail different databases which can read the storage formats, or require complex custom software which controls and commands different softwares to process parts of a solution.

Connection	Protocol or Communication Technology				
Host	SNA	IDSN	HLLAPI	APPC	CPIC
LAN	Token-Ring	Ethernet	FDDI	Zero-slot	ARCNET
	NFS	TCP/IP	UDP		
Network Operating Systems (NOS)	LAN Server	LAN Manager	Novell NetWare	Banyan	U-B Access1
	LANTastic	XNS	OSI	OS/2 LAN	
Interop Solutions	OSI	HLLAPI	TCP/IP	NDIS	ODLI
	IPX/SPX	Serial	Parallel	Etherlink	RS-232

Figure 11.2 Typical organizational networking protocols and software.

For example, a mainframe database should be readable and possibly changeable from a networked PC or workstation. In fact, mainframe databases can be converted to client/server operation, or even the mainframe data storage farms can be connected directly to networks servers. IRMA links over Token-Ring, Ethernet, and FDDI are effective for providing a simple terminal emulation from a PC, or from within a GUI window. Within an advanced environment, the mainframe database should be completely available for processing on a PC; in actuality, database products, including Oracle, Progress, Sybase, and Ingres, do provide data file portability. These and other tools, such as Gupta and Powerbuilder, function within certain heterogeneous network constructions by specific design only.

Interoperability does convey the notion that software application code will be portable across platforms and networks as well. In other words, code written for one platform should work on others across any number of bridges, routers, and gateways. Additionally, interoperability implies that data distributed across multiple platforms, formats, and processes can be globally manipulated. Interoperability has been termed *code portability, portable applications, code migration, transportability, platform transparency, open systems,* or *architecture-neutral distributed format* (ANDF) by the Open Systems Foundation (OSF). Unix and most high-level computer languages have thrived because of this interoperability vision, albeit more promise than premise. Each revision and upgrade of Novell NetWare includes a connection for a new operating system as a client: Windows for Workgroups, DOS, OS/2, Macintosh, Unix, RISC, to name but a few. Interoperability also represents the solution for a serious training problem.

The enterprise-wide network can include and embody other features as well. It can include distributed processing with a host computer servicing end-user computers. It can incorporate networked computing where idled devices are accessed for their capacity either to speed completion of a process or to add sufficient parallel computing capacity to solve the problem. It can also include downsizing host mainframes—replacing them with desktop machines—and the addition of global network management controls.

The enterprise-wide network concept is such a new threshold that the literature includes minted terminology and concepts to define the technology and add precision where little exists. For example, *cooperative processing*[1] and network computing concepts recognize the increasing distribution of locations where the user physically interacts with the computer, where the processing power is supplied, where files reside,

---

[1] John Gantz, "Cooperative Processing and the Enterprise Network," January 1991, a *Networking Management* White Paper.

where data resides, where output devices reside. This concept can be presented as a sharing of networked resources. Trends for sharing resources across a network show a clear need for faster networks, more complicated network management tools, and correspondingly more experienced network managers. This network is no simple LAN; it is an extended topology of interconnected and interoperating LANs forming the enterprise-wide network.

Enterprise-Wide Potential

Enterprise-wide networks are an outgrowth of many separate LAN installations. The application of extended networks also reveals the need to communicate between dispersed and multiple sites with some immediacy and with a complexity exceeding that of wide area networking. Enterprise-wide networks represent a means to prosper by cutting DP costs through downsized operations or to provide a competitive advantage achieved with rapid and comprehensive information access and connectivity. Be wary when presenting cost-savings as the primary benefit. If it is the only benefit, the organization is building a mentality of mere survival rather than seeking excellence and better results. Organizations link distributed sites together for the basic reasons listed in Figure 11.3.

Enterprise-wide networks are not merely data communication pathways. They may also transport voice and continuous motion video, too. The

- Downsizing opportunities
- DP operational consolidation
- Better control and management of subsidiaries
- Distributed client-server computing
- Mission-critical computing
- Consolidation of information management
- Preventing fragmentation of organizational information
- Integration of voice, data, and image carrier services
- Interconnectivity for LANs
- Electronic mail (E-mail) and network facsimile (FAX)
- Remote procedure calls (RPC)
- Remote processing
- Remote file transfer
- Terminal services and remote terminal emulation
- Source code control
- Online document (image) storage and retrieval
- Object-oriented tools
- Work-group computing
- Name services
- Executive information systems (EIS)
- Strategic vision

Figure 11.3 Reasons for enterprise-wide networks.

disparate technologies of information are converging together. Indeed, most networks can transport data, image, video, and voice using the same mechanisms; it is only necessary to packetize the information representation within a transmission protocol. Data processing, communications, networking, and information management are slowly becoming consolidated into a new concept. This centralization is reflected in the management and authority of these functions. The enterprise-wide network is a new rubric to bind functions together, as Figure 11.4 denotes.

Downsizing to LANs

The technology and the cost-benefit ratio of host mainframe-based computing have been superseded by microprocessors, client/server environments, and network-based computers. The data processing economics favor downsizing and networking for all but the most specialized applications. Various research reports conclude that organizations save 40 to 60 percent with microcomputer and LAN-based applications over the cost of mainframe-based operations. This cost savings derives from the fierce margin competition in PC hardware and software and the open systems available on engineering workstations and desktop microcomputers. Nearly every computer manufacturer has developed a line of desktop computers and these prices are pressured by clone makers. It also accrues from the quicker software development times typical of PC or Unix environments. Debuggers, graphical user interface (GUI) tools, interactive third generation language (3GL) and fourth generation language (4GL) databases, spreadsheets, screen painters, and code generators halve development, maintenance, and upgrade time. Most of the ancillary "savings" above 40 percent are amassed from pushing as much of the cost as possible to the end users. This shifts budgets and manpower from centralized DP departments to operational groups.

- Data communication
- Voice communication
- Facsimile (simple and broadcast) transmission
- Multimedia
- Telecommunications
- Office automation
- Production automation
- Data processing
- Image processing
- Motion video
- Video conferencing
- Information storage and retrieval
- Command and control
- LAN and WAN management

Figure 11.4 Enterprise-wide information management.

FDDI for Enterprise-Wide Networks 237

Literally, the cost basis favors networks of client/server processing over mainframe applications for all but very specialized or very entrenched data processing activities. While microcomputers have matched the raw processing speed of mainframes for years, accessibility, interconnectivity, and interoperability have limited most organizations from downsizing DP operations. While downsizing is an extraordinary difficult undertaking— one full of risks and problems—the risk of not considering and trying downsizing is that competitors will try it, and will succeed. Even entrenched DP activities should be reviewed for potential and significant changes. Such consideration is particularly relevant to organizations creating computer applications; they should worry that more cost-efficient competitors will erode their markets.

Microprocessors assembled as minicomputers represent direct and immediate replacements for mainframes. Digital Equipment Corporation (DEC) MiniVAXes and MicroVAXes replace the VAX mainframes. Midrange IBM AS/400 series machines replace 30XX mainframes. Microcomputer-based "superservers" and disk-based high-performance subsystems challenge the outdated notion that thousand transaction-per-second mission-critical applications are the domain of $3 million mainframes. Although the central processing unit (CPU) box may change, tape, disk, and other peripheral devices may not. Computer room requirements or space needs rarely shrink; cost savings are within reach because expansion can be planned to utilize a more cost-effective technology. When there is need to expand existing entrenched mainframe services, substitutions with downsized platforms provide significant cost savings. However, the real benefit in downsizing occurs when mainframe environments are replaced with client/server networks, microcomputers, and the superservers. Ethernet and Token-Ring are the major client/server networks, with Ethernet leading, given its interconnectivity and interoperability components, as well as its large entrenched base. However, the corporate culture embodied by IBM and long-ingrained buying habits provide an enormous market share for Token-Ring.

When organizations must link many departments over medium distances, neither of these protocols can provide the necessary service. While FOIRL links can provide 2 km point-to-point connections between two single points, this technology does not really provide a true MAN interconnection. FDDI, of course, does. If ISDN and frame relay, or T-1 is available in the area, these services can provide a good means of connection. Some of these services are available on demand only with bandwidth from 56 kbits/s to 1.536 Mbits/s. When bandwidth must be managed and the cost for wiring many sites for these common carrier services is factored in, FDDI may present a better choice.

With the advent of faster microcomputer bus structures such as *extended industry standard architecture* (EISA) and *microchannel architecture*

(MCA), personal computers have overcome a significant bottleneck. EISA provides 32-bit pathways whereas the *industry standard architecture* (ISA) found on most IBM AT-compatible PCs supports a more limited 16-bit channel. Wider pathways for data transfer and data communications mean that personal computers performing as file servers can match the storage performance of the mainframe for a fraction of the cost. Superservers and "disk farms," a concentration of storage disks, address the data storage, input/output, and data bus bottlenecks inherent even in the MCA or EISA architecture. This has created a distinct and viable opportunity for many organizations to rethink their data processing policies. This does not mean that the mainframe is dead, altogether replaceable by PCs. Mainframes too are getting more powerful and faster with emphasis toward specialized processing. This trend for installing PCs in place of mainframes only points to restructuring and a new emphasis toward end-user and ad hoc activities.

Bottlenecks and extraordinary expenses required to build the new mainframe applications—those perceived as providing a strategic advantage for an organization—have compelled many within the organization to try new approaches in desperation. Users of information want control and responsibility for it; they do not want it held by a technical department divorced from their needs. Personal computers with electronic spreadsheets, fully functional databases, and ingenious and effective user interfaces have seemed a simple and possible alternative. Indeed, this technology has thrived not merely because of the wide distribution and lower entry costs. The organization-wide distribution of identical tools enhances productivity and the value of any computer work. Better tools speed development. Implementation times for critical but simple projects are hours or days instead of months or years. Intermediate concepts can be tested as a spreadsheet or a database. Later, they can be fully programmed, data entry and validation routines can be overlaid, and the implementation can be extended for multiple users. Intermediate results (rarely seen in mainframe applications) encourage management and bolster this shift to microcomputer solutions.

The actual differentiation among the computing power of PCs, client/server workstations, and mainframes is not really at issue. The proposition is shaped more by perception than any true differentiation. This mentality is driven by MIS managers, computer organizations, and vendors. While most platforms, in addition to host mainframes, can support extensive disk farms with gigabytes of storage, implementation risks and the perceptual "ideal" architecture are encouraging the notion that mainframes are best as the host repositories for corporate data; network channels merely convey it to the workhorse PC platforms.

In part, this notion is driven by an outdated mentality and the inertia of elaborate organizations supporting mainframe activities. In part, it is also driven by the reality that time-sharing mainframes provide exceptional security, stability, reliability, and honed backup procedures whereas networks in practical observance do not. Most organizations *do* have insecure ad hoc networks lacking disciplined password policies and off-site file backup procedures. While not universally true, it usually is. Perhaps, this differentiation is best until the majority of organizations attract and promote communication managers, network managers, and information specialists to the same executive levels as that attained by mainstream MIS managers. Then, downsizing will not represent such a technical and collective risk to an organization.

One important point is that downsizing should not be undertaken merely to upgrade technology. Consider the disparagement one might make to defeat the proposal for replacement of terminals with networked PCs: "You are going to spend thousands of dollars per person to make an intelligent microcomputer into a dumb terminal?" *High-level language application program interface* (HLLAPI) is only a front-end mask to give a PC terminal connectivity to a host mainframe; it may not be cost-effective to replace or expand an installed base. A fundamental benefit must drive the shift from host mainframe DP operations to a distributed network environment. For example, PC-based data entry and data retrieval may benefit from reduced transaction processing times; when data filtering and verification can occur locally the time lag from a remote host is reduced. Building a network of PCs for terminal emulation so that a few users can get data from the mainframe is a misuse of the technology. Data conversions and "sneakernet" is cost-effective for minor applications. While it is not as convenient to ask the mainframe group to prepare a floppy disk when you want it, it is certainly more convenient than maintaining a network. Instead, consider replacement of failed star-configured wiring to the host with networked PCs and terminal emulation; this augments basic data access and file manipulation with superior PC-based tools. Keep the need for enterprise-wide networks within perspective; new technologies are no panacea.

It takes time for any technical knowledge and its ramifications to be fully realized. While personal computer advertisements and press reports initially touted that the power of these then newly-introduced microcomputers matched that of many mainframes, the concept that they could replace a mainframe was perceived. As a result of this oversimplification and mindless promotion, the potential for the PC was actually disbelieved. *Customer information computing system* (CICS), *system network architecture* (SNA) applications, and *virtual sequential access method* (VSAM) are just not transportable to or as easily interoperable on a PC, although OS/2 CICS without rollback functionality, VSAM record structure with PC COBOL, and SNA attachments are available for personal computers—subject to performance limitations.

The structure, the perception of the task, expectations of outcomes, responsibilities for control, the methodology—all these must be modified for the personal computer environment. Software development tools for personal computers have also superseded the power, complexity, effectiveness, and efficiency of the mainframe counterparts. This, too, has shifted the perception that downsizing is a strategic endeavor since it provides not only a cost reduction but also significant technological advances.

Client/Server Computing

Client/server computing represents the establishment of a host computer to provide services, including data storage and retrieval, software application file storage, printing, and mail delivery to end users. The host is the *server*. An end user is the *client*. Typically, a server is a file server, a database server, a mail server, or a print server. Generically, a PC-based file server performs all these functions concurrently within a multiuser format.

The benefit of client/server computing is that typical mainframe applications can be redeployed within a distributed database environment with *structured query language* (SQL). SQL is the PC-based successor to CICS, Cullinet, COBOL, and most other typical mainframe data processing development tools. Do not infer that SQL is the only or brightest option for a distributed database connectivity tool; many others exist, too. Many applications developed for NetWare utilize a B-tree *indexed sequential access method* (ISAM) developed by Novell called Btrieve. In fact, many SQL front ends form a shell for Btrieve including Novell's XQL. While the cost of the client/server hardware with the required local area network connections is far less than the mainframe and the software is also cheaper to buy (build or customize), the client/server environment provides ancillary services with minor additional investment. These include word processing, animation and multimedia presentations, desktop publishing, spreadsheets, databases, graphical charting, illustration, time and billing, accounts receivable (A/R), accounts payable (A/P), payroll, project management and task scheduling, and other PC applications. The important perception is that you get extra performance and functions without (or for a relatively small additional) cost.

Mainframe connectivity implies a large distributed geographic network—only a limited number of users physically sit in the computer room and the information the mainframe contains has a generic and universal value throughout the organization—adding a new user (node) often is as easy as adding a modem and terminal. On the other hand, a LAN is geographically limited to within a few thousand meters. Client/server computers within LAN environments encourage the growth of networks, which become enterprise-wide and raise the thorny specter of interconnectivity and interoperability conflicts. Downsizing is best planned with foresight.

Interconnectivity and Interoperability

Software integration and the physical and logical management of networks are critical networking issues because people "interoperate" and share information. There is a gap between what is viewed as necessary and what is available. There is a gap between what technology promises and what can be achieved. There is also a gap between what technology can provide and what value can be understood for actual usage. While the concept of linking local area networks into a single enterprise-wide network is paramount, the difficulty in logically connecting them is extraordinary. Not only do transmission media vary, data link protocols, transport methods, and data presentation limit interconnectivity; but also software application disparities complicate the task. Additionally, local networks may be managed through ad hoc management efforts. Each individual network may be controlled as a fiefdom with total independence from MIS operations or even other peer groups. It is unprofitable for this chaos to spill over to the enterprise-wide network. Duplicate node names, file partitions, user logons, and different levels of security or electronic mail protocols can limit interconnectivity and interoperability. For these reasons, standards such as *open data interface* (ODI), *network device independent specification* (NDIS), X.400, X.500, and the complete OSI communications model are so important. Even when different LANs conform to the OSI model, there is no guarantee that these LANs can even interconnect, let alone interoperate. The gray area in interpreting standards and implementing hardware and software creates disfunctionality.

Interconnectivity has become a sought-after service. The ensuing network complexity has made many networks nearly unmanageable. Networks with multiple servers or backbones with multiple subnets represent complex managerial tasks. This vacuum has attracted vendors to provide complex internetworking products and management tools to link different types of networks and provide file services independent from the underlying platform or network protocol.

The selection of competing vendor products has widened and diverged. Corporate users have opted for STP or UTP Token-Ring for its simpler wiring demands while software developers have selected Ethernet for its interconnectivity. These choices were often predicated by software requirements or simple preferences. While Token-Ring networks and Windows applications have provided effective access to mainframe processes and data, high-end workstations (like Sun-, HP-, and Unix-based systems) providing specialized turn-key solutions are now manufactured with integrated Ethernet connections. This has created a stalemate. Neither network controls the market. However, the convergence of many protocols to a single multimedia transport protocol—that is, IPX—shows that the users want to simplify internetworking. Furthermore, the site wiring is also converging to a single medium as well. 10BASE-T, Token-Ring, RS-232, and FDDI all share a common copper-based option.

In fact, as previously mentioned, many common PC-based network operating systems will work atop either Token-Ring or Ethernet. This relatively new development indicates network integrators' interest in supporting a large number of products. Indeed, vendors are responding both to their support limitations and the customers needs for network interconnectivity and interoperability through the introduction of *hybridware*. Hybrid devices include intelligent hubs, multimedia and multiprotocol routers, network concentrators, and multiprotocol management software. For example, 3Com Corporation now provides irregular drivers for their Ethernet boards and 10BASE2 hardware. EtherDisk transports protocols, which are typically run on Token-Ring, atop Ethernet. These popular Token-Ring protocols include NetBEUI, NetBIOS, LAN Manager and OS/2 LAN (Communication Manager).

Although the network software might be successfully transported on either standard medium, getting the different softwares to route and gateway through to each other is a serious problem, as Chapter 10 established. LAN Manager packets on Ethernet will not necessarily provide the TCP/IP interchange desired; Ethernet is merely the transport mechanism. Additionally, the economics and apparent ease of unshielded twisted-pair cabling has created extensions to the Token-Ring family while higher-performance optical networks such as FDDI are increasing the complexity of network integration and management.

Bridges, multiprotocol and multiport bridges, more advanced multiprotocol and multiport bridges, and complex gateways are only the physical links. Software and management control tools are frequently required at a minimum to link mainframes, heterogeneous networks, and the actual workstations to accomplish file transfers and data sharing. On the other hand, TCP/IP is media-independent. TCP/IP runs on Ethernet, NetWare, RS-232, serial or parallel wiring links, X.25, and other common media and connections. In many cases, activating reliable and functional interconnections with TCP/IP drivers is impossible. The memory requirements for multiple protocol stacks saps so much system memory that ordinary software applications cannot fit into active memory. This is prevalent for MS-DOS, less so for OS/2 and Unix. When multiple stacks fit within system memory, name or memory range conflicts frequently disable all network links; the protocols do not coexist.

For example, it is a feat of system integration and installation for LAN Server and Novell to coexist. Nonetheless, NDIS drivers are believed to be efficient with PC- and MS-DOS memory (requires about 80 K) and are only 20 percent slower while providing generic access to media and protocols. Because NDIS supports multiple protocol stacks simultaneously, this new protocol is gaining support for LAN interconnectivity. Many hardware vendors will provide an NDIS vendor for their network interface cards upon request; this is a good place to start when linking diverse LANs.

Usually though, remote access, file transfers, and mail forwarding simply will not work. In such cases, X.25 modem links provide slow but reliable TCP/IP file transfers and Internet mail connections, as Chapter 10 explained. When mail services work, files can be transferred as part of the mail message or attachments to the mail message. The lowest common denominator, the one interconnection method available for every computer system and hardware configuration, is the RS-232 modem controlled by terminal emulation software. Terminal emulation software (public domain software such as Xmodem and Kermit, or commercial products such as Attachmate or Crosstalk) includes text and file send and capture features. Mail and files are thus transferred at speeds ranging from 300 to 9600 characters per second (chars/s), and even higher—to 38,000 chars/s, with special CCITT V.32 data compression methods.

Furthermore, terminal emulation provides some powerful remote control functions and remote processing capabilities. PC Anywhere and similar remote network support tools provide terminal emulation with the processing at the remote site with only screen updates and keystrokes transmitted to local PCs. With terminal emulation running within MS Windows, *object linking and embedding* (OLE) and *dynamic data exchange* (DDE) hot links are feasible; minimally, MS Windows provides a textual or graphical cut-and-paste facility. Other operating system extensions, including the graphically-based X Windows and the character-based Desqview (also available with X Window supplements) support cut-and-paste capability for any character-based application. This means that any PC- or MS-DOS-based terminal emulation can be enhanced for a basic remote interconnection.

Although terminal emulation does not provide true LAN interconnection, it is a slow but functional WAN interconnection. The bandwidth is, of course, limited by the modem transmission speed and common carrier line clarity. While modem connections affected within a single building might represent a continuation of an internal LAN, modem connections are actually independent of distance. As such, they therefore represent a WAN configuration. At any rate, enterprise-wide networks built around RS-232, T-1, T-3, or X.25 "pipes" are apt to exhibit severe traffic bottlenecks at those pipes. When the bandwidth of these links inhibit effective operations, frame relay, ATM, SMDS, and SONET may provide incrementally and constantly adjustable connectivity for remote LANs. Note that FDDI and NetBIOS packets require complex protocol translation or encapsulation to match the format of these WAN protocols.

Interconnectivity is only the forefront of the problem. Interoperability is more complex and functionally important. *Interoperability* is a NATO term expressing the concept that military forces could standardize and share ammunition. Within the computer and network environment, the computer system is the weapon, data is the ammunition, and the structures and manipulations must be standardized. Although OS/2 supports DDE, the stunning success of Windows 3.1 is due in part to its advancing facilities to share information through the DDE and OLE interfaces. Second party suppliers provide robust network DDE. Note well that while any such creation of compound documents, processes, and objects radically promotes interoperability, it *also* increases the inherent fragility of the very specific linkages. DDE and OLE require an application name, topic name, and specific item name. This represents a one-way linkage from the client program to the server application. The server knows nothing about the client program and retains no information that any such linkage is in effect or has been established. Removal of a file linked through OLE or an insertion of rows and columns into a spreadsheet cell linked through DDE can potentially break the chain. Failure of any single cell, OLE object, or networked DDE cells and objects could undermine the very intent of the enterprise-wide network. When such a network provides mission-critical operations, consider *not* establishing and depending upon linkages that are one-way. Any loss of the DDE or OLE information (type of link, location for insertion, availability, or means to grab the cells) is not easily restored. Moreover, such linkages are not easily restored or repaired from backups since the linkages are time-critical; effective restoration assumes that backup has been performed within the *same* time periods on *all* LANs, servers, remote hosts, export disk partitions, and local user disks. The essential risk is that simultaneous backup is a highly unlikely proposition and a very serious management problem.

Recognition that fragility is a management problem is not new; it has been studied. Products do exist to address it. For example, Hewlett-Packard's New Wave interface for MS Windows in part addresses the limitations of the DDE and OLE linkages by maintaining cross-tabulated lists to prevent such likely errors. Not only does the client program link to the server application or file, but a server or file retains information describing these secondary uses. As another example, while simple database languages provide data dictionaries to show how fields are used, named, and linked, distributed databases also maintain details about location and state.

The essential risk for any distributed processing or client/server operation is, in fact, reliance upon resources not directly managed or controlled with the framework of the network setting. This is particularly prevalent with peer-to-peer networks, such as MS Windows for Workgroups, where data and application file storage is distributed across many computers; this data is not always uniformly backed up.

Despite the risks inherent in distributed processing, interoperability is only gaining in importance. Establishment of a file transfer path does not guarantee effective utilization of the network. For example, consider the problem of a Lotus 1-2-3 spreadsheet containing important data that should be uploaded to a mainframe or another PC database. While the interconnection for copying the file is established and functional, what is the format for that file? Should it be a 1-2-3 version 2, 2.2, 3.0, or 3.1 file? Assuming that you could determine an appropriate application file format, even that is not necessarily useful. Transfer of data between applications may require a comma-delimited or Lotus-style *stream data format* (SDF) file. Although these are common formats for transferring the actual data between different application software, the construction of such a file loses the logical interrelationships (that is, the cell formulas) between rows, columns, and cells within the worksheet to cause a significant loss of interoperability.

In spite of this divergence and complexity, the demand for internetworking increases. Organizations performing multiple platform software development require connectivity. This becomes increasingly important when a development source code control system must be reliable and available. Consequently, solutions which integrate and manage heterogeneous networks have extraordinary value. For example, Banyan provides peer-to-peer file access for a variety of machines including MS-DOS-based PCs and Macintosh computers through a file server based upon their proprietary Streettalk software.

Public domain (free or nearly free, copyrighted) software, such as the Clarkson drivers, provide TCP/IP interconnection for a variety of mainframe, Unix, and workstation platforms, as well as the ability to support multiple communication stacks for concurrent connectivity to multiple LANs. Commercial products such as Atlantix Axxess provide multiuser file servers which simultaneously handle MS-DOS, Macintosh, Unix, Xenix, LAN Manager on Token-Ring, ARCnet, and OS/2 with little regard for the underlying network. Although files are stored and named differently under each operating system, both Banyan Streettalk and Atlantix provide a transparent interface consistent with the expected norm for each operating system. Novell NetWare not only supports homogeneous clients operating its own *network operating system* (NOS), it also provides client access for OS/2 and DOS stations. Increasingly, other NOSs will support such hooks into heterogeneous systems to integrate the diverse LAN and WAN world.

LAN and WAN linkage is only part of the interconnectivity issue. It is also relevant to reach mainframes and other traditional host computing environments. *High-level language application programming interface* (HLLAPI) turns PCs into "smart" terminals running over *synchronous data link control protocols* (SDLC). HLLAPI with SDLC illustrates an old and limited connectivity tool. LAN gateways, including Rumba, AS/400, and other host-based gateways, tend to be both more effective and cost-efficient since the host mainframe attachment is just one more device on the network. The alternative is for *each* PC to support an IRMA card or modem for terminal connectivity with limited interoperability; Goldengate, IRMALAN, and Attachmate are among the many PC-based terminal emulation softwares which provide interconnectivity to host mainframes. These tools do not merely allow a modem-connected or networked PC to access mainframe data in the manner of a terminal, additional tools capture, transform, upload and download, and interactively and interoperatively manipulate application information.

Other tools such as IBM's advanced *program-to-program communication (APPC)* running on LU 6.2 is frequently advanced as IBM's strategic interconnection for host-to-PC networking. It is *system administration architecture* (SAA) compliant with th *common program interface communication* (CPIC) protocol. CPIC is an application programming interface (API) designed so that applications can multitask and interoperate without regard for the underlying computing platform, much like DDE and OLE link disparate objects. Standards do promote interconnectivity; slowly, the interoperability need is being reviewed and addressed. Manufacturers, vendors, and interested users can and do establish consistent standards. The IEEE committees, ECMA, CCITT, OSI, and NTSC set and establish standards for interoperability. For example, CCITT has defined X.400 for universal mail delivery via unique and differentiable addresses akin to international telephone numbers. CCITT, similarly, is considering an X.500 proposal for a universal file directory structure. This would promote accessing, viewing, and modifying files across networks and heterogeneous computing platforms.

Although manufacturers and buyers want to buy into standard computing solutions, there is little hope that stable long-term solutions will emerge and endure any time soon. Technology and its applications change dramatically and suddenly. TCP/IP has a protocol called *user datagram protocol* (UDP), which does not route well and defeats even networks that appear homogeneous. Novell and IBM have subscribed to the NDIS data-level protocol that is likewise not fully OSI compliant. Operating systems such as Unix, OS/2, and MS-DOS, while "standardized," show disruptive variety. There are multiple flavors of Unix including BSD, AT&T, X Windows, OSF, OpenLook, Xenix, and each hardware manufacturer bundles a slightly divergent version with the hardware. OS/2 exists as 1.1, 1.2, 1.3, and 2.0, along with base and extended editions and special file server versions. OS/2 even provides a LAN Server-like software for AS/400 interconnection not directly functional with IBM's own LAN Server. Even MS-DOS, the single most widely distributed software product, exists as a multivendor, multi-tiered product. There are intermediate numbered versions from 1.0 through 5.0, as well separate IBM PC-DOS and MS-DOS versions to support hardware BIOS differences.

Significant competition for these products exists with DR. DOS, Multiuser DOS, and 4DOS. Even MS Windows 3.1 provides another substantial API for networking development. Since networking is not an integral aspect of MS-DOS, it is extended with network software such as NFS, PC LAN, Novell NetWare, Banyan Vines, software and hardware drivers to support network attachment, and application software including network-smart Microsoft Windows. Microsoft is promoting Windows NT, even more than Windows 3.1, as a product that will transparently provide a network interface. Both Banyan and Novell provide a DOS-derivative network operating system that is not MS-DOS, Unix, nor OS/2. These are NOSs geared for server support of the client architecture networks. Drivers, boot configurations, memory management software such as QEMM.SYS and memory resident TSR software alter performance and compatibility to create a jungle of problems that infringe upon network operations and integrity.

Performance and response time is another quasi-compatibility issue of pertinence to client/server and host connectivity. Frequently, now, large data agencies install PC-based front ends to improve performance of host mainframe data collection and retrieval operations. Data validation and data entry are performed on a client PC without assistance from the host. When the record is validated, it is then shipped to the mainframe. Better performance in terms of response time for retrieval of a record means that the single data record only is fetched for viewing on the PC. Some systems that are designed to optimize processing may transmit blocks of master records with many unnecessary detail records. This clogs the network and creates bottlenecks at the host. This is particularly true for such new products as network fax, client/server database products, and any server-based software. This client/server technology is relatively new and not optimized to the same degree as host mainframe-based applications. Also, organizations spend considerable time and money to unify the data formats. Data is then transmitted using *electronic data interchange* (EDI).

Network Facsimile

One new concern for internetworking is facsimile reception. Network fax distribution has become quite good. In general phone lists, distribution lists, E-mail/modem/fax/voive mail delivery integration, automated cover sheets, timed delivery, time/cost minimization, image compression, higher resolutions, and other features are normally included in network software for handling outgoing materials. Incoming faxes represent a hassle and an as-yet incomplete solution. Conversion of fax into text via optical character recognition (OCR) is immature at best. It requires human interaction and is error-prone. Currently, routing incoming faxes requires separate phone lines, special routing codes, or human help. Human help means that faxes are not confidential, that faxes can be lost, and that dead storage can accumulate quickly.

Integration of user IDs, login IDs, or network mail system user names is far from complete. Universal addresses, as might be provided by X.400, could solve this issue. However, the use of universal addresses requires that these addresses be available universally. New problems will arise when this possibility is realized. Specifically, junk faxes, voice messages, E-mail, and modem downloads will clog systems with unwanted connect times, unwanted storage requirements, and the burden of sorting through the important information from the junk. As a result, the technology of network fax, while very cost-effective, is not costless and will unlikely be free from management concerns.

Consolidation of Information Management

Network management has become information management, a prevalent and critical concern for enterprise-wide networking. Network management encompasses data processing, management information systems, imaging (as in image storage and retrieval, multimedia, and image processing), telecommunications, data communications, networking, and information management as well. Information management will subsume all these functions and is increasingly being perceived as a critical function that cuts across business lines, management levels, physical locations, and organizational structure. Management is a distributed process with participants spread throughout the organization. What makes information management so difficult is that it represents so broad an area with no functional paradigms.

Even where organizations have installed integrated information systems (including enterprise-wide networks), the sheer complexity and difficulty in explaining the benefits and training users how to achieve organizational goals limit the very success of large network projects. Maintaining enterprise-wide networks is significantly more complex than running a small Token-Ring. One of the biggest hurdles is the assumption that when local networks are effectively maintained at the local level, the interconnections will function smoothly. Unfortunately, traffic spills onto local networks. Maintaining reliable internetwork links may persist as a substantial ongoing challenge. Files shared or applications distributed on an enterprise-wide network may not be available or may effect internetwork performance. Additionally, internetwork maintenance falls into the category of a patching activity rather than a proactive discipline.

Such comprehensive networks tend to represent critical elements for an organization. In the literature, important networks are ostenta-

FDDI for Enterprise-Wide Networks

tiously called *mission-critical networks*. Any failure, however time-limited, represents a serious threat and financial loss to the organization. Enterprise-wide networks perform more than the transmission of computer data from point to point; the changing perception that voice, video, and data require different networks is underscoring the importance of consolidating networks into a single paradigm. As such, network management is important, essential, and critical.

Additionally, the technologies and choices made for mission-critical networks are profound. Any interconnection or interoperation increases operational fragmentation; success depends upon the weakest links. Internetworking links themselves are distributed, but only because the data, the processes, the people, and the locations where results are required themselves are distributed and fragmented. Although it seems feasible to create standby, redundant, or fault-tolerant backup arrangements for both these weakest and even the strongest links, it is still a ruse. The enterprise-wide network is a complex organism. Some connections may seem cheaper, faster, or more reliable; the cost is bought in terms of complexity. A lack of skilled management and operational personnel quickly can unravel any gains. Mission-critical networks are not necessarily improved by redundant components, fail-safe links offered by multiple spanning-tree bridges, or fault-tolerant computers. Redundancy is a reliability "red herring." Statistical reliability and enterprise-wide networks represent complex analytical problems requiring experts.

Many problems can easily undermine enterprise-wide networks. These include the lack of skilled management and crisis teams. Operations may be disrupted by reliance upon a singular and overlooked DDE, network DDE, or OLE linkage. Even nonredundant network monitoring and control systems or malfunctioning fault switching components may cause widespread network failure. The best policy is to build networks with common components (Token-Ring, Ethernet, NetBIOS, TCP/IP, Novel LAN Workplace, T-1, and *simple* routers and gateways) and simplify operations wherever possible. Retain bright, resourceful, and competent network managers.

Although network management paradigms are becoming available as real products, vendor variety, entrenched mentality, and a lack of *management information database* (MIB) agency limit SNMP or CMIP utility. Protocol analyzers remain the generic tool of choice because they capture and count packets with minimal error. The analyzer forms the basis for more complex internetworking management tools. Again, information—primarily traffic volumes, transmission delay and transit times, and error conditions—is the most basic requirement for network management. This is useful for locating faulty workstations, workstations which are saturating the network and perhaps best segregated to subnets, and optimizing work output and network performance. In fact, analyzers, which have traditionally been sold as hardware, are now software products. These tools form the basis for minimal distributed network management and pass captured information to mapping and statistical software that runs on generic MS Windows PC platforms. This is paramount to any consideration to implement a campus network or an enterprise-wide network.

New management tools include blueprinting tools, PC-resident information gathering packages like protocol analyzers and net usage software (specifically, SNMP and CMIP), as well as new invasive tools which allow an authorized person to remotely control a networked PC (Control Room or Carbon Copy, for example). Such tools are merely the vanguard. Network managers require more complex tools to simplify enterprise network management.

Enterprise-Wide Linkage Products

Interconnecting local area networks should be a planned process. It is no quick fix or the solution to file access limitations. It is likely to create as many or more problems than solved, particularly when unmanaged or unmanageable local area networks are included in the grand plan. For example, see Chapter 10 for a discussion about gateway complexities. LANs that are out of control, overloaded, badly installed, or failing to achieve objectives can be integrated successfully into enterprise-wide networks under certain conditions. First, local networks must be controlled and local problems resolved prior to providing connectivity. Second, poor LAN performance issues must be understand before large storms of broadcast traffic are passed to the larger network. FDDI will still jam when enough local networks pass all their traffic, all the broadcast routing requests, and all the UDP messages and SNMP management requests.

Spanning-tree bridges and multiprotocol routers which filter traffic can actually improve LAN performance and reliability, if properly tuned. Gateways can translate incompatible protocols at a price of time, brute force, and overhead. Third, standards for the enterprise-wide network must be pushed down to the LANs and rigorously enforced; naming conventions (for users, nodes, and addresses) are a key reason more complex networks fail. Fourth and last, management must be convinced of the concept and provide sufficient motivation, encouragement, strategy, and funding to insure that the new linkage networks will have a fair chance to succeed; users must understand the strategy, too, and not feel alienated by this technological overhaul.

Nonetheless, given this favorable environment, maintenance, consistency, reliability, user access, and security will be more difficult issues with enterprise-wide networks. However, once the decision is cast to construct network linkages, software and hardware will be required.

FDDI hardware frequently provides a plug-and-play capability, whereas software and hardware or software-only products require complex installation and tuning. The true test remains in the intangibles such as determining strategy, matching user stated needs with objects and rationality, and maintaining a reliable and consistent network environment. Figure 11.5 shows a tabular consolidation of enterprise-wide linkage products. For additional information regarding the utility, performance, and limitations of these enterprise-wide network building blocks, refer to Figure 10.17.

Device	Attribute	Interop	Internet	MGT Notes
Repeater	Expand net	None	Lobes	Adds load
Bridge				
Multiport	Expand net	None	Rings	Adds load
Multiprotocol	Expand net	Protocols	Rings	Adds load
Router				
Multiport	Expand net	None	Rings	Adds load
Protocol	Expand net	Protocols	Rings	Complicated
Spanning trees	Fault tolerant	Minimal	Networks	Better reliability
Packet switch	Net trunk	None	Networks	Improves performance
Gateway	Software	Applications	Networks	Unreliable
FT protocol	Transfer files	Minimal	None	Improved sneakernet
MS Windows	GUI	Concurrency	None	Useful front end
Terminal emulator	Software	Cut-and-paste	Cut-and-paste	Useful within MS Windows
T-1	WAN	None	LAN/WAN	Decouple net
X.25	WAN	None	LAN/WAN	Decouple net
Frame relay	WAN	Adequate	LAN/WAN	Faster than X.25
ATM	LAN or WAN	Too new	LAN/WAN	to 6 Gbits/s
X.400	Common files	None	LAN/WAN	Uniform file and path names
X.500	E-mail	None	LAN/WAN	Basic need
VSAT	WAN	None	Global	Faster than T-1
SNMP	Local Mgt	Minimal	Marginal	Connectionless
CMIP	Global net Mgt	Adequate	Adequate but slow	Heavy toll on performance
CMOT	Net Mgt	Marginal	Marginal	Stop gap tool
Packet injector	Testing tool	Usually	Usually	Test network loading
Protocol analyzer	Necessary	Usually	Usually	Verify accuracy

Figure 11.5 Enterprise-wide linkage products.

Part 3
Practical FDDI Management

This section presents rules of thumb and suggestions for successfully applying FDDI. The formal CCITT, IEEE, ANSI, and ISO specifications do little to explain the hows and whys of success and failure with FDDI. Therefore, this part presents the design, planning, implementation, operational, and strategic issues. Emphasis is placed upon the practical issues that are often overlooked; therefore Chapter 12 concentrates on operational management.

Chapter 12

Managing an FDDI Network

For most situations, FDDI has been selected because it is the only connective medium with greater capacity than existing protocols. In other situations, FDDI has been selected for its its relative simplicity, its growing site installation, or its compatibility with many host computing platforms and software applications. In all cases, enterprise-wide management becomes a critical and necessary task. Figure 12.1 lists the categories of network management from the simplest survival mentality to the most complex, forward-thinking processes.

Rules of Thumb

FDDI is not necessarily a simple conglomeration of parts, nor is it easily upgraded or maintained; because it is apt to provide campus connectivity it is often a critical and necessary organizational component. However, some simple steps and foresight can ease the burden of those who maintain that network. Building on an understanding how FDDI works and how it is physically assembled, as presented in Chapters 1 through 10, this chapter addresses the practical and realistic expectations of an experienced network manager in the design and installation stages. Figure

Survival	At this level, the emphasis is to maintain a functioning network and keep critical applications working.
Response	At this level, network usage, performance, and future requirements are collected and analyzed.
Added value	At this level, network management seeks to improve the organizational benefits that accrue from the network and networked data and software.
Strategic value	At this level, network management is integrated into how the organization evolves to meet competition.

Figure 12.1 Levels of network management.

12.2 outlines the organizational and implementational items detailed in this chapter.

Sisyphus would have made the ultimate network manager. The job is never-ending, and each improvement—when finally accomplished—begs additional upgrades, changes, and fixes; uncovers oversights; and encourages new user requests. Moreover, as is the case for any service organization, major work and excellent improvements rarely yield recognition. The expectation is that service will always be provided flawlessly and invisibly. Unfortunately, human nature is such that the only time network service is visible is when it fails. To be successful, network managers must enjoy the accomplishment for its own sake, and succeed at building bridges, exploring the technology, recognizing the needs of the organization, and faithfully executing those requirements.

All networks require a great deal of babying. An irascible network requires extraordinary craft. Good work habits, good network documentation, and good technicians can keep any network functioning. With sufficient funds and an astute eye for applying those resources, a network will provide growth capability and reliability to yield significant advantages for the organization. As Chapter 2 explored, extracting significant competitive advantages from networks is no longer simply a matter of having a network. The network must integrate into operations

- Network administration
- Understanding user needs
- Resource allocation
- Financial planning and assessing budgetary allocations
- Evaluating resource allocation decisions
- Setting priorities
- Security
- Environmental problems
- Failures and repairs
- Downtime
- Crashes
- Planning for catastrophes
- Staging upgrades
- Upgrade policies
- Locating potential failure points
- Pilot projects
- Long lead times
- Replacement parts
- Ethernet monitoring
- Backup
- Coordinating network disruptions
- Moving equipment
- Tape backup and storage
- Questions to ask prospective vendors
- Squeaky wheel versus problem resolution
- Short-term versus long-term planning

Figure 12.2 Implementational and operational issues.

and provide services and information; it must be fundamentally important to operations.

Network Administration

Network management is a subservient role, and the players must be responsive in a timely manner to the network user community and to network problems. The manager must determine the acceptable level of services required to meet the community needs, the level of resources available to fulfill them, and the effort required to sustain them. Until these parameters are defined—often through consensus of many quarters—network administration will be a hodgepodge geared to crisis-level maintenance, instead of a controlled, foresighted team.

Network administration is a supportive activity just like data processing. As a consequence, network management is very much a vendor in a vendor-buyer relationship, the buyer in this case being the network user community. The audience is captive; the network may be the only game in town, like any monopolistic utility, because alternatives are difficult to implement when substitutes don't exist in the short term. Consider the breakdown in Figure 12.3 of the typical activities required for effective network management.

Because a network intertwines hardware, software, and procedural and labor components, resources must be available to assess and repair each of these layers. Not only does a network include these layers, but the network interacts with almost every layer within the organization. This is particularly the case with FDDI when an enterprise network connects an entire campus. Figure 12.4 illustrates the matrix organization often confronted by network managers. Frequently, the network manager and the support team are the most visible persons (other than mail room clerks or front desk guards) within an organization. With this visibility comes responsibility. The support team is not a secret organization. The support team does not directly bring revenue to the company; in fact, it is a cost center, which is a euphemistic way to say that

Core Services	Operations	Management
Cable laying	Network management	Network design
Hardware installation	Performance analysis	Network planning
Additions	Network optimization	Network analysis
Changes	Cost analysis	Network selection
Moves	Configuration	Network implementation
Updates	Network expansion	Network configuration

Figure 12.3 Categorization of network management.

	Network Mgnt.	Groups	Junior level	Senior level
Network Management	x	x	x	x
Groups	x			x
Junior personnel	x	x		x
Senior level	x			

Figure 12.4 Matrix management.

network administration is a large and difficult-to-manage overhead expense. With FDDI, that overhead may transcend many groups, departments, and even separate organizations. Ownership and responsibility is murky. Also, the network is a support function that rarely creates a discernible value to the organization. Like a telephone switchboard, the network provides a basic support service that defies easy quantification.

The network, like a telephone switchboard, is noticeable only when it doesn't function correctly. When it works well, users assume that they have a right to its resources; when it fails, then and only then do users take notice of the (bungling) efforts of the network administration team. The job is a service-related task: fix and repair, replace and maintain. Planning and implementation for the future are not perceived to be as critical as the immediate functionality; the team must maintain the fragile service. This breeds a reaction to crisis mentality and an emotional bent to avoid any change that could upset the fragile equilibrium. This breeds management conservatism, which can lead to failure of the organization by atrophy.

Understand Network User Desires

A flattened, decentralized organization fits well with a enterprise-wide network strategy because the network provides service to a wide range of people. Some will have computer experience, whereas others will not. Also, users will have expectations brought from other experiences and organizations, or will generate expectations from analogous situations. One example is the data processing (DP) department. The services of a network are somewhat similar to those of the DP department, and users may expect the same respect, response, or results. Understand the user community, respond to those needs, and if necessary, educate that community to the benefits, processes, and limitations of the newer networking technology. Nail down specifications for users and your vendors. Ask them the important questions first—not later. Communicate policies to all affected by the network. This will build credibility and respect, and alleviate some of the inherent work overload.

Resource Allocation

Because enterprise-wide network management is a service organization catering almost exclusively to widely distributed internal needs, it is a money hole. As suggested above, the network is a cost center, unless the network is large enough to service many departments within a sizable organization or provides enterprise-wide services and support activities to suppliers, allied field offices, and customers. In that case, it may be feasible to assess each department for the cost of network services rendered and establish a suitable charge-out policy for customer activities. Such a strategy generates an income for the network administration team, and thus a clearly defined market. Increases in service to a particular department can generate valid requests for a larger allocation for networking operating costs.

Many Fortune 1000 firms encourage profit center orientation for computer centers, in order to control and contain the rampant growth of a support group. Unfortunately, this orientation is more often used to assess "true" costs for the purpose of slashing the workforce and trimming expenses. The accounting is not used to assess possible competitive breakthroughs and more strategic uses of the networking technology. As such, it is seen as means to shave costs, rather than to make strategic investments. In past years, computer service organizations have sought continuous improvement to the basic installation, adding to cost with new equipment and people. Benefits from such growth never coincide with the addition of equipment and people. This accentuates the cost to the organization of any new resources.

The "black art" of data processing management, the difficulty in attracting qualified people, and the leverage held by such experts provided enough intimidation in the past to increase DP budgets at rates inconsistent with company growth. It is a fine line. Most organizations add DP resources when growth is clearly constrained by the lack of adequate systems. Few organizations yet perceived DP as a necessary investment component and critical to long-term growth.

Eventually, the investment problem can be resolved by assigning administrative responsibility for budget issues to the DP manager, vice president, or director, and basing the performance evaluation of such a manager on budget and profit issues. As a consequence, mainframe software and services usually support user accounts and charges; a fee-chargeback policy can be directly implemented. Because networks are geographically distributed and network services tend to be more nebulous and intangible, there is no directly applicable fee structure. However, there are clear, concise, and fair methods for assessing network uses and assigning user or departmental costs.

Financial Planning

Four major factors affect the implementation and usage of an FDDI network: reliability, organizational growth, coverage, and technological change. These four items determine the level of service achieved and the success of the network administration group. The solution used by many companies for any network constraint is the addition of more resources. Unfortunately, unlimited DP budgets no longer exist, and networks are usually derived from a different mentality than host services.

Networks are new resources to most organizations, and despite the many similarities, neither appear as glamorous nor are held in as high esteem as the DP groups were in the 1950s, 1960s, or 1970s. In the 1980s, personal computers often supplemented overloaded DP departments. Even now, distributed data processing and improved user-layer software have achieved a higher user sophistication, greater user expectations, and less reliance on a DP department. Also, distributed processing power with superservers allows the addition of less costly computers incrementally rather than a single, indivisible mainframe to cope with trickle growth; this better coordinates needs with resources. As the new networking technology unfolds, communication networks complement the desktop "toys." As a result of this perception, network budgets are modest and more tightly controlled than DP budgets are.

Good network management requires self-imposed financial controls. External controls devalue the esteem of network administration; it makes the network management team look like their first concern is to get more toys. It is vitally important to justify the expense of every aspect of a network. You cannot add up the numbers and ask management to sign a blank check. Intangible benefits of a network do not carry much weight when money can be spent on something else. Check signers want sophisticated cost-benefit analyses. Demonstrate the project payback. Calculate the net present value of the network over time. Show how downsizing DP operations will actually generate money in the present year. Show how the return on the networking project exceeds the organization's cost of capital.

For these reasons, a planning mechanism is necessary to address the existing network and to acquire additional resources to match organizational growth and technological change. Financial planning can be ad hoc in an environment in which there is a cost-plus mentality, or zero-based budgeting. Either method is better than none. Zero-based is better politically than ad hoc because every expense has been justified.

Ad hoc planning devalues the decision-making process, because needs are addressed sporadically and without clear controls. Each newly identified need becomes a battle for budget. Zero-based budgeting schemes are difficult to implement, since they require more management time. All hardware, software, and labor costs are addressed up front, and organizational change becomes a detailed, preplanned finan-

Managing an FDDI Network

cial issue. Growth in head count becomes a known quantity, and technological advancement is no longer an unknown quantity with nebulous ramifications, but rather a clearly stated and clearly controlled financial cost. Figure 12.5 contrasts the advantages and pitfalls of each financial tracking method.

Resource Allocation

Financial planning encompasses the entire network. Very often, resources are allocated to many individuals and groups within the framework of the network. When the network is a "free" resource, like telephone, secretarial services, desk space, or other utilities, the network is devalued. After all, it is free. Financial planning provides that first step for understanding the resources applied to intercommunication. A budgetary methodology builds that first stage for inventorying network uses. The second step is to gain an understanding of user needs. A network supplies easily discernible services, some of which are listed in Figure 12.6.

Understanding the consumption and depletion of these resources completes the picture of network management. Additional resources certainly will be procured to alleviate network overloads. What types of resources, to which sets of problems these resources will be targeted, and how much will be allocated are, in part, within the purview of the network manager.

Setting Priorities

Resource allocation decisions hinge upon the size of the network budget and user demands for services. Unilateral decisions are inappropriate, since the user community mirrors a vendor-buyer relationship. Ignoring the needs of the user is tantamount to a service failure. Applying technical skills without responding to the full measure of user questions, requests, and complaints is certain to breed resentment and distrust. Only two-way dialogue can simplify the resource allocation process.

	Ad Hoc	Zero-Based
Advantages	Specific goal orientation	Nonspecific
	Easy	Concise
	Fast	Informative
	Accurate	Prestigious
Disadvantages	Devalues management	Inaccurate (assumptive)
	Creates surprises	Time-consuming

Figure 12.5 Network budgeting choices.

- Communication
- Electronic mail and network fascimile
- File and print service
- Centralized coordination
- Centralized maintenance

Figure 12.6 Network services.

Users must feel that their issues are recognized and understood. Silent and unpublicized repairs (as though accomplished by the proverbial "elves") may solve network problems per se, but create a public relations nightmare. Therefore, all users must be able to voice their concerns and pet interests and see how this information adjusts the priorities of the network administration group.

While network managers may technically and politically understand the problems on hand, these problems must be clearly presented to the user community as well. The prioritized list of network administration goals and charters must logically match the perception of the identified and acknowledged network problems so that the community "buys into" any plan. The political complexity of an campus FDDI network is different from mainframe management. Network services and activities may be critical to users and, any changes, however subtle, may impinge upon them in ways not anticipated.

This inclusion in the problem identification and resolution process and in task prioritization will yield a better perception of the network group and a more satisfied community. The priorities should be delineated clearly to avoid possible misunderstanding.

Assessing Budgetary Allocations

If it is preferable to establish a profit center mentality, network costs can be allocated in several ways. All methods require determining a cost basis for equipment, software, labor, and repairs. Additionally, a basis should be established for a matching service level. Figure 12.7 lists some common network costs that form a cost basis.

Fixed costs include overhead such as inadequate and insufficient space, heat, power, and management salaries. This includes semivariable, fixed-cost items, like the initial cable, transceivers, and node equipment. Consumable materials include file space, paper and other media, and replacement and repair parts. Labor includes a portion of overhead, all network administration labor, and consultants. It also includes the fair cost of training sessions, shows, and documentation purchased. A cost basis should reconcile growth or shrinkage, since new users within a department require additional resources, place additional loads, and often request new types of services not previously provided.

Managing an FDDI Network

- Overhead
- Equipment
- Depreciation
- Labor
- Maintenance
- Media
- Consumables
- Training

Figure 12.7 Network costs.

The service level is the yardstick for prorating the network costs listed. Fee application schemes for allocating costs of the services are difficult because network service is the pie that all users and groups share. The costs for providing network services are black and white, whereas the value of the services rendered is not as clear. It is usually unreasonable to charge for each individual event because the accounting system will grow large and cumbersome, and will itself affect the level of network service. Complex schemes will win no friends, either.

Therefore, the cost charge-out system should be simple. Some possibilities include assigning costs by head count. This is immediately simple, but may shortchange the demands some groups place upon network load or network administration services. Another method might apply node counts as an appropriate measure. Either file space or paper output could form a prorated basis. Another basis could be built from the network traffic level. In fact, Chapter 14 includes an example in which frames are counted and used as a measure by which to assign costs. Figure 12.8 represents these and other possibilities.

Carefully weigh which measure is to be used as the fee basis since each user will adjust network usage so as to minimize statistics in that area. Users will optimize their usage and play against the system. This can, however, be applied to advantage. If it is important to minimize the growth or utilization of certain resources, the fee basis can be changed to encourage conservation. If a network is too busy and it is important to decrease load until upgrades are installed, arbitrary increases in the fee basis will compel users to conserve. Frequency of reassessing the fee basis is also an important consideration, since users will shift usage during the measurement period. Secret measurements that cannot be validated will infuriate everyone. The system must be open and honest, in addition to being simple. It will be necessary to defend the internal pricing strategy.

Licensing and Warranty Issues

Many organizations assume that the purchase of a software product guarantees the right to use that product in any manner, including multiple-site installation. This is rarely the intent of the software

- Head count
- Node count
- File space usage
- User connect time
- CPU time
- Prorated traffic level
- Service requests
- Individually negotiated
- Replacement part costs

Figure 12.8 Basis for prorating network costs.

vendor. Personal computer software is particularly vulnerable to this type of pirating; a single master copy gets installed on all the computers. Most organizations today, however, are too mature for this behavior.

Because networks are often installed as an organization grows, there is usually an installed base of existing tools and products. Software is often sold under a precondition that it is to be used on a single machine. It may not be supported within the context of a distributed network or multiuser environment, not because of legal issues, but rather from technical limitations and complexities in the networking environment. Therefore, it is important to consider whether a software package your organization depends upon is guaranteed to work within a networked environment, will be supported within that environment, or even, whether the product can be legally licensed for your use within a networked environment.

Security

Security is a factor that needs to be built into the initial network design. It is far easier to add security earlier than later. Security encompasses many aspects, including limits to physical equipment, such as access to the optical fiber cable and network communication hardware, and software access to machines, file storage media, and information replicating devices like tape drives, floppy disks, and cartridge tape units.

As a rule of thumb where security is desirable, the physical network as a whole should be as inaccessible as possible. The use of optical fiber certainly adds to network integrity since it is harder to tap and breach without some indications of tampering. Additionally, as many software keys as possible should be applied to the network. The role of network administrator is a conservative role, and such conservative security measures are best instituted. Therefore, all media backup devices should be locked up to prevent theft of information on portable media. Network servers that provide global services should also be removed from public access in order to curtail marginally qualified network users from trying to fix server problems. Access to power service, fuses, circuit breakers, and

Managing an FDDI Network

any other network transformers should be secured. The cable itself should be difficult to access for most people. Building managers regularly lock access to such building power panels; it is a safe and reasonable procedure. Figure 12.9 illustrates these simple and wise steps. Details and rationale for these policies are examined in Chapter 18.

Environmental Problems

FDDI is mostly inert media, although certain environmental factors will disrupt communication and network data processing. As stated in Chapter 6, electrical or magnetic interference in proximity to twisted-pair can adversely affect network impedance or color packets with random noise. Additionally, many wires side by side may cause mutual crosstalk interference despite internal shielding; this is not a proven assumption for minimum networks, but has been verified by independent sources for long parallel runs of cable. It may cause problems when voice, serial, and other data lines share UTP bundles. Optical fiber does sidestep these issues by using light rather and glass rather than electricity and copper.

Users may unconsciously force a workstation against a wall to create more desktop space and place pressure on modular or hermaphroditic connectors. Also, extremes of temperature can distort magnetic disk alignment, thus rendering a disk useless. High temperatures can overheat computer chips and cause premature node equipment failure. Likewise, temperature extremes can damage NIC electronics. Low humidity will cause static electricity to build up, static being a likely candidate as the cause for chip failure (particularly PROM chips) and a contributing factor to momentary power surges.

Figure 12.10 illustrates these environmental concerns. Solutions include installing climate control, securely installing cable to building structures or installing wiring conduits, and selecting a site carefully. Also, many facilities install monitoring devices that track deviations from acceptable operating conditions. It is reasonable to track temperature, humidity, smoke levels, security and facility access, system failures, and network failures.

- Limit access to physical network equipment and wiring
- Limit access to physical equipment
- Limit access to physical network servers
- Limit access to physical backup media devices
- Limit network access to servers and nodes
- Limit access with password protection
- Limit access to backup media and store it off-site
- Shread reports and old media

Figure 12.9 Rule-of-thumb security steps.

- Excessive temperature or temperature fluctuations
- Low or excessive humidity
- Vibration
- Stray and static electricity
- Fire, smoke, steam, and water
- Crosstalk and radio-frequency (RF) interference
- Electromagnetic interference (EMI)
- Security
- Construction mistakes
- Cable access through public property

Figure 12.10   FDDI environmental concerns.

Standards

American National Standards Institute (ANSI) generates a list of acceptable standards for computer languages, character sets, connection compatibility, and many other aspects of the computer industry. Adherence to a standard in network design may ease maintenance, spare parts, and upgrade problems. Non-ANSI components should be viewed with a healthy skepticism, but not necessarily ignored. However, some standards exist only because they were accepted as de facto before better or more rational solutions existed. Similarly, nonconformity to EIA/TIA-568 wiring standards may preclude simple protocol upgrades in the foreseeable future. Plan accordingly and build networks to standards.

Wiring Mechanical Integrity

Rules-of-thumb encompass those soft issues that a practiced manager discusses with peers over lunch. These include hard-learned solutions, as evidenced by this next item. As presented in Chapter 3, the hardware is specified by rigorous ANSI and IEEE descriptions. However, some mechanical features of that specification should be improved. Specify wire from recently manufactured and not recycled stock. Check optical fiber for performance at 850 or 1300 nn. There are other frequencies too. Check that the fiber will function at the one(s) you want. Qualify recycled or existing wiring with a scanner prior to use. Furthermore, twisted-pair wiring should be installed far from electrical signals and tied to a firm support or installed within a cable tray. When planning for aerial connections, assess the risks of installing what is effectively a lightning rod. Twisted-pair will certainly conduct lightning strikes. Fiber may if it is armored or bundled with secondary metallic lines.

Maintenance and Repairs

All networks require maintenance and repairs. *Maintenance* is defined as repairs performed before a problem exists; they are often preventive

Managing an FDDI Network

measures. Repairs are effected when the network fails. While maintenance often saves repairs, some maintenance causes problems which will require unexpected repairs. Understand the consequences of maintenance and that the consequences can be far-reaching, possibly including network downtime. Mechanical and software components require repair work. Parts fail, software malfunctions, and power surges or failures corrupt both hardware and software. Likewise, network configurations change in subtle ways, requiring hardware and software work-arounds, DIP switch resets, and component changes. Failures in these components create downtime.

Downtime

Network downtime is costly. Local area networks tend to limit the effects of the downtime, while FDDI enterprise-wide networks often globalize the effects of downtime. Although it is possible to assume that a ring wrap will bypass the problems, install optical bypass switches, self-healing circuits, and bridges and routers that isolate failing segments, effects are nonetheless likely to ripple throughout the organization. Various consulting organizations have calculated that downtime costs the average networked organization at least $15,000 per year in lost revenue, and $200,000 in productivity costs. Larger organizations can see these values in $1 million and $15 million ranges. These numbers translate into $1000 per person in lost revenue and $15,000 in productivity costs.

Problems are endemic even in the best of networks. At the first symptom of trouble, do you simply clear the network of users and determine the problem? That halts production and may cause the problem to vanish with the network load only to return when conditions ripen again. First, determine if the problem is localized or system-wide. Network downtime is part of the "excitement" of managing any network. FDDI is no exception. There are many reasons for a network to fail; some of these have been explicitly stated in prior chapters, while other reasons will follow in concise detail.

Network problems can, in part, be avoided with good initial design, compatible equipment, installation according to specification, and appropriate vendor post/sale support. Additionally, network segmentation and planned preventive maintenance may forestall such events from incapacitating the entire network. Enterprise networks should be designed so that loss of primary stations and connection segments will not halt operations completely. Servers can be localized and spanning tree bridges based upon modem technology can maintain linkages, albeit with lesser performance. Nonetheless, most operations can be retained. Preplanned downtime for upgrades and maintenance is preferable to system crashes. Users do not like surprises or the drama that accompanies a forced network halt. Connections, filters, software, device drivers, and the devices themselves can be checked for functionality on a periodic basis. While unplanned crashes are unpredictable, a stated policy for resolving crises and answering user questions can lessen the severity of a crash's impact as well as build confidence in the network team.

Crash Policy

Crashes are inevitable. Although optical fiber, dual-ring FDDI provides automatic ring wrap and reconfiguration feature and is particularly reliable, the network will crash. Hardware and software will malfunction, and many known or totally new problems will incapacitate network sections, segments, or the entire network installation. Since these cannot be prevented with complete success, it is best is to have a crash policy. The network management team must know what to do to solve the problem, and they must also know what to say. Panic responses undermine credibility. Even when the problem seems beyond hope of immediate repair, outline the problem. Describe the situation with a positive light. No matter how bleak things look, the users want to be reassured that you are in absolute control.

Users who depend on the network for completing their jobs might prefer to leave for the day if the problem will not be resolved in a reasonable amount of time. Show the proper respect to people's time. Groups may seek to hold meetings during this dead spot of activity. Activate spanning trees or reconfigure the network around the flaw.

While FDDI network crashes are certain to occur, far-reaching ramifications can be diverted with clear and concise explanations and open answers. The user community has few alternatives to the network administration group, and while the network team may feel pressured and overworked, they should also realize that the user community depends wholly on them. The network team should answer the questions in Figure 12.11 for each user.

- How long will service be unavailable?
- Why am I affected?
- Who else is affected?
- Will I be able to work?
- When will service be restored?
- What causes the downtime?
- What solutions exist?
- Will the solution be stable?
- Will the problems reoccur?
- What can users do to help?
- What should a user expect?
- What alternatives exist to complete my work?

Figure 12.11 Typical user questions during downtime.

Managing an FDDI Network

Planning for Catastrophe

The network manager is responsible for the security and continuing operation of the network. When the network crashes or when node equipment that is under network administration management malfunctions, the manager is pressed to restore service with rapidity. Minor software or hardware fixes are the grist for daily operations, but network disaster could make or break careers, the livelihoods of many people, and the very continuation of the organization. Catastrophe could be the result of a natural disaster, arson, accident, or sabotage. While any one of these is a rare event, the disruption is too massive to ignore.

Information backups, alternative emergency sites, redundant sites, and spare parts are the basics for restoring service after a disaster. Additionally, skilled and prepared people, a plan of action, an understanding of the critical needs, and a staged implementation are necessary components for network restoration. Figure 12.12 outlines these factors.

Most organizations prefer for business reasons not to make public disclosures of disasters or interruptions of operations. Likewise, recovery plans are kept secret. Whatever the recovery plan, the procedures should be pretested to ensure the completeness of the plan and to uncover any existing weaknesses, as well as those operations most critical to the business. Some commercial corporations provide "hot sites" and staff and support services for a fee. While this may be advisable for some organizations, others may prefer to plan their own disaster recovery procedures. At a minimum, keep an up-to-date list of the phone numbers of key personnel for users to contact in cases of network emergencies. This is a no-cost solution to many problems, and it generates goodwill as well.

Staging Upgrades

The use of paging beepers and network paging software can increase the effectiveness of the network management and alert network management to problems as they are occurring before users even become aware of the problem. Alphanumeric beepers can even convey concise

- Information backups
- Network status information answering service
- Alternative emergency sites
- Redundant sites
- Spare parts
- Strike team
- Plan of action for recovery
- Understanding of critical services
- Stated implementation plan

Figure 12.12 Data recovery components.

information so that all pages do not seem like crises and do not require a sudden scurry to the network in the middle of the night. With a message like "Frame relay link down," someone may merely need to call US Sprint or Williams Telecommunications (Wiltel) from any convenient phone. "Disk space out on Accounting Server" may mean that a support person logs into that computer from home on a modem and cleans up temporary files. The messages can convey severity, location, possible problem, and a user name. Many such calls can be repaired remotely, an important consideration when the network may be spread over many city blocks.

Planned downtime can include fixes and improvements to the network. Although these are often noncritical, they may be far from trivial to network operations. Such changes are usually tested and verified prior to their application, and are best applied off-hours or concurrently with the repair of an unplanned crash. Notification to the users of planned changes is good public relations because it forewarns users of possible negative side effects, as well as service improvements. It also serves to remind users of the events that happen behind the scenes, to their benefit. Common courtesy and savvy management dictate that you give users as much lead time as possible before implementing changes.

Upgrade Policy

The time for staging upgrades must be carefully orchestrated, and the user community must be made to understand and accept the inherent risks beforehand. Additionally, there should be an upgrade policy coordinated with all vendors. Fixes, improvements, and changes in technology should be applied where optimally beneficial, although technological changes at times may obsolete network components. Vendors should stand by their sales, and they should be willing to support all network equipment. There should be a policy on handling minor upgrades that would not unnecessarily outdate components. Also, it may be that secondary sourcing of so-called commodity items may breed incompatibilities later when a network is upgraded.

Be aware that prime vendors may alter their equipment or software, and third-party solutions may no longer be ideal. Some upgrades and installations might require a year of planning and several years of gradual implementation (while the old hardware and software are gradually phased out). This is particularly true when critical operations are transferred from a mainframe to a LAN, or from a nonessential LAN to a mission-critical client/server operation. A common problem with upgrades is that some components create a domino effect of necessary second-order upgrades, as with DOS 6.0, OS/2 2.01, and MS Windows 3.1. Do not dismiss the opportunity to roll back a bad upgrade.

Managing an FDDI Network 271

Locate Failure Points

The last four chapters expressed a need for network blueprinting. Possible network failure points should be located. While the maintenance logs suggested later in this chapter document what has gone wrong in the past, it is also appropriate to consider what might go wrong in the future. This preparation might encompass listing failures theorized but not actually experienced; it may be mentioned in trade journals or books. When a failure occurs that defies the usual solutions and is not listed in the troubleshooting section of this book pertinent to your network, peer table talk and theorized solutions are invaluable.

The normally recurring trouble spots might also be added to such a list. If the user community has access to such information, it can lend its diagnostic skills when failures do occur. Often, users have more information readily available than any member of the network administration team and can narrow the possible problem set, thus saving time.

Pilot Projects

It is anathema to test on unwilling and unknowing users. Few users want to be guinea pigs, and certainly no one should ever be an unknowing test subject. Major network changes, cable rerouting, or upgrades are best pretested and not indiscriminately applied with only a vendor's guarantees. As a consequence, it is is often difficult to test changes. Pilot projects are an appropriate solution. They certainly lower the risk of failure and localize the test to an observable network subset.

Pilot projects remove the effect of changes from the daily operational or manufacturing environment of the larger network. Isolated tests concentrate problems in a select and willing group and lessen the risk all will face when such changes are later applied to the complete network. Try changes using spare machines. Build a small network and test on that. Find willing users who want to feel that they are in the thick of things and like to talk about what they do and what the network team is doing. Locate a subnet that provides less critical services. Select a time when a segment is unused, perhaps after hours. Weekends or after hours may be the best time to effect global changes so that, should unforeseen side effects surface, all changes can be reversed without affecting the user base. Figure 12.13 illustrates when it is best to implement changes with test pilots.

Long Lead Times

Most projects on the network have long lead times. Either the parts are difficult to obtain, senior-level management is slow to understand and respond, or manpower is in short supply to complete the workload. Projects with long lead times are best launched immediately so that crises and

- Network extensions
- Gateway Installations
- Network bridges
- Repeater installation
- Subnetworks
- Superservers
- RAID and disk farms
- New types of node equipment
- New network configurations
- Host downsizing
- Shift to a new primary database management system

Figure 12.13 Pilot projects.

constraints will not deteriorate network performance. Such projects might include installation of parallel networks, gateways, faster machines, and optical fiber. The continued employment of network management may not only be at risk; a competitive advantage might be at stake as well.

Replacement Parts

In the normal course of network operations, components will fail. There are two policies for restoring service. The first is to swap parts from other working equipment to restore service. The second is to have an inventory of spare parts. Either method is reasonable, although in actual operation, some combination of the two will actually be applied sooner or later. Most managers prefer to maintain a parts inventory because repairs are simpler, do not affect functioning network users, and do not require duplicate efforts, that is, repairing the defective components as well as later repairing the unit that was the source of the problem. When a network uses old, antiquated, or unusual equipment, a spare-parts policy is recommended, because parts can be very difficult to obtain. If the equipment is more common and parts are nonetheless difficult to obtain from the manufacturer, a spare-parts inventory is critical.

Most upper-management teams seek to trim expenses. Replacement parts are nonfunctioning items, usually expensive in the quantities sought, and therefore rarely stocked. Convincing upper management that a spare-parts policy is absolutely necessary requires a mathematical analysis. Compare the costs of inventory against the costs of downtime, both partial and complete. Determine through consensus how often this might occur. Figure 12.14 presents the mathematics for such an analysis.

Audit the replacement-part inventory as the network evolves, new equipment is purchased, and other equipment is sold or antiquated. A spare-parts inventory must reflect the current network, and not the network as it was months ago. Turn over the inventory with regularity, and replace all parts in the inventory that are defective. Bad inventory

Managing an FDDI Network

```
+ Hourly network costs
+ Hourly network user costs
+ Loss of goodwill
+ Loss of network access
─────────────────────────
= Total hourly network costs

  Spare inventory valuation
÷ Lifespan and turnover rate
─────────────────────────
= Depreciated cost of spares
```

Network failure rate
(number chosen by consensus
or the past failure history)

$$\frac{\text{Total hourly network costs} \times \text{network failure rate}}{\text{Spare inventory valuation}} \leq \text{depreciated cost of spares}$$

Figure 12.14 Spare-parts inventory justification.

will fail not only to solve a network failure, it will seriously degrade network management's credibility.

The inventory should cover the expected loss of network downtime in the event that spare parts are unavailable. The spare-parts inventory does not need to equal the suggested inventory valuation if the organization is willing to accept some risk of downtime. Note also that an inventory does not guarantee that the necessary part is always in stock.

Consider acquiring used parts for the spare inventory. It is also possible to build new networks with used parts. As organizations replace 4 Mbits/s FDDI components with 16 Mbits/s or with FDDI, old NICs, workstations, servers, and MAUs are often sold as scrap. Buy these parts. They are likely to be cost-effective. Needless to say, test these components carefully. Refer to Chapters 12 through 16 for testing methods.

However, avoid recycling the wiring. It will have a significant number of bends and scrapes, and may have sustained injury in the removal process. Recycling NICs, PCs, and workstations as routers and gateways may also be unwise and represent a false economy. Four Mbits/s NICs provide the same upgrade path for you as for the original owner. Routers and gateways are critical and nonredundant network components. While it may be possible within the FDDI-based LAN Manager to establish primary and backup *domain controllers*, which provide services such as file services, exported disk partitions, electronic mail, and print support, duplicate servers and spanning trees actually providing intelligent (hot) redundancy are very difficult to establish. Also, recycled components tend to represent last generation equipment with lower levels of performance. Because routers and gateways often become traffic bottlenecks, these nodes often require the highest performance of all network components.

FDDI Monitoring

Network monitoring is good policy. The network management should know how the network is performing and should see problems before users are aware of them. While this is often impossible, traffic monitoring and performance analysis can yield information about the state of the network that will aid in design, planning, implementation, and control over network operations. User complaints can be answered with an informed response such as that the network is overloaded, that certain nodes have failed, or that a network server has malfunctioned. Answers like those breed trust, respect, and a happy user community. Channel load and TRT time are basic requirements. FDDI monitoring is possible with node software or special network monitoring equipment. This equipment is the subject of Chapters 13 through 15.

Maintain a Network Profile

Every organization requires a good inventory system. This holds true for network management as well. Not only must spare-parts inventories be maintained so that component failures do not hamper network access, but network node component inventories should be maintained. Many vendors provide automated inventory programs that capture PC node information, such as total disk space, free disk space, CPU type, memory configuration, boot file configurations, and monitor resolution and type. Since these tools do not provide database fields or even capture machine types, serial numbers, performance statistics, and user names, the manual method is still necessary until vendors provide more robust software. These high-profile items are partially outlined in Figure 12.15.

A network manager finds a complete hardware-software profile invaluable. Network failures can often be traced to incompatible equipment, mismatched revisions, outdated standards, or any number of other configuration differences. Furthermore, when a component is suspect and there are no replacement units, swapping such a part with a comparable item from another node is an efficacious method of verification.

It is worthwhile to track network equipment and node locations. Include in the node profile such information as part revision codes, versions, dates of installation and repairs, plus any maintenance information. Additionally, it is sound procedure to track software versions, installation dates, and dates when patches of test code were applied, since "tests" that work become permanent. Furthermore, certain networks allow nodal interlinking with ease, and this accessibility should be tracked at least for performance evaluation, if not for security reasons. Some of these items are documented with blueprints and notebooks, as the next sections discuss.

- Distributed files and databases
- Users
- Spare parts
- Network support equipment (printers, faxes, backup units)
- Node equipment
- Hubs, central wiring, and interconnectivity devices
- Software variations

Figure 12.15 Maintain a network profile.

Blueprint the Network

A complete network profile includes a schematic rendition of the network, with cable, electronics, node equipment, repeaters, and any other device which might need to be located at a later time. Several styles of physical blueprinting were presented in Chapter 7 and are repeated elsewhere, and Figure 12.16 lists common network items that are tracked and managed.

Managing Change

Although some organizations actually relish change, new technology, and constant shifts in priorities, most organizations, in fact, do not. Deviation from the status quo is perceived as a threat to the power structures, to the patterns of group interaction and interpersonal behavior, and a risk to successful results. Change is usually perceived as a threat by higher-level supervisors and the top executives since it threatens their power base and the flow of information which they have developed. Most others within the organization see change as a challenge to their abilities and the comfortable knowledge of how things work. Some see change as a means to further their power base, their indispensability, and a chance to advance.

Networks are especially disruptive since they alter access to information. Networks—LANs, WANs, and enterprise endeavors—as well as software applications represent a pattern of accomplishing results. View this as a complex production process, much like any assembly line,

- Location of wiring
- Connection points
- Location of patch panels
- Paths and lengths of lobe cables
- Location of node equipment
- Location of MAUs
- Location of repeaters, bridges, routers, and gateways
- Lengths of all wiring, sections, and segments
- Cable stress points and repair points

Figure 12.16 Common items to blueprint.

where the end product is information. Changes to this production structure tend to produce precipitous results. Changes foisted suddenly create explosive responses. It is a political and process problem, that once created, is nearly impossible to rectify.

Without support from users, network management authority is likely to be severely undermined and challenged. At the very least, trust and support will be broken. As such, communicate the reasons for considering changes *in advance* to all users and supervisors. Integrate responses and suggestions. Acknowledge concerns, fears, and needs. This insures that users in the network community feel that their needs are being understood and addressed, not ignored. While it may be necessary frequently to reject and deny user requests since resources are bounded and technology has its limits, still it is courteous and important to recognize the users. The network is, after all, for the benefit of the users and not for aggrandizement of the network manager and the network team. Chapter 21 elaborates on these issues and addresses some of the political ramifications as well.

The Problems of New Networks

The installation of a network changes the nature an organization in unanticipated ways. While it provides substantial benefits in terms of providing interconnection for mail, application and file access, and workgroup flow, a network is also an extraordinary investment in time, effort, and money. It is easy to see the benefits; frequently, new network managers and work groups fail to see the required effort until problems arise. A typical network is installed to provide uniform application access to a work group.

For example, a publishing group wants to use the same word processor and page composition program and so purchases site licenses. This software is installed on a single centralized server for automatic distribution by the network to the clients. The server is now an application server for its user group clients. Since it is also useful to streamline the writing and editing process in order to share files, all work is stored on the same server for shared access. The server is a file server, too. A database coordinates production schedules, stores name and address information, and provides a consistent source of scanned photographs (maintained as binary database field data). Since information is stored in a multiuser database on the server as well, it is also a database server. This server also has a Postscript printer attached since it is cheaper to buy one printer for everyone's use. As such, the server is also a print server. This machine is a critical and multifunctional component.

Since this network is likely to be an enterprise-wide FDDI backbone, assess the needs of other groups to require the same type of resources. Doctoral students at a university may have as much need for desktop

Managing an FDDI Network

publishing software as the official university publishing group. The database that is needed by the economics department may be useful for the geology department. The dean's office overseeing student grades may need just as much access to student billing and address information as the accounting and registrar's office. When these requirements and resources as viewed organizationally rather than parochially, there may be economies of scale. For example, it may be cheaper to maintain that legacy mainframe for CICS databases and new database repositories than acquire a specialized solution for each department. On the other hand, acquiring 4500 Sybase site licenses and some large superservers may represent a better investment than allowing each department to purchase a general purpose database and create a unique programming staff.

Networks tend to work as envisioned for a while. Then they evolve. Software must be added. A computer must be replaced because the printer port has failed. Each of these events requires that the server be removed temporarily from network service. When that occurs, the client/server network is not functional. If the clients are personal computers, they could be run in stand-alone mode to perform other work. However, when the network server or (the network cabling) is unavailable, then all access to the printer, the database, the site-licensed application software, or any of the files residing on this machine are lost. Simple changes to the server that were supposed to take five minutes require several reboot cycles, several editing changes to configurations files, and the five minutes is now easily an hour. The work group members go to a hastily planned meeting after 30 minutes in order to salvage the morning while the server administrator fixes the network.

Suddenly, the critical nature of the network and the network components because apparent. Off-hours and lunch become important time slots for server administration and file backup. The server cannot be disabled for changes without informing users. A sudden loss of the server may leave work in progress in an unstable state or damaged. It may leave the user with little means to detached himself from the network to use the PC as a stand-alone. This depends upon configuration. PC-DOS CONFIG.SYS and AUTOEXEC.BAT files should provide selective access to the network. OS/2 supports similar files as well as a STARTUP.CMD. Consider establishing client network access as an option rather than as a certainty.

Server backup is an important function. It is no longer a matter of backing up single-user machines; the work and success of an entire department reside in the server. Data distributed throughout a peer-to-peer network is only as safe as the latest complete *network-wide* backup. Configuration files, database files, scanned photographs, and page makeup files should be duplicated to another medium on a regular basis and relocated to a physically remote and protected site. Rare as it might be, consider what would happen if the hard disk crashed with all that work?

It is important to recognize that a new network rapidly becomes a key cog. As such, the ad hoc approach to managing a dozen personal computers will not work so well with a network and server. It becomes a critical and central focus of operations. A network is a system, and creates its own work routing. A successful new network should be consistent in its behavior, available during work hours, functional in what it provides, and reliable, as Figure 12.17 illustrates.

Log Work Requests and Network Changes

An organized network manager keeps a network notebook. The organized manager tracks all wiring, network communication hardware, and node hardware, and logs many other aspects of the physical network. These include wiring closet changes, work currently in progress, a wish list of major or minor network improvements, and both a problem log and a problem resolution log. The network notebook is represented in Figure 12.18.

Databases and MIS

Often all these lists can be maintained across the network on a database for rapid access from any node. The database also coordinates information and simplifies the data entry and data tracking requirements, and concise reports can be generated to provide otherwise unavailable insight into local or global causes of network problems. Figure 12.19 shows the interrelationship among several tracked components and suggests the power inherent in database tracking.

- Reliable
- Consistent
- Available
- Functional

Figure 12.17 Attributes of a successful network.

- Work completed on twisted-pair
- Work completed on hubs and central wiring
- Work in progress
- Wish list
- Problem log
- Problem resolution log
- Network traffic level log
- Network TRT log
- Symptom—solution workbook
- Version—compatibility workbook

Figure 12.18 Network administration notebook.

Managing an FDDI Network

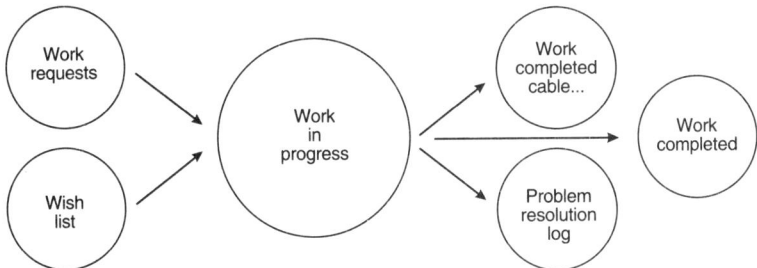

Figure 12.19 Database interrelationships between work logs.

Management information systems (MIS) yield flexibility to deal with change and uncertainty through information technology. They foster creative thinking and innovation, because information can improve both performance of the organization and the manager's ability to solve operational problems. "What if?" becomes easily tested when the data have been collected over time. Tools and the experience to use them are also already in place. MIS can also reduce the need for other problem-solving activities, because the tools and methodologies are already in place. It also requires additional resources not necessarily available.

However, the basic MIS technologies can be bootstrapped with networking technology to provide new opportunities otherwise not available within the narrow context of the network team. Figure 12.20 lists these possibilities, while the next several illustrations represent database output or typed pages that a network manager might maintain. Changes to the network connections (Figure 12.21) and node-site lobes (Figure 12.22) are logged on separate files or pages. Work in progress (Figure 12.23) provides a managerially inspired progress check on the status of all user-or management-initiated requests. A wish list (Figure 12.24) compiles those nonessential repairs or changes that should be completed. A problem log (Figure 12.25) tracks all network failures, and the problem resolution log(Figure 12.26) reflects the work actually completed.

Recurrent problems and users that seem prone to destroy equipment or software may regularly appear within the database reports. A database

- Define the implications of network technology
- .Construct relevant business scenarios
- Evaluate alternative network architectures
- Select a technical direction
- Establish a review process
- Uncover otherwise unknown relationships

Figure 12.20 MIS and networking benefits.

Work Completion Log: cable and wire

#	Date	Location	Repair	Tested
34	4/6/91	30 m from PC	replaced lobe	good

Figure 12.21 Work completion: coaxial cables.

Work Completion Log: MAUs and NICs

#	Date	Location	Repair	Tested
~~107~~	~~4/6/91~~	~~@ soft lab~~	~~beacons~~	~~marginal~~
108	4/6/91	no transmit		not yet
109	4/7/91	@ soft lab	beacon?	still off
110	4/8/91	@ soft lab	hub 2, jitter?	

Figure 12.22 Work completion: taps and transceivers.

Work in Progress

#	Date	Location	Repair	Status
34	4/6/91	30 m from PC	new lobe	good
108	4/6/91	no transmit		not yet
109	4/7/91	@ soft lab	beacons	still off
110	4/8/91	@ soft lab	bad jumper?	

Figure 12.23 Work in progress.

Wish List

#	Date	Location	Repair	Due Date
35	4/6/91	node 32	defragment disk	4/11/91
36	4/6/91	node 48	defragment disk	4/11/91
37	4/6/91	node 48	upgrade sftwr	4/11/91
38	4/6/91	node 48	test perf...poor	4/14/91

Figure 12.24 Wish list.

Problem Log: Users

#	Date	Location	Repair	User Name
34	4/6/91	30 m from PC	new section	SNOOPY
108	4/6/91	no transmit		MAWN
109	4/7/91	@ soft lab	beacons	JSL
110	4/8/91	@ soft lab	bad jumper?	JSL

Figure 12.25 Problem log.

Problem Resolution Log

#	Date	Location	Resolution	Date
34	4/6/91	30 m from PC	user happy w/fix	4/6/91
108	4/6/91	no transmit	OK	4/24/91
109	4/7/91	@ soft lab	user on net	4/7/91
110	4/8/91	@ soft lab	OK	4/11/91

Figure 12.26 Problem resolution log.

pays off by providing comparisons among network traffic statistics not otherwise noted. Maybe, that database will be the same Sybase tool that the rest of the example university chose above. Correlations between collisions, volume, peak volumes, particular equipment manifestation, and cross-linked malfunctions are more easily recognized. Figure 12.27 maps this relationship. Figures 12.28 and 12.29 illustrate two important traffic reports that can be generated from an on-line database. Other pertinent statistical information and formulas to generate such information are presented in Chapter 16.

Backup

Backup of information, services, hardware, and labor, and sometimes even backup processing are important functions of network management. No network is fail-safe; malfunctions and invasions happen. In order to protect the organization, a backup policy is suggested. Chapter 18 details backups and redundancy issues at length.

A good portion of any network is resident in unique files that define the relationship of nodes on the network, the operations of the network itself, and, quite possibly, scripts that have been programmed to automate many arcane processes that have become complicated over time. This information usually has value to the organization. Network backup is, therefore, a crucial procedure to ensure network integrity and security. Chapter 18 details network backup, including data, equipment, and software, as critical operational concerns.

Note that an FDDI backbone is a global service. Responsibility for subnet support and local resources must be clearly demarcated. Backup of user data and department resources is usually the responsibility of the individual users and departments. Responsibility for individual data on databases is generally less clear. Make it clear. Publish backup operation schedules with times, partitions, coverages, and clear indications of what isn't covered. If only databases on distributed servers are backed up because this information is critical for the entire organization, make clear that this backup does not protect user files, the network operating system, boot files, and departmental user accounts. If user accounts are administered globally, make it clear that user files are the users' responsibility—or, that network management does perform remote backups of user data on a published regular schedule. The details are specific to each organization, the budget and performance constraints, and political activities.

Coordinating Network Disruptions

Network disruptions happen mostly by surprise, although some are planned. Those few times when downtime is actually planned, it is a

Managing an FDDI Network

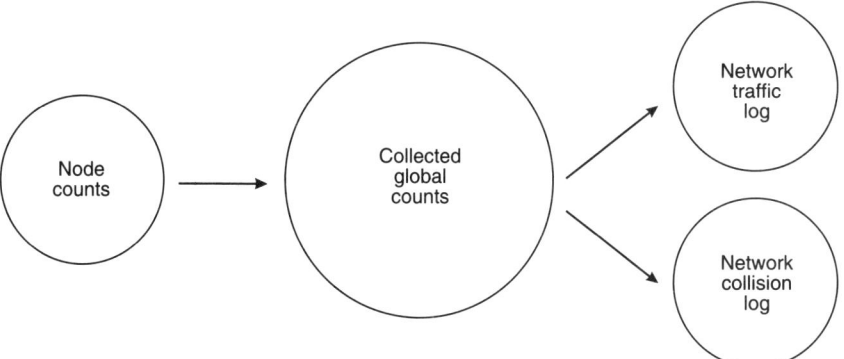

Figure 12.27 Databases provide insight into network traffic problems.

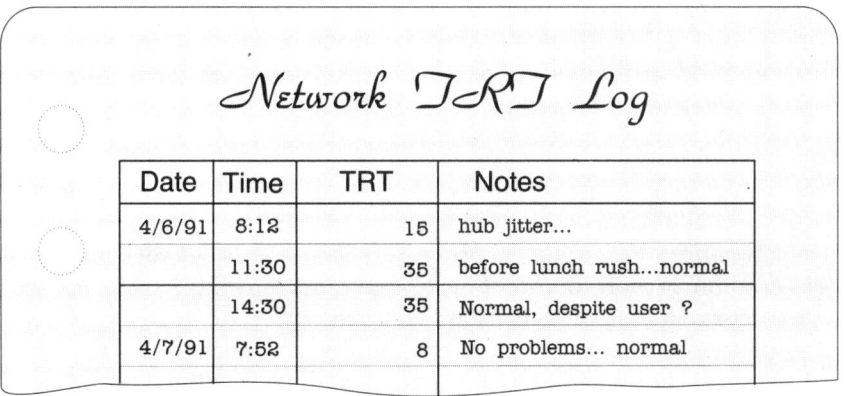

Figure 12.28 Network TRT log.

Node	Date	Packets	Percent	Notes
34	4/6/91	525,678	0.110	hub problem?
108	4/6/91	34,580	0.005	
TOTAL	4/6/91	4,457,820	1.000	What a busy day!

Figure 12.29 Network traffic log.

good policy to inform the user community. It is a common courtesy. Users do not like surprises. If the user work schedule is disrupted by the network management team when advance notification was possible, users have every right to shout their displeasure. Also, the power the user community wields in part affects the courtesy that the network administration group shows. For example, when digging up a parking lot to build that new science center, communicate that the FDDI backbone will need to rerouted away from the construction zone; publish the crossover time and that reconnection may take an entire day. Coordinate such disruptive events so that professors entering final grades during vacation will not be affected, or that the large test of a new remote billing system is not disrupted. Propose first, and then plan accordingly.

If the user community has control over operations common to many DP departments, almost no courtesy will be shown. Whatever policy is applied, remember to be consistent. Users will assume that each change is a permanent improvement. A downtime schedule should include the actual period of downtime, warnings beforehand, and notification if the duration of downtime will exceed the initial schedule. Courtesy wins respect. Consistency breeds trust.

Moving Equipment

Physical equipment moves can be planned events and, like scheduled downtime, should be coordinated with the user community for minimal disruptive effect. Few other events can erode valuable network management credibility more than bungled prearranged events. Problems are apt to occur and simple transitions are rare.

Inform those affected in the user community how much time is required for the actual change, what can go wrong, and what will happen if such problems arise. In order to achieve successful equipment relocation, set up parallel installations. Figure 12.30 illustrates one example in which a node connection can be installed and tested in advance of the actual node move. Other events, too, can be performed with such foresight. Also, moves may require extra parts, software tapes, extra hands. Plan for all exigencies, any surprises. Be aware that equipment or network configuration changes may have small but significant side effects. A little forethought will preserve that hard-earned respect.

Vendor Support

Network installation and management is by nature becoming less of an ad hoc activity. Hardware and software components are rarely acquired from the same sources, and frequently do not coexist well together. Advanced network devices such as bridges, routers, and hybrid brouters require complex installation and continual monitoring and configuration. Vendor support is all too critical, and before building or expanding

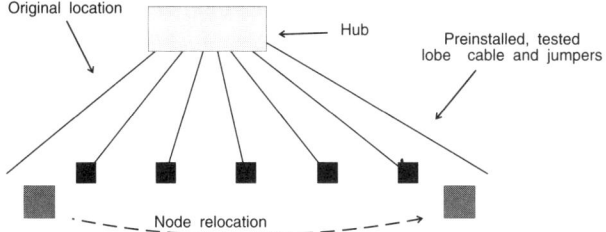

Figure 12.30 Preplanned equipment relocation and parallel setups.

networks with a hodgepodge of components, consider the questions listed in Figure 12.31. Additionally, if you are considering leasing equipment or hiring a vendor to install and maintain your local area networks and enterprise-wide networks, give full weight to each of these questions. Poor vendor selection creates lasting conflict.[1]

"Squeaky Wheel" versus Problem Resolution

As the squeaky wheel gets the grease, so, too, the loudest voice often gets the most response. In many situations, responding to the loudest voice lowers tension, cools tempers, and makes more people happier. As a side effect, however, such attention side tracks normal planning and problem resolution. It diverts attention from fixing critical failures, performing preventative maintenance, and attending to a controlled agenda. Responding to the squeaky wheel may undermine management initiative, degrade the credibility of network administration, and ultimately strip decision-making responsibility from the network administration team. Therefore, the better policy is to plan network needs, assess network resources, determine both short-term and long-term network direction, and last, reach a detailed agreement with users as to network problem prioritization and resolution.

Short-Term versus Long-Term Planning

Attention to the squeaky wheel underscores an attention to crisis-level response. While management of a new network or changeovers in management of a problem network may require crisis resolution, long-term success requires a long-term outlook. A manager should seek to maintain his or her job long term, seek to retain the management people on a long-term basis, and plan for long-term network growth, service growth,

---

[1] Modified from *Information Center Quarterly*, winter 1991.

- How often are preventive (maintenance) services, such as new software releases, delivered, and how often are problems with these services reported?
- How long does it take to correct problems?
- How important is customer service for your company? Where does customer support fit in your organization's hierarchy?
- How many people provide support?
- How is the support function structured?
- Is support provided from many locations or a central site?
- Are product developers available for consultation?
- Do barriers to direct communication with developers exist?
- During what hours is support available?
- Can you talk to support personnel immediately? Do you have to make an appointment? Do you have to leave a message and wait for a return call?
- How are support calls passed along? For example, do you speak to an administrative person for customer identification, talk with first-level support, and then wait for a return call from second-level support?
- How is support handled during off-hours and holidays?
- What are the vendor's standards and goals for support? Areas to look for are the times for returning calls, code repairs, and successful completion of calls.
- What procedures are followed if the product doesn't work?
- Do support members have online access to notes made from prior conversations with other support members?
- Are reference numbers provided for verified program problems?
- Does the vendor provide a support brochure?
- Does the vendor follow up on all calls?
- Are there differences between pre- and postsale support? Ask current customers as well as the vendor.
- Is training offered? If it is, request a copy of training policies, schedule of classes, and an overview of course content. Check out references (past attendees) as to the quality, focus, and suitability for the courses.
- If the need arises, will the vendor work with other vendors?
- What procedures will be followed if the vendor must work with other vendors?
- What information must users have in hand before calling for support?
- Does the vendor supply a list of common questions typically asked to prepare the caller to answer questions and perhaps solve the problem with the typical answers?
- What ways, in addition to the telephone, can you communicate with the support department? By fax? Telex?
- Does the support staff have the ability to mirror a sequence of steps while they talk on the phone with you? Can they dial into your system and provide remote diagnostics?
- Is there a technician experienced in enhancing performance?
- Are they authorized to sell and repair the equipment and software for which your organization foresees a future need?

Figure 12.31 Questions to ask your vendors.

and technological change. Short-term planning resolves only immediate issues. Long-term planning attends to the configuration of network services over years. Figure 12.32 illustrates why neither of the areas covered by short-term and long-term planning can be overlooked for long.

Easier Said than Done . . .

Network management is a difficult task. Matrix management impedes easy control of people and resources. It also raises the specter of squeaky wheel problem resolution, a policy apt to undermine network management and divert attention from more pressing problems. The complexity of a network, the sheer size of a network, the number of possible failures and malfunctions, the overloading, and the technical complexity of not only the network but also the devices accessing that network, create a difficult job. Stress is often the norm. Furthermore, senior management usually is unwilling to allocate sufficient resources to resolve even the most pressing network problems; resource scarcity is likely.

For these reasons, network management is a difficult task. Respect is won grudgingly and lost easily. Radical changes, unless always successful, will undermine the network manager's authority; management conservatism will erode any authority to fix, change, or improve the network, the communication channels within the organization, or the satisfaction and status due the management team. Work hard for credibility. Maintain that credibility with carefully chosen words, respect, understanding, and accuracy. Promises are easy to make, but they are easier made than kept.

Short-Term Planning	Long-Term Planning
Repairs	Preventative maintenance
Upgrades	Performance problems
Equipment relocation	New technology
Labor problems	Strategic application of networking
Performance overloads	Labor and resource concerns

Figure 12.32 Network short-term and long-term planning issues.

Dos and Don'ts

Figure 12.33 concludes this chapter with a general-purpose list of management dos and don'ts. Add to this list as your experience dictates. Copy it and affix it to your wall, if you are so inclined. However, don't regard these few items as all there is to network management; "feel," experience, and other intangibles are learned with time.

Do	Don't
Design a segmentable network	Overdesign
Adhere to specifications	Isolate specifications
Pretest new components	Assume component functionality
Define an overall strategy	Mix standards
Define a user pricing policy	Forget to create LAN usage policies
Define a repair policy	Scrimp on technical labor
Install extra wiring	Install "just enough" wiring
Identify potential failure points	Mix untested equipment
Experiment before implementing	Ignore user requests
Gain experience	Assume that users understand
Search for trouble spots	Look for complicated solutions when simple ones may suffice
Promote preventative repairs	Overlook the organization's culture

Figure 12.33 Network dos and don'ts.

Part 4
Network Troubleshooting

When the network fails there are various techniques to identify, locate, and repair problems. Many techniques are time-consuming without specialized tools like a wire scanner, an optical signal tester, and a network analyzer. Because each of these tools is indispensable on a large, busy, or very critical network, the knowledge needed to use them and interpret their results is presented in separate chapters complete with photographs, illustrations, and tables.

Chapter 13 suggests practical tools that test, monitor, and analyze network status. When the network fails there are various techniques to identify, locate, and repair problems. Some techniques require specialized tools like a multimeter, a twisted-pair wiring scanner, and time domain reflectometer for copper-based media and a light meter, light source, feature detector, and optical time domain reflectometer for optical fiber, and a network analyzer for all FDDI-based networks.

Chapter 14 details the usage of the copper-based and optical time domain reflectometer, the feature detector and light meter, and twisted-pair scanner and the practical steps to check the usability of network hardware, and to verify correct installation. These tools also provide a highly desirable method to benchmark a network.

Chapter 15 describes the necessity for network management software, the network protocol analyzer, and how to identify, locate, and isolate suspected network problems.

Chapter

13
Network Monitoring Tools

A network manager who administers a large or growing enterprise-wide network is certain to experience slowdowns, bottlenecks, or downtime. In order to combat these common problems, a network manager should have network monitoring tools. Chapter 8 mentioned the need for certain installation equipment including cable cutters, pliers, screwdrivers, tap set, crimp set, soldering iron, integrated circuit (IC) extractor, flashlight, hammer, cable ties, and other such tools. Because the FDDI network is both a mechanical, optical, and software entity, complex analytical tools are needed to evaluate that installation. This network-monitoring tool kit which supplements the normal installation tools should include a media-level tester, and network traffic-analysis software or a protocol analyzer. Not only are tools needed, but an understanding of how to use these tools and interpret their results is critical for effective network installation and maintenance. FDDI, unlike other "pipes," transmits invisible contents. While a plumber can see current water leaks and the results of past problems and see that a pipe is plugged up or running slowly, FDDI carries signals invisible to the eye without special viewing tools. Even laser signals at either 780, 850, 1300, and 1550 nm are effectively invisible to the naked eye. Actually, it is unsafe to try and view FDDI signals without tools. Tools make signal leaks and bottlenecks visible.

Media Testers

A media tester is a generic name referring to a multitester, continuity tester, a telephone line tester, scanner, light meter, optical feature detector, time domain reflectometer, and optical time domain reflectometer. FDDI media may be both electrical or optical within the same organization. You may need tools for one media, several media, or all. It is also likely you will need tools for Ethernet, RS-232, Token-Ring, and T-1. The next sections will discuss the tools required for each media.

Twisted-Pair Testers

Twisted-pair must be tested electronically. Generally, you will want to test that the pairs have no breaks, shorts, or open circuits. You will want to test that the wire itself provides the correct qualities to transmit signal properly. This usually means that the media conforms to specification for speed, signal quality, and resistance to signal and crosstalk. Simple tools that provide this capability are called *multitesters* or *ohmmeters*. The *time domain reflectometer* sends out signal pulses to test for shorts, breaks, and open (or incomplete) circuits. *Cable scanners* are more complex handheld tools that merge many of these features together with circuitry to display and simplify the analysis.

Figure 13.1 illustrates a typical multitester. The multitester measures ohms, volts, and thus shows the basic condition of the wiring in terms of shorts, breaks, and other bad connections. This is a useful tool to check continuity of patch cord or panel connections. The continuity tester is even simpler and measures whether the two probes contacting metal form a complete circuit. The telephone line tester is a specialized tool for verifying that a modular plug is a live telephone circuit with a dial tone and that all pairs are connected in the proper places. Although a multitester or continuity tester is useful in jam, it does not compare to the utility of a scanner. The pair scanner is the most useful of these tools. It is basically a handheld time domain reflectometer and is outlined in the next section and subsequent chapter.

The time domain reflectometer (TDR) uncovers breaks, shorts, and similar cabling anomalies. Figure 13.2 shows a typical bench-type unit with a built-in oscilloscope. *Time delay* refers to the radar-like process

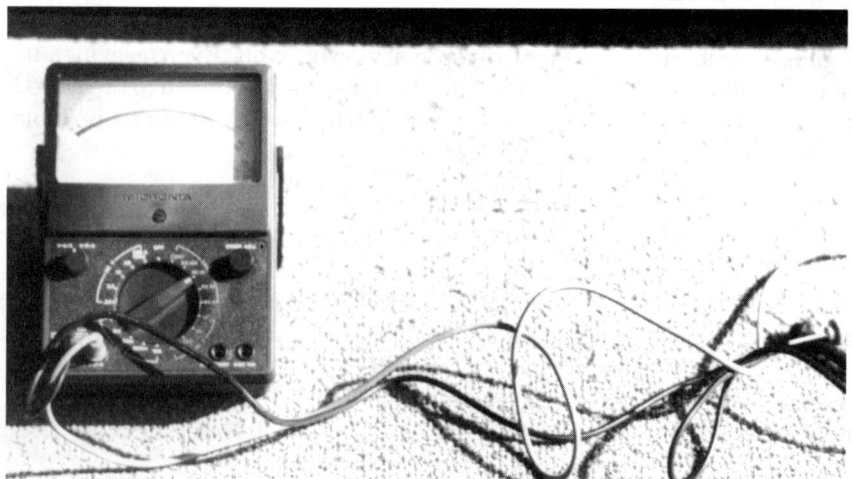

Figure 13.1 A typical multimeter. (Tandy Corporation)

Network Monitoring Tools

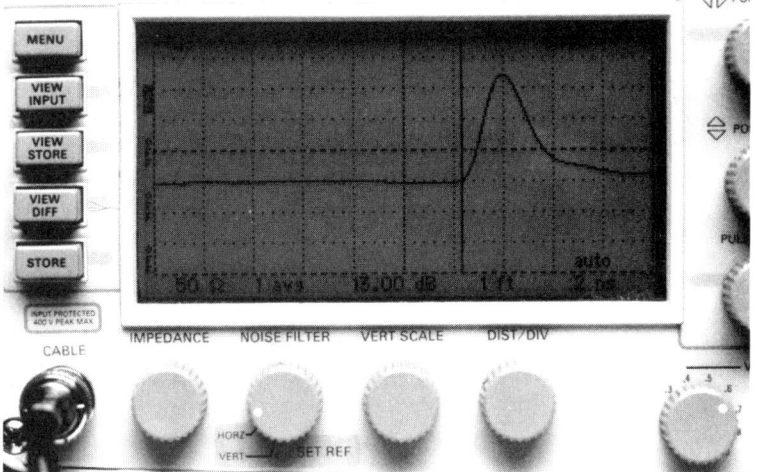

Figure 13.2 A time domain reflectometer. (Textronix)

employed to display the properties of wiring and location of any cable breaks. This technology is a significant refinement over continuity checkers and multimeters.

For example, the scanner or TDR will indicate whether a lobe cable is correctly wired, is attached to an active ring, and how long that lobe can be and still provide adequate network support.

The scanner is the emerging tool of choice for network media management. The few units for FDDI are handheld units, as shown by Figure 13.3. Not all vendors of Token-Ring or Ethernet scanners sell scanners for FDDI and 100 Mbits/s or greater wiring. However, they will certainly be forthcoming as higher speed media is specified by forward-thinking network managers and building designers. Unlike a multitester, the scanner is specialized for a particular media; typically twisted-pair (datagrade, UTP, and STP). Because it is specialized and developed solely for data communications networks, it is simpler to learn how to use these tools, interpret results, and define action plans. The typical scanner will indicate with LCD displays locations of problems and viability of different lobes and trunk wires. Some even will download information to a standard parallel port (in a PC or engineering workstation) for secondary analysis or documentation purposes. Chapter 14 specifies procedures for using these media analysis tools.

Optical Fiber Testers

The tool corresponding to the multitester for optical fiber is called the *light meter* or *optical power meter*. The light meter reads lumens of light

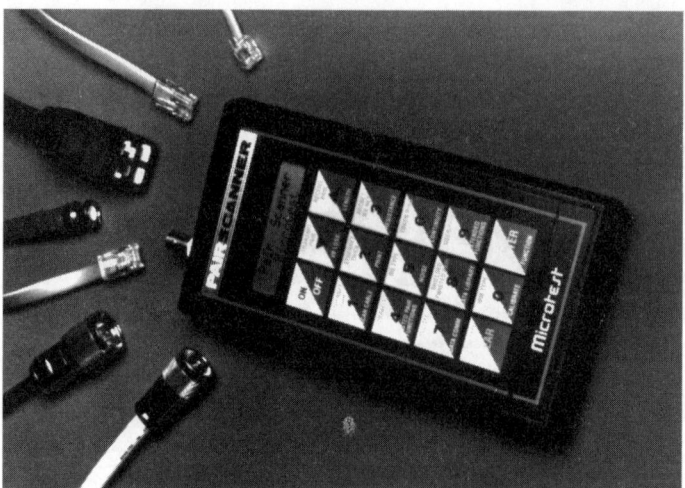

Figure 13.3 A handheld FDDI scanner.

in the appropriate wavelength for optical signal transmission. By using the light meter, you can interpret signal loss from splices and connectors, clarity of the optical media, and the light scatter or effectiveness of a length of fiber. However, the light meter must be paired with tool that will generate compatible signals. This is called a *light source, signal inserter,* or *optical signal generator.* These tools create *stabilized* light for the light meter to read and interpret. The reason the generators must be stabilized is so that the signal will represent a known brightness and frequency. Typical light sources created from electricity are sensitive to voltage, wattage, temperature, and the stabilities of those items. You do not want the light source to flicker and dim and mislead the light meter.

Some companies provide a tool called a *feature detector.* This device is basically a light meter and light source in single package. It also has some simple electronics to decode what it sees and apply labels to the anomalies. The feature basically indicates what features exist on a segment of fiber. It will show where the connectors, splices, and scatter occurs within the cable. This device is very similar to a scanner, but borrows some of the capabilities of the time domain reflectometer. Figure 13.4 shows a typical optical feature detector.

The *optical time domain reflectometer* (OTDR) uncovers breaks, leakage, and similar optical anomalies. It is analogous to the TDR, but for optical media. Time delay refers to the reflective process employed to display the properties of the fiber and location of any breaks. While it is a refinement of the light meter and light source, many managers may choose not to acquire the OTDR because of its expense and limited utility for FDDI, which generally works without glitches on optical fiber. OTDR

Network Monitoring Tools

Figure 13.4 A optical feature detector. (Noyes Fiber Systems)

functionality in a handheld scanner unit was not available at the time of writing. Chapter 14 specifies procedures for using these optical media analysis tools.

Network Protocol Analyzer

The protocol analyzer verifies correct operation of LANs, WANs, and MANs based upon capture and parsing tokens, frames, and encapsulated packets. A network manager is blind to network performance, capacity levels, and software transmission problems without such traffic monitoring capability. These tools can be either hardware-based or software applications which run on a standard node platform.

The analyzer performs the following functions. It computes *token rotation time* (TRT), channel utilization as a percentage of the transmission capacity, frame sizes, defective frames, frames with bad *cyclic redundancy check* (CRC), duplicate frames, and frames with user-defined parameters. Some decipher beacons to indicate a likely source of the ring failure. Most such tools can collect statistics around the clock to trace intermittent problems that are suspected but difficult to localize without constant supervision. Chapter 15 details the many additional features of a protocol analyzer and explains how to use this tool. One major note to realize is that few such tools exist that can trap 100 percent of network traffic at any single time. If they can, the storage requirements for capturing 30 to 100 Mbits/s for any length of time is very substantial. One minute alone can represent 8 Mbytes of disk storage.

CMIP and SNMP

Since the functionality of SNMP, CMIP, and CMOT somewhat overlap the functionality of a protocol analyzer, these software-based protocols are also discussed in Chapter 15. Although SNMP is a protocol monitoring and traffic-analysis tool, it is an effective database that is in effect a protocol analyzer. CMIP and transition CMOT also provide the ability to set alarms, establish automatic events, and initiate activities. Since most hardware-based analyzers can perform these tasks, CMIP represents more intelligent network monitoring and analysis software with the associated cost of a hardware-based analyzer. Refer to Chapter 5 for definitions and Chapter 16 for information on applying captured LAN statistics.

Network Tool Application

FDDI is simple in design and increasingly complex in terms of daily operation. The scope of a small FDDI network will likely include more square footage and floors than previously experienced with even the largest of LANs. The network manager faces hardware, software, and traffic problems. As of yet, no network has been free from installation, operational, and mechanical problems. Without these problems, there would be no justification for a network manager. The complexity of these problems and the ability of the network manager to solve them justify the existence of that job. Some problems will be camouflaged. It takes an astute manager and network team to trace these problems and maintain a functioning network. A good tool is surely indispensable.

A multitester or continuity tester is a necessity given its insignificant cost and versatility. Optical media requires a light meter, unless the NICs provide built-in loopback test functionality as they are increasingly likely to do. A full-featured TDR with video display screen and Polaroid camera is expensive and, as such, best employed by specialists who frequently install networks. The time spent learning how to use this tool well is usually unwarranted for most small corporate LANs. Instead, a scanner is cost-effective and utilitarian even for small FDDI networks (10 to 50 stations). This tool provides the most value when expanding an existing network, adding linkages, or when debugging a network that is not reliable. This use of this tool is best learned before actually installing the network; in reality, it will probably be learned within two or three hours in crisis mode.

The protocol analyzer is a tool best ignored on small LANs unless problems are endemic. When FDDI provides bridging, routing, and gateway services for many LANs, particularly for enterprise-wide FDDI networks, the protocol analysis should be able to decode all seven OSI layers for all transmission-level protocols or higher in use on the network. The beacon is a sufficient message to indicate ring hardware

Network Monitoring Tools

failure and provide some insight as to the location of the segment or lobe failure. Concentrator or hub indicator lights are more effective for debugging UTP and STP wiring failures. If necessary, the scanner is sufficient to expedite isolation of wiring failures. Since training time and costs for learning the analyzer will easily equal or exceed the cost of the protocol analyzer, this tool is best suited for large networks with many internetwork hops, busy campus backbones, or LANs supporting multiple protocols, or for an organization with multiple LANs and LANs of more than 70 nodes.

This should not to suggest that a protocol analyzer is useless on small LANs. The tool is designed to disassemble the protocol information from FDDI frames (and other protocol packets). Rather, the comprehensive tools—the suitcase-sized, full-featured $15,000 tools—are complex and generally unwarranted. A low-end model, generally under $2000, is sufficient for occasional use on the small LANs. A protocol analyzer is a good instrument for optimizing performance, uncovering LAN deficiencies, and for stressing the network.

These tools have overlapping functions. This section provides some insight into the overlapping functionality and limitations of each tool, as Figure 13.5 indicates. The multitester or continuity tester is a quick tool to demonstrate that a problem exists, while the scanner also indicates the

	Multi-tester	TDR	OTDR	Tester	Analyzer	SNMP	CMIP
Optical fiber			.	⊗	.	.	.
Lobe cable	⊗	⊗	.	⊗	.	.	.
Twisted-pair	⊗	⊗	.	⊗	.	.	.
Optical connector			⊗	.	.	.	.
Wiring hub (TP)	⊗	⊗	.	.	.	.	.
Photonic switch			⊗	⊗	.	.	.
Controller	.	.	.	.	⊗	⊗	⊗
NIC	.	.	.	.	⊗	⊗	⊗
Repeater	.	.	.	.	⊗	⊗	⊗
Bridge	.	.	.	.	⊗	⊗	⊗
Router	.	.	.	.	⊗	⊗	⊗
Gateway	.	.	.	.	⊗	⊗	⊗
Node level config.	.	.	.	.	⊗	⊗	⊗
Network config.	.	.	.	.	⊗	⊗	⊗

Figure 13.5 The overlapping functionality of network test equipment. The small solid bullets indicate a primary testing function, whereas the crosses indicate that the unit can provide minimal testing functions.

exact position of that problem. The protocol analyzer provides strictly software information based upon information contained in FDDI frames. This reveals software problems, channel overloading, configuration errors, or software flaws. It can in some cases pinpoint the source of a beacon or failed node—if the ring is still physically complete. Although FDDI SMT should indicate the location, source, and reason for a wring wrap or station failure, these ancillary tools are valuable for the time they save. Since there are many conditions that will break a ring, the scanner is an important tool to locate those failures. Note that a protocol analyzer for FDDI will not work on a broken ring, unless it wraps and you can access the wrapped segment; the isolated segment(s) are likely to be inoperative. Figure 13.6 shows how each tool is best utilized.

FDDI can fail to perform for a variety of reasons, as shown by Figure 13.7. Any of these conditions can severely affect the overall network response time. Some may cause a station or several stations to fail, even when stations are on different rings. An overloaded file server and a network fax saturating the network with images could overload the 100 Mbits/s FDDI bandwidth. The next two chapters show how to decipher such common problems using the media testers and the protocol analyzer.

	Hardware	Software
Physical level	Multitester	TDR
	TDR	CMIP
	OTDR	SNMP
Transmission level	Tester	Protocol analyzer
		SNMP
		CMIP

Figure 13.6 Network test equipment utilization.

- Poor cable connections
- Faulty MAUs and hubs
- Faulty Token-Ring controllers
- Improperly configured network
- Excessive network traffic
- Overloaded node devices
- Overloaded servers
- Improperly configured software
- Defective software
- Overlapping network addresses

Figure 13.7 FDDI failures uncovered by network test equipment.

Chapter 14
Media Testing

This chapter describes the scanner and time domain reflectometer for twisted-pair, and the light meter, light source, feature detector, and optical time delay reflectometer for optical fiber. This chapter shows the history, the functionality, usage, and alternatives to these technologies. The time domain reflectometer (TDR) supersedes the multitester and continuity tester because it can provide the same electrical feedback as the multitester. The optical time delay reflectometer (OTDR) supersedes the light meter and light source in terms of performance, but where cost is an issue, the other tools are nonetheless effective. Of note, the TDR is not a time *delay* reflectometer, as some people suggest. The scanners are just TDRs in a hand-held format. The electronics and complex display capabilities are replaced by simpler LED displays; in some products, the display features are available through a downlink to a standard PC.

Twisted-Pair FDDI Tools

In addition to basic wiring continuity tests, the TDR will precisely locate a wiring short, open, or break relative to a wire endpoint. Furthermore, this test instrument, when used in conjunction with a camera, or serial port attachment to a PC, can blueprint a network. This aids in debugging the all-too-common network failure. The TDR locates twisted-pair wire perforations and twisted-pair wire shorts, and can identify an electrically defective modular or genderless connection. For FDDI networks, a *short* circuit means the TX- wire is somehow connecting or touching the TX+ wire, the RX- wire is somehow connected to the RX+ wire, or the TX wires are in contact to the RX wires. Signal is therefore diverted from its proper station. An *open* circuit means that there is a cut through one of the four wires (or eight UTP) or that one of the four (or eight UTP) FDDI signal wires is not attached correctly to a connector. A *break* means that all four (or eight UTP) of the FDDI signal wires are open, and thus not conducting signal. The break is usually indicative of

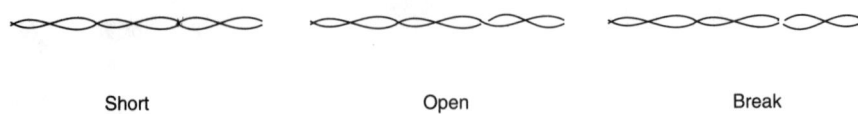

Figure 14.1 Twisted-pair wiring circuit short, open, and break.

a patch panel or connector failure, or damage to the twisted-pair wire. Figure 14.1 illustrates these three common wiring failures.

The scanner also can categorize the signal clarity of STP and UTP, the signal strengths, and wavelengths in use and any NIC transmitter on the fringes of those ranges. Since copper-based FDDI networks are star-configurations rather than true ring architectures as found in the optical media variant, the scanner can verify that each node can accurately repeat and relay signals.

Time Domain Reflectometer

Refer to Figure 13.2 for a photograph of a typical bench-type time domain reflectometer unit. This unit contains an oscilloscope display, a TV-like screen which displays a trace curve on a grid. The technique applied by this tool was developed in the early 1950s for locating cabling breaks in high-tension wires. The TDR was further refined specifically for use in tracing cable television broadband problems. It was used to locate shorts, breaks, cable impedance variances, and overloads on city-wide installations, but has been modified for use in baseband and broadband computer communication environments; the problems encountered are identical. Figure 14.2 shows handheld scanners.

The TDR unit connects onto the network in place of a node. The standard TDR or pair scanner will not send out phantom voltage and will not repeat signals. It will just view the lobe wire (or a trunk wire). It thus can remain connected onto the network at all times. Unless the twisted-pair hub automatically disables the lobe which you are testing, or you manually disable the lobe from the hub, the scanner will disable the network; logically downstream nodes should institute beacons to indicate a failed upstream node. It is an important tool in a crisis when a network fails completely. At such times few other tools, especially network software tools which depend on a functioning network, can operate; only noncomputer, nonsoftware tools operate when a network is broken.

The TDR operates somewhat like radar. It sends a voltage signal pulse from the attachment point (typically at the hub or NIC connector) down the network media, as illustrated in Figure 14.3.

Media Testing

Figure 14.2 Typical handheld scanners. (Microtest)

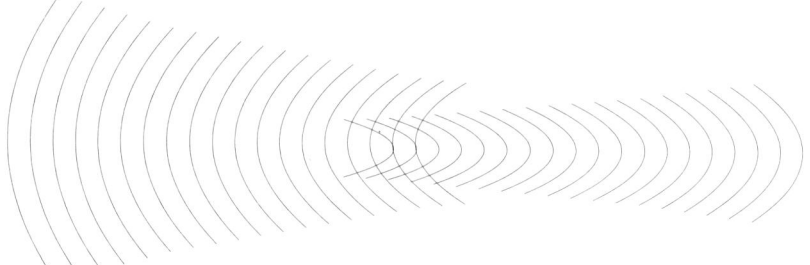

Figure 14.3 The TDR sends a signal which reflects from anomalies.

Note well, however, that this pulse is not compatible with most network protocols. The pulse may match normal network voltage levels or use a different voltage and wavelength. In any event, it will disrupt normal network traffic if the hub remains enabled. In other words, testing a live network is apt to spawn continuous beacons. Because the TDR knows nothing about network protocols, for example in the case of FDDI, the TDR signal will override token and data traffic. Any node that is transmitting a valid frame will soon see that the frame was corrupted. As a consideration to network users, before attaching these devices to a network, inform them that network performance may degrade due to the testing. On the other hand, an individual lobe can be tested without network repercussions if the line is bypassed from the hub or concentrator.

Propagation Velocity

The TDR must be set for signal propagation velocity, wire ohms and voltage, and signal degradation over distance. Some pair scanner units will sense the impedance and signal speed and assess whether the cable is of sufficient quality for use in FDDI. Some units will assess whether a lobe is qualified, and if not, why not, or determine the maximum qualified length for that lobe. Be sure to set the correct propagation velocity for the wire that you are testing. Pulses travel at different rates on different media, on different ages of wire, and on networks with excellent connectors and installation. Note that STP increases signal attenuation (signal strength decay and dispersion), but minimizes the crosstalk inherent on UTP. Measurements displayed by the TDR will be inaccurate if this information is not correctly set.

Optical Fiber FDDI

In addition to basic continuity tests, the light meter, feature detector, and OTDR will precisely locate an open or break relative to a cable endpoint, or bad splices, poor connections, and signal transmission problems. The difference between these tools is that the light meter requires a source light with a known and stable quality at the opposite end of the segment being tested. The feature detector is not a general purpose tool as the light meter is. The OTDR, on the other hand, generates its own source and reads the light scatter to make an assessment of the fiber. Light sources are generally available in 780, 850, 1300, and 1550 nm wavelengths, standard for optical fiber. Some OTDRs require a reflective terminating connector be placed at the opposite end of the cable or a second OTDR. While testing from both ends may be more precise, it is less convenient since it requires a second person at the other end, or potentially at least two 4 km (or 72 km) trips to set up the other end. By the way, this generally breaks the network during the test period unless you switch the primary ring to the second channel while you test the primary channel and hope that the ring does not wrap for any reason.

Furthermore, the OTDR when used with a camera, or a scanner with a serial port attachment to a PC, can blueprint a network. This aids in debugging the all-too-common network failure. For optical dual fiber FDDI networks, only a handful of things go wrong. The primary and secondary fibers can be wrongly connected at one end. One of the fibers can be broken. Or, the signal can be weakened by scatter, optical degradation, poor splices and connections. Neither the light meter or the OTDR will show that the cables are reversed. That is something best solved with good documentation and use of keyed shielded dual connectors.

If the signal degrades more than the acceptable 3 dB FDDI loss, something is wrong somewhere in the length of the fiber. While the light meter and the OTDR both will indicate this problem, the light can help

Media Testing

you find it unless you can track it to a separable segment of the cable. If the cable goes bad due to a physical failure, the light meter can only confirm that a problem exists.

The OTDR, on the other hand, can tell you exactly where the flaw occurs. You can follow these length readings to a bad connector, bad splice, or failure of the fiber itself. Connectors can be replaced, splices redone, and cable failures excised from the fiber and respliced. Resplicing is subject to signal loss; the newly spliced cable must remain within specification. Note that when dual fiber is spliced to remove a bad section in one fiber, check both fibers for conformity to specification after completing the splice. You do not want to introduce a new problem on another line.

Either of these tools—light meter and OTDR—are effective for qualifying breakout bundles of optical fiber. It is not difficult to tell if a fiber will work or fail. Either it works or it fails for the length and application; both tools can tell you that. Typically, though, a failed fiber in a large bundle is not repaired or spliced, simply ignored. It is too risky to risk damaging the other fibers. If too many fibers fail, the bundle is replaced in full or a single new line or new bundle is added to pick the load. Figure 14.4 illustrates these three common optical fiber failures.

The OTDR unit connects onto the network in place of a station. It rarely checks duplex fibers at the same time. Thus, you may need special connectors or adapters to connect the device to the ring. Also note that these jumpers and connectors tend to fail often from wear and abuse. While the OTDR remains connected onto the network, it breaks the ring. If you can establish the other fiber of a dual pair or a backup fiber, you can maintain full network operation. Otherwise, FDDI should wrap around the disabled segment.

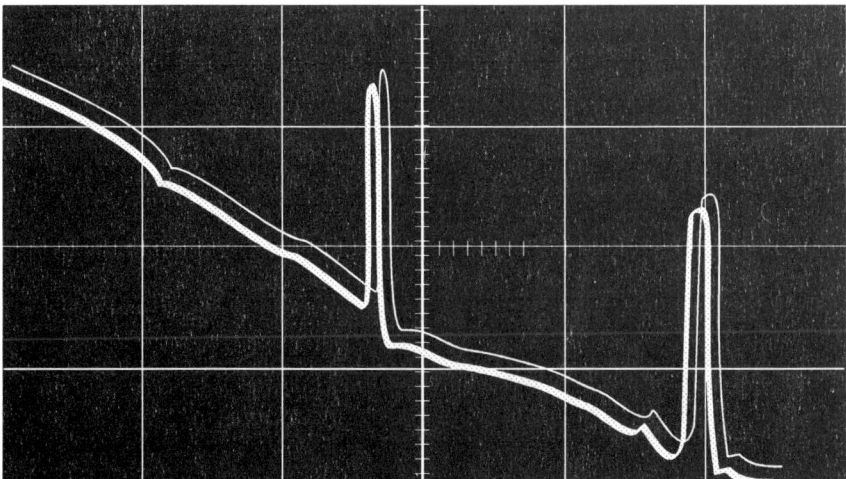

Figure 14.4 OTDR display of common fiber flaws.

Signal Characteristics

The light source, light meter, and OTDR must support and be set for the signal "color" that the NICs expect. If you qualify the network or the cable with the wrong bandwidth, it will work for that bandwidth but possibly not for the bandwidth in question. Although multimode fiber will usually support the full range of possible frequencies, single mode fiber is usually manufactured with optimal signal clarity at the specified signal propagation frequency. Typical FDDI wavelengths are 1300 and 1550 nm; other optical fiber frequencies in general use are 780 and 850 nm. One other caveat is when testing from opposing ends of a segment, make certain both the light source and light meter are set for the same frequency, or that both OTDRs are expecting the same frequency. You could have the right tools, but use them improperly.

Interpreting Results

All obstructions reflect the signal with various signatures which are read from a light meter, oscilloscope, or numerical display. These signatures must be learned as their interpretation is an art. Patch panels, splices, connectors, different grades and ages of cable, and, of course, breaks and shorts in the wire are visible. The same holds true for optical networks. Connectors, media attachment units, media breaks or shorts, excessive bends, and segments that are too long are visible in the display. On a digital TDR unit (typically the handheld scanner) lacking a visual display, these anomalies are visible as deviations from the normal numerical display or by a red indicator light.

See Figures 14.5 through 14.6 for samples of TDR and OTDR results. The reticule grid—vertical and horizontal lines that run through the middle of the oscilloscope display—is set to discriminate at 200 m. Each horizontal grid line is about a meter. The large spikes represent the test lead.

Figure 14.5 shows a break in a cable. Breaks caused by overextending the bending radius of twisted-pair wire or cuts through a wire pair, or radio-frequency interference from powerful sources (such as transformers, high-intensity lamps, and other electrical cables) show as large bends, spikes, and kinks in the display. Faulty NICs or hubs show up as a waveform different from that of a functioning unit—it usually lacks a large spike. If nonstandard or old media is inserted to replace a defective or damaged section of twisted-pair, the TDR will show this with a large pulse deflection. The test pulse wave will reflect with a dramatic difference in height, and with sufficient art one can interpret these deviations. The hand-held scanners will indicate these anomalies with indicator lights or by reports downloaded to a PC. The oscilloscope CRT also shows distance to the anomaly which is overlaid in the photographic samples. Figure 14.6 shows this common installation problem.

As another example, if the display indicates the network length is longer than specified, the genderless connectors may be stuck open. The

Media Testing

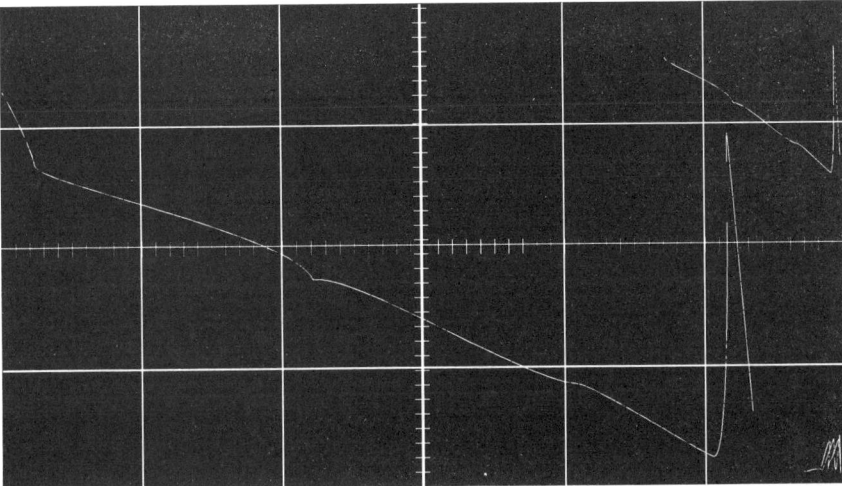

Figure 14.5 A break in the fiber.

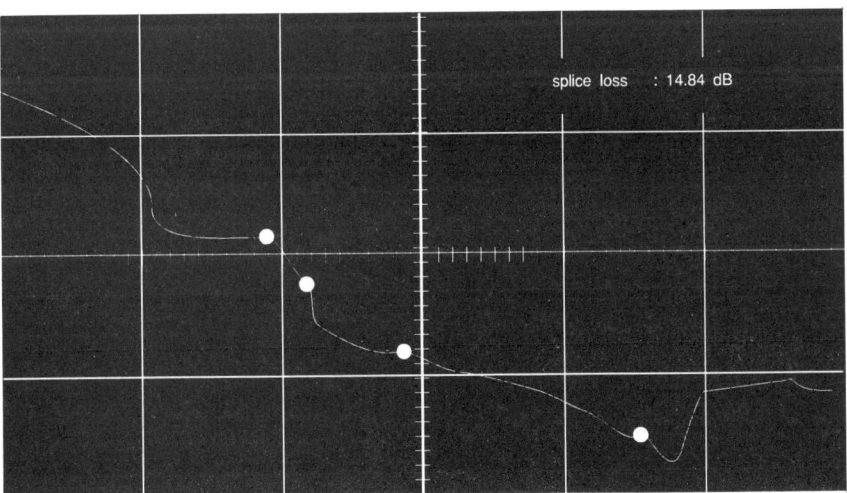

Figure 14.6 The OTDR display shows insertion of nonstandard media.

open ring will fail the length test. A second indication of missing ring closure or improperly installed connectors is a display that is mirrored beyond the blueprinted segment length, as Figure 14.7 indicates. This happens because the wave strikes the end of the wire, finds a medium with a different transmission quality, and reflects back down the cable inversely as shown. This is similar to the transmission characteristics

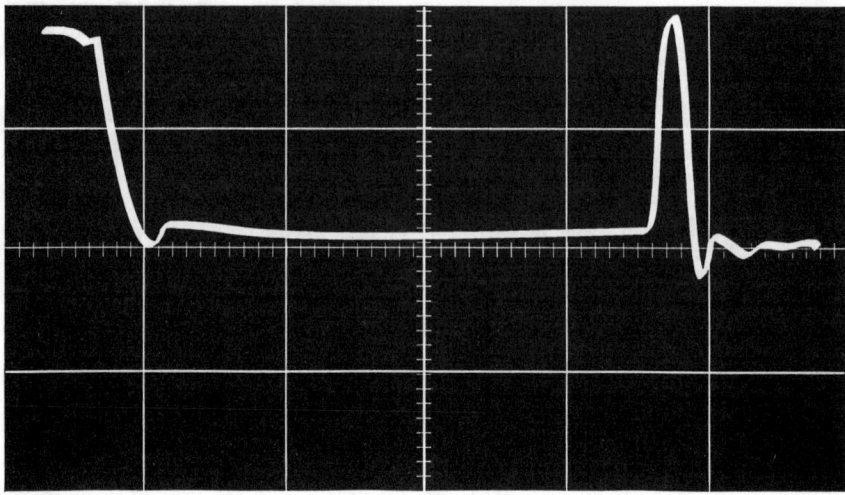

Figure 14.7 TDR display of a missing connector.

of light when it passes from one medium, like air, through another medium, like glass, and back into air. Depending on the reflective angle of incidence, the image will be deflected. A mirror image occurs at the 90° deflection of an improperly terminated end; the image will cease at hubs or stations. Handheld scanners usually will indicate a lobe flaw on a loopback test. The loopback test requires that a special genderless connector is attached at the opposite end of the lobe wire to *loopback* signal originating from the scanner back to the scanner.

Series inductance (evident as a scrape or break through the STP wire shield) shows as a positive pulse followed by a negative pulse. The last common waveform shows that the network cable impedance is out of specification, as would happen when improper cable is installed. This is typical when voice-grade UTP of insufficient quality is applied for FDDI lobes for runs longer than 30 to 50 meters. A series of alternating pulses would suggest this problem. Figure 14.8 details a TDR image caused by spliced twisted-pair wire with different transmission characteristics.

It is important to realize that since FDDI is logically a ring, any break or short in the ring will halt all network operations. This does include failure to properly attach the RI/RO cables to a single hub or to improperly connect them when there are many hubs. Breaks are more common than shorts. Pairs that cross over will break the network, a live telephone circuit in place of the proper LAN lobe certainly breaks the circle, and partial media connections or failed punchdown ties will halt the network. While node beacons may provide general indications where the break is, the scanner or TDR is the superior tool for actually locating and fixing short circuits, open circuits, or breaks. These tools supersede the multitester

Media Testing

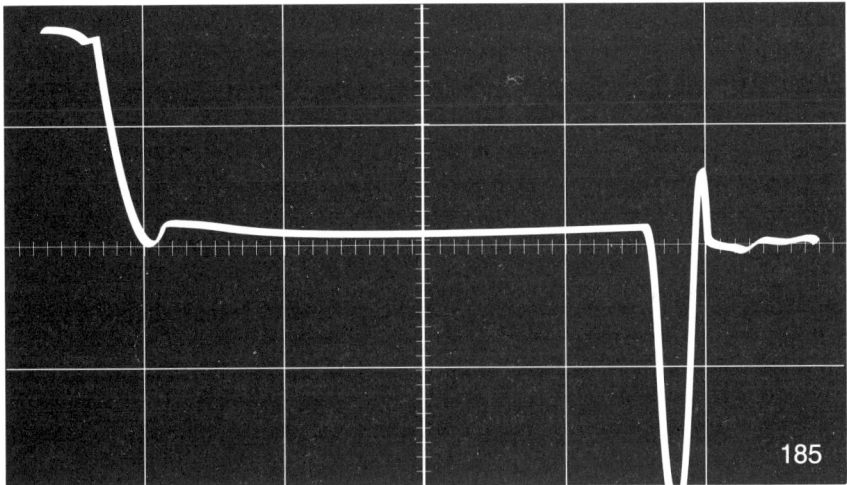

Figure 14.8 The TDR display of a missing connector.

because they accurately position the problem. There are also certain problems that cannot be diagnosed by just a multitester with any immediacy. These include bad wire, wrong grade of wire, radio-frequency interference, internal flaws, and mismatched sections. While a multitester will identify that one of these problems exists, it will not pinpoint the problem so that it can be categorized or localized, and diagnosed.

Without a TDR, the course of action would be to segment the ring progressively until the problem is localized sufficiently. Since FDDI is a star, each lobe or trunk is accessible and can be individual removed from the ring. Power-off workstations and they will be logically removed from the ring. Disconnect lobe cables or remove jumpers at the patch panel to physically remove workstations from the ring.

Visual inspections are time-consuming and often fruitless. The time requirement for such a search is excessive and demonstrates why the scanner is the tool of choice. A full-featured TDR will also send pulses continuously down the network twisted-pair wire. While jabber and signal jitter can be diagnosed with the TDR, there is no ingenious means to locate a NIC with the TDR other than as an endpoint on a lobe cable. As with a multitester, more complex problems require more complex tools. In this case, a software or hardware problem requires more than a hardware solution. This is best solved with a protocol analyzer.

Blueprinting

The time domain reflectometer and handheld scanner with serial downlink capability are the best available instruments to effect physical network blueprinting. The TDR or OTDR, in conjunction with a film recorder or screen camera, can illustrate the internal workings of the network wiring or optical fiber. These photographs or data downlinks (from scanner to PC) form a record against which future problems can be compared. It is a map of permanence. Figure 14.9 demonstrates the type of information that could be logically included in a careful ring scanner analysis. Note, however, that the Token-Ring scanner suitable for testing 4 Mbits/s and 16 Mbits/s will not adequately test the performance of STP or UTP for FDDI. A hand-held scanner specifically designed for FDDI is necessary. Figure 14.10 shows a representative cabling blueprint with notations.

Last, note that many integrated and specialized communications chips may incorporate TDR functionality within the chips themselves. Examples include several chip sets from Intel and National Semiconductor. Although software to utilize this function is not yet available, expect that it will become an important selling feature because it can simplify network management. Specifically, when the TDR function is combined with protocol analysis, building true topological (although linear) maps representing the network is simple. Reflectometry provides distances to wiring anomalies for each node lobe that can be matched against sent and return protocol frames. The frames provide node names (OSI or Internet addresses) that are matched to physical locations for network nodes. Some anomalies will be connectors, minor flaws, or true faults. Not only is the combination of information provided by these two tools useful for intelligently blueprinting the network, but also it is useful for indicating potential failure points as well.

In actual practice a network manager and an assistant might use two OTDRs to analyze the network and move them around from location to

Lobe Pairs	Length	Status
1	70.4	OK
2	66.2	OK
3	56.0	OK
4	56.0	OK
5	56.0	OK
6	56.0	OK
7	46.8	Ok
8	98.2	Atten.

Figure 14.9 Ring scanner data downloaded to PC.

Media Testing

location. Bad frames, duplicated addresses, and loss of tokens or frames require a protocol analyzer. The next chapter, Chapter 15, details the use of this tool and how it works. For more precise verification of network software errors, the protocol analyzer is the tool of choice. The workings of this instrument are described fully in Chapter 15.

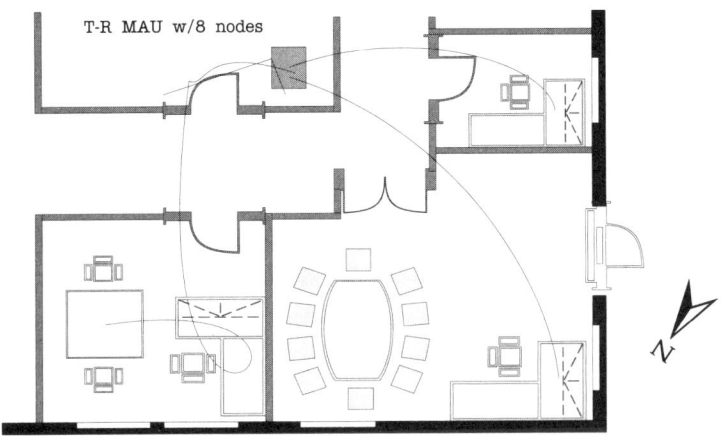

Bldg. 4, North Corner, 2nd floor   (4-15-1991)

Figure 14.10 This annotated instant photograph shows network documentation appropriate for a careful blueprinting.

Chapter 15
Debugging with the Protocol Analyzer

The last chapter explained how to test the mechanical layers of FDDI. The handheld scanner or feature detector and larger TDR and OTDR test wire for proper functioning. These simple tools are limited to resolving hardware problems on single-ring FDDI networks; few tools provide real insight into malfunctions across multiple ring networks because bridges, routers, and gateways are effective "firewalls" to isolate network activities. The protocol analyzer is one tool that transcends these limitations.

However, the protocol analyzer is not an essential FDDI debugging tool. The protocol analyzer will not solve all critical FDDI problems. It will not resolve many hardware problems. It is required only for large LANs, multiple ring LANs, LANs with hops or WAN segments, newly installed or expanded LANs, networks with many protocols, or networks with many problems. While the protocol analyzer is useful for performance analysis, balance its high cost, difficulty in learning how to use it, and the infrequent need to use it against the possibility of borrowing or renting the tool for brief periods or paying an expert with an analyzer for a few days. Since the FDDI protocol is deterministic in that a token circulates around the ring with some consistency, a protocol analyzer is necessary *only* in special cases; most FDDI failures are hardware-based or wiring-induced. When FDDI enterprise networks support multiple protocols—examples include NetWare, IPX, UDP, TCP/IP, encapsulation of other protocols such as Ethernet and Token-Ring, and OSI—the need for protocol analysis increases. Large and multiple segment FDDI networks may benefit from the exclusive use of a specialized hardware-based protocol analyzer.

In fact, the firewall is seen as increasingly representative of the operational mentality applied when interconnecting multiple LANs. Although the firewall is effective for isolating individual LANs from the effects and failures in other segments, the firewall may also, as a result, limit the scope of protocol analysis. SNMP is generally limited within each network and will not necessary pass through bridges, routers, or gateways. To some degree CMIP overcomes the firewall, while some vendors provide *remote probes* for incorporation in the rings or segments of interconnected LANs. Such management protocols do come at the cost of the network bandwidth they use.

Many network failures can be traced to software that transcends the physical layers of FDDI, network loading characteristics, and firmware, which is software loaded into a specialized hardware processor. This type of failure requires network management software and protocol analysis. The management process is based upon the collection of relevant network operating statistics like throughput rates, errors, beacons, ring recoveries, source and destination addresses, and overhead. Protocol analysis is a process where you view the transmission protocols, most likely IEEE 802.2 LLC or FDDI frames, IPX or NetBIOS data layer elements like MAC-level frames and datagrams.

The tools available consist of network communication protocol-based "software" such as Simple Network Management Protocol (SNMP), Common Management Information Protocol (CMIP), and the CMOT implementation, workstation-based tools, including Sun Microsystem's NFS-based *NETSTAT, PERFMON*, TCP/IP-based *PING*, NetView, or a protocol analyzer, which is a stand-alone computer, network interface card, and data collection and analysis software. Increasingly, as the sophistication of networks and software improves, expect to see more protocol analysis software, including tools such as the Teletek ChameLAN. They empower the network communication hardware to perform loop-back tests, add scanner and TDR functionality, and correlate this information with performance metrics.

The process of locating intermittent transmission failures with hardware testers is a random proposition. Such failures require more analytical techniques and a different network monitoring tool. A generic network monitor, also called a *protocol analyzer*, is the right tool for locating such software-based failures. It provides information to solve network problems. The protocol analyzer collects network traffic data, reports the network status, and many different variables, and converts that data into statistics, while some analyzers with sophisticated statistical packages can chart numerical results for visual analysis. The protocol analyzer confirms perceived performance degradation with hard evidence. This is a very important tool to verify bridge, router, and gateway functionalities, particularly now that they are so complex.

Network Management Protocols

Hardware protocol analyzers may become antiquated as network management protocols are incorporated into networks and as FDDI hubs become more sophisticated in debugging media- and performance-level

Debugging with the Protocol Analyzer

errors. Protocols such as SNMP, CMIP, and the CMOT overlap many of the features provided by stand-alone analyzers; in some cases they provide even more powerful features. Chapter 5 described these important three protocols. All these tools, including the protocol analyzer, collect and retain network performance statistics. Such information is important to assess reliability, work throughput, and functionality of any network, whether simple or enterprise- wide. Nonetheless, network management protocols often have blind spots, fail to route across bridges, routers, and gateways, or ignore FDDI hardware and signal encoding variants. Additionally, older networks and mixed networks with wired and wireless components likely lack the required network management protocol *agents* required for complete data capture and performance analysis. This comprises the major difference between hardware analyzers and software counterparts. Networks with components in excess of 20 percent unmanaged are best monitored with external protocol analysis tools; do not rely upon SNMP-or CMIP-derivative protocols with an agency requirement.

Network Management Software

Network management software represents a new application area. These utilitarian tools automatically map the network matching station numbers with the corresponding addresses. They also determine the physical layout of the network by using the built-in TDR functions found in most network access chip sets (such as are found in the Intel or National Semiconductor integrated network chips). Network blueprints are otherwise very time-consuming to construct. Perhaps the most important feature provided by network management software is an ability to interpret captured network statistics. These assessments and suggestions are valuable for tuning networks, recognizing physical limitations, and uncovering any violations of the network specifications. Additionally, some network management software can intelligently act upon alarms to segment the network, reroute network traffic to underutilized alternate paths, and perhaps even disable malfunctioning (chattering or jittering) network devices.

Protocol Analysis

The protocol analyzer is a computer workstation (or specialized software running on a standard network station) that is a network station. It requires access through one connection as a station, or through a multiport access unit or hub. The analyzer can send and receive FDDI frames just as any other workstation or node does. Figure 15.1 shows one such unit. The analyzer watches the network for all FDDI frames, not just for signals directed to its station. The protocol analyzer is said

Figure 15.1 A protocol analyzer. (Tekelec Corp.)

to be "promiscuous" because it "eavesdrops" on all stations in the network and potentially can capture any frame. It is a complicated tool in order to match the full network bandwidth and compile relevant statistics in real-time. Many such tools cannot maintain data collection at the full FDDI rate of 100 Mbits/s; some may only maintain burst-level tracking to 20 Mbits/s. Also, some tools may maintain the full bit rate of FDDI but be unable to interpret the frames in realtime. These tools may not be less expensive, but are less capable.

Commensurate with the protocol analyzer's complexity, it provides detailed information to trace complicated problems. A protocol analyzer listens to the signal on the network and finds a frame with known source and station destination, a multicast, or a broadcast destination. Frames with improper addresses, logical addresses for other rings or subnets, and nonresponsive addresses represent network errors and inefficiencies. The analyzer must also listen and identify jitter, beacons, ring recoveries, and misaligned signals on the local network. Furthermore, this tool must be able to identify frames derived from and destined for remote gateways. Anonymous frames must be filtered and captured for analysis and eventual problem resolution.

An FDDI network carries traffic for many different purposes, as outlined in Figure 15.2. The consistency of traffic varies by load rate, by source and destination, and by peak characteristics. Control of the

Debugging with the Protocol Analyzer

- Virtual terminal support
- File transfer
- Electronic mail
- Network file services
- Network print services
- Network station and node data backup
- Network file system support
- Database client/server
- Network utilities
- Network programs
- Network output services
- Network facsimile
- Distributed processing applications
- Phone integration
- Voice and image transmission
- Online conferences
- Workgroup meeting scheduling and calendar functions
- Image storage and retrieval
- Internetwork management information
- Point-to-point linkages
- LAN status reports

Figure 15.2 Typical FDDI traffic activities.

network and proper management require an understanding of the flow of frames. Since hardware testers only indicate the status of the physical plant, another tool like the protocol analyzer provides input for network use, load, consistency, resource distribution, and implied resource allocation decisions.

Thus, the protocol analyzer is an important tool for network management. Although software tools, such as PERFMON or NETVIEW, are invaluable for network analysis, a full-function protocol analyzer is a safe investment for a network of significant size or complexity; generally, this means multiple rings, or networks with multiple protocols (e.g., hardware protocols, such as ARCnet, Ethernet, FDDI, and Token-Ring; network and transport protocols, such as NetBEUI, NetBIOS, UDP, and TCP/IP; and vendor-specific encapsulation protocols). This tool is useful for collating error rates, performance levels, and interstation traffic. Such statistics, when above normal ranges, provide direct correlations to network problems.

For example, a high rate for CRC errors for a specific source station might indicate a faulty FDDI controller, whereas a high jitter rate may indicate that its NIC is not sensitive enough or that the twisted-pair lobe wire is too long. In general, rates as captured with the protocol analyzer correlate to specific problems that are easily matched to their sources for quick diagnosis.

However, the protocol analyzer does have its limitations. It does not provide a model for understanding network loading, give specific indications of why a network is performing badly, or offer suggestions about how to improve the performance of bottlenecked segments within the context of a larger enterprise-wide network. The complexities of networks linked with bridges, routers, and gateways, or connected through WAN X.25, T-1, or modem linkages generate complex interactions. Although expert systems software is increasingly provided with protocol analyzers so that the average technically trained person can make informed judgments about LAN performance and flaws, internetworks challenge our ability to comprehend the interactions and complexities.

The protocol analyzer frequently is unable to track networks supporting multiple protocols, such as IPX/SPX, TCP/IP, XNS, NetBIOS, and NetBEUI, although they are all much alike. It often ignores useful information from networks with multiple segments or extensions provided by routers and gateways. Although some vendors are adding expert systems to their protocol analyzers to address some of these shortfalls, true network analysis requires a performance queueing model, as described in Chapter 16. This network performance model, however, requires extensive network information, as might be gathered with a protocol analyzer. Despite the protocol analyzer's limitations, for all of these other reasons, it is a critical tool for network management on large rings.

Network Information

Network management software or a stand-alone protocol analyzer dedicated only to the task of watching the network is an important tool for network maintenance and evaluation. FDDI communication is a deterministic process. Basically, the token goes around the ring. A station that wants to transmit must get that token. If the token does not circulate once during the *target token rotation time* (TTRT), it is a certainty that something is wrong. Most problems on FDDI are obvious. Downstream stations *beacon* when an upstream neighbor does not function correctly. Stations and hubs *wrap* when segments fail. An intelligent hub will drop misbehaving nodes and nodes that it thinks are misbehaving. Even when network traffic increases to extraordinary levels, it is still impossible to break the ring. The TRT will be longer and users will be unhappy with ring latency and application response times. Nonetheless, the network will still provide communications, albeit at a reduced speed.

Network Performance Questions

In order to resolve higher-level network bottlenecks and FDDI traffic failures, the network administrator must view the network as a highway carrying data traffic. The network administrator seeks to answer opera-

Debugging with the Protocol Analyzer 317

tional questions as outlined in Figure 15.3 in order to evaluate the operational efficiency of any network. Understanding why these questions are relevant is the subject of the next section.

Heisenberg Uncertainty Principle

If the monitoring equipment actively requests and captures information, the process itself skews the results. Since every station on FDDI must capture, regenerate, and rebroadcast the frame signal, and since a protocol monitoring station is an active device, the inserted monitoring station will add between .0025 and .0200 μs delay to the TRT. It is also quite likely that file service requests, information probes, and process swap requests performed in the pursuit of network status data will generate network loading in addition to that of the base-level network traffic. The essence of the Heisenberg Uncertainty Principle is that the active process of observing an event alters the outcome of that event. Passive monitoring, on the other hand, watches each broadcast frame without accessing or affecting the network. This eliminates performance losses and potentially obviates any speed limitations that the monitoring actually seeks to chronicle. Unlike most vendor-supplied software tools, most protocol analyzers provide passive monitoring.

Vendor-Specific Limitations

Most vendors of network workstations provide resident software tools to track network access and usage for individual workstations. Some vendors even provide software that will measure network usage. Choose

- What stations transmit on the network?
- Do stations correctly transmit?
- Do stations respond correctly to transmissions?
- Do stations defer to the busy network?
- What is the traffic volume?
- What is the traffic consistency?
- What is the length of messages?
- What is average peak loading?
- What is full capacity?
- What is the average intermessage timing (latency)?
- What is the average wait delay (response time)?
- Which stations talk to each other?
- Do messages have frame errors?
- Can some stations not reach other stations?
- Which stations and nodes cause problems?
- Which rings or segments are overloaded?
- Do all stations comply to FDDI specification?
- Are gateways and routers performing to specification?

Figure 15.3 Questions answered by the protocol analyzer.

software and hardware that conforms preferably to the SNMP rather than CMIP standards or proprietary vendor tools. SNMP is more likely to be supported. Either SNMP or CMIP provides an agency address for SNMP or CMIP data collection. Hardware and software lacking in this regard are effectively invisible to the management protocols.

However, vendor-supplied network monitoring software tools will exhibit the same flaws and faults as their workstations and overlook some types of problems. Therefore, a specialized device is required to capture and parse all types of network frames. This is particularly pertinent for mixed protocol and multiple hop networks. The protocol analyzer fills this function because it is protocol-independent. The analyzer can view all IEEE 802.2 (MAC), LLC packets, IEEE 802.3 (Ethernet), IEEE 802.5 (Token-Ring), TCP/IP or UDP frames and FDDI frames that conform to TCP/IP, HPnet, XNS, DECnet, OSI, OSI (FDDI), NetBIOS, NetBEUI, SPX, or any other "standards." The tool passively captures a burst signal containing a FDDI frame, then parses this frame to whatever the encapsulation, upper-, or lower-level protocols dictate. Within this framework, SPX information and IPX control information, for example, can be viewed without reliance on questionable network-level software.

Some workstation vendors build analyzers as part of their product line. In general, it is a good management practice not to rely on single solutions in this specific case; it is desirable generally to install networks with components from a single vendor. Test equipment is sometimes better acquired from a competitor. These backup and alternative methods are reasonable. Therefore, consider purchasing a protocol analyzer from an independent vendor so that any vendor-specific problems or incompatibilities to "standard" FDDI can be uncovered.

The Role of Network Monitoring

Although FDDI can be viewed as analogous to a party-line telephone network, at other times a highway analogy is more appropriate. Since FDDI is a deterministic medium, certain traffic models represent FDDI's capacity, throughput, and timing attributes with a high degree of accuracy. These statistical models are presented in Chapter 16, but in this chapter the emphasis is placed upon the methodology for analytically tracing network problems by deciphering transmission frames, counts, and rates.

Understanding Network Performance

FDDI is a purely deterministic transmission medium. Network station stations transmit when they capture a token, transmit for a duration not to exceed the token hold timer, and finally release that token. [Should you foresee a need to improve multiple hop performance by adding burst mode, or maintain a large ring populated with very small acknowledgment

Debugging with the Protocol Analyzer

frames (under 200 bytes), specify a protocol analysis tool that supports these protocol enhancements.] Additionally, traffic speed is enforced at 100 Mbits/s. Overloads and traffic problems tend to occur at the stations themselves, barring wiring or hardware problems. Network problems can be grouped in a hierarchical progression. It is usually worthwhile to check for station hardware problems before searching for network hardware failures. Likewise, it is usually best to search for station software problems before searching for more global network bottlenecks, incompatibilities, or failures.

In order to monitor network performance, it is important to know how many stations there are on the network, and which actually transmit. The first order of network problems occurs when stations do not transmit correctly. This is generally a hardware-problem which FDDI will directly indicate by isolating failed stations. Hardware problems should not occur without beacons and ring wrap. FDDI is a robust third generation networking architecture (Ethernet is first generation and Token-Ring is a second generation LAN), and it manages hardware problems quite well. The analyzer gathers measurements to pinpoint these packaging and application-oriented problems.

Once the deterministic network hardware problems are resolved, the second order is to compute the actual traffic load. Each and every piece of equipment may function correctly. Systems may be reliable. Nevertheless, a network may perform slowly and erratically. This is usually indicative of an overloaded transmission channel or choke points at critical stations and network devices.

The most significant network measurement is the frame count, which tells how many frames, good or bad, have been transmitted on the network. This count can be subdivided into good frames and bad frames, by source and destination, by characteristics of frame length, type, frequency, or by error condition. Figure 15.4 groups these items in a matrix framework with practical implications.

Basic network monitoring is the process of capturing frames during a known time interval since problems occur within an interval of time, or can be pegged to a certain event in time. Therefore, frame volume (or throughput) is an important measurement. The consistency of volume is another important unit because inconsistency creates traffic bottlenecks that frequently do not clear; traffic consistency will be discussed in the next chapter. If network problems occur and the assumption is that the network is overloaded, volumes and peak volume statistics may validate this theory. However, it is important to compare observed volume to a theoretical capacity.

Other areas of network transmission problems are the degenerative transmission situations that occur when frames are defective, long, short, misaligned, wrongly addressed, or incompatible with the network

Good Frames	Bad Frames
Length	Beacons
Type	Overruns
Frequency	Encapsulation and translation errors
	Misaligned frames
	Frame errors
	FCS errors
	Protocol errors
	Stray signals

Figure 15.4 Network frame measurements. These measurements are also useful when subgrouped by frame source and destination.

standard. FDDI will usually isolate a station creating degenerative frames. However, good frames with bad data represent a second-order problem, best resolved with the protocol analyzer. This is a Charlie the Tuna conundrum; whether the tuna fish tastes good or the tuna fish has good taste. The play on words and word order should not hide that the meaning is different. It is important to recognize that the FDDI frames themselves conform to protocol, but that data within the FDDI data field—whether encapsulated as FDDI data, containing a LLC, MAC, TCP, or UDP packet, or as a translation from another networking protocol—is scrambled and defective. The search for the cause of these problems transcends statistical measurements because frames with bad data have to be repeated until they are received and interpreted correctly. Frames with bad data can flood a network and halt its effectiveness. In order to expose any sources for bad frames, defective frames must be examined for content, and the frame fields should be parsed and viewed, as Figure 15.5 illustrates.

In fact, protocol variances usually show in address discrepancies, length or type of field variations, or the LLC and upper-level protocol fields contained within the actual FDDI data field. If underlying causes for corrupted protocol formats, address discrepancies, or mismatched upper-layer protocols are to be exposed, frames must be captured and dissected.

Corrupted Frames

Comparisons of rates for short, long, and corrupted frames are important statistics, also. Damaged frames imply a hub, station, or lobe wire problem, a defective FDDI NIC, late acquisition of the frame or lack of synchronization, problems with signal regeneration or crosstalk, or outside noise. A damaged frame usually has a bad checksum, or *cyclic redundancy check* (CRC). Short, long, or damaged frames imply faulty

Debugging with the Protocol Analyzer

```
Source:        6:0:34:1:12:5F
Destination:   6:0:34:1:E4:FD
Length:        4212
CRC:           okay
```

Data: | DSAP | SSAP | Control | Data fields |

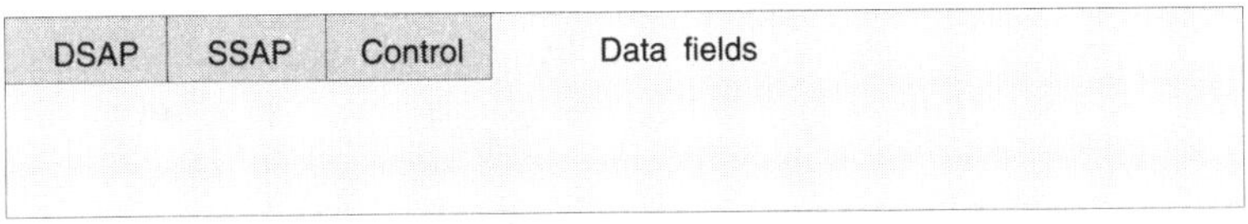

Figure 15.5 View of the decoded frame, data field only.

hardware at a workstation. This should correspond to ring wraps or requests to reinitialize the ring.

Statistics on corrupted frames should focus attention on the root causes of problems rather than on some ephemeral "global" problem. Excessive numbers of short, long, or defective frames could imply that transmission from a NIC was interrupted or that the transmitting workstation did not have the token but still transmitted. These corrupted frames could also indicate that the ring is supporting a NIC with a bad clock crystal or a problem synchronizing with the token or frame preamble.

A protocol analyzer with a robust software package (such as the Network General tools) eases the difficulty in calculating these items because it will automatically tally frame counts, calculate percentage rates, and graph trends. Graphic display of these items lends more meaning and can show trends not otherwise noticeable. However, even with a less satisfactory software package, the basic information can be collected and downloaded or rekeyed to a spreadsheet program for the same results.

Frame Counts

At a minimum, some metrics are required to compare network performance over different time frames. Another network status indicator, in addition to the TRT and the error rate, is a frame count. This number can be compared against a count from another day to see if unusually heavy traffic is the reason for perceived performance problems. For example, if there were 15,000,000 frames today versus 12,000,000 frames yesterday—a 20 percent increase—the magnitude of this difference would explain why performance has suffered, assuming no significant change in the TRT. On the other hand, 15,000,000 frames at FDDI speeds may represent only 50 *seconds* of normal loads. Such a load might be high for 4 or 10 Mbits/s protocols, but certainly not for FDDI. Assertions that a 20 percent load increase has caused the degraded performance is incorrect because the context is flawed. The statistics must be represented within an accurate context.

However, performance could be quite poor is this traffic was concentrated within the time frame. It all depends on the "burstiness"—a general term describing the sudden requirement to transmit large numbers of frames on a network with an otherwise predictable load—and time of day distribution of that extra workload. Sometimes, although less frequently, burstiness can also refer to a network load with great variance in frame sizes. An even more useful statistic would be a frame transmission rate per time period, called a *traffic rate*. While a frames-per-day rate is useful for comparison, more immediate frame counts are better. Counts per second, per minute, or per hour constitute a traffic rate. These counts allow comparisons during the shorter intervals within which most FDDI problems occur.

Statistics for Network Planning

By combining the number of frames transmitted (rather than the total frame count) with either the lengths of each frame or average length of transmitted frames, a transmission-level count is generated. This is a *bits-per-second* (bits/s) figure. Other literature uses a "bps" acronym. Every manager needs an indication of how much work is actually accomplished for planning growth, managing new tasks, and maintaining a functioning network. The TRT is practical since it increases linearly as a function of frame size and number of stations, and is a linear proxy for network latency, or response time. Latency is a better measure, but is usually too difficult to calculate. Usage rates aid planning by providing a nearly independent statistic. It is nearly independent because as the network grows and the load increases, response time decreases and less work can be completed within any interval. Consequently, usage rates are apt to be lower per station on a saturated network than on a nonsaturated network. Usage rates are a more consistent measure.

The usage rates also show type and quantity of work by station. They provide the necessary data to make informed network planning decisions. Chapter 18 presents many options to tune network performance. A difficult problem is identifying what should be tuned—whether the station, the database, the indexes, the clients, the bridges, the routers, or the "window" during which frames are transmitted before a confirmation of status is expected.

Network Traffic Composition

A subset of stations will have higher rates of usage than other stations as a consequence of the work performed, or as a result of those stations' need to access network resources. Different users work different hours, perform various duties that load a network differently, and generate different consistencies of FDDI frames. Also, too many users and sta-

Debugging with the Protocol Analyzer

tions clearly can overload a network and create bottlenecks and slow network response. Indicators of station-specific overloads are outlined in Figure 15.6. Figure 15.7 lists symptoms of a network-wide traffic performance problems. To understand the root cause of uneven traffic problems, it is important to understand the composition of that network traffic. The pie chart in Figure 15.8 summarizes data from captured frames. Of 330,000 frames, 50,000 were mail messages, 30,000 were follow-on frames for mail messages, and 240,000 were applied to other uses. Only 10,000 frames were identified as transport layer defects. The graphs imply that 25 percent of all network traffic in this sample is mail. Because there were follow-on mail frames, 60 percent of all mail messages average longer than a kilobyte. Note that 40 percent of all messages are brief. It is possible that one message is 0.3 megabyte (Mbyte) in length (and

- Overloaded network
- Too many stations, devices, and nodes (exceeding specification)
- Too many workstations
- Too many lengthy transmissions
- Chattering, jittering, or jabbering NICs
- NICs set to wrong transmission speed
- Mismatched hardware
- Defective application or network software
- Nonspec equipment

Figure 15.6 Typical causes for station- or node-specific overloads.

- High density of frames (high-level load)
- Lengthy transmissions (high peak demand)
- Maximum token rotation time
- Slow user response (overloads)
- Slow server response

Figure 15.7 Indicators of network-wide traffic problems.

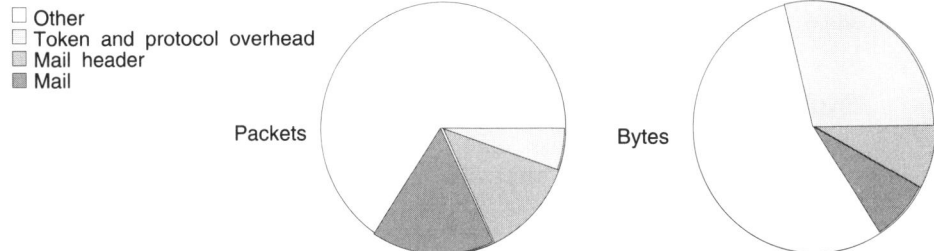

Figure 15.8 Indicators of network traffic composition problems. The pie charts detail the percentage of network traffic allocated to a particular function. In this example, most of the frames are small, but a few large mail packets correspond to most of the network utilization.

requires all 30,000 follow-on frames). This would skew the statistics and is one hypothesis to investigate.

The analysis does show that most mail messages are fairly brief, and 50,000 messages are a fairly significant number. If they come from a single station, it may imply that one user is broadcasting globally, and this may be unacceptable. Perhaps this type of transmission should be restricted to certain hours. If most messages are transmitted to a single station, perhaps this transmission level may imply the need for a bulletin board system rather than a mail broadcast.

Some processes may demand a significant portion of network traffic. Electronic mail, for example, may be a hidden use of network resources. The implication in this example is that mail is disproportionately overloading the network; while frame counts for mail are not large, the effect of actual traffic is skewed toward servicing mail requests. Likewise, data file uploading and downloading may be a significant load; this can be verified by examining the contents of the long trains of frames sent between specific pairs of stations. Time-stamping of frames would aid in this type of investigation. Perhaps, like mail, this type of transmission should be restricted to certain hours, too.

A solution, if usage-specific traffic is deemed a problem, may be to identify the need for electronic mail. Another similar source of network traffic is graphic paging, sometimes known as "screen refresh." This condition may imply that large blocks of high-density graphic information are being transferred with frequency from one machine to another. Several solutions to these types of problems are possible. First, transfer could be accomplished by tape or floppy disk rather than by the network. Second, a special link might be constructed to remove the burden from the main network, for example, a dual homing FDDI link, solely to support this transfer channel. Third, mail could be posted on a passive bulletin board rather than broadcast or multicast across the network. This last option not only reduces the load on the network, it also reduces disk storage space for multiple copies of identical messages. Furthermore, there is a double performance hit when mail is stored on and accessed from a file server since mail access requires network resources.

Global and Node-Specific Data Collection

Network software tools are sometimes available on the workstations, network servers, or PCs that are connected to the FDDI network. Network software tools may count frames, TRT, and sometimes identify sources and destinations with frame counts. Most often this software provides only single-station information and not global information about all stations. Both station-specific and global information is required for the best results in network maintenance. This information must be accurately acquired and displayed in useful formats. Figure

Debugging with the Protocol Analyzer

15.9 presents the minimum functionality for monitoring transmission-level network operations required to answer the network manager's questions.

Unless single-station statistics can be captured inexpensively and analyzed globally, network software tools are only transient indicators of network problems. Single-station statistics may pinpoint a problem with a particular station without indicating a specific station as the source of problems. Global counts may indicate a local or global problem, but rarely will pinpoint the cause. Unless global information with station-specific corroboration is available, problems cannot be isolated to a specific station. Even a problem as common as a jittering NIC cannot be resolved without such corroboration. Without the specific station information correlated to the global information, excessive transmissions of meaningless frames cannot be traced to their hardware sources except by trial and error or a binary search with physical test equipment.

The network statistics in Figure 15.10 show a high TRT. This global statistic would lead one to believe a problem exists everywhere. Node analysis from simple station-specific software would suggest that both stations 1 and 3 are faulty, whereas in fact only a single station may be causing problems, since a doubling in the TRT is significant. One station may be demonstrating that it is having difficulty communicating with the other station by the IPX protocol.

If usage rates seem localized to certain groups of stations, or localized to a certain manufacturer's parts, or certain types of users, then it might be desirable to localize those groups on subnets, or allocate special resources to the groups. Often, those groups may not warrant the extra costs associated with the additional resources, or it may be politically

- Count packets: all frames—overruns, corrupted, and good
- Display length of each frame
- Display average size of frames on network
- TRT and TTRT
- Store frames to memory (and/or disk)
- Monitor traffic levels
- Monitor individual stations, look for: high levels of traffic, high rates of retransmission, type of traffic, corrupted packets

Figure 15.9 Statistical values and functions needed for network analysis.

	Station 1	Station 2	Station 3	Network
Output frames	124000	150000	150000	424000
Input frames	60000	220000	9000	370000
TRT				0.6723 ns

Figure 15.10 Station-specific data bring global analysis into perspective.

unfeasible. It is important to note that FDDI is a public and potentially enterprise-wide resource without locks or accounting statistics. The added resources may be applied to improve the global performance incidentally in the attempt to improve performance for a selected group of stations and users. Capacity is a global constraint, not a configurable resource. Understand your goals before making performance assumptions for FDDI within your environment.

General Purpose Network Flow Information

Figure 15.11 lists some typical questions and corresponding network statistics by name. This listing, by means complete, is representative of the most expedient manner to answer each question posed.

Figure 15.12 lists some important counts, rates, and calculated statistics by name. This is not by any means a complete listing, just representative of information generally provided by protocol analyzers and network management software. The equations for these, or the methodology to generate them, are explained in the next chapter. This list included here to annotate several of the next charts.

Typical Network Questions	Statistics of Relevance
What stations transmit on the network?	Source and destination costs
Do stations correctly transmit?	Eliminate frames with error and analyze
Do stations repeat transmissions?	Simulation; utilization rate
Do stations acquire tokens correctly?	TRT
What is the traffic volume?	Counts, rates and utilization rate
What is the traffic consistency?	Capture packets; source and destination
What is the length of messages?	Size distribution
What is average peak loading?	Utilization rate; capacity rate
What is full capacity?	Frame counts or rates ; packet sizes
What is the intermessage timing?	Interarrival times
What is the average wait delay?	Latency distribution
Which nodes talk to each other?	Source/destination matrix
Do messages have frame errors?	Analyze and sort frame errors
Can some stations not reach other stations?	Analyze pattern of frames; simulation
Which nodes cause problems?	Frame counts, error counts
Which rings are overloaded?	Rates, TRT, interarrival times
Are gateways and repeaters to spec?	Rates, TRT, interarrival times

Figure 15.11 Typical management questions and corresponding statistics.

Debugging with the Protocol Analyzer

Frame Counts:
   All frames on networks
   Frames transmitted
   Frames received
   Frames deferred
   Frames per station
   By source
   By destination
   By source to destination
   By encapsulation method
   By translation source
   Size distribution in bytes (-, 3, 13, 64, 128, 256, 1024, 4024, 4474, 4486, +)
   Network period peaks station period peaks

Frame Errors:
   All packet/frame errors
   Alignment errors
   CRC errors
   Short frames
   Long frames
   Invisible frames
   Incompatible frames
   Misaddressed frames

Channel Utilization:
   TRT
   Throughput
   Peak rate
   Utilization as a percent of capacity

Capture:
   All frames
   Frames during an interval
   Frames with errors
   Frames with specific errors
   Frames with certain data types
   Frames from specific source station(s)
   Frames directed to a specific destination
   Station and node(s) frames with specific source/destination
   Frames with a certain size
   Frames without a protocol
   Frames with a specific protocol
   Rerouted, switched, and encapsulated frames
   Frames under UDP or TCP/IP
   Frame fragments
   Frames with SNMP information
   Frames with CMIP information
   Broadcast frames from routers and gateways (storms)
   Alarms

Figure 15.12 The protocol analyzer collects these common counts and rates, filters frames for specialized content, and calculates statistics useful for network analysis.

Statistics:
  Network usage as a percent of capacity
  Interarrival times (0 to 100 ms)
  Latency distribution
  Frame size distribution
  Station usage as a percent of capacity
  Station usage as a percent of network utilization packet
  Rate per second
  Bits/s
  Bytes/s
  TRT
  Retransmission rate
  Delivery error rate

Figure 15.12 The protocol analyzer collects these common counts and rates, filters frames for specialized content, and calculates statistics useful for network analysis. *(continued)*

Network Performance Data

Having identified statistics of interest, a measurement methodology needs to be developed. The worksheet in Figure 15.13 includes sample data for a large, complicated network, and the necessary steps to convert the collected data into applicable information. In this sample, the users experienced a network that was slow and unresponsive; they have complained to the network manager, who must validate or discount the users' claims. As a consequence of a thorough analysis with a protocol analyzer several unrelated problems were uncovered.

In this example, information has been captured during a 24-hour period on a network with 26 stations. The column headings represent each station, the number of frames input (i.e., received), the number of errors at the transport layer for these input frames, the number of frames output (that is, transmitted), the number of errors at the transport layer for these output frames, and two columns for rates. The first column shows input errors as a percentage of frames received. The second column shows output errors as a percentage of frames transmitted. The last two columns cannot be calculated until all the other information has been completed since these rates require network totals. These two right-hand columns show a method to compare station usage against network usage.

The following seven graphs and one table (Figures 15.14 through 15.20, and the table in Figure 15.21) compress a large number of network statistics into a clear picture. The network represented is a complex network with one main segment interconnecting four lesser segments; it has 172 stations in total. The rate of utilization reaches saturation levels so that typical problems are presented to the reader. Figure 15.14 subdivides the network load by source machine type. In this sample, a conclusion to be drawn is that the Xerox equipment is providing a baseline activity during the course of the day, perhaps data backup, coprocessing, global modem, or mail

Debugging with the Protocol Analyzer 329

Node	Input	Error	Output	Error	%input	%output
A	89897	261	37307	5	0.29	0.01
B	2492034	0	6116816	5	0.00	0.00
C	192212	251	129838	11	0.13	0.01
D	561151	0	415580	10	0.00	0.00
E	15987246	0	10022484169	362252	0.00	48.39
F	812002	446	747493	25	0.06	0.00
G	42862	0	44130	2	0.00	0.00
H	611480	1923	42840	14	0.31	0.03
I	115363	38	64289	1	0.03	0.00
J	103	0	84478	867	0.00	1.03
K	82097	234	40996	14	0.29	0.03
L	65316	346	10880	2	0.53	0.02
M	153256	0	120172	94	0.00	0.08
N	618	452	3140	3	73.14	0.10
O	1040322	1824	604794	48	0.18	0.01
P	1334398	347	1315634	9	0.03	0.00
Q	44748	0	53752	0	0.00	0.00
R	91380	0	32778	4	0.00	0.01
S	476121	266	483599	59	0.06	0.01
T	80594	0	72483	4	0.00	0.01
U	79780	0	71956	4	0.00	0.01
V	92126	0	21619	1	0.00	0.00
W	141428	0	108958	0	0.00	0.00
X	6018	0	501	3	0.00	0.60
Y	116901	150	66893	9	0.13	0.01
Z	33	2	59	7	6.06	11.86
NET	24709488	6540	20713472	1370		

Indicator	Stations	Solution
Busy stations:	B, E	Sub-net or filter
Bad hardware	N, Z	Check out the hardware

Figure 15.13 Statistical network worksheet.

services. The load on the IBM equipment is countercyclic to the normal workday, suggesting some planned off-peak process, whereas the Sun and DEC equipment appear to be servicing users during the normal workday. Such assumptions could be verified by frame capture techniques or learning about the specific processes on the network.

This same information is displayed in a different format by network service usage in Figure 15.15. Most of the peak load is created by user demands during the normal work hours.

The graph in Figure 15.16 presents loading on the main network segment that interconnects with four other segments. This traffic is identical to that represented in the above figure, although some of the load is localized on the subnets and therefore does not appear on the

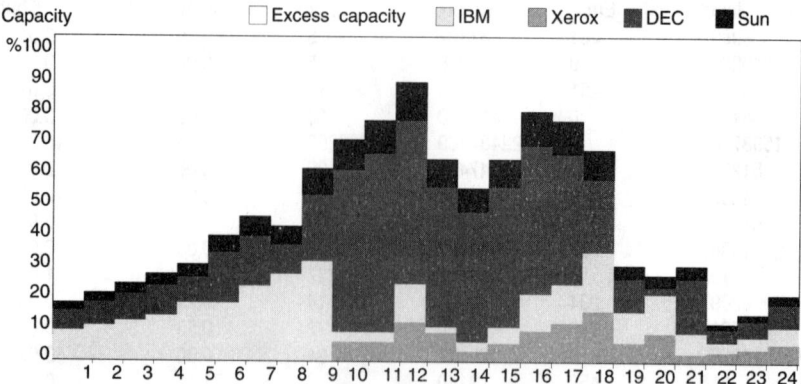

Figure 15.14 Peak load by source computer during a 24-hour period.

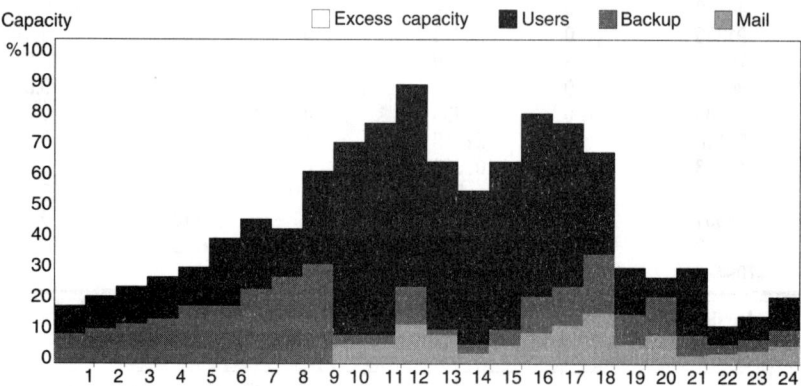

Figure 15.15 Peak load capacity by usage during a 24-hour period.

main net. The data used to construct the graph in Figure 15.16 are repeated by the histogram in Figure 15.17, which displays traffic by frame size. Several upper-level protocols and errors are overlaid to indicate the common frame sizes. In this sample, Novell NetWare at 16 Mbits/s with IPX is the upper-layer protocol. Errors are represented by frames that are less than the 13 bytes minimum that represent tokens, or those frames that exceed 4204 bytes that represent NIC jabber.

Each different size represents a different type of purpose. The high loading is obvious during peak business hours, and drops off during lunch and afternoon slack times, as Figure 15.18 illustrates. Interarrival times should be a minimum of the TRT at 45 ms. Interframe spacing of less than that represents signs of hardware defects. The network interarrival time in Figure 15.19 implies a TRT of 45 ms rate, thus duplicating information in Figure 15.18 converted to another format.

Debugging with the Protocol Analyzer

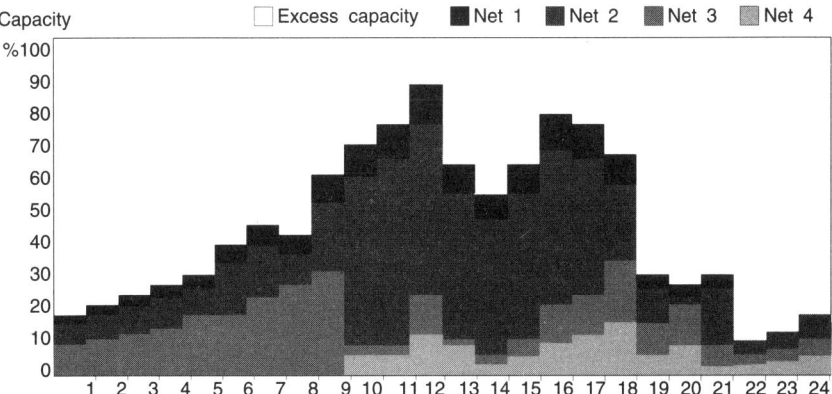

Figure 15.16 Peak load by network source during a 24-hour period.

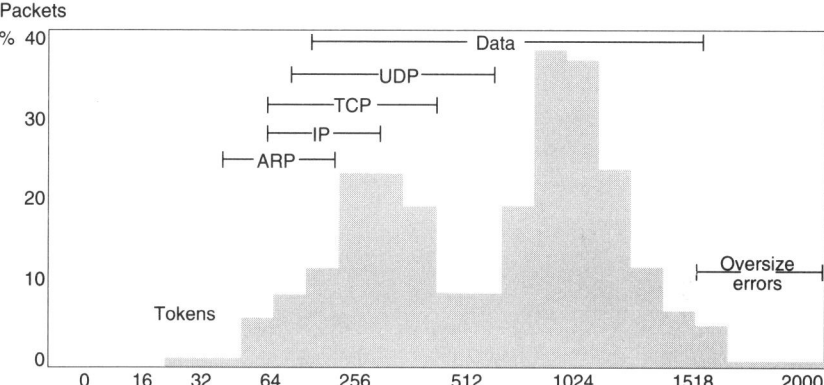

Figure 15.17 Distribution of packets by size, and packet protocol or usage.

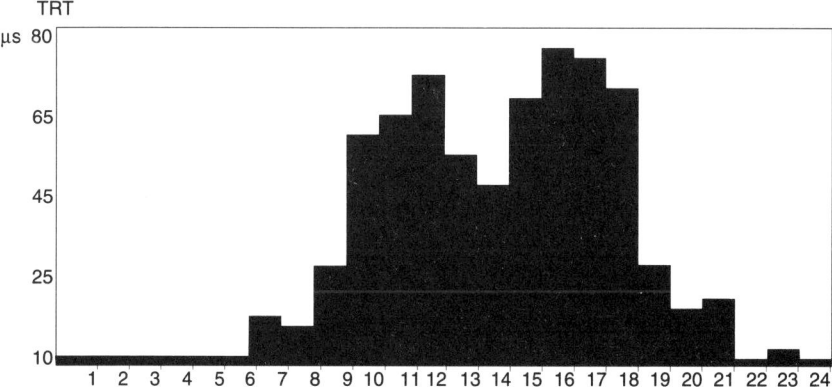

Figure 15.18 TRT during a 24-hour period.

Network access latency, as shown in Figure 15.20, is the time required for a request to be filled. The information is superimposed on the interarrival time for comparison. Latency times provide less important information than do collision rates or error rates, although they can confirm whether the problem is overload or hardware. In this case, since the latency shows a bell curve, the implication is that the network functions correctly except when the traffic load is too high, and latency shifts outward.

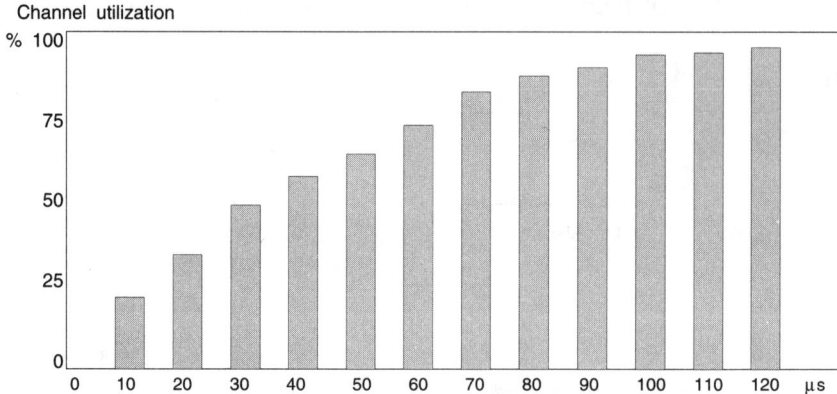

Figure 15.19 Histogram of interarrival times in μs.

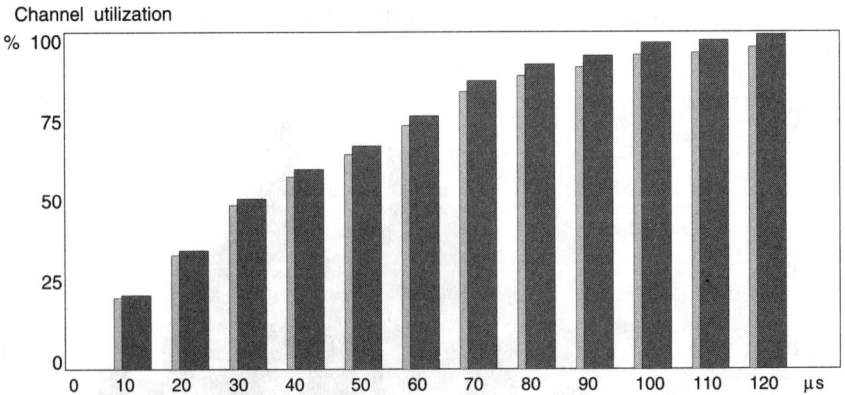

Figure 15.20 Histogram of network access latency (i.e., response time).

Network Load and Traffic Simulation

When statistics fail to identify network problems, station simulation on a protocol analyzer is a powerful methodology. Specialized software constructs frames of any length and content. A frame could thus contain any combination of errors, sources and destinations, and actual data content. Furthermore, network loading could be artificially increased to saturation levels—if the protocol analyzer cannot actually generate enough frames to saturate FDDI, consider running two units or a few cooperating stations also—to exercise the ring and station software or develop statistics otherwise unavailable within a specific network situation. This is useful, for example, to test network conditions with the addition of 250 stations. Figure 15.21 suggests the types of frames that can be built and the types of tests possible with station simulation. The delay and utilization characteristics of a network under various load conditions is an important consideration in design and planning stages.

Network Usage Assessments

While an analyzer can chart network performance, it also performs other esoteric duties with some imagination. Its functions might include preparing usage statistics for accounting and billing purposes. These statistics could then be used as a basis for charging users and groups for network utilization. Take as an example the information in Figure 15.22. User f in group B is the major user of network resources. Although it may be politically unfeasible to charge group B for that user's utilization, it might be important to demonstrate demand for network resources. It is certainly the case that should the network become saturated and unable to meet the demand for services, network access for user f may need to be changed. Group C might, for example, be the accounting department that provides the paychecks, payables, and receivables. Network utilization is minimal; however, relative value of this work is certainly maximum. This example indicates an implicit

Simulation	Anticipated Test Indications
Short frames	Beacons, ring wrap
Long frames	Beacons, ring wrap
Corrupted frames	Beacons, ring wrap
Duplicate tokens, nonrepeat of tokens	Ring recovery
Percentage network loading	Network performance/growth capacity
Misaligned packets	Controller hardware
Specified sources	Station functionality

Figure 15.21 Network simulation for preconceived theories.

Group	User	Daily Average Frames	Utilization	Network Utilization	Network Share
A	a	1,000,000	10	0.47	
	b	4,000,000	40	1.88	
	c	5,000,000	50	2.35	
		10,000,000			4.7%
B	d	40,000,000	20	18.94	
	e	70,000,000	35	33.15	
	f	90,000,000	45	42.62	
		200,000,000			94.7%
C	g	100,000	10	0.05	
	h	200,000	20	0.09	
	i	700,000	70	0.32	
		1,000,000			0.47%

Figure 15.22 Budgetary allocation by prorated network usage. Frames were captured and collected by global network FDDI source address in order to generate the utilization percentages. These percentages can be used to allocate network overhead to the appropriate groups or even individual users.

resource allocation decision, and perhaps the means to establish a realistic audit and cost charge-out system as well.

Capture and Store

Another key feature of a network analyzer is the tool's ability to intercept and retain frames. It should be able to capture every frame, although on a busy network available buffer space may prevent more than seconds or minutes of data to be stored. Some analyzers are too slow to capture every frame; they may capture one in five frames. This is statistically sound if the tool is capable of identifying and tracking each and every frame without storing the frame's contents. Many analyzers are just too slow to recognize all frames, a prevalent problem with FDDI. This means that frame counts do not accurately represent traffic; this is not sufficient. At a minimum, the statistics must be collected accurately. Each station often has resident software to track transmission information for the station itself. Some station workstations provide software for global tracking. If this information is accurate and not just approximate, a protocol analyzer may be unnecessary. The ability to filter selected frames or extract only header information is a powerful tool for statistical compilation, usually available only with a protocol analyzer. Also, time stamping of frames is a desirable feature for matching individual frames with function as demonstrated in the

Debugging with the Protocol Analyzer

mail example. Time stamping also provides latency and interarrival statistics and a reality check on the accuracy of these statistics.

Several analyzers store from 0.5 Mbyte to 4 Mbytes of frames. They take a "photograph" of the network activity. On a saturated network, 4 Mbytes may represent only 0.3 s of activity. Captured frames can be stored on disk and analyzed later with word processing tools. For example, 4 Mbytes of network traffic could be stored to disk. A quick view might indicate many mail frames as in the earlier example. Electronic mail, imaging, client/server database transactions, and network fax seems to require considerable disk space (confirmed by other tools) and now it seems to require a large portion of the network. How large is a matter for estimate unless the 4 Mbytes can be analyzed and measured by content. If the file can be edited and parsed, an accurate percentage figure can be compiled. Unix tools like GREP, WC, and AWK are especially competent for this analysis; otherwise edits and sorts with line counts are appropriate.

Snooping with the Analyzer

A protocol analyzer allows anyone who understands the use of this tool to monitor transparently and unobtrusively. By capturing and parsing frames, it is possible to decipher what users are doing on the network, particularly who is doing things illegally, unethically, or against policy. One use is to see who is using what resources on the network. While this seems Machiavellian, it can prevent unwarranted use of organization resources. It can uncover thefts, breaches in security, or hidden intrusions via unauthorized stations or a splitter or hub replacing a single station access. Another use of the protocol analyzer, if it has the ability to build specified frames at the bit or byte level, is to falsify frame designs and break whatever security is in place. If this tool can break security, this would indicate that others could undermine the security systems as well. Chapter 18 details these and other security issues.

The ability to capture and view frames adds a level of sophistication to network performance tuning. It also promotes spying. TRT, frame counts, defective frame counts, and any counts by source stations are information of value and useful to tuning a network. However, at higher levels of sophistication—when all other problems have been identified and resolved—it becomes important to understand the mix of information actually transmitted. Informed guesses may indicate a particular set of stations are used for long-haul uploading and downloading of large files. Other stations with heavy but sporadic network loads may indicate large electronic mail requirements. By visually inspecting selected frames, it is possible to confirm these hypotheses.

This chapter explained the workings of a protocol analyzer, the types of information it can collect, and how to analyze and apply those data. The next chapter derives the mathematical underpinnings for traffic analysis with an emphasis on degenerate network performances. Chapter 17 will apply this practical understanding to the logic of tuning networks.

Part 5
Network Management

This section explores the management and strategic issues of FDDI networking. Performance tuning, security, backup, and human aspects are covered since these are critical management concerns. As network technology evolves, competition and the usage of widely distributed enterprise-wide networks for strategic advantage is increasingly an organizational concern. This section provides the reader with an understanding of FDDI technology and operations.

Chapter 16 calculates the statistics of FDDI transmission protocols and the deterministic characteristics of token passing protocols. This information is useful in order to understand why bottlenecks and slowdowns occur and why performance becomes suboptimal. Chapter 17 builds upon the information in the preceding chapter and shows how to tune network performance. This chapter also builds upon the knowledge from the chapters on installation, configurations, network traffic, and statistics for the same purpose. It also discusses optimal planning, network loads, and alternative solutions for overloaded rings. This single chapter can be invaluable when network trouble occurs, when no solutions are self-evident, and when there appear to be no options for locating network failures. Chapter 18 discusses security issues, explains why the networking model contains no references to either data or physical security, why FDDI is not secure, and what precautions can be taken to protect a network from outside prying and unauthorized access. It also discusses what specialized hardware and judicious management procedures help maintain security. Chapter 19 explains backup procedures and suggests what hardware, software, or operational procedures can be implemented to produce a nearly fault-tolerant network. Issues and redundancy for the important network services—file storage, printing, tape backup of network data, shutdown of failed segments—are discussed in this chapter. Chapter 20 illustrates why trained and qualified people are an important resource for network administration. FDDI depends on people with expertise and experience. Without knowledgeable people, the network will perform below capacity, cause severe operational problems, constrain organization growth, and in extreme cases, even fail to function.

Chapter

16

Statistics for an FDDI Network

The last chapter detailed the workings of the protocol analyzer. This chapter derives the mathematics behind it and reveals further insights into FDDI mechanics by confirming rules-of-thumb with statistics. The assumptions are that FDDI networks perform well until the TRT degrades. The TRT is a proxy indicator for poor performance, and suggests that these problems can somehow be solved. The statistics show that a large TRT does impair efficiency, but that FDDI is efficient when understood and tuned.

Network Traffic

FDDI relies on a deterministic transmission process with token-passing priority enforcement as defined by the ANSI standards. As a preface to the statistical presentation in this chapter, let us review some of the characteristics of FDDI. Firstly, note that in most computer nomenclature megabits (Mbits) and megabytes (Mbytes) are usually octal numbers and are rounded for convenience. A megabit is actually 1,048,576 bits (2^{21}), and a kilobit is 1024 bits (2^{10}), but these numbers are not pertinent here. FDDI is an exception to this generic computer nomenclature as all of its numerical calculations are based on a decimal (base 10) count; transmission rates are based upon 125 MHz, or 125,000,000 clock cycles per second. Therefore, 125,000,000 bits can be transferred each second on FDDI. However, raw user data bits are not transferred at this rate. Certain bit sequences that do not provide a clear transition between 0 and 1 are disallowed by protocol. Hence, since all station addresses, checksums, and user data are encoded by the NRZI coding scheme four bits to five bits (4B5B), as outlined in Chapter 5, this cycle yields 100,000,000 bits/s in data transmission terms.

For the purposes of analysis, we can use either the 125 MHz or 100 MHz as the basis for transmission speed. Since protocol analysis is based upon frame data values, because the data is most measurable unit in the frame, and because all signal encoding is provided in hardware by the NICs, it is easier to use the 100 MHz basis. Furthermore, 100 makes a simpler divisor than 125. All measurements must be converted and presented in terms of this format for the calculations to work correctly. Similarly, the use of FDDI symbols and bytes is also confusing. This chapter will present each. In the simplest terms a byte with 8 bits requires 2 FDDI symbols for transmission. 32-bit bytes require 8 FDDI symbols.

Packets are transmitted only when a station holds a token, which is a 24-byte frame (3 FDDI encoded symbols) that gives one and only one station permission to transmit. Frames from the sending station are broadcast downstream to the next station, which in turn repeats the frame to its own downstream neighbor. When the frame completes a circuit of the logical ring, the original sending station does not repeat that frame. In a refinement over the token passing protocol in IBM Token-Ring, the station holding the token may send as many frames as it wants to during the token holding time. Upon concluding data transmission—either upon sending all its frames or if the THT expires first, the token is released to the next downstream neighbor on the network. The basic presumption is that the FDDI error is nil, and that the single data frame or many frames do not have to return to the sender before the token is released. This should appear similar to the 802.5 Token-Ring early release enhancement; in fact, it is performing the same function. Hence, there may be many frames on the ring, but nonetheless only one token at any time. Since FDDI transmission is unidirectional on the logical ring, always in the same logical direction on the ring, and frames are repeated by each station to the next logical station, stations are represented as *upstream and* downstream stations. An upstream station always transmits to the next active downstream station. Many disabled (unpowered or bypassed) stations may physically intersect the upstream and downstream stations. Optical bypasses or the active hub configuration determines the logical relationship of upstream and downstream stations. If a station wants to transmit, it captures a token and sends a frame. Otherwise, it sends just the token to its immediate downstream neighbor. It is the responsibility of the receiving station to accept, acknowledge, and reply to those transmissions within the allotted time window. Coresident transmission is actually allowed, much as it is with 802.5 Token-Ring supporting the *early token release enhancement*. The preamble, token transmission time, and NIC set up times effectively prevent frames from rear-ending each other.

This token-passing method is efficient and fair for high traffic loads, as Figure 16.1 illustrates. It is inefficient for low network loads, less efficient than the Fast Ethernet being considered as IEEE 802.3 GV. However, FDDI capacity and performance is predictable for all loading levels. It is virtually impossible to saturate the channel or overwhelm FDDI. Data delivery becomes slow, although consistently slow for all

Statistics for an FDDI Network

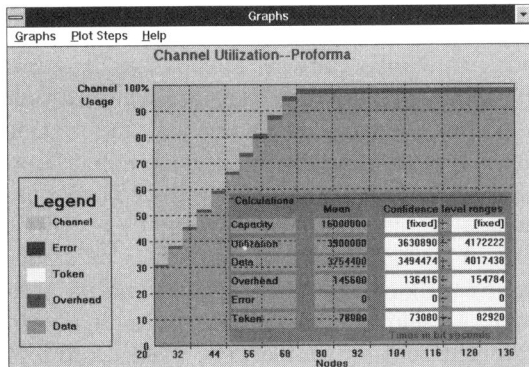

Figure 16.1 FDDI network model plotting efficiency as a function of traffic load. The best application is in the range of 20 to 65 percent channel utilization, although this protocol does not fail or saturate with increased traffic levels. (Courtesy of Network Performance Institute)

stations. There is no priority enforcement for FDDI stations. All equally have access to the token.

There are two exceptions where priorities on FDDI are possible. The forthcoming FDDI-II enhancement is intended to support asynchronous traffic to support real-time voice, images, and multimedia. Whether the 100 Mbits/s transmission speed will provide sufficient capacity for splitting bandwidth for data and these other operations is questionable. It may not become a viable product. The second exception is a feature of network configuration. By establishing a primary FDDI ring with secondary gatewayed networks that are either FDDI or other protocols, priorities can be established as a property of two (or more) token waiting times or network access times. Although priority access can not be established with the precision accorded to applications in the traditional mainframe time-sharing environment, it can be rigged by placing servers and key stations on the primary FDDI ring while loading up the secondary networks with varying numbers of nodes. The secondary networks with more nodes or more traffic will thus be accorded less priority to the primary ring.

Nonetheless, FDDI performance does become unacceptable when the station count increases toward the maximum and all stations have data to transmit. Utilization grows with load, but it also grows merely with an increase in network station count. It is almost impossible to fully utilize the FDDI bandwidth unless every station wants to broadcast all the time and the network primary station and secondary node count approaches exceeds protocol limitations. With more load, the token rotation time get slower.

FDDI Bottlenecks

Some high-level network processes do not know how to respond to multicast frames addressed to a subset of network stations, or broadcast messages addressed to no specific station. Such a situation creates a lot of network "noise," increased traffic levels, and some sending stations frustrated for lack of a reply. A typical blind spot many network managers will need to understand is the router- or gateway-induced broadcast storm. Multicast and broadcast messages are propagated by routing or gateway devices to update their routing tables. It also occurs as devices conforming to a spanning tree configuration test the functionality of the primary routing path. Devices lacking compatibility with a routing subprotocol—and many different routing protocols do exist—and lacking SNMP or CMIP agency will not respond to the broadcasts. Naturally, NetBIOS, NetBEUI, TCP/IP, Appletalk, or UDP broadcasts and global requests for responses could load the transmission channel; rather, it is more likely to stress the network nodes initially issuing or responding to these requests by saturating disk I/O or CPU time.

Rate Statistics

Some simple statistics decode the operating efficiency and generalized status of an FDDI network. This information is generally collected from application-layer software, SNMP, CMIP, or the protocol analyzer. The most applicable is rate information. *Rates* are the counts of a specific type of event during a fixed time interval. Rates are useful statistics for determining efficiency. For example, three types of rates to look for are the *frame rate*, sometimes called a *transmission rate* or *traffic rate*, a *token rotation time rate, token holding timers,* and *error rates.* Figure 16.2 lists some operation tracking formulas. *Error rates* represent transmission errors as a percentage of total frames transmitted, and these rates should be calculated in this way for uniformity. FDDI specification basically states

Transmission Rate	Traffic
	# of frames sent/time period
Transmission rate/sec	# of frames sent/second
Transmission rate/min	# of frames sent/minute
Transmission rate/hour	# of frames sent/hour
Beacon rate	# of beacons/ # of packets sent
Oversize frame rate	# of missized frames/ # of frames sent
CRC error rate	# of CRC errors/ # of frames sent
TRT	(Provides ring length, latency, network load)

Figure 16.2 Formulas for basic network statistical calculations.

Statistics for an FDDI Network

that the stations providing more than 1 bit error in 10,000 bits will be disabled. Effectively, FDDI transmission is error free, and the FDDI transmission error rate will 0 percent. Errors may occur through station timeouts, overloads, upper-level protocols, and other station problems. What this states is that a frame will be delivered intact on FDDI although the contents of the frame and the application of the frame data may contain errors. Most network managers make decisions based upon these simple rates.

It is important to note that rate statistics are most useful for diagnosing specific types of network bottlenecks and problems, plus both logical and physical locations for active network breakdowns. Additionally, rate statistics are good predictors of network performance when stations are added or traffic rates are increased. Rates are good for analyzing specific performance conditions subject to existing network configurations. When analysis is limited within this context, there is a one-for-one utility for solving network problems with rates. However, planning network growth or configuration changes requires a more complex model based upon non-deterministic mathematics. Such a model is defined and developed later in this chapter. This model is particularly effective for mixed protocol networks, networks of LANs, and enterprise-wide networks.

The count for frames transmitted will match the count for frames received. All FDDI access is performed in the first three layers of OSI model. Any disparity between these two numbers—number of frames output and the number of frames received—indicates a network hardware problem. Problems on top of FDDI are indicative of a software problem.

More complex network performance and traffic bottleneck problems do not necessary require more complex information. In fact, the data required for a queueing model (described later in this chapter) is nothing more than the times when frames are transmitted and those frame sizes. The relevant information usually requires the capture of information about *all* frames; this would require collection and collation of frame sizes, source and destination addresses, errors, and a time and date stamp. The frames themselves are rarely captured—just details about them to calculate accurate interarrival and service time statistics, network loading, and performance metrics. Additionally, expanded LANs and enterprise-wide networks may require service levels and throughputs for repeaters, bridges, routers, frame switches, gateways, and any other special pipes including ATM, FDDI, SMDS, SONET, T-1, X.25, and VSAT.

Definition of Abnormal States

FDDI statistics are not necessary on a network where all works well. Compulsive managers may collect such information just as a matter of

Packet Counts:	Process
Packets transmitted per node	Count outgoing packets
Packets received per station	Count incoming packets
TRT	Time for token to pass a node twice
Packets deterred	Requires special node-resident software
Packets per station:	Count outgoing and incoming packets by source
By source	Count incoming packets and filter by source
By destination	Count all packets and filter by destination
By source and destinations	Count into matrix
Size distribution	Extract length and plot
Network period peaks	Track highest transient network loads
Station period peaks	Track highest transient node load
Packet Errors:	**Process**
Alignment errors	Filter and count
CRC errors	Filter and count
Short packets	Filter and count
Long packets	Filter and count
Invisible packets	Capture packets and sort
Incompatible packets	Capture packets and sort
Misaddressed packets	Capture packets and sort
Channel Utilization:	**Process**
Throughput	Summation of packets by packet size
Peak rate	Highest transient load
Utilization as a % of capacity	Throughput (Mbits/s)/ transmission speed
Capture:	**Process**
All packets	Filter by specific parameters
Packets during an interval	Filter by specific parameters
Packets with errors	Filter by specific parameters
Packets with specific errors	Filter by specific parameters
Packets with certain data types	Filter by specific parameters
Packets from selected node(s)	Filter by specific parameters
Packets to selected node(s)	Filter by specific parameters
Packets with selected source/destination pairs	Filter by specific parameters
Packets with a certain size	Filter by specific parameters
Statistics:	**Process**
Interarrival times (0-100 ms)	Subtraction between clock times of arrivals
Latency distribution	Average waiting time to transmit
Packet size distribution	Sort sizes and count
Node usage as % of capacity	Packets/node/transmission speed x average packet size
Node usage of channel	Packets/node/throughput
Packet rate per second	Packets transmitted/second (exclude fragments)
Bit rate per second	Packet rate x average size x 8 (bits)

Figure 16.3 Common statistics applied to network analysis.

Statistics for an FDDI Network

course. As such, that information pays dividends when a problem does occur, and benchmarks, just like cable blueprinting, are valuable as measuring sticks. The statistical information in Figure 16.3 will provide useful results in suboptimal networks. There are also other situations indicative of malfunctioning hardware that can be tracked through statistics.

Transmission errors are classified as cyclic redundancy check (CRC) errors, alignment errors, under- or oversized frames. A *CRC error* is a checksum error on the FDDI frame and is usually discovered in conjunction with other types of errors. An *alignment error* occurs when a frame is not a multiple of 8 bits and is usually indicative of a framing error, NIC clock error, or the inability of a station to maintain the full FDDI speed. Some errors may be indicative of an error in the point-to-point optical link, or typical jitter and jabber problems in copper-based segments. Typically, these statistics are not kept by the network devices since defective stations and nodes are quickly purged from the ring by other stations or hubs.

Jitter or the *jitter budget*, though principally indigenous to FDDI on copper-based transmission media, affects all protocols. It represents variance from the acceptable signal characteristics. Signal frequency variability, strength, stability, deficiency in the square form signal, and a lack of differentiation between "0" and "1" are all characteristic of jitter. Jitter is most pronounced with FDDI transmission on UTP, less so with STP. It is important to note that although all computer logic is based upon discrete values, ultimately all network traffic is based upon analog waves. Figure 16.4 shows how signals lacking differentiation decay to become unstable.

This instability is important when signals are regenerated and repeated at each FDDI station or regenerated by repeaters, bridges, routers, and gateways. Since the repeating stations cannot interpret the meaning of the signal, only the CRC checksum bits can decay. This may force frequent retransmissions. When jitter errors occur, the obvious

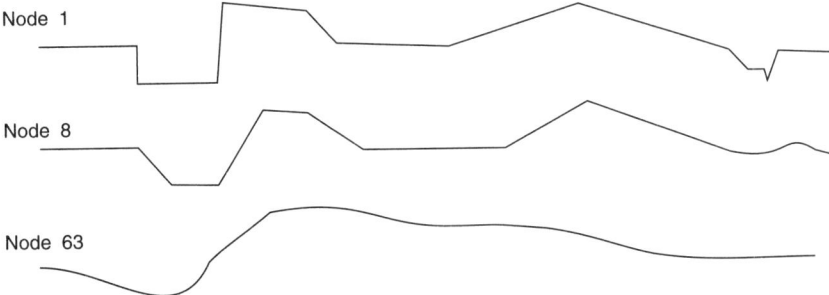

Figure 16.4 Crosstalk, EMI, RFI, and excessive cable lengths cause signals to decay; this causes signal jitter, especially given the high signal frequency of FDDI.

test is to capture and compare the same frames at different parts of the network. When there are obvious differences, tighten the gap between protocol analyzers until the offending repeating device is localized. Although this is not an infrastructure error per se, it is a hardware error that should be resolved efficiently using this technique.

A *short frame* contains less than 24 bytes (the frame size for a token, and thus, the minimum frame size). Long frames result when a NIC *jabbers* or *jitters* beyond the end of the frame or ignores THT protocol limitations. They could also result from software protocol errors, multiple ring hops, multiprotocol routing flaws, or retransmission problems. A network should experience no beacons and no abnormal preambles. A *beacon* means that a downstream station thinks that there is a break in the connection after the immediate upstream station. When a frame is improperly repeated, it is received at the next downstream station with either a CRC or an alignment error, if it is received at all. Long delays—anything longer than 8 μs—may initiate a *ring recovery*, which is a request to generate a new token and reestablish the network access protocol. An *abnormal preamble* occurs when the first few symbols of a frame do not match the expected starting delimiter synchronization pattern. Symbol mismatches are checked in the NIC hardware. No network load is passed to the station CPU.

Theoretical and Obtainable Capacity

Another useful statistic measures obtainable (or realistically achievable) performance against a rated capacity. See Figure 16.5 for theoretical and attainable transmission rates. The difference relates to server and station performance; a superserver could conceivably obtain the theoretical rate. The theoretical capacity of FDDI is 100 Mbits/s. Sustained traffic rates on a real FDDI network have not yet been observed since no vendor has constructed CPUs and NICs that can maintain a sustained transmission

Rate of Transmission	Bits	Bytes
Specified rate/sec	100 Mbits/s	12.5 Mbits/s
Attainable rate/sec	45 Mbits/s	5.6 Mbits/s
Specified rate/min	6 Gbits/s	750 Mbits/s
Attainable rate/min	2.7 Gbits/s	337 Mbits/s
Specified rate/hour	360 Gbits/s	45 Gbits/s
Attainable rate/hour	162 Gbits/s	80 Gbits/s
Specified rate/8-hour shift	2880 Gbits/s	360 Gbits/s
Attainable rate/8-hour shift	1309 Gbits/s	164 Gbits/s

Figure 16.5 FDDI transmission rates for two-station networks.

rate. Sustained traffic rates have been tested in laboratory situations and benchmarking tests. Attainable rates are in the 20 to 65 Mbits/s range. This yields a difference between the theoretical rate and actual throughput. The difference relates to upper layer protocol overheads, bottlenecks at the CPU, bus, disk, and NIC. However, do not assume that an FDDI network can handle all the traffic thrown to it. It will saturate with enough stations and interconnected unbuffered LANs. Calculated and plotted graphs detail this later in the chapter.

Token Rotational Time

The token rotational time (TRT) is the time it takes for the token to make a complete circuit of the network. This is true for a true physical circuit or for a logical circuit of a star-configured structure such as TP-PMD. This statistic is difficult to acquire without special equipment since a ring without stations inserted means that there are no tokens on the loop; it can be estimated fairly accurately with a simple formula. Generally, this value represents the time for a signal to propagate around the network and is solely a function of the hub switching delays, NIC electronic delays, station-to-station or lobe distances, and arrival frequency and size of frames.

As stations are actually activated and inserted into the network, TRT slows by the delay imposed by the electronics in each NIC unit. This also explains (one reason) why some networks perform well with stations activated and badly with fewer live stations. Realistically, this represents the minimum TRT most network managers will ever see. When all stations are quiet and the token circulates, TRT is signal propagation time plus approximately .02 ms (2000 bit times) electronics delay at each station's NIC unit.

Under an ultimate load—when every station wants to transmit full-sized frames and exercises that right when it acquires the token—TRT degrades to signal propagation time, approximately .0025 ms electronics delay at each station, plus the bit times for the data in the frame, with preamble and delay. The absolute minimum TRT represents the time it takes for the token to complete a rotation on the network with no stations inserted. The maximum TRT is 1.612 ms.

FDDI networks are controlled by the token passing protocol. Token errors include a lost token and duplicate tokens. While it is functionally difficult to see these problems, the proximate method is to count claim tokens. The *claim token* is a station's attempt to claim access to the network in lieu of a token passing within two average TRT units, or the average TTRT. After 8 ms the assumption is that the token has been lost. The claim token is generated after a satisfactory response to a station's ring recovery request. The protocol for *asserting* authority—based upon the claim token—is to issue a new token. This may require

- Number of network stations and subnetted nodes
- Network connection lengths
- NIC electronic delays
- Transmission and signal propagation time
- Frame size and protocol-based size limitations
- Frequency of station and node requests to transmit

Figure 16.6 The six components of the token rotational time (TRT).

four or five average TTRT units. When stations insert into the network (usually when they are powered on and the passive bypass in the network NIC becomes active and now repeats signals), the sudden signal noise or disruption may corrupt a few frames or tokens during that brief interval. An excessive number and continuing incidence of purge and claim tokens usually indicates protocol errors, faulty NIC units, or other basic hardware problems.

TRT remains one of the most useful FDDI statistics, and one generally not understood. Specifically, the TRT comprises the time for the token to complete a revolution on the network during which time all stations may capture the token and transmit bits for the duration of *token capture timer*. The token capture timer, or *token hold timer* is determined by the transmission speed or overridden by the NOS. Specifically, the token hold time permits a station to transmits a 9000 symbol (5000-byte) frame; this is reduced by NetWare to a full frame size of 4202 bytes (or less for multiple hops). As such, this TRT is a total of all NIC electronic delays for all network stations, the time for the transmission signals to complete a ring circuit, and the time to transmit a frame or the token itself. In other words, channel utilization, station counts, the network wiring length, and the TRT are parameters in a single equation that can be solved.

The TRT consists of the six components. These include transmission time and signal propagation time. Figure 16.6 lists the six components. The actual TRT times vary by protocol, media, and network length. The example in this section is based upon calculations on the fixed-sized IBM FDDI token of 3 symbols (24 bits). Furthermore, the *target TRT* (TTRT) varies by network load. Therefore, it is useful as input for utilization and network length calculations.[1] Specifically, the TRT can be extrapolated to network load and channel bandwidth utilization, as well as *total* network cabling lengths, as the following equations detail:

Utilization = Number tokens/second

---

[1] Derived from ANSI X3.169 specifications.

Statistics for an FDDI Network

Utilization = Maximum number of tokens/second

Since each token indicates a token revolution:

Number tokens/second = 1/Token Rotation Time (TRT)

These two equations reduce to the following useful formula:

Utilization = 1 - Ring latency/TRT

Additionally, the basic latency and utilization equations can be rewritten in another format to solve for the overall network length (when latency, TRT, and utilization values are available):

Ring delay = TRT (1 - Utilization)

where

Ring delay = latency + number of stations   x (jitter and electronic or optical delay) + network sections   x 4 μs/k

or

$L = 8 \ (TRT)(1 - U) - 7 - 5/8N) \ \ x \ 100'$

where

L = Length of the network connections

U = Network utilization

N = Number of network ring stations

The ring latency represents the minimum time for the token and all data frames to go around the ring. Think of this value as the waiting time for station that wants to transmit. For FDDI running at 100 Mbits/s, the minimum latency is the TRT for an unloaded network. Thus, the minimum latency is sum of all token rotation components. Figure 16.7 charts these values.

These basic formulas were modeled in Lotus 1-2-3 to generate graphs contrasting TRT with channel utilization. Figure 16.8 shows FDDI at 100 Mbits/s. This plot was generated with the Lotus graph option.

The graph illuminates two important points. First, FDDI very rarely saturates. Any free bandwidth is filled by idle token rotation. Second, additional stations increase the base latency time by adding to the jitter loss and electronic signal repetition, but do not necessarily affect the average latency time. The McGraw-Hill/Tab book, *LAN Performance Optimization,* includes Lotus 1-2-3 models on disk to show performance levels under varying LAN conditions. Anyone who is interested in the complete equations can decompose the spreadsheet equations.

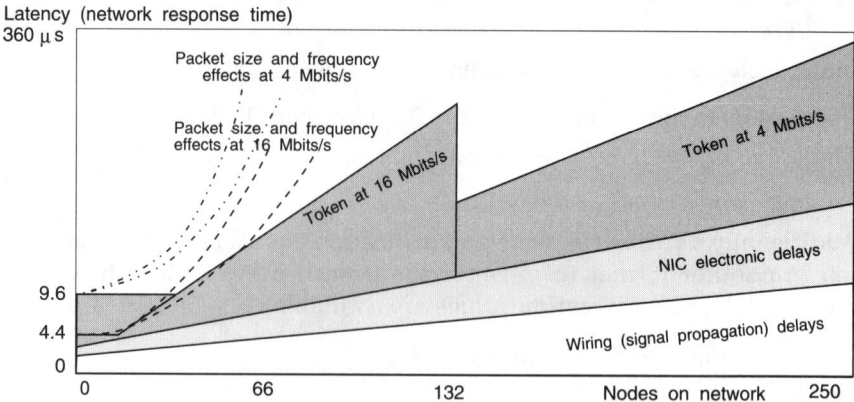

Figure 16.7 The minimum latency components for FDDI.

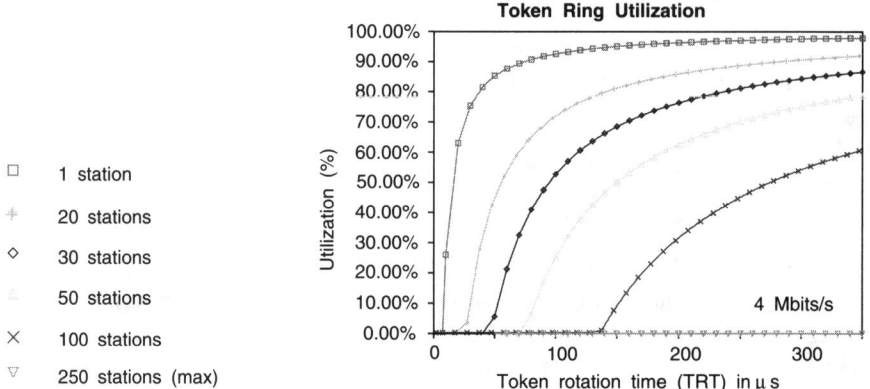

Figure 16.8 FDDI traffic load as a function of TRT.

Transmission Efficiency

Frame size is inversely proportional to frame rates, as Figure 16.9 illustrates. The false implication is that FDDI is more efficient with smaller frames. However, each frame requires a fixed-cost overhead that detracts from "efficiency" and the TRT is wasted channel time. The TRT, frame delimiters, and addressing and checksum overhead represent the least overhead for the largest frames.

While gross transmission efficiency is a linear function of frame size as Figure 16.10 displays, other events alter efficiency. For example, transmissions that exceed maximum frame length are parsed and broadcast in multiple frames with the overhead toll of multiple frames. While the gross evaluation suggests reasonable efficiency, the internal and external control information often demanded by IPX/SPX, UDP,

Statistics for an FDDI Network

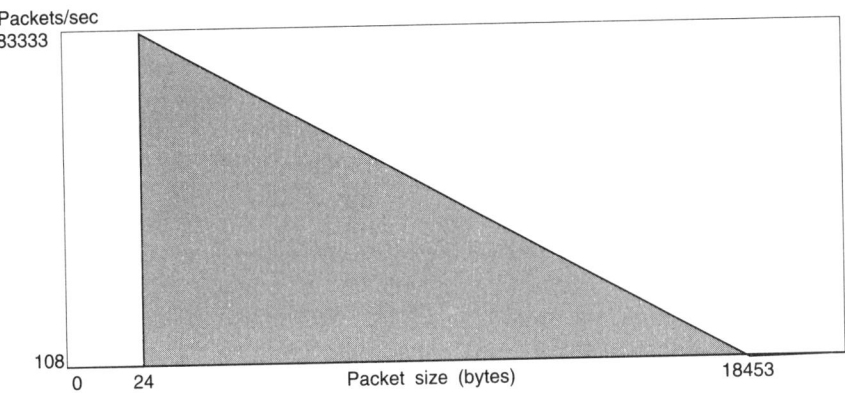

Figure 16.9 FDDI throughput as a function of frame size.

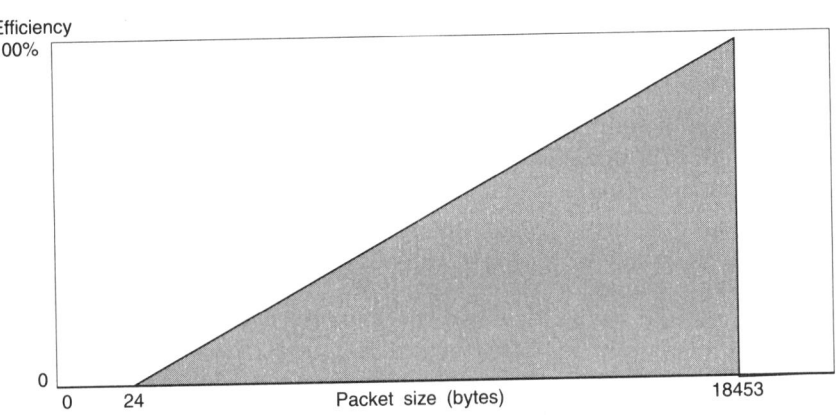

Figure 16.10 FDDI channel efficiency as a function of frame size.

Appletalk, NetBIOS, NetBEUI, or encapsulation lowers these figures. If the reader recalls, the IPX protocol requires a confirmation.

Transmission *efficiency* is defined as the percentage of data actually transmitted to the effort applied. FDDI frame sizes vary from the 3-symbol (24 bits) token minimum to the 9000-symbol (5000 bytes) maximum. As a result or the preamble, addresses, CRC and other other fields, the FDDI data frame maximum size is 4478 (or exactly 4486 when shortened preamble idle and addresses are used) bytes. While physically feasible according to the FDDI protocol, these frames sizes are not achievable under NetWare IPX. If you recall, maximum frame size is limited to 4202 bytes for compatibility with other networking protocols. While the frame does contain data, anywhere from 1 byte to 4478 or exactly 4486 bytes, each frame also contains a minimum of 24 bytes of

	Minimum Frame Size	Maximum Frame Size
Address	12 bytes	4 bytes
Overhead	32 bytes	10 bytes
Data frame	0 bytes	4486 bytes
TRT	.0005 μs	1.612 μs
Total Frame	44 bytes	4500 bytes
Tokens-packets/second	284,090	2777
TRT time	Ring minimum	1.612 μs
Overhead	99,999,980	977,775
Data frame	0	98,994,496
TRT delay	450,000	1,882,071
Efficiency	0.00%	98.99%

Figure 16.11 Frame transmission efficiency by frame size. The data frame is the variable-sized element with a minimum of 0 bytes to a maximum of 4478 bytes or 4486 when shortened preamble and addresses are used.

address and accounting information. Additionally, upper-level protocols such as TCP/IP or IPX demand control information fields. Even UDP, which is connectionless, maintains a packet format within each FDDI data field. Because overhead items are fixed sizes for each frame transmitted, efficiency is higher for larger frames, as Figure 16.11 charts.

Obviously, this information represents theoretical capacity. In actual usage, average frame size and the distribution of frame sizes affect network performance, data throughput, and data transmission efficiency. The capacity and the detrimental effects of errors and beacons must be developed with a completely different type of mathematics.

FDDI Modeling

Since FDDI station count and frame size are the major limitations to channel capacity and network utilization, it is important to model this. Because transmission requests are statistical and interdependent with many factors like frame size, station count, or average transmission rate, nonlinear methods are required to understand the transmission mechanics. The probability of a station actually transmitting is difficult to determine. First, a load level must be determined for each and every station. Second, that load must be applied independently for each station despite the possible correlation between events and the nonuniform loading often experienced on a network. This is often impossible since station transmission is dependent on what the network or other stations are doing, and transmission often synchronizes due to the frame waiting times and processing times required for each transmitted frame at the destination station. Additionally, the mathematics assumes station and traffic independence which is not usually provided. For example, users work during the hours of 9 a.m. through 5 p.m., attend meetings, and work in parallel, therefore requesting the same services. Also most FDDI NOSs require acknowledgments, and such confirmations are not processed independently.

The Queueing Model

The *queueing* (or, variously, "queuing") *model* describes waiting lines (hence queues), service response times, and throughput. It is an appropriate FDDI model because stations wait in line for slot time to transmit. Queueing theory provides a large number of alternative mathematical models for predicting different real-world events such as airplane arrivals, gas station servicing time, and metropolitan traffic jams. The traffic jam analogy is appropriate here. The queueing model defines process steps, waiting times, service times, service fulfillments, and service request denials (e.g., errors and beacons).

The three features of the FDDI mechanism are the arrival process, the waiting queue, and the service mechanism, as shown by Figure 16.12. This waiting line design illustrates the major mathematical groupings, which include the source distribution, the waiting queue, and throughput as represented by serviced requests. Because interconnection of LANs is an important data communications issue, expansion of this model is particular effective for mixed protocol networks, networks of LANs, and enterprise-wide networks.

The FDDI Model

Figure 16.13 shows the single-server mechanisms of FDDI transmission fulfillment. FDDI is a single server—one mechanism services all re-

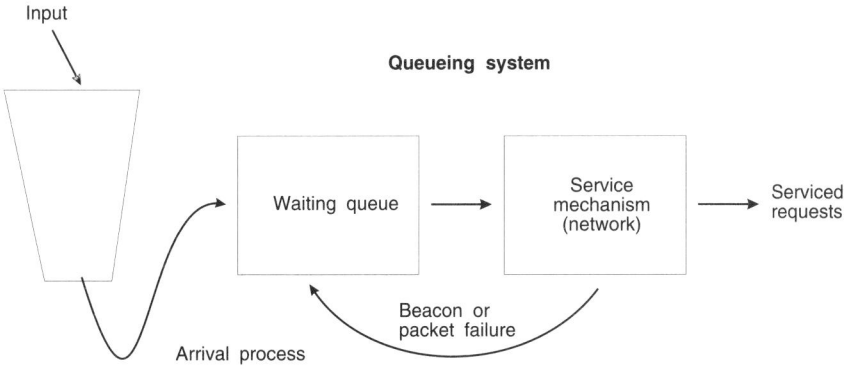

Figure 16.12 The queue service model.

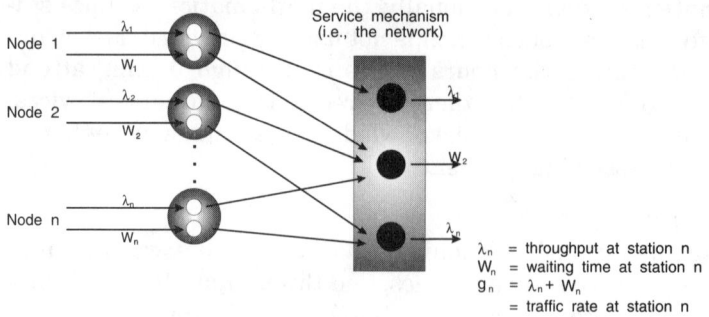

Figure 16.13 The classical queueing model architecture for FDDI.

quests for transmission throughout a network—and this designation is independent of the station or machine count, or the actual network configuration. Only one frame request can be serviced at a time; this remains as true for dual rings, single rings, as it is for nodes as FDDI trees or hubs. There is no other alternative. This model shows the process rather than the waiting times, lines, and throughput as in Figure 16.12. This design simplifies the mathematical rendering into a queueing model architecture where the three basic statistics are introduced: successful throughput, error, and traffic, which is the sum of tokens, throughput, and errors. The queueing model assumes an infinite number of stations and a fixed arrival time. This is virtually true for FDDI. While the maximum number of stations on the primary ring is 1000, the FDDI address supports numbers to 48 bits.

The model shows that as service times increase, all waiting times increase. Therefore, the key conclusion is that consistency of station service and the number of stations in the ring has as important a bearing on network performance as average service speed. In other words, if the network is erratic, performance will be that much worse. A key result of these equations shows that as arrival times approach service times, the users' waiting time (latency) increases as expected.

The model shows that higher utilization rates will not actually saturate FDDI, but in the end, larger numbers of stations will halt efficient use of the network as the sheer number of transmitting stations raises the probability (and actuality) of waiting time to unacceptable levels. Performance degrades as the channel saturates, either through larger numbers of stations, more frequent transmission requests, or larger frames. Despite the fact that the channel is a single server and the multiple station requests from a single station appear to correspond to single requests from multiple stations, multiple stations more readily degrade performance. This is akin to the familiar highway crawl not merely because too many cars use the highway during the day, but because there is too much traffic during selected intervals and the bottleneck never clears; every automobile is different and can't be likened to a bus even though a bus logically provides a similar distribution service. Mathematically, the reason for this observable phenomenon is that the standard deviation for transmissions (or, frame arrivals) increases as the number of stations increase. Additionally, more stations generally provide a proxy for a longer physical network or larger frame size. There is no proxy for greater variability in frame arrivals or with frame sizes. Variability tends to increase latency for users very dramatically, as the statistics support.

Conclusion

In conclusion, when all is said and calculated, it is clear that FDDI is a very predictable medium. Protocols such as FDDI, which are basically deterministic, provide a uniform utilization based upon station counts and frame sizes. FDDI is not deterministic insofar as early token release is supported and multiple transmissions can overlap. As FDDI is overloaded, the network will merely get slower until performance is unacceptable. But, it will not saturate to provide no throughput whatsoever, as Ethernet does around 30 percent of channel capacity. One note: Ethernet can provide a full 10 Mbits/s and many vendors provide attachments and software so that two channels between two nodes are established for simplex transmission on each channel.

The performance is interesting when considering other protocol-enhancement devices and higher-speed alternatives, such as Ethernet matrix switches, routers, gateways, ATM, SMDS, and SONET. Additionally, the statistics and modeling confirm the practical limits that network designers and managers have learned by trial and error. Plan for a maximum of 50 primary stations per FDDI channel. Establish bridges for connected subnets for better performance since bridges are faster than other linkage devices; the latency for transmission is less. When traffic on the primary ring becomes unacceptable, upgrade some or all of the bridges with buffering routers to screen the unnecessary subnet traffic from the primary enterprise-wide ring. Routers will handle a heavier traffic level at the expense of increased latency.

A fully populated FDDI with 1000 DAS stations is fine if the network is sparsely used, or provides only minimal functionality. However, realize that the longer token rotational time will reflect the longer physical ring wiring and the electronics delay from the many stations which must repeat each signal. For practical application, the original graphs in this chapter provide a measuring stick against which to measure a network's performance, health, and load. Should you desire better information of the performance and functionality of a data communications network, acquire and apply protocol analysis software and a hardware analyzer; feed these statistics into an *appropriate* network queueing model. The next chapter applies this information to network performance enhancements.

Chapter

17
Tuning Performance

While the last chapter detailed the mathematics of FDDI in terms of the queueing mathematics of performance models, this chapter explores methods to rechannel overloaded networks, improve throughput, increase network speed, and improve network reliability. Most network managers eventually experience network performance degradation as network software functionality decreases or workload increases. Improving performance usually implies providing a faster server, faster server disks, or better input/output (I/O) performance. I/O is the culprit in most network performance bottlenecks 40 percent of the time. Violation of specifications and poor network design, installation, and management account for another 40 percent. Rarely is network performance so dependent upon frame throughput and the consistency of the transmission rate. This is particularly true when few devices exist that can singularly transmit or receive more than 10 percent of the channel bandwidth. Performance also encompasses network reliability and efficiency.

Performance Solutions

There are several ways to solve network problems, including adhering to specification, providing faster protocols, optimizing servers and clients, rechanneling heavy FDDI loads with dual homing, installing routers and gateways, as well as implementing more exotic technologies. A very sophisticated software solution requires establishing priority enforcement. Unfortunately, no FDDI NOS supports priority transmissions, although FDDI-II may if it becomes a viable product. Best solutions are usually based on a clear understanding of the network problems and the available, simple, and relevant technologies.

This chapter details the techniques necessary to tune an FDDI network. These techniques include monitoring system performance, analyzing network statistics, and understanding the condition of that network. Figure 17.1 outlines performance tuning methods in a time-saving list.

- Monitor network load
- Monitor network performance
- Analyze network statistics
- Apply a queueing model
- Verify that the network matches Token-Ring specifications
- Ensure component consistency
- Install alternative channels for specialized needs
- Install multiple channels to balance loads
- Isolate segments with gateways
- Remove network repeaters
- Install "smart" repeaters and routers
- Provide fan-out units to improve configuration
- Buffer messages with store-and-forward devices
- Disable active SNMP or CMIP software

Figure 17.1 Performance tuning methodology.

Network Performance and Bottlenecks

FDDI networks exhibit poor performance for many reasons. Saturation of transmission channel capacity, while the most obvious, is only one of many and an unlikely possibility in the near term. In fact, authentic FDDI channel saturation is rare except in cases where there is a flaw. It is impossible to saturate FDDI; the latency just becomes longer and longer until network performance is unacceptable as the backlog grows at each station. It is important to differentiate that while the network may be within specification, the load waiting to transmit from each station may be an obstacle. Usually performance problems result from other component failures or overloading, hardware performance bottlenecks, or installation flaws. Component failures including chattering, jabbering, and jittering, optical signal scatter, as well as poor wiring, faulty installation, signal interference, and networks breaching specification. Performance is also a function of the speed of service for each individual component. Slow network cards, overworked file or application servers, disk-bound file servers, excessively large databases, queries to a distributed database that are not optimized locally, and slow computer memory also create bottlenecks that impair not only network performance but also the performance of individual network nodes. When FDDI is the backbone for an internetwork or enterprise-wide network, that backbone could be functioning perfectly, but the performance problems are obscured by the complexity of the subnet architectures and *their* ability to transmit the messages to the backbone.

For example, bridges passing all packets to the backbone and accepting all packets from the backbone may flood the subnets with needless chatter. It is possible that the bridges cannot handle the full load of all the packets sourced from all the other subnetworks that they must repeat. Installing a router will not necessary resolve the performance issue. While a router will reduce the backbone traffic level and will likely

Tuning Performance

reduce the traffic levels on all subnets, because routers are slower than bridges, they may be unable to route all frames at the necessary sustained speeds to clear the waiting backlog. Substitution of routers for bridges tends to reduce the amount of nondeliverable traffic, but causes a frame delivery backlog on the subnets. In terms of performance, gateways combine the worst features of routers while also adding a translation or encapsulation delay to data delivery. Gateways can, however, provide a performance improvement if they buffer traffic by offsetting output with existing traffic gaps.

The solution of breaking networks apart into subnets and connecting these to a matrix switch or backbone generally works for Ethernet and Token-Ring. In fact, this has been the most used method for regaining network performance as networks and organizations grew. However, it is not likely to work with mixed protocol networks and networks with mixed speeds. The technology for routing packets between different protocols and packets packets onto different networks is slow, and doesn't work at FDDI speeds. Imagine what would happen if an FDDI network overwhelmed an Ethernet subnet, as shown in Figure 17.2. While it is possible to bridge and route from one FDDI network to another, and though it is far simpler than converting protocols also, the network loads and speeds of transfer will likely be bottleneck.

Repeating an important point, FDDI networks never become saturated with too much traffic. They simply become slower until they reach the maximum TRT. Of note, the maximum TRT is simply a calculation of the station count times the maximum preamble synchronization times plus the NIC transmission setup times, plus the time to transmit the longest possible data stream. Should this value be exceeded, the clear implication is that the ring is out of specification. Too many users, too many file transfers, too many requests for data from a remote or

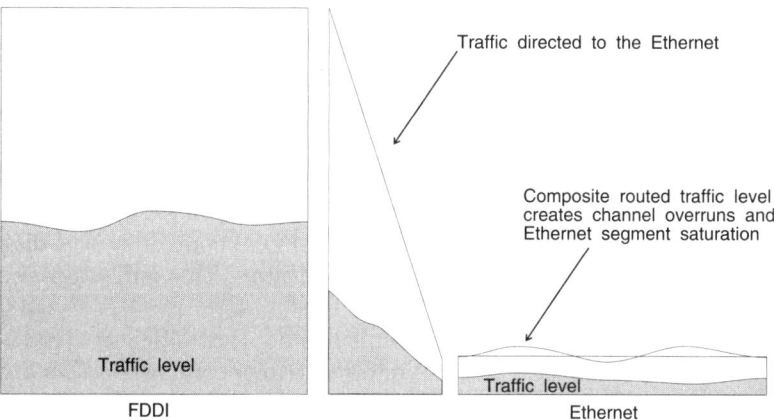

Figure 17.2 FDDI overwhelming an Ethernet segment.

distributed database, and too much reliance upon slow client/server processing are the most common causes for poor network performance.

Other more likely causes for poor network performance exist in addition to channel saturation. The transmission channel is only one component of the network. Most FDDI controllers provide an average burst transmission throughput of about 20 Mbits/s, which is 20 percent of the channel capacity. (Note that the FDDI NIC always sends signals at 100 Mbits/s, as per FDDI specification, but few PCs or even engineering workstations can sustain that transmission rate for more than a few seconds per minute. A time delay exists for gathering the data, assembling it into data fields, transmitting frames, and verifying acceptance by the recipient.) Although these processes occur in hardware on most FDDI adapters, moving that much data from disk or CPU memory to the card represents a bottleneck. Additionally, few file servers have hard disks that can transfer 8 Mbytes of information from disk into memory per second, let alone buffer a significant portion of that full image in memory at any one time while waiting for the controller to construct frames at its capacity. Most PCs (with ISA disk controllers) can achieve the slow disk transfer speed of 256 K (or 0.25 Mbyte) per second. Even if the file server with an SCSI-2 disk drive and controller were to sustain the data transfer speed of 4.4 Mbytes/s, the receiving PC may not be able to handle more than 256 Kbytes/s. Similarly, although "superservers" or specialty I/O backplanes may provide outstanding rates of I/O (25 to 38 Mbits/s), the recipients may be overwhelmed. Although this per se may seem like a bottleneck, this data transfer rate is faster than most FDDI controllers can encode or decode even when they have significant onboard buffer space and coprocessors. Floppy drives create bottlenecks due to their slower transfer speeds.

Consider the following example. Transfer of a 10-Mbyte graphics file on a two-node network nominally requires .3618 s across the communications channel. The time is derived by dividing 10,000,000 by 4478 (maximum data frame size) to find the number of frames required. This figure is then multiplied by the maximum token rotation delay. This ignores stack or protocol overheads. Additionally, higher-level protocols expect a one-for-one acknowledgment of each frame sent. This could increase the transmission time by 0.3618 s assuming an additional 2244 minimum-sized FDDI frames (and the maximum token rotation delay). Recall, however, that the slower of the local FDDI controller and disk I/O channel can sustain a maximum only 3 Mbits/s. This will suggest a transfer time around 4 s.

In fact, in reality upper-layer protocols are not that efficient. This is particularly true when OSI, TCP/IP, or other transport-level stacks are layered on top of FDDI to provide multiplatform routing and multiprocol connectivity. The application software will need to monitor transmission

Tuning Performance

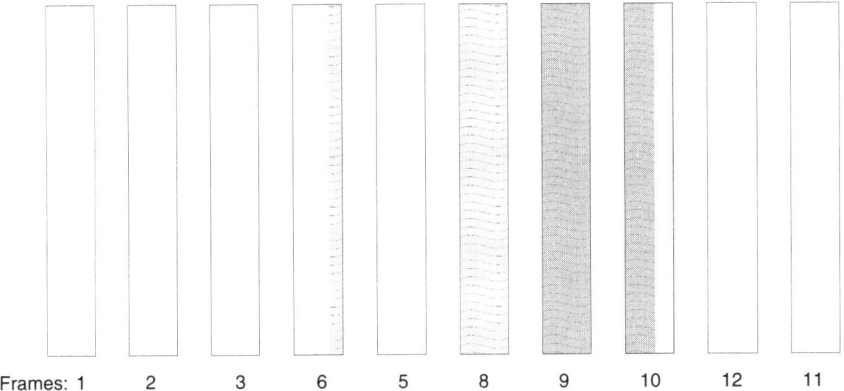

Frames: 1 2 3 6 5 8 9 10 12 11

Figure 17.3 Sequence error for block image transmission.

if only to count frames received and administer the sequence of data parsing and transmission. The graphic image in this example is a complex delivery, and the frames must be reassembled like a puzzle. Failure to reassemble the graphics data in sequence at this application level will result in a processing problem, as illustrated in Figure 17.3.

Furthermore, recall that the OSI level 2 MAC and LLC protocols require space within the data buffer of each frame. This is easily overlooked since these bits and meager bytes are hidden at the lowest levels. Since they are encoded as bit information, decoding the MAC and LLC parameters requires some effort. However, the point is that each OSI or NOS protocol layers add control blocks and bytes to the actual FDDI frame, thus decreasing throughput efficiency. Transmission of the 10-Mbyte image at FDDI speeds may require 8 s. An FDDI under normal load (25% channel load, .5 μs TRT) will actually require more than 1 minute to transfer the image. A 24-bit color TIFF image for a two-page magazine spread or a typical medical imaging CAT scan (that is illegal by FDA rules to compress) comprises about 55 Mbytes. Under such conditions, image transfer times could easily exceed 6 minutes.

Few networks consist of a mere two nodes; most have many nodes. Nonetheless, the controller transfer limitation implies that about 10 nodes (ignoring collisions) could probably transmit at constant capacity to 10 other receiving nodes before approaching the 100 Mbits/s FDDI channel capacity. A bottleneck at the server level may masquerade as poor FDDI channel performance. Bottlenecks will occur when multiple nodes send to or request information from a single node at once. The single node becomes a bottleneck despite excess channel capacity. This occurs not because this node simultaneously receives 10 frames at once. In fact, it cannot. If you recall, frames are in a train-car-like sequence by definition. The bottleneck occurs because this node must process the requests associated with each transmission.

For example, a file server handles user (or application) requests for data from files; an application server overlays sequential or program overlays for client users. Each request requires the server to interpret and process this. A client requesting an SQL view wants the server to extract specific information from a database and formulate that view for transmission to the client. That processing is not simple and is usually CPU-, bus-, and disk-intensive. Similar multiple requests from clients will cause a performance bottleneck at the server. This contrasts the issue of maximum network performance against maximum server performance. While these requests may necessitate some higher-level protocol transmission, network load may reach only 35 percent of capacity. By comparison, the file or application server may have reached 100 percent of CPU, controller transmission, disk access, or bus capacity.

One solution for poor client/server LAN performance is to replace existing servers with faster units. Often, this means that a standard high-end PC is replaced by a so-called "superserver" from a company such as Netframe, Parallan, and Tricord. These machines are designed with wider bus channels than standard MCA, EISA, or ISA PCs. For example, while MCA supports a 50 MHz bus and EISA supports a 33 MHz bus, Tricord provides at least 135 MHz. Because all data I/O, *direct memory access* (DMA), and control signals are passed across the bus, widening the bus usually improves performance dramatically. When disk access is the performance limitation on the network, high performance "disk farms" from a company such as Core International or Sanyo-Icon may relieve the bottleneck. Since the speed of the read/write heads are the limiting factors now in disk performance, disk striping, data spanning multiple disks, and even access to redundantly written data (i.e. shadowing) improves the data transfer rates by providing simultaneous access to the sequential blocks of data. These techniques are usually applied to provide a mission-critical safety net; RAID (redundant array of inexpensive disks) and shadowed disks also tend to yield a performance enhancement as well, as Figure 17.4 shows. Note that when these I/O bottlenecks are resolved, performance will improve. The next performance problem that surfaces after such I/O bottlenecks are resolved is the CPU. Bottlenecks tend to move to new places as the network is optimized.

Client/server network performance also is adversely affected by full disks. Traditionally, Unix-based FDDI networks require file servers to have a minimum of 10 percent free disk space. In fact, a Unix disk is not actually "full" until it is 110 percent full. This extra 10 percent freedom provides room to maneuver large files while confusing novice system administrators with new math. DOS-based, NetWare, and OS/2 systems also require the same disk freedom, particularly when providing data-

Tuning Performance

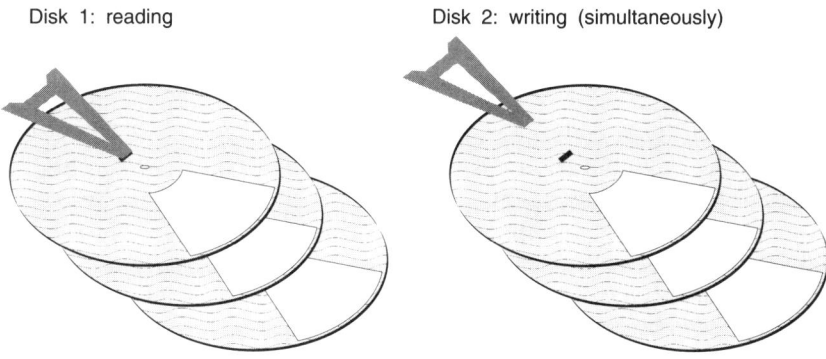

Figure 17.4 Shadowed disks tend to be faster to read and write.

base file service. As files grow under most disk operating systems, the file is rewritten over the old disk tracks while additions are chained and stored wherever free disk space is available. This is more efficient than creating a new file without discontinuous extents. It is particularly relevant for database record reads, creation, and updates. This is efficient when writing data on a mostly empty disk, but inefficient when this data is reread multiple times. The chains must be followed to termination and this requires multiple reads and repositions of the hard-drive heads, as Figure 17.5 indicates.

When a disk becomes very full, finding free disk space becomes a slow process as well. This is true for most operating and network systems. The free chains of space must be traced. Additionally, when large blocks of free space are required, minimum 4-K blocks may be chained together

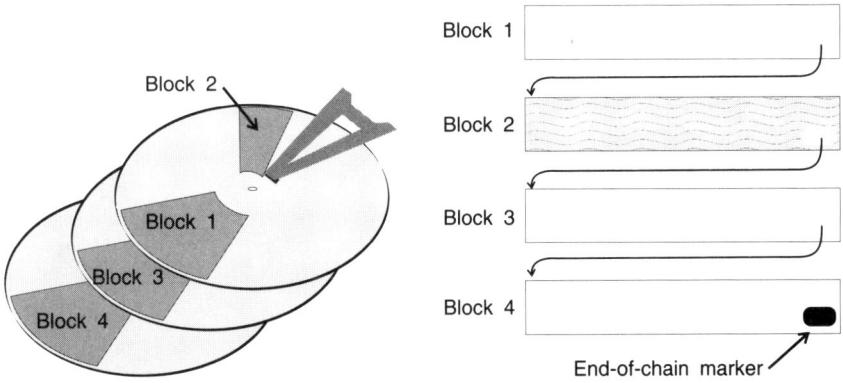

Figure 17.5 Chained files are inefficient to read.

to provide it. This makes for a slow writing process. While it would be prudent to provide a disk with at least 10 percent free space (and 30 percent would be even better), it is also important to realize that the fragmented files and free space waste disk access time and create bottlenecks. Tools including Norton Utilities, Mace, and PC Tools provide disk defragmentation software that gather all the files together into efficient contiguous segments. These tools also gather all the free space together into contiguous spaces as well. This dramatically improves disk performance for operations where files are continuously read, such as application software, system code, and database files, as Figure 17.6 indicates. The net result is faster server performance and potentially a better functioning network.

Network Load and Performance Monitoring

Network management is responsible for knowing what happens on the network. Ideally, the management will see the load approach unacceptable levels and take the necessary precautions to maintain high-quality service before users are aware of traffic overloads. Few tools other than a protocol analyzer or specialized frame-counting software tools provide sufficient services to monitor network performance with any accuracy. Small networks supporting limited file transfers and mainframe to personal computer downloading and uploading, usually avoid capacity problems. Larger or more utilized networks often demonstrate a creeping traffic growth, and eventual and sudden network capacity constraints. While it is possible to localize and resolve network overloads without understanding the composition of the network traffic, network load and performance monitoring pinpoint locations of problems and provide the network manager with information necessary to correctly implement repairs.

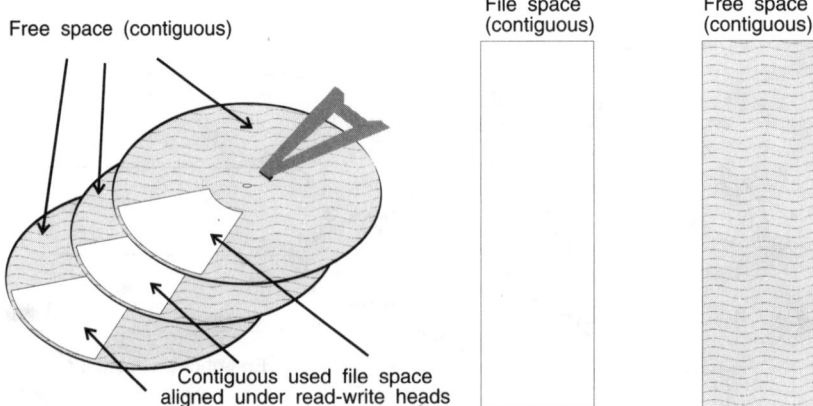

Figure 17.6 Defragmented files provide faster disk access.

Network Statistical Analysis

The mathematics are a curiosity unless understood and applied. Proper network load and performance analysis are most efficient with an understanding of the basic equations. Traffic rates (relative and absolute), waiting times, collision rates, and request resolution time (interframe timing) are based upon some of these important equations. Any rates that exceed a "normal" load imply a possible problem situation. If all rates vary, but do not vary logically, this, too, can be a clue to performance problems.

Verify Configuration to FDDI Specification

On small networks, the prevalent causes of network performance problems are misspecification problems. The network limitations were detailed in Chapter 4. Station-to-station segment and lobe length violations, node count excesses, and subnetted rings with too many hops are frequently causes for performance problems. It is important to realize that segments exceeding length specifications will not necessarily cause a performance problem but rather are *likely* to create signal bit decay, mistimings, and crosstalk, especially with copper-based media. Violations of specifications are not clear indicators for performance problems, but they certainly suggest it. To insist that network violations are the cause of performance problems may be to miss the true causes. Furthermore, installation flaws may exist if violations exist. Figure 17.7 reviews common network misspecification problems.

Other root causes include sloppy installation, faulty wiring, badly installed optical connections, too many optical connections, loose connections at jumpers or patch panels, poorly configured software, or mismatched cable components. Lobe and trunk wires, particularly the case with copper wire, often "work" on FDDI until the network becomes overloaded; mismatched wiring raises the impedance above acceptable levels. It is also very easy to exceed copper-based length limitations. If you suspect one of these problems, consult Chapters 4 and 5 for configuration information, or review Chapter 8 for installation suggestions.

- Maximum interstation segment length exceeded
- Maximum station count exceeded
- Maximum ring length exceeded
- Lobe grounding incomplete
- Poor electrical or optical connections
- Low-quality components
- Mismatched components
- Sloppy installation

Figure 17.7 Critical parameter violations.

Component Consistency

Another common cause for degraded network performance is noncompliance with a single FDDI standard. Optical FDDI shares the same encoding and signal characteristics with STP FDDI, but different encoding and signal characteristics from UTP FDDI. None will work efficiently across a bridge if the bridge frame limitation is 512 bytes. While NetWare *burst mode protocol* may overcome some of the routing limitations imposed by Novell NetWare, it may conflict with the THT requirements of FDDI.

The same argument can be made with NetBIOS, NetBEUI, Novell IPX, and TCP/IP derivatives. When multiple system software architectures must interface on the same network, the different systems can be isolated on separate network segments, as Chapter 8 suggested. At a minimum, monitor mixed networks specifically for transmission deficiencies. Other specialized interfacing equipment such as routers, gateways, or bridges can adequately protect network users from performance degradation due to mismatched standards and minor operational or component variations.

FDDI components, too, can create intractable problems. Different vendors may supply NICs with transmission rate clocks with subtle timing differences, or marginal signal quality. This equipment, while tuned for single-vendor usage, may communicate with other vendors' equipment unpredictably. A vendor may not subscribe to NITS testing to ensure standard compatibility. Therefore, maintain consistent network node configurations for best performance.

Network Slowdown Solutions

Most FDDI networks experience performance degradation when the traffic level is too high. The last chapter developed the mathematics and explored the methods to track and confirm this problem. If the traffic level is too high, and it cannot be reduced through user incentives (like peak time toll charges), there are several other methods to divert traffic for better performance including off-loading, installation of "local disks" for client/server applications, additional or alternative channel installation, and specialized routers. Load, traffic consistency, peak volumes, capacity, node location, recabling, and network extension techniques are a few of the issues covered within the next few sections to aid in resolving performance problems.

Distribute Load

The most economically available method to lower network usage is to charge for network service at graduated rates and offer users incentives to avoid prime-time network access. This is what a telephone utility does to

Tuning Performance

reduce daytime traffic and encourage off-peak usage. Since any network is built to handle a peak load, and since a peak load may be several times larger than off-hour usage, there is a built-in network excess capacity. Unfortunately, any extra capacity is generally useless during nonprime working hours. Figure 17.8 illustrates this principle by graphing network load during the progress of a normal day. Harried users often implicitly understand this principle and reorient their work schedules to reduce the impact on the overloaded network. Publish a graph of daily network loads to encourage off-peak usage if financial incentives are impractical.

When this last option is unavailable, the next-easiest method to reduce traffic levels is to filter the traffic and not allow certain vehicles on the network during peak usage. The network administration group, for example, doesn't need to perform data backups when the network is overloaded. Electronic mail can be stored and forwarded when the network shows a lull, or else saved for distribution during nonpeak hours. Other processes may be hogs of network resources. Curtail such processes. Figure 17.9 illustrates a typical distribution of network traffic. Note that this display represents volume percentages each hour of the typical day. Mail and graphics paging is a minor component in this sample.

Electronic mail often starts as a 10-line memo containing 1000 characters, but then is directed to 150 users. Since each user receives a separate copy, 150,000 characters plus the mail addressing information and FDDI frame information must be included. That simple mail message therefore requires upward of 300,000 characters of network transmission. A bulletin board with a single posting reduces this "junk mail" load almost fully. Side benefits include a reduction of "temporary" mail disk storage, temporary because each day's new mail will require that old space.

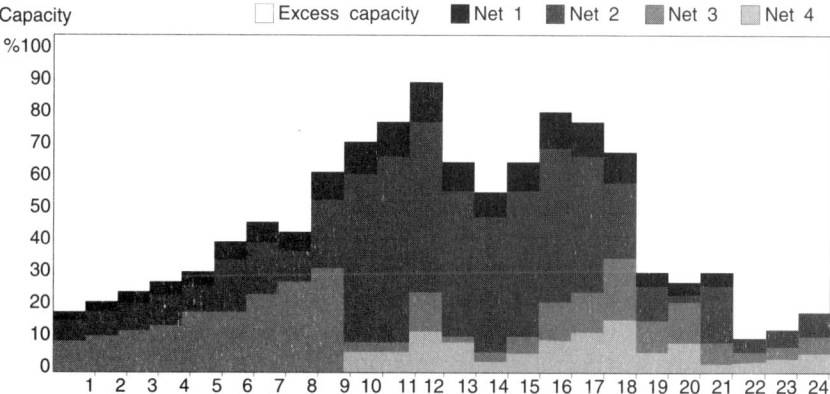

Figure 17.8 Peak network load capacity.

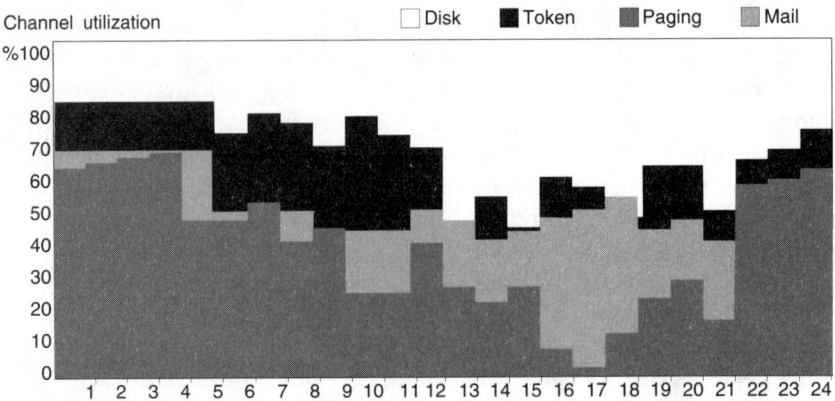

Figure 17.9 Traffic composition.

Data backup could be banned from the network and performed exclusively from the station bus. Such a policy may entail additional backup devices; it shifts financial costs from network communication channel improvements (infrastructure) to node-specific upgrades (depreciable usage-specific equipment), and thus to specific departments that subscribe to the enterprise-wide network. Departments can be encouraged to perform local backups with a financial chargeback system. If reliability and frequency of backup are concernd when users and departments are excluded from internetwork backups, managerial solutions may be necessary. One other point related to data backup is that LAN requirements for information storage is increasing rapidly. The processing time and time required to move Gbytes of data to a DAT storage device can exceed the hours in the day. As such, faster and more efficient backup devices may resolve a backup bottleneck.

Provide Local Resources

Since network traffic often consists of paging information, graphics display, or mail transmissions throughout a facility, a solution is to install local resources. Network printing can be relegated to local nodes, as can file storage. Determine the composition of the network traffic and rebuild the network to optimize for local solutions. Local disks and segregated backup channels might be an appropriate step to improve the performance of the sample networks illustrated in Figures 17.10 and 17.11. This type of analysis is ideal before embarking on any network reconfiguration. The down side to partitioning a network into clusters of local resources is that the concentration of resources originally available through networking is reversed and shifts financial costs. Management load increases, and costs increase, with the addition of local

Tuning Performance

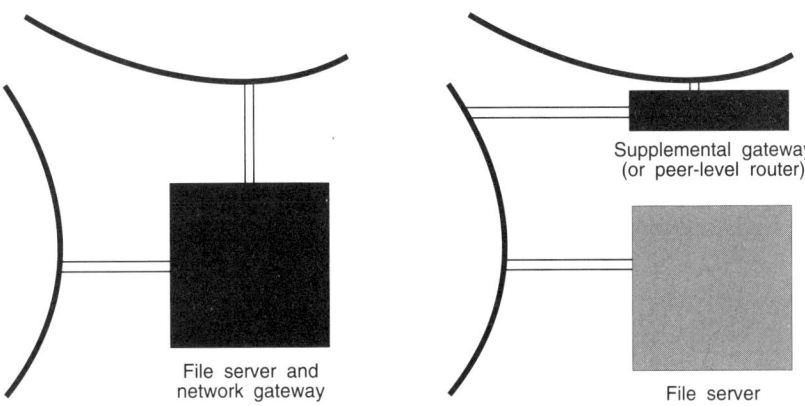

Figure 17.10 Gateway provides dedicated service to reduce a bottleneck.

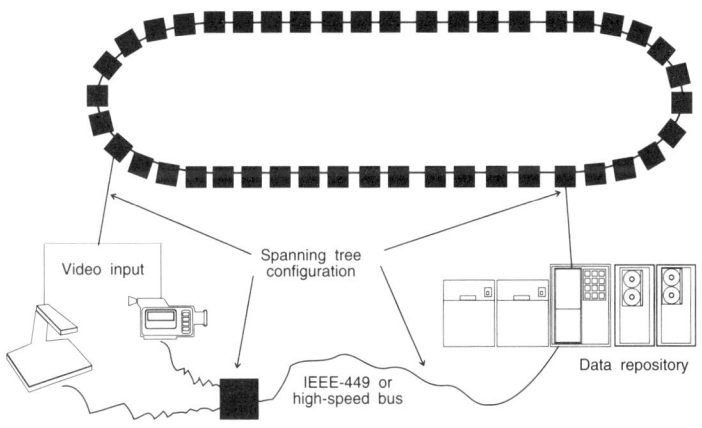

Figure 17.11 Alternative channels (dual homing) or a spanning-tree configuration provides a relief mechanism for a channel bottleneck.

resources because local units are generally more expensive than the public "bulk" versions. This reverses the economies of scale available through network resources. While this alternative may be more expensive, or take too long a time to install, it is an option.

Specialty Controller Hardware

There are more sophisticated and expensive methods to resolve FDDI bottlenecks. It is possible—but unlikely for most network users—to modify TCP/IP or build a new operating system to provide for priority transmissions. There are also specialized hardware implementations that can improve FDDI performance. Controllers with more buffer space or coprocessing chips increase throughput for slow workstations by caching large transmissions. Specifically, FDDI controllers are a growing tuning option. As an example, *bus mastering controller* is almost a necessity for FDDI in order to offload disk and network activity from the CPU to local processors on the expansion board. Other controllers that compress data achieve more efficient network utilization, while some vendors are designing hardware that will provide optimized protocol translations faster than software.

Optimize Station Bottlenecks

Unloading overburdened stations is another simple method to improve network performance. A common example is a workstation connected between two networks that provides gateway service. If this workstation is heavily used for processing, it will not have enough power to provide protocol translation and data rebroadcasting. Note, too, that the FDDI controllers are usually bound to the station's bus speed or to the disk I/O speed. Solutions include installing a faster CPU, dedicating a workstation to gateway service, installing a more potent NIC, or adding a specialized gateway to supplement the workstation.

There are three possible performance gains from substituting specialty gateway or bridge units for dual-ported stations. First, there is better individual station performance. Second, there is faster throughput by off-loading suspect station controller hardware or constrained bus configurations. Third, there is better signal quality and interconnectivity for multivendor installations; the workstation providing multivendor gateway service is likely to perform better for its native information than for other vendors' information.

Reiterating an important performance issue, a typical performance bottleneck may actually be a bridge, router, or gateway. If a unit is rated at 12,000 frames per second, it should handle 6000 frames *per side* under optimal conditions. This does not mean it will handle 9000 frames on one side and 3000 frames from the other side. Do not overlook this as a potential bottleneck on extended enterprise topologies. Also, consider that the interpretation of a higher-level protocol can slow the repeating process. As a consequence, a simple repeater in turn is faster than a bridge. Bridges are faster than routers. Routers are faster than gateways. None can maintain full FDDI frame speeds of nearly 300,000 frames/s.

Provide Alternative Channels

When an FDDI network carries a traffic volume at design capacity, performance deteriorates proportionately with more load, as illustrated mathematically in Chapter 15. This is true for FDDI, since FDDI is a deterministic process, but not true for 802.3 Ethernet networks, which are random. Alternative channels provide additional communication

Tuning Performance

paths, much as local side roads and highway "shoulders" relieve a highway bottleneck after a traffic accident. Alternative channels lower the demand on the network in much the same way that local devices lessen the number of requests for network access. An alternative channel might provide specialized high-speed disk-to-disk file transfers, imaging information transfer, or terminal services. Performance improvements are, however, limited by a station's ability to support multiple channels. Some Sun Microsystems workstations not only support dual homing for mission-critical applications but also they can be configured to use one NIC for outgoing data, a different NIC for incoming data, and other NICs for standard support on the different networks. Separate duplex channels with duplex transmission is effective for high-speed server-to-server connectivity. Any gain decays totally as the CPU load increases with the network load.

Terminals (DTE) or IRMA links require full frame transmission for each key stroke and are an overlooked FDDI resource hog. Terminal equipment transmissions reveal efficiencies of less than 0.2 percent when most network traffic may experience 60 percent efficiencies or higher. RS-232 lines—twisted-pair serial connections, for example—yield a better match than FDDI for such low-speed transmission. Conversely, an imaging camera or scanner often digitizes upward of a megabyte of information from a single picture. At FDDI speeds, 1000 or more frames will need to be built and transmitted. Such a load could jam an unloaded network completely for 0.4 s, or a network at capacity for a minute while the involved stations wait for tokens. Direct device-to-station bus connection improves transfer rates and transfer success rates. Many managers recommend hybrid networks and tune performance in just this manner.

Remove Bridges

Bridges generally create performance problems by extending the token rotation time since they represent a network station awaiting many tokens. This increases the waiting for all network stations, but basically backs up source and destination subnets. In situations where a network is grossly overloaded, disconnection of bridges may solve the traffic bottleneck by decreasing the electronics delay, as shown in Figure 17.12. This obviously defeats the purpose of the network by cutting intercommunication channels. There are other alternatives, but this iconoclastic solution can be quickly implemented to solve short-term overloading until more reasonable (and expensive) options can be implemented. A router with a filtering technology, a high-speed frame switch, or a backbone in a bus are superior alternatives—if they do not move the bottleneck from merely the inability to catch enough tokens to an inability to forward enough frames.

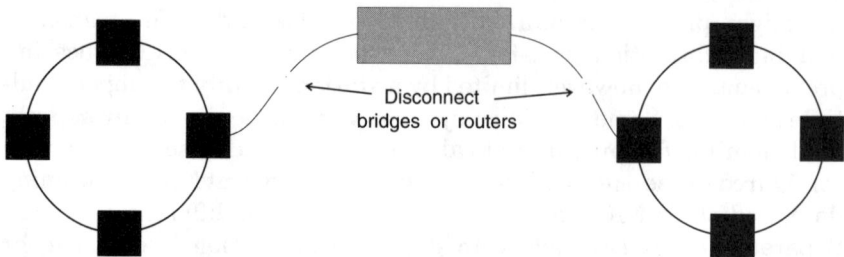

Figure 17.12 Unlink rings on an overloaded network.

The router transmits only those frames with a destination on another ring segment. Figure 17.13 illustrates the function of a smart repeater or OSI level 3 router.

While a ring of 100 stations may generate, for example, 100 units of global traffic, a network segmented in three smaller rings connected with two bridges will generate the same volume of traffic because the bridges will be forwarding the complete 100 units of traffic. If the network is correctly designed, the load originating on each ring is perhaps as low as 33 units (the average). If routers are installed instead, the result is a possible reduction in network load of 66 percent, although a more reasonable expectation would be about 50 percent. In point of fact, this separation may yield even better gains since protocol and frame overhead affects actual throughput. End rings (sections on the figure) will experience a lower traffic level, while the middle ring will often be forced to repeat traffic bound for the other end ring. This economy is illustrated in Figure 17.14.

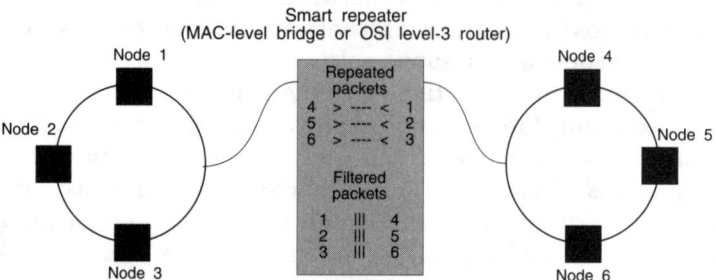

Figure 17.13 Install smart repeaters (routers) on an overloaded network. Only packets sourced from nodes 4, 5, or 6 destined for nodes 1, 2, or 3 are repeated across this gateway. Only packets sourced from nodes 1, 2, or 3 destined for nodes 4, 5, or 6 are repeated. Traffic is thus reduced.

Tuning Performance

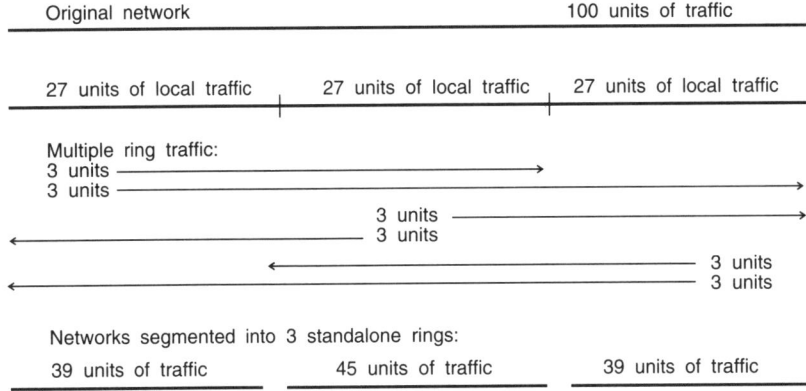

Figure 17.14 Routers reduce network load by isolating traffic to the necessary sections. Three sections of a single segment have an average of 33 units of traffic, of which 27 are local and 6 are destined for other segments. When these segments are subdivided with smart repeaters, traffic volume decreases by 55 to 61 percent. Note that latency will increase.

One other approach for improving FDDI network performance is to subdivide the ring with multiple network controllers in the server or merely add additional network controllers to the server, as Figure 17.15 illustrates. The extra frame buffer space and multiple controllers level the load, thereby improving performance. This is an effective approach only when the server bus is not at its capacity. Typically, a second controller card improves performance about 5 percent for client/server networks, from 7 stations to about 35 stations; there is no improvement outside that range. There is a mere 0.5 percent improvement for the third card and some performance degradation for subsequent cards due to DMA and bus waiting time conflicts.

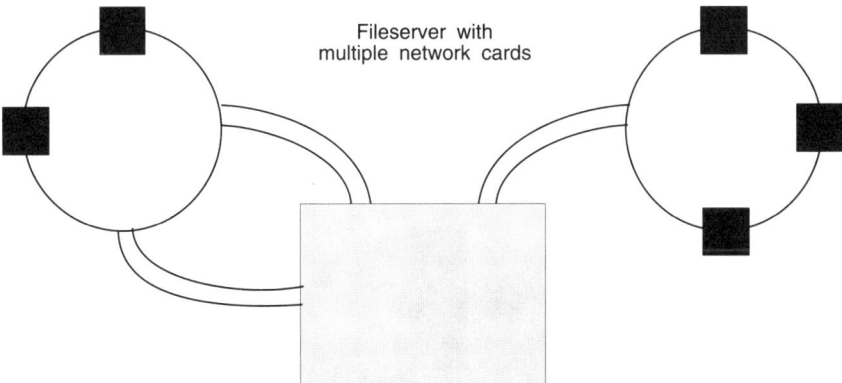

Figure 17.15 Multiple controllers can improve FDDI performance.

Buffer Networks with Store-and-Forward Gateways

The store-and-forward mechanism duplicates some of the filtration functionality of the router. It also understands the concept of waiting for a token and will store a message frame for an unlimited amount of time until network slot time is available; it might save the message frame until off-peak hours. This store-and-forward technology is used for long-haul optical fiber networks and microwave links to overcome the inherent weaknesses of realtime data communications transmission, because long-haul connections cannot function efficiently in real time at FDDI speeds. In effect, the token frame is converted to another protocol and medium, as outlined by Figure 17.16. Recall that store-and-forward mechanisms require that network protocols be decoupled from a return receipt message.

This is an expensive technology usually installed as an ISO gateway. It is, however, suitable for low-volume, low-priority transmission. It is dependent upon the robustness of the network software and effective protocol conversion or encapsulation. In fact, receipt confirmation may not be supported except at the mechanical level of the store-and-forward gateway. The concept is akin to a receptionist taking a message when the telephoned party is already busy; no message receipt confirmation is provided to the caller and the intended recipient of the call never knows he or she was wanted until a message is received, or until a follow-up call is accepted.

Rechannel with Additional Rings

When network bottlenecks are endemic, the best solution is additional FDDI rings. This implies that new cable and additional FDDI access hardware will have to be installed. This option is costly, and the deci-

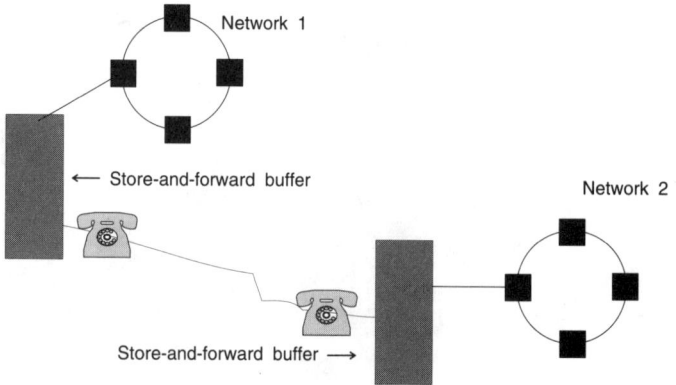

Figure 17.16 Store-and-forward buffering relieves bottlenecks by holding nonessential packets until the network is less loaded.

Tuning Performance 375

sion-making process must contrast the financial costs, maintenance issues, and the risk of acquiring a new technology. It is important to realize that multichanneling is no panacea; sufficient capacity must exist on each channel to provide transmission for local traffic and the detoured traffic.

Expand Conservatively

When other expansion options have been applied as deemed appropriate, the actual recabling should be planned in stages to minimize downtime and disruption. For example, the overloaded original network is left intact *until* a new channel is designed, built, and tested. Changes proceed in simple stages until successful operation is assured. If subtle problems arise in the early stages of the transformation, the changeover can be reversed until resolved. This philosophy is useful for new installations, and also for revisions and repairs of existing networks.

Tuning Performance

There are two basic conditions requiring tuning. These are an extended network bus topology and network overloading, conditions which are encountered by the network manager on all but the simplest networks. Even a network with five personal computer stations could create FDDI performance issues. For example, all five units might be within the same office and require 250 m STP lobes to a wiring closet. As another example, these five personal computers could be sited 1500 m apart, requiring special repeater hardware. While such design problems are possible on the minimal network, bus and disk I/O overloading is a more common network constraint. Network extension options for FDDI include adding bridges and routers, or installing gateways which can arbitrarily extend the length and width of the network topology. Longer networks tend to increase the loading and strain on FDDI, and therefore any extensions require careful analysis as part of the design phase. This is particularly prevalent with routers and other devices that create broadcast storms or forward SNMP data to a centralized repository.

Expand Reach with Wider Area Networks

As technology advances, most organizations discover that information becomes a critical component to their success. Information gathered from distant and occasional sources assumes a transmission technology different from local area networking. Modem, satellite, infrared or microwave transmission, T-1, frame relay ATM, and PBX are viable options to service those wide area networks. These technologies connect into FDDI via ISO bridging and routing.

FDDI

FDDI performance for FDDI backbones and links is complex when it serves a multipurpose internetworking role. Consider the following complications. When FDDI is installed to bridge Ethernet or Token-Ring networks, these packets are translated for optical fiber transport into the FDDI *subnet access protocol-service access point* (SNAP-SAP) frames. Major complications of this process arise in that the data translation must be performed in real time to keep up with the 100 Mbits/s FDDI speed, but also maintain the timing requirements of all interconnected local FDDI LANs. Encapsulating bridges operating at less than 4 (10 or 16) Mbits/s will cause bottlenecks. Additionally, traffic jams caused by saturated segments on either end of the FDDI link will create a bottleneck that will spill back to other subnetworks. It is unlikely that the FDDI link will approach a function capacity unless it becomes an uncontrolled public channel.

Ethernet, Token-Ring, UDP, Appletalk, and TCP/IP packets often are encapsulated for transport over the FDDI bridge or routerouter. Encapsulation is necessary to handle the FDDI protocol addressing scheme and ensure FDDI frame integrity. However, there is apt to be a loss of compatibility since the encapsulation scheme is proprietary to each FDDI bridge and router vendor. It also limits the ability of a workstation on FDDI from directly addressing any file server or workstation residing on the FDDI network, or the reverse. In such cases, FDDI is merely a faster piggyback carrier of the FDDI signal and provides no internetworking access. Internetworking requires a translating and addressing processor to correctly route these more complex service demands. Translation becomes necessary and becomes more complex when FDDI is used to "bridge" (e.g., multiprotocol route) Token-Ring to Ethernet and ARCnet, or any other LAN and WAN protocols, including X.25 and T-1. True protocol translation requires RISC and other optimized hardware to minimize this routing bottleneck. Since FDDI becomes the high-speed backbone, it must be a bridging and rerouting server. Hodgepodge bridging (actually, OSI-level routing) would only increase the data delivery times, increase the odds of delivery failure, create a wide variety of performance and traffic bottlenecks, and leverage the chance for incompatibilities.

Performance is complicated further by differences in frame sizes. Encapsulation works well for FDDI frames shorter than the 4456-byte FDDI data frame maximum. It can be a problem for 18,456-byte Token-Ring frames. Although there is a loss in efficiency since each Token-Ring frame carries a single FDDI frame, the greater channel speed mitigates this problem. The distribution of FDDI frames is not uniformly maximum-sized frames; it regularly includes collision signals from Ethernet, return receipts, and even data fragments from other protocols encapsulated in the FDDI data field. It is advantageous to filter extraneous frames before encapsulating them to avoid performance degradation on

Tuning Performance

the FDDI link. Despite its high throughput, FDDI could be swamped with meaningless and empty FDDI noise. Routers (or hybrid bridges) filtering source and destination addresses minimize this problem, assuming that they can process the frames in real time. Segmenting long Token-Ring packets into multiple FDDI frames also creates the potential for several performance hits. Potentially, each Token-Ring frame could be disassembled into three or more FDDI frames, a large burst of FDDI information could oversaturate the translation speed of the bridge, overwhelm the slower Ethernet or Token-Ring transport mechanism, and saturate them with fragmentary frames. This two-way process must occur in real time with expert tuning to prevent a traffic bottleneck.

However, TP-PMD provides a direct method to upgrade an STP Token-Ring network that does not meet performance requirements. The wiring is the same. The NOS is the same. The NICs and NIC drivers need to be upgraded. The MAUs are replaced with a junction box or hub. Although this may be an expensive undertaking, FDDI on STP bypasses the requirement to install FDDI optical fiber and the marginally more expensive NICs.

Solve Traffic Overloading Problems

On a overloaded network, the immediate problem is to lower network demands, or rechannel that load. Figure 17.17 outlines the steps necessary to alleviate this problem.

Tuning Recommendations

Network tuning encompasses more than remedial repairs. FDDI should be designed to service current loads with expansion points for future growth. Chapters 8, 9, and 10 detailed many of the planning and operational concerns. Another of those concerns is building a network

- Reschedule peak loads
- Remove repeaters
- Remove bridges
- Segment network with routers
- Install alternative channels with dual homing links
- Gateway busy sections
- Install more channels
- Install a high-speed backbone or switching backplane
- Install faster controllers or bus-mastering units
- Localize remote tasks
- Replace dual-purpose nodes with gateways
- Upgrade Ethernet and Token-Ring subnets with FDDI

Figure 17.17 Steps to relieve a saturated network.

with enough foresight to meet the user community's future communication needs. The last figure in this chapter, Figure 17.18, lists tuning recommendations.

- Plan for capacity
- Plan for overloads
- Set options to resolve in short term
- Set options to resolve in long term
- Provide the network with automatic "firewall" mechanisms
- Provide local access only when the network is saturating
- Disable all active SNMP or CMIP routines
- Educate users
- Increase fileserver data access speeds
- Increase the performance level of global stations

Figure 17.18 Network tuning recommendations.

Chapter 18
Network Security

This chapter confronts the issues of physical and data network security. Approaches that combat threats, strengthen vulnerabilities, and lessen risk are exposed to the reader. It is critical to differentiate computer system security from network security because computer security is possible without network security. LANs and enterprise security in general complicate security issues by extending the computer architecture to a physically distributed area and undermining basic textbook data security procedures. There is a basic fundamental contradiction between the need to provide distributed access to information and, at the same time, to provide controlled and restricted access to information.

As a consequence, the need for networks should be carefully investigated in light of security concerns. For any network installation, the ramifications of open network architecture should be understood, and the many alternatives to network security should be learned. The chapter outlines security vulnerabilities, and offers security measures for the reader's evaluation.

Security Overview

Attitudes about computer security are changing, not because theft and abuse are so common, but because the stakes have become so high. Computer processing and networking technology are no longer simply tools isolated from organizational operations; they are the lifeblood of many organizations. For these reasons, a concerted effort is required to divert attacks on networks.

Literature and movies have long had a special fascination with computer crime and abuse. Reports of yet another clever intrusion, massive "white collar" theft, or another computer virus scare is the grist of good reading. Like everyday burglaries, breaks in security are something that happen to someone else. In general, only minimum protection measures are applied, although such steps provide a false sense of security.

"Security" is hard to define. What one software or hardware designer invents, another can crack given enough incentive. Computer system and network users invent new problems because they hit upon novel methods to attack the protection mechanisms, just as viruses and the designers of viruses adapt to new protection measures. Hardware security has been the traditional route for control because it has been possible to limit physical access to equipment. Yet, with the increasing distribution of equipment onto the factory floor, or into individual offices, and with remote links via networks and enterprise-wide communication systems, the cost and difficulty of applying security has increased significantly. Traditional security is a secluded room; but that is no longer possible with networks. Physical restrictions prevent physical attacks to the computer. Levels of access rights restricted the logical access to the computer. However, *the computer* is no longer the monogeneous object it once was as *the mainframe*.

The mainframe has given way to tens, hundreds, or thousands of computers. Many units are important; but perhaps even more important than those few units is the structural integrity of the network, the value of the operations, and the value of the data as a whole. Attacks upon one unit can propagate problems throughout the whole network. The acceptance of networks raises the organizational cost and significance of a careless, dishonest, or disgruntled employee damaging the machinery and information, or stealing information. Figure 18.1 cites common reasons for security breaches.

FDDI Lacks Inherent Security

FDDI itself provides no security, neither network security nor data security. FDDI is designed as a simple and open physical medium for data transmission. Furthermore, FDDI is not immune to snooping and spying, nor diversion of information. Figure 18.2 outlines these basic vulnerabilities. This startling limitation may surprise some; how could a network exist and succeed where security is either virtually impossible, or comes at very high cost? However, FDDI transmission protocols are straightforward, and thus allow for transparent transmission of encrypted data.

- Inadequate physical security
- Inadequate indication of "sensitive" material
- Lack of locks on workstations
- Lack of organizational security policy
- Inadequate password systems
- No access logs or journals
- No records kept of efforts to penetrate security
- Lack of end-user security education

Figure 18.1 Common security breaches.

Network Security

- Open architecture
- Repeated (thus "broadcast") communication
- Easily spliced and "tapped"
- No hardware security measures
- Easily jammed transmissions

Figure 18.2 FDDI security vulnerabilities.

FDDI, like Unix, has begun its rise to be the enterprise-wide connectivity solution because of its speed, area coverage, and wide range of uses. While some specialized networks succeed solely because they meet strict government security criteria, or enforced contract bidding specifications, other networks have succeeded because they are simple enough to promote equipment interconnection and a generic platform. FDDI fills this description admirably. FDDI is simple and consequently, robust. It does, however, face security threats.

Threats to the Network

There are four categories of network security threats: internal and external vulnerabilities, and physical- and data-related risks. Externally, an organization is at risk from events that might compromise the physical integrity of the network. An organization is at risk from external threats posed by modems, and network, microwave, or PBX telephone tapping performed by computer "hackers," the occasional career crook, and motivated competitors.

Internally, the organization is vulnerable to profiteering employees and contractors, disgruntled employees, and the random disaster. Unless the network is perceived as a toy, data never have value, and all users perceive that work accomplished on the network is totally exposed and expendable and agree to this, then and only then is security an unnecessary constituent of network design and administration. Figure 18.3 illustrates those items at risk in a simple matrix.

External Threats

A network is exposed to external threats from physical attacks, and to a significantly greater degree, from data tapping. Most networks are contained within a single building, and as a result are usually secure from physical affronts. FDDI presents a broader risk because the FDDI channel is apt to run between buildings, through city blocks, and thus be fairly exposed. A saboteur cannot cut network wire or cable if it is locked away, nor disrupt power if power lines are underground and similar in appearance to many other lines. While this issue is often overlooked by many organizations, computers, in particular mainframes, have been attacked by terrorists and competitors. A destroyed main-

	External	Internal
Physical	Power lines	Power supplies
	Data lines	Data lines
	Network facilities	Network facilities
		Access units
Data	RF signals	RF signals
	Dial-up lines	Network nodes
	Microwave links	File server data
	Line links	Output devices
	Wastepaper	Wastepaper

Figure 18.3 Network items at risk and vulnerable to attack.

frame or severed network is not only an expensive item to repair or replace; the data or time lost can bankrupt a business, especially when data are the lifeblood of the business. Think of the effects to a university should a student group protesting a political decision (e.g., racial attacks, investment in the Republic of South Africa, or tuition grants or fee increases) decides to cut the FDDI network in multiple locations. Last, do not discount the possibility of catastrophe: computer damage from chance events such as fire, flood, hurricane and tornado, explosion, lightning and power surges or power deficits, or a collapsed building, could set the organization back more than need be under such extreme circumstances. Fire damage is not merely the direct damage from the fire and heat itself, but also fire axes, foam, debris, and water. FDDI links are also at risk from construction, excavation, and poor documentation.

While extrinsic damage to a network might occur (it is best not overlooked), dial-up modem and remote connections are the more frequent avenues of assault on a network. Most networks, even FDDI, often see the external world through telephone connections, T-1 links, and wireless signals. There is no reason to prohibit such contact, although there are many reasons to control it. Most organizations have local offices and satellite facilities, and communicate professionally and academically with others off-site. The problem is to prevent unauthorized entry onto the network that would allow a "user" to delete files, modify files, power down the network, spread viruses accidentally or maliciously, access privileged information, copy information for profit, or disseminate information to the public to discredit or supplant the organization. Figure 18.4 lists the potential dangers that must be guarded against.

Network Security

Physical	Data
Catastrophe	Network jamming
Power disruption	Network tapping
Terrorism	Theft/destruction of information
Network jamming	Data "diddling"
	Data tampering
	Misappropriation of data

Figure 18.4 External network threats in need of protection.

Computer Viruses

Of relevance to many FDDI network managers is the Internet virus propagated by a computer science graduate student. This virus replicated itself without causing overt damage other than filling disk space and memory with its copies. It propagated by reading the Internet address tables and reached out across networks to infest all the other machines on the LANs and WANs. Some network managers may rightfully argue that the Internet virus did substantial damage. Not only did it halt networks, it also caused the attached machines to attend to the high-priority processing of the virus itself. Note, that it did cause loss of use of the computers, lost time, and data loss, which amounted in aggregate to tens of millions of dollars. While PC networks are prone to destructive viruses like "PC is stoned," the Jerusalem virus, Michaelangelo, "Ping Pong," the "disk killer," and the disk boot sector virus from Pakistan called "Joshi," other networks with other types of platforms could easily be damaged by viruses specific to their hardware or software, or be a carrier for PC-based viruses. While personal computer viruses are disruptive, a network expands the damage by providing an easy path for infection. A new virus infects Postscript-PDL printers and damages the CMOS setup configuration. Other new viruses, called *stealth viruses* attempt to hide themselves to outwit virus-detection software.

The availability of object-oriented programming and menu-driven virus design tool kits have simplified the process of creating new viruses. Even shrink-wrapped software from reputable vendors is not immune to these attacks. Sometimes attacks create no effects to the primary attack site. DOS viruses can propagate fairly innocuously on OS/2 and Unix networks. While these diseases will change files and corrupt data when executed, the results tend not to be as immediate. However, when these viruses reach DOS stations through the network or through disk masters of software, the damage is immediate. To date, no one has died as a result of a virus; that may change as computers control more activities and as the next generation of air traffic control computers are based upon nonproprietary computing platforms. It is easy to imagine a situation where a computer is monitoring a patient, controlling aircraft, a nuclear power plant, or chemical additions on an assembly line. A virus could unwittingly and unintentionally halt the computer with devastating effect.

Virus damage protection and access prevention is available through software and hardware. Virus prevention and protection is not costless. In addition to the obvious cost of the virus software or hardware, there are costs for storing it, times to execute it, and the overhead related to running TSR and background operations. Some software creates extensive checksum and encoding tables so that in the event damage does occur, the damaged files can be replicated. As such, the overhead and process required to track viruses may be in effect worse than the virus. Additionally, some software that "cures" virus infestation is not innocuous itself in that the cure may corrupt files and damage the contents. Assess the requirements and access to the network accordingly.

Novell NetWare users should be aware that there are programs that unravel the security system and provide an entry point for unauthorized users. One such program, called HACK.EXE developed by students Leiden University in the Netherlands, makes NetWare think the user has supervisor privileges. Another program, called KNOCK.EXE, was distributed over Internet that provided unauthorized users access to a NetWare network. Novell has patches to prevent KNOCK.EXE from working, and a SECURFX.NLM to defeat HACK.EXE. These were developed in response to security breaches; this may not prevent future programs for NetWare, or for other ID and password systems, from being developed to defeat network security. As of yet, there have been no reports that anyone has decoded the password tables for many mainstream network operating systems. It is certainly possible, and when so much is at stake, it is a certainty that it will happen.

Internal Threats

A network is under scrutiny from the inside. Once the basic physical security of the network is breached, as often is the case, the network equipment is at risk. Unauthorized access to information is simplified, and prevention and detection are progressively more difficult to achieve when there is an amorphous "intrusion." The simplest security flaw is caused by users not logging off their machines. This is akin to leaving a door ajar, so that anyone can enter. While remote network links can be tapped between buildings regardless of the media, internally the network can be physically tapped like a common telephone eavesdrop. FDDI, as explained above, expands the horizon for eavesdropping since FDDI repeats the transmission packet globally to all network nodes. Although the technology for tapping FDDI is more difficult and costly than Ethernet or Token-Ring, it is not impossible. An intruder with a means to promiscuously read packets can intercept information without anyone being much the wiser.

Network Security

A protocol analyzer can tap the network. An optical signal splitter will do the job too.

A highly sophisticated user can override any software protection by directing falsified FDDI packets to a target station or node; this scheme progressively modifies those software protection schemes for an eventual intrusion. The source and destination addresses could both indicate the target node, and few protection schemes are designed to protect a user from harm. This level of power is possible because FDDI is open, and most operating systems key upon frame address information. As a consequence, protection stops far short of top security.

While eavesdropping has its many risks—breach of organizational secrets and theft of information—modification of data can be more devastating because it can remain hidden indefinitely, or be propagated and disseminated before errors are detected. Money can be siphoned from a payroll and redirected to other pockets, trade secrets can be tampered with, private files can be read, development efforts can be hindered, and "ironclad" results can be scrambled, discrediting the innocent. Figure 18.5 lists ways that security can be breached internally.

Physical access to the network equipment raises the possibility of sabotage from a disgruntled employee or an authorized visitor. The physical network cabling and devices, the station and node equipment, and the data residing thereon are at risk. Most organizations assume no need to protect the equipment from employees. Unfortunately, this is often an expensive assumption.

Protection Countermeasures

There are some straightforward measures which will protect the network. These include physical network isolation, standard password protection, limits applied to outside access, occasional changeovers in network operating policies, data encryption, and last, the monitoring of access channels, both physical and logical. Loss-limiting measures include fall-back provisions and a good network backup policy. Figure 18.6 indicates these progressive countermeasures.

Physical	Data
Power disruption	Network jamming
Network sabotage	Network tapping
Equipment damage	Theft/destruction of information
Network jamming	Data "diddling"
Network tapping	Data tampering
	Misappropriation of data

Figure 18.5 Internal network threats in need of protection.

- Physical network equipment and infrastructure isolation
- Identification *and* password protection
- Limited external access and internal subnetwork isolation
- Occasional policy changeovers
- Spread-spectrum technology (for wireless)
- Access control for network monitoring devices
- Vandal detection and incorrect password logs
- Application access and usage limitation
- Hierarchy of access (user, group, and limited file access)
- Fall-back countermeasures
- Network backup

Figure 18.6 Security measures applicable to FDDI.

Physical Network Isolation

The most effective network protection is simply to lock up the network and make it unavailable. Obviously, this severely cripples its usefulness. However, when more emphasis is placed upon physical security, and when access to the network is controlled, the network is more secure. This holds true for both physical and logical devices. Therefore, the best medicine is to limit access to the network where feasible. Unfortunately, most networks provide necessary communication channels for business, usually as electronic mail, change notices, meeting announcements, and other normal messages; and thus such draconian measures are inappropriate. Furthermore, many E-mail and groupware packages are not encrypted; the data is publicly accessible in spite of any physical security. While Lotus Notes and Novell NetWare provide security and encryption tools, the use of them is not assured; users tend to ignore them.

However, the concept of physical security through access limitation can be extended as far as necessary to meet requirements. The rule is to lock up as much as possible. Mainframe and network file servers should have limited and controlled access. If printed or drafted output (fighter plane plans, for example) is confidential, then certainly lock up the printers and delegate one person to burst, collate, and distribute all network output. For additional confidence, bond that person and shred paper and magnetic trash. Since data storage mechanisms often use removable media-like tapes, disks, punched output, or removable magnetic or optical platters, a cautious approach is to restrict access to these classes of devices and their active media. Log all mountings, and catalog all purchases, uses, disposals, and distributions of storage media.

If more security is required, lock up the transmission channels. Place cables beyond reach, in a plenum, in locked corridors, or restricted areas. Position multiplexing fan-out units beyond occasional reach and protect the FDDI connections. If this is unfeasible or impractical, then at the minimum, restrict access to as much of the physical network as possible. Run external optical cable in armored bundles. Establish alarms, with

Network Security

beeper activation if necessary, to provide notice of *any* loss of connection on these vulnerable links. Even a brief—two minute—loss could indicate that someone may have installed a tap or optical signal splitter on the segment. As such maintain documentation with fiber feature indicators.

The station node equipment is always vulnerable, although on a broadcast transmission medium like FDDI, each station and node provides a window of vulnerability to all other network node equipment, including file servers, hosts, and data storage farms.

Multiports and hubs not fully populated because some ports are not utilized offer a ripe invitation. The lobe is already in place, and the additional repeater or other multiport hub is invisible to the network monitoring tools. Therefore, it is wise to disable the extra unused ports where security is an issue, and periodically inspect all lobes for unauthorized tinkering. A lobe cable could be diverted from a single station node via a concentrator without anyone being wiser unless a periodic physical inspection is actually performed. Figure 18.7 illustrates a common node with an added hub. This illustration also demonstrates how even a fiber optical cable can be intercepted with a signal splitter for nearly invisible interception, subject to signal loss limits.

Password Protection

At the software level, password authentication protection is the most effective mechanism for network protection. Passwords prevent unauthorized access to files and network devices, and protect information from "diddling" and tampering. Unix is one of many operating systems where security can be breached when physical access is granted to the equipment. However, for most novice users, passwords keep prying eyes out. Most serious data thefts have been perpetrated by novices who exploit a hole in the system. Password protection limits software access to a node, thus limiting access to the network. Additionally, contingent upon the network operating system and support services, password protection may lock individual files. In situations where security is of utmost concern, tools that analyze files at the bit and byte levels can be entirely removed from the system or locked away from the casual user. Such tools can invalidate bit-level protection mechanisms.

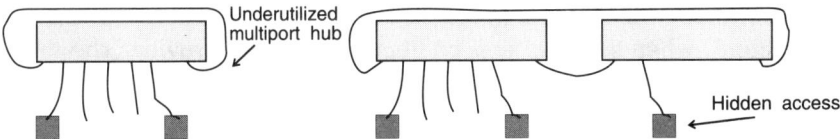

Figure 18.7 Hubs and concentrators provide a hidden opportunity to spy.

Password protection is only as strong as the weakest link. User login names and passwords that are freely disseminated ease access to the system. Common passwords that everybody knows breach the security. Hired consultants with external dial-in privileges can be a serious security problem. Prudent management of security requires that passwords be changed regularly, and that when an intrusion is indicated, passwords be deleted from the log until ownership of a login is requested again by a user. Good policy also requires that when people leave a company, their passwords be removed from the log, especially when a person has left under questionable circumstances. New user logins not matched with people, multiple logins for the same people, and guest logins possibly point to a breach of supervisory access and security.

Password protection is the most readily available network protection. Most networks provide password protection as a minimum security measure. It is also the most easily applied countermeasure, although it requires vigilance.

Encryption

Encryption is the transformation of data into a format that is not readable by anyone who does not have the key for decoding it. There are various formats for encryption which include substituting bytes with a code from a code table, replacing byte values with calculated mathematical value, or by transforming entire blocks of data through a key encryption algorithm. This later method is finding the most use today since it is virtually impossible to defeat. The DES method is one such system, while Internet has defined a new standard called the privacy enhanced mail (PEM) which relies upon a two part key; a published public key and the users private key. The problem remains how to assure the authenticity of the public key.

Although anyone who desires complete privacy should encrypt data, files, and mail messages, there are problems which generally preclude this. For example, it takes time to convert the information into and from the coded format. Additionally, it may require more space in terms of storage space or transmission time. The loss of a key also precludes recovery of the information contained by an encoded message or file. Consider what would happen if a person lost their code key. Consider what would happen if an employee encoded all his data, and when fired refused to reveal the key or code. The administration of messages and files containing gibberish is made that much more complicated. On the other hand, when secrets must be kept, encryption provides the most reliable method to do so.

Network Security

External Access

Most published security breaches have occurred through phone access modems. The most often perpetrated breaches occur through trusted employees or careless procedure and password controls. A phone line is a doorway into the network, the modem is a lock, and the password is the final key. Therefore, the best protection is not to have any protection, but also not to have any external phone access to the network. When phone lines are necessary, several precautions are relevant. Do not publish the phone number. Change the phone number frequently. Use modems that wait for a tone from the caller. This has the advantage of not accidentally informing a dialer that a computer exists at the number dialed. Install call-back modems that do not accept calls without verifying the identity of the caller, the phone number, and the password. Install specialized modems that are difficult to use (many modems talk only to others identical to themselves), or that scramble transmission. While data encryption usually adds a dramatic overhead, it may provide assurance for external links. Additionally, where feasible and available, install Caller ID technology to verify the actual number of the calling party at the time of the call. Note that there is some concern that Caller ID can be defeated so that no identifying telephone number is provided, or that a phony phone number is supplied. Install Caller ID to log the originating numbers of all callers. While Caller ID can be disabled with a few widely-known tricks, or given a fake phone number, the phone call without a number or with an unknown number is likely to represent a problem. Until these concerns are resolved, Caller ID should be installed in conjunction with other security measures. Figure 18.8 outlines these crucial procedures.

Where a network runs between buildings, lock up the cable, or install optical fiber which, at least for the present, is expensive to tap. If these possibilities are unfeasible, inspect the connections daily for signs of possible intrusion. If microwave or a radio frequency is used, scramble those transmissions. There are few legal remedies once an eavesdropper is detected spying on "public" RF signals. Select sideband or multiband transmitters rather than single frequencies. Be aware of the possible security leakages at time of installation, understand the need for organizational security, and weigh the benefits of applying the necessary security countermeasures. Figure 18.9 outlines these items.

Networks isolated by bridges, routers, and gateways provide additional security. Every step taken to isolate a network from public access increases the inherent security. While internetwork access is frequently required, subnets add a buffer when they filter the frames that are forwarded. All transmissions destined for nodes on the originating network are not globally broadcast beyond that originating network. A router or gateway filters only that traffic which must

- Avoid dial-up connections
- Don't publish the dial-up phone numbers
- Change the phone numbers frequently
- Use modems that don't supply a carrier tone
- Install call-back equipment and/or Caller-ID
- Control distribution of logons and passwords
- Change passwords frequently
- Install specialty modems

Figure 18.8 Limit dial-up access.

- Lock up access to wiring closets and hubs
- Check for intrusions
- Install optical fiber
- Alter transmission frequencies
- Apply SST and sideband transmission methods
- Scramble or encode transmissions
- Root out anomalies
- Remain vigilant
- Maintain network blueprints

Figure 18.9 Limit physical access.

be transferred to the other networks; source or destination address-explicit forwarding effectively retains sensitive material. As noted previously, this does not preclude the conveyance of "doctored" packets unless transmission is a one-way process. In this way, a network could be constructed with a centralized and rigorously secured network facility. This secured network would lock out all remote links and dial-up access. On the other hand, the central secured network could reach out and remotely access the other networks and their resources, including dial-out telephone communication lines. Many such secured subnets could be constructed with access to a general-purpose network backbone. Once one-way transmission is established from the core area, a vulnerability is nevertheless established.

Occasional Policy Changeovers

The best security relies upon sudden change. The most complete physical security systems, the best password and encryption systems depend upon new people, new passwords, new keys. You cannot bribe someone who is new and cannot break what you do not know; any security system is improved by constant and unpredictable variety.

Computer network security can implement such changeovers. Access codes, passwords, sign-in procedures, and front desk guards can be rotated with frequency. Change upsets best laid plans, and improves the odds that

Network Security

a trail of evidence will remain if an intruder actually breaches the network. Figure 18.10 outlines security measures that should be changed frequently.

Data Encryption

FDDI transmits anything placed in the data fields. FDDI easily supports data encryption. As stated in Chapter 4, FDDI, like the party-line telephone system, is blind to the nature of the conversations. Anyone who wants to listen to a party-line conversation is welcome, but unless the listener understands the key, the conversation is privileged. Just as a telephone will handle foreign languages, FDDI will transmit "foreign" data. Even promiscuous capture of packets will prove valueless if the data are properly encrypted. Data encryption is the most easily implemented security measure. It is, however, expensive in terms of computer time to encrypt and decrypt data, and should be applied judiciously. Furthermore, a motivated intruder could break almost any encryption scheme. The DES encryption code is a good tool for use within the continental United States; DES is not for export. Therefore, in those situations requiring encoded data transmissions and encoded data storage, other security measures should also be applied.

Wireless networks pose a serious transmission risk. While infrared signals rarely function through even clear glass windows, radio-frequency signals pass through just about everything. SST signals make interception that much more difficult. In fact, SST and randomly shifting frequencies represent the transmission technology of choice for secure communications.

Access Control for Network Monitoring Devices

Certain monitoring devices like the protocol analyzer allow promiscuous access to all FDDI traffic. The push from vendors supplying analyzers is for full OSI 7 layer decodes for virtually all transport layer protocols. When such a tool is easily available, the data payload is easily read unless encrypted. With such a device, mail, file transfers, in fact all network traffic,

- Sign-in procedures
- Access process
- Guard personnel
- Location of computer
- Door keys
- IDs and passwords
- Codes
- Network links
- Remote access
- Locations and names of files

Figure 18.10 Security measures that should be changed frequently.

can be passively, selectively, and silently captured. All mail, all data, all files can be cracked, read, and understood (unless encrypted). While the traffic may provide only a glimpse into the full information desired by an intruder, such a device can clearly unlock private secrets. Hidden connections that are not authorized are more difficult to spot, but once noticed are obvious for what they are. Not only is such a monitoring device highly effective at uncovering secrets, its presence is easy to hide. It is a suitable piece of network equipment, and it belongs.

An analyzer, or network software like SNMP, CMOT, or CMIP with certain packet capture features, will allow anyone with enough skill to capture and analyze FDDI frames transparently and unobtrusively. This promiscuous data capture technique raises a first-line security issue. Additionally, many protocol analyzers will allow a sophisticated intruder to build falsified FDDI frames or any other protocol packets that could crack security locks by forging valid keys. However, if a network administration removes, limits, or monitors usage of all such tools, a minimal measure of security can be achieved. Other measures are required for more certain protection.

A protocol analyzer's inherent danger is so obvious that it can be overlooked. While there is a clear need for it, unauthorized usage constitutes an invasion of privacy and breach of network security. Therefore, lock up such devices, and when they are in use, monitor their usage.

Application of Monitoring Devices to Detect Intrusions

While the protocol analyzer can actually intrude on private communications, it can uncover unauthorized network access. Nodes that shouldn't be on the network will appear as unknown FDDI addresses, or will transmit at unusual or unauthorized times. Furthermore, access to unauthorized devices, supposedly prevented but actually achieved, can indicate vandalism, and so be disclosed. One of the best features of FDDI is that optical signal decay and scatter are easily documented. Several inexpensive tools (relative to an OTDR), such as the feature detector, can show where all the connectors, splices, splitters, and bypass switches are on the network.

If transmission facilities on the analyzer were disabled to prevent such inadvertent data diddling, the snooper would still seek network access. This access is most often provided through an unauthorized connection or secondary hub. The feature detector, TDR, or OTDR would show that the network is longer than it should be. When security is an issue, precise network blueprinting becomes critical. Furthermore, a detailed impedance chart should indicate any present or past unauthorized tapping. The vampire clamps leave marks and increase the parallel impedance, and end connectors or cuts into the network coaxial cable are impossible to hide, becoming clues to tampering if detailed blueprinting is maintained.

Network Security

Although data encryption will foil some vandals, time works against data encryption. The key can be lost, passed around the office as passwords often are, broken with enough time and poor key recycling procedures, or broken by a clever person. There are additional techniques to thwart data theft. While the network monitor allows a sophisticated user to capture and read packets, it also can indicate who is utilizing network resources and thus indicate the possible presence of a spy. While the promiscuous mode of data capture is invisible to the network because the FDDI signal is a global broadcast, certain clues can correlate excessive CPU load with limited network access. Sooner or later, an unauthorized node is bound to request a retransmission. This, however, requires good detective skills to uncover.

Vandal Detection

A crook does not play by the rules. This is the prime danger, of course. In order to counter such danger it is important to understand the value of the data on the network and the damage that can be perpetrated; knowing this will point to the possible danger and to the people who will benefit from such intrusion or damage. The information resident on a network has no value except to certain parties. There are usually warning signs in security breaches. Train the network operators to spot anomalies since they often monitor all network traffic and could uncover problems as they happen.

Most of the administrative emphasis should be applied to prevent vandalism. The original network design should factor in security as a basic configuration constraint. Daily operations should be altered occasionally to disrupt the norm. Such strategies protect the network in anticipation of vandalism and snooping, but in no way completely preclude them. After most intrusions, there are traces that can be analyzed to prevent further access. These traces include log files, packet traces, time stamps, improper network impedances, unusual network interference, computer server problems, and missing or changed data files. The traces are outlined in Figure 18.11. The TDR in conjunction with network blueprints, administrative information, and good detective work can reveal electrical improprieties, while the network analyzer can indicate other software and traffic disparities as explained above.

- Network logon times
- Network logon names
- Node impedance or station optical scatter differences
- Network transmission interference
- Unusual entries on log and error files
- Missing output
- Missing or altered data files
- Unusual network activity

Figure 18.11 Clues to network intrusion.

Hierarchy of Access

There are several categories of security access created to clarify and evaluate the growing number of protection methods and escalating "secure" operating systems. To address this problem, the National Security Decisions Directive lists a framework for security evaluation.[1] This framework is outlined in Figure 18.12. The highest level is the verified subcategory under the verified protection level. To date, these exotic systems are merely in the design stages. Previous attempts at complete security failed either through excessively slow response time or under the concerted efforts of expert system crackers. Unix and MS Windows NT, for example, are both C_2, although with a little effort can meet the higher C standard. Multics, CMS, VMS, and other like systems also fail at C_2. CP/M and PC-DOS are clearly minimally protected and are classified as D.

Fall-Back Countermeasures

Network access audit trails and network security audits are standard procedures when security is an important network concern. Often, the logs will indicate an anomaly suggesting an intrusion. If an intrusion has been detected, it is necessary to act. If the intruder is known and the access point revealed, the problem is solved, although damage may already have been done. If the intruder is unknown, there are two courses of action. The first is to watch and wait, and trap the intruder. The second is to lock up the network without hope of catching the intruder. Which course of action appears best depends upon the costs of continued damage, repair of that damage, and the vindictiveness of the affected organization.

- A: Verified protection
  - A_1: Verified design
- B Mandatory protection
  - B_1: Labeled protection
  - B_2: Structured protection
  - B_3: Security domain
- C Discretionary protection
  - C_1: Discretionary security protection
  - C_2: Controlled access
- D: Minimal protection

Figure 18.12 Hierarchy of access.

---

[1] National Security Decisions Directive (issued September 17, 1784, no. 14).

Network Security 395

There are clear detective methods for trapping an intruder. The TDR, OTDR, and network analyzer provide one method of electronically locating snooping. Sherlock Holmes' style of observation is likely to reveal more cautious intruders. However, when the danger is clear and acute, and the identity of the intruder is less important than protecting the network, a staged shutdown of network doors is the best course of action.

There are elements of both hardware and software that can be shut down. These steps are outlined in Figure 18.13. From the hardware viewpoint, change as much as possible and disconnect as much as possible while retaining the required minimum functionality.

The procedure is as follows: disconnect all dial-in lines and change the access numbers to prevent future intrusions. Power down all remote transmitters and alter the transmitter frequencies. Inspect all twisted-pair, coaxial cables, optical fiber cables, and connections for signs of tampering, splicing, and all other indications of line tapping. If you suspect that the intruder may have discovered information derived from wastepaper, or from stolen printed material, make rapid plans to alter paper disposal methods and output distribution. Lock up the printers and hand-deliver printed output. Shred wastepaper. Certainly, data storage media hold the entirety of the organization's secrets. Lock up those media, both online and on backup tapes. Furthermore, log the disposition of the data storage media. Change keys, codes, and access procedures.

Many steps can be taken in software to locate signs of tampering. They may appear as missing or altered data files, or unusual log entries. Restore whatever damage is discovered. Additionally, change the password access. Purge outdated password entries. Limit remote access to

- Disconnect modems
- Change dial-in telephone numbers
- Shut down remote transmitters
- Alter radio or microwave frequencies
- Inspect cables and links for tapping, tampering, or intrusion
- Inspect network software and files for tampering
- Change ID and password file and purge outdated entries
- Alter executive code file ownerships
- Relocate and/or rename critical data files
- Disconnect bridges and gateways
- Cut hard-wired connections
- Change wireless frequencies
- Lock up printed output and storage media
- Reduce network user access
- Restore physical or data damage
- Limit access to remote devices
- Change door keys
- Alter entrance codes

Figure 18.13 Security roll-back countermeasures.

other network nodes and network devices. Change the access to network software that might allow data tampering and data snooping. This includes programs that read "protected" disks or files at the bit and byte levels and programs that override disk- or file-level protection schemes. Restricted access is possible to security-sensitive materials by moving them or changing their names.

Access to any machine in the network where sensitive data reside might require a magnetic access card like an automatic teller machine or credit card. Additionally, keyboards might have software locks to deter casual use. In any event, physical cases of networked machines should be locked securely to prevent replacement, removal, or temporary installation of hardware components, including floppy disk drives, tape archival units, hard disks, security components, serial or parallel ports (used to link to a laptop computer for downloading data), or nonsecured output printer.

These are generic techniques and work equally well when initially installing a network or at any time the organization suspects a problem. If the network is insecure, it is prudent not to tarry and wait until a problem is revealed before applying such countermeasures. Security entails a cost in time, materials, labor, and aggravation.

It is important to have adequate protection mechanisms; tight security could mean that it will be forever unnecessary to repair damage or prevent damage from happening again. Security is a series of applied techniques that are disruptive, inconvenient, and rarely transparent. The hope is that such techniques will never be required, but they are instituted purely on a prophylactic basis.

Network Backup

The network is hardware, software, and the data. If the hardware were damaged, it could be replaced more easily than the information it contained. Despite this relative ease of restoring hardware, do not overlook the need to have spare parts on hand. File servers and keyboard-level components are good candidates for the spare inventory. Assess the damage if a key component failed and were irreplaceable for a period of time. Keep spares of those units that could create a crisis if broken. Do not limit backup procedures solely to the data and software.

Many organizations are critically dependent upon data. Either they are the organization's product, or they provide records of funds payable and receivable. Data also can explain critical production or operational techniques. Network backup procedures provide a means to repair software and data damage. If a catastrophe occurs, backup media may change a catastrophe to merely a major inconvenience. As trite as that sounds, backups are a standard policy for most organizations with mainframe computer facilities. "Mainframe computer facilities" is referenced here mainly as an example of the attitudes and policies that have developed

Network Security

from the experiences now affecting the new network technologies. Many networks, however, developed from small components and therefore the organization and its managers lack the realization of the network's crucial importance. Enterprise-wide networks tend to include many subnetworks where management jurisdiction is local. Backup, as such, may be locally administered and incomplete. As a result, backups are nonexistent, infrequent, or applied to that minimum of personally owned files deemed important. A critical portion of any network is resident in unique files that define the relationship of nodes on the network, the network operations itself, and scripts automating arcane processes that have become complicated over time.

In the final statement, braggarts will often reveal their activities and indicate problems and a security breach. Listen well, be vigilant, and evaluate the level of security required. Cleverness will undermine all security systems, and ruthlessness will sway the most secure. Note well that the strongest security program will fail if the network operators and network users who are assigned to protect the resources are compromised.

This chapter has presented the issues surrounding network security. Threats and real dangers have been outlined, and practical and effective countermeasures have been proposed. Additionally, fall-back measures including backup procedures were prescribed when the preventive measures failed. These backup measures are detailed in Chapter 19.

Chapter

19

Backup and Redundancy

The last chapter introduced the subject of file backup and network component redundancy within the context of network security. Backup and redundancy are also operational concerns since users' work, organizational information, or products may reside on network equipment. Prophylactic concern is warranted; only in those situations where the network is a toy, simply a communications backbone, or where network users are responsible for their own work will such backup concerns be moot. Therefore, most network managers will discover that backup and redundancy are crucial aspects to their success and continued employment, and thus are best disclosed in a concise and clearly communicated policy.

Network Backup

The FDDI network is an amalgamation of hardware, software, and network data. The hardware is more easily replaced than the information contained within. Despite the relative ease of restoring hardware, do not overlook the need to have backup spare parts on hand. Assess damage to the organization should a key component fail and remain unavailable for an indefinite period; hubs units, file servers, and keyboard-level components are good candidates for the spare inventory. Superservers often provide a level of redundancy with paralleled power supplies, busses, CPUs, NICs, and *redundant arrays of inexpensive disks* (RAID). Do not limit backup procedures solely to the data and software aspects; also, consider the human aspect.

As explained in the preceding chapter, data diddling—the act of adjusting information from outside the normal systems and protections—and tampering can disrupt operations and cause manifold problems. Examples of data diddling include editing accounting files with a bit editor, adjusting school grades by changing exam scores, or recreating and altering a backup tape which is then used to restore a file "error." Backups and the network redundancy procedures explained in this chapter provide a time limit for the propagation of damage. If an intruder deletes or alters a file and this is discovered, backups provide recovery. Very few problems can be created that cannot be repaired from backup. Backups have value for the data they contain.

Since backup media are very portable, they should be tightly controlled and protected; damaged media may prevent restoration. Because catastrophe may strike a site, or an entire region, or sabotage may be very extensive and thoughtfully planned, backups should be removed off-site for additional security.

Backup and redundancy are necessary processes to ensure continued and consistent network operations. Backup and redundancy encompass more than tape or disk duplication of critical files; they imply duplication of critical data files, configuration files, software, password keys and access codes, physical wiring, hubs, station and node equipment, FDDI devices, and network servers. When a network provides the unique infrastructure to link different departments and functions within an organization, the network assumes an importance far in excess of its real value. The network's ability to disrupt the normal ebb and flow when it breaks justifies expensive procedures to maintain that network. A network may be indispensable; for those short periods of time when it cannot be used, it must be preserved. To this end, backup and redundant procedures are the corrective action.

Backup and redundancy exceed duplication of data. Any component with the power to disrupt operation should be duplicated. This includes software, hardware, data, and human labor. Figure 19.1 illustrates the elements warranting this attention.

The Value of Information

Many organizations depend upon electronic filing. It is either the organization's product, or it provides records of funds payable and receivable. Data in the form of lists of detailed instruction sets (CAD/CAM programs) may direct production or operational process. Network backup provides one of the few available and certain means to repair software and data damage. Should disaster strike, the backup may change a catastrophe to

Hardware	Software	Data	Labor
Gateways	System software	User data	Administration
Connectors	User-level software	Configurations	Planning/analysis
Backup devices	Network software	Procedural scripts	Software repair
Hubs	Utility programs	Network data	Debugging
File devices		Backup scripts	Repair
Wiring plant			

Figure 19.1 Network components that require periodic backup.

Backup and Redundancy

merely an inconvenience, as trite as that phrase may seem. Backups are a standard policy for most organizations with mainframe computer facilities. Many networks, however, are outgrowths of the free-form and independent personal computer environments, and therefore the organization and its managers lack experience with the cost of a network shutdown. As a result, backups are nonexistent, infrequent, or personally performed without clear or detailed instructions and without a fixed interval between backups. Network backup is a crucial procedure to ensure the continued operations of the network.

Media Backup

Most networking organizations create, modify, or disseminate software or data. The network provides the conduit for information. Since this information is easily damaged or lost, and not easily recovered if lost, much attention is given to preserving its integrity. Media backup is the usual form for duplicating and saving data. Magnetic media—floppy disks, cartridge tapes, cassette tapes, disk packs, reel tape, videotape or video cassettes—and paper copies or punch cards are the usual format for backups. The SEC may even require write once read many (WORM) optical storage for filing of critical documents and revisions of events. The data and software are copied from the source hierarchy to this archival media for long-term storage. Figure 19.2 presents a sampling of stable data storage media.

There are many issues to address about media backup. Figure 19.3 outlines some of these. Questions often asked include what data should be saved, and on what media should they be saved. It is also common to weigh how frequently data should be backed up, and during what time of the day, or before and after what operations should information be duplicated. Because there are security concerns, where the information is stored is a pressing issue. Since backup media are both expensive and eventually bulky, media are often recycled. How media are reused could have long term ramifications if they are prematurely recycled.

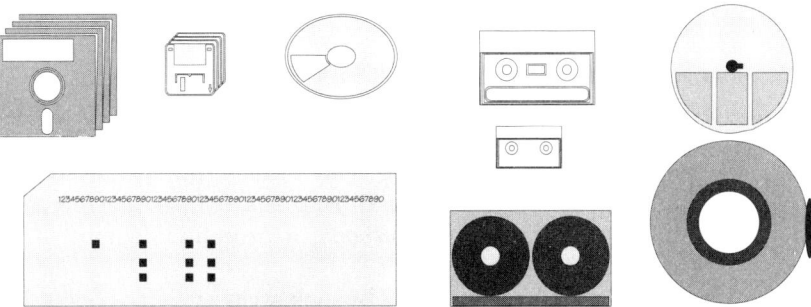

Figure 19.2 Data storage media.

- What should be saved?
- How often should data be saved?
- Where should the media be used?
- How should the media be stored?
- Where should the media be stored?
- What access precautions should be applied?
- How should data recoveries be instituted?
- What happens when the media are incompatible?
- How often should data be saved?
- How long should backup data be kept?
- What legal requirements must be fulfilled?

Figure 19.3 Data storage questions.

Not infrequently, customer commitments, venture-capital development agreements, and other legal agreements require media backup, including storage of software releases, and research data sets to be stored in escrow and financially insured. The IRS requires that financial records be retained for a number of years. Backups that fail to restore damaged or lost information are obviously worthless. This raises the issue of verifying backup media for content and accuracy.

In fact, many NetWare-based backup programs do not function adequately. Many bugs have been reported where the backup procedure has required literally hours but only a handful of files of the thousands on the volumes would have been successfully copied. Errors or software bugs in the backup software prevented a complete procedure. Furthermore, the errors uncovered or generated were not reported during or at the conclusion of the backup process. Other failings include backup up servers and other critical data sets, but backing up the files peer-to-peer clients, the system configurations, or process files, such as batch files, macros, or command sets. Another backup disaster includes a full file-level backup lacking directory path names, security rights, or ownership information; such a backup is almost useless when files with similar names overwrite each other.

Special consideration should be given to any distributed databases, distributed processing, peer-to-peer networks (such as LANtastic or MS Windows for Workgroups), or extended or linked file structures. When operations are so intermeshed, the data integrity is not only ensured through sporadic or carefully planned physical backups, integrity is also a factor of timing and sequencing. For example, SQL transactions are not *committed* until such time as there is assurance that all databases can be accessed and updated. Failure during the transaction process otherwise results in a *transaction rollback*, a procedure whereby all intermediate results are flushed.

This concept is critical for files linked by disk striping across disks, by applications across a network, by MS Windows object linking and embedding (OLE) or dynamic data exchange (DDE), remote procedure calls (RPC), and for distributed databases. The backups must coincide for all these elements; otherwise, data integrity is breached. For example, consider the failure of a distributed database. Timely backup was available for the master server, but was outdated for the slave servers. Consider that the database was corrupted for an unspecified reason. Restoration was performed only for the master because it was available. This results in an addition of a master record to a distributed database on one machine without comparable supporting detail records that were distributed to the slave servers. Such disparities create reporting errors, patient record oversights, products delivered but never billed, and other costly problems.

It may be far-sighted to consider the ramifications for linkage and coprocessing techniques and the absolute requirement for them. Perhaps—until the management technology for distributed data has evolved more—consider dissuading organizational implementation of OLE, DDE, networked DDE, distributed databases, and object files linked across networks.

What to Save

The simple answer is to back up all information that the organization cannot afford to lose. Software and network information that can't be replaced easily, or is expensive to replace, should be duplicated. Data and financial records should be saved. System software rarely changes and can be saved infrequently. Purchased software is often provided on media that are suitable as the backup in their own right, and a working copy should be made from the original while the vendor's master becomes the backup. Note however, the cost of replicating an entire file system from backup tapes of data, backup tapes of system, and the multitude of 3.5 inch application distribution disks, rather than from say a single master backup tape. That may blow a day or two, and the lost details (e.g., paths, configuration, unnecessary files) may take weeks to sort out correctly.

A backup procedure has costs, too. Media are expensive. The labor required to duplicate the information on a periodic basis is expensive. The backup process itself requires computer time, and often increases the level of network traffic, slowing other operations. These costs, which would be incurred for each and every backup, can be quantified as Figure 19.4 demonstrates. One way to determine how much should be saved is to calculate the costs of a backup strategy against the replacement value of what could be lost. Lost data can be recreated at some cost in time. This cost can be calculated. The work lost while the data are reconstructed can be assigned cost. These costs, which would be averted by a backup, can be aggregated and valued.

Tangible	Intangible	Long Term
Media	Network time	Storage costs
Labor	Network traffic load	Security risk
Storage costs	Network downtime	Media degradation

Figure 19.4 Network backup costs.

A direct comparison between averted costs and periodic backup costs is not necessarily correct. The backup procedure is an insurance policy. Direct comparison between averted costs and incurred costs implies a need for 100 percent coverage; however, an organization must determine an appropriate level of risk (of potential data loss) which it is willing to assume. This risk may be 0 percent (no risk) or 100 percent (all the risk). Generally speaking, daily, semiweekly, or weekly backups are adequate. Even a daily backup does not avert all risk since there is a window of risk. A daily backup might imply a 5 percent risk, whereas a weekly backup may imply a 10 percent risk. Risk is difficult to assess because it factors in such items as the probability of a data storage device failing and a data loss, and also the probability that recovery will take a certain amount of time. Since any backup scheme can fail—backup tapes could be corrupt, for example—risk is always inherent. Even "fault-tolerant" networks still exhibit a likelihood of failure.

Last, how much risk the organization is willing to assume must be considered. Some organizations will bet that the computers and the network will never fail, whereas others recognize that the business livelihood could be jeopardized by data loss. This simple mathematical relationship will determine the frequency of backup and the type of information to back up.

Who Provides Backup Services

Once a backup policy is determined—how often and how much—it is necessary to determine who actually provides the backup service. The network manager or network administration group provides these services if global network resources exist for network backup, if few other events disrupt the routine of the administration group, and if time is not an issue. However, FDDI network management provides a new problem. The network may be huge. Subnetwork backup may be beyond the scope, possibility, or politics of a central network management group. The FDDI may represent merely the interlink conduit, a service for all, but not the means for centralized backup. Responsibility for backup would rightly fall to a local administration.

Backup and Redundancy

Personal information could be saved globally, or saved by the individuals to whom it has value. Most mainframe environments perform global data backups since the data are stored in a single, concentrated location. This may be the case on a network which has centralized file servers. Where a network is distributed, as in the example of a personal computer network, and few facilities exist for global data backup, individuals are responsible for personal backup. Where users provide their own network service, users often are exhorted to provide their own backups. Impress upon users that doing their own housekeeping is in their best interests, but the network administration group will help as needed.

What Media

The media that are regularly available to the network machines should be the backup media of choice. PC networks generally have floppy-disk drives. This is adequate. Where storage of local fixed disks exceeds the size of the floppy disks, cartridge disks or streamer tapes are suitable devices for data redundancy. Also, data can be easily copied to another machine. It is less probable that both fixed disks will fail at the same time. (Probabilities of dual failures are generally factors of individual failures plus any correlated risks such as power surges, overheating, or sabotage.)

When data backup is a frequent and disruptive event floppy disks or streamer tapes may have insufficient capacity and speed. Reel units with 8-in or 11-in reels provide higher density and larger storage capacities. *Digital audio tape* (DAT) provides 5 gigabytes (or more) in a micro-cassette format. Cache space for backups also moves the process off line. Convenience and capacity are usually the most important criteria for selecting backup media.

The media should also be long-lived. When the computer is powered off, the information should not be lost. Therefore, electronic memory is not appropriate. Cartridge or reel tape, floppy or cartridge drives, punch tape or cards, and disk packs are common backup media. Furthermore, the medium chosen should be stable in the environment in which it will be stored. Do not choose paper or cards if they are liable to be eaten by insects or mold. A sealed disk pack is more secure for such a hostile environment. In addition, if electrical or magnetic interference is apt to erase data, paper stock is more appropriate as a medium. Most media will endure if care is exercised.

The media should be selected for compatibility with other machines. If a catastrophe does occur, destroying the entire facility, overspecialized media may complicate data and network recovery, or force network hardware replacement decisions that are not completely forward-thinking. Technology does change; do not allow a disaster to have ramifications for the network restoration. Also, make sure that if a backup unit fails for any reason, the organization will not be exposed to unnecessary risk. For example, if a tape drive fails, another unit should provide continued backup procedures and lost data recovery.

Last, obscure media provide both benefits and potential problems as suggested above. Although obscure media add a level of security to the network, they make external data recovery more difficult; unusual disk or tape formats raise the cost of information theft. Likewise, the selection of a large tape reel or a disk pack instead of a disk or tape cartridge makes it less likely that information will be removed from the building. However, obscure formats may increase the risk of losing information should equipment fail and be difficult to repair.

How Often and When to Back Up

A frequent question is how often should backups be made. The answer is twofold. First, back up as frequently as necessary to protect the work and data you are unwilling to lose. Vendor software may not need backup since it is available on the original installation media, although site specific installation information does. Network configurations change infrequently and can be duplicated whenever a change is made. Data files that change with regularity such as personal workspaces and account information might be backed up once a week, once a day, or even two or three times a day. Networks that provide commercial transactions, such as air-traffic control, real-time manufacturing control, or financial transfers might need support in parallel with an entire duplicated network and file spaces. Again, the cost of loss must be balanced against the cost of providing protection. Backup frequency depends on an organization's view of risk.

Second, perform a cost-benefit analysis. Determine the cost of providing the backups: include media (which can be recycled after a time), time, network degradation and downtime, labor, and storage costs. Compare those costs against the value of the lost work, or the value of recreating the lost work. Include the social, publicity, and aggravation damage wrought by loss. Choose whichever is least. Note that backup is an insurance cost, and the comparison between backup costs and possible material loss should be a fractional factor. In other words, if the possible loss is X, it is appropriate to apply only $X \times n$ where $n > 1$ reflects only the probability of loss. It is too expensive to insure the actuality of loss except when deemed necessary. If you think that data loss costs customers, respect, and other intangibles, and that it is necessary to completely insure against the loss, consider that the value of X should include the value of such soft costs. Figure 19.5 outlines the mathematics for such a calculation.

Backup and Redundancy

Figure 19.5 Network backup insurance analysis.

Where to Store

Backup media should be stored in a "safe" place. This means that the media should not deteriorate from elements, nor should it be subject to theft, misuse, or loss; it would be a serious management concern if backups were missing or corrupted. Backups should also be conveniently located. To insure security in the event of a far-reaching disaster such as a fire, flood, hurricane, or theft, backups might also be stored off-site. Consider as a possibility a bank vault or a warehouse that specializes in storage of computer media. Generally, a locked off-site room with restricted access and an entry log provides an adequate location. Note that precautions for safe media storage should be followed. Figure 19.6 lists these precautions.

Recycling Policy

Generally, backup media are recycled after a time. Backup media are expensive and when information has been superseded, the media can be used again. Also, the media are bulky, and require adequate storage space. Over time, this can be expensive and can precipitate a decision to recycle. Figure 19.7 depicts a recycling policy where media storing monthly backups are recycled after 2 months and media storing daily backups are recycled after each month. Note that quarterly media storing backups are not recycled until a year has passed.

- Dry
- Cool
- Upright
- Static-free
- No magnetic fields
- No electrical fields
- Easy access
- Timely access
- Secured

Figure 19.6 Precautions for safe media storage.

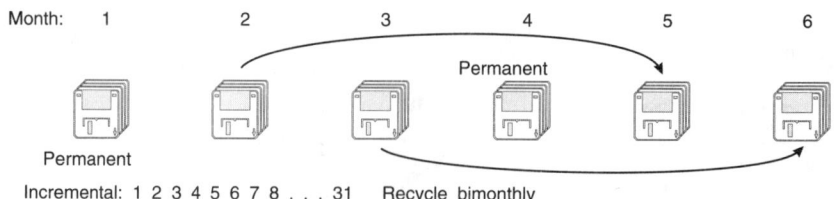
Figure 19.7 "Leap-frog" media recycling policy.

Value of Stored Information

Stored data have value to the organization and potentially to others, such as competitors. Thus, it may be important to take all measures necessary to insure their safety and usability. Many organizations cover the value of their data with an insurance policy. While many media storage service companies do insure readability and safety of the physical media, they may not insure the data on the tapes. In fact, without reading the tapes to verify that information actually exists, the service company could not know what exists on the tapes it stores. It guarantees the physical safety of the media only, not the logical content. Therefore, when information is a key constituent of a business it is important to evaluate and insure the monetary worth of that information. As elsewhere, insurance costs are high. Most organizations insure only what they cannot afford to lose. Assess the level of risk your organization is willing to assume and insure the remainder. Decrease risk with insurance on the media.

The caveat is that media dependability may fade over time as the media are used again. This can be checked, but note that wear on the media and the equipment tends to degrade performance and longevity.

Verification of Backup

Once a data backup and media recycling policy is implemented, the process should be tested occasionally to verify that it is effective and working as anticipated. It is appropriate to audit the library and ensure that the inventory of backups matches expectations. Sometimes, a backup will complete on an unformatted tape with no indication of errors, but nonetheless be invalid and incomplete. It is prudent to verify that the policy governing access to the information is actually enforced so that backups are not lost, corrupted, or stolen. Those who should have access should know how to locate pertinent media and perform the necessary tasks. Those without access privileges should be denied access to the media. The data backup should be usable. A crisis could be compounded unnecessarily if lost information was discovered after the fact to be irretrievable. A lot of trust rides upon the network management when the team establishes a disaster recovery plan. A periodic audit of the backup media

Backup and Redundancy

and their accuracy is a simple but effective measure to ensure that implementation matches planning, a crucial step for any manager.

Hardware

Duplicate data backup devices in case a backup or data restoration unit fails, forcing extensive work-arounds. The choice of the backup hardware should be predicated upon the choice of media, media reliability, media compatibility, and interchangeability. If disaster strikes and the backup media are unreadable, not only has a lot of time and effort been wasted, but the organization has been unduly put at risk. The hardware selected for backup procedures should meet certain standards for reliability, speed, ease of use, and ability to be repaired. Other concerns include storage density and dropout, recycling, and compatibility.

Certainly, a medium that is specific to a single unit has marginal worth; should that unit ever fail, the medium is useless. Therefore, media should be interchangeable from one machine to another. Also, consider that should a network catastrophe occur, it may be critical for the continuation of the organization that the data backups be accessible by another organization or another network site. Data backup compatibility, in media format, media density, track alignment, and physical accessibility, is an underlying criterion. Likewise, data density has some bearing. The higher the density at which information is stored, the higher the risk that it will erode, be damaged by time, or experience dropout. *Dropout* is when information on media degrades from usage and time. Dropout is often seen on much-used videotape; it occurs with all magnetic media. Laser-burned media are usually immune from such problems while also serving to meet the Securities and Exchange Commission (SEC) regulations for permanent retention of security transactions.

However, whatever the media actually selected, the speed raises secondary concerns. As the density of storage is increased, the media are more prone to dropout and media failure. At the same time, storage space is reduced, labor and media handling costs are reduced, and potentially, backup time is saved. Additionally, higher densities often place a higher transmission load on the network because the storage device services a faster rate of data transfer. The media transport mechanism is usually the limiting factor on speed. Thus, by increasing the media density, higher speeds and efficiencies are achieved. Common reel tape densities include 800, 1600, 3200, and 6250 bits/in. The media for each density are identical, although total information storage increases by nearly a factor of 4 from the lowest to the highest density. Cartridge tapes often store from 1.2 to 6.0 Gbytes (gigabytes) on a small format cassette. This is a distinct improvement over the larger format magnetic storage supporting from 20 to 40 Mbytes by a factor of 100. Not only are they more reliable; they also minimize operator time jockeying tapes since one tape replaces 100.

Also, contemplate redundancy in communication channels. Consider what might happen should a phone line wiring bundle be cut within the organization by a careless contractor or damaged under the street by an errant backhoe or broken water main. These unexpected events do happen and thus need to be anticipated. Likewise, wide area X.25, PBX, PDN, microwave, and VSAT links do fail. AT&T data lines could be brought down by a storm 2,000 mi away, while a satellite battery system could go dead or the satellite could drop into the atmosphere. Where is the redundancy?

The IEEE 802.1 spanning tree configuration provides automated switching of data communications pathways to alternate routes in the event of a channel failure. Note, however, that the time required for the spanning tree bridge—100 ms or more— to recognize a channel failure and establish a remote dial-up phone link—120 s—may be insufficient to maintain real-time operations. Add firewalls between networks, local or otherwise, so that security or network failures do not undermine an enterprise-wide network. This is especially relevant for mission-critical networks, too, when the financial basis of entire organization depends on one or more file servers. Spare servers may seem expensive—until they are actually needed.

Lack of expertise is a risk. When personnel is untrained, processes will be inefficient, slow, or poorly administered. Problems that might be simple for trained personnel attain an air of catastrophe and confusion when handled by a staff that is too inexperienced. Expertise, both technical and managerial, mitigates rough edges inherent in any network. Expertise is expensive. It gravitates to the most interesting jobs, the ones with the most salary or enjoyment. As elsewhere, assess the level of risk an organization is willing to assume uninsured.

Labor

A network administration team is generally employed where a network is large and distributed, where the problems are many and complex, and where the network fulfills a critical role within the organization. In critical situations it is important to have backup for all key components. Not only does this mean software, data, and node and network hardware, it also includes the people that maintain the network. Sickness, vacations, consistently long work days, job dissatisfaction, and other factors can mean that labor is not always available. If 24-hour network response and problem coverage are required, then extra resources must be available for around-the-clock coverage. If only one person knows the answers, the crisis-level discomfort is increased, breeding mutual distrust. Adequate resources resolve such issues.

Disasters

Man-made and natural disasters verifiably do occur. Redundancy and secondary sites are important considerations when operations depend upon having a working network. Hurricane Andrew hit south Florida in August 1992 and caused at least $65 billion in damage mostly in rural and suburban areas. It missed most of the Miami-metropolitan area by a mere ten miles, and did little damage to the central city and office towers. Nonetheless, several major corporations were severely affected. Many suspended operations since they were without basic facilities and services. Others relocated in desperation to survive. Most—at the least—were inconvenienced for more than three weeks due to lack of power, phones, water, and people who could not commute because of roadblocks, downed power lines and trees, or concern over their own wrecked homes.

For example, the Burger King corporate headquarters sustained heavy structural damage. Networks were literally washed away and PCs were blown through the windows and up to several miles away by storm-induced secondary tornadoes. Backup media stored on site in filing cabinets or inside plastic desktop storage boxes became inundated with seawater and rendered unreadable, thus lost. Backup paper copies also suffered water damage and mildew before they could be salvaged. Original software, manuals, and ownership licenses suffered similar fates. The site itself was rendered unusable for nearly nine months. Since the extent of the storm covered a wide geographic area and many vacant offices were destroyed as well, alternate sites were not readily available either. Replacement PCs (without software or hardware) were unavailable locally and had to be ordered from out-of-state mail-order operations for two-day delivery.

Realize that a system delivered in two days does not mean operations were restored to normal in two days. Without software, backups, installation disks for owned software, networks, and the preexisting data, it is unclear that the operations will ever return to the pre-storm configuration or any sense of the previous normalcy. In all likelihood, something similar has been be reestablished. Although the manufacturers of engineering workstations outdid themselves and diverted units from other customers, this specialty hardware and unusual software required nearly two months to restore to operation.

Homes were destroyed and people were dispersed to new living situations. As a result, computer operations were lost for an extended period. Operations were suspended without the necessary electrical power, critical people were lost by attrition as they became unable to cope with extended commutes from new housing locations, and efficient procedures that had developed over time atrophied. The organization required emergency sites. Although multiple emergency sites were established within days, new phone lines for T-1 or modem connections did not represent a priority for the Southern Bell. The disaster was just so widespread that Southern Bell did not have sufficient resources to immediately repair existing lines and install any new circuits at the same time. Although this hurricane was an unusually powerful one, the message should be clear to many organizations: backup and redundancy is absolutely critical to the continued operation of an organization.

If this last example seems too singular, consider a more common accident like the flood that halted activity in parts of Chicago during February 1992. (The Chicago flood occurred when a maintenance diver broke through a wall between an old underground passageway and Lake Michigan. This inundated subterranean passageways throughout much of the old city and flooded out sub-basements, electrical systems, and underground mass transportation.) This example is similar to the previous one; but more likely to occur: new construction on a nearby building is proceeding without prior incident when a bulldozer strikes an underground water main. While the accident does not straight-away affect business operations in nearby office towers and office complexes, it ultimately does halt business at those sites for an extended time. First, building sprinkler systems and local fire hydrants are crippled. This renders the nearby buildings unsafe. Second, lack of functioning sanitary facilities renders the buildings functionally uninhabitable. Third, concern about the safety of underground power lines renders the now flooded street areas unsafe until the power is shut off. This lack of electrical power now halts elevators, and computer and network operations. Since most new energy-efficient buildings do not have windows that open, this subsequent lack of ventilation prevents any usage whatsoever of the office space. Businesses in the buildings can not even inform calling customers by phone that the system is shutdown; they have been ordered from the building by concerned city safety officials.

Consider also the case of the World Trade Center Complex bombing in Manhattan. As Chapter 18 explained, terrorist attacks in the past have been aimed at mainframe operations. Mainframes are not as important anymore; communications centers are. While the direct damage of this 200 lb C-4 explosive car bomb directly affected the underground parking garage beneath the Vista and a attached underground subway station, the guts of the complex operations, including power supplies, public address, communication systems, water, heating, and cooling systems, were damaged by the explosion. Back-up generators failed. Operations in these related buildings and all access to these buildings (even for tenants to reclaim important documents and information) were limited while the police investigated the accident scene. Furthermore, the damage undermined the structure of the building. This prevented normal use of the complex until repaired. If you are responsible for the continuation and survivability of computer opera-

Backup and Redundancy 413

tions for your organization, you cannot ignore the possibility—albeit very remote—of a significant disaster whether natural or man-made. Your own salary as well as other people's livelihood depends upon effective and comprehensive disaster planning.

Had the bomb been split into multiple charges and placed at strategic building supports, the explosive might have toppled the building. Adjacent buildings might have been hit or damaged; certainly the entire Wall Street area would have been affected for a significant period. While this would have killed operations personnel on-site and effectively crippled ongoing and recovery operations, there are certainly limits to your responsibility for ordinary network operations. However, some organizations cannot tolerate disruption for any reasons at any cost. Could a rescue group, the Coast Guard, a police organization, the Army, or the Federal Reserve System withstand such a disaster? How would its constituency view the failure to provide services despite the scope of the disaster?

Tape backups are useless—they alone are not enough. What is needed is a secondary site with water, electricity, phones, and network wiring. The backup tapes might be useful if the secondary site were to have a server and client machines, although any work accomplished since the time of those backups might be inaccessible. If phone lines were still functioning in the primary site, a LAN-to-LAN by WAN update could speed resumption of operations without lost work. An astute organization would try to enable temporary call-forwarding or call-routing to a secondary location. Think of the effects to the Sun Microsystems distributed financial systems, as described in Chapter 1, should an event disable headquarters operations. Worldwide operations depends on those FDDI networks.

Although this is book is about FDDI networking per se, phone access is probably more important to most businesses than their networks. When billing operations are network-based, affected organizations can always move the servers, a handful of nodes, some jumpers, a MAU or two, some power strips, and the Rolodexes to a new site, and thus have operations online within a few hours. More involved operations with onsite mainframes and host-based linkages may still find operations hampered despite backup power supplies or generators for the mainframes since the other site failings prevent full use of the integrated computer operations. The message should be clear to many organizations: backup and redundancy is absolutely critical to the continued operation of an organization. Backup and redundancy may require a secondary site somewhat distant from the base operations. When disaster requires it, move the operation to the secondary site and put people in hotels until the primary site is restored.

Redundancy

In prior chapters, maintaining equipment redundancy and a parts inventory were proposed as parts of an operationally astute policy. The issue here is backup, and when parts fail it becomes important to have replacement units available to solve the problem. This is particularly relevant for FDDI since it so often is a mission-critical connective network. All stations and secondary nodes ultimately connect into a central ring. Failure of this central resource will disable the network unless properly configured and constructed to provide fail-safe rerouting. No amount of rewiring or inventive actions can bypass such critical components. Maintain spare hubs, or have plans to rewire master stations into whatever is still functioning. This same philosophy must be extended to other single sources. This includes servers, server disk space, and any other critical devices. Failure of the database server or server for a client/server network will render the network dead. Loss of parts of striped files or total loss of files will render the network dead. When OCR, FAX, or printing are part of mission-critical operations, duplicate those nodes and their functionality.

Media backups, in part, provide a measure of security. The storage equipment and the device drivers are equally liable to fail and require replacement. Redundant parts are suggested. In addition, the people who maintain the network will occasionally be at home, on vacation, out sick, or leaving for a new job. The expertise to complete a repair should be available in duplicate to prevent a knowledge shortage. The level of redundancy maintained should factor in the level of risk an organization is willing to assume uninsured, since redundancy of parts and labor is an expense.

Parts cataloged as inventory and backups prepared and saved should be available and usable. Moreover, that inventory should be functional as well as available. Test the parts. Test the media. Prepared disaster recovery plans that fail are worse than having no contingency plans, since there is an expectation for an acceptable recovery. Such a failing tends to shorten careers suddenly.

Chapter 20
Human Factors

Communication has become a sophisticated management role. An organization inexperienced in communications technology faces a credibility problem because so much of business and management is based upon rapid and effective communication. FDDI becomes a complex issue because it represents an enterprise-wide complexity, a coverage of a vast geographical area, and because it tends to integrate operations no one can imagine when it first is installed as a connectivity solution.

Therefore, qualified people who can design, plan, install, and maintain a communications network are very important. The role is a difficult one because a network manager is a vendor to the user community. Responsibilities include responding to user and network problems, enhancing the information flow, and installing new applications, as well as maintaining network resources and costs within an established range.

There is never a lack of problems. There is always a lack of time to get things done and a shortage of staff to do all that needs to be done. Frequently, this results in a poor image and puts undue stress on the staff. The use of more people is unacceptable to upper management, and a reduction in the level of network service is unacceptable to everyone in the user community. Therefore, a significant part of any network management, including FDDI, is a clear understanding of these stresses and a means to cope with this supportive role.

The charters for network management, whether issued formally or developed over time and never verbally expressed, are compatibility, credibility, security, and stability. Figure 20.1 reiterates these charters

- Compatibility
- Credibility
- Security
- Stability

Figure 20.1 The network management charter.

fulfilled with a network team, experienced management, and administrative control of the network resources.

Network Management

While a manager cannot control certain types of events, a manager can respond to events beyond control. Failure to accept events and responsibility for their impact, or reluctance to act and compensate for detrimental effects is a clear sign of management failure. Action, concerted and focused, is a clear sign of acceptance and control, whereas a reluctance to finalize decisions is an indication of a technical vacuum, a lack of clear lines of authority, or a basic interpersonal communication weakness. On the other hand, frantic and undirected action imparts disharmony to the user community. A network is a critical cog in the communications pathway; action and results consistent with the culture and requirements of the organization in time of crisis are imperative.

Required Management Skills

The network manager's administrative abilities should encompass record-keeping, inventory-tracking, technical, diagnostic, interpersonal and analytical abilities. The ability to clearly explain complex ideas and reassure people at all levels in an organization is a key success factor. Little can overcome weak administrative control of resources. Figure 20.2 outlines these management needs.

Administrative Control

Administrative control is an important factor for a large, growing, or critical network. Otherwise, self-taught experts or members of an ad hoc committee will provide such expertise. When a network provides development

- Administrative control
- Record-keeping skills
- Inventory-tracking skills
- Technical management skills
- Ability to make decisions
- Ability to establish priorities
- Means to cope with staff shortages and burnout
- Ability to provide recognition
- Skills to train and develop employees
- Team building skills
- Evaluation skills
- Ability to reassure people
- Effective communication skills

Figure 20.2 Network management skill set.

services, enterprise-wide communications, or critical services such as financial accounting, the network requires backup, daily maintenance, and a reliable team to control its operations. The network administrator provides planning, network design and configuration expertise, maintenance and upgrade abilities, and also serves as the arbiter of file space, network access, and performance disputes. The most important role may be that of a clearinghouse for information and liaison to the user community.

Note, however, that responsiveness does not mean saying "yes" to everything. A negative reply is just as responsive as a positive one; no administrator can afford to forget this, nor the meaning of "yes" and "no." Resources are always limited. While this may often imply that a new file server, a bridging router, or a new hire that will exceed available budget, limited resources could mean that one more meeting, one more evaluation, or even one more "of course I'll take a look at it for you" will exceed the available time resources. Responsiveness is necessary, but it must be tempered with reality.

Lone wolves, the ruthless, aggressive types, are not effective managers despite the long-standing stereotype. A good administrator must be a team player. The traditional, autonomous "chief" is not effective in a service environment, and is counterproductive in today's workplace. This is particularly relevant when the responsibility for information systems and computer networks is guided by a pyramidal reporting structure while actual MIS and network management is a matrix obligation. Team orientation, responsiveness to subordinates, and a service ethic are personality traits that people welcome in an administrator today.

Distance from peers and subordinates results in an inability to hear constructive gossip. The gap also undermines administrative authority which should be based upon the nonegalitarian principle of information sharing and coordination rather than rank and command. The principle of "we are all in the same boat" is not a farce if actual rather than authoritarian control is desired.

Record-Keeping and Inventory-Tracking Skills

Since the network is composed of many parts—hardware, software, data, and personal node equipment—accounting and inventory skills are required to track components and maintain an adequate inventory of spare repair parts. Records should indicate the status of software and hardware, and node configurations of all network components. A manager must know how to blueprint the network and track the status of work orders and job completions.

Technical Skills

A serious issue for most organizations is finding a technical manager with the right mix of technical and organizational abilities. Often skilled technicians are elevated to management roles solely because of their demonstrated expertise, or skilled managers will find their talents at odds with the culture of a technical organization. These mismatches need to be corrected quickly for the good of all. Sometimes, when a qualified administrator is placed in the position of managing highly qualified technical personnel, the "troops" test and bait the manager in order to evaluate the manager's technical skills. When they find the technical ability lacking, they generally assume that the manager will not be competent. Network administration is a bifurcated need requiring both clear and ordered administration abilities and well-honed technical skills.

In the case of the technically competent manager, the administrative and interpersonal skills will present a valid challenge. This challenge must be confronted squarely, not avoided. A technical manager will certainly resolve the technical problems with ease, but may often fail to meet the expectations of subordinates and peers for handling issues, or disappoint the high expectations of network users. The solution, as proposed by copious managerial literature, is to map out the organizational interrelationships in order to understand the hidden needs, agendas, and expectations, and to build a power base within the organization. Listening to gossip is also suggested, although this implies a sufficiency of time to chat with and listen to people. Such a power base opens conduits of information, and provides for both formal and informal sources of answers, help, and organizational support.

In the case of the skilled manager who lacks the necessary technical skills, the problems will be in locating resources to solve problems and gaining the respect of the "troops." The skilled manager usually brings a power base and organizational contacts as a matter of course.

Technical Managing Skills

Part of any job is regulating and influencing people. For the network team, this is a two-way process. Not only must the network manager manage the network team; all members of the network team must manage expectations company-wide, since the entire company is often the team's client. Management is not only from the top down, but also from the bottom up. The required skill set comprises more than the technical skills to maintain the physical and operative well-being of the network. Users must be satisfied that they are receiving adequate and equal (to any fee basis, if applicable) service. Because this skill set is so large, a single person might not succeed at the job. Perception of the workload usually determines who and how many people constitute the management team. If more than a single person is required—in fact, several might be required to provide hardware, software, maintenance, and administrative support—the internal dynamics of the group increase management workload. Adding more people to a problem does not always hasten the solution.

A good manager knows how to manage and control a situation. This does not imply that a good manager controls his or her team; rather, it means that the manager is able to control the situation and derive consensus goals and communicate them clearly to the team for implementation. The manager might feel distinctly out of control because of a dependence on the network team for implementation and technical skills. Here, as elsewhere, success will depend upon building consensus.

Interpersonal Communication Skills

Organizations spend money on technology, not on the basic skills of how to be a good employee; this issue must be addressed. While technical skills are clearly necessary to resolve the technical network problems, a honed communication skill is a prerequisite. Reiterating an earlier point, there is a vendor-user relationship in the network maintenance role. A manager can do a top-notch job in the mechanical side of the network, but still fail if the targeted user community is ignored. People slated to use the system are often removed from the planning process and find that plans made for them really don't solve their problems. Exclusion from the planning process is also a political sleight that suggests that the users are neither intelligent enough nor important enough. Such ignorance rapidly erodes any manager's effective authority and ultimate success. Additionally, a manager should know how to prepare all the paperwork that goes with being a manager. Honed presentation skills help convince others that you know how to design, plan, implement, and manage.

Making Decisions

Think big: realize that the consequences of many decisions may not become apparent for years. New administrators tend to err on the conservative side, finding it difficult to leap from their petty circumstances to the big picture. The game could be lost on this relative inaction.

Often the network administration team will be constrained to repair only those items that show clear failures. While individual problems may be innocuous, a number of marginal problems may combine to produce a global effect. Because the network management role is a repair, replace, and restore role, forward-thinking action is difficult to achieve. Upper management rarely encourages potentially disruptive risk taking. Radical changes are frowned upon, and network changes are filtered through a conservative screen of consensus. This policy can be the death of the success of a network manager, because growth, technological change, and proliferating problems may undermine that person's authority, perceived competence, and ability to institute large-scale repairs. It can also create a dead-end job. This tendency should be resisted. Not only will conservatism ultimately devalue the network manager and the team, but the organization as an entity may slip behind the competition, as new technology supersedes the old.

Conservatism boxes a manager into a suboptimal position and limits the options otherwise available. When decision making is indecisive and risk taking has been avoided as a matter of policy, taking even moderate chances raises eyebrows because others have become accustomed to the norm. Breach of the norm, no matter how risky or risk-adverse, will cause objections. Establish your credibility soon. The pattern of risk taking is established early on and success with those risks builds a consistent confidence in the network administration team.

Setting Priorities

The best action is to negotiate with the user community. If users are denied a say in network management, you will have a poor user-vendor relationship. Users clearly will not get the type and level of service which they desire. The important point is that service is not merely network performance and computer resources, it also comprises personal reassurances, attention to people as individuals, and recognition of users' deadlines and problems. It is erroneous to assume that you or your team can determine needs and priorities. Users feel slighted and out of control when decisions are made for them. Certain projects or certain users may be key to the organization. For example, their network welfare is more critical than the welfare of other users. Unless this circumstance is communicated to the user community, other user groups might feel shortchanged when resources are applied to resolve problems not affecting them personally.

Working around Staff Shortages

Extra staffing is always needed and difficult to obtain; staffing is always a real management issue. A high level of skill in small part counterbalances the paucity of staff. Good management, good organizational skills, and clear communication with the user community almost make up for threadbare resources. Involve the user community in the planning process; users know what they want. If consulted and apprised of events, they will help the process. If users are uncomfortable, they will reflect and magnify this insecurity over time. The users will understand resource limitations if clearly expressed. Involve them, and they will be part of your team.

Burnout and Recognition

"Burnout" is a common result of understaffing. The level of network problems and the workload imposed are often beyond the control of the network team or the manager. Lack of control is a situation that can be rectified, but the daily pressures magnify the difficulty of the job. Without adequate recognition of accomplishments, the team members will feel frustrated, undervalued, and often, angry.

A manager who communicates well with the user community has solved part of this problem by explaining the limits of the resources within that manager's control and the level of service that can be provided. This will lessen the daily pressures, thus diverting episodic burnouts. More important, however, is attributing credit where it is due. Provide positive feedback to the team members and be certain that the user community is aware of the value of the services rendered.

Employee Development Skills

Since staff shortages are a certainty, it is important to recognize the desires of the employees for technical achievement and accomplishment and help the employees to develop new skills. In order to construct an effective network management team it is important to provide a defined framework within which the group functions. Demonstrate policies by example and maintain a clear and concise model. Avoid sudden shifts in demands, needs, and policy. Practice and rehearse the policies until the group is competent and confident. By all means, provide feedback, demonstrate by example, reaffirm correct and incorrect procedures, reaffirm the developing skill sets, and fine-tune any newly acquired skills. Train on all levels. Role models acting differently will undermine any "positive" results. Figure 20.3 lists team development suggestions.

Team Building Skills

It is a given that there will be staff shortages and that the staff will experience burnout. In order to cope with these problems it is imperative

- Define a framework
- Demonstrate by example
- Practice for confidence and competence
- Provide immediate feedback
- Allow time for job-related education
- Express satisfaction with performance publicly
- Express dissatisfaction with performance privately
- Listen

Figure 20.3 Team development steps.

that the manager understand how to encourage the staff to develop new skills, and how to foster initiative and a team approach.

Evaluation Skills
Part of the job of manager includes hiring, firing, specifying the pay scale for each job, and evaluating the team members. Good evaluation skills are important for maintaining each team member's sense of fair pay for work performed. Effective evaluation encourages superior performance by outlining what the expected goals are, and how each team member has performed relative to these goals. Failure to present clear and concise goals will discourage good team spirit and confuse the team members and the user community. Additionally, inability to evaluate team performance will create disgruntled employees.

The Network Team
Crucial to any FDDI is an experienced network team. The assumption that FDDI is just like Token-Ring or Ethernet is correct insofar as most of the technical aspects go, but incorrect for the politics and reach of information control. While optical fiber networks may represent a new technology to the organization, it is well within the paradigm of LANs. The aspect of FDDI that provides global services is apt to be new, politically charged, and ripe for power struggles. A network team would not be needed if FDDI were a simple hook-up-and-run type of LAN. Instead, the link requires shared resources that offer both load limitations and a complex architecture. The simplified wiring of FDDI eases the burden of maintaining a network in contrast to the star-coupled mainframe environment. As a consequence, the technical skill set for the network team should be different from that of a mainframe support team; the interpersonal skill is much the same. The network team must understand the diverse needs and varied equipment in use within the network community. It also must recognize the interrelationship that a network creates. A good team can make a crucial difference between a functioning network and an unmitigated disaster. A good team makes a manager look good.

Team Skill Requirements
Several skill sets are required to keep the link of that network up and running. Figure 20.4 lists some of these needs. The physical layers of FDDI need to be maintained, and the software link layers need management.

- Technical knowledge
- Diagnostic skills
- Analytic skills
- Interpersonal communication abilities

Figure 20.4 The network team skill set.

Human Factors

The station equipment, consisting of nonspecialized computer hardware, needs physical maintenance. The node equipment can range from simple and reliable personal computers to more fragile and complex engineering workstations, file servers, and print servers. This application layer requires software, physical, and preventive maintenance.

Technical Knowledge

The network team applies mechanical and computer knowledge to plan, design, implement, and repair the network. Alternatively, if the group has a firm organizational charter, hired outside experts ease the load when problems exceed the abilities of the in-house crew.

Diagnostic and Analytic Skills

As important as good technical skills for the success of a team member is the ability to uncover network problems in a FDDI environment. Problems are not solved with textbook knowledge. They often transcend the vendor manuals and the scope of any book. It is therefore important that all team members know how to think through a situation given the relevant facts, and apply technical knowledge to solve problems.

Interpersonal Communication Skills

Organizations spend money on the people who bring to the company technical skills but not necessarily the basic skills of how to be a good employee. Furthermore, the skills to succeed managing a fundamental organizational resource—the same skills a controller or financial officer should have—are perceived as necessary for network management. They should be.

However, although technical skills are clearly necessary to resolve the technical network problems, a honed interpersonal communication skill is prerequisite, not only for managers, but for the technicians as well. A technician can do a top-notch job in developing and repairing or implementing the mechanical side of the network, but still fail if the targeted user community is ignored. People slated to use the system are often removed from the repair process and find that plans made for them really don't solve their problems, or even negatively affect their work.

Hierarchy

Organizations are political. Even nonprofit organizations are not immune to ambition. Hierarchical structures are established to achieve effective results and also to put people into controlled positions. No organization escapes the chains of authority. Authority is rooted in the power of money, voting stock, seniority and titles, fear, knowledge, and expectations that develop over time. For example, the authority to reroute the network is based upon not only title but the expectation from users that since you have moved the cable before, you can do it now.

Electronic mail and fax services are useful tools to layer on top of a network. Electronic mail provides a useful capacity for people to share memos, schedule complex meetings, and sidetrack phone tag. Anyone can communicate with anyone else. Management may perceive this as a breach of the chain of command, an undermining of traditional authority, and a serious problem since they may not have the time or the knowledge to control the network. The network installation must not undermine the normal organization culture or threaten the reporting hierarchy of an organization—or else the network technology becomes a serious threat. LAN fax services provide network users with the ability to send an outgoing facsimile with less labor, or see incoming faxes automatically routed without a security breach, misplacement of the fax, or lost pages. Additionally, *optical character recognition* (OCR) provides the means to translate a facsimile into a data format with a minimal labor component.

Fear of Technology

Networks represent a complex technical installation. More than that technology, they represent a profound organizational and management integration that is perceived as a complex technology. This results in a fear of change, distrust of technical innovation, and suspicion of the people who manage the computer systems and networks. Instinctively, this fear translates into a battle to remove, disrupt, and destroy the computer systems and the networks. While most users can merely disrupt and sabotage operations, top management can fire people and remove equipment. Disruptions and sabotage are annoying or expensive although resolvable problems.

Fear from top management can undermine network operations and your own personal success. These fears represent a serious nonverbal risk that must be recognized and addressed with effective communication skills. Users can be trained and helped so that the network doesn't threaten them. Top management can be trained in network lore, too, although more likely the need and time for it is minimal. Instead, top management must be shown that the network benefits them in the myriad of ways listed in Chapter 2. Any perceived threats must be addressed quickly and resolved.

Squeaky Wheel versus Problem Resolution

Users shout and scream for their share of the pie. Each user wants more attention, faster service, and better results. Some shout louder than others, and clearly some users have more political clout as a consequence of their position, length of service, or network of friendships. While it often is necessary to resolve problems within a political framework, this should be moderated by clearly stated policies. A network by its design is an interrelated organism; thus certain problems need solutions as a prerequisite to repairing others. A service policy is a must.

Set up a policy. For example, respond to problems on global resources before those of user-specific workstations. Repair global failures that inhibit the work of a larger group before attending to a single user's complaint. Repairs or changes that are upgrades or minor modifications should command less priority than a total failure of a user workstation. Such a setting of priorities requires a clear policy from the network manager. Adhere to that policy.

The Effects of Change

There are two successful ways of organizing a company: centralized and decentralized. There are valid reasons for going either way. Most managers and consultants know the textbook reasons: a decentralized company focuses the power in the hands of those who can best apply that power, whereas a centralized organizational structure returns control to a select few. But reasons for choosing a particular structure are irrelevant when facing problems. Sometimes, simply changing the organization from one structure to any other achieves results. Changes compel people to reconsider how they do things, indicate that performance is being evaluated, and also that their needs for attention are being fulfilled.

A network manager would do well to remember this concept when a situation seems out-of-hand: a simple change of organizational structure, policy, and reporting relationships may restore control. Furthermore, FDDI is apt to bring change itself. Groups formerly without any knowledge or interaction with other groups may find themselves sharing or fighting over control and information. The change in access to resources is a fundamental change provided by MAN and WAN networking.

Political Feasibility

All networking tasks—whether new designs, fundamental implementations, upgrades and expansions, solutions for performance problems, or even mechanical repairs— are subjected to external scrutiny and political examination. Even the most basic repairs require a reallocation of resources, if only a technician is shifted from one ongoing project to the repairs. Although the repair might be as critical as restoring *some* network service to the entire organization, the reassignment is seen by those immediately affected as a loss. A typical response sounds like, "I guess I am not important enough!" Unfortunately, the answer really is "no" because the repairs are indeed more important to the organization as a whole. The real issue is how people within the organization perceive the allocation of the network manager's consideration to their own needs as it affects them.

Although this seems like a resource allocation problem, the communication of how and when resources are distributed is really a political problem. Technical questions such as network standards, physical media, acceptable protocols, and what is the best solution to fulfill the needs of an individual group are not always answered with the best technical answer. That may not be what people want to hear from the network manager. Technical evaluations are actually *loaded* questions that are tempered by judgment.

Successful network managers, ones who gain credibility and thrive, address every question with multiple answers, as Figure 20.5 prioritizes. There is the sensitive political answer, the technical qualification, the evaluation of utility and plausibility, a presentation of period time for implementation, and a response factoring in the availability of resources, including labor, equipment, and money.

Sometimes, complex and sensitive questions are answered bluntly with unfortunate political and interpersonal consequences. For example, "Every other department will aid the effort and wants to see this accomplished. But that backward DP department obstructs every effort to connect their precious mainframes into the proposed enterprise-wide network...."

Other times, answers will be, and must be, discreet. This tends to achieve better results and earns the respect and confidence of the DP department. The contemptuous overtones should not be expressed, rather cleverly skirted or masked. How remarkable or how backward the DP department actually is represents an relatively inconsequential issue. Furthermore, derisive remarks, though offered privately, often are rumored and embellished in the grapevine. Certainly, expressing personal views will tend to restrict any future success with the DP group and alienate the scorned individuals. Instead, consider, for example, "An FDDI backbone connecting all FDDI and Ethernet LANs is certainly the answer that matches your needs; it only needs the support and encouragement from the DP people." Both quotes reflect the same sentiment, the same technical evaluations,

- Politically viable
- Monetarily achievable
- Technically possible
- Skills congruent with objectives
- Realistically plausible
- Realizable within timetable

Figure 20.5 The priorities of exigencies that conflict with networking projects.

and plausibility within a timetable, but provide critically different political and interpersonal insights.

By the same token, the network manager should not respond to a network user with emotional statements or escalate an already heated discussion. If that happens, the disagreement is lost. Realize that the issue probably involves a resource allocation request that has not been fulfilled. Also, there might be a reason divorced from anything related to the network, and the network manager is an easy target or a person the user knows will argue needlessly; that may be very satisfying. The user may be under stress to perform up to par, to complete an overdue task, or be angry at a spouse. Assess the motivation for the user's hostility. Whatever that motivation, the user is angry at the *role* of network manager, but not personally at the network manager, per se. It is likely that the user would probably have the same discussion with any other person filling the role of network manager.

The outcome of the discussion in terms of emotional satisfaction for the user may be different even while the realities of time and resource limitations might not. In other words, the outcome may be the same regardless of how the discussion progresses, yet the user may feel that the network manager has listened to the stated complaints, understood these complaints, responded to these complaints and also to the underlying frustration, and defused any political or personal reasons for the controversy.

Additionally, emotional statements or gestures undermine the effectiveness of the manager. Respect is lost. Instead, respond to the anger and frustrations of the user. This does not mean that the network manager must concede; rather the manager must politely respond and explain the limitations imposed upon that network management and budgeting role. Solicit ideas. Ask what the user would like accomplished. Demonstrate the priorities and listen to any thoughts about reassessing those priorities. As the final word, nonetheless, that may mean saying "no." At least, the user's frustration might be rechanneled with the result that a once angry user becomes an ardent supporter and ally.

Easier Said than Done. . .

Most plans are more easily derailed, than easily completed. Communication and negotiations with the user community establish a credible relationship, while priorities determine which problems will be resolved and when they will be resolved. Despite the best of intentions, the workload usually outstrips available resources and the complexity of network problems often taxes the technical expertise and time availability of the network team. Things just will not get done. As long as the user community is apprised of these delays and gets clear feedback, options for temporary solutions, and/or revised time schedules, the relationship will flourish. Communication is key to successful human interaction.

Part 6
Troubleshooting Reference

This part contains practical and concise information for the network manager to facilitate debugging FDDI network failures. Instead of text and graphics, this part uses a methodology that progressively isolates the suspected component. The prescribed procedures encourage good work habits and help network managers develop a logical approach to solving network failures. Chapter 21 is a detailed troubleshooting manual that describes techniques to isolate hardware, software, and network overloading problems. Chapter 22 summarizes the contents of this book with a tool usage manual. This chapter supplies ideas and information on when to analyze the network with a multimeter, light meter and light source, a pair scanner or TDR, a feature detector or OTDR, and a protocol analyzer to solve network problems.

Chapter

21

FDDI Troubleshooting Sequence

Isolation Techniques

The first step when network failure occurs is to eliminate the obvious and isolate the problem for diagnosis. Figure 21.1 illustrates a logical step-by-step search pattern. The first step is to determine if failure is network software-, network hardware-, station-, or node-specific. Seek to physically localize the problem. Unfortunately, experience with the reader's specific network provides the best basis for categorizing the failure. The only rule of thumb is that hardware failures are intermittent or transient and generally inexplicable, whereas software failures are reproducible and more logical. Software failures most often provide log messages which can help debug the trouble.

However, as network operating systems become more complex, supporting hot server activation, disk mirroring, disk striping, as well as multithreading and multiprocessing, the chances that memory could be overrun increase. Such sudden software failures are often inexplicable and not easily resolved. Any memory-resident monitoring software or diagnostic tool alters the memory mapping. As a result, such tools may not provide any insight into the failure. Additionally, the tools themselves may *stave off* the software failure. In either event, if a wrong assumption is made, the step-by-step isolation technique will eventually indicate that the reader incorrectly diagnosed the failure.

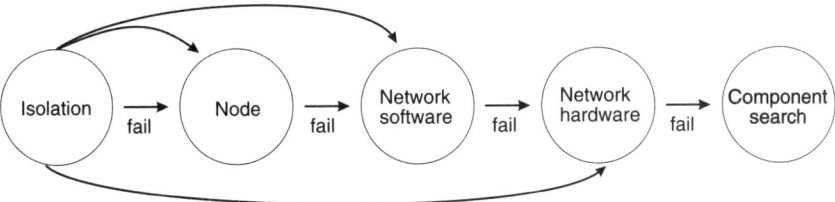

Figure 21.1 The logical FDDI troubleshooting sequence.

Station Hardware and Software Failures

If the failure has been isolated to a single station, follow the steps to accomplish repair. The station may have failed, and this could cause network-wide failure. Assuming that the problem has been isolated to a failed station, follow the outlined steps in the tables. The sequence progresses with less likely causes of network failure. If all checks succeed, the problem is probably global, although individual stations are more likely to fail than the entire FDDI network and consequently they should be tested first. In fact, a failed node on a subnetwork and an irate user are usually the first indicators of a hub, primary station, or global network problem. If the network fails as a unit, even though hardware is a more frequent cause of network loss than software, software should be explored first, if at all possible, because the diagnostic tools are comprehensive.

If all stations seem to be working independently, ascertain if network-level devices are suspect. While FDDI, IPX, UDP, NetBEUI, NetBIOS, TCP/IP, and many other upper-level communication software are supposed to be "stateless," some condition has likely occurred to lock the software into a perpetual waiting cycle. Assuming that the problem has been isolated to failed network software, follow the steps outlined in the accompanying tables. The sequence progresses with less likely causes of FDDI failure. Should all software, both node-level, station-level and global, seem to be functioning correctly, it is probably a hardware malfunction that is causing the inconvenience. The "server" side of a link shouldn't retain "state" before or after a transaction, although it frequently does. Therefore, every network transaction implies an open and close of a file and the network link. (This is not always true for client/server database transactional processing, or, when transaction commit and rollback features are enabled for SQL, DB2, and similar full-featured relational databases.) If state is maintained, the system is said to be jammed. Not only can this process halt the network, but it can also cause a gradual and progressive degradation in normal network performance as network operating software creates gratuitous loading.

Network Hardware Failures

At this stage in the isolation process, the problem is probably a global network hardware problem. For example, a main connection is broken, or a crucial router or bridge has failed. Assuming that the problem has been isolated to a failed network hardware component, follow the steps outlined in the accompanying tables. The sequence progresses with less likely causes of FDDI failure. If the network defies these standard debugging strategies, there may be a hidden component that is at fault.

FDDI Troubleshooting Sequence

Progressive Search for Hidden Component Failure

If all network components and devices appear to meet FDDI specifications, the final alternative is to power down the network piece by piece, section by section, until the problem is uncovered. If the problem can't be resolved quickly and the user community is willing to endure a complete network shutdown, a sequential shutdown of the network in conjunction with a binary or sequential search pattern will ultimately uncover any network problem. Note that the binary search is more efficient than random, guesswork methods networks. Follow the steps outlined. This is a last resort, and should be performed only with cooperation from the user community.

Isolation Techniques for Enterprise-Wide Network Failures

For either hardware or software problems, isolate the location:
- Apply binary search method or apply sequential search method.
- Check for failed segment operation.
- Check station or hub mechanisms for correct functioning.
- Check bridge mechanisms and sustained capacity.
- Check router mechanisms and sustained capacity.
- Check gateway mechanisms and sustained capacity.
- Check the network management statistics (SNMP or CMIP) and FDDI SMT information.
- Check the software indicators.
- Apply the multimeter, continuity tester, feature tester, or light meter to physical connections.
- Apply the ring scanner, TDR, or OTDR.
- Gather statistics and diagnose with protocol analyzer.

On location:
- Verify operation of all subsegments or rings (secondary networks in isolation).
- Check to confirm that components are plugged in.
- Jiggle components in case of short circuit, lack of optical connection, dirt in connections, or corrosion.
- Trace a beacon signal upstream on ring or hub.
- Check for electrical shorts or breaks and optical failures.
- Replace failed components or interchange suspected components.
- Reroute traffic through other bridges, routers, or gateways.
- Check for failed packet encapsulation or translation.
- Check for overloaded components (bridges, routers, gateways).
- Check for station and addressing errors.

Note: Step through each check. If the test shows correct network operation, proceed to the next item. Each item is progressively less likely to occur. If all checks succeed, widen the search pattern to a larger subset of the network. If a node has failed without clear reason, check the network. If the network has failed without clear reason, check the network software.

For a software problem, isolate the location:
- Check the network management statistics (SNMP or CMIP).
- Gather statistics and diagnose with the protocol analyzer.
- Analyze the network software.
- Locate failed or nonoperative stations in the ring and subnets.
- Check the software indicators.
- Root out nonfunctional stations and physically remove them from ring or isolate them with a remote switch.

On location:
- Isolate segments.
- View station memory maps.
- View software state.
- Reboot devices, stations, or nodes selectively.
- Restart software.
- Replace software.
- Debug and/or fix software.
- Check for overloaded components (bypasses, signal splitters, bridges, routers, and gateways).
- Power down hubs, bridges, routers, and gateways.
- Power cycle individual hardware components.
- Reroute traffic and bypass failed sections or components.

Note: Step through each check. If the test shows correct network operation, proceed to the next item. Each item is progressively less likely to occur. If all checks succeed, widen the search pattern to a larger subset of the network. If a node has failed without clear reason, check the network. If the network has failed without clear reason, check the network software.

FDDI Troubleshooting Sequence

Isolation Techniques for Network Failures

For either hardware or software problems, isolate the location:
- Apply binary search method or apply sequential search method.
- Check for failed, nonoperative station.
- Check the software indicators.
- Apply the multimeter, light meter, feature detector.
- Apply the pair scanner, TDR, or OTDR.
- Gather statistics and diagnose with the protocol analyzer.

On location:
- Check to confirm that components are plugged in.
- Jiggle components in case of short circuit, dirt, or corrosion.
- Check for electrical shorts or breaks.
- Replace failed components or interchange suspect components.

For a software problem, isolate the location:
- Gather statistics and diagnose with the protocol analyzer.
- Analyze the network software.
- Locate failed or nonoperative station.
- Check the software indicators.
- Root out nonfunctional stations and other critical devices.

On location:
- Reboot stations and workstations selectively.
- View station memory maps.
- View software state.
- Restart software.
- Replace software.
- Debug and/or fix software.
- Power cycle individual hardware components.

Note: Step through each check. If the test shows correct network operation, proceed to the next item. Each item is progressively less likely to occur. If all checks succeed, widen the search pattern to a larger subset of the network. If a node has failed without clear reason, check the network. If the network has failed without clear reason, check the network software.

Decreasing Likelihood Search: Station Failed

If a station has failed, check that:
- The node or station unit is plugged in.
- The node or station has electrical power.
- The node or station is functioning.
- The device inserts into ring (ring noise on protocol analyzer).
- The workstation sees FDDI and NOS.
- The station connections and lobe connections are secure.
- The hub connection is correct.
- The FDDI controller electronics function with dual homing or on the right channel.
- The FDDI address is correct.
- The Internet or IPX address is correct.
- All other stations are working.
- Some other stations are working.
- That FDDI versions, variations, and signaling characteristics match.

If all checks succeed =>
........you have a network software failure or
........you have a network hardware failure or
........you have a device driver conflict or
........you may have experienced electricity spikes or stray voltage, or
........you have a hidden component failure.

Decreasing Likelihood Search: Network Software Failed

If network software has failed, check that:
- The network software is correct.
- The network is not overloaded with traffic.
- The "state" of FDDI is not jammed.
- All stations are set to the same speed.
- Each software station is compatible and repeats tokens and data packets.
- FDDI specifications are met.
- FDDI versions and protocols are uniformally supported.
- The network software is performing tasks.
- The operating network software is not corrupted.
- The software is compatible with physical devices.

If all checks succeed =>
........you have a network hardware failure or
........you have a device driver conflict or
........you may have experienced electricity spikes or stray voltage, or
........you have a hidden component failure.

Note: Step through each check. If the test shows correct network operation, proceed to the next item. Each item is progressively less likely to occur. If all checks succeed, widen the search pattern to a larger subset of the network. If a node has failed without clear reason, check the network. If the network has failed without clear reason, check the network software.

FDDI Troubleshooting Sequence 437

Decreasing Likelihood Search: Network Hardware Failed

If network hardware has failed, check that:
- The network software is correct.
- The network print and file servers are online.
- The network is not overloaded with traffic.
- The ring is intact.
- Lobes are correctly installed.
- Hub connectors are tightly connecting.
- No lobe sections are broken.
- There are no cable breaks, cuts, or abrasions.
- The "state" of FDDI is not jammed.
- STP or UTP FDDI is not connected to a live telephone circuit.
- STP or UTP FDDI wiring is not crossed over.
- STP or UTP FDDI wiring bundle also does not support RS-232.
- STP or UTP FDDI wiring bundle also does not support serial communication.
- STP or UTP FDDI wiring polarity is maintained properly.
- STP and UTP FDDI wiring is not interconnected.
- The gateways and routers are functioning.
- Devices and hubs units are not jammed.
- Individual network rings are functioning.
- Repeated segments (rings) are functioning.
- Gateway segments (rings and other structures) are functioning.
- Individual network wiring sections are operational.
- Controller components are functioning.
- Controllers are not jabbering, jittering, or chattering.
- Controller electronics are operational.
- There are no software station incompatibilities.
- FDDI versions and variations match.
- There is no outside electrical or radio-frequency interference.

If all checks succeed =>
........you have a device driver conflict or
........you may have experienced electricity spikes or stray voltage, or
........you have a hidden component failure.

Note: Step through each check. If the test shows correct network operation, proceed to the next item. Each item is progressively less likely to occur. If all checks succeed, widen the search pattern to a larger subset of the network. If a node has failed without clear reason, check the network. If the network has failed without clear reason, check the network software.

Progressive Search for Hidden Component Failure

To shut down the entire network, follow these steps:
1. Power down all stations.
2. Power down all hubs, bridges, routers, and gateways.
3. Power down all file servers, print servers, and auxiliary devices.
4. Disconnect all network segments.
5. Check specification on all individual station segments, lobes, or auxiliary segments.
6. Electrically and/or optically test wiring components for electrical incompatibilities.
7. Electrically test controllers for electrical incompatibilities.
8. Disconnect all network sections and rings (institute binary search).
9. Electrically and/or optically test wire components for electrical incompatibilities.
10. Electrically test controllers for electrical incompatibilities.
11. Power up each individual network ring or section.
12. Complete to specification all individual components.
13. Reconstitute rings.
14. Power up each individual network ring or segment.
15. Electrically test wiring components for electrical incompatibilities.
16. Electrically test lobe lines for electrical incompatibilities.
17. Power up all stations on each individual ring.
18. Power up all file servers, print servers, and auxiliary devices.
19. Power up devices and hub units.
20. Power up bridges.
21. Power up routers.
22. Power up gateways.
23. Reconstitute network and reconnect all rings.
24. Power on all stations.

If all checks succeed and the network remains dysfunctional =>
........you have traffic overload or
........you have a device driver conflict or
........you may have experienced electricity spikes or stray voltage, or
........you may have experienced an act of vandalism

If all checks succeed and network now provides complete service =>
........you had traffic overload or
........you had a network "state" problem or
........you had corrupted memory or
........you had a user application crashed network software or
........you may have experienced electricity spikes or stray voltage, or
........you had software incompatibilities or
........you may have experienced an act of vandalism

Note: Step through each check. If the test shows correct network operation, proceed to the next item. Each item is progressively less likely to occur. If all checks succeed, widen the search pattern to a larger subset of the network. If a node has failed without clear reason, check the network. If the network has failed without clear reason, check the network software.

Chapter

22

Tool Usage Reference

The network tools—network hardware indicator lights (on hubs), the multitester, the twisted-pair scanner or time domain reflectometer, light meter and light source, feature detector, or optical time domain reflectomter, and the protocol analyzer—have overlapping functionality. The accompanying tables coach the network management team in the hour(s) of crisis by suggesting appropriate uses for each tool. These uses and the listed sequences direct the reader to a careful investigation; the aim is to discover the causes of possible network malfunction. The ideal values are repeated here for the reader's convenience.

Additionally, there are two sections detailing the sequence of tools and the best tool to apply in cases of hardware or software failures. While hardware problems are often easier to locate and repair than software problems, search for problems at the highest, most comprehensive, level; this is often a statistical search with a protocol analyzer, or a software search. Note also that software-level searches are generally noninvasive.

As each test succeeds, select a more basic component until the problem is traced. Certain types of problems, including hardware malfunctions, may be clearly pinpointed with this software search. A software search with a protocol analyzer or network management software like SNMP or CMIP is apt to provide comprehensive diagnosis. In some serious cases network faults necessitate TDR, scanner, or multitester testing of twisted-pair or OTDR, light meter/light source, or feature detector testing of optical fiber because the network traffic is halted, precluding the use of the protocol analyzer. Check the network globally first. Contrast any visible conditions with experienced events or network statistics. Check if any stations or nodes are functioning in a stand-alone mode, or analyze any patterns of failed stations or nodes. Check key servers for functionality. Localize the search to a common area, or common subset of possible problems, and test accordingly.

If the problem cannot be localized, consider the possibility of a hardware malfunction and, as with the software tests, start with a major component and select progressively more basic components until the problem is traced. Unresolved problems may necessitate a complete shutdown and network restart as detailed in the preceding chapter.

Functionality of Network Tools

Indicator lights (on intelligent hubs)
- Is network functioning?
- Check for proper network configuration and station of ring wrap, optical splitters and bypasses switches
- Check network device receiving electrical power.
- Check for correct network device installation.
- Check for proper transmission speed settings.
- Does device transmit?
- Does device receive?
- Does device recognize token?
- Does device jabber, jitter, or chatter?
- Does device pass loop-back test (may need scanner)?

Multimeter
- Check network voltage: 0 V on halted network, within -4.5 V to +4.5 V when transmitting (actually refer to vendor specifications for STP or UTP signal volatge level)
- Check network resistance (negligible).
- Check network impedance (approximately 16 ohm/100 m).
- Check connector conductivity.
- Check network wiring for continuity and polarity.
- Check probes for conductivity and pairwise isolation.
- Check lobe pinout continuity.

Pair scanner or time domain reflectometer (TDR)
- Check network lobe conductivity (16 ohm/100 m).
- Check lobe cable continuity.
- Check controller and connector installation.
- Check controller repeats signal.
- Perform a signal spectrum analysis.

Optical scanner, light meter/light source, feature detector, or optical time domain reflectometer (OTDR)
- Check station fiber continuity.
- Check lobe fiber continuity.
- Check connector and fiber end continuities.
- Check controller and connector installation.
- Check controller repeats signal.
- Perform a signal spectrum analysis.

Note: Step through each check. If the test shows correct network operation, proceed to the next item. Each item is progressively less likely to occur. If all checks succeed, widen the search pattern to a larger subset of the network. If a node has failed without clear reason, check the network. If the network has failed without clear reason, check the network software.

Tool Usage Reference 441

Functionality of Network Tools (*continued*)

Protocol analyzer and network managemet software (SNMP, CMIP, and CMOT)

- Check for network traffic overload (>80% channel utilization).
- Check for exceptionally busy stations or nodes (>20% network load).
- Check for chattering or jabbering controllers.
- Check for long TRT (> 2 ms).
- Check for high CRC error rates.
- Check for small or oversized frames.
- Check for good frames with nonsense data field values.
- Check for interconnectivity device failures and overloads.

Note: Step through each check. If the test shows correct network operation, proceed to the next item. Each item is progressively less likely to occur. If all checks succeed, widen the search pattern to a larger subset of the network. If a node has failed without clear reason, check the network. If the network has failed without clear reason, check the network software.

Troubleshooting Sequence for Software Failures

If the network is functioning:

Indicator lights (on intelligent hubs)
- Check that station or node is online.
- Perform loop-back tests.
- Check that network is online and available.
- Check for operational dial-up, PBX, or PDN interconnectivity.
- Check that station or node is transmitting.
- Check that station or node is receiving.
- Check that configuartion devices are online and switched properly.
- Check that station or node is detecting token and retransmiting the frame as received (no overruns).
- Check that twisted-pair node is not jabbering, chattering, or jittering.

Protocol analyzer: partial network service
- Perform a network-wide statistical evaluation:
  Traffic load
  Frame counts
  Frame defect rate
  TRT times
  Rates of beacon exceeding number of ring insertions
  Missing frame addresses
  Duplicate station and node addresses
  Jittering twisted-pair NICs
  Nonresponsive hubs
- Check for interconnectivity device failures and overloads.

Server software functioning with partial network service
- Perform a network software and hardware evaluation:
  Check for any new changes
  Software functioning
  Version numbers
  Version compatibility
  File service
  Memory levels
  Source
  Check for overloads

Note: Step through each check. If the test shows correct network operation, proceed to the next item. Each item is progressively less likely to occur. If all checks succeed, widen the search pattern to a larger subset of the network. If a node has failed without clear reason, check the network. If the network has failed without clear reason, check the network software.

Tool Usage Reference

Troubleshooting Sequence for Software Failures (*continued*)

If station or node subset halted:

Indicator lights (on intelligent hubs)
- Check that stations and nodes are online.
- Check that stations and nodes are receiving tokens.
- Perform loop-back tests or check ring for integrity.
- Check that network is online and available.
- Check that network devices are online, available, and configured properly.
- Check that stations or nodes are transmitting.
- Check that stations or nodes are receiving.
- Check that any hubs are online and configured correctly.
- Check that any twisted-pair node is not jabbering, chattering, or jittering.

Protocol analyzer: partial network service
- Perform network-wide statistical evaluation:
  Traffic load
  Frame counts
  Frame defect rate
  TRT and TTRT
  Missing frame addresses
  Nonresponsive stations or nodes, nodes upstream from beaconing stations or nodes

Station or node software functioning with partial network service
- Perform a station or node software and hardware evaluation:
  Check for any new changes
  Software functioning
  Version numbers
  Version compatibility
  File service
  Memory levels
  Source
  Overloads

If network halted and no network service is available:
- Power down hub concentrators and remove lobes.
- Power down network and restart all stations and nodes individually.
- Check hardware for proper installation and functionality.
- Or, as a last resort, apply a progressive search.

Note: Step through each check. If the test shows correct network operation, proceed to the next item. Each item is progressively less likely to occur. If all checks succeed, widen the search pattern to a larger subset of the network. If a node has failed without clear reason, check the network. If the network has failed without clear reason, check the network software.

Troubleshooting Sequence for Hardware Failures

If the network is functioning:

Indicator lights (on intelligent hubs)
- Check that station or node is online.
- Perform loop-back tests.
- Check that station or node is receiving and retransmitting.
- Check that switches and bypasses are configured correctly.
- Check that twisted-pair node is not jabbering, chattering, or jittering.

Protocol analyzer: partial network service
- Perform a network-wide statistical evaluation:
    Traffic load
    Frame counts
    Frame defect rate
    TRT
    Missing frame addresses
    Jittering twisted-pair NICs
    Nonresponsive stations and nodes

If a station or node subset is halted:

Indicator lights
- Perform loop-back tests.
- Check that station or node is online.
- Check that network is online and available.
- Check that station or node is receving and retransmitting.
- Check that twisted-pair node is not jabbering, chattering, or jittering.

Protocol analyzer: partial network service
- Perform statistical evaluation on suspect stations and nodes if possible:
    Traffic load
    Frame counts
    Frame defect rate
    TRT and TTRT
    Missing frame addresses
    Jittering twisted-pair NICs
    Nonresponsive stations and nodes

Note: Step through each check. If the test shows correct network operation, proceed to the next item. Each item is progressively less likely to occur. If all checks succeed, widen the search pattern to a larger subset of the network. If a node has failed without clear reason, check the network. If the network has failed without clear reason, check the network software.

Tool Usage Reference 445

Troubleshooting Sequence for Hardware Failures (*continued*)

Scanner and TDR: erratic or no network service

- Check the cable for continuity in terms of:
    Breaks
    Shorts
    Abrasions
    Parity errors and cable crossovers
    Misspecified cable
    Excessive bends
    Impedance errors
    RFI/EFI errors
    Excessive crosstalk
- Check the connectors for:
    Poor installation
    Shorts
    Breaks
    Genderless contacts with metal fatigue and nonrelease
    Dirty or greasy fittings
- View the twisted-pair NICs for:
    Jabbering or jittering electronics
    Signal interference
    Poor installation
    A signal spectrum that is out of specification

Note: Step through each check. If the test shows correct network operation, proceed to the next item. Each item is progressively less likely to occur. If all checks succeed, widen the search pattern to a larger subset of the network. If a node has failed without clear reason, check the network. If the network has failed without clear reason, check the network software.

Troubleshooting Sequence for Hardware Failures (continued)

If the network is halted:

Optical scanner, light meter/light source, feature detector, and OTDR: erratic or no network service
- Check the cable for continuity in terms of:
    Breaks
    Fiber crossovers
    Misspecified fiber
    Wavelength errors
- Check the connectors for:
    Poor installation
    Breaks
    Fibers ends do not meet, mesh, or align
    Fibers ends are different sizes
    Chips or scratches on fiber ends
    Dirt or grease on fiber ends
- View the twisted-pair NICs for:
    Poor installation
    A signal spectrum that is out of specification

If the network is halted:

Indicator lights (on intelligent hubs)
- Check that station or node is online.
- Check that station or node is receiving and retransmitting.
- Perform loop-back tests.
- Check that twisted-pair node is not jabbering, chattering, or jittering.

Note: Step through each check. If the test shows correct network operation, proceed to the next item. Each item is progressively less likely to occur. If all checks succeed, widen the search pattern to a larger subset of the network. If a node has failed without clear reason, check the network. If the network has failed without clear reason, check the network software.

Tool Usage Reference

Troubleshooting Sequence for Hardware Failures (*continued*)

TDR: no network service
- Check the cable for continuity in terms of:
    Breaks
    Shorts
    Abrasions
    Misspecified cable
    Impedance errors
    RFI/EFI errors
    Excessive crosstalk
    Excessive bends
    A signal spectrum that is out of specification
- Check the connectors for:
    Poor installation
    Shorts
    Breaks
    Upside-down installation
    Genderless contacts with metal fatigue and nonrelease
    Dirty or greasy fittings
- View the transceivers for:
    Jabbering or jittering electronics
    Poor installation
- Test the lobe cables for:
    Bad pin-out
    Misspecified cable
    Impedance errors
    Shorts
    Breaks
    Crossover
    Connection with live phone lines (48 V, 96 V when ringing)
    Dirty or greasy fittings
    Poor installation

Note: Step through each check. If the test shows correct network operation, proceed to the next item. Each item is progressively less likely to occur. If all checks succeed, widen the search pattern to a larger subset of the network. If a node has failed without clear reason, check the network. If the network has failed without clear reason, check the network software.

Troubleshooting Sequence for Hardware Failures (*continued*)

OTDR: no network service
- Check the fiber for continuity in terms of:
    Breaks
    Fiber crossovers
    Misspecified fiber
    Length errors
    Splicing failure
    Wavelength errors
    Switch or bypass errors
- Check the connectors for:
    Poor installation
    Breaks
    Fibers ends do not meet, mesh, or align
    Fibers ends are different sizes
    Chips or scratches on fiber ends
    Dirt or grease on fiber ends

Optical Scanner: no network service
- Check the fiber for continuity in terms of:
    Breaks
    Fiber crossovers
    Length errors
    Misspecified fiber
    Splicing failure
    Wavelength errors
    Switch or bypass errors
- Check the connectors for:
    Poor installation
    Breaks
    Fibers ends do not meet, mesh, or align
    Fibers ends are different sizes
    Chips or scratches on fiber ends
    Dirt or grease on fiber ends

Note: Step through each check. If the test shows correct network operation, proceed to the next item. Each item is progressively less likely to occur. If all checks succeed, widen the search pattern to a larger subset of the network. If a node has failed without clear reason, check the network. If the network has failed without clear reason, check the network software.

Tool Usage Reference

Troubleshooting Sequence for Hardware Failures *(continued)*

Light meter/light source or feature detector: no network service
- Check the fiber for continuity in terms of:
    Breaks
    Fiber crossovers
    Misspecified fiber
    Splicing failure
    Length errors
    Wavelength errors
    Switch or bypass errors
- Check the connectors for:
    Poor installation
    Breaks
    Fibers ends do not meet, mesh, or align
    Fibers ends are different sizes
    Chips or scratches on fiber ends
    Dirt or grease on fiber ends

Multimeter: for serious cabling failures or isolated testing
- Test the cable for:
    Breaks and shorts
    Misspecified cable
    Impedance errors
- Test the connectors for:
    Poor installation
    Breaks and shorts
    Crossover
    Wrong connectors
    Genderless contacts with metal fatigue and nonrelease
    Dirty or greasy fittings
    Adherence to specifications

Part 7
Appendixes

The glossary lists local area network, data communications terms, and FDDI terms used within this book and cross-references them by their all-too-common acronyms. The bibliography lists references and some suggested additional readings and sources.

Appendix

Glossary

AC: Alternating current. Electricity.

Active Monitor: A network node, usually the first unit to attach to the network, which initiates **Ring Polls** and **Ring Purges** when the ring is perceived to be broken or the token has been lost for longer than the TTRT. All stations serve as active monitors on FDDI.

Adapter Board: A PC board that plugs into any computer, including mainframe, minicomputer, personal computer, or workstation. Within the networking context it often refers to the network access unit, network interface card (NIC), or a network controller adapter.

Address: A reference to a source or destination station on a network.

Address Error: A frame is improperly labeled with either source or destination information.

Adjusted Ring Length: The driving transmission path length for a ring architecture when a station or segment fails, and the ring wraps to provide network service without interruption.

Alignment Error: A frame that has not been synchronized correctly. It usually is uncovered as a frame that is not a multiple of 8 bits.

American National Standards Institute: A governmental agency that maintains standards for science and commerce that include a list of acceptable standards for computer languages, character sets, connection compatibility, and many other aspects of the computer and data communications industries. Also known by the ANSI acronym.

Analog: Something that bears a similarity to something else.

Analog Signal: A transmission in which information is represented as physical magnitudes of electrical signals.

ANSI: See **American National Standards Institute.**

453

Application Level: The seventh layer of the OSI Reference Model which supports identification of communicating partners, establishes the authority to communicate, transfers information, and applies privacy mechanisms and cost allocations. It may be a complex layer. The application layer supports file services, print services, and electronic mail.

ARL: See **Adjusted Ring Length.**

Asynchronous Transfer Mode: ATM. A cell relay packet network providing from 155 Mbits/s to gigbytes/s from central offices to central offices, and perhaps even to the desktop.

ATM: See **Asynchronous Transfer Mode.**

AUI Cable: Attachment Unit Interface cable that connects a workstation to an Ethernet transceiver or fan-out box. Often called a **drop cable.**

Average: The statistical value representing the middle point in a sample distribution. Also, the sum all sample values divided by the number of samples.

Bandwidth: The range (band) of frequencies that are transmitted on a channel. The difference between the highest and lowest frequencies is expressed in hertz.

Baseband: A transmission channel which carries a single communications channel, on which only one signal can transmit at a given time.

BAT: Abbreviation for a batch file; usually refers to an MS-DOS or OS/2 script containing commands to execute. The file extent for an MS-DOS or OS/2 script file.

Bayonnet Connector: See **ST Connector.**

Beaconing: A term used to describe a malfunctioning station on a FDDI network that has not isolated itself from the ring. A constant signal which collapses the ring.

Benchmark: A measuring standard. network performance benchmarks include **Mbits/s, throughput, error rates**, and other less formal definitions.

Bits/s: See **Bits Per Second.**

Bits Per Second (bits/s): Rate at which data is transmitted over a communications channel. Sometimes abbreviated as bps.

Bit Time: The time for a network to transport 1 bit of data. It is equivalent to the reciprocal of the network transmission rate and is a convenient measurement in performing network performance calculations.

Block: The smallest unit of paged data read from memory or from disk.

BMP: See **Burst Mode Protocol.**

Glossary

Boot: A small rubber or plastic cup that fits over the ends of unconnected optical fiber cable and ceramic ferrules to protect the fiber from dirt, scratches, and breakage.

Break: A physical break (electrical or optical) in the network media that prohibits passage of the transmission signal. See also **Open**.

Breakout Bundle: A single package containing multiple optical fibers, wires, and cables supporting extraction of single wires at intermediate places along the full length of the wiring package.

Bridge: A device that interconnects networks using *similar* protocols. The bridge provides service at level 2 of the **OSI Reference Model**. See also **Gateway** and **Router**.

Broadband: A transmission cable with a wider frequency range (than baseband) that carries individual multiplexed communications channels.

Broadcast: The transmission from one station on a network to two or more stations on a network, or a frame with a destination broadcast address.

Brouter: Combination or hybrid derived from **Bridge** and **Router**. A device that performs the function of a bridge while filtering protocols and frames specifically destined for a station on another interconnected network.

Buffers: A temporary memory structure allocated for containing data. Usually refers to a memory structure for containing a block read or written to a hard disk.

Burst Mode Protocol: A NOS enhancement implemented in Novell NetWare that optimizes the performance of intensive file transfer operations.

Bus: A network topology in which nodes are connected to a linear configuration of cable. The data transfer path with a computer.

Bus Master: A specialized CPU and interface unit that controls the data transfer path and bypasses the computer CPU.

Bus Width: Refers to the size of the data units that the computer system needs to move through I/O. Usually represented by 8, 16, 32, or 64 byte units.

Cable Scanner: A testing tool which verifies the integrity and performance of network wiring and cable. It tests for electrical breaks, shorts, impedance, capacitance, as well as for signal crosstalk and signal attenuation. These tools are sometimes called pair or ring scanners when designed for FDDI.

Cable Tester: A testing tool which verifies the integrity and performance of network wiring and cable. It tests for electrical breaks, shorts, impedance, capacitance, as well as for signal crosstalk and signal attenuation. These tools are sometimes called pair or ring scanners when designed for FDDI.

Cache: A temporary memory structure that **buffers** data movement in computer system to provide faster access to information and improve overall performance.

Caching Controller: A storage interface device that improves disk performance. See **Cache**.

Capacitance: The electrical properties of the network cable and hardware.

Carrier Sense Multiple Access with Collision Detection (CSMA/CD): A communications protocol in which nodes contend for a shared communications channel and all nodes have equal access to the network. Simultaneous transmissions from two or more nodes results in random restart of those transmissions.

CCITT: See **Consultative Committee for International Telephone and Telegraph**.

CDDI: See **Fiber Data Distributed Interchange**. Twisted-pair wiring option from Crescendo.

CDMA: See **Code-Division Multiple Access**.

Cell Relay: A packet switching network providing a nondedicated logical transmission pathway. See **Asynchronous Transfer Mode**.

Chained Files: Files on disk stored in discontiguous **Blocks**.

Channel: An individual path that carries signals.

Channel Logic: The logical functions between the transceiver cable and the data link layer which support the defined interface between the system and the hardware,

Chatter: The condition resulting when NIC electronics fail to shut down after a transmission, and the NIC floods the network with random signals.

CI: See **Confidence Interval**.

Claim Token: The signal propagated by a station which determines that a token is overdue, lost, or corrupted.

Client/Server Processing: The establishment of a host computer (server) to provide end-user (client) services.

Client: A network "user," often a device or workstation.

Client Layer: The collective term that is used to refer to the data link and physical layers of the **OSI Reference Model**.

Glossary

CMIP: See **Common Management Information Protocol**.

CMOT: CMIP on TCP/IP.

Code-Division Multiple Access: Wireless transmission technology that employs a range of radio-frequency wavelengths to transport multiple channels of communication signals. See also **Spread-Spectrum Technology**.

COM: The file extent for an MS-DOS executable command application.

Common Carrier: Companies which provide communication networks (like AT&T).

Common Management Information Protocol: A network management protocol compatible with the OSI Reference Model. Also called **CMIP**.

Common Network Interface Protocol: A contender for standard network management protocols specified by **ISO**. This protocol provides a standard for managing large networks across bridges, routers, and gateways. See also **Simple Network Management Protocol**.

Computer Virus: Man-made software designed to disable, damage, or destroy computer hardware or read/write storage systems. Sometimes the term virus should refer instead to *worms*, *trojan horses*, and *trap doors*.

Concentrator: A wiring hub.

Confidence Interval: A statistical range surrounding the average value.

Congestion: A slowdown in a network due to a bottleneck.

Consultative Committee for International Telephone and Telegraph: An international organization that makes recommendations for networking standards like X.25, X.400, and CCITT facsimile data compression standards.

Contiguous File Blocks: Storage units in a hard drive that are logically positioned next to each other.

Corrupt Data Error: Condition resulting when hardware components fail.

CRC: See **Cyclic Redundancy Check**.

Crosstalk: A technical term indicating that stray signals from other wavelengths, channels, communication pathways, or twisted-pair wiring have polluted the signal. It is particularly prevalent in twisted-pair networks or when telephone and network communications share copper-based wiring bundles.

CRC Error: See **Cyclic Redundancy Check Error**.

CSMA/CD: See **Carrier Sense Multiple Access with Collision Detection**.

Cyclic Redundancy Check: A checksum—an error checking algorithm—that the transmitting station includes within a frame. The receiving station generates its own CRC to check against the transmitted CRC. If the results are different, the receiver usually requests a retransmission of the frame. This encoded value is appended to each frame by the data link layer to allow the receiving NIC to detect transmission errors in the physical channel. Also **Frame Check Sequence** (q.v.).

Cyclic Redundancy Check Error: An error caused by alignment errors, 8-bit-multiple shortages, under- or oversized frames.

Cylinder: Refers to a collection of tracks within a hard disk that are co-located on multiple platters.

DAS: See **Dual Access Station**.

Data Compression: A method of reducing the space required to represent data, either as bits, characters, or graphic images.

Data Link Layer: The second layer of the **OSI Reference Model**. It manages transmissions and error acknowledgment and recovery. Technically, the mechanical devices map data units to data link units, provide physical error detection and notification, and link activation and deactivation.

Data Processing: Computer operations which are geared to the entry, manipulation, and dissemination of information.

Data Terminal Equipment: A computer terminal which connects to a host computer. It may also be a software session on a workstation or personal computer attaching to a host computer.

Datagrade Twisted-Pair: Telephone-type wire twisted over its length to preserve signal strength and minimize **Crosstalk** and **Electromagnetic Interference** for high-speed data communications networks.

DC: Direct current. Electricity.

DCE: Abbreviation for **Distributed Computing Environment**.

DDE: Abbreviation for **Dynamic Data Exchange**.

DDL: Abbreviation for **Dynamic Link Library**. The file extent for an MS-Windows or OS/2 application overlay and executable code library.

Decouple: A gateway (OSI application layer) process to notify an application that transmission will not be completed within the roundtrip delay limitations of a network protocol. Instead, a completion message (for transmission success or failure) is given at some later time. This feature is critical for WANs, heterogeneous networks, and enterprise-wide facilities.

Glossary

Defragment: The process of rewriting files stored on disk in discontiguous **Blocks** into a contiguous format to improve disk performance.

Delni Unit: A type of fan-out box from DEC for DECnet (Ethernet).

Destination Address: The receiving station's address. See **Address**.

Device: Any item on the network. This includes logical addresses that refer to software or hardware processes. It is refers to any physical station, including a PC, **workstation**, mainframe, minicomputer, **bridge**, **router**, **gateway**, remote probe, **repeater**, or **protocol analyzer**.

Digital: A representation of information by a unit of length or size.

Digital Transmission: A transmission of information represented by electrical units.

Distributed Computing: The technique of maintaining application software and data files on a centralized server for access by individual users on network stations. See also **File Server**.

Distributed Computing Environment: See **Distributed Computing**.

Disk Farm: A collection of inexpensive hard disks which provide significant data storage facilities.

Disk Head Seek Time: The average time required for the read/write heads on a hard drive to reach a random **block** and **sector**.

Disk Mirroring: See **Mirroring**.

Disk Shadowing: See **Shadowing**.

Disk Striping: A technique which writes sequential data blocks simultaneously over several physical storage units to provide greater integrity of data and faster read and write access to the data.

Disk Transfer Time: Average time required to read or write a block to a hard disk.

Downsizing: The replacement of computer equipment (and the operating environment) with a less expensive version.

DP: Acronym for **Data Processing**.

Driver: A software program to control a physical computer device (q.v. NIC, printer, disk drive, or RAM disk).

Dropped Frames: Frames or packets lost in transmission.

Drop Cable: Generally an 802.3 Ethernet transceiver cable. May also refer to the Token-Ring lobe cable, or the cable from a hub to node on FDDI.

DTE: Acronym for **Data Terminal Equipment**. A computer terminal.

Dual Access Station: An FDDI station which attaches to dual FDDI rings.

Dual Fiber Connector: See **Dual Fixed Shroud Connector.**

Dual Fixed Shroud Connector: Original name (now a trademark by AMP) for the duplex connector designed for FDDI that shrouds (i.e., extends over and protects) the fragile fiber ends. See **Media Interface Connector.**

Duplex: The method in which communication occurs, either two-way as in full-duplex, or unidirectional as in half-duplex.

Dynamic Data Exchange: Also called **DDE**. A method introduced by Microsoft with MS Windows to link cell information into a master document, spreadsheet, or other compound process running within the same CPU processor and memory stack. The cell content is not altered or duplicated, merely temporarily inserted for the master.

Dynamic Link Library: Code overlays loaded into memory as requested by application programs or operating systems.

Electromagnetic Interference: Signal noise pollution from radio, radar, or electronic instruments.

EMI: See **Electromagnetic Interference.**

EMS: Abbreviation for *either* **Enhanced Memory Services** or Expanded Memory Services. Refers to a remapping and utilization of memory beyond the 640 K normally accessible to MS-DOS.

Enhanced Memory Services: A MS DOS memory specification allowing memory mapping for addresses above 640 K.

Enhanced Small Device Interface: A specification for attaching subservient computer devices to a computer processor bus.

Enterprise Networks: A wide area network that services all (or most) organizational sites. See **Enterprise-Wide Networks.**

Enterprise-Wide Networks: A wide area network that interconnects networks at multiple sites.

Error: A functional violation of a network protocol.

Error Rate: The number of errors during a period of time divided by the number of *frames* tranmitted during that same interval. Errors may be reflected as a single bit error, but the rate should reflect errors as a basis not of bit throughput, but rather of frame throughput. See also **Throughput.**

ESCON: Abbreviation for IBM dual fiber connectors called Enterprise System Connectors.

ESDI: Abbreviation for **Enhanced Small Device Interface.** A disk storage specification.

Ethernet: A popular example of a **local area network** from which the IEEE 802.3 standard was derived. Ethernet applies the IEEE 802.2 MAC protocols and uses the persistent CSMA/CD protocol on a **Bus** topology. Transmission rate is a maximum of 10 Mbits/s. Ethernet is a persistent transmission protocol.

EXE: The file extent for an MS-DOS or OS/2 executable application.

Facility: A WAN connection provided by a common carrier (such as Sprint, MCI, or AT&T).

FAT: Abbreviation for **File Allocation Table.** Refers to the MS-DOS, OS/2, or Unix table structures that maintain file directory information (q.v., size, name, placement, and block chaining).

FCS: See **Frame Check Sequence.**

FCS Error: See **Frame Check Sequence Error.**

FDDI: See **Fiber Data Distributed Interface.**

Feature Detector: A device for measuring lengths, objects, scatter, and probable performance in optical fiber.

Ferrule: The ceramic or machines metal tube used to center, align, and support the thin optical fiber.

Fiber: Optical fiber. A network signaling medium based upon plastic or glass transporting optical signals.

Fiber Data Distributed Interface: Optical fiber network based upon the ANSI X3.139, X3.148, X3.166, X3.184, X3.186, or X3T9.5 specifications. FDDI provides 125 Mbits/s signal rate with 4 bits encoded into 5-bit format for a 100-Mbit/s transmission rate. It functions on single or dual ring and star network with a maximum circumference of 250 km, although copper-based hardware is an option. See **CDDI, SDDI, TP-DDI,** and **TP PMD.**

Fiber Optical Interface Repeater Link: The interconnection protocol required for point-to-point repeater links based upon optical fiber in LANs.

Fiber Optics: Thin, lightweight glass or plastic cables that transmit data by modulating light pulses.

File (Buffers): A temporary memory structure allocated to contain names, locations, sizes, and other information about a file residing on a hard disk.

File Allocation Table: Refers to the MS-DOS, OS/2, or Unix table structures that maintain file directory information (q.v., size, name, placement, and block chaining).

File Server: A device that provides file services for other stations and nodes. It is a shared resource often with higher speed, larger capacity, or better economies-of-scale than remote data storage.

Firewall: A mechanism to protect network stations, subnetworks, and channels from complete failure caused by a single point.

Firmware: Software which is encoded into a ROM BIOS or PROMs.

Fixed Shroud Connector: Original name (now a trademark by AMP) for the duplex connector designed for FDDI that shrouds (i.e. extends over and protects) the fragile fiber ends. See **Media Interface Connector.**

FOIRL: See **Fiber Optical Interface Repeater Link.**

Frame: A self-contained group of bits representing data and control information. The control information usually includes source and destination addressing, sequencing, flow control, and error control information at different protocol levels.

Framing: The process of assigning data bits into the network time slot.

Frame Check Sequence: A checksum value to verify correct receipt of the data frame. The checksum is based upon a cyclic redundancy formula. The encoded value is appended to each frame by the data link layer to allow receiving controllers to detect transmission errors in the physical channel. Also called a **Cyclic Redundancy Check.**

Frame Check Sequence Error: The condition occurring when the encoded value appended to each frame specifies the received frame as corrupt. See also **Cyclic Redundancy Check Error.**

Frame Relay: A packet switching device. See **Packet Switching Network.**

Frame Relay: A switching interface to get **frames** or **packets** over parts of the network as quickly as possible.

FSD Connector: See **Dual Fixed Shroud Connector.**

ft: Abbreviation for an SAE foot.

Full-Duplex: A two-way transmission method that echoes characters to ensure proper reception.

Gateway: A device that routes information from one network to another. It often interfaces between dissimilar networks and provides protocol translation between the networks. A gateway is also a software connection between different networks; this meaning is not implied in this book. The gateway provides service at level 7 of the **OSI Reference Model.** See also **Bridge** and **Router.**

Gauss Meter: A device that measures the strength of a magnetic field.

Glossary

GIS: Abbreviation for **Graphical Information System.** Generally refers to a database of graphical data, although it also can refer to an image storage and retrieval system.

Global Resource: Any hardware, software, server, or other resource generally available to all processes and users on a network.

Graphical Information System: Generally refers to a database of graphical data, although it also can refer to an image storage and retrieval system.

Half-Duplex: A one-way transmission method that does not support characters' echoes.

Handshaking: The exchange of signals between transmitting and receiving devices or their associated modems to establish that each is working and ready to communicate, and to synchronize timing. See also **Protocol.**

Hertz (Hz): A unit of frequency that is one cycle per second. FDDI is 125 million hertz, or 125 million cycles per second. 5/4 cycles are required to represent a bit transition with FDDI **NRZI** encoding.

High Level Language Application Programming Interface: Also called **HLLAPI.** An IBM standard for interconnecting processes running on host computers for data transfer and user display.

High Memory Area: An MS-DOS memory region generally corresponding to any memory above 640 K and below 1024 K. Device controllers and VGA drivers can be loaded into this area for PC performance enhancement.

HLLAPI: Abbreviation for **High Level Language Application Programming Interface.** An IBM standard for interconnecting processes running on host computers for data transfer and user display.

HMA: See **High Memory Area.**

Hub: A network interface that provides star connectivity for FDDI nodes. See **MAU.**

Hunt Group: A series of telephone numbers in sequence that permits the calling party to connect with the first available line.

Hub Adapter: A network interface board that provides access for additional network nodes. This **Network Interface Unit** essentially doubles as a concentrator unit.

I/O: Abbreviation for input and output from a computer. Refers to all memory movement with the **bus,** data moved to and from disks, user and screen presentations, and data frames placed to and from the network channel.

IDE: Abbreviation for **Integrated Drive Electronics.** A composite unit consisting of a disk drive and controller components.

IEEE: The **Institute for Electrical and Electronic Engineers.**

IEEE 802: An IEEE standard for interconnection of local area networking computer equipment. The IEEE 802 standard describes the physical and link layers of the **OSI Reference Model.**

IEEE 802.1: A specification for media-layer physical linkages and bridging.

IEEE 802.2: A specification for media-layer communication typified by Ethernet, FDDI, and Token-Ring. See also **Logical Link Control.**

IEEE 802.3: An Ethernet specification derived from the original Xerox Ethernet specifications. It describes the CSMA/CD protocol on a bus topology using baseband transmissions.

IEEE 802.5: A token ring specification derived from the original IBM Token-Ring LAN specifications. It describes the token protocol on a star/ring topology using baseband transmissions.

IES: An acronym for **Inter-enterprise Network System.** See **Enterprise-wide Networks.**

Impedance: The mathematical combination of resistance and capacitance that is used as a measurement to describe the electrical properties of the coaxial cable and network hardware.

In: Abbreviation for an SAE inch.

Inductance: The property of electrical fields to induce a voltage to flow on the coaxial cable and network hardware. It is usually a disruptive signal that interferes with normal network transmissions.

Institute for Electrical and Electronic Engineers: An membership-based organization based in New York City that creates and publishes technical specifications and scientific publications.

Integrated Drive Electronics: Also abbreviated as **IDE.** A composite unit consisting of a disk drive and controller components.

Intelligent hub: A hub device that connects Ethernet, FDDI, and Token-Ring nodes and manages nodes and traffic while it also isolates failing lobes, trunks, and nodes.

Interface: A device that connects equipment of different types for mutual access. Generally, this refers to computer software and hardware that enable disks and other storage devices to communicate with a computer. In networking, an interface translates different protocols so that different types of computers can communicate together. In the OSI model, the interface is the method of passing data between layers on one device.

Glossary

Interface Error: An indicative of hardware or software incompatibilities.

International Standards Organization: Abbreviated as **ISO.** An international organization that sponsors the development of unified standards for measurements and data communication.

Internet: A government-sponsored mail communication network that gave rise to TCP/IP protocols.

Internetworking: Communication between two or more different networks through a bridge, a gateway, a modem, or other routing equipment.

Internet Address: An address applied at the TCP/IP protocol layer to differentiate network stations from each other. This is in addition to the station hardware or protocol address.

Internet Packet Exchange: A common network-level protocol proposed and applied by vendors, including Novell. IPX is based upon the original Xerox **XNS** frame specifications.

Internet Protocol: See **Transaction Control Protocol/Internet Protocol.**

Interoperability: The process of different network protocols, network hardware, and host mainframe systems to communicate.

IPX: Abbreviation for **Internet Packet Exchange.** A Novell specification for OSI level 3 data exchange.

IPX: See **Internet** and **Internet Packet Exchange.**

ISO: **International Standards Organization** which created the **OSI Reference Model.**

Jabber: To talk without making sense. The condition when a NIC's timing electronics malfunction, and the unit broadcasts in excess of the specified token holding timer limit and creates an oversized frame.

Jitter: A network failure that occurs when a FDDI network segment preamble and the frame signal are out of phase. The jitter shows up as transmission signal distortion, decay, frequency, and timing errors on a token-based LAN.

Jitter budget: The allowed range for signal distortion on a token-based LAN.

km: Abbreviation for a metric kilometer, or a unit representing a 100 **m.** It also may be represented by k.

Kbytes: Abbreviation for kilobytes (1024 bytes) of memory. Also, K.

LAM: Acronym for **Lobe Attachment Module** (q.v.).

LAN: Acronym for **Local Area Network** (q.v.).

Latency: The waiting time for a station desiring to transmit on the network.

LAN Operating System: See **Network Operating System.**

Learning Bridge: A smart device that interconnects two local area networks using similar protocols. It learns what stations are on each connecting segment and routes only that information which is destined for the other segment, therefore improving network performance. The learning bridge is a simple router that provides service at level 3 of the **OSI Reference Model.**

Lease Line: A dedicated common carrier circuit providing point-to-point or multipoint network connection. Also called a private line.

Light Meter: A device for measuring available light; wavelength sensitive in FDDI applications.

Light Source: A device for creating a stable light source of a defined wavelength (color) for testing optical fiber segments and connections in FDDI applications. Also, a device for generating a stabilized light with a known wavelength and strength (brightness).

Linkage Product: Any unit that provides an interface between network segments. This includes gateways, bridges, and other specialty components.

Link Control Field: A data field contained within an an Ethernet packet as part of the Internet Protocol.

LLC: See **Logical Link Control.**

Load Balancing: A technique to equalize the workload over peer and client network components. This includes workstations, storage disks, servers, network connectivity devices, and network transmission channels.

Lobe: A section of cable or wire extending from a MAU, hub, or concentrator to a network station.

Lobe Attachment Module: A type 3 media filter which provides signal retiming and filtering so electrical signals will function correctly on unshielded twisted-pair media.

Local Area Network: Also referred to by the acronym, **LAN.** A network limited in size to a floor, building, or city block.

Local Echo: A host implementation for capturing and display individual keystrokes on terminal or serial connections.

Logical Device: A description that lists how the network references **Physical Devices** (q.v.).

Logical Link Control: A data link control field occupying the first few bytes of the data field that initiates, maintains, and terminates any communication.

Glossary

Long Frame: A frame that exceeds the specified protocol length maximum of the FDDI maximum hold timer.

Loop-back Test: A test for faults over a transmission medium where received data is returned to the sending point (thus traveling a loop) and compared with the data sent.

Low-Level Format: A process which creates (or overwrites) the pattern of **Tracks** and **Sectors** on a hard or floppy disk while the disk head is moving across the spinning media.

m: Abbreviation for a metric **Meter** (39.25 SAE in).

MAN: Abbreviation for **Metropolitan Area Network.** A network that spans buildings, city blocks, a college or corporate campus. Optical fiber repeaters, bridges, routers, packet switches, PDN and PBX services usually supply the network links.

Manchester Encoding: A digital encoding technique in which there is a transition in the middle of each bit time period. A "1" is represented by a high level during the first half of the bit time period whereas a "0" is represented by a low level during the first half of the bit time period.

Mating surface: The critical polished end of the optical fiber and support **Ferrule** where butting fibers connect to transmit signal.

MAU: See **Media Access Unit.** Also called a (passive) **Hub.**

MB: Abbreviation for a megabyte (1024 kilobytes) of memory.

Mbits/s: Abbreviation for a megabits per second. Sometimes abbreviated as Mbps.

Mean: See **Average.**

Media: The physical material used to transmit the network transmission signal. It is either some form of copper wire or optical fiber. However, wireless networks use infrared, microwaves, or radio frequency signals through the ambient air as the media.

Media Access Control: A hardware-level protocol for networking corresponding to ISO level 1.

Media Access Unit: Media Access Unit connects directly to a lobe and broadcasts and receives information over that cable and switches the signals to the next active downstream station. It is often called a **MAU** or **Hub.**

Media Filter: A passive (unpowered) electrical device which provides signal retiming and filtering so that FDDI will function correctly on unshielded twisted-pair media.

Media Interface Connector: The dual connector with locking tabs specified by the ANSI FDDI specification.

Memory Paging: The process of moving memory within the CPU or temporary computer memory to other parts of memory, to screen, or to a disk.

Metal Oxide Varister: Typical electrical device included within backup power supplies, surge suppressors, and power filters to protect electronic equipment from electrical surges. Abreviated as MOV.

Meter: Unit of measurement equivalent to 39.25 SAE in, or 3.27 ft. Meter is abbreviated as **m**.

Metrics: A formal measuring standard or benchmark. network performance metrics include **Mbits/s, throughput, error rates**, and other less formal definitions.

Metropolitan Area Network: Abbreviated as **MAN**. A network that spans buildings, city blocks, a college or corporate campus. Optical fiber repeaters, bridges, routers, packet switches, PDN and PBX services usually supply the network links.

MFM: Abbreviation for **Modified Frequency Modulation** encoding method used for storing data on a hard disk. A disk storage specification.

MIC: See **Media Interface Connector**.

Microsecond: 1×10^{-6} second, abbreviated ms or μs.

Millisecond: 1×10^{-3} second, abbreviated ms.

Mirroring: A technique which writes the same data to multiple disks simultaneously to minimize the chance that data is lost due to a malfunction. See also **Shadowing**.

Misaligned Frame: A frame that trails a fragmentary byte (1 to 7 residual bits), and has an FCS error, or a packet that was framed improperly by the receiving station and therefore a **Synchronization Error** (q.v.).

MLT-3: See **Multi-Level Transmission-3**.

Modem: A device which converts digital to analog signals and restores analog signals back into digital signals for transmission over a network.

Modified Frequency Modulation: Abbreviated as **MFM**. This is an encoding method used for storing data on a hard disk. A disk storage specification.

Monitor: See **Protocol Analyzer**.

Monte Carlo Experiments: Repetitive experiments using sophisticated variance reduction techniques to approximate the behavior of a random process.

MOV: See **Metal Oxide Varister**.

MPS: Megabits (1,000,000 decimal units) per second (Mbits/s). This is a channel bandwidth. See also **Bandwidth** and **Mbits/s**.

ms: Abbreviation for a **millisecond**.

Multicast: The ability to broadcast to a select subset of stations and nodes.

Glossary

Multi-Level Transmission-3: A signal encoding method used on FDDI on twisted-pair which randomizes data to reduce electrical emissions and also equalizes the signal levels.

Multimeter: A test tool that measures electrical voltages (units in V) and resistances (units in Ω). It is also called **Multitester**. It is sometimes called an **ohmmeter**.

Multitester: A test tool that measures electrical voltages (units in V) and resistances (units in Ω).

Multithreading: A concurrent processing of messages commonly implemented in OS/2, UNIX, and VMS operating systems.

Multimode Fiber: An optical fiber optimized in construction for transmitting various wavelengths of light within a single or multiple channels for data communications.

Nanosecond: 1×10^{-9} second, abbreviated as ns.

NAU: Network Access Unit. This term represents the network controller as found in most FDDI adapter boards. See also **Controller**.

NDIS: See **Network Device Independent Specification.**

NetBEUI: Abbreviation for network **NetBIOS Extended User Interface.** A version of NetBIOS from Microsoft (LAN Manager).

NetBIOS: Abbreviation for **Network Basic Input Output System.** The first level of network software which controls network hardware. A specification for OSI level 1 data exchange.

NetBIOS Extended User Interface. Abbreviated as **NetBEUI**. A version of NetBIOS from Microsoft (LAN Manager).

NETBLK: Network Block Transfer Protocol.

Network: Hardware and software that allow computers to transmit data over both local and long distances.

Network Access Unit. Another term that represents the network controller as found in most FDDI adapter boards. See also **Controller**.

Network Basic Input Output System: Abbreviated as **NetBIOS**. The first level of network software which controls network hardware. A specification for OSI level 1 data exchange.

Network Block Transfer Protocol: A protocol used to transfer large units of data at the operating system level over a network. Abbreviated as **NETBLK**.

Network Computing: The ability of underutilized workstations to broadcast their status and provide automatic, parallel computing power.

Network DDE: See also **Dynamic Data Exchange.** A method for linking cell information (such spreadsheet cells, text blocks, audio or graphic elements) into master documents, spreadsheets, or other compound processes accessible by LAN, WAN, or enterprise-wide networks. These TSR or shell processes define the location of the cell, type of information, method of access, complete address, or frequently the means to establish remote links and initiate remote processes to fetch the cell contents.

Network Device Independent Specification. Some vendors define it as Network Driver Interface Specification. An effort to create a standard for bridging different types of network adapter cards and multiple protocol stacks. This network-level protocol is supported by IBM LAN Manager and new Microsoft networking products, such as MS Windows for Workgroups.

Network Interface Card: The network access unit which contains the necessary hardware, software, and specialized PROM information for a station to communicate across the network.

Network Interface Definition Language: IEEE proposed model for parallel processing and logical process partitioning across a distributed network. See also **Network Computing.**

Network Interface Unit: See **Ethernet Controller.**

Network Layer: The third layer of the **OSI Reference Model** which activates the routing with network address resolution and flow control in terms of segmentation and blocking. Also, this layer provides service selection, connection resets, and expedited data transfers. The **Internet Protocol (IP),** or **IPX,** both common network softwares, runs at this level.

Network Monitor: See **Protocol Analyzer.**

Network Operating System: A platform for networking services that combines operating system software with network access. This is typically not application software but rather an integrated operating system.

NIC: See **Network Interface Card.**

NIC: See **Network Interface Card.**

NIDL: See **Network Interface Definition Language.**

NIU: Abbreviation for **Network Interface Unit.** See **Controller.**

nm: Nanometers. 1×10^{-9} meter. Generally refers to the color or wavelength of optical signals on a data communications network.

Node: A logical, nonphysical interconnection to the network that supports computer workstations or other types of physical devices on a network. Alternatively, a node may connect to a fan-out unit providing network access for many devices. A device might be a terminal server, or a shared peripheral such as a file server, printer, or plotter.

Glossary

Noise: Electrical signal interference on a communications channel that can distort or disrupt data signals. Generally, this refers to **electromagnetic interference (EMI)** or **radio-frequency interference (RFI)**.

NOS: See **Network Operating System**.

NOSystem: See **Network Operating System**.

Network Operating System: The software required to control and connect stations into a functioning network conforming to protocol and providing a logical platform for sharing resources.

Non Return to Zero, Invert on Ones: The FDDI optical encoding standard for tranforming 4 bits into a 5 bit code.

NRZI: See **Non Return to Zero, Invert on Ones**.

ns: Abbreviation for **Nanosecond**.

Object Linking and Embedding: Also called **OLE**. A method introduced by Microsoft with MS Windows not merely to link specific data cells but also to include the latest versions of entire documents, graphic images, full-motion video, and sounds into a master document, spreadsheet, or other compound process or object. Changes made to objects linked thusly within this master framework are simultaneously reflected and updated within the individual and original cells, processes, or objects. Additionally, other masters, including objects with multiple OLE links, would see such changes simultaneously. See also **Dynamic Data Exchange** and **Network DDE**.

ODI: See **Open Data-Link Interface**.

Ohmmeter: See **Multimeter**.

OLE: See **Object Linking and Embedding**.

Open: A partial physical break (electrical or optical) through one or more signal conductors in the network media that prohibits passage of the transmission signal. Open circuits usually do not refer to a complete cut of the media. See also **Break**.

Operating System: The software required to control basic computer operations (q.v., disk access, screen display, and computation).

Open Data-Link Interface. Also called **ODI**. An interoperability standard. Novell has proposed this network-level protocol and built IPX/SPX with this protocol specification. This is the LLC control standardized by Novell.

Open Systems Interconnection Reference Model: A specification defination from the International Standards Organization (ISO). It is a data communication architectural model for networking.

Optical Bypass: A mechanical device for redirecting optical signals past a segment, station, or ring on an optically-based network.

Optical Fiber: A thin, lightweight glass or plastic material drawn into a cable that carries data communications via light modulation.

Optical Power Meter: A **Light Meter**. A device for measuring wavelengths, features, and transparency of optical fiber.

Optical Switch: A mechanical transistor-like device for rerouting optical signals on different pathways.

Optical Time Domain Reflectometer: Test equipment that verifies proper functioning of the physical components of the optical fiber network with a sequence of time-delayed optical pulses. Primarily, this tool checks for contiguity and signal carrying capacity of optical fiber for data communications.

OSI Reference Model: Open Systems Interconnection Reference Model defined by the International Standards Organization (ISO), which has determined a data communication architectural model for networking.

OTDR: See **Optical Time Domain Reflectometer**.

Overhead: CPU, disk processing, and/or network channel bandwidth allocated to the processing and/or packaging of network data.

Oversized Frame: A frame that exceeds the maximum frame size defined by a protocol.

Packet: A self-contained group of bits representing data and control information. The control information usually includes source and destination addressing, sequencing, flow control, and error control information at different protocol levels. See **Frame**.

Packet Buffers: A structure created in computer memory to build, disassemble, or temporarily store network data frames.

Packet Burst: An overwhelming broadcast of frames requesting network and station status information, source or destination addresses, or indicating panic error messages.

Packet Switching Network: A network transmission methodology that uses data to define a start and length of a transmission for digital communications. A process of sending data in discrete blocks.

Paging: See **Memory Paging**.

Pair Scanner: A testing tool which verifies the integrity and performance of network wiring and cable. It tests for electrical breaks, shorts, impedance, capacitance, as well as for signal crosstalk and signal attenuation. These tools are sometimes called pair or ring scanners when designed for FDDI.

PBX: See **Private Branch Exchange**.

PDN: See **Public Data Network**.

Glossary

Peer-to-Peer Exchange: The ability of computer workstations from the same or different vendors to interconnect and communicate.

Persistence: A statistical term refering to a protocol's method of accessing the network. Ethernet is *persistent* in transmitting, while other protocols are *nonpersistent* and wait for a permission token.

Physical Address: The unique address associated with each workstation on a network. A physical address is devised to be distinct from all other physical addresses on interconnected networks. A worldwide designation unique to each unit.

Physical Channel: The actual wiring and transmission hardware required to implement networking.

Physical Device: Any item of hardware on the network.

Physical Layer: Level 1 of the **OSI Reference Model** which insulates the data link layer from the medium-dependent physical characteristics.

Ping: A protocol request to poll a subset of network stations for an active status. See **Ring Poll.**

Polling: An access method involving a central station asking each station in a predetermined order if it has data to send. This is often used in mainframe environments, and the order is often determined as a function of priority.

Position-Dependent Unfairness: A situation common to networks where some stations receive better service due to proximity to other stations or a central location in a bus-structured LAN.

Premises Network: See **Enterprise-Wide Network.**

Presentation Layer: This is the sixth layer of the **OSI Reference Model** which transfers information from the application software to the network session layer of the operating system. At this level, software performs data transformations, data formatting, syntax selection (including ASCII, EBCDIC, or other numeric or graphic formats), device selection and control, and data compression or encryption.

Print Server: A device that provides print services for other stations. It is a shared resource often with higher speed, larger capacity, or better economies-of-scale than local printers.

Private Branch Exchange: Also called a PBX. A telephone system used to connect calls between offices in the same complex, and to switch calls between the site and a larger phone network.

PROM: Abbreviation for programmable read-only memory. A computer chip with software designed into its structure.

Protocol: A formal set of rules by which computers can communicate. This includes session initiation, transmission maintenance, and termination.

Protocol Analyzer: Test equipment that transmits, receives, and captures data frames to verify proper network operation.

Public Data Network: Also called a **PDN**. An analog or digital wide-area communication link. This term usually refers to a common carrier such as AT&T, Sprint, or MCI.

PVC: Polyvinyl chloride. An extensively used insulator in cable coatings and coaxial cable foam compositions.

Queueing Model: A statistical model describing a system of event arrivals (q.v., frames or transmission requests) and service times (q.v., tranmission delivery times, network channel loading, and performance levels). Also *Queuing Model*.

Radio-Frequency Interference: Electronically propogated noise from radar, radio, or electronic sources. See **Electromagnetic Interference**.

Radio-Frequency Switch: A remote radio-frequency trigger relay that electrically switches sections of network wiring or coaxial cable and alters network topology. Sometimes called an isolation switch or a **Firewall**.

RAID: Acronym for **Redundant Arrays of Inexpensive Disks**. Functions as a large, fast disk drive.

Random: A statistical term referring to a process with outcomes in a defined sample space. Random does not mean chaotic, indiscriminate, or arbitrary.

Random variable: A numerical function defined over a sample space.

Redirector: A software driver that diverts commands to access local devices and routes them to network devices for data storage, retrieval, and printing.

Redundant Arrays of Inexpensive Disks: A disk farm with data volumes traversing multiple disks.

Repeater: A device that boosts a signal from one network lobe or trunk and continues transmission to another similar network lobe or trunk. Protocols must match on both segments. The repeater provides service at level 1 of the **OSI Reference Model**.

Resistance: The measurement of the electrical properties of the wiring and network hardware that describes their ability to hinder passage of electrons.

RF: Acronym for **Radio-Frequency** (q.v.).

RFI: Acronym for **Radio-Frequency Interference** (q.v.).

Ring: A network topology that has stations in a circular configuration.

Glossary

Ring Poll: An FDDI protocol whereby each station sends out a broadcast signal to every active station to see if it is functioning correctly.

Ring Purge: An FDDI protocol operation where a station initiates a request to create a new token.

RLL: Abbreviation for the run length limited data encoding method used for storing data on a hard drive. A disk storage specification.

ROM: Abbreviation for read only access memory. Refers the basic information required by most computers to check memory, initialize the bootstrap, and load operating systems and networks.

Router: A device that interconnects networks that are either local area or wide area. Routers often provide intercommunication with multiple protocols. Routers provide service at level 3 of the **OSI Reference Model.** See also **Bridge** and **Gateway**.

RS-232: A standard for interfacing data communications between peripheral devices and the computer.

s: Abbreviation for a second.

SC Connector: The AT&T designed push/pull connector for single strand optical fiber. This connector is improved over the **ST Connector** because the flanges entend beyond the fiber and protect the fragile mating surfaces.

Scanner: A testing tool which verifies the integrity and performance of network wiring and cable. It tests for electrical breaks, shorts, impedance, capacitance, as well as for signal crosstalk and signal attenuation. These tools are sometimes called pair or ring scanners when designed for FDDI.

Scatter: Optical signal interference and distortion on a communications channel that can distort or disrupt data signals.

SCSI: Abbreviation for **Small Computer System Interface.** A hardware device controller specification.

SDDI: See **Fiber Data Distributed Interface.** Twisted-pair wiring option backed by vendors such as Synoptics and IBM.

SEF: See **Source Explicit Forwarding.**

Sector: A pie-shaped structure on a hard disk.

Server: A dedicated processor performing a function such as printing, file storage, or tape storage. See also **File Server** and **Print Server.**

Service Address Point: A data link status value contained within the logical link control field of each frame data field that initiates, maintains, and terminates any communication.

Session Layer: The fifth layer of the **OSI Reference Model**. It recognizes the stations on the network and sets up the tables of source and destination addresses. It also establishes, quite literally, a handshaking for each session between different stations. Technically, these services are called *session connection, exception reporting, coordination of send-receive modes,* and of course, the actual *data exchange.*

Shadowing: A technique which writes the same data to multiple disks simultaneously to minimize the chance that data is lost due to a malfuntion. See also **Mirroring.**

Shield: A barrier, usually metallic, within a wiring bundle that is intended to contain the high-powered broadcast signal within the cable. The shield reduces **electromagnetic interference (EMI)** and **radio-frequency interference (RFI),** and signal loss.

Shielded Twisted-Pair: Pairs of 22 to 26 gauge wire clad with a metallic signal shield.

Short: A physical discontinuity (usually electrical, rarely optical) such that one or more signal conductors in the network media leaks signal into other conductors. Usually, a short refers to an electric short circuit between signal conductor and the shield or grounds. It can also refer to a short between receive or transmit pairs.

Signal: A transmission broadcast. The electrical or optical pulse that conveys information.

Signal Quality Error: A background indicator, or "heartbeat," signal that provides a carrier signal.

Signal Splitter: A partial mirror or optical signal repeater that splits an incoming signal in two or more identical outgoing signals.

Simplex: A transmission standard that does not echo characters.

Simple Network Management Protocol: A contender for standard network management protocols becoming widely implemented by NIC hardware and software vendors to provide management of heterogeneous networks. See also **Common Network Interface Protocol**.

Simulation: A technique to model or represent a real-world situation using computerized tools.

Single access station: An FDDI station which connects into a concentrator, but not into the dual optical fiber ring.

Single Mode Fiber: An optical fiber optimized in construction for transmitting a single wavelength of light within a single channel for data communications.

Small Computer System Interface: A hardware device controller specification. Abbreviated as **SCSI.**

Glossary

SNA: System Network Architecture. IBM host connection protocol.

SNMP: See **Simple Network Management Protocol.**

SONET: See **Synchronous Optical Network.** A common carrier fiber-optic transmission link providing basic bandwidth in blocking units of 50 Mbits/s. Multiple streams can support bandwidths up to 18 billion bits per second.

Source Address: The transmitting station's logical address.

Source Explicit Forwarding: A security feature provided by a bridge, router, or gateway that permits only frames from a specified list to be forwarded to another network.

Spanning-Tree Algorithm: IEEE 802.1 standard that detects and manages logical loops in a network. When multiple paths exist, the **bridge** or **router** selects the most efficient one. When a path fails, STA automatically reconfigures the network with a new active path.

Spectrum Analysis: A technique that tests the radio, electrical, or optical signal frequencies to ascertain that the transmission signal conforms to requirements.

Splice: A mechanical connection made in optical fiber by fusing the media together with heat.

Spread-Spectrum Technology: Wireless radio-frequency signal transmission that utilizes multiple frequencies to transmit an identical signal to defeat jamming, background noise, and lower the required power requirements.

SPX: Abbreviation for **System Packet Exchange.** A Novell specification for OSI level-4 data exchange.

SQE: See **Signal Quality Error** heartbeat.

SST: See **Spread-Spectrum Technology.**

ST Connector: The BNC twist-on connector for single strand optical fiber.

STA: See **Spanning Tree Algorithm.**

Stable: A description of the consistency for a network protocol, infrastructure, or application subject to error condition and traffic loading levels.

Star: A network topology where nodes join at a central location.

Station: A logical, nonphysical interconnection to the network that supports computer workstations or other types of physical devices on a network. Alternatively, a station may connect to a fan-out unit providing network access for many devices. A device might be a terminal server, or a shared peripheral such as a file server, printer, or plotter.

Station: A single addressable device on FDDI, generally implemented as a stand-alone computer or a peripheral device such as a printer or plotter. This sometimes refers to a **Node** or **Workstation**.

Stochastic: A process that is random, or probabilistic.

STP: See **Shielded Twisted-Pair**.

Subnet: A ring that is a portion of a larger network.

Swap File: A temporary file established on a local workstation to buffer network data access, provide rapid storage for image displays and work files, and to provide a linearly mapped memory for construction of database views and complex data processing.

Synchronization: The event occurring when transmitting and receiving stations operate in unison for very efficient (or inefficient) utilization of the communications channel.

Synchronization Error: An FDDI frame that is framed improperly by the receiving station or overruns the controller.

Synchronous Optical Network: SONET. A common carrier fiber optic transmission link providing basic bandwidth in blocking units of 50 Mbits/s. Multiple streams can support bandwidths up to 18 billion bits per second.

Target Token Rotation Time: The expected time in which a station can next acquire the token after transmitting.

TCP/IP: Acronym for **Transaction Control Protocol/Internet Protocol**. Although commonly referred to as TCP/IP, a complete implementation of this networking protocol includes Transaction Control Protocol (TCP), Internet Protocol (IP), Internetwork Control Message Protocol (ICMP), User Datagram Protocol (UDP), and Address Resolution Protocol (ARP). Standard applications are File Transfer Protocol (FTP), Simple Mail Transfer Protocol (SMTP), and TELNET which provides a virtual terminal on any remote network system.

TDR: See **Time Domain Reflectometer**.

Teflon: Trade name for fluorinated ethylene propylene. A nonflammable material used for cable foam and jacketing.

Telco: A reference to modular telephone wiring.

Terminate and Stay Resident: Also called **TSR**. A PC- and MS-DOS program that is permanently loaded into memory for access by a unique key-stroke sequence or event sequence. It can be likened to an extension to the operating system functionality.

Terminal Server: A computer device that provides low-speed DTE network access. A device for connecting terminals to a network.

Glossary

Throughput: A measurement of network work accomplished. Measurements are presented in percentages, bits/s, frames/s, or other user-defined gauges.

Time Delay Reflectometer: An incorrect reference to a device called a **Time Domain Reflectometer**.

Time Domain Reflectometer: Test equipment that verifies proper functioning of the physical components of the network with a sequence of time-delayed electrical pulses. Primarily, this tool checks for contiguity and isolation of STP and UTP wiring.

Time Domain Reflectometry: The process of testing transmission lines for proper electrical functioning.

Time-Division Multiplexer: A method using specific time slots to access a communication link. This is accomplished by combining data from several devices into one transmission.

Token: The protocol-based permission that is granted to a station in a predetermined sequence. The permission allows that station to transmit on the network.

Token Acquisition Time: The waiting time for a station awaiting permission to transmit to acquire the token.

Token Hold Timer: The time measurement and measuring device that sets the time a station may hold a token (while transmitting data), and thus implicitly refers to the size of the longest possible legal frame.

Token ring: A physical networking configuration.

Token-Ring: An IBM network protocol and trademark.

Token-Ring: A popular example of a **local area network** from which the IEEE 802.5 standard was derived from original IBM working papers. Token-Ring applies the IEE 802.2 MAC protocols and uses the nonperistent token protocol on a logical ring, although a physical star topology. Transmission rate is a 4 Mbits/s, with upgrades to 16 Mbits/s and options to release a token upon completion of frame transmission, early token release, and burst mode option.

Token Rotation Time: The time for a token to circulate once around the network. See **Token**.

Topology: Layout of a network. This describes how the nodes are physically joined to each other.

Track: A circular (ring-shaped) structure on a hard disk.

Traffic: A measure of network load which refers to the frame transmission rate (frames per second or frames per hour).

Transaction Control Protocol/Internet Protocol: Common communication protocol servicing the network and transport layers that provides transmission routing control and data transfer. This represents logical connectivity at levels 2 and 3 of the **OSI Reference Model**, although the protocol does not conform in fact to this model. Also known by its acronym, **TCP/IP**.

Transmission Error: Catch-all term for a CRC Error. Such errors are caused by **Alignment Errors, Undersized Frames,** or **Oversized Frames** (q.v.), plus a variety of application and system software, or hardware failures.

Transport Layer: The fourth layer of the **OSI Reference Model** which controls data transfer and transmission control. This software level is called **Transaction Control Protocol (TCP)**, the common network software.

TRT: See **Token Rotation Time.**

TSR: See **Terminate and Stay Resident.**

TTRT: See **Target Token Rotation Time.**

Twisted Pair Physical Layer Media Dependent (TP-PMD) is the official ANSI designation for FDDI supported by twisted-pair wiring. See also **Fiber Data Distributed Interchange.**

Twisted-Pair: Telephone-type wire twisted over its length to preserve signal strength and minimize **Electromagnetic Interference.** May also be spelled as *twisted pair.*

Type Error: A frame that is improperly labeled with protocol information.

TP-DDI: See **Fiber Data Distributed Interchange.** Twisted-pair wiring option acronym.

TP-PMD: See **Twisted Pair Physical Layer Media Dependent.**

UDP: User Datagram Protocol. A simplified version of the **Transmission Control Protocol (TCP)** for application-level data.

UMB: See **Upper Memory Blocks.**

Undersized Frame: A frame that contains less than 64 bytes, including address, length, data, and CRC fields.

Unshielded Twisted-Pair: Pairs of 22 to 26 gauge wire usually in bundles of 25 pairs installed for telephone service and occasionally for data networks. Referred to as voice grade twisted-pair or VG wiring.

Upper Memory Blocks: An MS-DOS memory area that is accessible above 1024 KB. MS Windows and some application software can be loaded into this memory when special memory access software is installed. Both *enhanced* and *expanded* memory services reside within UMB. Expanded memory tends to provide the better MS-DOS performance, although it provides the more restricted utility.

UPS: Uninterrupted Power Supply. A backup power supply in case the main electrical source fails.

UTP: See **Unshielded Twisted-Pair.**

Virus: See **Computer Virus.**

VSAT: Very-Small-Aperture Terminal. Synonymous with satellite data communication.

WAN: Wide Area Network. A network that spans cities, states, countries, or oceans. PBX services usually supply the network links.

Wiring Concentrator: See **Wiring Hub.**

Wiring Hub: Central wiring concentrator for a series of FDDI stations.

Workstation: A single addressable site on FDDI, generally implemented as a standalone computer or a peripheral device, connected to the ring with a controller. Also termed a **Station.**

Appendix B
Additional Reading and References

Barry, Diane, Marketing Communications, Cabletron Systems, Rochester, NH.

Baum, Michael, Manager of Optical Interconnection Technology Group, AMP Incorporated, Harrisburg, PA 17105.

Bickel, Peter J., and Kjell A. Doksum, *Mathematical Statistics: Basic Ideas and Selected Topics*, Holden-Day, San Francisco, CA, 1977.

Cherupalla, Shyam, Codenoll Technology Corporation, Yonkers, NY 10701.

cisco Systems, *Routing Protocols: cisco Technology Brief*, Menlo Park CA.

Cutler, Scott, SE Area Manager, MicroCom, Atlanta, GA.

Dauber, Steve, Product Marketing Manager—Network Analysis Products, San Jose, CA.

Eggers, Barry, Major Accounts, Business Development Manager, Cisco Systems, Orlando, FL.

Fetterolf, James, New Product Business Development, AMP Inc. Valley Forge, PA, 01776.

Fogarty, David, Editing Manager, McGraw-Hill, New York, NY 10011.

Foster, Denise, Sales Communications, BT&D, Kennett Square, PA 019348.

The *Fiber Optic LAN Handbook*, Codenoll Technology Corporation, Yonkers, NY 10701, 1990.

Fiber Optic Training Videos, The Light Brigade, Kent WA.

Glasser, Jeanne, Editor, McGraw-Hill Computer Science, New York, NY 10011.

Additional Reading and References

Grieser, Elizabeth, Marketing Coordinator, Triplett Corp., Bluffton, OH 45817.

IEEE Standards for Local Area Networks: Logical Link Control Procedures, IEEE, New York, 1985.

Internet Protocol Transition Workbook, March 1981, SRI International, Menlo Park, CA 94025.

Kilker, Jeanne, PR Manager, Microtest, 3519 E. Shea Blvd. Suite 134, Phoenix, AZ 85028.

Kirby, Scott, Area Support Manager, cisco Systems, Orlando, FL.

Lee, Ronald, Senior Consultant, Novell, Inc. 122 East 1700 South, Provo, UT 84606-6194.

Ley, Keith, Fiber Optic Sales Manager, Integrated Communications, Mt. Arlington, NJ 07856.

Morrel, Grif, Account Manager, BT&D, Kennett Square, PA, 019348.

Nershook, James, Laser Precision, Albany NY.

Network Performance Institute, Inc. PO 41-4371, Miami Beach, FL 33141-1350.

Noyes Fiber Systems, Laconia, NH 03247.

Paine, Jeff, Manager of PR, cisco Systems, Menlo Park, CA.

Rohan, Perry, South Florida Territory Senior Sales Manager, Cabletron Systems, Rochester, NH.

Rossie, Reeza, Manager of Network Systems, University of Miami School of Medicine, Miami, FL 33018.

Shannon, C. E., *The Mathematical Theory of Communications,* University of Illinois Press, Urbana, IL, 1964.

Shuman, Barry, Codenoll Technology Corporation, Yonkers, NY 10701.

Sparks, Chuck, Area Sales Manager, cisco Systems, Orlando, FL.

Schneider, Mike, VP Sales and Marketing, Noyes Fiber Systems, Laconia, NH 03247.

Stiegel, Tony, Technical Sales, Beach Wire & Cable, Huntington Beach, CA 92649.

The Supernet Family for FDDI, Advanced Micro Devices, Sunnyvale, CA., 1991.

Turner, Dave, Senior Technical Consultant, Cabletron Systems, Rochester, NH.

Wallach, Jeff, Sales Support Engineer, Network General Corporation, Miami, FL.

Additional Reading and References

Wilcom, Inc., PO Box 508, Laconia, NH 03247.

Woodling, Dave, USNET, Dallas, TX.

Zernick, Hava, Tekelec, Calabasas, CA 91302.

Index

Abnormal preamble, 346
Adapter, 106, 107, 108
Adapter, definition of, 107
Address resolution protocol, ARP, 78, 126
Administrative control, 75, 416
Administrator, 362, 419
AIM, 9
Altair, 220
American Airlines, 12
American National Standards Institute, ANSI, 73, 93, 266
APOLLO, 10
APPC, 246
Ardis, 221
ARP, *see* Address resolution protocol
Arson, 269
AS/400, 246
ASCII, 77, 82
ATM, 99, 103, 147, 355
Automated image management, 9
AUTOXEC.BAT, 209

Backbone, 45, 88, 225, 376, 377, 390, 399
  definition of, 36
Backup, 38, 40, 52, 256, 277, 282, 328, 367, 368, 386, 396, 397, 399, 400, 401, 402, 403, 404, 405, 406, 407, 408, 409, 411, 413, 414, 417
Bandwidth, 85, 88, 99, 218, 221
Banyan, 205

Baseband, 197
Baseband cable, 193, 195
Beacon, definition of, 123, 346
Beepers, 163
BICC, 220
Blackouts, 139
Blueprinting, 156, 169, 183, 184, 271, 308, 309, 313, 345
  benchmark, 183, 184
BNC connectors, 170
Bottlenecks, 83, 238
Breakout cable, 148
Bridge, 79, 80, 85, 94, 188, 190, 193, 196, 197, 198, 199, 200, 201, 203, 284, 366, 370, 371, 376, 377, 395
  encapsulating, 376
  intelligent, 200
  multiprotocol, 204
  performance, 370
  smart repeater, 192, 193, 194, 199, 202
British Caledonia, 21
Broadcast, 342
Broadcast storm, 202, 342, 375
  definition of, 199
Brouter, 284
Brownout, power, 139
Buffer, 120, 121, 194, 389
Bulletin Board Services, 17
Burglaries, 379
Burst mode protocol, 366
Burstiness, Definition of, 322
Bypass switch, 45

Cable length errors, 139
Cable:
  estimating lengths, 139
  Kevlar reinforced, 102
  length errors, 139
  PVC, 103, 138, 168
  radius, 154
  routing, 152
  securing, 154
  shorts, 176, 300
  Teflon, 102
  ties, 169
  Tray, 266
Caller ID, 389, 390
Cancellation yolk, 68
Catastrophe management, *see also* Disasters
  269, 381, 407, 422
Category 5 wiring, 147
CATV, 62
CCITT, 136, 246
CDDI, 226
CDPD, 221
Ceiling plenum, 139
Cell relay, 99, 139
Chatter, 180
CICS, 239, 240
cisco Systems, 199
Claim token, definition of, 347
Client, definition of, 240
Client/server, 34, 134, 208
  computing, 12, 37
Climate control, 139
CMIP, 96, 97, 313, 318, 342
CMIP over TCP/IP, CMOT, 95, 313
CMS, 394
Coaxial cable, 91
  Teflon, 103
Codenoll, 76
Coding, 4B5B, 339
Collapsed backbone, 31
Collision, 46, 47, 194
Collision detection, 46
Collision retry, 370

Common Management Information Protocol, CMIP, 32, 91, 93, 94, 95, 96, 195, 202, 250, 312
Compass, magnetic, 69
Compatibility, 128
Computer-aided design, CAD, 23, 24, 40, 77, 400
Computer-aided manufacturing, CAM, 23, 24, 40, 77
Computer-aided publishing, CAP, 23, 24
CONFIG.SYS, 209
Configuration, 88, 101, 177, 183, 195, 199, 218, 224, 228, 229, 230, 267, 277, 354, 358, 366, 406, 417
Configuration, safety, 66
Connectivity, Dynamic Data Exchange, 244
Connectivity, Object Linking and Embedding, 244
Connector, 147, 165
  bayonet (ST), 148
  DB-9, 173
  failure points, 185
  fiber optic, 148
  fixed shroud duplex, 148
  FSD, 171
  genderless, 102, 173
  hermaphroditic, 102, 173
  installation, 169
  MIC, 171
  modular, 171, 172
  pinout, 151
  RJ-11, 110
  ST, 170
  testing installation, 176
  wiring scheme, 151
Continuous motion video, 235
Controller, 69, 107, 120, 121, 122, 125, 182, 203, 360, 369, 370
  NIC, 106
Coprocessing, 40
Coprocessor, 120
Countermeasure, 388, 397
CPIC, 246
Crescendo, 76
Cross-point switch, 200
Crosstalk, 52, 103, 320

Index

CSU/DSU, 140
Cyclic redundancy check, CRC, 118, 122, 320
  definition of, 118
Cylink, 220

D-connectors, 110
DAS, 101
DAT, 405
Data capture, 94
Data diddling, 387
Data dropout, definition of, 409
Data payload, definition, 82
Data processing, 7, 8, 9, 19, 20, 21, 25, 33, 236, 240, 248
Data storage, 22, 24, 41
Database, 7, 34, 37, 38, 93, 94, 95, 117, 233, 238, 240, 245, 277, 278, 360
DB-9 connector, 173
DC voltage, 114
DDE, 243, 244
DEC, 76
DECnet, 318
Decouple, definition, 194
Dedicated lines, 139
Destination service address port DSAP, 118
Device, definition of, 35
Diagonal cutters, 161
Digital data communications protocol, DDCMP, 78
Direct memory access, 362
Disasters, 411
  backhoe, 87
  bulldozer, 87
  windstorm, 87
Disruption, 103, 282, 375, 424
DMA, 362
Domains, definition of, 97
Downsizing, 7, 12, 235, 236, 240
Downstream station, definition of, 340
Drive distance, definition of, 109
Dropout, definition of, 409

Dual attached station, definition of, 35
Dual homing, definition of, 106
Duplex, 41, 88

E-mail, 367
Early token release, 340, 355
Early token ring, 122
Eavesdropping, 223, 225, 226, 227
EBCDIC, 77
ECMA, 246
EDI, 77, 247
EIA/TIA, 44, 102, 147, 155, 177, 195, 266
Electricity, 139
Electromagnetic interference, EMI, 60, 163, 168
Electronic data interchange, EDI, 77
Electronic Industry Association, *see* EIA/TIA
Electronic mail, 6, 18, 24, 38, 40, 77, 125, 126, 241
EMI, 59, 60, 63, 67, 68, 69, 103, 139, 153, 265, 407
  RF, 59, 65
Encapsulation, 114
  definition, 82
  packet, 33
Encryption, 388, 390, 393
Ending delimiter, 118
Enterprise-wide networks, 3, 7, 32, 49, 97, 142, 195, 197, 204, 212, 219, 223, 231, 232, 233, 234, 235, 237, 239, 240, 241, 243, 245, 247, 248, 249, 250, 251, 313, 417
  definition of, 232
  maintenance, 285
  security, 379
Error, 354
ESCON connector, 141, 147, 148
Ethernet, 81, 83, 128, 135, 195, 205, 220
  specifications, 110, 112
ETR, 122
Expert system, 16

Facilities, 139

Facility, 104, 368, 405
Facsimile, 9
Failures, common, 184
Fan-out
  Multiport, 80
Fast Ethernet, 135, 340
FastNet, 135, 340
Faults, 110
FCC, 63, 66, 67, 69, 218, 221, 222
FDDI, 31, 32, 33, 34, 45, 76, 81, 83, 88, 96, 195, 200, 219, 226, 376
  compatibility, 141, 142, 144
  definition of, 84
  failures, 92
  incompatibility, 48
  limitations, 46, 81, 88, 99, 135, 144, 163, 176, 177, 217, 302
  management, 255, 257, 259, 261, 263, 265, 267, 269, 271, 273, 275, 277, 279, 281, 283, 285, 287
  performance bottlenecks, 291, 319, 358, 364, 369, 370, 376
  specifications, 266
  transmission methodology, 120
  transmission process, 113
  utility, 29, 31, 33
FDDI-II, 219
Feature detector, definition of, 294
Fedders, 16
Fiber, breaks, 50
Fibre channel, 147
Fire, 180, 266, 382, 407
Flashlight, 161, 291
Flood, 382, 407
FM radio
  AM/FM, 163, 168
Frame, components, 114, 115, 117, 118, 119, 120, 121, 128, 198, 318, 376
  components, 114, 117, 118, 119
  definition of, 82, 107, 115
  fields, 117, 119
Frame check sequence, FCS, checksum, 118, 121, 122, 125, 320
  definition of, 118, 121
Frame relay, 139, 198, 205, 216, 227
Fusion splicer, 162

Gateway, 82, 83, 94, 108, 188, 190, 193, 198, 200, 202, 203, 204, 210, 233, 242, 275, 317, 342, 370, 372, 374, 375, 377, 389, 395
  definition of specialized gateways, 202
  functionality, 108, 209
  performance, 370
Genderless connector, 173
GOSIP, 205
Graphic user interface, *see* GUI
Greenbook specification, 76
Grounding, 175
GUI, 32

HACK.EXE, 384
Half repeater, 193, 194
Hammer, 291
Handshaking, 77, 115
HDLC, 78
Health risks, 51, 53, 55, 57, 59, 61, 63, 65, 67, 69
Hermaphroditic connector, 173
HLLAPI, 239, 245
HPnet, 318
HSC, 15, 16, 17, 18
Hubs, 108
Hurricane, 382, 407
Hybrid devices, 200

IBM, 12, 17, 76, 83, 237
  PC LAN, 128
  PC, 238
  SNA, 195
IDE, *see* Information data exchange, 15
IEEE, 73, 78, 200, 266
  802.1, 191
  802.3 GV, 340
IGRP, 199
Imaging, 31
Impedance, 147, 177, 180, 184, 306, 307, 392
Inductance, 168
Information data exchange, 15
InfraLAN, 220

Index

Installation,
  equipment, 161, 162
  failure points, 184
  optical fiber, 164
  testing, 181, 182
  twisted-pair installation, 165
Institute for Electrical and Electronic Engineers, see IEEE
Interconnection, 210
Interconnectivity, 32, 204, 231, 232, 233, 235, 237, 240, 241, 243, 246
Intermediate to intermediate, 199
International Standards Organization, ISO, 73, 74, 75, 78, 91, 93, 94, 119, 168, 193, 202
Internet, 243
  address, 79, 125, 127
  definition of, 127
  origination, 126
  protocol, 126, 128
Internet Packet Exchange, see IPX
InterOp, 141
Interoperability, 84, 126, 128, 202, 204, 210, 231, 233, 237, 241, 245, 246
  derivation of, 243
Inventory, parts, 156
IPX 78, 119, 122, 125, 152, 78, 312, 330
  IPX/SPX, 117, 204
IRMA, 213
ISDN, 217
ISO, 73

Jabber, 180, 330
  definition of, 123, 346
Jacket, 167, 168, 184
Jams, 47, 353
Jitter, 178, 180, 325
  definition of, 346

KNOCK.EXE, 384

Ladders, 54, 55
LAN, local area network, 12, 24, 35, 35, 36, 40, 41, 46, 78, 83, 87, 99, 219, 232, 235, 240, 241, 247
  definition of, 35

maintenance, 285
security, 379
LAN Manager, 83, 205, 208, 242
LAN Server, 83, 205
LANtastic, 136
Lease/buy decisions, 133
Light meter, 146, 162
Light scatter, 147
Link failure mode:
  wiring hubs, failures, 181
Lobe, 91
  definition of, 109
Local area network, see LAN
Log, 271, 278, 281, 388, 394, 407
Logical link fields, 119
Logical ring structure, 109
Loopback test, 306

MAC, 77, 84
Management information system, MIS, 278
Manufacturing automation protocol, MAP, 124, 129
MAPS, 205
Matrix switch, 135, 191
MAUs, 104
Media access control, 77, 84
Media connectors, 110
Media interface connector, 101, 148, 171
Memory limitations, 205, 206
Metallic oxide varister, 140
MIC, 141, 147
MIC connector, 171
Microsoft, 32
Mission-critical concerns, 45, 414
MLT-3, 142
Modem, 41, 91, 140, 195, 197, 232, 246, 328, 389, 390
  call-back, 389
  caller-ID, 389, 390
Modular connector, 171, 172
Motorola, 61, 220, 221
Moving equipment, 256
MS-DOS, 207, 242

MS Windows, 31, 32, 241
Multicast, 342
Multics, 394
Multimedia, 31
Multimeter, 181
Multiplexing, 42
Multipurpose devices, 194, 195
Multitester, 54, 163, 167, 168, 176, 181, 299, 307

Narrow channel transmission, 222
NDIS, 32, 241, 246
NetBEUI, 242
NetBIOS, 242
NetWare, 32, 83
   Novell, 207, 242
   security breaches, 384
Network:
   addresses, 182
   administration, 160
   backbone, 143
   benefits of, 8, 35, 37, 39, 41, 43, 45, 47, 49
   blueprinting, 156
   compatibility, 33, 45, 73, 75, 76, 90, 91, 99, 101, 255, 266, 409, 415
   configuration, 104
   definition of, 35
   file transfers, 245
   grounding, 175
   health risks, 51, 53, 55, 57, 59, 61, 63, 65, 67, 69
   installation, 160
   latency, 332
   limitations, 137
   management, 32, 76, 96, 160, 231
   operating systems, 206, 207
   overload, 193
   performance, 32, 49, 210, 211
   planning, 131, 133, 135, 137, 139, 141, 143, 145, 147, 149, 151, 153, 155, 157
   protocols, 84
   requirements, 132
   sections, 146
   segments, 146
   software, 6, 7, 12, 23, 33, 35, 37, 48, 50, 75, 76, 77, 83, 84, 91, 93, 94, 95, 96, 106, 108, 113, 115, 117, 119, 121, 122, 123, 124, 125, 126, 127, 128, 129, 159, 194, 197, 199, 202, 203, 204, 228, 229, 230, 233, 240, 241, 245, 255, 257, 260, 268, 270, 277, 282, 298, 307, 312, 313, 318, 364, 365, 370, 374, 396, 400, 410, 417, 419, 423
   shutdown, 401
   testing, 50
   topology, 45, 198, 229, 230
   WAN management, 99
   wireless, 313
Network access unit, NAU, 107
Network file system
   NFS, 247
Network interface card, NIC, 107
Network interface definition language, NIDL, 42
Networking management, 32, 76, 96, 160, 231
Network operating systems, NOS, 206, 207
Networktesting, 50
Network World, 141
New York Stock Exchange, NYSE, 20
NFS, 205
   Sun Microsystems, 208
NIC, 106, 122, 184, 366
   jitter, 325
NITS, 366
Node, definition of, 35
Noise, 48, 69, 87, 89, 90, 175, 178, 223, 265, 320, 377
Nonreturn to zero code, *see also* NRZI, 111
Nonreturn to zero, invert on ones, *see* NRZI
NOS, 206, 207
Novell, 32
NRZI, 86, 90, 111, 141, 339

OCR, 247
OLE, 243, 244
Open shortest path first, 199
Open systems interconnect model, OSI, 33, 73, 74, 75, 76, 78, 79, 80, 81, 82, 83, 84, 91, 94, 95, 96, 108,

Index

115, 124, 127, 198, 202, 203, 246, 318
Optical bypass, 340
Optical bypass switch, 146
Optical fiber, 66, 67, 76, 79, 81, 85, 87, 88, 99, 179, 195, 219, 224, 226
 cable, 85, 87
 limitations of, 136
Optical time domain reflectometer, 167
OS/2, 208, 209, 242
OS/2 Communication Manager, 242
OS/2 LAN, 242
OSF, 234
OSI, 31, 96, 205, 361
OTDR, 162, 395
Overheating, 182, 405
Overload, 118, 300, 319, 323, 364
Ozone filters, 57

Packet rate, 342
Packet switch, 191, 200, 204
Packet transmission losses, 211
Packet: *see also* Frame
 83, 105, 106, 107, 115, 116, 125, 127, 129
 fields, 352, 391
 header, 80
Pagers, 163
Passwords, 380, 385, 386, 387, 388, 389, 390, 391, 393, 395
PBX, 22, 41, 46, 140, 194, 226
PC, 27, 66, 83, 120, 205, 234, 246, 239, 240, 242, 245, 250, 277, 324
PC-DOS, 247, 277
 MS-DOS, 245, 246
PDN, 198
Peak load, 182
Peer-to-peer, 34, 36, 37, 218, 245
Pennsylvania Power and Light, 61
Performance, 32, 80, 83, 95, 99, 102, 120, 135, 137, 178, 191, 199, 202, 203, 211, 218, 225, 228, 229, 230, 248, 250, 255, 272, 318, 319, 333, 339, 352, 354, 355, 357, 358, 359, 360, 361, 362, 363, 365, 366, 367, 369, 370, 371, 373, 375, 377

Performance Analysis
 Monitoring, 25, 50, 75, 125, 126, 256, 274, 317, 318, 364
Performance degradation
 Network performance degradation, 224
Performance problems, 92
Performance, improvements, 193
Pliers, 161, 291
Power failures, 139
Power protection, 139
Power surges, 265, 405
PP&L, 61
Premise wiring standard, 102
Priority enforcement, 123
Processor, definition of, 35
PROM Extractor, 291
Proteon, 205
Protocol:
 analyzer, 162, 391, 392, 393, 395
 Advanced Program-to-Program Communication, APPC, 246
 Common Program Interface Communication, 246
 comparisons, 97
 CSMA, 45
 CSMA/CD, 46, 47
 High-Level Language Application Program Interface, HLLAPI, 239
 incompatibility, 246
 NDIS, 241
 ODI, 241
 OSI, 241
 simulation, 333
 SNMP, 99
 Synchronous Data Link Control, SDLC, 245
 System network architecture, SNA, 239
 TCP/IP, 242
 translations, 205
 User Datagram Protocol, UDP, 246
 X.400, 246
Public data network, 198
Punchdown blocks, 174
PVC cable, 138

Radiation, 58, 59, 60, 64, 65, 67, 69, 85, 180
Radio-frequency, 391
  RF, 59, 60, 63, 64, 66, 67, 139, 153, 180, 220, 221, 265, 304, 407
  interference, 90, 304
RAID, 362, 399
  disk farms, 272
RAM mobile data, 221
Receipt, 115, 122
Rechanneling, 357
Reconfiguration, 368
Record-keeping, 416
Redundancy, 118, 201, 399, 401, 403, 405, 407, 409, 411, 413, 414
Redundant array of inexpensive disks, see RAID
Repeater, 78, 83, 108, 192, 193, 200, 202, 358, 372
  simulation, 192
  smart, 200
Resistance, 103, 181
Resource
  Budgeting, 260
Retransmission, 96, 107, 108, 114, 121, 179, 393
Retrofit, 54
Retry, 124
Ring:
  structure, 223
Ring recovery, 123
  definition of, 346
RJ-45, 110
Router, 80, 81, 88, 117, 188, 198, 199, 200, 201, 204, 284, 342, 370, 372, 374, 377, 417
  definition of, 201
  dynamic tables, 212
  hybrid, 202
  multiport, 212
  multiprotocol, 212
  performance, 370
  routing tables, 212
Routing information protocol (RIP), 199
Routing table, definition, 212
RS-232, 136, 137, 195, 243

SAA, 246
Sabotage, 424
SABRE, 10, 22
SAS, 101
Scaffold, 163
Scandia Airlines, SAS, 21, 22, 88
Scanner, 89
Scanning, 31
SDLC, 245
SEC, 401, 409
Security, 21, 87, 102, 149, 199, 221, 224, 226, 227, 229, 230, 256, 264, 266, 335, 379, 380, 381, 383, 385, 386, 387, 388, 389, 391, 392, 393, 395, 397, 399, 400, 407, 414, 415
  breach, 335
  countermeasures, 394
Segmentation, 77, 95
Self-healing, 45, 88
Server, definition of, 240
Server, terminal server, 137
Signal, definition of, 107
Signal decay, 147
Signal noise, 107
Signal propagation delay, 106
Simple Network Management Protocol, see SNMP
Simple repeater, 192
Smart repeater
  learning repeater, 193
SMDS, 218, 227, 355
Smoke, 266
SNA, 239
SNAP-SAP, 376
Sneakernets, 14
SNMP, 93, 94, 95, 96, 120, 127, 195, 202, 312, 313, 318, 342, 375, 392
Soft error, 123
Software, 83
SONET, 219, 355
Source Code Control, 245
Source explicit forwarding
  routing tables, 199
Source route transparent, 199

Index

Source service address port, SSAP, 118
Spanning tree, 81, 201
    definition of, 200
Spanning-tree bridge, 191, 249
Spare parts, 161
Specifications:
    CDDI, 76
    greenbook, 76
    SDDI, 76
Speed of light, 107
Spread-spectrum technology, *see* SST
Spreadsheets, 238
SQL, 240
SST, 220, 222, 386, 391
ST connector, 141, 147, 170
Stabilized light source, 146, 162
Starting delimiter, 118
State, 95, 194
Static electricity, 52, 266
Station, definition of, 35
    unauthorized, 335
Statistics, 202, 312, 326, 335, 339, 342, 345, 357, 358
Store-and-forward, 194, 202
STP, 76, 86, 99, 102, 225
Strategic necessity, 22
Strategic value, 25
Strategy, 3, 5, 7, 8, 9, 11, 13, 15, 17, 19, 21, 23, 25, 27
Stray voltage, 52
Sun network file system, NFS, 247
Supercomputing, 41
Superservers, 238, 260, 272, 399
Surge suppression, 140
Synchronization, 119, 121
Synchronous data link control, SDLC, 78
Synoptics, 76

T-1, 136, 139, 195, 218
Tampering, 387, 395
Tapping, 381, 392, 395
Target token rotation time, 316

TCP, 91, 93, 94, 95, 96, 117, 119, 122, 126, 127, 128, 204, 242, 246, 318, 352, 366, 369
    definition of, 127
TCP/IP, *see* TCP
TDR, 89, 313, 395
    Scanner, 168
Teflon, 89, 90, 168
Teflon cable, 138
Telecommunications Industries Association, *see* EIA/TIA
Telephone equipment, 140
Terminal emulation, 246
Terminal server, 137, 195
Test equipment, 163
Theft, 387, 393, 406, 407
TIA, *see* EIA/TIA
Time domain reflectometer, TDR, 168, 183, 307
Token, capture of, 106
    definition of, 106
Token capture timer, definition of, 348
Token hold timer, definition of, 348
Token ring, 205
Token-Ring, 81, 128, 190, 220, 340
Token rotation time, definition of, 108
token rotational time, definition of, 347
Tool kit, 55, 56, 161, 163, 167, 168, 170, 291
    AM/FM radio, 69
Tools, vacuum cleaner, 139
Topology, 42, 43, 73, 78, 185, 228, 375
    bus, 32, 36, 45, 222
    definition of, 42
    mesh, 218
    ring, 44, 45, 81, 88
    star, 42, 180, 191
    Token ring, 88
Tornado, 382
TP, 110
TP-DDI, definition of, 43
Traffic, 45, 48, 49, 50, 79, 80, 87, 105, 106, 117, 124, 168, 193, 199, 202, 203, 224, 298, 323, 324, 334, 339,

359, 364, 367, 372, 373, 375, 391, 403
Traffic jam, 211
Traffic rate, definition, 322
Transaction control protocol, *see* TCP
Translation, definition, 82
Transmission rate, 342
Troubleshooting, 115, 202
TRT, definition of, 347
Trunk, definition of, 109
  network, 143
TSR, 207
TTRT, 348
  definition of, 316
TWA, 10, 11
Twisted-pair, 31, 102, 138
  failure points, 184
  wiring tips, 178, 179, 180
Type 1, 89

UDP, 119, 204, 246
  User Datagram Protocol, 78, 95
Uninterruptable power supply, UPS, 139, 140
Unix, 7, 208, 209, 241, 242, 245, 246, 381, 394
UPS, 139, 140
Upstream station, definition of, 340
US Sprint, 270
User Datagram Protocol, 95
UTP, 76, 86, 99, 102, 110, 225

Vandal detection, 393

Vandalism, 392, 393
Video, full-motion, 31
Vines, 83, 205
Virus, 383
VMS, 394
Voice grade twisted-pair, 138
Voltage, 64, 65, 67, 113, 178, 179, 185, 302
VSAM, 239
VSAT, 217, 227

Waiting time, 50, 354
WAN, 46
  definition of, 38
  management, 99
WaveLAN, 220
Wide area network, WAN, 46
WilTel, 270
Wire stripper, 161, 170
Wireless, 219, 222, 386, 391, 395
Wireless networks, 138
Wireless, limitations, 220
Wireless, point-to-point, 220
Wiring, concentrators, 108
  definitions, 89
  limitations, 155
  shorts, 50, 161, 299
  standards, 155

X Windows, 31, 32, 243
X.25, 12, 205, 215
XNS, 318